Advancements in Socialized and Digital Media Communications

Gülbuğ Erol
Iğdır University, Turkey

Michael Kuyucu
Alanya University, Turkey

IGI Global
PUBLISHER of TIMELY KNOWLEDGE

A volume in the Advances in Media, Entertainment, and the Arts (AMEA) Book Series

Published in the United States of America by
IGI Global
Information Science Reference (an imprint of IGI Global)
701 E. Chocolate Avenue
Hershey PA, USA 17033
Tel: 717-533-8845
Fax: 717-533-8661
E-mail: cust@igi-global.com
Web site: http://www.igi-global.com

Library of Congress Cataloging-in-Publication Data

Names: Erol, E. Gülbuğ (Ebru Gülbuğ), editor. | Kuyucu, Michael, editor.
Title: Advancements in socialized and digital media communications / edited by Ebru Gülbug Erol, Michael Kuyucu.
Description: Hershey, PA : Information Science Reference, [2024] | Includes bibliographical references and index. | Summary: "This book includes all the new media practices related to communication. This publication aims to offer both empirical and theoretical information focused on the current situation and future expectations of digital communication and social media"-- Provided by publisher.
Identifiers: LCCN 2023051768 (print) | LCCN 2023051769 (ebook) | ISBN 9798369308554 (hardcover) | ISBN 9798369308561 (ebook)
Subjects: LCSH: Information society. | Internet--Social aspects. | Information technology--Social aspects. | Digital media--Social aspects.
Classification: LCC HM851 .A275 2024 (print) | LCC HM851 (ebook) | DDC 303.48/33--dc23/eng/20231129
LC record available at https://lccn.loc.gov/2023051768
LC ebook record available at https://lccn.loc.gov/2023051769

This book is published in the IGI Global book series Advances in Media, Entertainment, and the Arts (AMEA) (ISSN: 2475-6814; eISSN: 2475-6830)

British Cataloguing in Publication Data
A Cataloguing in Publication record for this book is available from the British Library.

Advances in Media, Entertainment, and the Arts (AMEA) Book Series

Giuseppe Amoruso
Politecnico di Milano, Italy

ISSN:2475-6814
EISSN:2475-6830

Mission

Throughout time, technical and artistic cultures have integrated creative expression and innovation into industrial and craft processes. Art, entertainment and the media have provided means for societal self-expression and for economic and technical growth through creative processes.

The **Advances in Media, Entertainment, and the Arts (AMEA)** book series aims to explore current academic research in the field of artistic and design methodologies, applied arts, music, film, television, and news industries, as well as popular culture. Encompassing titles which focus on the latest research surrounding different design areas, services and strategies for communication and social innovation, cultural heritage, digital and print media, journalism, data visualization, gaming, design representation, television and film, as well as both the fine applied and performing arts, the AMEA book series is ideally suited for researchers, students, cultural theorists, and media professionals.

Coverage

- Communication Design
- Cross-Media Studies
- Visual Computing
- Data Visualization
- Design Tools
- New Media Art
- Digital Media
- Film & Television
- Environmental Design
- Products, Strategies and Services

IGI Global is currently accepting manuscripts for publication within this series. To submit a proposal for a volume in this series, please contact our Acquisition Editors at Acquisitions@igi-global.com or visit: http://www.igi-global.com/publish/.

The Advances in Media, Entertainment, and the Arts (AMEA) Book Series (ISSN 2475-6814) is published by IGI Global, 701 E. Chocolate Avenue, Hershey, PA 17033-1240, USA, www.igi-global.com. This series is composed of titles available for purchase individually; each title is edited to be contextually exclusive from any other title within the series. For pricing and ordering information please visit http://www.igi-global.com/book-series/advances-media-entertainment-arts/102257. Postmaster: Send all address changes to above address.

Titles in this Series

For a list of additional titles in this series, please visit:
www.igi-global.com/book-series/advances-media-entertainment-arts/102257

Digital Space in the Wake of Shrinking Traditional Media
Alfred Okoth Akwala (Technical University of Kenya, Kenya) Denish Ouko Otieno (Kenya Institute of Mass Communication, Kenya) and Amos Moraro Marube (Technical University of Kenya, Kenya)
Information Science Reference • copyright 2024 • 300pp • H/C (ISBN: 9781668493564) • US $225.00 (our price)

News Media and Hate Speech Promotion in Mediterranean Countries
Elias Said Hung (Universidad Internacional de la Rioja, Spain) and Julio Montero Diaz (Universidad Internacional de la Rioja, Spain)
Information Science Reference • copyright 2023 • 364pp • H/C (ISBN: 9781668484272) • US $215.00 (our price)

Examinations and Analysis of Sequels and Serials in the Film Industry
Emre Ahmet Seçmen (Beykoz University, Turkey)
Information Science Reference • copyright 2023 • 389pp • H/C (ISBN: 9781668478646) • US $215.00 (our price)

Using Innovative Literacies to Develop Leadership and Agency Inspiring Transformation and Hope
Limor Pinhasi-Vittorio (Lehman College, CUNY, USA) and Elite Ben-Yosef (The BYEZ Foundation, USA)
Information Science Reference • copyright 2023 • 287pp • H/C (ISBN: 9781668456149) • US $215.00 (our price)

Music and Engagement in the Asian Political Space
Uche Titus Onyebadi (Texas Christian University, USA) and Delaware Arif (University of South Alabama, USA)
Information Science Reference • copyright 2023 • 254pp • H/C (ISBN: 9781799858171) • US $215.00 (our price)

Handbook of Research on the Relationship Between Autobiographical Memory and Photography
Mark Bruce Nigel Ingham (London College of Communication, University of the Arts London, UK) Nela Milic (London College of Communication, University of the Arts London, UK) Vasileios Kantas (University of West Attica, Greece) Sara Andersdotter (University for the Creative Arts, Sweden) and Paul Lowe (London College of Communication, University of the Arts London, UK)
Information Science Reference • copyright 2023 • 636pp • H/C (ISBN: 9781668453377) • US $295.00 (our price)

Contemporary Manifests on Design Thinking and Practice
Gözde Zengin (Karabük University, Turkey) and Bengi Yurtsever (Mugla Sıtkı Kocman University, Turkey)
Information Science Reference • copyright 2023 • 277pp • H/C (ISBN: 9781668463765) • US $215.00 (our price)

IGI Global
PUBLISHER of TIMELY KNOWLEDGE

701 East Chocolate Avenue, Hershey, PA 17033, USA
Tel: 717-533-8845 x100 • Fax: 717-533-8661
E-Mail: cust@igi-global.com • www.igi-global.com

Special thanks to the beloved people we lost during this long and thin way called life.

Table of Contents

Detailed Table of Contents

The music industry underwent a radical transformation with the emergence and widespread adoption of the MP3 concept along with the digital transformation. Digitalization, which first caused the decline and then the disappearance of physical music sales, has changed the access to music in the music industry by 100%. This study examines the transformation of the music industry on the axis of digitalization. Before digitalization, music was listened to on vinyl records, CDs, and cassettes, but with digitalization, music has started to be listened to only through MP3. In 2000, Steve Jobs opened the first digital music platform iTunes, and this study examines the 20-year development of digital music platforms, emphasizing the economic effects of digitalization on the music industry. At the end of the study, inferences are made about how digitalization will affect the music industry in the 2030s, and predictions are made about the future music industry.

Cinema has replaced every story. This study tries to reveal the filmographies of Turkish directors living abroad in the contemporary Turkish cinema period. This study is important in that it tries to reveal how socio-cultural and economic events experienced on a global basis are reflected in the director's cinemas. The directors in question are names that are affiliated with both Turkish culture and the culture of the country they live in, so what they reflect in their films is important not only in terms of the culture in which they live and grow up, but also in terms of the culture they carry in their genes. The starting point of the study is how the directors try to express themselves in terms of narrative features and the subject covered. In this context, five Turkish directors who have lived and are living abroad were selected by purposive sampling method, and their films were analyzed using the qualitative case study method. As a result, directors reflected their feelings, thoughts, dreams, and the realities in their films.

Recently, research on the discovery and use of local data sources that can be used in hyperlocal journalism has gained importance. In this sense, this study includes a literature review on data journalism practices in hyperlocal media organizations. In the study, the importance of data journalism and social media use in hyperlocal journalism in the field of communication is emphasized, and how data journalism can be used in the fields of digital journalism and digital newspapers, its contributions, and solution suggestions are discussed. This study aims to contribute to presenting the news more effectively and meeting the information needs of the society by shedding light on the developments in the field of communication.

We can use neuromarketing to understand how consumers feel, think, and behave. Eye-tracking also gives us clues as to whether the tools we use in marketing communication can actually achieve the results we want. In this way, our messages will reach the masses much more easily and at less cost, making marketing communication more effective. Did the person receiving the message really notice the brand, logo, product, or was it just a fun activity for them? Eye-tracking can answer this question much more easily and with less cost, making marketing communication more effective. This chapter explores eye-tracking in marketing.

Advances in digital media have affected consumer preferences and tendencies as they have impacted the field of marketing. Whilst digital marketing becomes more effective every day, influencer marketing has taken its place among the most popular marketing strategies of recent times. Defined as a personality that alters and influences the way other people behave, influencers have tried to shape consumers' preferences and purchasing behaviors by obtaining and evaluating information in different ways and promoting products and services. Although influencers have an impact on their followers' preferences, consumer opinions towards influencers are equally significant. This study aims to analyze consumers' views on the concept of influencers, why they follow influencers, and their perspectives on influencers' earnings and status. In addition, the study focused on how influencers' product and service promotions affect consumers' opinions about brands and companies and their purchasing behaviors.

With the rapid development of technology, we are exposed to the ease and challenges of the digital age in all aspects. Technological revolutions are leading to rapid transformations in the global system. These developments can also bring crises. Therefore, it is necessary to be prepared for crises in the digital transformation. Anticipating and taking precautions for crises is one of the most important issues in the digital age. Effective tools are needed to rapidly and effectively solve crises through digital processes. This study will address the management of crises in the digital world and convey important notes to the reader on topics such as management, crisis, leadership, digitalization, and the digital age. The study will conclude with recommendations for solving crises in the digital field.

This study addresses the critical role of organizational apologies in crisis management, focusing specifically on their impact on corporate reputation and stakeholder behavior. Recognizing that crises can severely damage an organization's reputation and legitimacy, the research explores the complexities of using apologies as a crisis response strategy. It builds upon existing scholarship that has predominantly analyzed the legal and financial aspects of organizational apologies to delve into the nuances of their effectiveness. The study's scope is narrowed down to crises for which the organization is highly culpable, as perceived by public opinion shaped by news media. The research thereby offers granular insights into the strategic utility of varying apology categories, particularly in situations where the organization faces intense media scrutiny and stakeholder skepticism.

The rise of digitalization has brought significant changes across various fields, including diplomacy. This has given rise to the concept of "digital diplomacy," which combines traditional diplomatic practices with digital tools and social media platforms. Digital diplomacy leverages social media's ubiquity to enable politicians to not only reach their constituents but also shape their public image effectively. This phenomenon offers politicians new avenues to enhance public relations, craft their image, and engage voters. Recently, a global trend known as "digital diplomacy" has emerged, with politicians using cat-related posts on social media platforms as a novel approach. In this study, researchers analyze the cat-related social media posts of politicians in Turkey, examining their potential roles in creating a charming image, influencing the audience, or garnering societal attention. The study employs content analysis and delves into socio-political contexts to explore this intriguing phenomenon further.

In today's world, technology has become central to human life, leading to the popularity of social media applications. Consequently, the interdisciplinary concept of communication has evolved and transformed. This transformation has rapidly integrated diplomatic practices into the digital world, contributing to the expansion and implementation of the concept of public diplomacy. States and non-state actors have actively used social media applications to bring cultural diplomacy activities, one of the tools of public diplomacy, into the digital realm to influence individuals and communities, change negative perceptions into positive ones, shape an image, create attraction, or convey desired messages. In this study, cultural activities shared on the Instagram official account of the U.S. Embassy in Bishkek (@usembassybishkek) are examined in the context of cultural diplomacy. The findings are evaluated based on the shared posts, interaction results, participation, and conclusions are drawn.

The main aim of this study is to explore the associations between acculturative stress, well-being, life satisfaction, and social media use among Turkish refugees in Norway. This study examines the results of an online survey of Turkish refugees living in Norway. The snowball sampling method was used to recruit respondents. A correlational analysis was used to explore the associations between variables. The study found that the level of acculturative stress was negatively correlated with both the level of well-being and the level of satisfaction with life. The level of well-being was found to be positively correlated with the level of satisfaction with life. The female refugee participants reported higher levels of acculturative stress than males. Another finding of the study was that being employed was positively correlated with the level of well-being. No significant correlation was observed between social media use intensity and other variables.

deep learning-enhanced controller to act quickly and wisely on behalf of their physical counterparts. The approach combines user content posting and like behavior for personality prediction. Depending on the application, digital twins can be represented virtually as a social humanoid robot or a software element without a physical replica. The status messages uploaded by each user are pooled as a document. The work enhances security by 17.4%.

Preface

In the expansive realm of communication, the evolution has been exponential, witnessing a revolutionary shift catalyzed by technological strides and societal adaptations. From the rudimentary forms in the 1900s to the pervasive influence of the internet today, this book navigates through the intricate tapestry of social media's impact across diverse domains.

Our aim is ambitious yet focused: to dissect social media's influence within the realms of communication science, public relations, advertising, journalism, and a myriad of related fields. The concept of "social media" stands as a cornerstone, deeply embedded in the fabric of modern human existence for the past decade. Its evolution, characterized by constant software updates and seamless integration with changing technology, continually reshapes not just daily routines but also the landscape of industries and businesses worldwide.

This publication endeavors to encapsulate the spectrum of new media practices, delving into empirical evidence, theoretical frameworks, research findings, and comprehensive analyses. From the transformative impact on business practices to its pervasive influence on individual lifestyles, this book aims to serve as a comprehensive guide illuminating both the current landscape and future trajectories of digital communication and social media.

Designed for a diverse readership encompassing scholars, researchers, academicians, students, and professionals across various disciplines - philosophy, sociology, economics, and more - this book aspires to be a compass guiding further exploration and understanding of this rapidly evolving field.

As editors, we curated an extensive array of topics, ranging from social networks like Facebook and Instagram to digital cinema, digital public relations, and emerging areas such as digital ecology. Each chapter reflects our commitment to presenting in-depth analyses, authoritative insights, and comparative studies, offering a holistic view of the expansive domain of digital communication.

We hope this book becomes an invaluable resource, inspiring curiosity, sparking discussions, and fostering deeper comprehension of the dynamic interplay between digital media and communication in our contemporary world.

ORGANIZATION OF THE BOOK

As editors of *Advancements in Socialized and Digital Media Communications*, we present an array of chapters that encompass the dynamic landscape of digital communication across various disciplines. Here is a glimpse into each chapter's thematic exploration:

Chapter 1: "Twenty Years of Digitalization in Music from Vinyl Records to Spotify Digitalized Music Industry" by Mihalis Kuyucu: This chapter unveils the transformative journey of the music industry, charting its course from physical sales to the digital revolution. It examines the economic impacts and forecasts the future of music in the digital era.

Chapter 2: "Turkish Origin Directors Living in Europe and Their Perspectives on Cinema" by Gülbuğ Erol and Mustafa Gülsün: This study delves into the filmographies of Turkish directors abroad, exploring how socio-cultural experiences influence their cinematic narratives.

Chapter 3: "The Impact of Social Media on Communication" by Azadeh Eskandarzadeh: Analyzing the profound changes in communication, this chapter evaluates the effects of social media on relationships, citizen journalism, and its role in shaping contemporary society.

Chapter 4: "Cyber Habitat of Digital Culture: A View on Political Economy of Culture" by Berna Berkman Köselerli: Addressing the cultural aspects of digital society, this study scrutinizes digital platforms' influence, reflecting on their role in shaping cultural identities within capitalist structures.

Chapter 5: "Brand Evangelism Within the Framework of Digital Labor" by Fikriye Çelik: Exploring the fusion of immaterial labor with digital platforms, this chapter investigates brand evangelism on Instagram and its implications for labor exploitation.

Chapter 6: "Data Journalism and Social Media in Hyperlocal Journalism" by Cihan Çakır: Focusing on data journalism's significance in hyperlocal media, this study emphasizes the role of data in enhancing news delivery and meeting societal information needs.

Chapter 7: "Using Eye-Tracking in Integrated Marketing Communication" by Turgay Oyman: Highlighting the significance of eye-tracking in marketing, this chapter evaluates its effectiveness in understanding audience perceptions and optimizing marketing communication strategies.

Chapter 8: "Consumer Perspective on Influencers, the Rising Trend of Digital Marketing Perspective" by Gülşah Akto: This chapter delves into consumer perceptions of influencers, analyzing their impact on brand preferences and purchasing behavior.

Chapter 9: "Perspectives of Digital Marketing for the Restaurant Industry" by Mohammad Talukder, Sanjeev Kumar, Iva Das: Examining digital marketing's role in the food industry, this chapter provides insights into leveraging online platforms for restaurant growth.

Chapter 10: "Digitalization in the Public Management: Turkish Public Institutions Example" by Salim Kurnaz, António Rodrigues, Osman Sunar: This study explores digitalization in Turkish public institutions, analyzing e-government usage and future social media prospects.

Chapter 11: "Public Relations and AI" by Hakan Irak: Exploring the intersection of public relations and artificial intelligence, this chapter examines AI applications in PR, shedding light on current applications and future implications.

Chapter 12: "Crisis Management in the Digital Age" by Hasan Yılmaz: Addressing the challenges posed by digital transformations, this chapter navigates through crisis management strategies within the digital landscape.

Chapter 13: "Mitigating Reputational Damage in Corporate Crises: An Examination of Apology Strategies" by Elanor Colleoni, Grazia Murtarelli, Stefania Romenti, Francesca Dodini: Investigating organizational apologies in crisis management, this study dissects their impact on corporate reputation and stakeholder behavior.

Chapter 14: "Cat Diplomacy: A New Approach to Digital Public Diplomacy Through Politicians' Cat-Related Social Media Posts" by Ayten Cansever: Analyzing the peculiar phenomenon of politicians using cat-related social media posts, this study explores its role in digital public diplomacy.

Chapter 15: "An Examination of Diplomatic Entities' Digital Communication: A Case Study of the U.S. Embassy in Bishkek's Use of Instagram" by Onur Kaya: Examining cultural diplomacy on Instagram, this chapter evaluates the U.S. Embassy's digital communication strategies in Bishkek.

Chapter 16: "Exploring the Associations Between Acculturative Stress, Well-Being, Life Satisfaction, and Social Media Use Among Turkish Refugees in Norway" by Ali Acilar: This study explores the relationships between acculturative stress, well-being, life satisfaction, and social media use among Turkish refugees in Norway.

Chapter 17: "Influence of Instagram as a Social Media Platform on Academic Routine and Schedule of Students" by Pritesh Somani, Ushmita Gupta, Rashmi Mahajan, Vishwanathan Iyer, Nitesh Behare, Meenakshi Singh: Delving into Instagram's impact on students' academic routines, this chapter investigates the platform's influence on educational patterns.

Chapter 18: "Competitive Data Use, Analysis, and Big Data Applications in Online Advertising" by Sinan Akseki: Focusing on big data applications in advertising, this chapter explores utilizing competitive data analysis for precise online advertising.

Chapter 19: "A Ludological and Narratological Analysis of Crime Representations in Digital Games" by Feridun Nizam: Examining crime representations in digital games, this chapter explores the portrayal of crime in the gaming industry, filling a gap in existing studies.

Chapter 20: "Machine Learning and Virtual Reality: Enabling Safety in Social Media Websites" by Ambika N: Highlighting safety measures in social media, this chapter explores the use of machine learning and virtual reality to enhance security on social platforms.

Each chapter in our edited reference book offers unique insights into the multifaceted realm of digital communication, covering a diverse range of topics, methodologies, and implications within this rapidly evolving field.

IN SUMMARY

As editors of *Advancements in Socialized and Digital Media Communications*, we culminate this comprehensive volume that unravels the intricate tapestry of digital communication in our contemporary world. The collection of chapters within this book, authored by esteemed scholars and researchers, encapsulates the dynamism, challenges, and transformative power of digital media across diverse domains.

From the evolution of the music industry in the digital era to the nuanced explorations of social media's influence on communication, cinema, marketing, public relations, diplomacy, and beyond, each chapter adds a distinct layer to our understanding of this expansive landscape.

We've traversed through studies scrutinizing the impact of influencers on consumer behavior, the strategic utilization of apologies in crisis management, the interplay between social media and academic routines, and even the portrayal of crime in digital games. These investigations serve as a testament to the vast array of facets that digitalization has woven into our lives.

Moreover, our contributors have navigated through the intricate dynamics of data journalism, artificial intelligence in public relations, and the transformative potential of cultural diplomacy through digital channels. The implications of social media on refugees' well-being, the changing landscape of public service broadcasting, and the evolving nature of digital marketing strategies for restaurants represent just a few of the many thought-provoking discussions encapsulated within these chapters.

This anthology not only reflects the current state of digital communication but also serves as a guiding compass for future exploration and understanding in this rapidly evolving sphere. The diverse perspectives and methodologies presented here offer invaluable insights and avenues for further inquiry.

As editors, we extend our gratitude to the contributors whose meticulous research, diverse perspectives, and scholarly rigor have enriched this volume. We hope this book serves as a foundation for ongoing dialogue, exploration, and innovation in the ever-evolving realm of socialized and digital media communications.

May this collection inspire curiosity, spark discourse, and pave the way for continued advancements in understanding the profound impact of digitalization on our interconnected world.

Gülbug Erol
Igdir University, Turkey

Michael Kuyucu
Alanya University, Turkey

Introduction

The coverage area of Digital Communication is gradually expanding; therefore, the need for the discipline also increases. Digital Communication is a result of the existence, and human beings unknowingly participate in and use digital communication environments while living. This study, which started to take shape in mid-2023, is designed to examine current events in the digitalized communication environment in the world and bring a new breath to the field. The dynamic structure of digital communication should be examined from a broad perspective.

The study includes the latest trends in digitalized communication environments, from the music industry to cinema. This work, which approaches communication environments with a new understanding, appeals to everyone, regardless of age and profession, who wants to make their lives more meaningful and understand the changing digital environments more easily. It is possible to see new titles such as music and digital games in the study, which is basically designed as five main sections: social media, radio-television, journalism, public relations and cinema.

It was a great benefit for us to be able to reach researchers from all over the world and study their works. We hope it will be useful to everyone who is interested in the subject. We would like to express our gratitude to all the employees of IGI Global who were always with us during the printing of the work.

Chapter 1
Twenty Years of Digitalization in Music:
From Vinyl Records to Spotify

Mihalis Michael Kuyucu
Galata University, Turkey

ABSTRACT

The music industry underwent a radical transformation with the emergence and widespread adoption of the MP3 concept along with the digital transformation. Digitalization, which first caused the decline and then the disappearance of physical music sales, has changed the access to music in the music industry by 100%. This study examines the transformation of the music industry on the axis of digitalization. Before digitalization, music was listened to on vinyl records, CDs, and cassettes, but with digitalization, music has started to be listened to only through MP3. In 2000, Steve Jobs opened the first digital music platform iTunes, and this study examines the 20-year development of digital music platforms, emphasizing the economic effects of digitalization on the music industry. At the end of the study, inferences are made about how digitalization will affect the music industry in the 2030s, and predictions are made about the future music industry.

INTRODUCTION

The digital development of the music industry over the past two decades has been dramatic. Music is being consumed on streaming services instead of vinyl records and CDs. Spotify, Apple Music, Tidal, and YouTube Music have democratized access to massive music libraries and changed the music industry's economics. These platforms use freemium, subscription-based, and ad-supported business models to attract users and make money. Beyond streaming, they have added live events, merchandising, and exclusive content to their revenue streams. A wealth of data is driving this digital growth, revealing user preferences, changing marketing methods, and redefining artist-fan connections.

DOI: 10.4018/979-8-3693-0855-4.ch001

THE BEGINNING OF THE DIGITAL MUSIC PLATFORMS

Digital music platforms have experienced technological innovation, commercial disruption, and changing consumer behavior. Explore these platforms' history and development. Vinyl, cassette, and CDs were the main music distribution methods before digital platforms. Although charming, these formats were limited in portability, durability, and capacity. MIDI files were the first digital music files utilized by musicians and producers for electronic instruments and software.

Creating MP3 in the 1990s was revolutionary. It reduced music files substantially without compromising audio quality. This enabled digital music storage and sharing. Napster was launched in 1999 (Yassin & Yassin, 2021). It made music sharing and downloading easy, encouraging piracy. Napster was shut down due to legal issues, but it showed customer demand for digital music. Apple introduced iTunes in 2001, allowing consumers to legally buy and download songs and albums. This site offered a legal alternative to piracy and started the digital music sales revolution. Platforms like Pandora, launched in 2000, introduced the concept of Internet radio. Users could listen to music stations curated based on their preferences but had limited control over song selection. On-Demand Streaming: Services like Spotify (2008) and Deezer (2007) introduced on-demand music streaming, allowing users to choose exactly what they wanted to listen to. These platforms often operated on a freemium model, offering both free (ad-supported) and premium (subscription-based) listening options.

Recognizing the demand from audiophiles, platforms like Tidal offered lossless, high-fidelity streaming, catering to those who prioritized sound quality. Platforms like YouTube Music combine audio tracks with a vast library of music videos, offering a unique blend of audio and visual content. SoundCloud emerged as a platform for independent artists, DJs, and creators to share their music, remixes, and live sets, fostering a community of indie music enthusiasts (Yassin & Yassin, 2021). As streaming developed, artist royalty payments were criticized. Many said the reimbursements were low, raising questions about the streaming model's sustainability and fairness. Some platforms acquired exclusive artist releases to differentiate themselves and entice members, although this practice has become controversial and rarer. Spotify expanded into audio entertainment services as podcasts and other audio content became popular.

Figure 1. CD-MC and LP for music distribution

Figure 2. The official logo of MP3

Digital music platforms are millions' main music consumption source. They have large libraries, tailored recommendations, and flexible subscriptions. Smart speakers and voice assistants have made streaming more interwoven into users' lives.

THE HISTORY OF GLOBAL DIGITAL MUSIC PLATFORMS

The digitalization of music in the past two decades has changed how we consume, distribute, and commercialize it. From vinyl albums and cassette tapes to digital platforms, the music industry has changed drastically. Let's give a look to the global digital music platforms that shaped the industry in the last two decades.

iTunes (iTunes-2001)

The late 1990s and early 2000s were turbulent for the music industry. P2P file-sharing services like Napster fueled music piracy (Kleinman, 2019). The industry faced falling CD sales and rising unauthorized downloads. Apple launched iTunes against this backdrop. iTunes was an online music retailer. Users could buy and download songs and albums to their computers and iPods. This was new at the time when CDs were bought physically. The iTunes pricing strategy was groundbreaking. Apple offered 99-cent tracks as a legitimate alternative to piracy. This price strategy made music more affordable and let users choose their favorite songs instead of buying an album. The iPod, Apple's portable music player, helped iTunes succeed. Users may easily buy, organize, and listen to music on the go because of their seamless connection. Apple added DRM to its music files to placate record labels and curb piracy. Songs purchased from iTunes could only be played on Apple devices. This method was abandoned in 2009, making tracks DRM-free and easier to utilize. iTunes popularized digital album graphics and provided digital booklets, mimicking CD purchases. iTunes was crucial to digitizing the music industry. It solved the piracy problem and changed how customers used music.

Apple Music (2015)

Another major music industry transition occurred in the mid-2010s. Spotify, which offered huge music libraries for a monthly charge, was growing. Apple launched Apple Music to capitalize on this trend. Over 100 million songs were available to Apple Music users (Apple Newsroom, 2023). This large library allowed users to stream their favorite songs, albums, and artists without buying them. Apple Music was

Figure 3. The appearance of iTunes music

Figure 4. The mobile screen of Apple Music

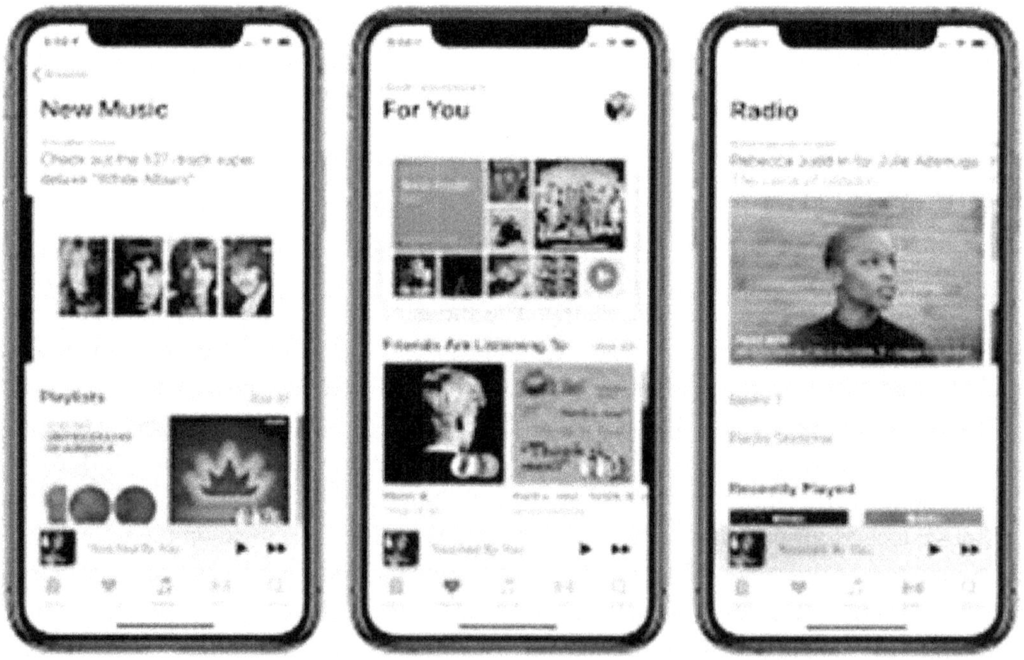

known for its tailored playlists. Apple hired music specialists to build mood, genre, and activity playlists. Apple Music stood out from algorithm-driven competitors with its personal touch. Another interesting feature was Beats 1, a 24/7 global radio channel. Beats 1 provided a dynamic, real-time element to streaming with famous DJs, exclusive interviews, programs, and song premieres. Apple embedded Apple Music into its ecosystem. It worked on all Apple devices and imported customers' iTunes library, making the switch easy for longtime users. Apple Music first offered "Connect," where artists could share images, videos, and other content with fans. Although this function was ultimately minimized, it showed Apple's desire to connect artists and listeners. Apple Music made streaming the main music format. Apple made Apple Music a prominent streaming provider by utilizing its massive user base and integrating it into its ecosystem.

Spotify (2008)

Daniel Ek and Martin Lorentzon, two Swedes, envisioned a platform with a massive music library in the mid-2000s when the music industry was still struggling with piracy and digital transformation (Forbes, 2023). They created Spotify in 2008, which revolutionized music streaming. Spotify's freemium approach revolutionized the music industry. Spotify's massive music collection was free with advertisements under this model. For an uninterrupted experience, pay monthly for the premium version. This method offered a legal alternative to piracy and exposed many users to music streaming. Spotify emphasized playlists, while iTunes focused on albums and music purchases. Users may create, share, and find playlists for any mood, activity, or occasion. Music consumption became more dynamic and individualized with playlists. One of Spotify's best features is "Discover Weekly," a weekly playlist based on user listening behavior. Every week, Spotify uses advanced algorithms to recommend songs to users. This tool and other tailored recommendations made music discovery fun and easy. Spotify created collaborative playlists to which various users contributed. Through similar musical tastes, this element-built camaraderie between friends, families, and even strangers. Spotify expanded globally, but its strategy was not uniform. The platform appealed to varied audiences with specialized material, playlists, and suggestions based on regional music trends and interests. Spotify has merged with smart speakers and game consoles over time. This ubiquity lets people listen to their favorite songs wherever. Spotify expanded into podcasts due to their popularity. Today, it broadcasts podcasts on a variety of topics in addition to music. Spotify has succeeded, but it has faced hurdles. The platform's royalty payments to musicians have been criticized as inadequate. Spotify also faces complicated license agreements and competition from other streaming companies. Spotify's influence on music is clear. It has democratized music access, promoted playlists, and introduced millions to streaming. User-centric features like personalized recommendations and collaborative playlists have set industry norms. Spotify proves the power of innovation in digital music with hundreds of millions of active users.

Figure 5. The logo of Spotify

Deezer (2007)

When music streaming was only starting out, a French business called Deezer debuted. Deezer, founded in August 2007 by Daniel Marhely and Jonathan Benassaya, pioneered music streaming before Spotify (Corporate Executives, 2020). In its early days, Deezer's web platform stood out. Deezer streamed music from browsers, unlike earlier services that required downloads. Its accessibility made it a popular streaming platform for beginners. Deezer started in France but aimed globally. As it expanded internationally, the

Figure 7. Logo of Deezer

deezer

platform launched in several nations. Deezer opened music streaming to previously underserved audiences. As music streaming competition increased, Deezer offered new features to differentiate itself. "Flow," a customized music stream, is one example. By mixing familiar and new tunes using algorithms and user data, Flow creates a unique listening experience every time. Audiophiles desire high-quality audio; therefore, Deezer created Deezer HiFi, which uses FLAC (Free Lossless Audio Codec). This maneuver targeted a tiny yet loyal audiophile audience. Deezer went beyond music. The platform included lyrics so users could sing along to their favorite songs. In response to podcast popularity, Deezer added them to its repertoire, making it a more complete entertainment platform. Deezer prioritized localized content to suit its broad global audience. Regional music charts, local artists, and market-specific editorials were on the site. Deezer resonated with users from diverse cultures thanks to this strategy.

Deezer struggled like other music streaming platforms. Competition from bigger companies, licensing agreements, and commercialization were continuous challenges. Deezer overcame these obstacles by forming smart alliances. They partnered with telecom companies to package Deezer subscriptions with mobile plans, increasing their user base. Deezer's impact on music streaming is tremendous. As a pioneer, it helped popularize music streaming, especially in new markets. Its user-centric features, local

Figure 6. Deezer music platform

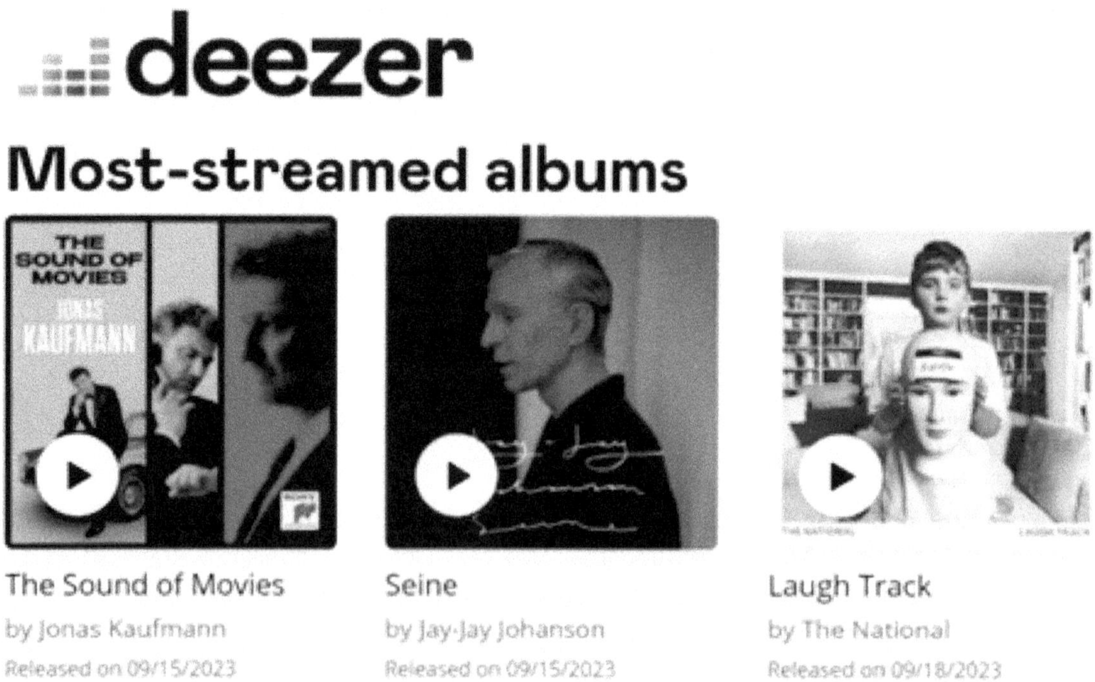

content, and high-quality audio have made it a top music streaming site. With millions of tracks and users, Deezer proves digital music's transformational power.

Amazon Music (2007)

Amazon has always been adept at diversifying and entering new markets. Amazon Music was created in 2007 to capitalize on the growing digital music business. Amazon's MP3 shop launched its digital music business. This DRM-free website lets customers buy and download MP3 songs and albums (Amazon, 2023). Amazon songs could be played on any device, unlike some iTunes tunes, giving users more options. Amazon's MP3 store rivaled iTunes. Amazon offered DRM-free songs at low pricing to compete with iTunes. This challenge for iTunes' digital music sales supremacy was substantial. Amazon responded when the music industry switched from downloads to streaming. Amazon Prime Music was established in 2014 as a free streaming service for Prime members. Its collection was small compared to other streaming services, but it offered value to Prime's shopping, video streaming, and other features. Amazon Music Unlimited was launched in 2016 to compete with Spotify and Apple Music. This monthly subscription service (Prime members get discounts) has a music library that rivals the industry leaders. Curated playlists, customized stations, and high-quality audio streaming are available.

Amazon Music's flawless integration with Alexa and Echo smart speakers is a highlight. Asking Alexa to play their favorite songs, albums, or playlists is simple and hands-free. Amazon Music HD, for

Figure 8. Amazon Music's Music Explorer

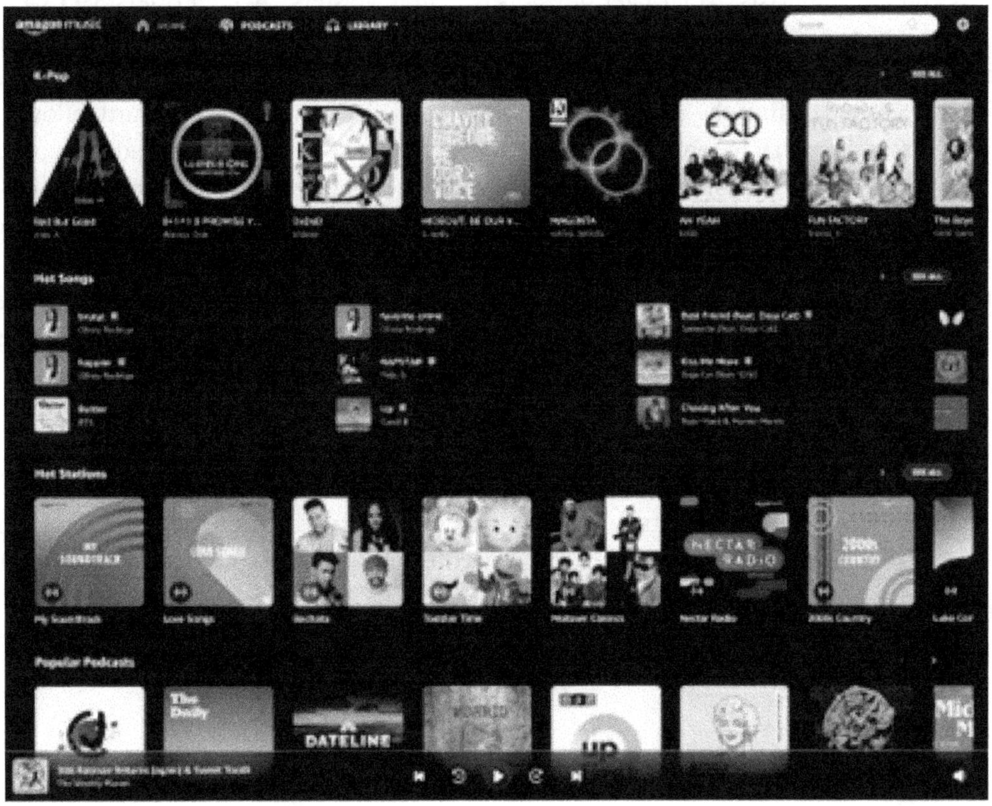

Figure 9. Logo of Amazon Music

audiophiles, has a greater bitrate and better sound quality than basic streaming. This action established Amazon as a music platform that values audio quality, appealing to a tiny yet loyal audience. Amazon Music has many features, yet it competes in a tough industry. Amazon uses its environment to differentiate. Alexa and Echo integration, Prime bundling, and competitive pricing for Prime members are purposeful attempts to attract and keep subscribers. Amazon Music's transformation from a digital retail to a streaming service reflects the music industries. Amazon Music has become a global music streaming leader by adjusting to market trends and exploiting its huge ecosystem. Amazon Music remains a digital music powerhouse with millions of members and a big repertoire.

Tidal (2014)

Tidal was founded in 2014 with a distinct identity and aim in a world dominated by Spotify and Apple Music (Fortune, 2021). Its fate changed in 2015 when a coalition of musicians led by Jay-Z bought it from Norwegian business Aspiro. This acquisition and rebranding made Tidal an artist platform. Sound quality was Tidal's main selling feature from the start. Lossless audio streaming on Tidal appeals to audiophiles and music purists. Tidal later developed "Tidal Masters," which offers MQA-encoded recordings, pushing streaming sound quality. Tidal differentiated itself by giving exclusive content from artists, primarily Jay-Z and the consortium that owned Tidal. Exclusive album releases, music videos, live performances, and behind-the-scenes information. Tidal was essential for diehard followers of these artists due to exclusives. Jay-Z rebranded Tidal to promote artist dedication. To address a major issue of streaming services, the site offered musicians and producers better royalty rates. In doing so, Tidal established itself as a platform that cherishes artist contributions and ensures fair compensation.

Beyond music, Tidal included high-quality music videos, documentaries, and interviews. Editorial information on musicians, albums, and the music industry was added to the platform. Tidal began live-streaming concerts, performances, and special events. This feature enhanced Tidal by adding material beyond music streaming. Tidal struggled in a competitive market despite its unique offerings. Some liked its exclusivity, but others saw it as fragmenting the music industry. Tidal's premium subscription price (supported by its high-fidelity streaming) made it harder to sell to the typical customer, especially compared to cheaper options with larger user bases. Tidal has changed music streaming in many ways. It promoted sound quality in the digital age, artist rights and compensation, and exclusive content as a differentiator. Tidal's artist-centric approach and focus on quality over quantity have made it a distinctive and vital music streaming platform.

Figure 10. The appearance of Tidal in desktop and mobile

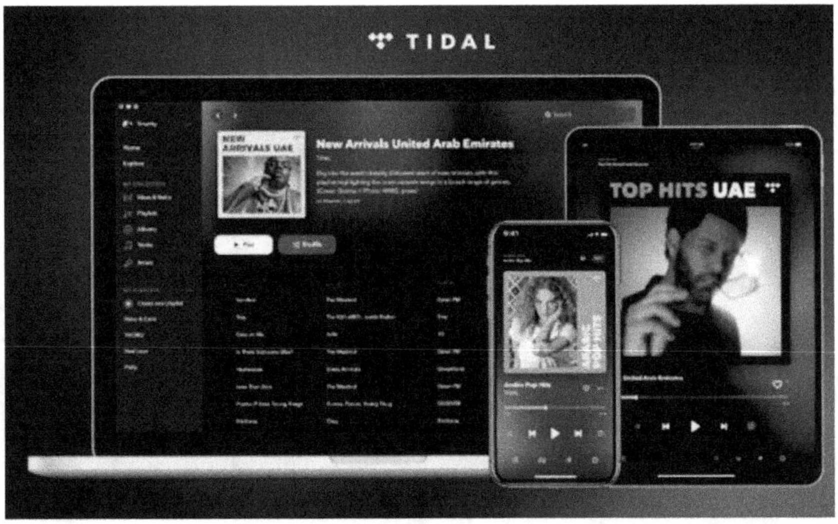

Figure 11. Logo of Tidal

YouTube Music (2018)

Since 2005, YouTube has been crucial for musicians, labels, and fans. From official music videos to live performance covers and fan-made material, YouTube has always been about music. Google, YouTube's parent company, launched YouTube Music in 2018 to capitalize on the platform's devoted music streaming potential (Snapes & Sweney, 2018). YouTube Music's flawless video-audio combination is a highlight. Users can switch between listening to a song and watching its music video with a simple tap. This dual mode offers a unique experience, catering to both passive listeners and those who want a visual accompaniment to their music. Leveraging YouTube's extensive content base, YouTube Music boasts one of the most diverse music libraries among streaming platforms. Apart from official tracks, users can delve into remixes, covers, live performances, and other content that's unique to YouTube.

Drawing from Google's expertise in AI and machine learning, YouTube Music offers highly personalized music recommendations. The platform considers listening history, search patterns, and even location to curate playlists and song suggestions tailored to individual users. Recognizing that users might not always remember song titles, YouTube Music introduced a "smart search" feature. Users can search for songs using vague descriptions, snippets of lyrics, or even by describing the music video, making the discovery process more intuitive. For premium subscribers, YouTube Music automatically creates an "Offline Mixtape" based on listening habits. This mixtape, which is regularly updated, can be accessed without an internet connection. Additionally, users can download songs, albums, and playlists for offline

Figure 12. YouTube Music Explorer

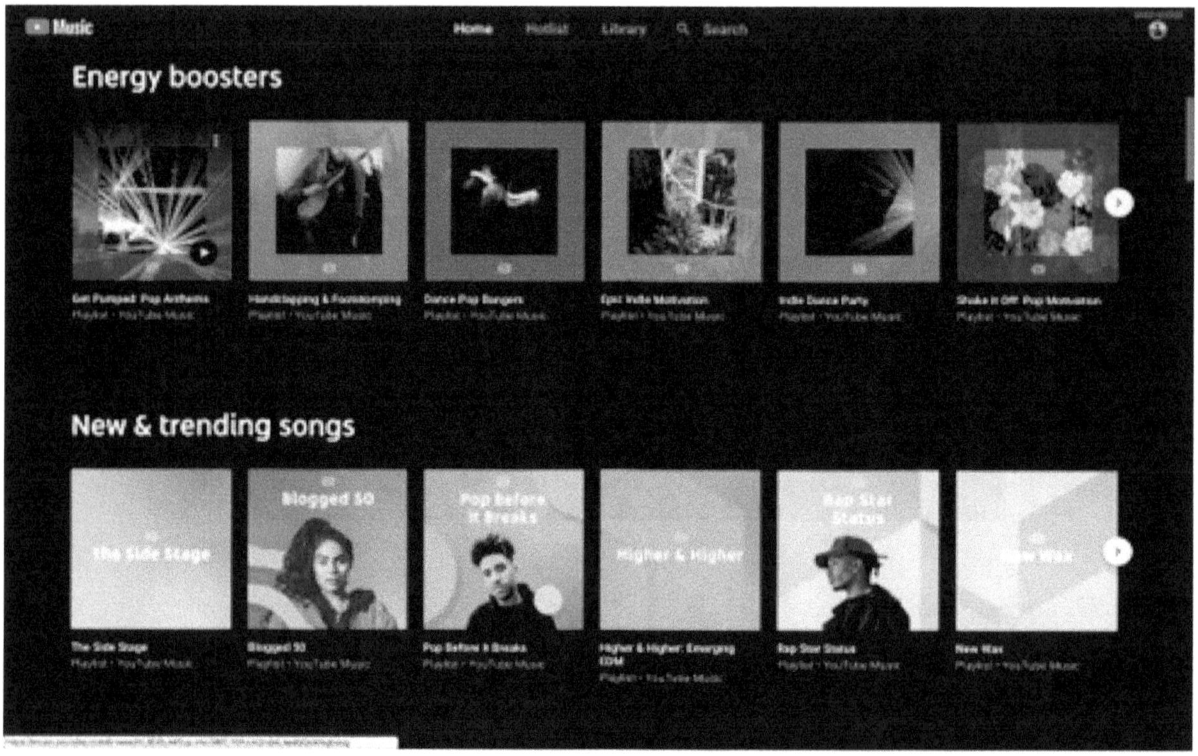

listening. YouTube Music Premium comes with YouTube Premium (previously YouTube Red), which allows background playback, ad-free YouTube, and YouTube Originals. This bundle includes music and video, adding value to members.

YouTube Music joined a market dominated by Spotify, Apple Music, and Amazon Music despite its vast feature set. YouTube Music relied on its video content, enormous catalog of unique tracks, and YouTube's user base to stand out. To recruit new subscribers, the site ran aggressive marketing campaigns and provided discounts. YouTube Music is new to dedicated music streaming but has quickly become a major participant. YouTube Music has established itself by using YouTube's large content base and adding features that suit modern listeners. It shows the changing nature of music consumption, where audio and video material are blurred.

Figure 13. Logo of YouTube Music

GLOBAL PLATFORMS AND THEIR GENERAL SPECIFICATIONS

Many global digital music platforms exist. Features, services, and specs distinguish each platform. Spotify is a Swedish freemium service with ad-supported and premium editions. Spotify is recognized for "Discover Weekly," a weekly playlist based on user listening behavior (Pasick, 2022). User-created, shared, and discovered playlists are its focus. Spotify Connect lets consumers stream music across devices. Spotify has added podcasts and other non-music audio programming in recent years. Apple Music, established by Apple Inc., is a subscription service with a trial period. Beats 1 Radio, a 24/7 global channel, is a highlight. Apple Music integrates with Siri and offers expert-curated playlists. Apple Music also offers music videos.

Deezer, from France, uses a freemium model like Spotify. Its "Flow," a customized audio stream, is distinctive. An integrated lyrics function lets users sing along on Deezer. The platform hosts podcasts and radio broadcasts. Deezer HiFi offers FLAC sound for audiophiles. Amazon Music offers multiple plans. Amazon Prime Music has a restricted repertoire, while Amazon Music Unlimited has a full streaming subscription. Amazon Music integrates with the Echo and Alexa. They also launched Amazon Music HD for high-quality streaming. Amazon Music has expert-curated playlists like others. Jay-Z headed a team that bought Norwegian startup Tidal (Leonard, 2015). Standard and hi-fi tiers are available via subscription. MQA tracks and high-fidelity audio are Tidal's specialty. It prioritizes fair pay and exclusive artist material. Finally, Google introduced YouTube Music as an extension of YouTube. The freemium model offers ad-supported and premium subscriptions. With its video integration, YouTube Music lets users smoothly navigate between audio tracks and music videos. The platform's "Smart Search" feature lets users search for music by lyrics or description. Personalized YouTube Music recommendations are based on YouTube and YouTube Music user history.

FACTS AND NUMBERS ABOUT THE GLOBAL DIGITAL MUSIC PLATFORMS

The digital music streaming landscape is vast, and several platforms dominate the scene with impressive subscriber and user numbers. Spotify boasts a massive user base with over 551 million total Monthly Active Users (MAUs) (Spotify, 2023). Of these, 220 million subscribers in more than 180 markets. Apple Music had reported surpassing 88 million subscribers by 2022 (Curry, 2023). This figure represents a significant portion of the dedicated music streaming market. Deezer, originating from France, has made its mark globally with over 16 million total Monthly Active Users (MAUs) (Gitnux, 2023). The platform's paid subscribers, those who opt for an ad-free experience with additional features, number over 7 million.

Amazon Music, with its various tiers from Prime Music to Amazon Music Unlimited, reported having over 82 million customers globally (Susic, 2023). This number encompasses all their service levels, making it a significant player in the music streaming industry. Tidal, known for its high-fidelity streaming and artist-centric approach, has seen debates regarding its exact subscriber count. However, estimates in recent years suggest that the platform has around 3 million paid subscribers worldwide (Rys, 2016). YouTube Music, an extension of the video giant YouTube had over 80 million premium subscribers (Forristal, 2022). This includes YouTube Premium and YouTube Music Premium members. YouTube has billions of users worldwide, and a large fraction utilize it for music, even if they are not paying subscribers.

THE BUSINESS MODELS OF DIGITAL MUSIC MARKET

The business models of digital music platforms had a change in the last two decades. The reason of this was the licensing problems that they had to challenge. The music companies were very hard for these platforms, and they always asked more and more but on the other hand he digital music companies wanted to give always less and less. The first and most popular model based on the advertising revenue, but this was not enough itself. They had to take some other revenues and this lead to start the premium subscription model. In this part of the article we will check the business model of the digital music platforms. How did they improve these model and what is the current situation now.

Freemium Model

In digital music streaming, the freemium model, a combination of "free" and "premium," is a popular strategy (Gerber, 2019). From free music streaming to premium experiences, it is geared for a wide spectrum of people. The free tier is an entry point. Platforms can attract many users by releasing much of their music catalog for free. Trade-offs occur with this access. Intermittent ads between songs generate money and encourage users to upgrade to the premium tier. Platforms may limit the free tier to encourage upgrades. Users may only be able to shuffle tracks or skip a certain amount every hour. These constraints make the free tier enticing but limit it enough to make the premium tier appealing. These platforms make most of their money at the premium tier. For a monthly or annual charge, customers can unlock many additional services. The first benefit is no ads, assuring uninterrupted listening. Premium members can also download music for offline listening, which is useful in locations with poor internet or during air travel. Unlimited skips let users customize their listening experience, and some systems offer audiophile-quality streaming. Premium subscriptions are essential for the platform's profitability and royalties to artists, songwriters, and record labels.

Subscription-Based Model

The subscription model is simpler than the freemium model. It offers a premium experience from the start without a free tier (excluding trial periods) (Li et al., 2016). Tidal and Apple Music have not maintained a free tier. This decision emphasizes their premium experience dedication. It emphasizes the value of music and fair artist compensation. Many sites without a free tier rely on marketing, commercial collaborations, and unique content to attract members. To mitigate the absence of a free tier and to give potential users a taste of the platform, many subscription-based services offer trial periods. During this time, users can access the platform's full suite of features without charge. These trial periods can range from a few days to several months, depending on promotions. The goal is to showcase the platform's value proposition compellingly enough that users opt to continue with a paid subscription once the trial ends. By default, users on these platforms enjoy all the benefits associated with a premium subscription on freemium platforms. This includes ad-free listening, offline downloads, unlimited skips, and, in some cases, exclusive content or higher audio quality. The consistent revenue from these subscriptions ensures a steady income stream for the platform, which can be reinvested into improving the service, securing exclusive content deals, or expanding into new markets.

Ad-Supported Model

Digital platforms in music and other media rely on the ad-supported model. It allows free content while making revenue. YouTube's free version and Pandora's original offer a huge music library for free. Advertisements occasionally interrupt listening. These adverts can be audio commercials between songs, video ads before music videos, or app or website banners. These platforms make money by charging advertisers to show their ads to users (Fuller, 2018). Ad impressions, clicks, and user activities can determine the advertiser's cost.

Targeting adverts is a benefit of these platforms. Music streaming platforms collect consumer data, from demographics to listening habits. This data lets advertisers target specific audiences, enhancing user engagement. Ad-supported platforms must balance user experience and revenue. Too much advertising repels users, while too few hurt profits. It is tricky to balance when competing with premium or subscription services.

Bundled Subscription

Platforms bundle complementary services to add value to users. This strategy can improve user retention, platform loyalty, and offering depth (Li et al., 2019). Amazon Music's integration with Amazon Prime is a classic example of bundling. Prime members, who primarily subscribe for benefits like free shipping and access to Amazon Prime Video, also get access to Amazon Music with a limited music library. It's a value addition that enhances the overall appeal of the Prime subscription. For those who want a more extensive music library, Amazon offers Amazon Music Unlimited at an additional cost. This tiered approach caters to casual listeners and music enthusiasts alike. YouTube Premium is a bundled offering that enhances the overall YouTube experience. Subscribers not only get access to YouTube Music Premium, which offers an ad-free music listening experience, but they also enjoy an ad-free experience on YouTube itself. Additional perks, like background playback, allow users to listen to videos even when their screen is off or when they're using another app. This bundled approach makes the subscription more attractive, as users get a multifaceted enhancement to their YouTube experience.

High-Fidelity and Niche Subscriptions

In the vast world of music streaming, most platforms prioritize accessibility and a broad music library. However, there's a segment of the audience with discerning ears that prioritize sound quality above all else. This is where high-fidelity and niche subscriptions come into play. Standard music streaming often compresses audio files to make them more manageable for streaming, especially on mobile data. While this is efficient, it can lead to a loss in audio quality. High-fidelity streaming, on the other hand, offers lossless audio, meaning there's no quality reduction from the original recording. This results in clearer, richer, and more detailed sound. Tidal is perhaps the most well-known platform that emphasizes its high-fidelity streaming, offering what they term "HiFi" sound quality. Deezer, too, offers a "Deezer HiFi" tier that provides FLAC (Free Lossless Audio Codec) quality sound (Earle, 2022). Given the additional data costs and the niche appeal, high-fidelity streaming options are often priced higher than standard subscriptions. They cater to audiophiles, professional musicians, and sound enthusiasts who have the equipment and desire to appreciate the finer nuances of high-quality audio.

Revenue Distribution

The music streaming industry, while lucrative, operates on relatively thin margins. A significant reason for this is the need to distribute a large portion of the revenue back to the creators and rights holders of the music (Wikström, 2022). When we talk about rights holders in the music industry, we're referring to a collective group that includes record labels (which might have their own contracts with producers, session musicians, etc.), artists, and songwriters. Each song streamed has multiple stakeholders who need to be compensated. Generally, streaming platforms pay rights holders based on the number of streams their songs receive. When a user plays a song, a micro-payment is made for that stream. Over time, micro-payments accumulate into large amounts that rights holders get. The cost per stream depends on numerous things. Its overall revenue, number of streams in a given period, and contractual agreements with record labels or independent artists are among these. Regional rates vary depending on advertising revenues, subscription pricing, and user activity. The income distribution strategy of streaming platforms is controversial. Many musicians and industry insiders worry that per-stream compensation is too low compared to traditional music sales. This has raised questions about the streaming model's viability and fairness, especially for independent and developing musicians.

CONCLUSION

The landscape of music consumption has been irrevocably altered by digital streaming platforms. Their innovative business models and strategies have not only provided listeners with unparalleled access to music but have also introduced new revenue avenues for artists, record labels, and the platforms themselves. As these platforms continue to evolve, leveraging data for personalized experiences and branching out into ancillary revenue streams, they underscore the dynamic and ever-evolving nature of the music industry. While challenges persist, especially around fair revenue distribution and competition, the symbiotic relationship between artists, platforms, and listeners hints at a future where music remains an integral part of our digital lives, resonating with us in more personalized and immersive ways than ever before.

Today looking globally there are only a few popular platforms. These are Spotify, Apple Music, Deezer and Youtube Music. Especially these four platforms are dominating the digital music industry. Regarding that people don't but any more music physically on MC, CD and LPs we can say these platforms are not only dominating the digital music industry but also all the music industry. Because today the distribution of music is done digitally. Of course, the rebirth of LPs brought a new breath to the market but still the 90% and more of the music listening activities are done from the digital platforms. Here these four platforms are the leader of this market. Spotify is the market leader based on subscriptions and number of users and Apple Music and Youtube Music is coming behind Spotify. There is a war between these three platforms. While this is a war for market leadership this is also an indicator of oligopoly. These three digital music platforms had created an oligopoly in the world. This is another issue that should be regarded as a thread for the music independency. Today music distribution is under the monopoly of digitalization and these digitalization has an oligopoly of three main global companies: Spotify- Apple Music and Youtube Music.

So the industry experts and the nations should start thinking about the disadvantages of this oligopolistic market to the local music industry of the countries and to the music business. This oligopoly has such a big power that they can change the trends in music and shape the popular music market because of their big reach and number of subscribers. The today and future of music listening behaviors is going to be shaped by the digital transformation and this oligopolistic structure of one Swedes and two USA companies can be a big challenge and a thread. Nations should try to encourage their national digital music platforms and motivate users to use and subscribe to them in order to create a balance between the global platforms and local national platforms otherwise all the nations and local music businesses will be the slave of this oligopolistic digital music market.

REFERENCES

Amazon. (2023). *Playback & DRM Overview*. https://developer.amazon.com/docs/music/playback_overview.html

Apple Newsroom. (2023). *Celebrating 100 million songs*. https://www.apple.com/newsroom/2022/10/celebrating-100-million-songs/

Corporate Executives. (2020). *Deezer*. https://corporate-executives.com/companies/deezer/

Curry, D. (2023). *Apple Music Revenue and Usage Statistics (2023)*. Business of Apps. https://www.businessofapps.com/data/apple-music-statistics/#:~:text=Statistics%2C%20Company%20data-,Apple%20Music%20users,million%20on%20the%20previous%20year

Earle, A. (2022). *High Fidelity (HiFi)*. Deezer. https://support.deezer.com/hc/en-gb/articles/115004588345-High-Fidelity-HiFi-

Forbes. (2023). *Martin Lorentzon*. https://www.forbes.com/profile/martin-lorentzon/

Forristal, L. (2022). *YouTube Music and Premium top 80 million paid subscribers*. Tech Crunch. https://techcrunch.com/2022/11/09/youtube-music-and-premium-top-80-million-paid-subscribers/?guccounter=1&guce_referrer=aHR0cHM6Ly93d3cuZ29vZ2xlLmNvbS8&guce_referrer_sig=AQAAAMAcNflnvqgfUUFdV-l2EQvA05k0QkQPi8b9UoR6eo1sKUzTdi-1NBSz1m1111CnbwvSo9O_HA-gCRNVDFPuxkg8631tNhyRTwsIfl8RDxOFtYnqe8GkbKTJ0mlca-NpUMMyXMbwpBimh9KMjmOFBXhRsxglnSiBuOLXRM_UfOr_c

Fortune. (2021). *A Quick Guide to Apple Music, Spotify, and More Top Music Streaming Services*. https://fortune.com/2017/09/11/spotify-apple-music-tidal-streaming/

Fuller, Z. (2018). *Spotify, Apple Music and Ad-Supported Streaming*. Midia Research. https://midiaresearch.com/blog/spotify-apple-music-and-ad-supported-streaming

Gerber, R. (2019). *The Freemium Model Is Coming To Music*. Forbes. https://www.forbes.com/sites/greatspeculations/2019/08/14/the-freemium-model-is-coming-to-music/

Gitnux. (2023). *The Most Surprising Deezer Statistics And Trends in 2023*. https://blog.gitnux.com/deezer-statistics/#:~:text=With%20over%2016%20million%20monthly,library%20of%2073%20million%20tracks

Kleinman, B. Z. (2019). *A brief history of Apple's iTunes*. BBC News. https://www.bbc.com/news/technology-48511006

Leonard, D. (2015). *Why Jay Z's Tidal Streaming-Music Service Has Been a Disaster*. Bloomberg. https://www.bloomberg.com/news/features/2015-05-28/why-jay-z-s-tidal-streaming-music-service-has-been-a-disaster

Li, S., Luo, Q., & Qiu, L. (2016). The Optimal Pricing Model of Digital Music: Subscription, Ownership or Mixed? SSRN *Electronic Journal, 1*(1), 1–60. doi:10.2139/ssrn.2884252

Pasick, A. (2022). *The magic that makes Spotify's Discover Weekly playlists so damn good*. Quartz. https://qz.com/571007/the-magic-that-makes-spotifys-discover-weekly-playlists-so-damn-good

Rys, D. (2016). *Tidal Claims Three Million Global Subscribers, Finally Releases Kanye's 'Pablo' Stream Numbers*. Billboard. https://www.billboard.com/pro/tidal-three-million-global-subscribers-kanye-west-pablo-streams/

Snapes, L., & Sweney, M. (2018). *YouTube to launch new music streaming service*. The Guardian. https://www.theguardian.com/music/2018/may/17/youtube-music-new-streaming-service-launch

Spotify. (2023). *About Spotify*. https://newsroom.spotify.com/company-info/

Susic, P. (2023). *31+ Fresh Amazon Music Statistics 2023: Revenue, Users, Subs*. HeadphonesAddict. https://headphonesaddict.com/amazon-music-statistics/#:~:text=How%20many%20people%20use%20Amazon,has%20around%2082.2%20million%20users

Wikström, P. (2022). *The Music Industry in an Age of Digital Distribution*. OpenMind. https://www.bbvaopenmind.com/en/articles/the-music-industry-in-an-age-of-digital-distribution/

Yassin, D., & Yassin, D. (2021). *A brief history of streaming services*. The Michigan Daily. https://www.michigandaily.com/music/brief-history-steaming-services/

Chapter 2
Turkish Origin Directors Living in Europe and Their Perspectives on Cinema

Gülbuğ Erol
Igdir University, Turkey

Mustafa Gülsün
https://orcid.org/0000-0002-1202-6246
Muş Alparslan University, Turkey

ABSTRACT

Cinema has replaced every story. This study tries to reveal the filmographies of Turkish directors living abroad in the contemporary Turkish cinema period. This study is important in that it tries to reveal how socio-cultural and economic events experienced on a global basis are reflected in the director's cinemas. The directors in question are names that are affiliated with both Turkish culture and the culture of the country they live in, so what they reflect in their films is important not only in terms of the culture in which they live and grow up, but also in terms of the culture they carry in their genes. The starting point of the study is how the directors try to express themselves in terms of narrative features and the subject covered. In this context, five Turkish directors who have lived and are living abroad were selected by purposive sampling method, and their films were analyzed using the qualitative case study method. As a result, directors reflected their feelings, thoughts, dreams, and the realities in their films.

INTRODUCTION

Cinema is an important communication tool that changes and transforms the societies in which it operates through a strong communication network (Hoşçan, 2015:17). Cinema emerges as an effective element in terms of helping people from different cultures get to know each other and destroying the prejudices in their minds (Özkan, 2014:340-349). Cinema, which is followed with interest by every member of the society, has become an art form by presenting changing lifestyles to the audience with different tech-

DOI: 10.4018/979-8-3693-0855-4.ch002

niques and has been in a constant development process. In our country, cinema, which is an important tool that enables the transformation of our society, whether in the pre-Republican or post-Republican period, has produced works that touch our culture and social structure (Karakaya, 2018:48-70). In today's world, which is described as a systematic century, there are very few people untouched by cinema. Even if there are no movie theaters in some places, there is internet, CD, television, etc. There is a place for cinema in every individual's world, with tools like these (Mencütekin, 2010:259-266). One of the main factors why cinema is seen as an art form and is loved so much is the directors. Each of the directors, who have large fan bases and whose works are followed with great curiosity, has brought a different breath to cinema. New era Turkish cinema started to make its presence felt in the world and in festivals since the mid-nineties. A new cinema world was created, going beyond the conventional Yeşilçam narrative. Young generation directors have a great share in creating this world (Hoşçan, 2015:21). The number of directors of Turkish origin who have contributed to the recognition of Turkish cinema, especially in Europe, is undeniable. In our study, these directors are discussed together with their cinema worlds.

According to data announced by the Ministry of Foreign Affairs in 2018, approximately 6 million Turkish citizens reside abroad. About 5.5 million of them live in European countries such as Germany, France and Italy. Immigrant Turkish citizens, called the third and fourth generations, have found a place for themselves in the societies they live in and have used the advantage of being members of two cultures. When looked at from a cinema perspective, the point that can be seen is that directors of Turkish origin act with a mixed identity when they transfer their experiences in the countries where they live and reside to cinema, and they also include their feelings and thoughts about Turkey in their works. In their works, they blended the past with the current time, touched on the ties with their country, and tried to present sections of the lives of immigrant citizens.

The common feature of such films is that they reflect the roles assumed by individuals in their immigration experiences in the context of their families and social environment relations. In these films, the directors try to convey their families' immigration experiences and lives, being immigrants within the traditional Turkish family, cultural and identity conflicts, and the break between generations. "In particular, films of this genre shot by directors identified as German Turks have achieved and continue to achieve significant success in the festivals they attend. (Özkoçak, 2019:431-452)

Based on this context, our directors and cinema worlds who successfully represent Turkey abroad have been examined.

METHOD

In the empirical part of the research, 5 directors living abroad were selected using the purposeful sampling method. The selected directors have created public opinion with their success abroad. They have received important awards at various festivals. Descriptive, thematic and categorical content analysis was preferred in the analysis study. Movies are analyzed in the light of data and converted into numerical data based on it; by looking at these data, inferences are made and generalizations are made.

FATIH AKIN

Originally from Trabzon, the director was born in Hamburg, Germany, in 1973. His interest in cinema started from an early age. This interest grew even more with the video films his family watched to satisfy their homesickness in the 80s (Kültür, 2017:3-17). Akın, who started his education at the Hamburg Visual Arts College in 1994 and completed it in 2000, won the "Audience Award" at the Hamburg International Short Film Festival with his first short film, "Sensin", which he wrote and directed in 1995 (Işıkoğlu, 2005:77). When defining himself, Akın says that he does not see himself as either Turkish or German, sometimes he feels like both, and sometimes he thinks he is neither. He has many interviews on this subject. In her interview with Ayşe Arman, she said the following:

Sometimes it is like that, sometimes it is like that. I am Turkish because I am very angry. You know, Turks get involved and fight; They are not calm, they always have a 'temper' and 'aggression'. This example sounds very familiar to me, but I also have German-like features. I was born and raised there and completed my education there. I speak German. The language that goes through my mind is German, the language in my dreams is German, I swear in German, I make love in German. Dude, I'm officially German! We are the new Germans. When does a German become a German? When she's blonde with blue eyes? Do I have to be like this? I don't believe in nationalities. I think this is a very old idea. (Sürmeli, 2017: 57)

The effects of the environment he lives in can be seen in Akın's films. He has witnessed the negative aspects of life since he was a child. Themes such as sexuality, violence, longing, anger, betrayal, passion, pain and fear are frequently encountered in his films. Along with these themes, characters who love living freely, clinging to life and pursuing happiness stand out in his films. Hıdıroğlu, İ., E., Yıldırım (20018:1369-1385). Akın, who is seen as one of the representatives of accented cinema, handled accented cinema in a way that made a difference in German cinema.

Table 1. Fatih Akın filmography

Year of Shooting	Title (Name) of the Film
2019	Altın Eldiven
2017	Paramparça
2016	Elveda Berlin
2014	Kesik
2012	Cennetteki Çöplük
2009	Aşka Ruhunu Kat
2008	Seni Seviyorum New York
2007	Yaşamın Kıyısında
2005	İstanbul Hatırası: Köprüyü Geçmek
2004	Duvara Karşı
2002	Solino
2000	Temmuz'da
1998	Kısa ve Acısız

Figure 1. Duvara Karşı film poster
Source: https://tr.wikipedia.org/wiki/DuvaraKarşı

FERZAN ÖZPETEK

Koçak, S., S., Tüplek, (2018:54-86) Ferzan Özpetek was born in Istanbul in 1959. After spending his childhood years in his country, he went to Italy in 1976 to study cinema history. The director, who immigrated to Italy with his family when he was 17, has been living there for 45 years (Şirin, 2019:77). Çinay, H., H., H., Sezerel (2020:111-136). Özpetek is a director known and followed with interest both in Italy and Turkey. Features of two cultures are frequently encountered in his films. Koçak, S., S., Tüplek, (2018:54-86) Local traces of Turkish culture attract attention in his films. For example, scenes about Mevlana in the movie Holy Shovel, scenes about the Ottoman Empire in the movie Harem Suare, and scenes of the Turkish Bath in the movie Hamam can be shown. Traces of Mediterranean culture are also blended in Özpetek's films. Subjects such as confrontation with the past and family ties are abundant in Özpeteğin's cinema. Özpetek, who prefers a simple presentation to exaggeration, uses comedy and drama together.

As a requirement of hybridizations in cinema, Özpetek Cinema was integrated into Mediterranean, Hollywood, and Italian Cinema. The analysis provides information about the process and change of global cultures meeting local culture through Ferzan Özpetek Cinema.

Özpetek, by making a bit of opposition in the context of traditions and customs, made gender impositions the subject of his films in the context of gender (İmançer, 2018). Far from gender, the director also used some orientalist representations in his films. The characters he created, the spaces he used, and the marginalizations bear traces of the east (Kaya, 2010).

Table 2. Ferhan Özpetek filmography

Year of Shooting	Name/Title of the Film
2019	Şans Tanrıçası
2017	Napoli'nin Sırrı
2017	İstanbul Kırmızısı
2014	Kemerlerinizi Bağlayın
2012	Şahane Misafir
2010	Serseri Mayınlar
2008	Mükemmel Bir Gün
2007	Bir Ömür Yetmez
2005	Kutsal Yürek
2003	Karşı Pencere
2001	Cahil Periler
1999	Harem Suare
1997	Hamam

Figure 2. İstanbul Kırmızısı film poster
Source: https://tr.wikipedia.org/wiki/%C4%B0stanbul_Kırmızısı

THOMAS ARSLAN

He was born in 1962. During his childhood, he lived in Ankara for a while because his father did his military service. He returned to Germany after staying in his homeland for 4 years. He started his cinema career with short films. He included the lives of immigrant families living in Germany in his films. He took his place among the important names of German new wave cinema with his film trilogy (Özkoçak, 2019:431-452). Arslan, a German filmmaker of Turkish origin, has a filmography consisting of many

Table 3. Thomas Arslan filmography

Year of Shooting	Name/Title of the Film
2013	Altın
2010	Gölgede
2007	Tatil
2001	Güzel Bir Gün
1999	Satıcı
1997	Kardeşler

Figure 3. Kardeşler film
Source: https://www.filmgalerie451.de/en/films/brothers-and-sisters

interesting works. The above-mentioned Berlin trilogy, consisting of The Brothers, The Salesman and A Beautiful Day, takes its subjects from the problems faced by the children of families immigrating to Germany. Recently, Arslan has been working against Hollywood cinema by using traditional film genres, which is one of the main aims of the Berlin School, of which he is known as a member (Reinhardt, 2013:6). Thomas Arslan, who saw himself as a writer, acted together with a group of cinema students who criticized the German approach to comedy. Later, after graduating from film school, he worked as a screenwriter and director. In addition to shooting many short films and documentaries between 1984 and 1992, Arslan has been working as a cinematographer and producer in many feature films in Germany since the early 1990s. (Whittier, 2007:24).

NECO ÇELIK

He was born in 1972 in Berlin, the capital of Germany. In addition to his director personality, he is also known for his writer personality. There are documentaries, short films and feature films. He worked hard to be accepted because he entered the community without any cinema education (http://kulturakademie-tarabya.de/tr/resident/neco-celik/).

He was born in 1972 in Berlin, the capital of Germany. In addition to his director personality, he is also known for his writer personality. There are documentaries, short films and feature films. He worked hard to be accepted because he entered the community without any cinema education (http://kulturakademie-tarabya.de/tr/resident/neco-celik/). Neco Çelik is considered among the second generation directors. His interest in cinema dates back to 1994. Before founding the film company, he was the leader of a gang called 36 Boys, consisting of Turkish youth, especially during the fall of the Berlin Wall. The main mission of this group is to fight against increasing fascism and hostility. Neco Çelik, whose first feature-length work, Urban Guerillas, received the Turkey – Germany Film Festival, Audience and Honorable Mention awards in 2004, deals with the stories of young people growing up in a multicultural and multi-identity environment. His other feature-length work, 15 Minutes in Low Fire, was shot in our country in 2006. In 2011, he became the first Turk to receive the Faust award, which is

Table 4. Neco Çelik filmography

Year of Shooting	Name/Title of the Film
2006	Kısık Ateşte 15 Dakika
2004	Şehir Gerillaları
2002	Günlük

Figure 4. Kısık Ateşte 15 Dakika film poster
Source: https://www.sinemalar.com/film/148/kisik-ateste-15-dakika

considered equivalent to the Oscar in German theater, with his opera interpretation of the movie Against the Wall (Özkoçak, 2019: 430-452). Neco Çelik is one of the German-born directors of Turkish origin who began to influence German cinema with his works since the 1990s. The subject of the films shot by these directors consisted of the daily life of Turks living in Germany. These films reflected the lives and experiences of Turks between their homeland and the country where they were born (Kaçmaz ve Yılmaz, 2014: 54-59).

BUKET ALAKUŞ

The director, who was born in Istanbul in 1971, settled in Germany since his childhood. After graduating from the Berlin Academy of Fine Arts in 1995, she started studying cinema. After graduating from the Berlin Academy of Fine Arts in 1995, she studied directing in Hamburg. Alakuş, like Fatih Akın, benefits from his past while creating his Works (Işıkoğlu, 2005:85).

The director, who was born in Istanbul in 1971, settled in Germany since his childhood. After graduating from the Berlin Academy of Fine Arts in 1995, he started studying cinema. Alakuş, like Fatih Akın, benefits from his past while creating his works. (Işıkoğlu, 2005:85). Buket Akkuş's films generally take their subjects from the lives of people who immigrated from Turkey to Germany. Akkuş is considered one of the leading producers of Turkish-German cinema. It has taken its place among the members of the German National Integration Plan. Because of this duty, it is important how harmony and integration come to life in his works. He received many awards with his first feature film called Anam. In his films, in parallel with gender, cultural and religious motifs, there is generally a representation of harmony that requires mutual and multifaceted responsibility (Kehya, 2023:34-50).

In an interview, Alakuş stated that the movie "Anam", which was screened for the first time at the Munich Film Festival in July 2001, received the "Audience Award". Reminding that "Anam" won the "Best Screenplay Award" at the Europe Grand Prize held in Genoa, Alakuş said that the film was awarded the "Max Ophüls Award" in January 2002 and the "Best Young Director Award" by the Otto Sprenger Foundation in February. He noted that he was deemed worthy. http://www.kameraarkasi.org/yonetmenler/buketalakus.html

The films of Buket Alakuş, one of the leading filmmakers in German-Turkish cinema, mostly represent individuals of Turkish immigration origin. It is important to see what kind of harmony and integration perspective is reflected in the films shot by Alakuş, who was among the delegations in the German National Integration Plan (2007). Starting with his multi-award-winning debut feature Anam – Meine Mutter (2001), Einmal Hans mit scharfer Soße [A Hans with Hot Sauce] (2013), Die Neu [The New Girl] (2015) and Der Hodscha und die Piepenkötter [The Hodja and The rise of integration is observed in the films Ms. Piepenkötter] (2016).

On the axis of gender, cultural and religious motifs in these films, there is generally a representation of harmony that requires mutual and multifaceted responsibility. When we analyze these four migration-themed films on the representation of integration, we move away from the cinema of sacrifice (those affected) and duty, and encounter socio-economically strong women with culture conflict, generation conflict, religious rights demands. It is important for us to consider Alakuş's films for the following reason: Conflicts and crises are generally turned into comedy or drama elements in these films, even if they arise from cultural reasons and certain fears and prejudices. Idealized representations and discourses are also necessary steps for integration by offering dialogue, discussion, listening and compromise.

Table 5. Buket Alakuş filmography

Year of Shooting	Name/Title of the Film
2006	Schnee im Sommer
2005	Başka Bir Lig
2001	Anam
1997	Schlüssel

Figure 5. Anam Film poster
Source: https://www.sinemalar.com/film/4895/anam

CONCLUSION

Cinema is one of the most important means of communication today. This art, which is followed with interest and curiosity by millions of people all over the world, is extremely effective in promoting countries and societies. Thanks to cinema, people have the opportunity to get to know countries or societies that they have not seen or know anything about, and they tend to change their opinions, whether positive or negative. Of course, it would be inevitable for an art of such importance to be of great importance. Quality productions, big budgets, and great efforts are indicators of this. Of course, many factors are involved in creating these works. One of the protagonists of these factors, perhaps the most important, is the directors.

In the process of intercultural communication and interaction, cinema is also at an important point as the intersection of cultures. The effective, fluid and dynamic structure of culture makes structural exchange and transition between cultures possible. Thus, transitions between cultural elements/elements with different dynamics may occur.

Turkish Cinema operates on certain controversial topics from time to time. Periods sometimes carry certain traces, but generally speaking, it is possible to examine Turkish Cinema in two main parts: traditional and contemporary. In this context, the second generation, that is, the directors of contemporary Turkish Cinema living abroad, have followed a path more commensurate with social developments, both with the subjects of their films and their narrative structures.

Their unique perspectives on cinema, the techniques they use, and the heroes they create bring with them their own fan base. People consider directors as an important criterion when choosing a movie. They can more or less guess what the movie they choose promises them. For example, when they decide to watch Fatih Akın's movie, they know that they will encounter scenes such as lust, pain and fear. From the perspective of our country's cinema, the role of directors is undeniable. The works they produce are important for the promotion of our country. In recent years, we have directors of Turkish origin who have successfully represented our country abroad. In our study, we had the opportunity to examine some of these directors.

REFERENCES

Çinay & Sezerel. (2020). Ferzan Özpetek Filmlerinde Gösterge Olarak Yemek: Mine Vaganti/Serseri Mayınlar Üzerine Bir İnceleme. *Journal Of Tourism And Gastronomy Studies,* (8), 111-136.

Cormican, M. (2013). Kültürlerarası Etkileşimde Sinemanın Rolü: Ferzan Özpetek Ve Fatih Akın Filmlerinde Kültürlerarasılık. *International Journal of Science Culture and Sport,* (1), 340-349.

Göktürk, D. (2004). Yüksel Yavuz's Kleine Freiheit / A Little Bit of Freedom. *TRANSIT, 1*(1)

Hıdıroğlu & Yıldırım. (2018). Fatih Akın Filmlerinde Geleneksel Simgelerin Temsili. *Atatürk Üniversitesi Sosyal Bilimler Enstitüsü Dergisi*, (3), 1369-1385.

Hoşçan, Ç. (2015). *Arzu ve İktidar: Ferzan Özpetek Sineması Üzerinden Eleştirel bir Bakış*. Doğu Kitabevi.

Işıkoğlu, D. (2005). Kültürlerin Kesişimi, Aksanlı Sinema ve Almanya'daki 2. ve 3. Kuşak Türk Yönetmenlerin Sinemasal Üretimi (Yayımlanmamış Yüksek Lisans Tezi). İstanbul Üniversitesi, Radyo, İstanbul, Türkiye.

Kacmaz, E. G., & Yilmaz, T. (2014). Fatih Akin Filmlerinde Gercekligin Temsili Representing Reality in Fatih Akin Films. Betonart: Concrete. *Architectural Design*, (41), 54–59.

Karakaya, H. (2018). Türk Sinemasında Din Adamı Tiplemesi. *Munzur üniversitesi Sosyal Bilimler Dergisi*, (12), 48-70.

Kehya, R. Ö. (2023). Alman-Türk Sinemasında Bir Entegrasyon Yönetmeni: Buket Alakuş. *Diyalog*, 34-50.

Koçak & Tüplek. (2018). Yönetmen Ferzan Özpetek'in İstanbul Kırmızısı Filminin Türkiye Tanıtımı Çerçevesinde İncelenmesi: Göstergebilimsel Bir İnceleme. *BUJSS,* (11), 546-86.

Kültür, N. (2017). Aksanlı Sinema ve Fatih Akın. *Maltepe Üniversitesi İletişim Fakültesi Dergisi*, (2), 3-17.

Mencütekin, M. (2010). Sinema Dili, Film Retoriği ve İmgelenen Anlama Ulaşma. *Arel Üniversitesi İletişim Fakültesi,* (34), 259-266.

Özgün Kehya, R. (2023). Alman-Türk Sinemasında Bir Entegrasyon Yönetmeni: Buket Alakuş. *Diyalog Interkulturelle Zeitschrift Für Germanistik, 11*(1), 34 – 50.

Özkoçak, Y. (2019). Göçmen Ve Sinema Avrupa Göçmen Sineması Ve Türk Asıllı Yönetmenler. *Stratejik ve Sosyal Araştırmalar Dergisi*, (3), 431-452.

Reinhardt, B. (2013). *Gold by Thomas Arslan: Always on the move but why, and where?* World Socialist Web Site.

Şirin, Y. (2019). *Oryantalizm Bağlamında Ferzan Özpetek Sineması (Yayımlanmamış Yüksek Lisans Tezi).* Maltepe Üniversitesi, Radyo, Sinema ve Televizyon.

Sürmeli, Z. (2017). *Sinemada Oryantalist ve Oksidentalist Fatih Akın Filmleri Örneği (Yayımlanmamış Yüksek Lisans Tezi).* Ordu Üniversitesi, Sinema ve Televizyon.

Vaganti, M. (2021). *Mine Vaganti (Losse Cannons).* Tr Beca Film Festival.

Whittier, J. B. (2007). *Representatıons Of Germans And The Use Of Language In Turksıhgerman Fılms By Fatıh Akın And Thomas Arslan* [Thesis]. The University of Georgia.

Chapter 3
The Impact of Social Media on Communication

Azadeh Eskandarzadeh
University of Canada West, Canada

ABSTRACT

This chapter delves into how social media has transformed the way we communicate with one another both on a level and on a scale. The authors analyze theories such as the uses and gratification theory and perspectives on communication. Additionally, they explore platforms like Facebook, Twitter, YouTube, and blogs. They evaluate the impact of media on forming relationships and building social connections. Furthermore, they assess how organizations utilize media for marketing, advertising, and engaging with customers. They also examine emerging trends in citizen journalism and changes in how people consume news. Critical examination is given to issues surrounding privacy concerns, surveillance, misinformation, activism, polarization, and filter bubbles. Finally, they highlight the influence of influencer marketing, social audio/video platforms, and the internet of things on forms of social communication.

INTRODUCTION

According to Boyd and Ellison (2007) social media has completely revolutionized the way individuals communicate profoundly impacting our interactions and information sharing, in todays era. It's truly astonishing to witness the popularity of platforms like Facebook, Twitter and YouTube as of January 2022. In fact Clement (2022) reports that there are over 4.5 billion users engaging with media globally. Over the decades communication technologies have undergone significant transformations due to the emergence and widespread adoption of digital media. The advent of media platforms has significantly transformed the landscape by facilitating connections and information exchange, between people (Kaplan & Haenlein 2010). As highlighted by Perrin (2015) billions of individuals now rely on media to connect stay informed and spend their lives. With its presence social media has become a part of our everyday routines enabling global communication and fostering connectivity. This paper will delve into examining how social media impacts our communication dynamics and interpersonal interactions.

DOI: 10.4018/979-8-3693-0855-4.ch003

In this exploration we will delve into theories and research surrounding topics such, as managing relationships, media consumption habits organizational strategies and the emerging challenges they bring. Our main objective is to understand the impact of media on communication from perspectives.

While social media offers opportunities it also presents challenges that require consideration from various angles (Tufekci, 2017). The purpose of this chapter is to examine this subject by utilizing theories and discussing current issues. Social media refers to platforms where individuals can create and share their own content. Popular examples include Facebook and LinkedIn for connecting with friends and colleagues through profile creation and interaction. There are also microblogging services like Twitter for sharing updates and following others. Additionally there are media sharing sites like YouTube and Instagram for uploading and viewing videos/photos (Obar & Wildman 2015).

The term "media" describes communication technologies that are connected, interactive and accessible, at any time (Jenkins, 2006).

This encompasses not platforms like Facebook and Twitter but other forms of online communication such, as websites, blogs, videos and podcasts (Deuze, 2006). Digital communication revolves around the sharing of information using media and technology. It encompasses ways in which people can interact using computers, mobile devices and the internet (Lievrouw & Livingstone 2006). The aim of this chapter is to examine the evolution of media and its impact on different aspects of communication. We will achieve this by exploring theories conducting real world investigations and analyzing examples. In the chapter we will delve into a range of intriguing topics that explore how individuals utilize media communicate within organizations engage in journalism practices and tackle emerging issues. These sections collectively offer an understanding of how social media's shaping and being shaped by communication, in the digital era (Boyd, 2014).

Evolution of Communication Models

Traditional Models

In the past, mass media used a broadcasting model where only a few organisations could share information with a large audience. According to Deuze (2006), newspapers and magazines were the initial types of mass media, giving publishers and editors control over the production and distribution of content. In the 20th century, this method was created to bring audiovisual content to people through radio and television. It allowed for the distribution of material to large audiences who could passively consume it (Papa et al., 2000).

Stages of Transition

The rise of technologies related to information and communication during the 20th century disrupted traditional ways of mass communication (Williams & Edge 1996). In the 1980s and 1990s individuals who were quick to adopt these technologies engaged in interactions through platforms, like BBSes, IRC and listservs that were primarily user driven (Cummings et al., 2002). Wellman (2001) suggests that the internets emergence as an easily accessible platform brought about a shift towards more open forms of communication and collaboration. Moving into the 2000s there was an increase in broadband and mobile internet access enabling consumers to both consume and create content referred to as prosumers (Jenkins, 2006). Platforms like blogs and wikis provided opportunities for individuals to share their thoughts and ideas freely while social networks such, as Friendster and Myspace introduced means of connecting with others (Boyd, 2008). Since then smartphones and applications have become ubiquitous worldwide resulting in these changes where digital connectivity has become a part of our daily lives for everyone involved (Boulos et al., 2011).

Converged Landscapes

According to Deuze (2007) the current communication landscape is a combination of channels and grassroots involvement made possible by Web 2.0 technology and mobile connectivity. New media places emphasis, on participation contributions from non professionals and interaction among participants (Jenkins, 2008). On the hand traditional media still focuses on curating and distributing content. This ongoing interplay between grassroots communication highlights the convergence of separate modes into integrated multiplatform environments (Bruns, 2008).

Boyd (2010) suggests that the rise of media exemplifies a shift towards models as it enables sharing experiences fostering connections and facilitating community exchanges on an unprecedented scale. Furthermore Benkler (2006) argues that new networked publics have emerged due to the redefinition of who can communicate how they can do so and for what purpose in response, to evolving arrangements.

Theoretical Foundations

People actively seek out forms of media to meet their needs, such, as gaining information socializing and finding entertainment (Katz et al. 1974). On media platforms individuals connect with others and share updates and content in order to feel validated and find a sense of belonging within communities (Whiting & Williams 2013). Theories on communication view these interactions as occurring through networks, where individuals take on roles like friends, followers and members of circles (Wellman et al., 2003). Convergence culture refers to the merging of media with user generated activities on emerging platforms (Jenkins, 2006). These theoretical perspectives provide insights into the underlying motivations and patterns of interaction facilitated by media.

Social Medias Impact on Relationship Maintenance

Ellison et al. (2007) suggest that social media makes it easier for people to maintain connections with networks thereby strengthening ties and building social capital. However it is important to note that excessive use of interactions can potentially weaken relationships as highlighted by Roberts and David in their study conducted in 2020. Putnam (2000) emphasizes that social media does not help strengthen relationships, within our circles but also encourages us to connect with a diverse range of people. Based on a study conducted by Bozicevic and Lüders in 2019 research has indicated that platforms can play a role, in facilitating connections with others be it for professional purposes. Nonetheless the task of managing networks can prove daunting due, to concerns surrounding privacy and the need to control information.

Organizational Uses of Social Media

Many businesses depend on platforms to connect with their target audience. They achieve this through methods such, as targeted ads, direct marketing, customer support, public relations and internal communication (Mangold & Faulds 2009). According to Trainor (2012) companies can boost brand loyalty by using real time messaging to interact with customers. Additionally providing customer service through media platforms can enhance service quality. However not having control, over publicity can pose various challenges as pointed out by Li and Suh (2015). Organizations rely on tools to improve engagement and evaluate the effectiveness of their strategies (Hoffman & Fodor 2010). Targeted advertising enables the targeting of audiences based on demographic, interest and behavior data (Kietzmann et al., 2011). Customized ad formats are designed to engage user personas.Direct social selling involves leveraging influencer marketing by collaborating with accounts and personalities to authentically promote brands within their follower communities (Freberg et al. 2011).When it comes to customer service handling issues publicly, on media platforms helps build trust while addressing matters privately can ensure better resolution. The quality of care can be assessed through sentiment analysis (Stieglitz & Dang Xuan, 2013). In times of crisis communication plans train spokespersons to monitor platforms respond promptly and turn publicity into positive outcomes using empathy, transparency and relationship building techniques (Coombs, 2007).

Internal collaboration tools facilitate work by enabling brainstorming sessions providing project updates and informal resource sharing opportunities. This enhances productivity and fosters innovation among team members (Treem & Leonardi 2013).

Analytics play a role in extracting business intelligence from metrics such as follower growth rate, engagement levels, referral traffic data and conversions (Hoffman & Fodor 2010). Setting goals aligned with performance indicators helps optimize return on investment.

Emerging tools utilize intelligence to deepen our understanding of consumers through modeling of future needs. Additionally they automate social media interactions, on a scale.

Emerging Issues and the Road Ahead

There are issues to consider including privacy violations, the potential, for widespread surveillance, reliance on technology the spread of false information the weakening of activism and increasing political divisions (Tufekci, 2017). According to Latzer et al. (2016) finding a balance in policy frameworks that allows for expression encourages innovation and ensures community wellbeing can be quite challenging. Gillespie (2018) emphasizes the need for collaboration between platforms, governments and civil society to effectively regulate media and empower its users. To fully harness the benefits of media while mitigating its impacts continued research is essential to understand its effects on areas such as technology advancement, economy dynamics and societal changes. The significant reliance of platforms on data collection for targeted advertising has heightened concerns, over privacy breaches and surveillance practices (Zuboff 2019). Various issues may arise from this practice including identity theft or profiling which could potentially lead to oppression or even the concept of "pre crime" (Lyon 2001).

Misinformation campaigns exploit technological vulnerabilities to sow doubt among the public confuse voters and hinder fact based discussions (Lazer et al., 2018). While platforms are striving to address this issue it remains challenging for policies to differentiate between propaganda and authentic political expression (Wardle & Derakhshan 2017).

As highlighted by Tufekci (2017) digital organizing plays a role, in empowering activism. However it is important to acknowledge that there are also movements that leverage the digital platforms to mobilize their own causes. Flaxman et al. (2016) establish a link between the amplification of viewpoints and the creation of "echo chambers," which subsequently contributes to heightened emotional polarization in the real world.

The design of technologies has the potential to diminish peoples engagement with their communities and families exacerbating health concerns—particularly among young individuals who are more susceptible to comparing themselves with others (Andreassen, 2015; Twenge, 2017). We require intervention models that strike a balance, between openness prioritizing well being and considering interests.

CONCLUSION

Social media has opened up possibilities for people to connect and communicate. However it has also brought about challenges and complexities. To navigate this landscape effectively it is crucial for researchers, companies and public authorities to collaborate with a focus, on rights and solid evidence. By making choices and being mindful of our actions we can fully enjoy the benefits of networking while safeguarding our democratic values and well being. In the future it will be important to monitor how people use technology to ensure that everyone can access its advantages in an inclusive manner. The impact of media on individuals, communities and society, as a whole has been significant. It has greatly improved our ability to connect with one another and participate in activities. However guiding these platforms towards inclusivity can be challenging.

By delving into the psychological and political aspects involved we can develop a better understanding of how technology can be designed to respect the dignity and universal rights of all humanity.

To develop policies it's essential to have an understanding of how platform business models function and consider the communication needs of regular individuals. To ensure navigation of the world public education should prioritize teaching fundamental digital and media skills. These skills empower individuals to critically analyze and engage with the messages we encounter online on a basis. As technology advances beyond our comprehension it may be worth considering implementing regulations or design focused measures, for added protection.

Developed governance frameworks offer a glimmer of hope in striking a balance between openness and security. They also address concerns regarding well being and accountability which's quite reassuring. Achieving this goal involves implementing these frameworks in a manner that fosters transparent partnerships with all parties. However, it's crucial to approach changes with humility and remain open to reassessing our objectives.

In general, as seen with transformative technologies, society holds the power to steer innovations, towards humanity's interests through wisdom, caution and collaborative efforts despite our differences.

The continuous evolution of media is yet to be realized and its future impact will depend on our ability to strike a balance, between various elements, including empathy, foresight and fairness for every individual, within virtual and real-life communities.

REFERENCES

Benkler, Y. (2006). *The wealth of networks: How social production transforms markets and freedom.* Yale University Press.

Boulos, M. N., Wheeler, S., Tavares, C., & Jones, R. (2011). How smartphones are changing the face of mobile and participatory healthcare: An overview, with example from eCAALYX. *Biomedical Engineering Online*, *10*(1), 1–14. doi:10.1186/1475-925X-10-24 PMID:21466669

Boyd, D. (2008). Why youth (heart) social network sites: The role of networked publics in teenage social life. In D. Buckingham (Ed.), Youth, identity, and digital media (pp. 119-142). The MIT Press.

Boyd, D. M. (2014). *It's complicated: The social lives of networked teens*. Yale University Press.

boyd, d. (2010). Social network sites as networked publics: Affordances, dynamics, and implications. In Z. Papacharissi (Ed.), *Networked self: Identity, community, and culture on social network sites* (pp. 39-58). Routledge.

Bruns, A. (2008). *Blogs, Wikipedia, second life, and beyond: From production to produsage*. Peter Lang.

Cummings, J. N., Sproull, L., & Kiesler, S. B. (2002). Beyond hearing: Where real-world and online support meet. *Group Dynamics*, *6*(1), 78–88. doi:10.1037/1089-2699.6.1.78

Deuze, M. (2006). Participation, remediation, bricolage: Considering principal components of a digital culture. *The Information Society*, *22*(2), 63–75. doi:10.1080/01972240600567170

Deuze, M. (2007). Media work. *Polity*.

Ellison, N. B., Steinfield, C., & Lampe, C. (2007). The benefits of Facebook "friends:" Social capital and college students' use of online social network sites. *Journal of Computer-Mediated Communication*, *12*(4), 1143–1168. doi:10.1111/j.1083-6101.2007.00367.x

Gillespie, T. (2018). *Custodians of the Internet: Platforms, content moderation, and the hidden decisions that shape social media*. Yale University Press.

Hoffman, D. L., & Fodor, M. (2010). Can you measure the ROI of your social media marketing? *MIT Sloan Management Review*, *52*(1).

Jenkins, H. (2006). *Convergence culture: Where old and new media collide*. NYU Press.

Jenkins, H., Ford, S., & Green, J. (2013). *Spreadable media: Creating value and meaning in a networked culture*. NYU Press.

Kaplan, A. M., & Haenlein, M. (2010). Users of the world, unite! The challenges and opportunities of Social Media. *Business Horizons*, *53*(1), 59–68. doi:10.1016/j.bushor.2009.09.003

Katz, E., Blumler, J. G., & Gurevitch, M. (1974). Utilization of mass communication by the individual. In J. G. Blumler & E. Katz (Eds.), *The uses of mass communications: Current perspectives on gratifications research* (pp. 19–32). Sage.

Kietzmann, J. H., Hermkens, K., McCarthy, I. P., & Silvestre, B. S. (2011). Social media? Get serious! Understanding the functional building blocks of social media. *Business Horizons*, *54*(3), 241–251. doi:10.1016/j.bushor.2011.01.005

Latzer, M., Hollnbuchner, K., Just, N., & Saurwein, F. (2016). *The economics of algorithmic selection on the Internet*. Springer. doi:10.4337/9780857939852.00028

Li, C., & Suh, A. (2015). Factors influencing information credibility on social media platforms: Evidence from Facebook pages. *Proceedings of the Association for Information Science and Technology*, *52*(1), 1–4. doi:10.1002/pra2.2015.145052010030

Lievrouw, L. A., & Livingstone, S. (Eds.). (2006). *Handbook of new media: Social shaping and social consequences*. Sage.

Mangold, W. G., & Faulds, D. J. (2009). Social media: The new hybrid element of the promotion mix. *Business Horizons*, *52*(4), 357–365. doi:10.1016/j.bushor.2009.03.002

Obar, J. A., & Wildman, S. (2015). Social media definition and the governance challenge: An introduction to the special issue. *Telecommunications Policy*, *39*(9), 745–750. doi:10.1016/j.telpol.2015.07.014

Papa, M. J., Singhal, A., & Papa, W. H. (2000). *Organizing for social change: A dialectical journey of theory and praxis*. Sage Publications.

Perrin, A. (2015). *Social Media Usage: 2005-2015*. Pew Research Center. Retrieved from http://www. pewinternet. org/2015/10/08/social-networking-usage-2005-2015

Putnam, R. D. (2000). *Bowling alone: The collapse and revival of American community*. Simon and Schuster.

Roberts, S. J., & David, M. E. (2020). *The social media party: Politics in a Facebook world*. Oxford University Press.

Trainor, K. J. (2012). Relating social media technologies to performance: A capabilities-based perspective. *Journal of Personal Selling & Sales Management*, *32*(3), 317–331. doi:10.2753/PSS0885-3134320303

Tufekci, Z. (2017). *Twitter and tear gas: The power and fragility of networked protest*. Yale University Press.

Wellman, B. (2001). Physical place and cyberplace: The rise of personalized networking. *International Journal of Urban and Regional Research*, *25*(2), 227–252. doi:10.1111/1468-2427.00309

Wellman, B., Haase, A. Q., Witte, J., & Hampton, K. (2001). Does the Internet increase, decrease, or supplement social capital? Social networks, participation, and community commitment. *The American Behavioral Scientist*, *45*(3), 436–455. doi:10.1177/00027640121957286

Whiting, A., & Williams, D. (2013). Why people use social media: A uses and gratifications approach. *Qualitative Market Research*, *16*(4), 362–369. doi:10.1108/QMR-06-2013-0041

Williams, R., & Edge, D. (1996). The social shaping of technology. *Research Policy*, *25*(6), 865–899. doi:10.1016/0048-7333(96)00885-2

Chapter 4
Cyber Habitat of Digital Culture: A View on the Political Economy of Culture

Berna Berkman Köselerli
Giresun University, Turkey

ABSTRACT

This study aims to reveal the cultural aspects of digital society by discussing the views of scholars in the field. In liberal digital culture debates, digital platforms are regarded as alternative meeting places and democratic user-friendly spaces. As it is known, cutural materials can be deployed easily, instantly, and globally through digital technologies. People build online communities and share photos, videos, images, opinions with others by using social networks. Critical digital culture studies pointed out that the digital platform companies dominate the digital culture industry. Digital culture is shaped by the capitalist accumulation, so the functions of digital platforms are limited. In this study, digital culture is defined to build common meanings, values, experiences, and practices via digital platforms. In addition, a dialectic model is developed to comprehend the digital culture together with the political economic structure that transform it.

INTRODUCTION

Digital technologies enable users to access information easily and diminish the cost of participation in cultural fields. In digital culture, people are both consumers and producers of cultural artifacts produced on digital platforms. Digital platforms are the new spaces of culture and allow the distribution of cultural artifacts, contents, and expressions.

The period when digital culture began to form in our daily lifes can be traced back to the 1980s after the invention of personal computers which are used in homes. As David C. Mowery and Timothy Simcoe cite that researches on computer networking began in the early 1960s, rougly 15 years after the invention of computer. Use of the Internet was primarly limited to researchers, computer scientists, and networking engineers through at least 1985. The commercial exploitation of the Internet that began in the 1990s after the Cold War era (Mowery and Simcoe, 2002: 1371-1385). It can be said that with the entrance of networks into commercial use in 1990s, digital culture has become established on a global level.

DOI: 10.4018/979-8-3693-0855-4.ch004

The framework of this study is based on digital culture debates in the past few decades. Digital culture studies can be gathered under two main approaches. First, liberal digital culture studies mention that technology has a binding effect on the culture and transforms the whole society. Technological determinists take part in liberal digital cultural studies.

According to Thomas V. Reed, technological determinists suggest that technologies are the most important force driving human history and society. Technological determinism ignores the fact that technologies emerge from various social and cultural groups. Culture creates technologies (Reed, 2019: 10).

The other main approach in digital culture studies is the critical view. As Reed says, critical digital culture analysis has a rejection of technological determinism. They argue that technologies and cultures never be neatly separated, since technical innovations are always created by individuals and groups shaped by cultural assumptions and biases, and technologies are always used in particular cultural contexts that reshape them even as they partly reshape the cultural contexts (Reed, 2019: 12).

Besides, there is a need for critical digital culture studies to investigate how political economy structures influence the field of digital culture. Digital culture studies generally neglect the activity of huge companies that dominate the digital culture platforms. Whereas cultural products, content creativity, and information flow are raised in a cyber habitat controlled by conglomerates.

There is a relationship between technological developments and the political economy of media, marketing, and entertainment fields. For instance, marketing firms are using digital technologies to assemble databases about consumers and to target campaigns based on information through their surveillance (Klinenberg and Benzecry, 2005: 9). New communication technologies have reduced the price of entry into a cultural field. Digital networks and infrastructure systems allow cultural producers to instantaneously transmit enormous amounts of information across the globe (Klinenberg and Benzecry, 2005: 8-11). Information flow in digital platforms is controlled by market forces. The field of digital culture has been shaped by concentrations in ownership. The largest media companies remain in possession of the market and cultural production. In this context, it is important to comprehend the cultural field in terms of the political and economic system.

Eric Klinenberg and Claudio Benzecry identify three organizing schools while explaining the character of cultural changes driven by digital technologies: digital revolutionaries, the cyber-skeptics, the cultural evolutionists (Klinenberg and Benzecry, 2005: 13). Digital revolutionaries (such as N. Negroponte, W. Mitchell, D. Haraway, and M. Castells) argued that new technologies have caused structural changes in cultural production. Cyber-skeptics (such as J. Turow, P. Howard, and Frankfurt School representatives) see digitization as a mechanism through which culture industries advance larger projects, thereby threatening the integrity of creative fields or the relative autonomy of artists and intellectuals. According to these scholars, technology is an effect of investments driven by economic, political, or cultural interests and not a basic force of change. Cultural evolutionists (such as P. Hirsch, R. Peterson, D. Berger, and C. Kadushin) emphasized the organizational and institutional change between periods of technological development (Klinenberg and Benzecry, 2005: 13-15).

Some scholars have branched out the concept of digital culture as cyberculture. Madhavi Malapragada as one of them, frames an interdisciplinary approach to cyberculture studies. According to this scholar, digital culture studies neglect the relationship between virtual life and real life, cyberspace and home (Malapragada, 2006: 200). On the other hand, there is a gap in cybercultural studies that engage with the different disciplinary formations of diaspora studies, gender studies, postcolonial studies, and media and cultural studies. Cyberculture studies are inadequate in addressing the diverse representations of home on the Web, the transnational social imaginaries, and the reconfiguration of home in the new global order (Malapragada, 2006: 201-202).

The framework of this study is based on the discussion of digital culture studies. In this study, the habitual features of digital culture are described. A definition of digital culture will be made and a dialectical model will be developed in the cultural field to comprehend the relation between the political economic system and digital culture.

BACKGROUND

The concept of culture is interpreted in different meanings in literature. Cultural relations and practices which are at the core of everyday life are produced in social formations. Culture is transferred to other societies and future generations by forms and means of communication. According to Raymond Williams culture, first, came to mean, the general state or habit of the mind. Second, it came to mean, the general state of intellectual development, in a society as a whole. Third, it came to mean, the general body of the arts. Fourth, it came to mean, a whole way of life, material, intellectual and spiritual. As Willams says culture is affected by the great historical changes which changes in industry, democracy, and class (Williams, 1960: XIV). Williams draws attention to its connection with daily life by calling culture a whole way of life and states that it has been shaped by historical processes.

According to Theodor W. Adorno and Max Horkheimer culture has become industrial after enlightenment. This development leads to the commodification of culture. Adorno and Horkheimer use the term 'culture industry' to describe the nature of mass production and mass culture. In their terms, culture has begun to infect everything with sameness. The use of standard products to meet the same needs in the culture industry. The technology of the culture industry confines itself to standardization and mass production. Technology is serving in favor of those with a strong economic position (Adorno and Horkheimer, 2002: 95). In this argument, technical rationality is the main feature of the culture industry in the 1940s. After the 1980s with neoliberal economy policies, technical rationality dominated in cultural field. Huge companies increased their investments in technological innovations. Capitalism continued to exist by spreading at a global level. Network technology has become a new tool for the control of market forces and state actors. State actors have become supporters of neoliberal policies which is to the benefit of market forces. With the commercialization of network technology after the 1990s, the culture industry turned digital culture literally into a field for profit.

Culture includes a society's art, beliefs, customs, games, technologies, traditions, and institutions. It also encompasses a society's mode of communication: the creation and use of symbol systems that convey information and meaning. Culture may be defined as the symbols of expression that individuals, groups, and societies use to make sense of daily life and articulate their values. The mass media are the cultural industries as the channels of communication that create and distribute cultural products to people (Campbell, Martin, and Fabos, 2014: 6). Digital platforms are the new field of the culture industry allowing the production of cultural artifacts and contents.

According to Reed, culture is the values, beliefs, and behaviors that are typical and define a group. Culture is fluid, not a neatly bounded entity. Cultural meanings are never settled, they are always subject to contestation (Reed, 2019: 2). New phase of globalization is the spread of digital communication networks. In other words, communication technologies are the key force of neoliberal globalization. Digital culture depends on the thinking and acting of users, including the decisions of citizens and consumers who are using new technologies (Reed, 2019: 3-5). Digital culture is mediated by not only the users but also the owners activity. Communication flow on digital platforms isn't linear, mediated by the dialectic activity of these actors. Digital platforms has become the field of struggle of these actors. Users create contents, share opinions, make comments by interacting with each other. Besides cultural activities of users are restricted, shaped and commodified by owners. Users are seperated by age, gender, ethnicity and class. However due to the conveniences brought by technology, class differences are invisible in network and they appear as equal citizens. Whereas inequalities are reinforced in digital platforms. So there is a contestation over the cultural meanings produced by actors.

Levin Ilya and David Mamlok discussed the concept of culture in their work in terms of human experience. Ilya and Mamlok considered culture as an experience of an information shell which is a human creation. According to them, in digital culture, the interaction of almost every human experience is mediated through a sophisticated shell connected to big data. The shell provides a person with context-oriented information. The restructuring of society and culture can be related to the transformation of the human experience (Ilya and Mamlok, 2021: 1-2).

In terms of time, the hyper-connectivity coupled with digital technologies led to the expedition of action. In terms of space, one can work, communicate, consume, and conduct many other actions from almost every place on the globe (Ilya and Mamlok, 2021: 3). Those changes reshaped how people interact with themselves and how they recognize their self-conceptions. Digital technologies stipulate new modes of action and reshape human experience.

According to Ilya and Mamlok digital culture is composed of a three-dimensional space of culture: spiritual culture, social culture, and technological culture. A characteristic feature of all forms of spiritual culture is that they have a combination of knowledge and values. Spiritual culture is the cognitive value of the cultural space. Spiritual culture consists of diverse forms of human activities in the network, including creating kinds of text, photos, and videos of various contents and forms (Ilya and Mamlok, 2021: 6-7). The spiritual culture also includes self-perceptions and identities. Personal identity in a hyper-connected world allows the person to present her/his identity differently than in reality (Ilya and Mamlok, 2021: 8). Besides, social culture is most expressed in the digital society in the new dynamics of public consciousness formation. A prominent feature of social culture in the network society is that people are both consumers and content producers. Informational openness is the basic feature of the social culture of digital society (Ilya and Mamlok, 2021: 9-10).

Spiritual and social cultures are aimed at creating values and ideals, while the technological culture focuses on what and how to do it. Technical values colonize its spiritual values. The economic organization which is based on technical developments reinforces the spread of consumerist society. Rationality plays an essential role in reshaping almost every field in the technological culture of digital society. Today's cyberspace can be understood as an effective tool for accessing information and knowledge. This affects human experience and worldviews (Ilya and Mamlok, 2021: 10-11).

Culture contributes to the formation of cultural identities which are shaped by beliefs, values, and cultural practices. According to Aiswaria G. Shajan, culture can be defined as the mouth of a community that speaks about the unique identity of a community which shows the cumulative deposit of knowledge, value systems, ruling bodies, experiences, perspectives attitudes, etc. Digital culture refers same qualities of a culture, yet the communication and practices are interacting on digital networks only in digital culture (Shajan, 2023: 31). Digital culture is a concept that defines the culture of humans that developed as part of technological interactions. Individuals and groups of society are interconnected and inseparable in digital relations of digital culture (Shajan, 2023: 34). Digital identities which are built in digital culture, are related to beliefs, values, practices, and individual expressions that can define a person or a group of society. Digital identity has two modes: the original and the fake. The original is attached with the personal identification that relates to national citizenship. The fake identity is used for dark deeds by hiding real identity on digital platforms (Shajan, 2023: 33). The disadvantages of digital platforms are fake identities, security issues, manipulation, and exploitation can be possible, plagiarism and copyright issues, social isolation, addiction, etc. The advantages of digitalization are as; less expensive, time savings, communication made easy, interactivity, social connectivity, distance never becomes an excuse, versatile working, learning opportunities are more, information at your fingertips, e-payments, e-purchases, in short everything is set with a click (Shajan, 2023: 32). Digital culture also can be explained by the negative and positive functions of digital technologies. Yet this view handles the construction of culture from a narrow perspective. There is a need to examine the cultural field together with the structures that transform it.

According to Mark Deuze, digital culture can be expressed as the interaction of humans and machines in the context of computerization and the digitalization of society. People produce and consume information in a way of interactive and gives meaning to their lives. The emergence of a fragmented, edited, connected, and networked worldview in itself is part of digital culture (Deuze, 2006: 66). As Deuze says, digital culture has three constitutive features: "participation" as the process of meaning-making, "remediation" as modifying and manipulating reality in the remix of old and new media, "bricolage" in terms of assembly, disassembly, and reassembly of mediated reality (Deuze, 2006: 66). Participation is a feature of digital culture, people produce cultural artifacts easily and interact with each other thanks to digital platforms. Digital platforms which have functions like traditional public spheres, circulate views and expressions. Yet this virtual sphere is fragmented and mediated. So the reality produced in digital platforms is mediated and is ready to be manipulated. The reality which consists of digital codes has become virtual. The virtual reality in digital platforms is different from daily life. Besides, manipulated information can be deployed by the users activity. So this leads ethical issues in terms of the use of digital platforms. Virtual reality appears as a edited reality which is accuracy can not be assured.

Charlie Gere sees digitalization as a marker of culture since it encompasses both the artifacts and the systems of signification and communication which include our contemporary way of life. Technology is a tool that has contributed to the development of our current digital culture (Gere, 2014: 16-18) According to Gere, new technology and a capitalist economy produce a new kind of capitalist techno-culture (Gere, 2014: 148). Network technology is a responsive tool for personal needs and niche concerns and a kind of bottom-up model of organization. Web as a space for collaboration and reciprocal communication. What Gere wants to point out is that, social network software such as Facebook, YouTube, and Flickr; peer-to-peer software for sharing digital music and video files such as Napster and BitTorrent; search engines such as Google; new forms of public debate and self-expression such as blogs and podcasts; new forms of organizing and distributing knowledge such as Wikipedia make the users more active (Gere, 2014: 212-218).

As Gere says, the emerging digital culture is an interlinked and participatory nature in an increasingly atomized society. There is an opposition between greater cooperation and increasing atomization in digital culture. We live in a world in which we are increasingly both bound together and separated by the globalized networks of information communication technologies. Traditional forms of community are eroded, and new forms of subjectivity and connection are being developed (Gere, 2014: 222). From this point of view, it can be said that while connectivity emerges thanks to digital platforms, people can get away from each other since they are detached from real places of daily life. Compared to real life, in digital platforms more artificial and superficial cultural relations can be established. Connectivity between users is temporary and solidarity is weak in digital platforms.

José Van Dijk investigates social media's impact on daily lives and also mentions the culture of connectivity in digital spheres and tries to explain how platforms have become central forces in the construction of sociality (Van Dijk, 2013: 23). For example Facebook interface allows its members to create profiles with photos, lists of preferred objects (books, film, music, etc.) and contact information, users can also join groups and communicate with friends. Flicker is an advanced tool that connects users via their content and gives users to control content. YouTube shapes the network for sharing creative practices and values, political arguments, and cultural products (Van Dijk, 2013: 47; 94; 115).

From a participatory culture to a culture of connectivity it occurs in network communication. Social media platforms lead to active participation and civic engagement (Van Dijk, 2013: 4). Implicit participation is the usage inscribed in the engineer's design using the coding technologies described. Explicit use refers to how real or actual users interact with social media (Van Dijk, 2013: 33). According to Van Dijk, digital platform owners have an interest in the side of users. They try to get information about users and share the information with third parties, to create value from data. Using this coding technology relationships become commoditized (Van Dijk, 2013: 16; 47). Social media tools enable their users to connect in real-time with others, yet users are tracked for what content they click on employing cookies (Van Dijk, 2013: 161-163). Digital platforms seem to provide participation, yet it has various limitations for users. Van Dijk, mentions commodification, however, neglects the structural constraints that stem from ownership in the field of digital culture.

Andrew Darley mentioned the forms and constitutive parts of digital culture. In Darley's terms, digital imaging technologies are vital components of modes of cultural production. Digital technologies support to creation of images which can be processed by the way of combining, recombining, animating, copying, and manipulating (Darley, 2000: 128). Digital technology is playing a role in image simulation used in cinema, animation, advertising, music videos, and video games. The mass-mediated forms, styles, and images are expanding the cultural horizon (Darley, 2000: 132). The computer-enhanced enhanced techniques of image simulation involve verisimilitude (Darley, 2000: 140).

Luke Tredinnick discussed the effect of digital information technology by addressing the concept of culture. According to Tredinnick culture involves three elements: social relations within a social system (lifestyles); idea systems that mediate social practices and social relations (value systems, traditions, and beliefs); and the material system which includes the products of social and cultural practices (art and literature) (Tredinnick, 2008: 3).

Digital technologies allow to access the virtual sphere for excluded individuals and groups which create and transmit knowledge. Digital technologies enable equal participation in the structures of discourse and reduce the marginalization of world views within society and culture (Tredinnick, 2008: 119). Alternative discourses and resistance efforts of excluded individuals and groups can circulate in digital platforms. But information flow and users activity are controlled by power actors.

Digital technologies decentralize control over knowledge and discourse. Structural changes emerged in the representation of power which is mediated by technology. Power relations emerge through the linguistic distribution of digital content (Tredinnick, 2008, 120-121). Digital culture has democratized participation for certain privileged groups and perpetuates the existing social inequalities within the wider social system. The ownerships of the network (digital media corporations) and state actors filter access to the web so the representation of inequalities carries on with this sphere (Tredinnick, 2008:

126). The field of digital culture is subject to power relations and inequalities. It is necessary to see the existence of power actors to interpret cultural relations.

THE MAIN FOCUS OF THE CHAPTER

In the scope of this study, a definition of digital culture will be made. Digital culture will be handled in this study with its physical, intellectual, and technological dimensions to comprehend its features totally. Digital culture can be separated into three main parts: First is the material culture, second is the symbolic culture, and third is the network culture. Material culture, which includes the production of cultural artifacts and contents, is the physical dimension of digital culture. Cultural artifacts and contents, which are distributed with digital codes, emerge with the circulation of information. Information circulation supports capitalist accumulation. Users' data is tracked by the cookies and is sold to the advertisement companies. So the owners of digital platforms get cost from the user's data. Data-driven economy dominates the material character of digital culture. Commodification is seen in material culture. Symbolic culture is about making sense of the environment. Symbolic culture includes the production of meaning in our lives, behaviors, practices, values, and artifacts. Symbolic culture is the intellectual dimension of digital culture. Besides, network culture is the technological dimension of digital culture. The network culture refers to the participation and interconnectivity. Users participate in digital platforms easily and cheaply at a global level and share various information. Besides, they are connected by links that are built into the network.

In this context, it can be said that digital culture is to build common meanings, values, experiences,relations and practices via digital platforms. Digital networks are the new cultural industries of society that are driven by capitalist market instruments working together with communication technologies in the global order. Developments in new communication technologies and market conditions are controlled by the ruling class. Thus, the digital sphere created by new communication technologies is subject to class inequalities. Market and government forces are the main actors controlling the circulation of cultural artifacts and contents in the digital sphere. Capital owners develop technology to expand their power in the area. Users are active by producing content in the digital sphere where the rules are predetermined by the owners.

The digital society which is encompassed by hyper-connected networks is constructed by the digital culture industry. The digital culture industry shapes the production and consumption of cultural products and determines the activities of virtual life. The area targeted by the digital culture industry is driven by market forces and state actors. In this study, the political economy of culture will be handled to depict the cyber habitat of digital culture concretely.

Digital platforms are a communication network and allow the transmission of data and the distribution of goods to the targeted demographic groups. Even though the Internet's open architecture, controlling authorities, and market incumbents prevent its widespread (Karaganis: 2007: 257-260). Content filtering is a tool of control for regulators and other actors. Content filtering on the Internet is a barrier to freedom of speech and cultural expression. Digital technologies shape the forms of cultural participation and freedom (Karaganis: 264-275). Digital technologies are created by market forces, therefore developments in political economy have a dominant possession on cultural participation and expression.

According to Kevin Robins and Frank Webster, in technoculture debates, digital platforms are regarded as an alternative that is creating new kinds of meeting places and user-friendly spaces for the global community. However, Robins and Webster draw attention to the determinant of the political economy in the definition of cyberculture. Robins and Webster consider the global political economy to encompass the new technocultural aspect. Global political-economic logic is mobilizing new information and communications media to create an extraterritorial space of enterprise (Robins and Webster, 2002: 240-243). They mention technological colonization emerging by the structure of political economy in the society. Robins and Webster refer to network capitalism functions, the hegemony of corporate interests, the information economy, and capitalist accumulation. In other words in the cultural field, the fundamental principles of capitalist society continue.

Aswin Punathambekar and Sriram Mohan point out that American digital platform companies dominate the world, and cultural identities and political processes are being transformed under the influence of digital platforms. Regulations and policies in capitalist global media systems lead to unequal flows of capital and content. Digital platforms are facilitating our social, cultural, political, and economic interactions and exchanges (Punathambekar and Mohan, 2019: 207-208). Hybrid forms (both global and local patterns) of cultural production and cultural identity occurred in digital platforms. Economic and political forces shape the digital media landscape. Transformations in the digital media sector involve the adoption of neoliberal economic policies and the deregulation and privatization of sectors in the economy (Punathambekar and Mohan, 2019: 210). The digital media economy has become tightly integrated with the advertising, marketing, print, film, radio, and television industries (Punathambekar and Mohan, 2019: 213). What their theory wants to draw attention to is the unequal character of the capitalist regime. Economic and political actors have the power to determine the field of digital culture. Neoliberal policies affect the development of digital platforms.

Some historical and social transformations have caused the formation of the digital culture industry. Neoliberal economic policies affect industrial development. Enrique Bustamante aims to define three basic processes that have produced important changes in the cultural industries during the past few decades. Deregulation, concentration, and globalization bring about wide-ranging transformations when it comes to creative products and their consumption (Bustamante, 2004: 803). Cultural industries are adapted to new technological innovations and networks. The cost of content creation and services is reduced, and openness and access to culture and communication are increased. However, the potential for democratization and expansion of creativity and expression is limited by the strategies of big conglomerates. Seeking profit in the capitalist system has pushed the cultural industries towards concentration (Bustamante, 2004: 806-807).

The diverse sectors of culture and communication have seemed increasingly united in the past few decades. Internet portals, search engines, content providers, and service providers concentrate on mass digital traffic (Bustamante, 2004: 807-808). New functions of commercialization and new value chains have emerged, on the other hand, new dependencies, barriers, and new powerful competitors have been created. These developments demonstrate the colonization of the new media and markets (Bustamante, 2004: 813). Increasing concentration in a few big conglomerates also raises the transition of culture and communication. Products and services are created produced and packaged transversally and globally according to niche markets (Bustamante, 2004: 814). The networks can be seen as a new public stage and global space, yet their unequal character fragments the world. Capitalist systems make a profit from every form of exploitation of time, format, prices, and the public by digital networks (Bustamante, 2004: 811-816). Bustamante refers to the global feature of the digital culture which is constructed by the big conglomerates. Besides, it can be said from this theory, people using digital platforms communicate with each other in a way of unequal due to class relations. Communicative forms are fragmented in communities of digital culture.

Digital technologies make it easier and less expensive to deliver words, music, symbols, and images to consumers around the world. Cultural artifacts can be produced, copied, transmitted, and stored digitally using technological developments in the cultural industries of digital society. Cultural industries had to adjust their business models and strategies to deal with the new technologies. New digital players are occurring in this new industry such as YouTube, Google, Vimeo, Pixar, Napster, and Amazon (Hart, 2010: 1-3).

The interactivity of digital technologies and file sharing of digital files via the Internet transform business models. The ability of new technologies to facilitate interactive exchanges among those connected to networks also makes it more difficult to differentiate consumers and producers as consumers share their writings, images, and music in the digital industry (Hart, 2010: 2). The boundaries between previously separating cultural industries are eroded. The digital production, storage, and delivery of entertainment, information, and education have changed. For example, infotainment and edutainment content emerge. Infotainment refers to the combination of information and entertainment, while edutainment refers to the combination of education and entertainment (Hart, 2010: 6). Digitalization and industrialization are the basic features of digital culture. Digital culture is deployed by the information exchange in the digital sphere. Data is processed and commercialized in digital platforms. That is, another characteristic of digital culture is informationalism. The information-based industry is dominant in digital culture to carry on capitalist accumulation.

Culture and communication are not excluded from the basic rules of capitalist economics, and commercialization and industrialization processes prevail in these fields. (Tremblay, 2015: 76-78). Cultural products and services have been integrated into commercial and industrial sectors. Commercialization and industrialization have two forms: the first is material reproduction, and the second is the use of communication networks. Cultural industries involve the production and distribution of books, newspapers, CDs, programs, films, and radio, or TV broadcasting. Media device industries such as TVs, cameras, video players, and book printing are the other aspects of cultural industries (Tremblay, 2015: 80). According to Gaëtan Tremblay, cultural industries are also digitized in the information society. Digital technology has an unlimited potential to support the freedom of creation and access, diversity of viewpoints and cultures, knowledge sharing, internationalism, and democratization. These cultural developments and information society models are seen in North America, Western Europe, and Japan (Tremblay, 2015: 82). Tremblay draws attention to the unlimited potential for digital technologies. On the contrary, communication circulation in digital platforms is filtered by the state and market actors. Forms of control differ under authoritarian and democratic regimes. In authoritarian regimes, more control efforts and content intervention are observed. According to Herbert Marcuse (2004: 41-49), the control capacity of technology can promote authoritarianism. Technological power tends to be the concentration of economic power. In this context, it can be said that technology is used to establish dominance and spread power.

According to Petter Törnberg and Justus Uitermark, while mass media is shaped by industrial mass production and mass consumption, social media is shaped by micromarketing and the accumulation of data. Consequently, both media structures are rising under the capitalist regime (Törnberg and Uitermark, 2022: 575).

The new structuring of markets causes specialization in which production, advertising, and media are all segmented and segregated. The rise of digital platforms enables the combination of fragmented and individualized targeting of audiences with an oligopolistic ownership structure (Törnberg and Uitermark, 2022: 578).

The digitalization of the economy has meant that capitalism is based on a new regime of accumulation. Production and advertising have become data-driven. Advertising revenue has thus moved from targeting a mass audience to targeting specific niche market segments and following the audience data (Törnberg and Uitermark, 2022: 579).

Digital media platforms become spaces for self-presentation, they are key stages for turning consumption into symbolic capital. Digital media as part of a flexible regime of accumulation depends on differentiation and lifestyle. The expansion of the symbolic dimension of consumption into new segments of life is part of flexible accumulation. Digital capitalism is the expansion of commodification, in other words, colonizing and commodifying new aspects of human life (Törnberg and Uitermark, 2022: 581-585). Törnberg tries to explain the cultural logic of digital capitalism and draw attention to commodification as a main feature of digital capitalism. In a digital society, capitalism continues to exist in its mechanism by transforming. Capitalism has become dependent on digital technology to expand its market. As a result, cultural relations and practices are affected capitalist mode of economy.

SOLUTIONS AND RECOMMENDATIONS

Network technology enables information to be organized and deployed. Digital information can be created, modified, stored, recombined, copied, and manipulated by using digital platforms. Network technology has hypertextual and data-based infrastructure, so allows us to connect and link people. Cultural implications and relations are mediated by digital means of communication. As Vincent Miller suggests, interactivity, hypertextuality, automation, and data-based actions are technical structures of computer-mediated communication. Interactivity can be seen as the exchange of messages and connectivity with users in a way of multidirectional flow (Miller, 2020: 20). Hypertext is a form of text that is composed of nodes or blocks of text that form the links between these blocks of content. Links embedded in web documents compose the hypertextuality. Digital products can be automatically modified or created through software and programs instead of being created by people. Databases consist of lists, tables, and structures that have discrete units, objects, or bits of information. A database system turns data into stored and organized meaningful information (Miller, 2020: 21-24).

According to Miller, every way of organizing information has cultural implications. Networked, digital, hypertextual, databased environments encourage the erosion of the distinction between producers and consumers of media. Digitalization allows the easy production of original works or the easy copying or manipulation of already existing works. Hypertextual environments allow an autonomy to the user to select his or her path through the materials available. Databases allow users to retrieve and recombine existing objects, texts, and data in an infinite number of ways (Miller, 2020: 25-26).

Time has become separated from space in terms of social action with others. The separation of space and time means that social relationships have become disembedded (Miller, 2020: 236). Digital technologies set individuals free from the constraints of space and time. Users can establish contact with anyone through communication networks. Members of online communities choose when and how to engage with other community members. By overcoming space and distance, online communities also overcome the problem of mobility (Miller, 2020: 239-240). Digital platforms are increasing mobility, establishing weak ties between individuals and groups. Digital technology is based on connectivity and choice. People are free to choose connections with others. There are no limits to establishing relationships via using networks. So groups are dynamic: adding members and creating new groups (Miller, 2020. 247-249). Miller refers to the transformation of space and time. So the way communities come together has changed. Online communities connect easily with each other and their mobilization has increased. Social relationships on the network are different from the real life. Since the way of interacting with reality has changed, the ties between users started to weaken.

The production of digital cultural materials is restricted by the logic of digital capitalism and accumulation regimes. Big conglomerates/ companies invest heavily in network technology to make a profit and increase their accumulation. The distribution of digital objects is affected by the capitalist mode of economy. As Micheal Betancourt says the digital object becomes the human-readable forms of image, movie, text, etc. through the actions of a machine that run the binary signals. Digital objects can be edited, compiled, combined, and distributed; copies can be reproduced further (Betancourt, 2015: 38-42). Digital reproduction becomes an inherent characteristic of digital objects. For digital technologies, the creation, storage, and distribution of information are not limited actions. The accumulation and management of digital files is an outcome of the development of digital technologies (Betancourt, 2015: 45-47). Auro of information in digital platforms has a role in the capitalist ideology of wealth accumulation. Auro of information is directed by the auro of digital capitalism. To maintain the circulation between production and consumption, accumulated capital is necessary. On the other hand, digital technology, its development, deployment, production, and access all demand a large expenditure of capital both to create and maintain (Betancourt, 2015: 58).

To grasp the relation between the political economic system and the cultural field, a dialectical model can be built up. In the sun theory model (Figure 1.), culture exists at the core of the social world cycle and affects (feeds) the political economic system like sunshine. Culture has leaked every aspect of the social world cycle. Culture and the system of political economy are both intertwined and autonomous areas. The political economic system also affects (organize/ control) the cultural field. That is, there is a dialectical determination relationship between them, society consists of this dialectical relationship. In the model, culture is the source and transforms the political economic system, besides political economic system is the constructive field that encompasses and transforms the culture, and society is the output. Culture has two sides; digital and traditional. Both these sides depend on human experiences, yet the digital culture occurs in digital platforms. As a result of this experience, symbolic meanings are produced while creating cultural materials, values, beliefs, and practices. In the social world cycle, micro-units and macro-units are constructed. For instance, network technology, and virtual communities (tools and actors) are the micro-units, and digital culture industry and capitalism (structures) are the macro-units. Actors are acting within the structures, therefore structures can't be ignored. Tools are constructed by the structures and structures are the units that transform the actor's activities as they exist in the field of digital culture. An actor-structure unity prevails in the social world cycle.

FUTURE RESEARCH DIRECTIONS

The views of some key scholars may guide future research. According to Pierre Bourdieu, culture which is produced socially and historically includes not only material production but also symbolic production. Symbolic production is the constitution of the meanings and values. Cultural production isn't independent of power relations and class relations. Although culture has an autonomous character, it is surrounded

Figure 1. Culture

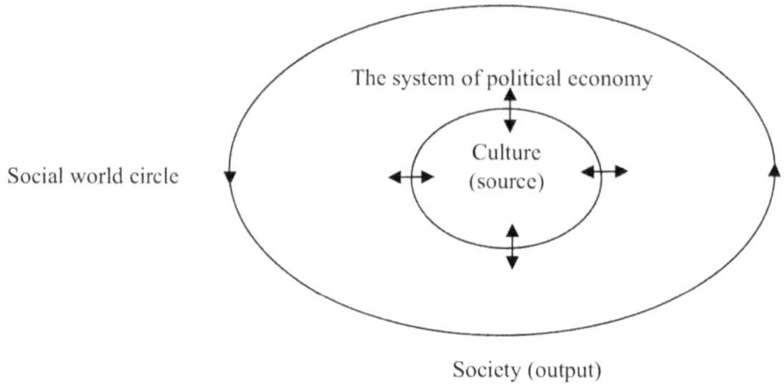

by the field of political economy (Bourdieu, 1993: 37-399). In this context, cultural relations should be comprehended with the developments in the political-economic system. In other words, cultural production depends on political and economic processes. Power relations stem from class relations are seen in the field of culture. Digital technology serves the dominant class which has economic power, so digital culture is shaped according to the needs and interests of this class. Power relations are also seen in the production of symbolic meaning. The symbolic dimension of digital culture involves a contestation over meaning. There are different and unequal actors struggling over meaning on digital platforms. Future research should consider this inegalitarian structure of the network.

A liberal perspective that evaluates network technology only as a democratizing tool may disrupt future research. According to Eran Fisher, the spirit of networks revolves around decentralization and dehierarchization. As he claims, the networks are more democratic tools which are empowering underprivileged and marginalized individuals. Networks have a participatory and inclusive manner and also allow for more individual freedom, emancipation, and authenticity. Networks contribute to individual empowerment by allowing individuals to come together in meaningful action (Fisher, 2010: 211-215). Although network technology leads to the participation of users, it is a hierarchal tool that centralizes power relations by giving control capacity to the dominant class. While the technology centralizes the structure of the network for owners, decentralizes this structure for users. Digital platforms allow access to information for users, so cultural materials can be created and transmitted quickly and instantly. Information is distributed in a decentralized manner among the users. However, information flow is controlled by the owners, and the units that are centralized continue in networks. Digital platforms such as social media should be considered hybrid structures. Consequently, digital platforms are not areas of unlimited freedom and democracy as is claimed in the liberal perspective.

CONCLUSION

People can share cultural information in different types such as text, sound, and moving images via networks. Interconnectivity and interactivity among users are constructed in the context of digital spaces. Multiple actors have a role in deploying cultural information by using network technology. State and market powers, non-governmental organizations, civil society organizations, local organizations, representatives of parties and associations, virtual groups and communities, and individuals are the actors that contribute to the empowerment of cultural transmission. Networks support the construction of virtual groups and communities by linking people. Digital platforms are not free public discourse spaces, on the contrary, they are driven by power actors such as governments and corporations. Digital culture must be understood through structures that transform it. As a result, not only users but also owners/ power actors of the network are the creater of the digital clutrual materials.

Social formations are based on class relations and are affected by the political-economic system. Power relations and inequalities are seen between the dominant class and the non-dominant class in the social formations. Digital culture rises above the capitalist economy, power relations, and inequalities. The dynamics of capitalism continue in digital society. The features of capitalism (such as competition, profit, and accumulation) affect the field of digital culture.

In this study, it is claimed that the cyber habitat of digital culture is shaped by the political-economic system. The political economy of digital culture contributes to comprehending the dynamic of cultural implications. As emphasized in this study, material culture, symbolic culture, and network culture are the components of digital culture. Digital culture is driven by the information-based culture industry. Cultural artifacts and contents are subject to the circulation of digital information. Information has become a commodity. While producing cultural artifacts and content, data of users are sold to advertisers. Besides, advertisements of companies are published on digital platforms where cultural exchange takes place. The commodification of cultural artifacts and contents refers to the material culture. Cultural artifacts and contents circulating on digital platforms have symbolic meaning. Therefore digital culture can be understood as producing common meanings. Human experience and relations produces common meanings, values, beliefs, and practices. Digital culture stems from human experiences and relations mediated by network technologies. A different perception of reality is constructed by human experience in digital culture, unlike traditional culture. Hence identity construction, group affiliations, and community ties are different than traditional culture. Digital platforms enable users to connect and participate easily, instantly, and globally. Briefly, the cyber habitat of digital culture can be listed as follows: digitized, networked, participatory, having connectivity, globalized, commodified, and symbolic.

REFERENCES

Adorno, T. W., & Horkheimer, M. (2002). The culture industry: Enlightenment as mass deception. In G. Schmid Noerr (Ed.), *Dialectic of Enlightenment: Philosophical Fragments* (pp. 94–156). Stanford University Press.

Betancourt, M. (2015). *The critique of digital capitalism*. Punctum Books.

Bourdieu, P. (1993). *The field of cultural production*. Colombia University Press.

Bustamante, E. (2004). Cultural industries in the digital age: Some provisional conclusions. *Media Culture & Society*, *26*(6), 803–820. doi:10.1177/0163443704047027

Campbell, R., Martin, C., & Bettina, F. (2014). *Media & culture mass communication in a digital age*. McMillan Learning.

Darley, A. (2000). *Visual digital culture*. Routledge.

Deuze, M. (2006). Participation, remediation, bricolage: Considering principal components of a digital culture. *The Information Society*, *22*(2), 63–75. doi:10.1080/01972240600567170

Fisher, E. (2010). *Media and new capitalism in the digital age*. Palgrave Macmillan. doi:10.1057/9780230106062

Gere, C. (2002). *Digital culture*. Reaktion Books.

Hart, J. A. (2010). *Toward a political economy of digital culture: From organized mass consumption to attention rivalry*. https://www.academia.edu/22951072/Toward_a_Political_Economy_of_Digital_Culture_From_Organized_Mass_Consumption_to_Attention_Rivalry

Ilya, L., & Mamlok, D. (2021). Culture and society in the digital age. *Information (Basel)*, *12*(2), 1–13.

Karaganis, J. (2007). The ecology of control: Filters, digital right management and trusted computing. In J. Karaganis (Ed.), *Structures of participation in digital culture* (pp. 256–280). Colombia University Press.

Klinenberg, E., & Benzecry, C. (2005). Cultural production in a digital age. *The Annals of the American Academy of Political and Social Science*, *597*(1), 6–18. doi:10.1177/0002716204270420

Malapragada, M. (2006). An interdisciplinary approach to the study of cybercultures. In D. Silver & A. Massanari (Eds.), *Critical Cyber Studies* (pp. 194–204). New York University Press.

Marcuse, H. (2004). Some social implications of modern technology. In D. Kellner (Ed.), *Technology war and fascism* (pp. 39–66). Routledge. doi:10.4324/9780203208311-6

Miller, V. (2020). *Understanding digital culture*. Sage Publications.

Mowery, D. C., & Simcoe, T. (2002). Is the Internet a US invention? An economic and technological history of computer networking. *Research Policy*, *31*(8-9), 1369–1387. doi:10.1016/S0048-7333(02)00069-0

Punathambekar, A., & Mohan, S. (2019). Digital platforms, globalization, and culture. In J. Curran & D. Hesmondhalgh (Eds.), *Media and Society* (pp. 207–224). Bloomsbury Publishing. doi:10.5040/9781501340765.ch-011

Reed, T. V. (2019). *Digitized lives: Culture power and social change in the internet era*. Routledge.

Robins, K., & Webster, F. (2002). Prospects of a virtual culture. *Science as Culture*, *11*(2), 235–256. doi:10.1080/09505430220137261

Shajan, A. (2023). Digital Culture and Digi-Relations. In S. Chakraborty (Ed.), *Dynamics of dialogue, cultural development, and peace in the metaverse* (pp. 30–39). IGI Global.

Törnberg, P., & Uitermark, J. (2022). Tweeting ourselves to death: The cultural logic of digital capitalism. *Media Culture & Society*, *44*(3), 574–590. doi:10.1177/01634437211053766

Tredinnick, L. (2008). *Digital information culture: The individual and society in the digital age*. Chandos Publishing. doi:10.1533/9781780631677

Tremblay, G. (2015). Cultural industries, the creative economy, and the information society. In L. A. Albornoz (Ed.), *Power media culture: Global transformations in media and communication research* (pp. 73–95). Palgrave Macmillan. doi:10.1057/9781137540089_4

Van Dijk, J. (2013). *The culture of connectivity, a critical history of social media*. Oxford University Press. doi:10.1093/acprof:oso/9780199970773.001.0001

Williams, R. (1960). *Culture & Society 1780-1950*. Anchor Book.

Chapter 5
Brand Evangelism Within the Framework of Digital Labor

Fikriye Çelik
Sivas Cumhuriyet University, Turkey

ABSTRACT

Renewed labor practices have linked immaterial labor to material labor processes. The creative power and activity connection of social media users, who are considered today's networked workers, as one of the stages of digital labor is one of the most important examples of this situation. Considering the appearance of labor in the new world, it is understood that brand evangelism is one of the forms of labor exploitation of contemporary capitalism. In this context, in the study, brand evangelism seen in Instagram was discussed within the framework of digital labor. The sample of the research consists of three Instagram user accounts with high followers who produce paid content in exchange for brand collaboration or advertising on social media. Forty images included in the research were subjected to content analysis. At the end of the research, it was concluded that Instagram stands out as the application area of brand evangelism and pointed out that the free labor culture that has become widespread in the digital environment covers labor exploitation.

INTRODUCTION

Today's contemporary global capitalism has taken traditional labor exploitation to a further stage. Labor has gradually moved away from its material nature. In other words, labor has now lost its visibility. Therefore, a form of labor that is completely disconnected from value has emerged. The distinction between labor and capital has disappeared. Today, in the age under the siege of communication networks, the form of digital labor is mentioned. As it is known, digital labor consists of stages. One of these stages is the creative power of social users and the intense activity connection it creates. Because these users are today's networked workers. Therefore, all products produced by these workers are within the scope of digital labor.

Undoubtedly, where there is labor involved, the existence of exploitation reveals itself. Contemporary capitalism differs from traditional capitalism with its forms of labor exploitation. Because the new

DOI: 10.4018/979-8-3693-0855-4.ch005

capitalism has now brought exploitation to the highest point. Brand evangelism comes first among these forms of labor exploitation. Both the people called brand evangelists and the people who listen to these people's experiences are cogs of capitalism. Undoubtedly, the object of labor exploitation here is brand evangelists. As a matter of fact, users who resort to sharing, especially on social networks and social media channels, maintain their position as digital labor producers with this evangelism they undertake. Therefore, on the one hand, these people are subjected to labor exploitation by global capitalism, and on the other hand, they become unpaid labor producers in brand promotion.

Brand evangelism is the new marketing logic. Evangelism marketing is a paradigm that develops when customers who believe in the brand and embrace the brand influence others. This is a high-level marketing practice that involves persuading potential customers to recognize the brand, purchase and use the product. Considering the new spaces created by the age and where daily life takes place, it is not difficult to say that social media inevitably reveals brand evangelism. Today, this is the form of marketing that most intensively motivates customers to engage in purchasing behavior. Because the brand evangelist is completely voluntary in the promotion and does not cooperate with the brand. Naturally, suggestions given by a person who has experienced the product, without seeking profit, reach a high acceptance among people.

There are many different definitions or concepts in the literature about brand evangelism. Brand ambassador, brand fanaticism, brand missionary are a few of them (Choudhury, Mishra and Mohanty, 2019, p. 3; Doss, 2014, p. 15; Singh, 2015, p. 5). Dedication stands where these naming points. Because as Doss and Carstens (2014, p. 13) said "a brand evangelist frequently exhibits a strong desire to influence consumption behavior." Therefore, as can be understood from the definitions, the customer profile that a brand most wants to gain or does not want to lose consists of evangelists with this dedication. As a requirement of the digital age we experience today, it is not surprising that the most prominent brand evangelists are digital content producers. The fact that users who are digital content producers on social media are part of the consumption network through brand evangelism and produce at the same time while consuming, emphasizes the cycle experienced in the new space. Because there is labor production here. This content production, each of which deserves to be evaluated in the context of digital labor, also stabilizes the monopoly status of global capitalist companies. Thus, while the user who becomes an evangelist grows the brand, on the other hand, the monopoly of the digital space, which is the place of content production, becomes absolute. Undoubtedly, the existence of endless exploitation here is too obvious to be overlooked. As a matter of fact, digital labor presents itself as a form that covers labor.

Digital labour that one of the forms of cultural labour is a specific form "that has to do with the production and productive consumption of digital media". It is known that today it is difficult to talk about a form of cultural labor that is not from the digital world (Fuchs and Sandoval, 2014, p. 492). One of the distinctive traits of digital labour is the disappearance of a clear distinction between labour time and life time. In this aspect digital labour introduces new forms of exploitation that go beyond the classical waged relationship. In this respect, digital labor leads to a new form of exploitation that goes beyond the classical wage exploitation (Fumagalli et al., 2018, p. 11).

This study illuminates the fact that internet users, who act as volunteer ambassadors on social media as part of brand evangelism, produce digital labor through their posts and face great exploitation through this labor. Fuchs and Sevignani's (2013, p. 251) claim that social media platforms use "a capital accumulation model that cannot work without the commodification of users' online activities" was an important starting point in the research. As a matter of fact, according to him (Fuchs, 2020, p. 135) the commodity-producing labor of the advertising model, which is among the capital accumulation models in the capitalist communication industry, is digital labour. Within the scope of the research, three Instagram user accounts with high followers, which had the power to exemplify the subject, were examined. Only the stories of three accounts that were followed for three months were taken into account and their posts were excluded. As it is known, the Advertising Board affiliated with the Ministry of Commerce published the 'Guide on Commercial Advertising and Unfair Commercial Practices by Social Media Influencers' on May 4, 2021. With the regulation made within the framework of this guide, it is obligatory to use a phrase indicating that the content is advertising in advertisements and collaborations on social media. The knowledge that collaboration or advertising agreements must be stated on the post has made it easier to access posts made for brand ambassador purposes. The data obtained was subjected to content analysis.

In order to ensure that the research results are evaluated in the correct context, the analysis of the findings was carried out around two themes that form the framework of the study. For this reason, instead of explaining the concepts of brand evangelism and digital labor, which are the two main themes of the study, under a separate heading, the information in the literature regarding these concepts was mentioned together with the findings.

METHOD

The primary aim of the study is to show that brand evangelism which rises through users who devote themselves to telling and promoting the brand they like or admire with a kind of devotion is actually a labour that social media users' shares and to point out the fact that social media users are exploited through this digital labour production. The research is important both because it focuses on a current issue and because it illuminates the fact that everyone is faced with the qualification of being a digital labour producer or brand evangelist in the virtual environment embedded in daily life.

The sample of the research consists of three Instagram user accounts with high followers who produce paid content in exchange for brand collaboration or advertising on social media. The latest situations of numerical data regarding the examined social media accounts as of October 2023 is given in Table 1.

These three accounts, which produced paid content in exchange for brand collaboration or advertising on social media, were followed for a three-month period between July and October. Only the stories of the mentioned accounts were taken into account and their posts were excluded. However, stories containing facial images that allow the account owner or another person to be recognized are excluded. For this reason, only forty images were included in the analysis. In determining the content to be included in the research, the Advertising Board's 'Guide on Commercial Advertising and Unfair Commercial Practices by Social Media Influencers' dated May 4, 2021 was taken into account. According to the aforementioned guide, the obligation to indicate cooperation or advertising agreements on the post was taken into account.

Table 1. Examined Instagram account info

User Account	Job	Follower	Number of Posts
X1	Digital content producer	966K	1284
X2	Digital content producer	547K	8105
X3	Fashion consultant	519K	4282

Table 2. Advertising indicators in examined Instagram accouts

User Account	Blank	Not Advertising	Not Cooperation	Obligatory Ad
X1	2	27	1	
X2		3		3
X3	4			
Total: 40				

Expressions such as 'not advertising' and 'not collaboration' were examined on the posts that should be evaluated within the framework of evangelism. As a result of the review, the phrase 'advertisement' was not found in 6 of the evaluated contents. Expressions such as 'not an ad' were found in 30 contents. However, the expression 'not cooperation' was seen in 1 post, and 'obligatory advertising' was found in 3 contents. The detected contents were stored by taking screenshots. The obtained images were categorized and subjected to content analysis.

FINDINGS AND ANALYSIS

The findings obtained as a result of the research were found to be important in terms of revealing that the research sample became digital labour producers despite being paid users as brand faces or brand promoters on social media. Undoubtedly, it is difficult to say that these accounts, which already produce high numbers of stories during the day for a paid, receive the reward of their labour within the framework of the labour-value theory. However, at a later stage, another exploitation situation attracts attention. What gives this remarkable result are the findings that reveal that the sample in question produced posts for brand promotion without any advertising or collaboration. In this context, the research findings are collected under two title. The data obtained were evaluated in the context of brand evangelism under the first title. In the second title the findings were examined around digital labour.

Brand Evangelism

Evangelism, which literally means 'to promote an idea', is actually a word with a religious reference. The word, derived from the Greek Evangelos, was first emerged in 300 BC. The original meaning of the word is found in the Bible. The term, which means spreading good news, is explained as "believers preaching to non-believers, exciting them and convincing them" (Goldfayn, 2011, p. 8). The concept also refers to the person who spreads morale-boosting news.

The concept of evangelism, which finds meaning as part of the religious context, entered the business world or marketing field thanks to the internet boom in the late 1990s (Kawasaki, 2015, p. 1). The concept, which entered the business world in the context of defending an idea, owes its popularity to Canva's evangelist chief Guy Kawasaki. Kawasaki's books 'How to Drive Your Competition Crazy' published in 1996 and 'Entrepreneur's Handbook' published in 2004 have enabled the concept to become a marketing term. According to Kavasaki, known as the father of evangelism marketing, this new marketing logic is based entirely on volunteers. Because these people undertake such volunteering with the hope of a better world and with full devotion. Evangelists who establish a relationship that is not based on any pressure or mutual exchange are accepted unconditionally by the people who follow them. Because here is a brand that has been experienced before and the person who recommended this brand talks about this experience with pleasure. These evangelists, whose feelings and thoughts are centered on experience and happiness or pleasure arising from experience, do not aim to gain profit from the brand. The aim of this action is to help other people benefit from the brand (Singh, 2015, p. 8; Saravanan and Saraswathy, 2017, p. 2). Especially the production of content praising the brand by social media accounts with high followers is seen as the strongest and most strategic marketing strategy by today's brands.

Based on the definitions that explain brand evangelism there is no doubt that brand evangelists have certain characteristics that distinguish them from ordinary consumers. Goldfayn (2011, p. 15-16) summarizes these under nine title.

1. They are the main customers
2. They are passionate customers
3. They are news hunters
4. They are communicators
5. They are buyers who believe in the brand
6. They are customers who forgive the brand's mistakes
7. They are consumers who show excessive repetitive purchasing behavior
8. They are public advocates of the brand
9. They are customers who are excited about the brand

In addition to these characteristics put forward by Goldfayn, Doss and Carstens (2014, p. 16) also underline the five-factor personality model known as the "Big Five" and draw attention to the characteristics of extroversion, openness to experience, neuroticism, conscientiousness and agreeableness, which they think are prominent in brand evangelists.

After all these explanation and meaning efforts, it has become easier to recognize brand evangelists in this research. In the evaluation made on three samples during a three-month period, 40 examples of brand evangelism, also called experience marketing, were found. These examples consist of posts of the social media account owner in question based on experience or suggestions. Expressions such as 'not an advertisement', 'obligatory ad' and 'not a collaboration' were searched on the posts. The accounts in question, which were determined not to be in any financial collaboration with the brand based on the contents examined, were evaluated in the context of brand evangelism. The images in Picture 1 and Picture 2 exemplify these contents.

In Picture 1 above, it can be seen that X3, with 519K followers, shared a brand image in her story without using any advertising phrases. While there is no warning on this image that it is not an advertisement, there is also no statement indicating that it is an advertisement. So the post is a clear example of brand evangelism. As a matter of fact, the brand name is framed in close-up. When we look at Picture 2, we see a post by X2, a digital content producer with 547K followers. In this content, instead of using an image that highlights the brand name, recommendations are made about the popular movie by tagging the Instagram account. The sharing of X3 has an image more like an ambassador with a reflection of brand love.

One of the images examined within the scope of the research can be seen in Picture 3. In this post, digital content producer X1 with 966K followers talks about the importance of collagen consumption for health and puts the brand in the frame. Right next to this example, in Picture 4, it can be seen that

Figure 1. X3

Figure 2. X2

Figure 3. X1

Figure 4. X2

Figure 5. X1

Figure 6. X1

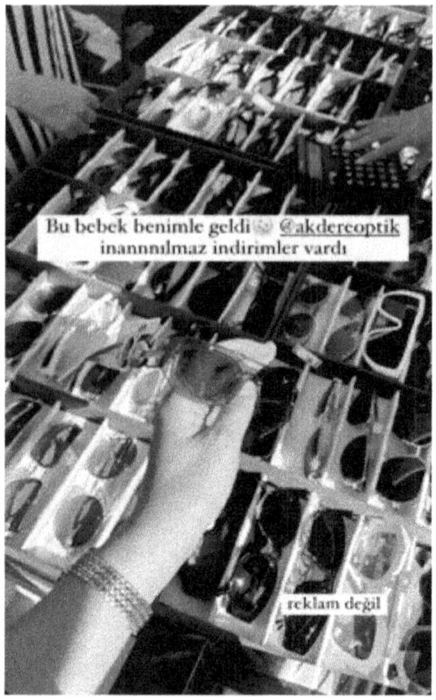

there is a sharing based on likes. In this story of X2, there is an example of an evangelism with pleasure. It is not difficult to say that the post produced with the discourse "it's not an advertisement, really" has the power to illuminate the place where brand ambassador meets brand love. Because in this example, the desire to share is remarkable despite the Ministry of Commerce rules. Undoubtedly, this situation needs to be explained with brand love. Brand love is a sign of passionate commitment. In other words, brand love is a kind of emotional expression that transforms the experience resulting in satisfaction into loyalty. In the literature review, many studies are encountered based on the nature of the deep relationship established with the brand. It seems that these studies mostly point to the basic emotion such as love, while talking about passion that increases the intensity of this emotion. At the same time, another common point of these studies is to draw attention to the connection of love with brand identity by associating it with two deep-rooted facts such as trust and commitment (Fetscherin and Conway Dato-on, 2012, p. 151; Thomson et al. 2005, p. 88; Albert and Merunka, 2015, p. 15, 17-27). However, brand love includes more than love, it includes the desire to declare love (Carroll and Ahuvia, 2006, p. 81).

At this stage, the contents in Picture 5 and Picture 6 are the clearest example of this situation. For example, in Picture 5, X1 introduces the brand she likes with the expression "my dear". Undoubtedly, brand love is clearly observed here. Because the expression "my dear" is, on the one hand, a word expressing love, and on the other hand, it is a personalized tool used for commodities. However, the expression "this baby came with me" seen in Picture 6 is an example of a similar picture. In this example picture, X1 approaches the brand with love and admiration with the word "baby" and displays an ownership of the brand. Because while the "baby" is known as a mean that is both loved and adopted, it is also a mean that is priceless. X1, which demonstrates brand love through analogy, personalizes the commodity with the expression "it came with me". These two examples show that it is a correct perspective for Carroll and Ahuvia to explain brand love within the framework of the desire to declare love.

Figure 7. X1

Figure 8. X1

Based on approaches to explain this issue, it is possible to say that brand love, which reveals brand advocacy, contributes to the process of creating a positive image of the brand. A similar but more advanced stage also applies to brand evangelism. In brand evangelism, there is an effort to affirm the brand in society within the framework of passion-based sentimentality. Over time, the effort turns into a commitment that cannot be separated from the brand. As a matter of fact, according to Matzler et al. (2007, p. 6) "if a consumer is passionate about a brand, he/she will engage in a much more emotional relationship with the brand and even miss the brand or feel loss when the brand is unavailable." The examples analyzed in the research make it easier to claim that the language used by the evaluated social media account users in sharing brands with which they are in professional business partnership and the discourse preferred in content indicating voluntary ambassador are different from each other. Using emotional expressions more intensely and choosing more sincere language confirms this idea.

In Picture 7, the persuasion method arising from a strong belief is seen in the post that draws an evangelist profile. In this image, X1 seems very confident about herself, her advice, and the brand, using a very clear and short expression, as well as a choice of saying a friend's recommendation. X1, who voluntarily demonstrates the practice of spreading the brand, not only shows the product but also shows a great desire to further spread and purchase the brand she likes. This example proves that brand evangelism is an enthusiastic practice. Similarly, the example seen in Picture 8 shows itself as a result of feelings of excitement and enthusiasm. In this content, X1 is not satisfied with persuasion through words alone, but has also chosen to use emojis. The heart, butterfly, and crying emojis in this example are actually a clear indicator of the sentimentality embedded in evangelism. The examined example confirms the statements that "brand evangelism is subjected to declaring intentionally rather likewise thoughts and sentiments in regards to a specific brand to others deliberately and regularly energetically" (Choudhury, Mishra and Mohanty, 2019, p. 3). Thus, these shares plan to greatly influence purchase behavior.

Figure 9. X1

Figure 10. X1

Kawasaki (2015), who was the first name to introduce marketing to evangelism, mentions that small actions are actually a series of actions that create a big movement in the digital world we live in. Indeed, the behavior that spreads throughout society does not occur easily or quickly. There is a need for some small but effective driving factors that enable this. Undoubtedly, Kawasaki is not wrong in his claim that one of the most effective ambassador techniques is social media. Because today we are faced with the fact that we live in a world that proves the truth of this idea.

Look around your office and you'll see evangelists everywhere—the EVP who regularly contributes to conference panels; the teammate who tweets about industry research; the executive assistant who puts photos of new products in her Pinterest feed. They are the kinds of leaders companies want in their ranks today. So you should develop the skills you need to join the club. In my experience, there are three ways to effectively evangelize: old-fashioned schmoozing, public speaking, and social media. (Kawasaki, 2015, p. 1)

The images above show online behavior, which Kawasaki describes as a kind of skill developed by evangelists. In this image, the user reveals an evangelist profile, happily explaining which products she purchased. Because the evangelist not only gets to be part of the free ad, but also enjoys this action. The explanations written on the shared photo show this. X1, who shares her shopping with her followers, chooses an encouraging language in Picture 9: "I bought an extremely beautiful skirt." Similarly, the expression "I bought so many beautiful things from here" in Picture 10 has an encouraging tone as required by evangelism.

Digital Labour

Producing free labour that poses the appearance of voluntary ambassador undoubtedly indicates the existence of exploitation. However, an internet user's sharing for a paid requires mentioning another form of exploitation. This is naturally labor exploitation. The sample of the research, which shows that they are producing digital labour through their posts and are not aware of the fact that they are facing great exploitation through this labor, has given many examples of this fact.

Hartley mentions that the dialogic communication model that emerged with the development of social networks includes everyone in the producer class (Hartley, 2012, p. 3; Quoted in Fuchs, 2014b, p. 50). This explanation brings Kawasaki to mind. As a matter of fact, according to Kawasaki, evangelism in the social age is everyone's job. When these two explanations are considered together, it is not difficult to say that the concepts of labor and evangelism are converging in social networks and social media channels.

As it is known, digital labour is one of the popular topics of the recent period. Fuchs, who takes Marx's concept of 'abstract labor' and focuses on the Autonomist Marxists' concept of 'immaterial labor', brings immaterial digital labour processes to the agenda on social media. Fuchs's concept of 'digital labour' is based on Lazzarato's (1996, p. 132-133) concepts of 'immaterial labor' and Terranova's (2000, p. 46-52) 'free labor'. According to Fuchs (2014a, p. 252), it is deceptive to describe labor as 'immaterial'. Such a conceptual explanation is the product of the dualist perspective. The distinction between the material and non-material world is not a correct way of seeing. Therefore, Fuchs carries out his conceptual efforts based on the practice of completely excluding this concept.

The issue we examine in this study can actually be considered as presenting an example of the outputs of the new media ideology. Today, it seems that technology has finally imposed itself and reached general acceptance. This fact indicates that there is a need for a correct literacy process, without excluding new media and without escaping from the fact that being on social media platforms is the result of the age. At this stage, it seems that the best option is to listen to Fuchs's (2020, p. 50) ideas. According to him, there is no doubt that the internet is controlled by capitalist companies. Because the capital structure of these platforms indicates monopolies. Both the owner of the means of production and owner of the products of labor show the same place: Capitalist. Fuchs thinks that the main focus of social media environments linked to monopoly interests is advertising based on microtargeting. The examples given under this title of the study support this conclusion.

For Fuchs, 'digital labour' is a labour that focuses on information production and is under the exploitation of capital. Considering its scope, it can be seen that the concept includes user actions that produce surplus value by sharing, liking and commenting in internet-based media, especially social networks. Undoubtedly, we are talking about a producer consumer profile here. The 'user commodity' emerges in this form of labor, where production and consumption processes converge simultaneously. It is not difficult to read Toffler's (1980) production-centered and Ritzer's (2009) consumption-centered views in Fuchs' explanations when he talks about the new human model conceptualized as 'productive'. Companies marketing the commodity consisting of shares, comments and likes to advertising companies brings the issue of digital labour to the agenda. Fuchs (2019, p. 15) emphasizes that the concept of digital labour has a broad meaning that includes all forms of paid and free labour required for the existence, production and use of digital media. This means that the main issue in this discussion is not the production of the commodity or the marketing of this commodity, but rather the seizure of a common social mine by capital.

Table 3. Three waves of digital labour research

Wave	Focus	Subjects
First	Digital labour as unpaid social media work	Prosumers
Second	Digital labour as unpaid social media work and also low-paid crowd- and gig economy work	Prosumers as well as workers and gig workers
Third	Digital labour as all work within the dynamic and fluid digital economy (understood as the ICT and platform sectors and their various supply chains)	Prosumers, crowd- and gig workers, as well as tech workers, digital service workers, digital hardware assembly workers, certain miners, and digital rubbish recycling workers

Source: Dorschel, 2021, p. 293.

As seen in the table above, it is understood that the topic of digital labor is based on "how power relations alter through the new forms of work". Dorschel (2021, p. 291-292) states that digital labor research consists of three waves. According to him, Fuchs, who advocated the third wave, has found a way to look at the issue of digital labor from a more expanded framework. Fuchs (2010, p. 188), who seems to insist that capitalist production relations reproduce themselves with technological developments in the means of production, mentions the capitalist nature of information production and claims that providing 'free labor' in digital spaces means being exploited endlessly. According to him, the productivity derived from internet users is producing value on behalf of capital. Fuchs seems to reject Marx's distinction between productive labor and non-productive labor. As it is known, Marx thinks that there is a direct relationship between capital and productive labor. However, this view, which Fuchs defends through new media, is not unfounded. Because the rules of new capitalism have relaxed the strict boundaries of traditional capitalism. Thus, the indirect or direct nature of the labor and capital relationship seems to be obscured.

The intertwining of material labor, which underlines exploitation, with the new form of labor that becomes abstract in the digital world, makes it difficult but also easier to understand the value production of digital labor. For example, the relationship between brand evangelism and digital labour on social media platforms, which we underlined in this study, is extremely important. In the examples given in the above title the effort to establish a deep connection with the brand, to gather fans for the brand and to post with love for the brand does not go unnoticed. This effort is undoubtedly also an indicator of digital labour. It would be correct to look at content that exemplifies both digital labour and brand evangelism under this title, which offers a way to understand the topic through this relationship.

It can be said that brands that prioritize brand evangelism and interact intensively with the consumer present a creative totality. Undoubtedly, this creative process is actually a result of the creative labor of the evangelist posing as a social media user. For example, as can be understood from X2's post in Picture 11, the user is not in the labor time of traditional capitalism. However, when viewed within the framework of contemporary capitalism, the meaning of the visual changes completely. This picture is a kind of evidence that capitalist production relations reproduce themselves under the instrumentality of new technology. As a matter of fact, with this content shared in free time, an evangelist is seen as devoid of the value he created. Right next to it, in Picture 12, an artistic effort in the content of X3 draws attention. It is not possible to think that this image has the appearance of a meaningless sharing. At first glance, the absence of any explanation or recommendation on the image may seem like a meaningless photo sharing. However, based on the previous posts of the user account coded X3, there is a brand that is liked and admired in this image. X3, which has previously shared a lot of praise about the brand and presented an evangelist profile, does not even feel the need to make any statement in this image. He

Figure 11. X2

Figure 12. X3

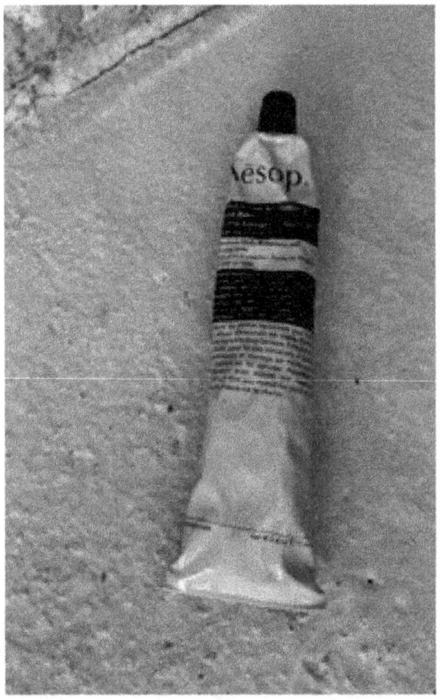

simply expresses his feeling with a post that reproduces his admiration. This inference is not just a guess, comment or assumption. This analysis is made possible by the information that the account in question, which has been followed for a long time, periodically produces content that praises the same brand and encourages its followers to purchase it. In fact, Picture 8, produced without the need for any words, is a complete prototype of brand evangelism and is a remarkable example of how strong the evangelist's loyalty and admiration is towards the brand.

There is no doubt that these two examples and the other examples examined in the study are indicators of digital labor. Likewise, these are examples of free labor. Thus, it is possible to see brand evangelism as a movement that endlessly exploits digital labor.

It is possible to evaluate the images above, which do not have the word 'advertising' or have the words 'not advertising', as a clear example of both digital labour and brand evangelism, as in the previous images. It is especially important to see the heart emoji in both images where emoji usage is seen. Undoubtedly, the heart emoji, which is seen as an indicator of love, love or loyalty towards the brand, can be considered a symbol of evangelism. As a matter of fact, it should be said that the existence of brand love was encountered in the previous stage of brand evangelism.

In some of the samples included in the evaluation in the research, an expression such as 'compulsory advertising' draws attention, as seen in Picture 15. As mentioned before, due to the Advertising Board's latest regulation regarding advertising collaborations on social media, users have the obligation to declare their brand collaborations. Looking at the example given above, there is a desire to produce free content even though there is no agreement. The account owner named X2, who underlines the obligation to write 'mandatory ad' in accordance with the legal regulation, is clearly acting as a brand ambassador. She is looking for a way to share a post that includes appreciation, love, loyalty or recommendation for a brand with which she does not seem to have a contract. At this stage, it is inevitable to comment that the user in question has bowed to technological pressure. Because in this age where it is not possible

Figure 13. X1

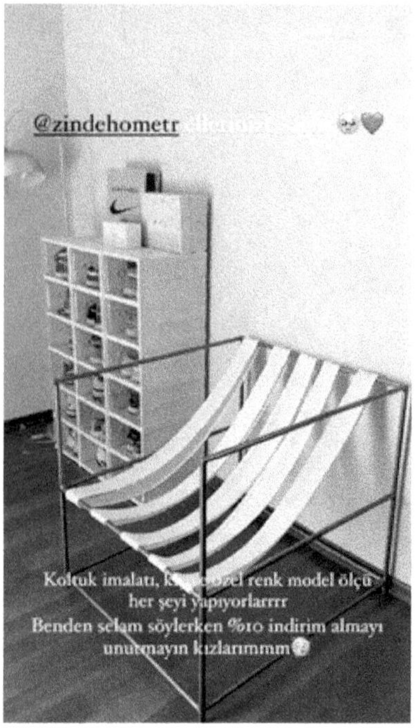

Figure 14. X3

Figure 15. X2

Figure 16. X2

to escape from the use of the internet or social media, users, specifically X2, are looking for legal ways to be exploited voluntarily. Even this search is actually strong enough to summarize the picture clearly.

Social media prosumption is just one form of digital labour which is networked with and connected to other forms of digital labour that together constitute a global ecology of exploitation enabling the existence of digital media. It is time to broaden the meaning of the term 'digital labour' to include all forms of paid and unpaid labour that are needed for existence, production, diffusion and use of digital media. (Fuchs, 2014a, p. 296)

Indeed, both the images shown above and the images below are evidence that social media prosumption are part of the global ecology of exploitation. The online behavior that appears as a kind of commitment and is placed within the framework of digital labor gives rise to an evangelist profile in the next stage. Because the labor that arises from and feeds digital media cannot leave the frame of capitalist capital.

In Picture 17 above, X3 gives the appearance of being main customers, which is one of the basic characteristics of brand evangelists. The absence of any explanation in this image indicates the existence of a remarkable evangelism. X3, who is seen sharing a favorite product of a brand she admires, finds it sufficient to place the product in the frame. It should be said that this inference did not only emerge in the context of this visual, but also that the same product of the same brand was encountered in the previous posts of this followed user account, which were outside the scope of the study. As can be seen, X3 has only tagged the brand in this sample image and benefited from the power of the heart emoji. It is possible to see the white color of the heart emoji as a message of pure and true love. When we look at the practice exhibited by X1 in Picture 18, we encounter one of the prominent qualities of brand evangelism. In this image, one encounters the practice of energetically expressing feelings about a particular

Figure 17. X3

Figure 18. X1

brand, known as the distinctive act of evangelism. As can be seen, the expression "incredibly good" is used enthusiastically here.

These two sample images examined specifically, in general, all other sample posts gain meaning as digital labour of brand evangelists. Thus, it has been concluded that the user accounts in question, which do not receive wages for their labor, allow the labor created during life time to be devalued, and allow the storage and marketing of personal data obtained from the shares, present examples that illuminate the reality of digital labor.

CONCLUSION

Labor, which has been the center of different discussions from past to present, is experiencing a new historical process today. Contemporary global capitalism has moved the concept of labor away from its traditional meaning and carried the extent of exploitation to a higher level. The new capitalism, which intensively reveals forms of immaterial labor, free labor and play-labor, has led to the emergence of a remarkable form of digital labor. Digital labour exemplifies labor production in contemporary spaces as a form that indicates the capitalist nature of information production.

The fact that the productivity derived from internet users produces value for the benefit of capital reveals endless exploitation. As a matter of fact, it is seen that this form of labor has its equivalent in different forms and contents. Brand evangelism, which has emerged as a necessity of the age, is one of these forms of labor exploitation. The space where evangelistic practice is exhibited necessitates an emphasis on digital labor. This study has managed to find evidence of the idea that there is no reason to disagree with Fuchs' critique of postcapitalist utopia. Content was found to prove that the three Instagram user accounts with high followers evaluated within the scope of the research were brand ambassadors other than advertising or collaboration. These user accounts engage in advertising or production of work in collaboration with brands. On the other hand, it has been observed that the same user accounts not only produce for a fee, but also create unpaid labor. Explanations such as 'not an advertisement' and 'not a collaboration' written on Instagram stories show this. Undoubtedly, this fact clearly exemplifies brand evangelism. However, the labor production process that operates with brand evangelism becomes even more remarkable.

According to the conclusions underlined in the research, technological developments in the means of production that determine the direction of capitalist production relations are the update of exploitation relations. It is clear that the idea of intellectual creativity is completely a cover for exploitation under the intense flow where knowledge is replaced by information. The contents evaluated in this study have illuminated the fact that brand evangelism, which develops accompanied by brand love and brand loyalty, has become a voluntary participation in capitalist production relations through digital labour production.

REFERENCES

Albert, N., & Merunka, D. (2015). Role of Brand Love in Consumer Brand Relationships. In M. Fetscherin & T. Heilmann (Eds.), *Consumer Brand Relationships Meaning, Measuring, Managing* (pp. 15–30). Palgrave Macmillan.

Carroll, B. A., & Ahuvia, A. C. (2006). Some antecedents and outcomes of brand love. *Marketing Letters, 17*(2), 79–89. doi:10.1007/s11002-006-4219-2

Choudhury, M., Mishra, B. B., & Mohanty, P. K. (2019). An empirical study of brand evangelism for recommending cars-a qualitative & Systematic review of literature. *International Journal of Technical Research & Science, 4*(3), 1–12. doi:10.30780/IJTRS.V04.I03.001

Dorschel, R. (2021). Reconsidering digital labour: Bringing tech workers into the debate. *New Technology, Work and Employment, 37*(2), 288–307. doi:10.1111/ntwe.12225

Doss, S. K., & Carstens, D. S. (2014). Big five personality traits and brand evangelism. *International Journal of Marketing Studies, 6*(3), 13–22. doi:10.5539/ijms.v6n3p13

Fetscherin, M., & Conway Dato-on, M. (2012). Brand love: Investigating two alternative love relationships. In *Consumer-brand relationships: Theory and practice* (pp. 151-164). Routledge.

Fuchs, C. (2010). Labor in informational capitalism and on the internet. *The Information Society, 26*(3), 179–196. doi:10.1080/01972241003712215

Fuchs, C. (2014a). *Digital labour and Karl Marx*. Routledge. doi:10.4324/9781315880075

Fuchs, C. (2014b). Karl Marx and the study of media and culture today. *Culture Unbound, 6*(1), 39–76. doi:10.3384/cu.2000.1525.14639

Fuchs, C. (2019). *Dijital Emek ve Karl Marx. Kalaycı, T. E. ve Oğuz, S. (Trans.).* NotaBene Yayınları.

Fuchs, C. (2020). *Communication and capitalism: A critical theory*. University of Westminster Press.

Fuchs, C., & Sandoval, M. (2014c). Digital workers of the world unite! A framework for critically theorising and analysing digital labour. *TripleC, 12*(2), 486–563. doi:10.31269/triplec.v12i2.549

Fuchs, C., & Sevignani, S. (2013). What is digital labour? What is digital work? What's Their difference? And why do these questions matter for understanding social media? *TripleC, 11*(2), 237–293. doi:10.31269/triplec.v11i2.461

Fumagalli, A., Lucarelli, S., Musolino, E., & Rocchi, G. (2018). Digital labour in the platform economy: The case of Facebook. *Sustainability, 10*(1757), 1-16.

Goldfayn, A. L. (2011). *Evangelist marketing: What Apple, Amazon, and Netflix understand about their customers (That your company probably doesn't)*. Benbella Books.

Kawasaki, G. (2015). The art of evangelism. *Harvard Business Review*, 108–111.

Lazzarato, M. (1996). Immaterial labour. In P. Virno & M. Hardy (Eds.), *Radical Thought in Italy: A Potential Politics* (Vol. 7, pp. 132–146). University of Minnesota Press.

Matzler, K., Pichler, E., & Hemetsberger, A. (2007). Who is spreading the word? The positive ınfluence of extraversion on consumer passion and evangelism. In *AMA Winter educator's conference proceedings marketing theory and applications* (pp. 1-22). American Marketing Association.

Ritzer, G. (2009). *Enchanting a disenchanted world: Continuity and change in the cathedrals of consumption*. SAGE Publication.

Singh, N. (2015). Evangelism marketing: The evolution of consumer fidelity. *Journal of Marketing Communications*, *11*(1), 5–16.

Terranova, T. (2000). Free labor: Producing culture for the digital economy. *Social Text*, *18*(2), 33-58.

Thomson, M., MacInnis, D. J., & Park, C. W. (2005). The ties that bind: Measuring the strength of consumers' emotional attachments to brands. *Journal of Consumer Psychology*, *15*(1), 77–91. doi:10.1207/s15327663jcp1501_10

Toffler, A. (1980). *The third wave*. William Morrow and Company, Inc.

Chapter 6
Data Journalism and Social Media in Hyperlocal Journalism:
Telling Local News With Data and Social Media Interaction

Cihan Çakır
https://orcid.org/0000-0002-4100-365X
Avrasya University, Turkey

ABSTRACT

Recently, research on the discovery and use of local data sources that can be used in hyperlocal journalism has gained importance. In this sense, this study includes a literature review on data journalism practices in hyperlocal media organizations. In the study, the importance of data journalism and social media use in hyperlocal journalism in the field of communication is emphasized, and how data journalism can be used in the fields of digital journalism and digital newspapers, its contributions, and solution suggestions are discussed. This study aims to contribute to presenting the news more effectively and meeting the information needs of the society by shedding light on the developments in the field of communication.

INTRODUCTION

The digitalization process resulting from technological progress has brought the media and journalism sector into a process of change and transformation. Reporting and journalistic practices are starting to take on new forms with this digital transformation. This process continues as a structure that constantly changes with technological developments (Picard, 2014). These developments in the field of journalism and journalism naturally affect the local media, and many processes such as digital progress, the development of the internet, the emergence of new media, local journalistic practices in collecting and writing news, and deciding which news to select and which to publish are changing. In other words, the internet paves the way for local media to transcend the physical and geographical boundaries that indicate their

DOI: 10.4018/979-8-3693-0855-4.ch006

locality. As a result, local media organizations are breaking their own locality and moving out of their local areas (Franklin, 2006, p.21).

In a way, hyperlocal media has emerged as local media exceeds its limits. Because, unlike the traditional understanding of local media, hyperlocal media can be understood as new forms of digital local media that include the amateurism of local media but offer a technologically opportune alternative to traditional mainstream media (Rodger, 2018, p.857). Dimensionally, hyperlocal media generally serves a population such as a city or town, and its financial strength, sustainability, professionalism and quality in news production processes vary from region to region (Dovbysh, 2020, p.2). Because, in addition to official and larger-scale local media organizations, hyperlocal media organizations represent smaller-scale and more amateur journalism institutions. In this sense, it is different from professional media organizations (Tenor, 2018, p.1065).

Recently, media organizations have been adding the concept of data to their journalistic practices. With the increase in open data sources and requests around the world, the inclusion of data analysis in news content, the rapid spread of presentation techniques with visualization, and data journalism becoming a global phenomenon, it has begun to be widely used in professional journalism practices in recent years and has affected both journalistic practices and social processes (Appelgren et al., 2019, p.1192). The use of data analysis in journalistic practices has a great potential for both the public to act more consciously and for objectivity, trust and accountability (Schudson, 2010, p.107). This situation also manifests itself in local and hyperlocal media organizations. Data journalism is also carried out in these media organizations, albeit to a limited extent, and it has an impact on their own communities.

Although there is an increasing number of research on hyperlocal media, whether or not data use and data journalism practices are used in this field, how they are used and how they are visible remains an issue that is ignored or not thought about much, and is not researched. Although hyperlocal media has a small-scale area and an amateur journalism approach, it also includes data journalism practices as a type of online journalism with the opportunities brought by digitalization. Therefore, analyzes of how digital technologies transform the media environment in a particular region are also gaining importance in terms of hyperlocal media and data journalism.

In this sense, this book chapter generally focuses on the importance and impact of using data journalism in hyperlocal journalism. The book chapter provides a literary review on the narration and presentation of local news with data. The chapter covers basic concepts such as how data journalism can be used in hyperlocal journalism and how local news can be presented more effectively through data analysis, visualization and interactive content. The chapter also addresses the relationship of social media to hyperlocal journalism and data journalism. Topics such as the impact of social media on news dissemination, interaction and reader participation, social media data sources and analysis, social media analytics and news production are also included in the content of the department. This book chapter contributes to researchers, journalists and communication professionals working in the field of digital journalism and digital newspapers by presenting the basic concepts, research areas and trends regarding the use of data journalism and social media in hyperlocal journalism. Additionally, it offers solution suggestions on how to enrich the data-based narrative of local news with the use of social media and how to ensure that the news reaches wider audiences. In addition, taking into account the developments in the field of digital journalism and digital newspapers, it is to discuss how data journalism can be used in these areas and what contributions it can make.

HYPERLOCAL JOURNALISM

Technological developments reduce the costs of content production and distribution on the internet and give more active roles to the audience, making it possible for new actors, including hyperlocal media, to enter the media field. In this sense, hyperlocal media exists as an increasingly expanding field of research, especially in recent years (Halvorsen & Bjerke, 2019, p.115; Downham & Murray 2020, p.257). Hyperlocal media is a form of community media defined as "online news or content services relevant to a town, village, single postcode, or other small, geographically defined community" (Radcliffe, 2012, p.6; Cook et al. 2016, p). .7). Since this definition includes web content in the understanding of hyperlocal journalism, it also comprehensively covers other understandings of news. In addition, not including web content, online media or new media and social media in the hyperlocal area makes it difficult to distinguish it from other news concepts (Harte et al., 2016, p.233). To overcome this challenge, Hess & Waller emphasized that hyperlocal journalism should be limited to the online space only. This both distinguishes it from the traditional journalism practices of the pre-internet era and causes it to include the traditional journalism practices in question by feeding on these practices (2016, p.196). This enables it to be conceived as a mixed form of local journalism or a unifying media approach that combines traditional journalistic practices with public participation. In other words, hyperlocal journalism is considered as a hybrid journalism that includes new and traditional journalism codes and is formed by a new community. This situation differs from traditional local journalism in the news production, practices, working styles and communication between people who work in hyperlocal journalism (Arnold & Blackman, 2021, p.2).

Hyperlocal media often gain visibility through websites founded or supported by community members, entrepreneurs, or former journalists (Tenor, 2019, p.130). These media outlets may be independent or operated by an individual or group. News published in hyperlocal media may be written in accordance with professional journalism codes, but it may also be unofficial news that is completely far from this, and in general, hyperlocal media organizations operate based on non-profit revenue models (Kurpius et al., 2010, p.360). For this reason, most hyperlocal media organizations go bankrupt and close down, and this situation alienates potential investors from these organizations (Metzgar et al., 2011, p.773). Failure to find investment and financing accelerates the closure of local news organizations. This closure affects the level of participation of the local community and opens it up to the disruption of democratic processes, causing local communities to fail to catch up with current public issues (Shaker, 2014, p.133). However, even if they are closed due to financial difficulties, hyperlocal media are important for the community. Because it can provide technological opportunities for the interaction and participation of local communities, the presentation of new news formats and the production of these innovative journalism practices (Lacy et al., 2009, p.1). These technological opportunities are also important in that they provide community members with the opportunity to participate in the news at a high rate. In hyperlocal media, rather than editing the content, newspaper editors pave the way for community members to create the content and increase participation (Chadha, 2015, p.6).

Hyperlocal media is a form of citizen-led online community media serving at the local level. It can be assumed that such spaces, which are frequently used on social media and result in high levels of audience participation, provide users with a civic and activist style (Turner, 2021, p.2236). This situation, which occurs with the widespread use of digital media technologies, makes it possible for ordinary citizens to become digital hyperlocal media participants in various places (Kim et al., 2022, p.1). Given the participatory nature of hyperlocal media, there is a certain expectation that this is equivalent to peoples coming together in practices of civic engagement and activism, and hyperlocal media communities can simultaneously provide points of contact for thousands of residents, local discussion, or information gathering (Metzgar et al., 2011, p.783). This, together with hyperlocal online media characterized by their coverage of more overlooked areas and their orientation and commitment to the community, is revitalizing the understanding of media with new approaches to information that are closer to society (Negreira & Lopez-Garcia, 2021, p.1).

Hyperlocal journalism involves using online tools to engage readers. Unlike traditional media, these online relationships with new media and social media are specific to this new field of journalism. When considered in terms of traditional local media, the potential of these media to create content together with their readers is mentioned (Baines, 2010, p.582; Zamenopoulos et al., 2016, p.105). However, the level of this potential is not at the level provided by hyperlocal journalism practices. Hyperlocal media followers generally approach an event with similar reactions and concerns. Hyperlocal media organizations that maintain permanence in the field are positioned more independently and interact with readers both through their own websites and social media. These organizations also show that journalism will be permanent by basing it on sincerity, establishing close relationships with the reader, and being guided by people in the local community (Barnett & Townend, 2015, p.333). In this sense, hyperlocal media organizations enable readers to interact with editors and each other, contribute to news and posts, and prepare the contextual process of the news together. Web pages that engage in hyperlocal journalism generally contain such areas for reader participation (Metzgar, et al., 2011, p.153).

At this point, since hyperlocal journalism highlights participation and is related to community members, it is also related to social capital and its elements, trust and reciprocity. These elements strengthen the bonds of members in the community, and this process continues as strongly online as it does offline. This situation is also important for journalists. Because, the journalist is seen not only as a creator of news content, but also as a person who interacts with the reader through social media and can create a community (Lewis et al., 2014, p.229). Due to the natural structure of social media, reciprocity in communication is achieved through elements such as likes, comments and shares, and contributes to the formation of digital communities. In this way, a network is created to convey local information to community members quickly and reliably, and a source of information is provided to community members. Thus, the social capital of community members increases (Harte et al., 2017, p.165).

Another issue in hyperlocal journalism is media ethics. Determining and complying with certain conditions related to media ethics is necessary for professional journalism. However, media ethics is becoming an ignored issue with digitalization (Tenor, 2018, p.1066). Ordinary citizens or amateur journalists may use journalistic practices in an unprofessional manner when covering the event in the news. In this sense, these individuals often present the news in a manner that lacks objectivity and editorial processes. This situation allows the presentation of news that is irregular, unprofessional and far from media ethics (Ward, 2014, p.457). This situation manifests itself in the concept of hyperlocal journalism. Because amateur people can produce news content in these areas both through social media and their own websites (Cook et al., 2016, p.9).

Although hyperlocal news sites are associated with the online space, their effects are formed by social and physical relations. As technology develops socially, internet technology offers a new form of communication to traditional communication environments. In other words, the effect of hyperlocal media cannot be considered separately from the social structure in which it exists, like traditional media, and is shaped by the culture of that society (Chen et al., 2015, p.712). Local news sites bring local communities closer to each other culturally and increase their participation in local media (Mersey, 2009, p.348). In addition, many of the institutions that deal with hyperlocal journalism face difficulties in terms of human and financial resources. In order to overcome this difficulty, communication among local readers along with word-of-mouth communication among themselves becomes important (Bobkowski et al., 2018, p.2). This situation also manifests itself in the online environment, and in accordance with the channel complementarity theory and the local character of hyperlocal news sites, word of mouth communication continues online by sharing the news they receive from these hyperlocal news sites on their own social media. In other words, people who are members of a local community receive news about the community from online media channels as well as traditional media (Dutta-Bergman, 2004, p.42). Hyperlocal media organizations are among these channels for local communities.

Hyperlocal media organizations differ from other mainstream news organizations in many ways. For hyperlocal journalism practices, citizen journalism is important (Carson et al., 2016, p.2). Because, while citizen journalists tend to write news based on their personal interests and experiences and cite themselves as sources, professional journalists tend to write news on topics that are considered more serious and rely on different sources, especially official institutions such as the police and courthouse (Paulussen & D'Heer, 2013, p.599). In this sense, hyperlocal journalism is in a position to eliminate the negative effects left on people by the serious news preferred by traditional media organizations. The negative content news constantly imposed on traditional media channels negatively affects people's view of themselves and the people around them in the local area. However, the hyper-participatory structure of hyperlocal journalism, specific to its locality, can minimize these effects and make the daily lives of local people easier through news (Meijer, 2013, p.25). In this sense, the aim of hyperlocal journalism is to make traditional media more accessible to the audience. Filling the empty space created by the decreasing rate of preference over media or digital media is seen as replacing traditional media in the local area. In other words, hyperlocal media is a more technology-based version of traditional media (Kurpius, et al., 2010, p.359). In light of these technological developments, the concept of "data" is becoming increasingly important in journalism and media practices. At this point, it is also important to use data journalism practices in hyperlocal media.

DATA JOURNALISM IN HYPERLOCAL MEDIA

The subject of data journalism is seen as one of the fastest developing areas when research in the field of journalism is taken as a criterion (Ausserhofer et al., 2020, p.952). Data journalism emerged as a result of the development of technology and computer-mediated journalism practices and with the understanding of sensitive journalism (Anderson, 2018, p.22). Data journalism represents a concept of journalism that is basically based on data that people have open access to, and the collection, processing and visualization of these data with very strong claims of accuracy based on them (Borges-Rey, 2020, p.917). In this sense, in order to apply data journalism, it is necessary to have a certain technological infrastructure and digitalization processes, the ability to process and store data and visualize this data (Loosen et al., 2020, p.1247). In other words, journalism is experiencing a quantitative transformation (Coddington, 2015, p.333).

The main purpose of data journalism is to transform complex and numerous numerical data into content that the reader can understand, and to give the reader the details of the event that is the subject of the news in a clearer and more memorable way. In other words, it means telling the story of the news in an understandable way through data. Understanding data journalism in this way also imposes duties on those who work in journalism, such as statistical analysis, computer knowledge, data visualization and good use of the internet (Mair & Keeble, 2014, p.27). In this sense, finding a data journalist is a very difficult process for media organizations.

When we look at the literature, it is said that data journalism mostly aims for the benefit of the public in terms of accuracy, precision, trust and accountability. In addition, these features are an important tool in data journalism that enables the public to participate in the news (Boyles & Meyer, 2016, p.945). The reliability of the data keeps a news created with data away from personal opinions, and it is said that the news can be created by adhering to the ethical principles of journalism along with objectivity. As long as journalists have access to data sources, they can independently research, find, verify, report and make news about the events that are the subject of the news. As a result, it activates the readers who read the news and ensures social participation with interactive graphics and visuals (Borges-Rey, 2016, p.835). However, open and complete access to data for both journalists and people in society varies by country and region. This situation shows that data journalism cannot always be realized positively in every region, as mentioned above (Camaj, 2016, p.347). In addition to this negativity, the quality of the data accessed, the timeliness of the data affect the reliability of the content of the news (Wiley, 2021, p.890).

These situations regarding data journalism also bring ethical problems. Because it is based on quantitative data, data journalism is seen as more accurate than traditional forms of journalism. However, this provides data journalism experts with a false sense of authority based on technological knowledge. In other words, not all of the data obtained is absolutely correct, the data needs to be verified and cleaned and sorted (Appelgren, 2018, p.310). While some data journalists pay attention to this situation, others ignore it and do not consult other data sources other than the data provided by the data sources, and may not perform data cleaning and sorting. In this case, it reduces the reliability and reader interest of data journalism (Loosen et al., 2017, p.1248). In addition, in order to avoid distortions that imply untrue facts, data should be given a clear meaning through data visualization and ways for the reader to access these data sources should be provided. Information about the source from which the data was obtained should be given and links should be left. That is, data should be made publicly available in an accountable manner. This is created thanks to hyperlinks (Tandoc et al., 2017, p.999). In this way, readers can find the data, see them, check their accuracy, and obtain information from them by copying them. Not sharing the data set used undermines trust in news organizations (Young et al., 2018, p.117). In addition, data journalism has an important position when considered in terms of privacy. Because data sets are large personal data pools. Individuals may have private information in a data set. In this case, it becomes important for these people to be informed about sharing their data. However, in most cases this permission is not obtained (Fairfield & Shtein, 2014, p.39). Since source confidentiality is one of the basic journalistic principles, it is also an important issue in data journalism. However, it is unclear whether this confidentiality can be protected in completely algorithm-based systems. In this sense, people who engage in data journalism are forced to disclose the source of the data due to its transparency (Craig et al., 2017). All of these create ethical problems of data journalism.

Data journalism is a part of technological opportunities and is generally seen as the monopoly of large media organizations due to the difficulty of finding personnel to work with. However, it is also visible in local and regional media organizations based on smaller-scale, daily and more local and even community-specific data. However, in some cases, local media organizations are unable to meet hyperlocal data applications. Again, these hyperlocal data applications are important for local readers to more effectively narrate noteworthy local events and agendas in their own regions and communities (Boyles, 2020, p.389). To benefit from this potential impact of data on news, hyperlocal organizations need to invest more in data and data journalism. However, the low budget of hyperlocal media creates problems especially in the employment of data personnel and the diversity of data-based news. Because data journalism involves a certain specialization process and its reflection on the news (Young et al., 2018, p.116). First of all, in order for data journalism to reach even very small-scale media organizations, it is necessary to regulate the prices of data applications. Because small local media businesses, especially hyperlocal media organizations, have limited budgets for data applications (de Limas Santas et al., 2020, p.2). When hyperlocal media cannot access data sources, people in the community are limited in their news about developments, and their potential to connect with other people in their communities decreases, social capital relations decrease, and the social relations of local communities may be endangered (Boyles, 2020, p.390). In addition, another factor that makes it difficult to do data journalism in hyperlocal media organizations is the difficulty of providing localized data sources and accessing these currently created data for data journalists (Lowrey et al., 2019, p.70). Despite all these negativities, there are increasing data units in Europe and they share data with local and hyperlocal news organizations (Stalph, 2020, p.3).

Data journalism is hindered not only by these negativities but also by the unique character of hyperlocal media. The unique nature of hyperlocal media means that the communities in the region where it is located are intertwined. This situation carries the potential that impartiality and the distance between the reader and the journalist may not be maintained while the data to be used are being converted into news, as the journalist and the community know each other, perhaps even being neighbors. Because hyperlocal journalists generally organize the content of the news to ensure interactivity with the local environment of the readers in the community. So, in a sense, the content is tailored to community members and does not provide too much negative news about readers' own local area (Stalph et al. 2023, p.1885). In this sense, in a sense, hyperlocal media organizations generally ignore the public discourse and accountability dimensions of journalism. Because what the local community expects from these organizations is primarily to be a good community member rather than a journalist. In this sense, the first duty of the hyperlocal journalist is to look after the interests of the community and ensure the development of the community and the region by providing solutions to community-related problems (Hess & Waller, 2017, p.20). In addition, being closed to innovations and technological developments inherent in the local area and financial impossibilities also affect the use of data journalism in hyperlocal media. The fact that there is resistance to the transition to the digital field and the slow progress of the process can be seen as one of the reasons why data journalism is visible in hyperlocal media.

CONCLUSION AND DISCUSSION

Journalists can deliver their news to large audiences via social media, interact with readers, and ensure the news spreads faster. At the same time, social media can be seen as an important tool for journalists to access news sources and data, and to research and verify news. Regarding the use of data journalism in hyperlocal journalism, social media platforms have great potential. Data, interactions, check-ins and other user activities shared on social media can contribute to telling hyperlocal news in a data-based manner. By analyzing data on social media, journalists can identify events, trends and problems in local communities and use this data in the news production process. The role of social media in journalism is not limited to just collecting data. Journalists can also actively use social media to distribute and spread news. Sharing news on social media can encourage greater participation from readers, enable news to reach a wider audience, and make it easier to receive feedback from readers. However, the relationship between social media and journalism also presents some challenges. Although social media allows news to spread quickly, it can be difficult to check the accuracy of the news and prevent the spread of fake news. Journalists should be more careful and work with reliable sources to verify information circulating on social media.

Focusing on the issues discussed as a result of the study, hyperlocal journalism generally has limited financial resources. Lack of sufficient funding can be a major obstacle to producing quality content and creating a sustainable business model. Limited financial resources, especially in hyperlocal media organizations, and the need for high-tech tools in data journalism can be seen as one of the biggest obstacles to hyperlocal journalism. In addition, when considered in terms of education and talent, deficiencies stand out. Because data journalism skills are often limited among hyperlocal journalists. Lack of training in this area can limit their ability to use and present data effectively. Finding well-equipped experts in the field of data journalism is a very difficult process for hyperlocal media. This situation causes hyperlocal media to use processes such as conveying the news with data, processing, interpreting and sorting the data, reporting it in a way that the reader can understand, and visualizing it by turning it into news content, in a very limited way. Providing basic journalism training for hyperlocal media and data journalism is crucial. The deficiencies in training covering topics such as news writing techniques, access to news sources, news evaluation and news design can be seen in hyperlocal media. Because employees in hyperlocal media organizations generally consist of amateur journalists and community members. In this sense, it is important to acquire basic skills for data journalism. Training should be provided on subjects such as collecting data from databases, analyzing data, visualizing and interpreting data. Likewise, training should be provided on how to evaluate and select local news in hyperlocal media. Issues such as newsworthiness, accuracy, impartiality and the importance of the news to the local community should be addressed. Training should be organized for hyperlocal media on how to communicate effectively with the local community and interview techniques. They should be taught how to collaborate with local resources. In terms of journalism education, these trainings and eliminating deficiencies will help journalists who will work in hyperlocal media and data journalism to develop the skills they need. In addition, it is also important that these trainings are constantly updated and supported with appropriate resources. In addition, the insufficient technological infrastructure required for data analysis at the national level restricts hyperlocal media organizations and communities' access to news and social media, making it difficult for people to follow and participate in data news in hyperlocal media. In addition, when ethical problems arising from the nature of data journalism and hyperlocal media are combined, there are certain problematic points in terms of the accuracy and reliability of the news. The rapid spread of news on social media can lead to the rapid spread of false or misleading information and may also affect the reliability of hyperlocal news.

A number of solution suggestions are offered within the scope of this study in order to carry out data journalism correctly in hyperlocal media. The first of these includes sustainable financial models. It is clear that efforts must be made to develop sustainable financial models for local journalism. Sustainability of hyperlocal media can be achieved through different income sources such as subscription models, donations, advertisements and grant funds. Hyperlocal media provides valuable information for local people. Creating subscription models to access this information can provide a sustainable source of income. While we offer free basic content, subscription fees may be charged for access to premium content and special benefits. It is important to generate advertising revenues by collaborating with local businesses and institutions. These advertisements can be provided by promoting the products and services of local businesses on the hyperlocal media platform. Income can be generated by organizing educational programs and events for local communities. Participation fees may be charged for these events and paid access to educational programs may be provided. Additionally, donations and fundraising campaigns can enable local communities to support the platform. Such campaigns can be organized in cooperation with non-governmental organizations and individuals. In addition, it is also possible to generate income by collaborating with local businesses or making sponsorship agreements. Such collaborations can be valuable, especially for local events, projects or special news. In addition, local data journalism can generate income by sharing the local data it collects and analyzes with different institutions or researchers. It can also create a sustainable source of income by providing data analysis services. Another solution can be to generate income by licensing the content created by the hyperlocal media platform to other media organizations. This not only allows the content to reach a wide audience, but also creates a source of income.

In addition, providing data journalism training to hyperlocal journalists is important to enable them to use data effectively and enrich their news. In this regard, organizing training programs and workshops in the context of data analysis and journalism of hyperlocal media organizations is important for data journalism practices in these media organizations. In addition, although limited, strengthening the technological infrastructure for local communities, increasing access to news and facilitating social media interaction are important for hyperlocal media. This helps reduce the gap between global and local. Additionally, accuracy and reliability should be emphasized in hyperlocal journalism. Editorial control and verification processes should be strengthened, and fact-checking practices should be encouraged to combat misleading information. Likewise, it is important for people in hyperlocal media to draw boundaries between themselves and community members and to create news content impartially.

Considering all this, the combination of hyperlocal journalism, data journalism and social media for the field of communication and journalism enables societies to participate more in news production and sharing. This encourages local communities to be heard more effectively and create their own news. Social media allows news to be shared instantly and quickly accessed by millions of people. Hyperlocal and data-driven news is shared on social media platforms to easily reach targeted local communities. Social media platforms enable news to reach a wide international audience, not just a specific geographical region. Thus, hyperlocal news can reach a wider audience at the national and even international level. Data journalism in hyperlocal media, when shared via social media, makes it easier for readers to engage with news, comment and share their opinions on news content. These interactions can help journalists better understand their readers' interests and shape their content accordingly. In addition, social media ensures that hyperlocal news remains up to date. These instantly shared news enable communities to react quickly to events and developments. The use of data journalism in hyperlocal media can ensure that news is presented on a more accurate, reliable and documented basis. By reducing the risk of misinformation and manipulation, data-based news can increase the accuracy of news and play an important role in gaining the trust of the society. In addition, news created with data can enable visualization. Data journalism can help make news more attractive and understandable by making complex data understandable through simple and effective visuals. This situation increases the readership potential of hyperlocal media. Visual tools such as graphs, maps, and infographics allow readers to better understand and interact with content. Additionally, because social media makes it possible to customize news based on individuals' interests and preferences, algorithms can recommend readers news that aligns with their interests, increasing the visibility and accessibility of local news. Hyperlocal media can use the data it obtains in a meaningful way for the community. Data journalism allows for a more in-depth examination of local news through methods used to extract meaningful information from large data sets. This helps to better understand the problems and needs of societies. In this way, by drawing attention to local communities through hyperlocal media, specific problems of that region can be brought to the national agenda. In addition, both social media and data journalism diversify news sources by using different sources. This allows hyperlocal news to offer a richer and more diverse range of content. Hyperlocal media, together with social media, enables individuals to share their own observations, news and events. This strengthens civic journalism and increases community participation. The development of civil journalism is important, especially in terms of rapid dissemination of news in local communities and delivery to hyperlocal media organizations.

The study also offers research topics for future studies, these are suggestions that are seen as lacking in the field and are believed to contribute. First, data journalism training programs should be created and promoted for hyperlocal journalists. These trainings will improve data collection, analysis and visualization skills and help journalists present news more effectively. In this sense, conducting studies on hyperlocal media and data journalism training and presenting detailed solution suggestions by revealing the situation is important for the expansion of the field. In addition, social media strategies of hyperlocal news platforms should be improved and updated. Social media management should be used effectively to ensure local news reaches a wider audience. For this purpose, it is also important to conduct research that measures the social media management and knowledge of hyperlocal media organizations. Additionally, hyperlocal media organizations should develop data-driven content strategies. These strategies should focus on creating content in which data plays a central role, engaging readers and ensuring understanding. In this sense, studies need to be carried out on what kind of data content strategies hyperlocal media should use. Likewise, in hyperlocal journalism, readers' opinions and feedback are taken into consideration. It is important for these media organizations to investigate the mechanisms that encourage the participation of readers and shape local news content and by what other mechanisms participation in hyperlocal media can be increased. In addition, future studies should develop sustainable business models for hyperlocal news platforms. Revenue sources such as advertising, subscriptions, donations, sponsorships and collaborations should be studied and innovative financial models should be explored.

As a result, this study explains the relationship between hyperlocal media and data journalism within its own limitations. It is expected that the study will serve as a resource for future studies. The combination of hyperlocal journalism, data journalism and social media can improve the quality of local news in the future, encourage participation and strengthen the connection between communities and journalists. It is thought that the studies and practices that have been done and will be carried out in these areas are of critical importance for presenting hyperlocal news more effectively in the future.

REFERENCES

Anderson, C. W. (2018). *Apostles of Certainty*. Oxford University Press. doi:10.1093/oso/9780190492335.001.0001

Appelgren, E. (2018). An ıllusion of ınteractivity. The paternalistic side of data journalism. *Journalism Practice*, *12*(3), 308–325. doi:10.1080/17512786.2017.1299032

Appelgren, E., Lindén, C., & van Dalen, A. (2019). Data journalism research: Studying a maturing field across journalistic cultures, media markets and political environments. *Digital Journalism (Abingdon, England)*, *7*(9), 1191–1199. doi:10.1080/21670811.2019.1685899

Arnold, C., & Blackman, S. (2021). Retrieving and repurposing: A grounded approach to hyperlocal working practices through a subcultural lens. *Digital Journalism (Abingdon, England)*. Advance online publication. doi:10.1080/21670811.2021.1880330

Ausserhofer, J., Gutounig, R., Oppermann, M., Matiasek, S., & Goldgruber, E. (2020). The datafication of data journalism scholarship: Focal points, methods, and research propositions for the investigation of data-intensive newswork. *Journalism*, *21*(7), 950–973. doi:10.1177/1464884917700667

Baines, D. (2010). Hyper-local: Glocalised rural news. *The International Journal of Sociology and Social Policy*, *30*(9/10), 581–592. doi:10.1108/01443331011072316

Barnett, S., & Townend, J. (2015). Plurality, policy and the local. *Journalism Practice*, *9*(3), 332–349. doi:10.1080/17512786.2014.943930

Bobkowski, S. P., Jiang, L., Peterlin, L. J., & Rodriguez, N. J. (2018). Who gets vocal about hyperlocal. *Journalism Practice*. Advance online publication. doi:10.1080/17512786.2017.1419827

Borges-Rey, E. (2016). Unravelling data journalism: A study of data journalism practice in british newsrooms. *Journalism Practice*, *10*(7), 833–843. doi:10.1080/17512786.2016.1159921

Borges-Rey, E. (2020). Towards an epistemology of data journalism in the devolved nations of the United Kingdom: Changes and continuities in materiality, performativity and reflexivity. *Journalism*, *21*(7), 915–932. doi:10.1177/1464884917693864

Boyles, J. L. (2020). Strength in numbers. In A. Gulyas & D. Baines (Eds.), *The routledge companion to local media and journalism* (pp. 389–397). Routledge. doi:10.4324/9781351239943-44

Boyles, J. L., & Meyer, E. (2016). Letting the data speak. *Digital Journalism (Abingdon, England)*, *4*(7), 944–954. doi:10.1080/21670811.2016.1166063

Camaj, L. (2016). From 'window dressing'to 'door openers'? Freedom of information legislation, public demand, and state compliance in south east europe. *Government Information Quarterly*, *33*(2), 346–357. doi:10.1016/j.giq.2016.03.001

Carson, A., Muller, D., Martin, J., & Simons, M. (2016). A new symbiosis? Opportunities and challenges to hyperlocal journalism in the digital age. *Media International Australia, Incorporating Culture & Policy*, *161*(1), 132–146. doi:10.1177/1329878X16648390

Chadha, M. (2016). The neighborhood hyperlocal. *Digital Journalism (Abingdon, England)*, *4*(6), 743–763. doi:10.1080/21670811.2015.1096747

Chen, N. N., Ognyanova, K., Zhang, C., Wang, C., Ball-Rokeach, S. J., & Parks, M. (2017). Causing ripples in local power relations. *Journalism Studies*, *18*(6), 710–731. doi:10.1080/1461670X.2015.1078738

Coddington, M. (2015). Clarifying journalism's quantitative turn. *Digital Journalism (Abingdon, England)*, *3*(3), 331–348. doi:10.1080/21670811.2014.976400

Cook, C., Geels, K., & Bakker, P. (2016). *Hyperlocal revenues in the Europe and UK*. Nesta.

Craig, D., Ketterer, S., & Yousuf, M. (2017). To post or not to post: Online discussion of gun permit mapping and the development of ethical standards in data journalism. *Journalism & Mass Communication Quarterly, 94*(1), 168–188. doi:10.1177/1077699016684796

de-Limas-Santos, S., M., A. K. & Bruns, A. (2020). Out-of-the-box versus in-house tools: How are they affecting data journalism in australia? *Media International Australia*, 1–15. doi:10.1177/1329878X20961569

Downham, S., & Murray, R. (2020). The hyperlocal 'renaissance' in Australia and New Zealand. In G. Agnes & D. Baines (Eds.), *The routledge companion of local media and journalism* (pp. 255–264). Routledge.

Dutta-Bergman, M. J. (2004). Complementarity in consumption of news types across traditional and new media. *Journal of Broadcasting & Electronic Media, 48*(1), 41–60. doi:10.1207/s15506878jobem4801_3

Fairfield, J., & Shtein, H. (2014). Big data, big problems: Emerging ıssues in the ethics of data science and journalism. *Journal of Mass Media Ethics, 29*(1), 38–51. doi:10.1080/08900523.2014.863126

Franklin, B. (2006). *Local journalism and local media:Making the local news.* Routledge. doi:10.4324/9780203969205

Halvorsen, L. S., & Bjerke, P. (2019). All seats taken? Hyperlocal online media in strong print newspaper surroundings. *Nordicom Review, 40*(2), 115–128. doi:10.2478/nor-2019-0030 PMID:33907698

Harte, D., Turner, J., & Williams, A. (2016). Discourses of enterprise in hyperlocal community news in the UK. *Journalism Practice, 10*(2), 233–250. doi:10.1080/17512786.2015.1123109

Harte, D., Williams, A., & Turner, J. (2017). Reciprocity and the hyperlocal journalist. *Journalism Practice, 11*(2-3), 160–176. doi:10.1080/17512786.2016.1219963

Hess, K., & Waller, L. (2016). Community anf hyperlocal journalism. A "sustainable model". In B. Franklin & S. A. Eldridge II, (Eds.), *The routledge companion to digital journalism studies* (pp. 194–204). Routledge. doi:10.4324/9781315713793-20

Hess, K., & Waller, L. (2017). *Local journalism in a digital world.* Palgrave. doi:10.1057/978-1-137-50478-4

Kim, Y., Chae, Y., & Kim, Y. (2022). Doing community: Digital hyperlocal media as care. *Digital Journalism (Abingdon, England)*, 1–15. Advance online publication. doi:10.1080/21670811.2022.2145330

Kurpius, D., Metzgar, E., & Rowley, K. (2010). Sustaining hyperlocal media. *Journalism Studies, 11*(3), 359–376. doi:10.1080/14616700903429787

Lacy, S. R., Daniel, R., Esther, T., & Margaret, D. (2009). Examining the features, policies, and resources of citizen journalism: Citizen news sites and blogs. *Web Journal of Mass Communication Research, 15*(1), 1–20.

Lewis, S. C., Holton, A. E., & Coddington, M. (2014). Reciprocal Jjournalism. *Journalism Practice, 8*(2), 229–241. doi:10.1080/17512786.2013.859840

Loosen, W., Reimer, J., & de Silva-Schmidt, F. (2020). Data-driven reporting: An on-going (r)evolution? An analysis of projects nominated for the data journalism awards 2013–2016. *Journalism*, *21*(9), 1246–1263. doi:10.1177/1464884917735691

Lowrey, W., Broussard, R., & Sherrill, L. A. (2019). Data journalism and black-boxed data sets. *Newspaper Research Journal*, *40*(1), 69–82. doi:10.1177/0739532918814451

Mair, J., & Keeble, R. B. (2014). *Data Journalism: Mapping the Future.* Abramis.

Meijer, I. (2013). When news hurts: The promise of participatory storytelling for urban problem neighbourhoods. *Journalism Studies*, *14*(1), 13–28. doi:10.1080/1461670X.2012.662398

Mersey, R. D. (2009). Online news users' sense of community: Is geography dead? *Journalism Practice*, *3*(3), 347–360. doi:10.1080/17512780902798687

Metzgar, E. T., Kurpius, D. D., & Rowley, K. M. (2011). Defining hyperlocal media: Proposing a framework for discussion. *New Media & Society*, *13*(5), 772–787. doi:10.1177/1461444810385095

Negreira-Rey, M.-C., & López-García, X. (2021). A decade of research on hyperlocal media: An international approach to a new media model. *Online Journal of Communication and Media Technologies*, *11*(3), e202111. doi:10.30935/ojcmt/11082

Paulussen, S., & D'Heer, E. (2013). Using citizens for community journalism. *Journalism Practice*, *7*(5), 588–603. doi:10.1080/17512786.2012.756667

Picard, R. G. (2014). Twilight or new dawn of journalism? Evidence from the changing news ecosystem. *Journalism Practice*, *8*(5), 488–498. doi:10.1080/17512786.2014.905338

Radcliffe, D. (2012). *Here and now: UK hyperlocal media today.* Nesta. https://media.nesta.org.uk/documents/here_and_now_uk_hyperlocal_media_today.pdf

Rodgers, S. (2017). Roots and fields: Excursions through place, space, and local in hyperlocal media. *Media Culture & Society*, *40*(6), 856–874. doi:10.1177/0163443717729213

Schudson, M. (2010). Political observatories, Databases & news in the emerging ecology of public information. *Daedalus*, *139*(2), 100–109. doi:10.1162/daed.2010.139.2.100

Shaker, L. (2014). Dead newspapers and citizens' civic engagement. *Political Communication*, *31*(1), 131–148. doi:10.1080/10584609.2012.762817

Stalph, F. (2020). Evolving Data Teams: Tensions Between Organisational Structure and Professional Subculture. *Big Data & Society*, *7*(1), 1–13. doi:10.1177/2053951720919964

Stalph, F., Hahn, O., & Liewehr, D. (2023). Local data journalism in germany: Data-driven reporting amidst local communities and authorities. *Journalism Practice*, *17*(9), 1882–1901. doi:10.1080/17512786.2021.2019089

Tandoc, E. Jr, & Oh, S.-K. (2017). Small departures, big continuities? Norms, values, and routines in the guardian's big data journalism. *Journalism Studies*, *18*(8), 997–1015. doi:10.1080/1461670X.2015.1104260

Tenor, C. (2018). Hyperlocal News And Media Accountability. *Digital Journalism (Abingdon, England)*, *6*(8), 1064–1077. doi:10.1080/21670811.2018.1503059

Tenor, C. (2019). Logic of an effectuating hyperlocal: Entrepreneurial processes and passions of online news start-ups. *Nordicom Review*, *40*(2), 129–145. doi:10.2478/nor-2019-0031

Turner, J. (2021). Someone should do something: Exploring public sphere ıdeals in the audiences of uk hyperlocal media facebook Pages. *Journalism Studies*, *22*(16), 2236–2255. doi:10.1080/1461670X.2021.1991837

Ward, S. J. A. (2014). Radical media ethics. *Digital Journalism (Abingdon, England)*, *2*(4), 455–471. doi:10.1080/21670811.2014.952985

Wiley, S. K. (2021). The grey area: How regulations ımpact autonomy in computational journalism. *Digital Journalism (Abingdon, England)*, *11*(6), 889–905. doi:10.1080/21670811.2021.1893199

Young, M. L., Hermida, A., & Fulda, J. (2018). What makes for great data journalism? A content analysis of data journalism awards finalists 2012–2015. *Journalism Practice*, *12*(1), 115–135. doi:10.1080/17512786.2016.1270171

Zamenopoulos, T., Alexiou, K., Alevizou, G., Chapain, C., Sobers, S., & Williams, A. (2016). Varieties of Creative Citizenship. In I. Hargreaves & J. Hartley (Eds.), *The Creative Citizen Unbound* (pp. 103–128). Polity. doi:10.2307/j.ctt1t89gk8.11

Chapter 7
Using Eye-Tracking in Integrated Marketing Communication:
Do They See What We Want to Show?

Turgay Oyman
https://orcid.org/0000-0002-4868-2229
Igdır University, Turkey

ABSTRACT

We can use neuromarketing to understand how consumers feel, think, and behave. Eye-tracking also gives us clues as to whether the tools we use in marketing communication can actually achieve the results we want. In this way, our messages will reach the masses much more easily and at less cost, making marketing communication more effective. Did the person receiving the message really notice the brand, logo, product, or was it just a fun activity for them? Eye-tracking can answer this question much more easily and with less cost, making marketing communication more effective. This chapter explores eye-tracking in marketing.

INTRODUCTION

The fact that many businesses producing products with similar features operate around the world has brought competition to a higher level. Although this situation includes many challenges for businesses, it puts consumers in a stronger position than ever before.

The ability of businesses to cope with these challenges requires going beyond classical methods. Businesses that need to overcome the challenges brought by technology by using technology have started to use methods such as customer relationship management, integrated marketing communication (IMC) and neuromarketing that will provide competitive advantage.

DOI: 10.4018/979-8-3693-0855-4.ch007

INTEGRATED MARKETING COMMUNICATIONS

The dizzying developments in production and transportation facilities and the spread of electronic commerce have saturated the market in terms of products and/or services. Businesses have now realized that they cannot gain competitive advantage due to the fact that the changes they will make in the marketing mix elements (product, price, place, promotion) can be easily copied. For this reason, integrated marketing communication (IMC) has become an important concept for businesses that want to get to know their existing and potential customers better and to establish and maintain long-term relationships with their customers (Mihaela, 2015:1149).

IMC was first proposed by Northwestern University in 1989 (Ivanov, 2012:538). It is defined as the transfer and sharing of information and meanings related to the product/brand in order to identify, stimulate or satisfy customers' wants and needs (Tuncel, 2009:118). With the development of communication tools, the fragmentation of traditional media channels and the rise of non-traditional channels, this definition has continuously evolved from a limited view of coordinating communication tools to a strategic process (Briggs et al., 2005:83; Mihatr, 2012:976). It was emphasized that IMC should cover the whole organization and should be stakeholder focused. From a more holistic perspective, it is emphasized to improve the integration of the whole of communication and messages produced by all departments, units and divisions of the organization (Porcu et al., 2019:147). A consistent message presented in this way will be able to draw a stronger image in the memory of consumers than contradictory or inconsistent messages. Regardless of the channels in which the consumer is exposed to the message, the brand image placed with consistent messages can also be protected. In addition, for the consumer who encounters consistent messages in different channels, this will be perceived as a quality indicator and will play an important role in creating customer loyalty (Šerić et al., 2014:148).

With an enterprise-wide strategic approach, IMC should deliver consistent messages from all communication sources, establish effective two-way communication with internal units and external stakeholders, focus on stakeholder-centered strategies by establishing long value-oriented relationships with them, and ensure high-level horizontal and vertical integration involving the entire organization. (Porcu et al., 2020:437).

In the implementation of the decisions taken according to the results obtained as a result of marketing researches conducted by businesses, the impact of IMC is communicated to the consumer through the marketing mix. Redesigning the packaging that will bring the business to where it wants to be in the eyes of the target audience, highlighting the features of the product or increasing marketing communication activities can also affect the emotions of the consumer by increasing direct or indirect experiences and mediate the establishment of a bond (Mihatr, 2012: 978).

IMC's aim to influence consumer behavior requires the study of how consumers think, feel, reason and choose between different alternatives. Understanding consumer response helps marketers to identify marketing objectives, structure goals and create coherent messages (Mihatr, 2012:976). Successfully implemented IMC provides cost advantages to businesses and helps to use resources efficiently and to do the right things. It also increases the impact of the work done by creating a synergy effect (Yolaç and Demir, 2004:124).

NEUROMARKETING

Neuroscience, which enables the observation of changes in the human nervous system and behavior due to psychological and physiological factors, has started to be used in the field of marketing with the contribution of technological developments (Hubert and Kenning 2008: 273). Neuromarketing helps us understand consumers' preferences and decisions by observing physiological and neural data (Harrell, 2019: 64). In traditional methods such as surveys and focus group interviews, which are widely used, consumers respond at their conscious level and unconscious data cannot be evaluated. (Harris, Ciorciari, & Gountas, 2018; Alsharif, Md Salleh, Baharun, et al. 2021). However, the assumption that consumers only make decisions rationally has changed and it has been revealed that emotions are effective in their decisions (Mileti, Guido, & Prete, 2016; Piccarozzi et al., 2021). Understanding consumer emotions allows us to better understand the choice and decision process (Blazquez-Resino et al., 2022). A better understanding of the consumer's cognitive processes through observation has the power to eliminate the misleading answers we encounter in traditional methods due to neighborhood pressure, fear of shame, or inability to express their emotions (Lim, 2018; Morin, 2011). This makes the use of neuromarketing widespread in both marketing research and marketing communication.

Figure 1. Common neuroscientific methods for neuromarketing
Source: Lim (2018:207)

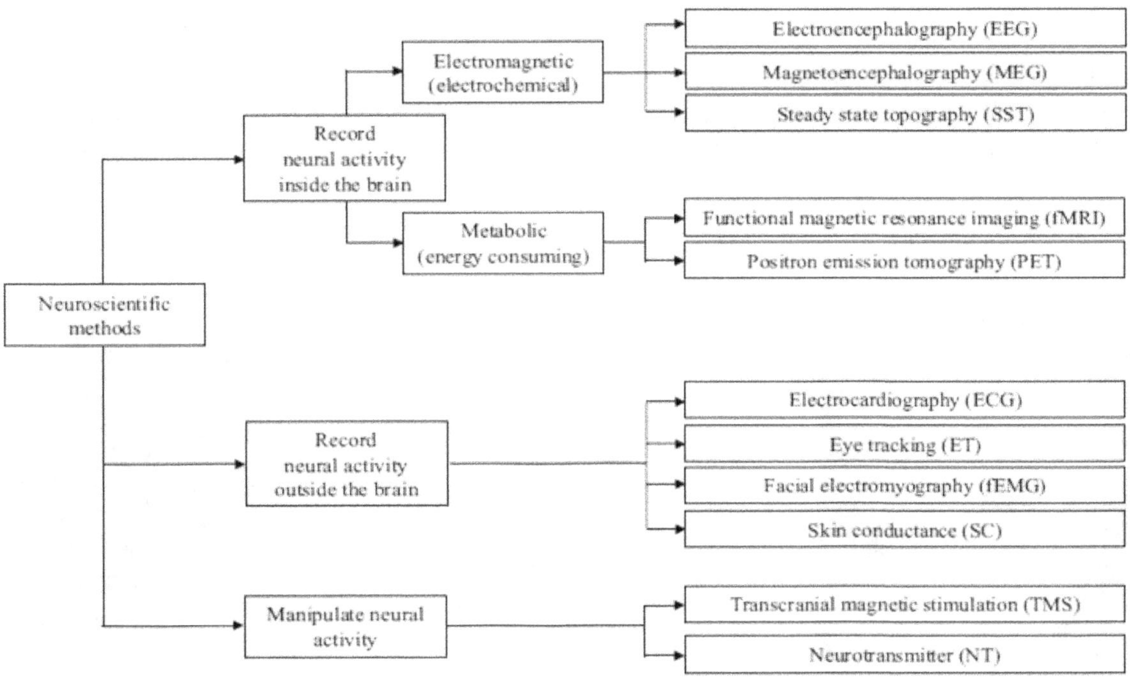

Methods Used in Neuromarketing

Neuroscience allows us to instantaneously observe, map and record the activities that occur in the brain and nervous system during responses to stimuli. We can classify the tools used in neuroscience under three headings (Figure-1).

- Tools that measure neural activities in the brain
- Tools that measure neural activity outside the brain
- Tools that manipulate neural activity (Lim, 2018:206).

Below, not all methods are explained, but only the most commonly used methods in neuromarketing studies are described.

Electroencephalography (EEG)

The electroencephalogram (EEG) allows us to observe the change over time in the electrical signals generated by the activation of brain cells in response to any stimulus (Blinowska & Durka, 2006:1). This measured electrical activity ranges from -100 to +100 μV (Read and Innis, 2017:2). EEG can be measured non-invasively with electrodes placed on the scalp or with probes placed in the cortex. The EEG signal that occurs when exposed to a stimulus is called an event-related potential (ERP) (Blinowska, & Durka, 2006:1). EEG signals are named as Delta, Theta, Alpha, Beta, Gamma and Beta waves according to their frequency ranges (Aktop & Seferoğlu, 2014:26). Figure-2 shows EEG devices and Figure-3 shows examples of data obtained from EEG.

Functional Magnetic Resonance Imaging (fMRI)

FMRI uses a magnetic field and radio waves to help us observe the brain in detail. FMRI can observe which areas of the brain are active when exposed to stimuli depending on the oxygen in the blood. Brightness in that area of the brain indicates increased neuro activity in that area (Özkaya, 2015:36). FMRI has a high spatial resolution, allowing us to observe the depths of the brain (Agarwal and Xavier,

Figure 2. EEG devices: Medical EEG device (left), Emotiv (center), ABM (right)
Source: Tunalı (2016:4).

Figure 3. P300 signal
Source: Tunalı et al. (2016:4)

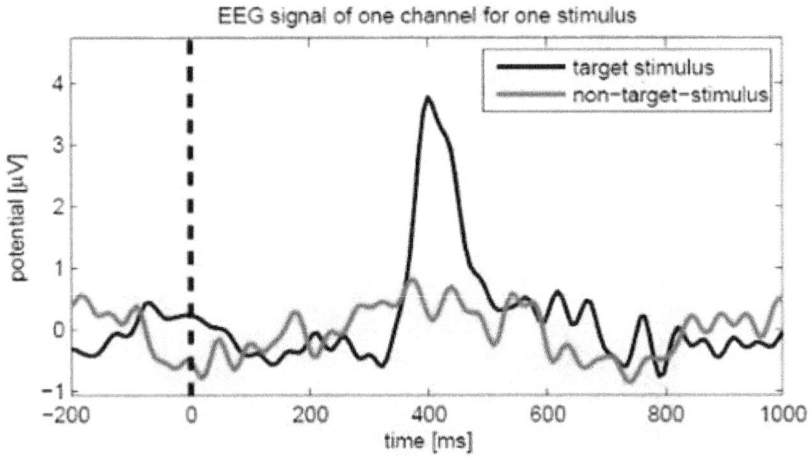

Figure 4. FMRI device
Source: https://www.jameco.com/Jameco/workshop/Howitworks/what-is-an-fmri-scan-and-how-does-it-work.html

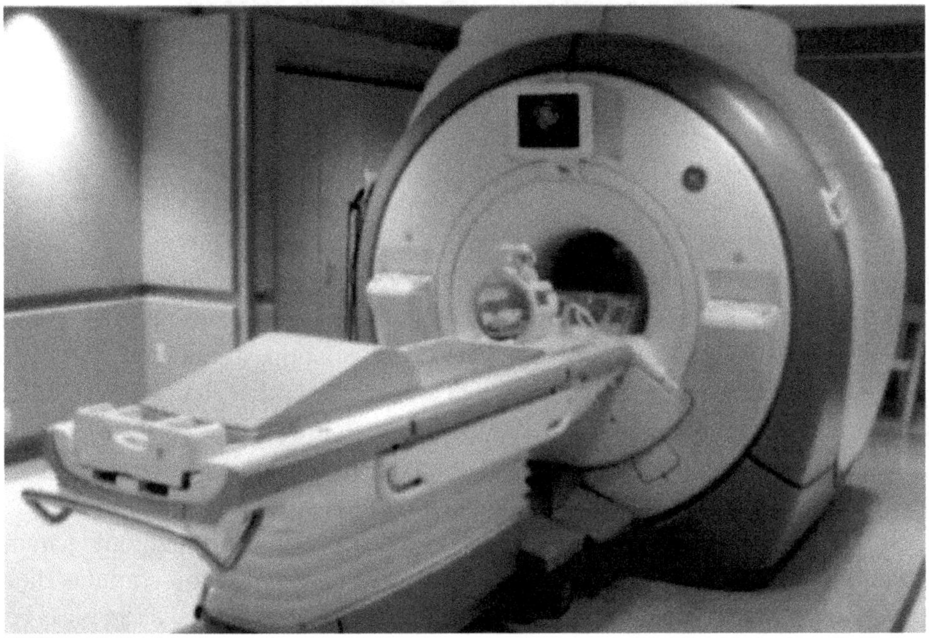

2015:28) and thus has an important position among other techniques. Figure-4 shows the fMRI device and Figure-5 shows examples of data obtained from fMRI.

Figure 5. FMRI brain scan result
Source: https://www.cognitivefxusa.com/blog/fmri-brain-scans-duke-study-implications

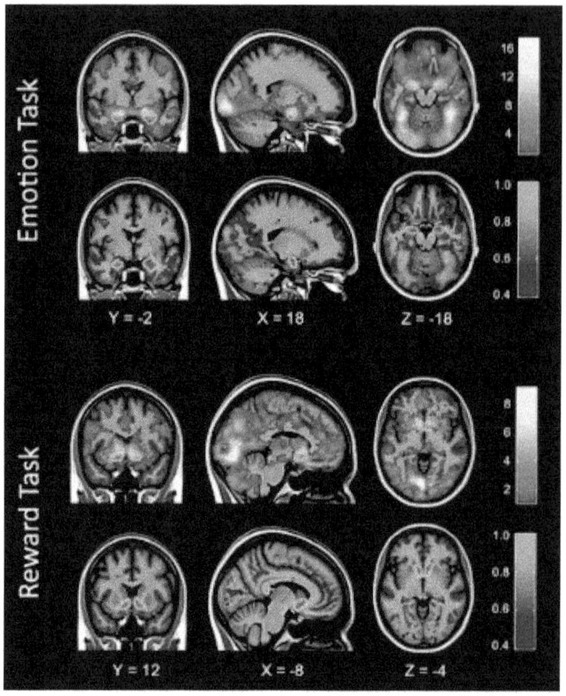

Skin Conductance (SC)

Galvanic Skin Response (GSR) is defined as a change in the electrical properties of the skin. Electric current can be used to observe the response of our autonomic nervous system through the eccrine sweat gland. The psychogalvanic reflex (PGR), also called galvanic skin response (GSR), is a change in the electrical properties of the body (skin) following noxious stimulation, stimulation that produces an emotional response, and, to some extent, stimulation that attracts the body (Sharmal et al., 2016:13). When individuals are presented with or exposed to a stimulus, their autonomic nervous system is activated. This process leads to sweat gland activity and thus a change in skin conductance (Li et al., 2022:2). This change cannot be consciously controlled as in other autonomic processes (Aytekin, 2019:1584). These changes measured by electrodes allow us to observe two different parameters: tonic parameters, which are naturally continuous, and phasic parameters, which occur in response to a stimulus such as advertising and express short-term activity (Kula and Süer, 2006:108). In this way, we can observe whether the stimulus affects the stimuli or not. Figures 6 and 7 show the GSR device and Figure 8 shows examples of the data obtained from the GSR.

Transcranial Magnetic Stimulation (TMS)

Transcranial Magnetic Stimulation (TMS) is a technique that aims to produce a small and transient electric current in the cerebral cortex by a very strong magnetic field generated by a stimulating coil. The stimulating coil is held very close to the scalp and focused on a specific area. The magnetic field

Figure 6. GSR device
Kaynak: https://eminaker.medium.com/n%C3%B6ropazarlama-ara%C5%9Ft%C4%B1rma-y%C3%B6ntemleri-gsr-galvanic-skin-response-2c9f5ac071ff

Figure 7. GSR device
Kaynak: https://eminaker.medium.com/n%C3%B6ropazarlama-ara%C5%9Ft%C4%B1rma-y%C3%B6ntemleri-gsr-galvanic-skin-response-2c9f5ac071ff

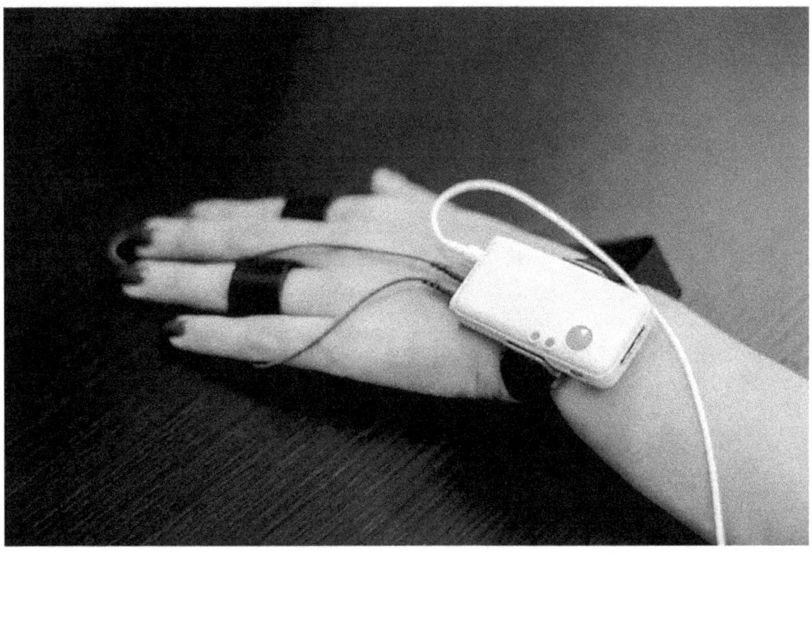

Figure 8. GSR data
Kaynak: https://www.noropazarlama.net/2020/05/04/gsr-deri-iletkenligi-nedir-nasil-olculur/

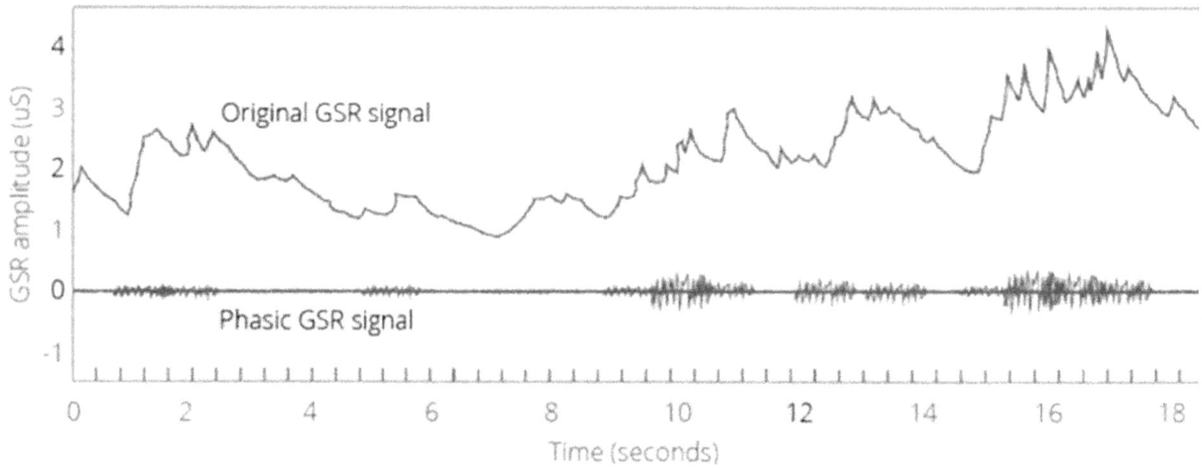

Figure 9. TMS operation simulation
Source: https://brainclinics.com/rtms/

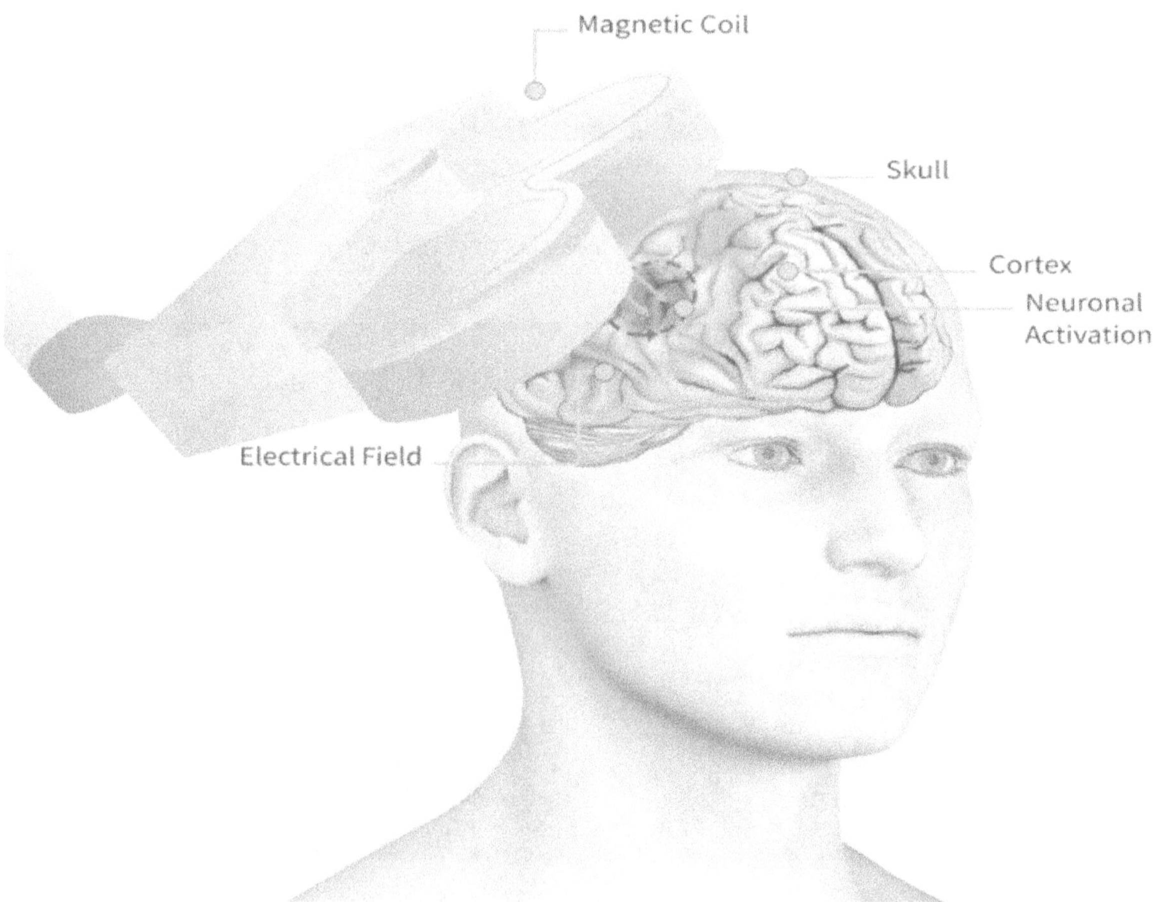

creates a localized electric current in the tissue. The patient is seated in a chair and the electromagnet is placed on the head. The magnetic field is applied as close as 5 cm to an area of 1.5 cm2. When TMS is applied to the cerebral cortex, depolarization of neurons occurs in the underlying electrical field. This depolarization spreads to related regions via synaptic pathways (Doksat and Aslan, 2006:93; Alpay et al., 2005.136. This depolarization is recorded by other methods that do not disrupt brain functions. In this way, it provides the opportunity to study causality and see its effects on behavior (Lim, 2018:209).

Figure-9 illustrates the working principle of TMS. Visual representation of the induction of electrical currents in the brain (gray arrows in the brain) through magnetic pulses applied via a coil (gray figure 8) placed on the head. The colors on the scalp reflect the electrical field, i.e. where neural activation is most focused (https://brainclinics.com/rtms/).

Eye Tracking

Eye tracking technique, one of the most common methods used in neuromarketing studies, was developed by Mowrer in 1936 (Özdoğan, 2008:135). It allows us to track where and for how long the eye movements are focused and how the eye follows a route. It offers the opportunity to make inferences about what the viewer/viewers actually see and what they focus on with the combination of hardware and software that allows us to track the data of a single user as well as the data of a group (Baş ve Tüzün, 2014:221).

There are three main methods used to track eye movements:

- Recording pupil responses, usually by directing infrared rays at the eye
- Measurement of electricity in the skin covering the eye area
- Monitoring movement with special lenses worn on the eye (Özdoğan, 2008:137).

The most widely used of these methods is the tracking of the pupil with infrared rays, which both does not harm the person and is not affected by environmental light sources.

Eye movements consist of eye jumps of 3-5° called saccades lasting 30 - 40 milliseconds and fixations (focusing) lasting approximately 200 - 300 milliseconds (Chandon, 2007:5).

Fixation; provides information about where the eye is at a given moment. Along with focusing, we can also learn the number and duration of focusing.

Leap; leap data, which refers to the transition of the eye from one point to another point,

With the combination of focus and jump data, we can obtain the route information that the eye follows (Erdemir ve Yavuz, 2016:101-106). The path of the eye is used to analyze visual perception, cognitive purpose and interest (Santos, 2015:34).

With this data, gaze plots, heat maps, cluster and area of interest data are created. With this data, gaze plots, heat maps, cluster and area of interest data are created.

We can say that the use of eye tracking in market research has two different focal points. The first is the identification of consumers and the study of their consumption behavior. The second is on the effectiveness and efficiency of products. The areas of use of the eye tracking technique, which provides deeper information about the cognitive processes underlying attention, learning and memory, are shown in Table 1.

Bebko et al. (2014) examined the attractiveness of text, face and brand/logo in print advertisements of non-profit organizations with eye tracking technique. Using first fixation duration, number of fixa-

Table 1. Usage areas of eye tracking technique

Görsel Testler	Kullanım Testleri
Ambalaj Testleri Logo, amblem, figür testleri Teşhir Ekipmanları Mağaza tasarımları, alışveriş alışkanlıkları, raf düzeni ve ürün yerleştirmeleri Basılı reklam (Gazete, Dergi v.b.)	Interaktif TV testleri Otomotiv ve uçuş simulasyon uygulamarı Web sitesi testi Yazılım kullanabilirlik testleri Bilgisayar oyunları ve etkileşimi El Terminali & Smartphone
Açıkhava reklamları TV Reklamları Online Reklamlar	Kullanıcı deneyimleri Mesleki performans ölçümleri Araştırmalarda vaka kullanımı Öğrenme ve eğitim uygulamaları Tıbbi araştırmalar (nörolojik, psikiyatrik

Source: Hür ve Kumbasar 2011

Figure 10. Heat maps wildlife conservation advertisement
Source: Bebko (2014:362).

tions, and total visit duration as metrics, they concluded that eye tracking measurements are an effective indicator of donor behavior (Bebko et al., 2014).

Figure-10 shows the use of kangaroos in an advertisement for an organization that collects donations for wildlife conservation. Bebko et al. (2014) found that the frequency of the subjects' repeated visits to the page and the length of the total time spent focusing on the face increased the likelihood of encouraging others to donate.

Figure 11. Heat map showing visual attention in the goal directed condition with an advertisement located at the top of the page
Source: Resnick and Albert (2014:213)

Figure 12. Heat map showing visual attention in the free-viewing condition with an advertisement located at the top of the page
Source: Resnick and Albert (2014:214)

Figure 13. Heat map showing visualattention in the goal directed condition with an advertisement on the right side of the page
Source: Resnick and Albert (2014:213)

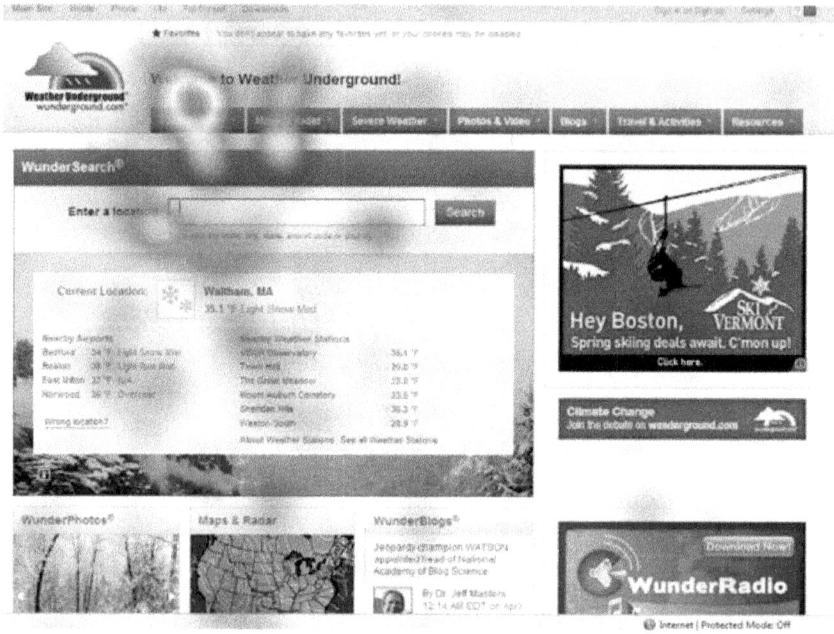

Figure 14. Heat map showing visualattention in the goal directed condition with an advertisement on the right side of the page
Source: Resnick and Albert (2014:214)

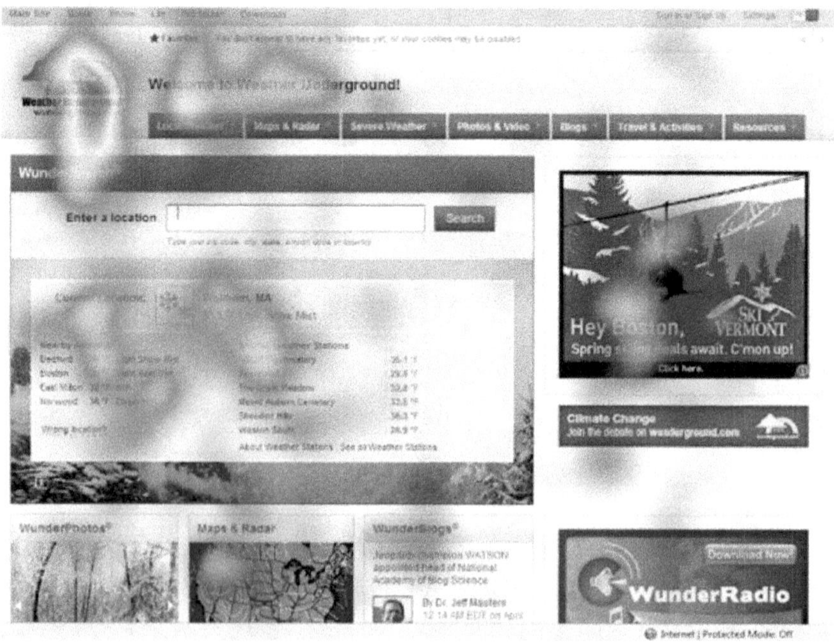

Figure 15. Evaluated ads
Source: Scotta (2016:636)

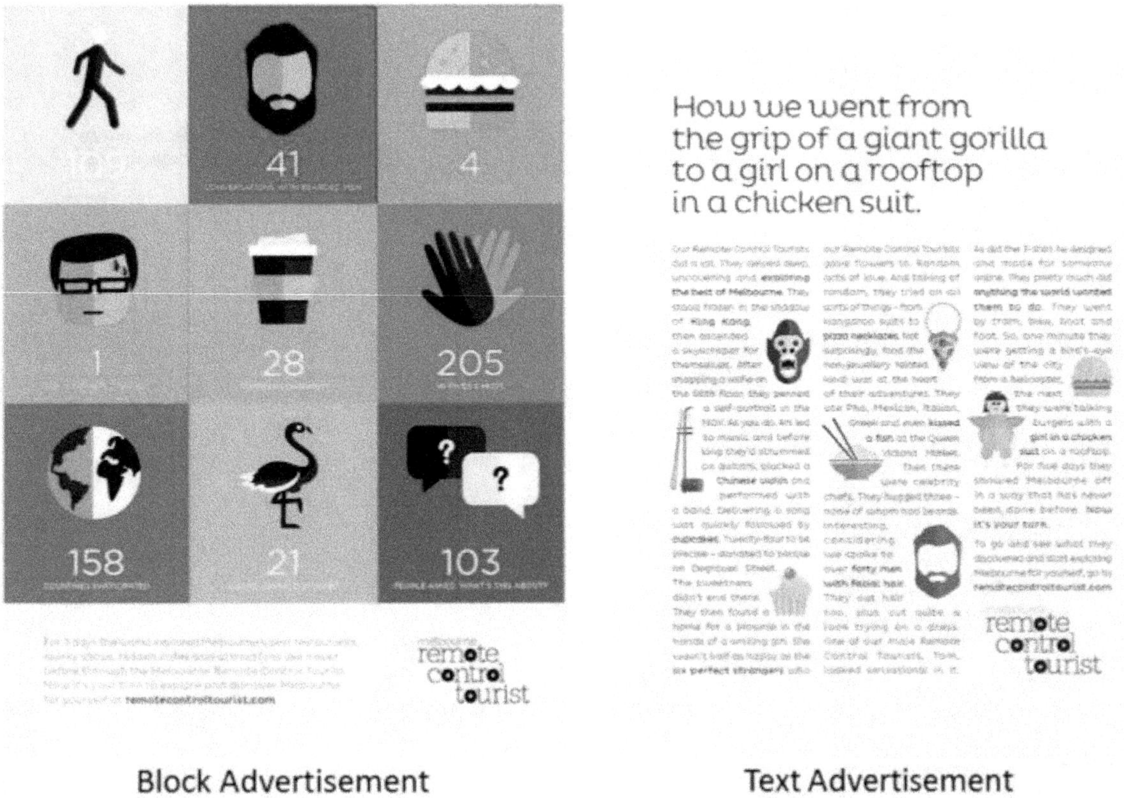

Resnick and Albert (2014) used analysis of variance and eye-tracking method in their study on the blindness of advertising banners on web home pages. With the eye-tracking method, they concluded that the position of banner ads has a significant effect on visual attention.

It is seen that the banner ad is placed on the top of the page in Figure-11 and on the right side of the page in Figure-13. They concluded that users tend to avoid ads when ad banners are placed on the top and right side, and they do not tend to avoid ads when in free viewing mode (Resnick and Albert 2014:216).

Scotta et al. (2016) examined the effectiveness of two versions of a tourism magazine organized as blocks and text using eye-tracking and self-report methods. They found that eye-tracking and self-report data were consistent with each other and that there were significant differences between the two ads tested.

To evaluate the ads shown in Figure-14, average duration time, number of saccades, heat maps, and first fixation path displays metrics were evaluated. It shows that the block ad is more successful in attracting and maintaining attention than the text ad, and it is understood that textual information should be presented in a more concise manner (Figure-16 and Figure-17) (Scotta et al., 2016:639).

Figure 16. First fixations on block ad
Source: Scotta (2016:639)

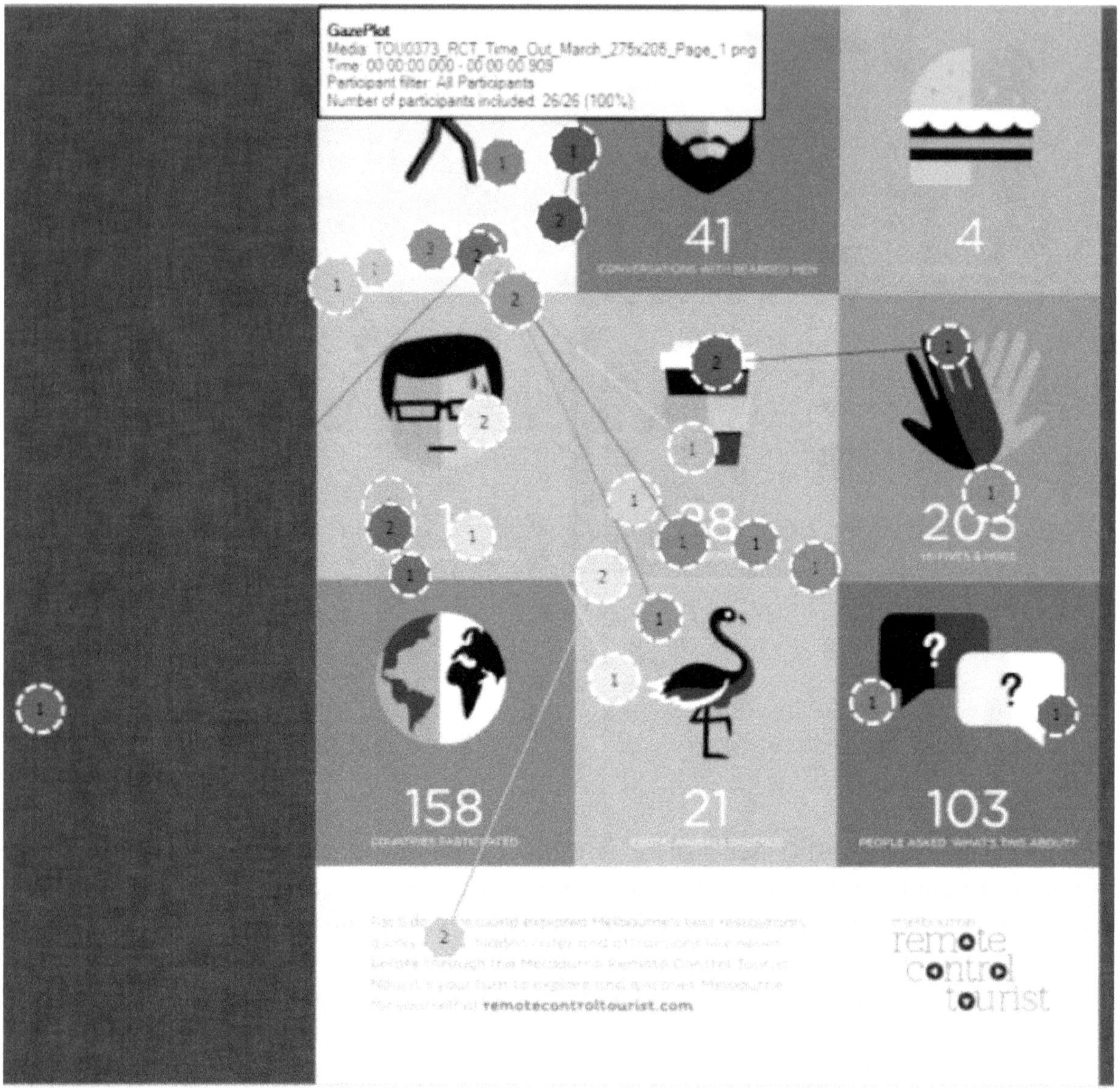

CONCLUSION

The fact that consumers' lives are filled with devices such as televisions, computers, cell phones and tablets has made them more accessible to businesses, and consumers have become immune to these messages. In today's complex, increasingly dense media environment, it is now much more difficult for commercial brands to differentiate themselves from their competitors, to explain their benefits to information-saturated consumers, and to convince them, compared to the times when there was no intense message bombardment. Businesses will be able to overcome this challenge with IMC and neuromarketing practices. As it can be understood from the studies presented in the study, the use of eye-tracking not

Figure 17. Scan paths on text ad
Source: Scotta (2016:640)

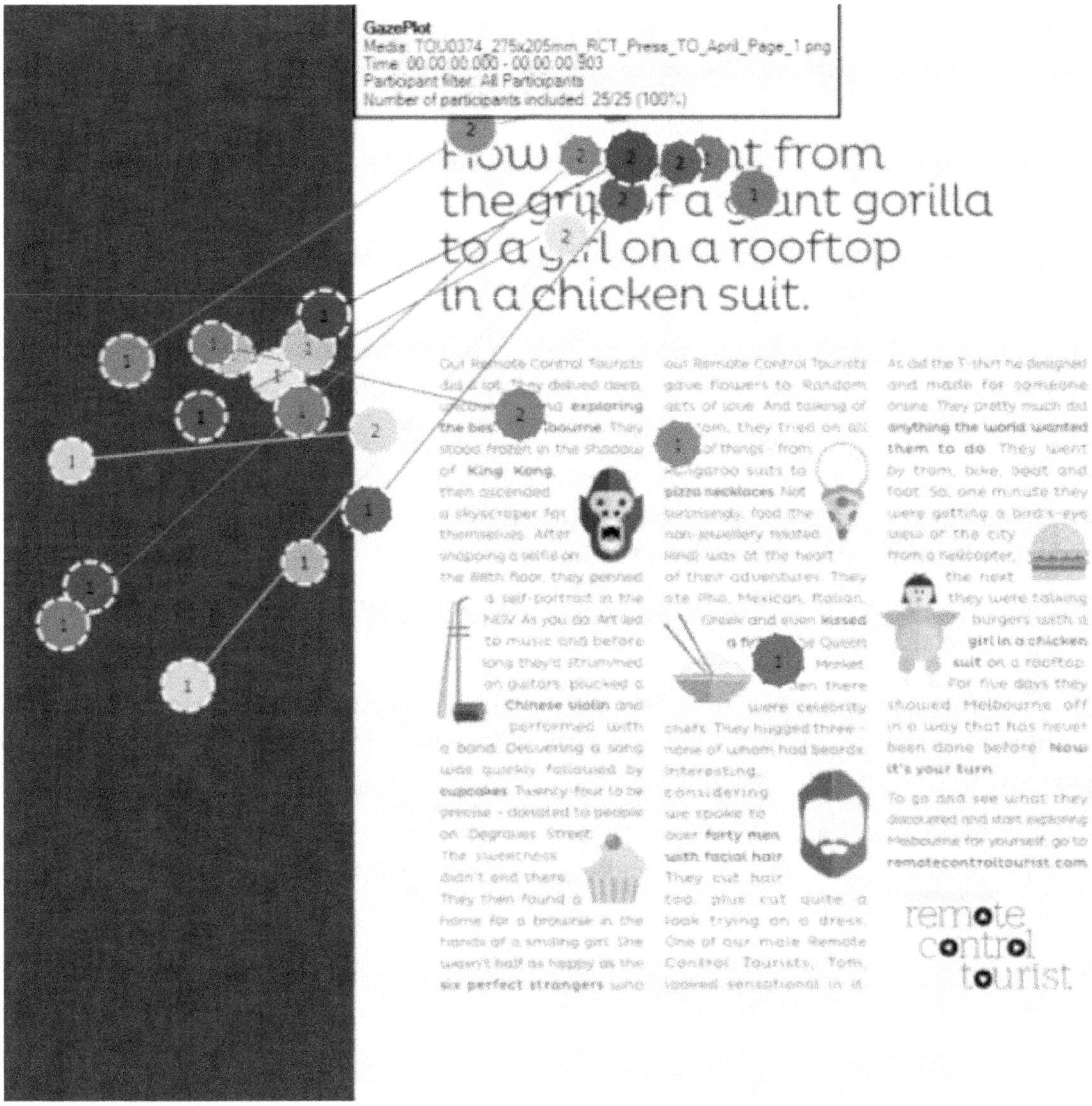

only increases the effectiveness of communication activities such as television commercials, which are prepared by spending large budgets, but also helps to make more effective and efficient arrangements, thus providing cost advantages.

REFERENCES

Aktop, A. & Seferoğlu, F. (2014). Sportif performans açısından nöro-geribildirim. *Spor ve Performans Araştırmaları Dergisi, 5*(2).

Alpay, N., Karşıdağ, Ç., & Kükürt, R. (2005). Transkranyal manyetik stimülasyon (TMS). *Dusunen Adam : Bakirkoy Ruh Ve Sinir Hastaliklari Hastanesi Yayin Organi, 18*(3), 136–148.

Alsharif, A. H., Md Salleh, N. Z., Baharun, R., & Yusoff, M. E. (2021). Consumer behaviour through neuromarketing approach. *Journal of Contemporary Issues in Business and Government, 27*(3), 344–354.

Aytekin, B. A. (2019). İzleyici ve içerik etkileşimi bağlamında yeni bir youtube fenomeni olarak otonom duyusal meridyen tepki (ASMR) etkisinin deri iletkenliği ölçümü (GSR) tekniği ile incelenmesi. *OPUS–Uluslararası Toplum Araştırmaları Dergisi, 10*(17), 1568–1600. doi:10.26466/opus.533789

Baş, T. & Tüzün, H. (2014). Tüketicileri (Kullanıcıları) ve ürün kullanımlarını analiz etmek için göz izleme yönteminin kullanılması. *Tüketici Yazıları*, (4), 217 – 234.

Bebko, C., Sciulli, L. M., & Bhagat, P. (2014). Using eye-tracking to assess the ımpact of advertising appeals on donor behavior. *Journal of Nonprofit & Public Sector Marketing, 26*(4), 354–371. doi:10.1080/10495142.2014.965073

Blazquez-Resino, J. J., Gutierrez-Broncano, S., & Gołąb-Andrzejak, E. (2022). Neuroeconomy and neuromarketing: The study of the consumer behaviour in the Covid-19 context. *Frontiers in Psychology, 13*, 13. doi:10.3389/fpsyg.2022.822856 PMID:35369189

Blinowska, K., & Durka, P. (2006). *Electroencephalography (EEG)*. Wiley Encyclopedia of Biomedical Engineering. doi:10.1002/9780471740360.ebs0418

Briggs, R., Krishnan, R., & Borin, N. (2005). Integrated multichannel communication strategies: Evaluating the return on marketing objectives—the case of the 2004 Ford F-150 launch. *Journal of Interactive Marketing, 19*(3), 81–90. doi:10.1002/dir.20045

ChandonP.HutchinsonJ. W.BradlowE. T.ScottH. (2007). *Measuring the value of point-of-purchase marketing with commercial eye-tracking data.* Faculty and Research Working Paper. Available at: https://ssrn.com/abstract=1032162

Doksat, M. K., & Aslan, S. (2006). Tekrarlanan transkraniyal manyetik stimulasyon (rTMS) ve depresyon tedavisi. *New/Yeni Symposium Journal, 44*(2), 92-99.

Harrell, E. (2019). Neuromarketing: What you need to know. *Harvard Business Review, 97*(4), 64–70.

Harris, J. M., Ciorciari, J., & Gountas, J. (2018). Consumer neuroscience for marketing researchers. *Journal of Consumer Behaviour, 17*(3), 239–252. doi:10.1002/cb.1710

Hür, Ş. & Kumbasar, S. (2011). Göz hareketlerine dayalı araştırma çözümleri eye-tracking teknolojisi. *Araştırmada Yenilikler Konferansı.*

Ivanov, A. E. (2012). The Internet's impact on integrated marketing communication. *Procedia Economics and Finance, 3*, 536–542. doi:10.1016/S2212-5671(12)00192-X

Kula, H., & Süer, C. (2006). Kısa süreli egzersizin antrene sporcularda deri iletkenliğine etkisi. *Saglik Bilimleri Dergisi, 15*(2), 107–115.

Li, S., Sung, B., Linc, Y., & Mitas, O. (2022). Electrodermal Activity Measure: A Methodological Review. *Annals of Tourism Research, 96*, 103460. Advance online publication. doi:10.1016/j.annals.2022.103460

Lim, W. M. (2018). Demystifying neuromarketing. *Journal of Business Research, 91*, 205–220. doi:10.1016/j.jbusres.2018.05.036

Mihaela, O. O. E. (2015). The influence of the integrated marketing communication on the consumer buying behaviour. *Procedia Economics and Finance, 23*, 1446–1450. doi:10.1016/S2212-5671(15)00446-3

Mihart, C. (2012). Modelling the influence of integrated marketing communication on consumer behaviour: An approach based on hierarchy of effects concept. *Procedia: Social and Behavioral Sciences, 62*, 975–980. doi:10.1016/j.sbspro.2012.09.166

Mileti, A., Guido, G., & Prete, M. I. (2016). Nanomarketing: A new frontier for *Neuromarketing. Psychology and Marketing, 33*(8), 664–674. doi:10.1002/mar.20907

Morin, C. (2011). Neuromarketing: The new science of consumer behaviour. *Society, 48*(2), 131–135. doi:10.1007/s12115-010-9408-1

Özdoğan, F. B. (2008). Göz izleme ve pazarlamada kullanılması üzerine kavramsal bir çalışma. *Gazi Üniversitesi Ticaret ve Turizm Eğitim Fakültesi Dergisi, 2*, 134-147.

Özkaya, B. (2015). Marka yönetiminde araştırma: Fonksiyonel manyetik rezonans görüntüleme tekniği. *Maltepe Üniversitesi İletişim Fakültesi Dergisi, 2*(1), 24–47.

Piccarozzi, M., Silvestri, C., & Morganti, P. (2021). COVID-19 in management studies: A systematic literature review. *Sustainability (Basel), 13*(7), 3791. doi:10.3390/su13073791

Porcu, L., del Barrio-García, S., Alcántara-Pilar, J. M., & Crespo-Almendros, E. (2019). Analyzing the influence of firm-wide integrated marketing communication on market performance in the hospitality industry. *International Journal of Hospitality Management, 80*, 13–24. doi:10.1016/j.ijhm.2019.01.008

Porcu, L., del Barrio-García, S., Kitchen, P. J., & Tourky, M. (2020). The antecedent role of a collaborative vs. a controlling corporate culture on firm-wide integrated marketing communication and brand performance. *Journal of Business Research, 119*, 435–443. doi:10.1016/j.jbusres.2019.10.049

Read, G. L., & Innis, I. J. (2017). Electroencephalography (EEG). The İnternational Encyclopedia of Communication Research Methods, 1-18. doi:10.1002/9781118901731.iecrm0080

Resnick, M. & Albert, W. (2014). The ımpact of advertising location and user taskon the emergence of banner ad blindness: An eye-tracking study. *Intl. Journal of Human–Computer Interaction, 30*, 206–219. doi:10.1080/10447318.2013.847762

Santos, R. O. (2015). Eye tracking in neuromarketing: A research agenda for marketing studies. *International Journal of Psychological Studies, 7*(1). doi:10.1080/13683500.2014.1003797

Šerić, M., Gil-Saura, I., & Ruiz-Molina, M. E. (2014). How can integrated marketing communications and advanced technology influence the creation of customer-based brand equity? Evidence from the hospitality industry. *International Journal of Hospitality Management, 39*, 144–156. doi:10.1016/j.ijhm.2014.02.008

Sharma, M., Kacker, S., & Sharma, M. (2016). A Brief Introduction and Review on Galvanic Skin Response. *International Journal of Medical Research Professionals, 2*(6), 13–17. doi:10.21276/ijmrp.2016.2.6.003

Tunalı, S. B., Ömer, G., & Göktuğ, Ö. (2016). Pazarlama ve Reklam Araştırmalarında Nöropazarlama Üzerine Yapılmış Araştırmaların İncelenmesi ve Etik Boyutunun Tartışılması. *Kurgu*, *24*(2), 1–8.

Tuncel, H. (2009). Halkla İlişkiler Anlayişiyla Bütünleşik Pazarlama İletişimi. İstanbul Üniversitesi İletişim Fakültesi Dergisi, (35), 115-136.

Chapter 8
Consumer Perspective on Influencers, the Rising Trend of Digital Marketing Perspective:
A Qualitative Research on Generation Y

Gülşah Akto
https://orcid.org/0000-0002-7616-4111
Fırat University, Turkey

ABSTRACT

Advances in digital media have affected consumer preferences and tendencies as they have impacted the field of marketing. Whilst digital marketing becomes more effective every day, influencer marketing has taken its place among the most popular marketing strategies of recent times. Defined as a personality that alters and influences the way other people behave, influencers have tried to shape consumers' preferences and purchasing behaviors by obtaining and evaluating information in different ways and promoting products and services. Although influencers have an impact on their followers' preferences, consumer opinions towards influencers are equally significant. This study aims to analyze consumers' views on the concept of influencers, why they follow influencers, and their perspectives on influencers' earnings and status. In addition, the study focused on how influencers' product and service promotions affect consumers' opinions about brands and companies and their purchasing behaviors.

INTRODUCTION

The type of interaction referred to as social media, which has rapidly spread on the Internet, has moved away from the traditional approach to advertising with the perspective of recommendation marketing. Promotional advertising practices of famous people through television, radio, or newspapers have been slowly replaced by digital media. Advertising and promotional activities by both celebrities and individuals who are recognized only on social media channels have come to the spotlight. At the axis of this approach were individuals with the ability to influence large masses of consumers, social figures, and

DOI: 10.4018/979-8-3693-0855-4.ch008

those with a following on social networks. Such practices have led to the emergence of a new marketing field called influencer marketing, and this has attracted attention with its rapid expansion in the world (Glucksman, 2017, p. 78).

Influencers represent a new type of independent, third-party advocate who molds the behaviors of an audience through the use of blogs, tweets, and other social media channels (Freberg et al., 2010, p.3). Through platforms such as Instagram, YouTube, Twitter, and Facebook, digital media influencers generate content promoting specific brands in order to raise brand awareness. The success of influencers, distinguished by their number of followers and status, is significant for brands. Therefore, gaining consumer trust is essential for influencers to establish their relationship with a brand or organization. The number of followers, comments, and likes on product and service promotions have assumed their place among the actions that support the sense of trust towards influencers. All mentioned points demonstrate key aspects of a social media influencer's success. Influencers on social media open a new channel for brands to scale with consumers more naturally and into their everyday lives (Freberg et al., 2010, p.5). Through channels within influencer marketing, consumers follow people who promote products and services and exchange ideas. Influencer marketing consists of companies that engage with people with followers in the digital world to communicate with them for a fee (Bakker, 2018, p. 80). The impact of influencer marketing, as a new marketing communication tool attracting attention, plays an important role in the purchasing behavior of consumers. Influencers are significant in the context of current consumer behavior as an intermediary between the brand and the consumer and as a source of information.

This study aims to reveal the perspective of Generation Y consumers towards influencers based on the information outlined above. This study aims to fill this gap in the literature. The research is valuable in the sense that it analyzes consumer perspectives on influencers and influencer marketing together.

In this respect, the following questions will be addressed.

- What do Gen Y consumers think about influencers?
- Why do Gen Y consumers follow influencers?
- Do Gen Y consumers consider influencer as a profession?
- Does the number of followers of influencers matter to Gen Y consumers?
- What do Gen Y consumers think about the social status of influencers?
- Do Gen Y consumers care about the opinions and suggestions of influencers?
- Do Gen Y consumers buy products shared by influencers without questioning them?
- What are the expectations of Gen Y consumers from influencers?

BACKGROUND

The consumers of the digital world, in need of consumption, want to get instant service, be more active, and get information about everything they experience. Consumers who demand more information about the product or service they want to buy acquire the information that they need by reaching out to the corporation or through influencers who have become digital representatives of word-of-mouth communication who have tried the product and commented on it. Companies, on the other hand, strive to attract consumers on social media through influencer marketing strategies using influencers they favor and trust.

In this regard, a review of the literature on influencer marketing reveals that there are a large number of studies focusing on the concept, historical process, and strategies of influencer marketing. (Gamage &

Ashill, 2023; Hudders & Lou, 2023; Dömbekçi & Erişen, 2022; Fariver &Wang, 2022; Kazancı, 2022; Zengin Demirbilek, 2021; Campbell & Farrell, 2020; Karataş and Eti, 2020; Mutluer, 2020; Ponirah, 2020; Stubb, Claesson, & Liungberg, 2018; 2019; Gross & Florian, 2018; Bakker, 2018; Mert, 2018; Gmachi, 2017; Braatz 2017.)

Seyyid et al., (2023), in their study attempted to understand influencer marketing from the perspective of brands. The study provides insights into how effective influencer collaboration can best be achieved. Lou & Hudders (2023), offer valuable insights into the current challenges of influencer marketing in their research. Addresses how and with which strategies they use marketing effectively. Gamage & Ashill (2022), investigated how influencer-generated publicity affects followers' willingness to inquire about the product. Bakker (2018), in his study, aimed to conceptualize influencer marketing. In his study, Mert (2018), investigated the development of influencer marketing, its application patterns, and economic dimensions. Kazancı (2022), examined the aspects of social media influencers' posts influencing university students' intention to browse and purchase products and services. In her study, Zengin Demirbilek (2021) explored the development process of influencer marketing practices, the tools through which they have become widespread, and the strategies used. As a result of the study, it was concluded that there is a transformation and change in the marketing channels of businesses with digitalization, and social media platforms are preferred more often compared to traditional marketing channels.

Evaluating the relevant research, there are limited studies that address consumers' opinions about influencers. Thus, this study aims to fill this gap in the literature. This research is important since it analyzes the consumer perspective on influencers and influencer marketing together.

Digital Consumers of Digital Marketing

The field of marketing, unable to remain indifferent to the changes in the global arena, has evolved into a new dimension, especially with the development of digital technologies. In the Globalizing world, the opportunities offered by the digital world have drawn the attention of companies and the concept of marketing has shifted towards digital environments (Aw & Agnihotri, 2023, p.1). Companies that endeavor to increase brand awareness through marketing by striving to find ways to reach more consumers faster and more effectively and to leave a positive impression in the minds of consumers have started to use social media platforms intensively. The rapidly developing technologies have accelerated the shift towards digital media as an alternative to traditional marketing techniques (Kazancı, 2022, p.59).

Companies use search engines and e-mail to communicate with consumers in digital marketing, which is conducted through electronic devices. The marketing strategy that has gained the most momentum in recent years has been using social media platforms. Search engine, social media, content, website, e-mail, and influencer marketing have taken center stage in digital marketing strategies (Panda & Mishra, 2022, p.1). Consumers responded to the changes in the field of marketing and increased their expectations from companies. In particular, consumers, who appear before businesses as digital consumers, wish to get information about products and services with different methods other than traditional marketing tools. (Gmachi, 2017, p.34).

According to Kotler, consumers used to be more interested in content in traditional media. Because they had no other choice. Digital media has changed everything. Through social networks, consumers have countless sources of user-generated content that they consider more appealing based on their interests. What makes them attractive is that they are tailored to the wants and needs of consumers (Kotler et al., 2021, p.168).

As consumer culture is directly and indirectly affected by the internet, social media, mobile applications, and devices, the concept of digital consumer has taken a place in the literature. Digital consumers can easily choose brands by searching for products and services on the internet (Dey et al., 2020, p.2). By reviewing and responding to comments made on social media about the brand, product, and service, the consumer is involved in the production and consumption. Digital consumer culture is thus created through repetitive and reciprocal interactions between the online and offline world through individual, social, and commercial behaviors and practices (Deuze, 2006, p. 63).

The Background of Influencer Marketing

As digital and technical developments have led to new marketing strategies, they have also led to differences in consumers' media preferences. Web technologies have provided individuals with the opportunity to contribute to the content. Technologies have accelerated the popularity of social media platforms such as Instagram, Twitter, Facebook, etc. by introducing mobile applications, allowing individuals to build an online following (Leung et al., 2022, p:230). Especially marketing 4.0 and 5.0 practices, changes in consumer media preferences and the shift of marketing strategies to the digital world have driven influencer marketing. The fact that consumers spend more time on digital media than traditional media has resulted in companies preferring influencer marketing over traditional marketing. Companies have turned to advertising and promotion of influencers as it is easier and more affordable to reach consumers through social networks (Gerdeman, 2019). Influencer marketing provides more sales and return on investment than traditional marketing, changes in the technological, economic, and social fields in recent years and differentiating consumer preferences have all brought influencers to the forefront. Digital transformations of the traditional marketing approach, changing behaviors and expectations of consumers have popularized influencer marketing (Ahmad,2018, p.24).

The Concept of Influencer and Influencer Marketing

The rapid development of modern technologies, and in particular the Internet in all its applications, offers both consumers and businesses a multitude of innovations and opportunities. Ever-updating social media platforms and blogs allow people to be active online and create content (Ewers, 2017, p. 1). Social media platforms such as Instagram, Facebook and YouTube have become a part of the customer communication of many brands with their intense user behavior. Influencer marketing is defined as a marketing practice that leverages well-followed online users who can affect consumers' attitudes and decision-making processes in favor of brands or ideas. (Femenia-Serra &Gretzel, 2020, p. 65).

Influencers, sometimes referred to as social media celebrities, have a large number of followers, can create purchasing motivation in their followers, and are considered reliable sources of information for consumers. Consumers who believe in and are impressed by the content produced by influencers can direct their followers to the content offered (Aktaş & Şener, 2019, p.405).

Freberg et al. defined influencer as a new type of social media phenomenon that molds the behavior of their audience through social media networks such as Facebook, Instagram, and others in exchange for a certain fee. These individuals often provide information and advice to followers; therefore, they are more likely to influence purchase behavior through word-of-mouth (Freberg et al., 2019). Carter, on the other hand, defines influencers as trusted personalities who have a large following on social media platforms and therefore have a wide reach and interaction capacity (Carter, 2016). Similarly, Agostino et al. define an influencer as an individual who is active on social media, empowered, listened to, and trusted by social media users (Agostino et al., 2019).

Social media influencers promote brands through their personal lives, making them more relatable to the average consumer. According to Ledbetter and Meisner, when a party tries to influence another to take specific actions, a dynamic process emerges that can change the course and content of relationships. In this context, influencers are the ultimate link between a brand and a consumer (Ledbetter & Meisner, 2021).

Influencer marketing is defined as a type of social media marketing that involves endorsements or product placements by social influencers or internet celebrities. The fact that well-known people or users on social media, called influencers, make certain product promotions by contracting with brands can be shown as an example of influencer marketing (Karataş & Eti, 2022, p.189). Instagram, one of the most prevalent social media tools in recent years, has also become one of the most widely used applications of influencer marketing techniques. Influencer marketing refers to the marketing of brands through social media influencers to reach their target audiences. This approach can enable brands to increase brand awareness and sales by offering their products and services directly to potential customers. As the opinions of influencers are considered significant, the individuals around them are affected by influencers in the purchasing process. Therefore, the more followers influencers have, the greater the importance of their opinions. (Stubb, 2019, p.12).

TYPES OF INFLUENCERS

Influencers by Follower Count

According to Kazancı, influencers are divided into 5 categories according to the number of followers: nano, micro, mid-level macro, and mega. (Kazancı, 2022, pp.55-56).

Nano Influencers: Influencers with a follower list of between 1,000 and 10,000 on social media channels. It can be assumed that they not only have a close relationship with their followers but also that they devote enough time to building this relationship. They can be recommended for medium-sized businesses with a small budget or as a way to reach a niche target audience. Instagram is a platform where these influencers can easily be found (Brown & Hayes, 2008, p. 49).

Micro-Influencers: Celebrities with less than 100 thousand followers who appeal to a niche target audience or influencers with 10 - 50 thousand followers in some classifications They have a direct impact on purchasing behavior with their authentic personalities that have their personal lives, are better informed in, and are appropriate to their area of interest. Micro-influencers are not celebrities in the traditional sense. They have a direct influence on purchasing behavior with their unique personalities having their own lives, more knowledgeable in their own field of interest, and suitable for their field of interest (Kazancı, 2022, p. 55).

Mid-Level Influencers: Influencers with 50 to 500 thousand followers. If this person is an expert in subjects other than television celebrities, series, and shows and has more than 50 thousand followers, they may be the right influencer for the brand Freberg et al., 2011, p.90).

Macro Influencers: Although there is no classification, people who have more than 100 thousand followers on social media, or between 40 thousand and 1 million followers according to some classifications, or between 500 thousand and 1 million followers according to others, can be considered in this category (Brown & Hayes, 2008, p.49). They are mostly in this category and have not appeared in major roles. Macro influencers are best suited for their reach. There is a natural density of followers.

Mega Influencers: Influencers with more than 200,000 followers are in this category. They are the influencers with the highest number of followers. These influencers may have more than 1 million followers on at least one social network. Many of the mega influencers produced shows on offline platforms and gained their fame in this way (Mert, 2018, p.1311).

Influencers According to Social Status

Friedman refers to media influencers as endorsers and identifies three types of endorsers commonly used in advertisements today (Kazancı, 2022, pp. 56-58).

Famous/Celebrity Endorser: Publicly recognized entertainers, actors, athletes, etc. The product they endorse is known for achievements in areas other than its class (Freberg et al., 2011).

Professional Endorser: They have a high level of familiarity with the class of product being promoted. They have acquired the knowledge they have through experience or studies as a result of a certain education (Kazancı, 2022, 56).

Ordinary Consumer Endorsers: People who do not have any particular knowledge other than what they have gained during the normal use of the promoted product (Kazancı, 2022, 57).

Considering this information, an influencer is one of the most intriguing and prominent professions in the world and in our country. Despite it is debatable whether this should be considered a profession or not, however, there is no denying that during the time spent on social media, users encounter many influencers. In such cases, Influencers, who are rising stars, become the target of brands (Mert, 2018, p. 1311). In the global movement scene, what matters more than a brand's origin, number of years of existence, or illustrious past are the ties it establishes with communities.

Gen Y and Influencer Marketing

According to Kotler, each generation has different ideas and perspectives on products and services. This has led businesses to create different strategies and business models. Generation Y, born between 1981 and 1996, is the first generation born when the internet was available. They are also the first generation to be closely linked to the use of social media. They are ready to express themselves on social media. Thus, they are highly susceptible to being influenced by what their peers and those they follow on social media say and buy. This generation, who can question everything, likes to consume fast (Kotler et al., 2022, pp. 34-35).

Generation Y consumers, who particularly stand in front of businesses as digital consumers, want to have information about products and services through different methods other than traditional marketing tools. Standing out with their fondness and commitment to technology, Generation Y's relationship with influencers is different compared to other generations. Generation Y is often exposed to the posts of influencers, which is naturally referred to as the new trend of digital marketing, while accessing information. Generation Y individuals, who can easily access digital media content, can communicate easily with digital influencers who use social media channels as an intensive means of communication and expression (Gmachi, 2017, p.34). These consumers, who use social media intensively, obtain information about products in a short time through influencers on social media platforms.. Generation Y consumers who have inquisitive characteristics search the product and service promotions advertised on social media before purchasing them. They take purchasing action by checking user comments about the product in digital media (Kotler et, al; 2022, p.50).

METHOD

Research Model

This study was designed in line with the Phenomenological (phenomenological) research model, which is one of the qualitative research designs, as it aims to analyze the perspective of Generation Y consumers towards influencers. The phenomenological model concentrates on phenomena that one is aware of yet does not have an in-depth and detailed understanding of. This approach aims to investigate phenomena that are not entirely unfamiliar and not completely comprehended (Yıldırım & Şimşek, 2005, p.78). Phenomenological studies investigate the opinions and perceptions of individuals towards a certain phenomenon. It examines perceptions of the phenomena observed by different individuals (Yalçın, 2022, p.217).

Working Set, Scope and Limitation

In this study, since the perspective of Generation Y consumers towards influencers will be evaluated, the study group of the research consists of Generation Y academic and administrative staff working at Fırat University. In light of previous studies in the literature, Generation Y consumers constitute the limitation of the research, as it is assumed that Generation Y values peer communication and user experiences in the final purchase decision and that they can also be influenced by the content of influencers from this point of view. Since influencers extensively use Instagram among other social media platforms and influencer marketing is mostly practiced on this platform, the research is limited to Instagram users. In this direction, the people to be included in the study were selected by purposive sampling method. Participants were selected by criterion sampling method among purposive sampling methods. Criterion sampling is the study of all cases that meet a predetermined set of criteria. These criteria can either be drawn from ready-made forms or created by the researcher (Yıldırım & Şimşek, 2005, p.135).

The criterion for this study was developed by the researcher as presented below.

- Generation Y consumers who actively use the internet and social media,
- Having an Instagram account on social media platforms.
- Following at least 2 Influencers on their Instagram account

As part of the study, Generation Y consumers who follow at least two influencers on their Instagram accounts were interviewed. In this study, the sampling period was terminated after the interviews with 10 people when it was decided that new data could no longer be obtained as the answers given in the interviews started to become repetitive. Within the scope of data collection, the relevant Ethics Committee Approval was obtained with the decision of Fırat University Social and Human Sciences Research Ethics Committee (2023-18389). The data were collected and evaluated through face-to-face, in-depth interviews.

Data Collection and Analysis

According to Yıldırım & Şimşek (2005), the primary data collection technique in phenomenological research is the interview. An interview can be defined as the activity of obtaining the thoughts and feelings of the participants about a subject or a situation. Interviewing is an effective technique for comprehending the feelings, thoughts, attitudes, perspectives, experiences, and complaints of individuals (Dömbekçi & Erişen, 2022, p.143).

In this study, the interview technique was used to collect data, and the participants were asked questions from the semi-structured interview form. As is known, semi-structured interviews are neither as rigid as fully structured interviews nor as flexible as unstructured interviews. It lies between the two extremes. In semi-structured interviews, the interviewer has a general road map. However, depending on the characteristics of the person interviewed, different dimensions of the subject are attempted to be uncovered by changing the questions in this general framework (changing the question, adding or removing new questions) (Karataş, 2017, p. 69). The semi-structured interview form was developed by the researcher based on the literature and the research questions. Then, the opinions of specialists in the field of communication sciences were taken.

The voluntary participation of the respondents was essential, and each interview lasted approximately 15 to 45 minutes. The interviews were audio-recorded with the permission of the participants. Before each interview, the purpose and method of the research were explained to the participant. Subsequently, these recordings were transcribed in full. The transcribed data were read several times and then coded by identifying frequently used expressions in the data by taking expert opinions, these codes were categorized and nine themes were formed. The statements of the participants are directly quoted. In the quoted statements, the ages of the participants were indicated and female participants were coded as Y1K (35), Y2K (36), Y3K (29), Y4K (27), Y5K (30) and male participants were coded as Y1E (38), Y2E (34), Y3E (40), Y4E (28), Y5E (32).

Descriptive analysis is a technique of analysis in which the data obtained are summarized and interpreted according to predetermined themes, direct quotations are often used to reflect the views of the interviewees in a striking way, and the results are interpreted within the framework of cause-effect relationships (Yıldırım and Şimşek, 2003). In this study, coding was created, and then themes that will form the outlines of the research findings were identified.

FINDINGS AND CONCLUSIONS

In this section, the views of Generation Y consumers towards influencers were divided into themes and analyzed based on the data collected through the interview method.

What Does the Concept of Influencer Mean to Consumers?

Generation Y participants have expressed varying views on influencers. Participants have defined the concept of an influencer in general and stated that an influencer is a person who earns money by affecting others. The consumer perception of influencers is centered on people who influence and make money. The perception of influencers among consumers is concentrated on people who affect and monetize.

Table 1. Information about participants

Participant Code	Gender	Age	Profession	Education Degree	Daily Time Expenditure on Instagram
Y1K	Female	35	Academic Staff	Doctoral Degree	2-3 Hours
Y2K	Female	36	Academic Staff	Doctoral Degree	2-3 Hours
Y3K	Female	29	Administrative Staff	Undergraduate Degree	3-4 Hours
Y4K	Female	27	Administrative Staff	Master Degree	2-3 Hours
Y5K	Female	30	Administrative Staff	Undergraduate Degree	4-5 Hours
Y1E	Male	38	Academic Staff	Doctoral Degree	3-4 Hours
Y2E	Male	34	Academic Staff	Doctoral Degree	4-5 Hours
Y3E	Male	40	Administrative Staff	High School Degree	2-3 Hours
Y4E	Male	28	Administrative Staff	Associate Degree	2-3 Hours
Y5E	Male	32	Academic Staff	Master Degree	3-4 Hours

The participant coded Y1K (35), *"I would call them people who promote something to convince someone."*

The participant coded Y2E (34), *"A promoter is someone who influences others."*

The participant coded Y5E (32), *"I can call influencers people who have achieved a on social media."*

The participant coded Y4K (27): *"They can be people who share their opinions on any subject, give advice, or promote products and services."*

The participant coded Y1E (38), *"I can define them as people who try to influence a specific audience with their choices and lifestyle and make a living out of it."*

The participant coded Y3K (29), *"I can say that these are people who promote products and services, share their knowledge and experiences, and make money."*

The participant coded Y3E (40), *"I think they are people who make easy money."*

The participant coded Y4E (28), *"I can define an influencer as a person who makes money by promoting and advertising."*

The participant coded Y5K (30), *"I can call them people who have achieved a great reputation fame on social media"*

Is an Influencer a Profession According to Consumers?

The participants' opinions on whether an influencer is a professional or not vary. Participants who expressed that it is not a profession stated that it cannot be a vocation unless certain training is obtained. Participants who considered it as a profession considered it as such because it involves effort, time, and especially because money is earned. Respondents Y1K, Y3E, Y3K, and Y4K certainly did not consider influencers as a profession. Participants who considered it as a profession believed that it can be a profession if there is effort and wages involved in the work. The participant, who views it as a profession even if they do not have training since they have found their audience, stated that influencers are a profession with courage.

The participant opinions indicating that influencers are not a profession are as follows.

The participant coded YK1 (35), *"I don't think influencer is a profession. For it to be a profession, there needs to be an effort. It may be more of a hobby, however, it is definitely not a profession."*

The participant coded Y3E (40),*"Absolutely not, influencer is not a profession. A profession is a talent, a personal skill. Being an Influencer should not be considered a profession. Anyway, the posts are copy and paste, there is no innovation and talent, so it is not a profession."*

The participant coded Y3K (29), *"Influencer should not be a profession, I don't think it is a profession and I don't support it."*

The participant coded Y4K (27), *"In my opinion, influencer is not a profession, it definitely shouldn't be. It doesn't make sense to consider product promotions as a profession without any training."*

The participants' opinions stating that influencers are a profession are as follows.

The participant coded Y2K (36),*"Influencer can be a profession, in an informal way. Even if it is not defined in the literature as a doctor or a pharmacist, it is unofficially practiced as a profession. Since we witness people who leave their actual jobs and become influencers, I can say that influencer is a profession."*

The participant coded Y4E (28),*"Influencer could be a profession. They both advertise themselves and make money by promoting products and services. I think it could be a profession since they make money."*

The participant coded Y5K (30), "Influencer can be a profession. It can be a profession if done realistically

The participant coded Y2E (34), *"I consider influencer as a profession. I think it is a very nice profession. Because they find their audience and become famous. They are making good money. It is a profession even if they are not trained. I think it is a profession that requires courage."*

The participant coded Y1E (38), *"It can be a profession, a profession that shares their knowledge and experience with people."*

The participant coded Y5E (32), *"Absolutely İnfluencer is a profession."*

The Consumer View on the Earnings of Influencers

In the answers given by the participants about the earnings of influencers, it was stated that it was an unfair gain, however, it was observed that the earnings were generally thought to be justified. Participants who say that individuals prefer to leave their main professions and become influencers think that the amount they receive from being an influencer is an important source of income. The view of the participant who sees it as a serious unfair gain is that young people are negatively affected by the earnings of influencers. It was stated that earning income by advertising and promotion without receiving formal education distracts young people from education and that making easy money by wanting to be an influencer negatively affects young people.

The participant coded Y1E (38), *"I think they deserve their earnings. They earn with the number of followers and the number of likes. So there is one thing, there are people who follow influencers and like their posts and stories."*

The participant coded Y4E (28): *"They make serious money, otherwise, why would they advertise and promote? I see it as a fair gain. They work according to their standards, they spend hours and days. That's why I think they deserve the money earn."*

The participant coded Y2K (36), *"I don't know the exact breakdown of influencers' earnings. But I think they made serious money since they quit their actual jobs and became influencers. "*

The participant coded Y3K (29), *"They make serious profits and make great efforts. They spend time promoting products and services. I especially find the earnings of influencers who share their brand's products justified. I consider the profits of those who do not have their brand but share the products they use and the services they receive as unfair earnings."*

The opinions that there are unfair gain are as follows:

The participant coded Y1K (35), *"I do not think well about the earnings of influencers and the wages they receive. Earning too much money has a negative impact, especially on young people. Making too much money from it alienates young people from education. Young people now think that why should they study for many years when they can become influencers and earn more money. I think they have made a considerable amount of unfair profit."*

The participant coded Y3E (40), *"They earn well in the medium term but there is no gain in the short term. Those who make a lot of money are definitely unfair profiters."*

The participant coded Y5K (30), *"They earn earning on social media shares. realistic social media posts can be a fair gain."*

The participant coded Y4K (27), *"I think some influencers earn a lot. It can be the subject of news reports and newspaper headlines. I think that influencers who make a profit without their own brand as a collaboration have unfair gain."*

The participant coded Y5E (32), *"I think well about the earnings of influencers and the wages they receive. They deserve their earnings."*

Reasons Why Consumers Follow Influencers

Although the reasons why participants follow influencers vary, in general, it is to get information about products and services. Getting information about the places they visit, discovering new places, and having fun are among the reasons for following influencers.

The participant coded Y4E (28), *" more about exploring places than promoting products and services. Having information about restaurants and accommodations in different cities is among the reasons for my interest."*

The participant coded Y2E (34), *"I usually follow influencers to discover and learn about new places. Service promotions are more important to me than product promotions. For example, I follow influencers who promote places to visit, campsites, and hotels to stay in a city."*

The participant coded Y5K (30), *"I follow influencers to get information about products and services."*

The participant coded Y1E (38), *"Product promotions do not catch my attention. I follow people who share content in the field of service, whether it's a course or a place to stay. Influencers who provide information on scientific issues especially attract my attention."*

The participant coded Y3K (29), *"I'm interested in influencers who promote products and share entertaining videos. I can say that I especially follow influencers for entertainment purposes."*

The participant coded Y3E (40), *"I follow influencers on my Instagram account. Rather than getting information about products and services, I follow influencers who share entertaining posts. It's entertaining and I follow them to pass the time."*

The participant coded Y5E (32), *"I follow İnfluencers to have a good time. It happens when we get information about products."*

The participant coded Y2K (36), *"I follow them to get information about products and services, especially products related to health, and I follow them for the information they provide about healthy living."*

The participant coded Y4K (27), *"I usually follow influencers to discover brands of cosmetics and clothing. I can find out about brands I have never heard of previously by following influencers."*

The Importance of the Number of Followers of Influencers for Consumers

Analyzing the opinions of the consumers about the number of followers of the influencers, the number of participants who stated that the number of followers has no importance was high. Some participants stated that they considered influencers with fewer followers more realistic. Participants who paid attention to the number of followers stated that influencers with more followers are more trustworthy.

The opinions of the participants who think that the number of followers is not important are as follows:

The participant coded Y1K (35), *"The number of followers is not important to me. The number of followers does not influence my opinion. Generally, people who have a great deal of knowledge and skills do not have a large number of followers. People who showcase their luxurious lives and share useless videos and stories have more followers. Influencers may have few followers, but the value they add to me and useful content are important to me."*

The participant coded Y3E (40), *"The number of followers is not important to me. The content of the images and videos shared is important. The correct content is important to me. I cannot claim that an influencer with a large number of followers reflects their true opinions about a product or service, so I don't care about the number of followers. I think those with fewer followers make more realistic posts to promote themselves and make their names known."*

The participant coded Y4E (28), *"The number of followers of influencers is not important to me. The number of followers does not influence my opinions about the product, service, or brand being promoted. I make sure that the brands of the products shared and advertised are reliable."*

The participant coded Y4K (27), *"The number of followers is not important to me, what is important is that the product and service being promoted is reliable and reflects the facts. I think people with fewer followers share more realistic content."*

The participant coded Y2K (36) stated the following that it is both important and unimportant, emphasizing quality.

"I can say that the number of followers of influencers is both important and unimportant. A high number of followers does not necessarily indicate that the content is of high-quality and reliable. A lack of followers does not affect my opinion of the brand or my buying behavior. Maybe that influencer is at the early stages, and the number of followers will increase over time."

The views of the participants who stated that the number of followers is important are as follows:

The participant coded Y1E (38), *"The number of followers of influencers is important to me. I value the opinions of people with a large number of followers. Product and service recommendations of influencers with few followers do not affect my buying behavior."*

The participant coded Y2E (34), *"I care about the number of followers. I believe that if the influencer's followers are greater, the products and services promoted by that person are better and of higher quality. The number of followers inevitably affects my opinion of the brand."*

The participant coded Y3K (29), *"A high number of followers definitely attracts my attention. A high number of followers means that there are people who trust that influencer. People will not follow if they are not satisfied with the product and service promoted if they do not trust them."*

The participant coded Y5E (32), *"The number of followers of is important to me."*

The Status of Influencers in Social Life and Consumer Perception

More than half of the participants stated that social status is unimportant, the opinions and suggestions of unknown people are considered rather than well-known famous people, and it is emphasized that non-celebrities products, services, and brands are more reliable. Sincerity and trust were more important than status.

The participant coded Y2E (34), *"Status in public life is not important to me. The posts of very famous people are based on self-interest. It's to make money. The way of presentation of service and product promotion is more important than status. The influencers I follow on Instagram are not very popular, but I care about their opinions and suggestions since I like their presentation style, and I think they are more sincere and trustworthy."*

The participant coded Y3E (40), *"Status in social life is not important to me. I am interested in the experiences and advice of people who are not famous. Because they act more naturally and spontaneously."*

The participant coded Y5K (30), *"Status in public life is not important to me. Trust and realty matters more."*

The participant coded Y4K (27), *"I tend to pay more attention to the opinions and thoughts of people who are not famous. The posts and suggestions of well-known people never influenced my purchasing behavior and trust in the brand. After all, celebrities make promotions for considerable amounts of money, I don't find it reliable."*

The participant coded Y2K (36), *"Social status is not the only criterion. Trust and sincerity matters more."*

The participant views highlighting the importance of social status focused on individuals who were self-educated, knowledgeable and created their brand, and these individuals were found to be more trustworthy.

The participant coded Y1K (35), *"Status in public life is important to me. I would say that I consider the suggestions, advice, and brand preferences of trained and informed experts. I am intrigued by the recommendations of widely recognized people, and I am affected by them even if I don't want to be."*

The participant coded Y1E (38), *"Social status is important to me. Recommendations and brand preferences of widely recognized athletes and artists are significant. I don't pay much notice to product promotions and recommendations from people who are not well known."*

The participant coded Y3K (29), *"I care about the social status of influencers. I have great respect for influencers who have educated themselves in quality of life and created their brand. This, however, does not mean that I would buy what they recommend with absolute confidence. I would first research, and then I think about buying."*

Consumers Who Consider Influencer Posts as a Source of Information

Most of the participants in the study stated that the product and service promotions shared by influencers are a good source of information and provide them with an idea about brand names. Among the participants, only Y3E (40) expressed that product and service promotions are not a source of information.

The participant coded Y3E (40), *"I don't pay attention to the product promotions shared by influencers. It is not much of a resource for me. If I want to find information about products and services, I research on the internet."*

The participant coded Y1K (35), *"I think that the posts of influencers are a resource for me in promoting products and services. I have come to know brand names that I have never heard of before. I can get information about products and services."*

The participant coded Y1E (38), *"They share products for promotional purposes. Should you buy everything they suggest? I don't know, but for me, shared product and service promotions are a resource. I would say that it is a resource for appropriate promotions according to my field of interest."*

The participant coded Y5K (30), *"I think that the posts of them are a resource for me in promoting products and services."*

The Consumer Profiles Who Question Influencers' Promotions

Consumers who question the posts of influencers emphasized that they do research before purchasing. Consumers, particularly consumers doing internet research, stated that they consider user comments.

The participant coded Y2K (36), *"I question the products and services promoted by influencers. I have never bought a product blindly on an influencer's recommendation. I purchase products and services I trust. I have never regretted my purchases. Because I had researched it online."*

The participant coded Y4K (27), *"I follow the posts of influencers. I watch their stories and videos. When there are brands that I have never heard of before, I immediately search for the brand name in search engines and read user reviews. I never buy products and services without an evaluation."*

The participant coded Y3K (29), *"I would not say that I question the products and brands shared by influencers too much. If I am following an influencer, that influencer has been questioned enough. I don't too much question the products and brand names that most people like and comment on."*

The participant coded Y3E (40), *"I question and research the products shared, I don't purchase without inquiring."*

The participant coded Y5K (30), *"Without doubt, I question and research the products shared, I don't purchase without inquiring."*

What Consumers Expect From Influencers

The expectations of consumers from influencers are focused on a sense of trust. Among the participant expectations are sharing accurate and reliable products, stating the truth about products and services without misleading information, and considering the consumer budget.

The participant coded Y1E (38), *"Sharing accurate information is important to me. Products and services should be promoted by objective evaluation and without undermining people's trust."*

The participant coded Y4E (28), *"My expectation from influencers is for them to be realistic. Promote affordable products and services by keeping the consumer's budget in mind."*

The participant coded Y3K (29), *"My expectation is to be fully served. I would particularly like them to promote their brands. Sharing truthfully, without deception. I would say that influencers should improve themselves and increase their number of followers with a sense of trust."*

The participant coded Y5E (32), *"My expectation from is for them to be truth and realistic."*

The participant coded Y2E (34), *"My expectation from influencers is that they should make realistic promotions by not prioritizing financial concerns. Creating confidence by promoting products and services with catchy strategies."*

The participant coded Y3E (40), *"Influencers should not abuse people's trust, or steal people's dreams. After all, consumers believe them, so they buy products and services and spend money. Life is expensive and people may not have money. I would ask them to have a conscience."*

The participant coded Y2K (36), *"Influencers should be objective. If they can tell the pros and cons of the products and services they promote, they can be more reliable. I expect them to empathize the most. They may as well be themselves in the position of us, the consumers. What would they think if they were misleadingly promoted a product?"*

SOLUTIONS AND RECOMMENDATIONS

- Since trust is more valuable for consumers than the number of followers, influencers should first explain the benefits of the products and services they use and the services they have received to make their names known to large masses.
- Since influencer posts are a resource of information about products and brands for consumers, different aspects of the promoted brands should be mentioned.
- The reality of consumers who are active in the questioning of the production and consumption system must be taken into account. Financial concerns should be shunned and misleading product and service promotions should be avoided.
- Companies and businesses can extend their brands and reputations to a wide range of consumers through influencers in different roles and statuses.

FUTURE RESEARCH RECOMMENDATIONS

The effect of influencer marketing on consumers' purchasing behaviors plays a significant role. Companies that use the opportunities offered by the digital world are trying to find ways to reach more consumers faster and more effectively. Companies that strive to increase their brand awareness and leave a positive image in the minds of consumers have started to use social media platforms intensively. With rapidly developing technologies, the trend toward product and service promotions by influencers as an alternative to traditional marketing techniques has accelerated. It would be useful for the literature to investigate the reasons why companies and brands prefer influencer promotions.

CONCLUSION

Consumers using digital media intensively acquire information about products in a short time through influencers on social media platforms. Due to their status among their followers, influencers play an effective role when a decision is to be made or a step is to be taken. Influencers are significant for businesses and brands as they have the power to steer perceptions and attitudes. On the other hand, consumer attitudes and perspectives are also effective in following influencers, and the production-consumption relationship continues with a two-way communication flow.

The study cluster of the research, which deals with consumer perspectives on influencers, consists of Generation Y consumers. In the study, the data obtained through face-to-face interviews were divided into themes and analyzed.

The concept of an influencer is widely defined in the literature as a person who makes money (Gamage & Ashill, 2023; Bakker, 2018; Percy & Elliot, 2016; Gönülşen, 2020; Ponirah, 2020.) The answers provided by the participants regarding the concept of influencers were similar to the literature. Participants defined the concept of the influencer as a person who has an impact, earns money, and gives advice. Furthermore, participants generally considered the earnings of influencers as justified earnings. Participants who consider influencers with unfair gain think that influencers negatively affect young people. It is among the opinions that young people move away from education to earn money in a short time, that they take influencers as an example, and that young people are affected in the opposite direction by this situation.

Kazancı (2022) concluded that influencer posts are considered informative and entertaining for consumers. Similarly, in this study,

participants stated that they follow influencers to get information about products and services. Discovering new places and having a nice and fun time were cited as reasons for following influencers.

The participants who stated that influencer is not a profession expressed that it cannot be a profession without certain training. Participants who considered it as a profession regarded it as a profession because money is earned.

Veriman et al. (2018) stated in their study that influencers with a high number of followers are more favored, consumers pay more attention to the opinions and suggestions of influencers with a high number of followers compared to those with a low number of followers, and they find them reliable. In this research, unlike Veriman et al. (2018), it was determined that the number of followers did not have much significance for consumer preferences. Most of the participants stated that they care more about the influencer's trustworthiness and sincerity than the number of followers and status of the influencer.

Participants stated that product and service promotions shared by influencers are a source of information and facilitate brand preferences. Participants who questioned the posts of influencers emphasized that they did research before purchasing products. The expectations of consumers from influencers are centered on trust.

As a result, a bidirectional communication flow can be argued to exist between influencers and the consumers who follow them. With the bidirectional communication flow, consumers who switch from a passive to an active position are included in the production-consumption system. Influencers try to influence people with their opinions and suggestions, the products and services they promote, they can also be influenced by their followers as well. Since the user comments of followers on products and services are references for other users, negative opinions against the products promoted may undermine the sense of trust in influencers. At this juncture, it is important for the influencer to promote with real information. Another important issue for influencers is whether they have a profession or not. Even though influencers have recently been considered a profession, it is still a matter of debate. Considering the data obtained in the research, the answers given by the participants show that this debate continues.

REFERENCES

Agostino, D., Arnaboldi, M., & Calissano, A. (2019). How to Quantify Social Media Influencers: An Empirical Application at The Teatro Alla Scala. *Elsevier. Heliyon*, *5*(5), 1–7. doi:10.1016/j.heliyon.2019.e01677

Ahmad, I. (2018). The Influencer Marketing Revolution. *Social Media Today*, *15*(2), 22–26.

Aktaş, A., & Şener, G. (2019). Nüfuz Pazarlamasında (Influencer Marketing) Mesaj Stratejileri. *Erciyes İletişim Dergisi*, *6*(1), 399–422. doi:10.17680/erciyesiletisim.477592

Aw, E. C. X., & Agnihotri, R. (2023). Influencer marketing research: Review and future research agenda. *Journal of Marketing Theory and Practice*, 1–14. doi:10.1080/10696679.2023.2235883

Bae, S., & Lee, T. (2011). Gender Differences in Consumers' Perception of Online Consumer Views. *Electronic Commerce Research*, *11*(11), 201–214. doi:10.1007/s10660-010-9072-y

Bakker, D. (2018). Conceptualising influencer marketing. *Journal of Emerging Trends in Marketing and Management*, *1*(1), 79-87.

Braatz, L. (2017). *#Influencer Marketing on Instagram: Consumer Responses Towards Promotional Posts: The Effects of Message Sidedness, Responses* [Master thesis]. University of Twente.

Brown, D., & Hayes, N. (2008). *Influencer marketing*. Routledge. doi:10.4324/9780080557700

Campbell, C., & Farrell, J. (2020). More Than Meets The Eye: The Functional Components Underlying İnfluencer Marketing. *Business Horizons*, *63*(4), 469–479. doi:10.1016/j.bushor.2020.03.003

Carter, D. (2016). Hustle and Brand: The Sociotechnical Shaping of Influence. *Social Media + Society*, *2*(3), 1–12. doi:10.1177/2056305116666305

Claesson, A., & Liungberg, N. (2018). *Consumer Engagement on Instagram: Viewed through the Perspectives of Social Influence and Influencer marketing* [Master thesis]. University of Lund, Lund, Sweden.

Coşkun, T. (2019). *Hedonik Ve Faydacı Tüketim Davranışları İle Tüketici Etnosentrizmi Arasındaki İlişki: Kuşaklara Yönelik Bir Araştırma* [Doktora tezi]. Muğla Sıtkı Koçman Üniversitesi.

De Veirman, M., Cauberghe, V., & Hudders, L. (2017). Marketing through Instagram influencers: The impact of number of followers and product divergence on brand attitude. *International Journal of Advertising*, *36*(5), 798–828. doi:10.1080/02650487.2017.1348035

Deuze, M. (2006). Participation, remediation, bricolage: Considering principal components of a digital culture. *The Information Society*, *22*(2), 63–75. doi:10.1080/01972240600567170

Dey, B. L., Yen, D., & Samuel, L. (2020). Digital consumer culture and digital acculturation. *International Journal of Information Management*, *51*, 102–157. doi:10.1016/j.ijinfomgt.2019.102057

Dömbekci, H., & Erişen, M. A. (2022). Nitel Araştırmalarda Görüşme Tekniği. *Anadolu Üniversitesi Sosyal Bilimler Dergisi*, (22), 141–160. doi:10.1177/20563051166663

Ewers, N. (2017). *#Sponsored –Influencer Marketing on Instagram An Analysis of the Effects of Sponsorship Disclosure, Product Placement, Type of Influencer and their Interplay on Consumer Responses* [Master thesis]. University of Twente, Enschede, Holland.

Femenia-Serra, F., & Gretzel, U. (2020). Influencer marketing for tourism destinations: Lessons from a mature destination. In *Information and Communication Technologies in Tourism 2020: Proceedings of the International Conference in Surrey, United Kingdom, January 08–10, 2020* (pp. 65-78). Springer International Publishing.

Freberg, K., Graham, K., McGaughey, K. A., & Freberg, L. (2011). Who are the Social Media Influencers? A Study of Public Perceptions of Personality. *Public Relations Review*, *37*(1), 90–92. doi:10.1016/j.pubrev.2010.11.001

Friedman, H. H., & Friedman, L. (1979). Endorser Effectiveness by Product Type. *Journal of Advertising Research*, *19*(5), 63–71.

Gamage, T., & Ashill, N. (2023). Sponsored-influencer marketing: Effects of the commercial orientation of influencercreated content on followers' willingness to search for information. *Journal of Product and Brand Management*, *32*(2), 316–329. doi:10.1108/JPBM-10-2021-3681

Glucksman, M. (2017). The rise of social media Influencer marketing on lifestyle branding: A case study of Lucie Fink. *Elon Journal of Undergraduate Research in Communications*, *8*(2), 77–78.

Gmachi, S. (2017). Der Einfluss von Influencer-Marketing auf die Generation Y. *Psychology & Marketing*, 32-55.

Gönülşen, G. (2020). Olumlu Marka İmajı Yaratmada Influencer Pazarlama Stratejisinin Marka Algısı Üzerindeki Etkisi: Foreo Türkiye Markasının Uygulamalarına Yönelik Bir Araştırma. *Akdeniz Üniversitesi Sosyal Bilimler Enstitüsü Dergisi*, (8), 9–34.

Gross, J., & Wangenheim, F. V. (2018). The big four of Influencer marketing: A typology of Influencers. *Marketing Review St. Gallen*, (2), 30–38.

Karataş, M., & Eti, H. (2022). Dijital Pazarlama Çağında Instagram Fenomenlerinin Tüketici Satın Alma Davranışlarına Etkisi. *Academic Journal of Information Technology*, *13*(50), 184–219. doi:10.5824/ajite.2022.03.005.x

Kazancı, P. (2022). *Influencer Marketing Uygulamalarının Üniversite Öğrencilerinin Satın Alma Niyeti Üzerine Etkisi* [Doktora tezi]. Selçuk Üniversitesi.

Kotler, P., Kartajaya, H., Setiawan, I. (2021), *Pazarlama 4.0 Gelenekselden Dijitale Geçiş* (Çev. Özata, N.). Optimist Yayıncılık.

Kotler, P., Kartajaya, H., Setiawan, I. (2022), *Pazarlama 5.0 Gelenekselden Dijitale Geçiş* (Çev. Taner, G.). Nişantaşı Üniversitesi Yayınları.

Ledbetter, A. M., & Meisner, C. (2021). Extending the personal branding affordances typology to parasocial interaction with public figures on social media: Social presence and media multiplexity as mediators. *Computers in Human Behavior*, *106610*(115), 106610. doi:10.1016/j.chb.2020.106610

Leung, F. F., Gu, F. F., & Palmatier, R. W. (2022). Online influencer marketing. *Journal of the Academy of Marketing Science*, *50*(26), 226–251. doi:10.1007/s11747-021-00829-4

Mert, Y. T. (2018). Dijital Pazarlama Ekseninde Influencer Marketing Uygulamaları. *Gümüşhane Üniversitesi İletişim Fakültesi Ekonomi Dergisi*, *6*(2), 1300–1328. doi:10.19145/e-gifder.431622

Panda, M., & Mishra, A. (2022). *Digital marketing*. https://www. researchgate. net/publication/358646409

Percy, L., & Elliott, R. (2016). *Strategic advertising management*. Oxford University Press.

Ponirah, A. (2020). Influencer Marketing as a Marketing Strateg. *Journal of Economicate Studies*, (04), 11–16.

Seyyid, T. A., & Mehmood, F. (2023). Brand–SMI Collaboration in İnfluencer Marketing Campaigns: A transaction cost economics. *Technological Forecasting and Social Change*, *192*, 1–15. doi:10.1016/j. techfore.2023.122580

Stubb, C. (2019). *The Gray Zone in Marketing Consumer Responses to Influencer Marketing*. Abo Akademi University.

Yalçın, H. (2022). Bir Araştırma Deseni Olarak Fenomenoloji. *Anadolu Üniversitesi Sosyal Bilimler Dergisi*, *22*(2), 213–232. doi:10.18037/ausbd.1227345

Yıldırım, A., & Şimşek, H. (2005). *Sosyal Bilimlerde Nitel Araştırma Yöntemleri*. Seçkin Yayıncılık.

Zengin Demirbilek, E. (2021). *Pazarlamanın Dijital Dönüşümü: Influencer Marketing Üzerine Bir Uygulama* [Doktora tezi]. İstanbul Üniversitesi.

Chapter 9
Perspectives of Digital Marketing for the Restaurant Industry

Mohammad Badruddoza Talukder
https://orcid.org/0000-0001-7788-2732
Daffodil Institute of IT, Bangladesh

Sanjeev Kumar
https://orcid.org/0000-0002-7375-7341
Lovely Professional University, India

Iva Rani Das
https://orcid.org/0009-0006-9805-4331
Daffodil Institute of IT, Bangladesh

ABSTRACT

Digital marketing tactics are now an essential part of the restaurant business. They offer a variety of ways to connect with customers, build a brand, and grow the business. This chapter examines the various perspectives on how digital marketing can be implemented in the food industry. It supplements our prior understanding of the subject by providing new and informative data. The chapter emphasizes the significance of cultivating a proficient online identity and brand, utilizing social media platforms for marketing and advertising objectives, actively managing online feedback and reviews, collaborating with influencers and food bloggers, integrating online ordering and delivery, and employing data analysis methodologies for tailoring marketing campaigns. A comprehensive analysis from all angles provides helpful insights into the best practices for digital advertising in the restaurant industry. In the digital age, restaurant owners and marketers can enhance visibility, attract new customers, and build long-term client relationships by adopting these approaches.

DOI: 10.4018/979-8-3693-0855-4.ch009

INTRODUCTION

The restaurant industry underwent an enormous shift recently due to the rapid advancement of digital technology. The significance of digital marketing in the restaurant business cannot be overstated, given customers' increasing reliance on smartphones and computers for dining suggestions, online booking, and food delivery (Nampoothiri, 2021). Restaurants have unprecedented chances to communicate with customers, establish connections with their desired consumer base, and enhance brand promotion through online platforms (Meek et al., 2021). This chapter explores the diverse perspectives on digital marketing within the restaurant industry to support restaurants in navigating the dynamic digital landscape and achieving success. Additionally, it provides practical guidance.

This chapter uses several sources and industry experts to review the critical viewpoints on restaurant digital marketing. The perspectives discussed cover a wide range of topics, including establishing an authoritative online identity, leveraging the power of social media platforms, effectively managing online evaluations and maintaining a positive public image, collaborating with influential individuals, utilizing email marketing strategies, optimizing localized search results, integrating online ordering and delivery services, and utilizing data analysis and personalization technology.

The chapter incorporates a range of market data, industry research, and case studies as references for supporting the presented viewpoints. These resources provide empirical evidence and real-life examples of restaurants across different markets and segments effectively employing digital marketing strategies. The references cited in this chapter will offer a comprehensive and evidence-based examination of digital marketing within the restaurant industry.

This chapter also recognizes the dynamic nature of digital marketing and the imperative for ongoing adaptation and experimentation. To maintain success during evolving technology and shifting consumer behavior, restaurants must continuously assess and enhance their digital marketing strategies (Kurdi et al., 2022). Also, this chapter provides a comprehensive analysis of various perspectives that can be utilized by restaurant owners, marketers, and industry experts to gain a deeper understanding of the current market behavior. By considering these perspectives, they can make informed decisions and develop effective strategies for their digital marketing activities.

The digital age has changed restaurants' marketing and consumer engagement techniques. This chapter examines the significant viewpoints on digital marketing in the context of the restaurant business in depth. By adopting these views and using the opportunities provided by digital media, restaurants may increase their brand recognition, client base, and customer retention (Valerio et al., 2019). The following chapters will go deeper into each viewpoint, providing essential insight and ideas to help restaurants efficiently navigate the complex world of digital marketing.

Digital marketing strategically implements various internet platforms and technology to promote restaurants and effectively engage prospective customers. The restaurant industry comprises diverse enterprises preparing and delivering food and beverages (Talukder & Hossain, 2012). This chapter explores various essential components of digital marketing, encompassing the establishment of an online presence, the utilization of social media marketing, the optimization of search engine visibility through SEO techniques, the implementation of content marketing strategies, the utilization of email marketing for customer engagement, the adoption of online ordering and delivery services, the management of customer reviews and ratings, the implementation of mobile marketing for enhancing smartphone experiences, the leveraging of online advertising for broader reach, and the utilization of analytics and data insights for making data-driven decisions to improve campaign effectiveness (Mohammad et al.,

2023). When these essential phrases are used together, it becomes clear how digital marketing tactics may be customized to meet the particular requirements of the restaurant business.

1. SUCCESSFUL ONLINE PRESENCE

In the digital age, restaurants must have a robust online presence to effectively communicate with their target audience and differentiate themselves in a competitive market (Lepkowska-White et al., 2019). The first half of this chapter includes a thorough literature review on the significance of building a strong online presence for restaurants and examining the essential aspects and methods involved in this endeavor.

1.1 A Strong Digital Footprint

Numerous academic studies demonstrate the importance of having a solid digital presence for restaurants. According to Gutierrez et al. (2023), people rely more on the Internet for information when making food choices. A restaurant's website can attract and retain customers better if it is entertaining and visually appealing. Furthermore, According to Farrar & Papies (2023) research, a restaurant's internet presence is critical in increasing its reputation and positively altering consumer impressions.

1.2 Online Presence Essentials

A strong restaurant's digital presence requires several vital features. Website excellence starts with a well-designed interface. Jin et al. (2022) found that intuitive user interfaces, attractive designs, and responsive layouts improve user experience and attract visitors. According to Hung & Wang (2021), websites must have current menus, hours of operation, contact information, and reservation alternatives.

Researcher Kurdi et al. (2022) also emphasize the importance of brand consistency across digital channels. Restaurants must keep their logos, color schemes, and imagery consistent. Potential buyers trust consistent brands more.

1.3 Effective Online Presence Strategies

Restaurants use many methods to build their internet presence. SEO is needed to boost internet exposure. Khan & Mahmood (2018) say optimizing webpages with appropriate keywords, Meta tags, and backlinks improves search engine ranks. Localized keywords also help establishments attract local customers.

Social networking is great for building a digital presence. Scholar Jariangprasert et al. (2019) suggest that eateries use Facebook, Instagram, and Twitter. By creating engaging content, answering customer questions, and using social media advertising, restaurants may reach their target audience.

Review websites significantly affect a restaurant's online presence. Researcher Gavilan et al. (2018) found that Internet reviews influence consumer choices. Restaurants can manage internet reviews by encouraging satisfied customers to leave positive feedback and quickly responding to negative or complaint-oriented comments. People can increase their online trust and reputation by doing this.

2. UTILIZING SOCIAL MEDIA PLATFORMS

Social media has changed how businesses interact with their target audience; the restaurant industry is no exception. The chapter's literature review delves further into the significance of using social media platforms for digital marketing in the restaurant business. This study examines the advantages, methods, and best practices for using social media platforms to boost brand recognition, interact with customers, and assist business growth.

2.1 Social Media Benefits

Numerous advantages have been found for restaurants that use social media marketing. According to Lima et al. (2019), restaurants can benefit from social media by expanding their client base, raising brand awareness, and building relationships with locals. Using social media, restaurants can interact with their customers in real-time, as Sashi et al. (2019) discovered, according to J. Li et al. (2021), social media marketing can save money. Restaurants are not charged to post their menus online, promote special deals, or share engaging content with their patrons. Small, independent restaurants don't have to break the bank to take advantage of the benefits of social media.

2.2 Tips for Making the Most of Social Media Networks

Restaurants employ a diverse range of methods to utilize social media platforms effectively. Selecting suitable platforms is of utmost importance, as it should be based on the specific characteristics of the target market and the nature of the restaurant in question. Facebook, Instagram, Twitter, and YouTube are widely recognized as prominent platforms utilized by restaurants, offering unique capabilities and targeting opportunities.

The provision of engaging content is a crucial element in social media marketing. Mao et al. (2020) underscore the significance of visually appealing images and videos in attracting social media users. Restaurants have the potential to effectively communicate their brand narrative by strategically presenting their menu offerings, providing insights into their internal operations, and highlighting customer interactions.

Active community management is crucial for achieving effective social media marketing. According to Leung et al. (2022), restaurants can cultivate a sense of genuineness and establish connections with their clientele through various means, such as actively interacting with their followers, promptly addressing messages and comments, and engaging in conversations. According to a study by Al-Abdallah et al. (2022), customers are urged to actively share their dining experiences, provide reviews, and upload images to enhance brand advocacy and establish credibility.

2.3 Best Practices in Making Use of Social Media

Restaurants must follow best practices for social media marketing. Scholars Talukder & Bhuiyan (2020) emphasize the importance of brand voice and aesthetic consistency across social media platforms. This consistent strategy boosts the restaurant's online brand recognition.

Social media marketing helps restaurants reach more people while targeting a specific audience. Strategic advertising methods, including location-based targeting, interest-based targeting, and remarketing, are crucial to social media advertising efforts, according to Tamer & Hussein (2020).

3. MANAGEMENT OF ONLINE REVIEWS AND REPUTATION

Managing online reviews and reputation in the current digital environment plays a crucial role in influencing consumer decision-making and shaping the overall perception of a restaurant. This section of the chapter offers a thorough analysis of the significance attributed to the administration of online reputations and reviews for restaurants within the digital marketing domain. This research examines the influence of online reviews, effective management strategies for handling them, and the importance of maintaining a favourable digital image.

3.1 Influence of Online Reviews

Numerous studies consistently highlight the significant impact that online reviews have on consumer behavior. The studies by Ruiz-Mafe et al. (2018) demonstrate that online reviews substantially influence customers' decision-making processes. Potential customers frequently utilize these reviews as a means to assess the quality and dependability of a restaurant. Negative reviews have the potential to deter potential customers and inflict damage on a restaurant's reputation. In contrast, positive thoughts can enhance customer confidence and attract new patrons.

According to a study conducted by Schultheiß & Lewandowski (2021), it has been found that online reviews play a significant role in influencing search engine rankings and local search visibility. Search engines often consider the quantity and quality of considerations when determining a restaurant's ranking in search results. To maintain a favourable online reputation and attract local clientele, it becomes imperative for restaurants to exercise control over online reviews.

3.2 Strategies for Managing Online Reviews

Restaurants employ various strategies to manage online reviews effectively. Engaging in proactive surveillance of online review platforms and promptly addressing client feedback is an essential strategic approach. The research conducted by Allard et al. (2020) demonstrates that responding to positive and negative evaluations can enhance a restaurant's reputation. The restaurant's prompt and customized responses to customer feedback exemplify its commitment to valuing customer opinions and ensuring a superior dining experience for patrons.

Furthermore, the De Pelsmacker et al. (2018) study underscores the importance of providing professional and constructive feedback in response to unfavorable evaluations. Restaurants must recognize any issues that arise and, if necessary, express remorse and provide a solution or extend an invitation to address the matter privately. This approach demonstrates a sense of accountability and a commitment to ensuring client satisfaction, which may mitigate the adverse consequences of the review.

3.3 The Significance of Maintaining a Positive Online Reputation

In the context of restaurants, maintaining a positive online reputation is of utmost importance due to its impact on the perceptions and trust of patrons. According to a study by H. Li et al. (2020), a restaurant's reputation can be enhanced through positive online reviews and a high overall rating. This, in turn, can lead to increased patronage and financial gains for the establishment. According to recent research conducted by Vajjhala & Ghosh (2022), it has been found that a favorable online reputation can potentially enhance search engine outcomes, thereby augmenting the online visibility of a restaurant.

According to recent research conducted by (2023), businesses should actively seek out positive online reviews to establish and sustain a favourable online reputation. Restaurants can employ diverse strategies to enhance customer engagement and satisfaction. These tactics may encompass the provision of rewards to patrons, the practice of sending post-visit emails to customers, and the placement of review requests near the point of sale. These strategies facilitate the generation of consistently positive reviews while mitigating any negative ones.

4. COLLABORATION WITH INFLUENCERS AND FOOD BLOGGERS

The adoption of influencers and food bloggers has recently emerged as a viable digital marketing technique for restaurants. This chapter examines the current literature on the usefulness of forming partnerships with influencers and food bloggers in the restaurant industry. This study examines the benefits, tactics, and most effective methods of leveraging influencer collaborations to increase brand recognition, attract potential customers, and encourage organizational growth.

4.1 Benefits of Collaborating With Influencers and Food Bloggers

Restaurant marketing research shows the many benefits of working with influencers and food bloggers. Talukder et al. (2023) found that influencers may connect with an extensive and engaged audience, mostly restaurant patrons. Restaurants can partner with influencers and bloggers to attract customers who value their endorsements.

Influencer relationships can also provide user-generated content that showcases the dining experience. Cassar et al. (2020) found that user-generated material influences consumer decision-making. Prospective diners actively seek realistic and authentic experiences when making dining choices. Restaurants may use their expertise and creativity to create compelling content for their target audience. Strategic alliances with influential food bloggers can achieve this goal.

4.2 Approaches for Engaging in Collaboration With Influencers and Food Bloggers

Restaurants employ various strategies to engage in partnerships with influencers and food bloggers successfully. According to a study by Prasetyo et al. (2021), it is imperative to identify influencers who align with the restaurant's brand values and target demographic. Restaurants can enhance the authenticity and appeal of their collaboration efforts by carefully selecting influencers with a genuine passion for food and dining, ensuring alignment with the influencer's audience.

Moreover, the research conducted by Cartwright et al. (2022) illustrates that providing influencers with a unique and memorable encounter can enhance effectiveness in collaborative endeavors. Restaurants have the potential to leave a lasting impact on influencers, who are motivated to share their experiences with their followers through the provision of unique tastings, behind-the-scenes tours, or customized dining opportunities. Consequently, the collaboration between the restaurant and the influencer yields mutual benefits, thereby establishing a mutually advantageous scenario.

4.3 Best Practices for Collaborating With Influencers and Food Bloggers

To optimize the outcomes of influencer engagements, restaurants should adhere to established best practices. The research conducted by Bhatt et al. (2021) emphasizes the significance of transparency and direct communication. Ensuring alignment and fostering effective collaboration among all parties involved can be achieved through establishing unambiguous expectations, comprehensive elucidation of content limitations, and provision of relevant business-related information.

Furthermore, restaurants must assess the outcomes of their partnerships with influencers. Scholar Talukder (2020) suggests that a comprehensive understanding of the effectiveness of influencer collaborations can be obtained by closely monitoring significant performance indicators, including social media engagement, website traffic, and conversion rates. Restaurateurs can make informed decisions regarding future partnerships by analyzing the provided data to evaluate the return on investment.

5. THE IMPACT OF EMAIL MARKETING ON CUSTOMER LOYALTY IN THE RESTAURANT INDUSTRY

Email marketing has become increasingly important in the restaurant and hotel sector to build customer relationships and inspire loyalty. This portion of the chapter provides a detailed analysis of the impact of email marketing on customer loyalty in the restaurant business. The study's overarching goal is to provide insight into the value of email marketing as a tool for attracting and retaining customers, encouraging repeat business, and cementing lasting connections.

5.1 The Advantages of Email Marketing in Enhancing Customer Loyalty

Numerous studies consistently indicate the efficacy of email marketing in enhancing customer loyalty towards restaurants. The study conducted by (2023) demonstrates that customized email campaigns positively impact consumer loyalty and repeat patronage. This is achieved by providing customers with a sense of exclusivity and value. The augmentation of customer engagement and the fortification of the emotional connection between patrons and restaurants can be achieved through email communication, wherein exclusive offers, incentives, and tailored suggestions are provided.

Furthermore, as evidenced by the research conducted by (Bonfanti et al., 2021), the implementation of email marketing strategies has been found to effectively maintain a prominent presence in the minds of customers for restaurants. Customers are incentivized to revisit the restaurant through periodic newsletters and updates, which keep them apprised of novel additions to the menu, upcoming events, and exclusive promotions. Restaurants have the potential to enhance their brand visibility and cultivate enduring customer loyalty through the establishment of regular email communication.

5.2 Approaches for Email Marketing and Establishing Customer Loyalty

Restaurants employ diverse strategies to leverage email marketing to foster customer loyalty efficiently. According to the research conducted by Tranberg et al. (2018), establishing an opt-in email list is of utmost importance. Restaurants can effectively target their desired audience by implementing a strategy that involves encouraging customers to subscribe to their email newsletters. The expansion of the email list can be achieved through various techniques, such as implementing incentive programs, incorporating sign-up alternatives on the website and in physical stores, and utilizing point-of-sale data.

Segmentation is a crucial strategy for achieving effectiveness in email marketing. According to a study conducted by Vo et al. (2021), restaurants can tailor their email content and offers to specific client segments by employing email list segmentation techniques that consider consumer preferences, behavior, and demographics. Implementing a customized strategy enhances the relevance of communications, leading to increased engagement and the cultivation of client loyalty.

5.3 Optimal Approaches for Email Marketing and Enhancing Customer Loyalty

Restaurants must adhere to optimal strategies to maximize the effectiveness of their email marketing campaigns. The research conducted by Sahni et al. (2018) emphasizes the importance of developing compelling email content. To enhance the overall quality of emails, it is recommended to incorporate an aesthetically pleasing design, maintain brevity, and ensure the presence of clear and conspicuous calls to action. Emails are more likely to be opened and read by recipients when they incorporate visually appealing food photographs, distinctive greetings, and relevant content.

Moreover, the research conducted by V. Kumar & Mittal (2020) suggests that restaurant emails must be optimized for mobile devices, given the substantial proportion of email recipients accessing their emails through mobile platforms. Customers are likely to have a smooth and captivating experience when viewing emails on mobile devices, thereby enhancing the likelihood of their engagement in desired actions such as making reservations or placing orders.

6. LOCAL SEO AND ONLINE VISIBILITY

In the digital world, restaurants require local SEO. This program aims to increase its web presence and attract local clientele. This chapter examines restaurant local search engine optimization (SEO) literature. Local search engine optimization (SEO) boosts online visibility and in-person customer traffic. This study investigates its advantages, tactics, and best practices.

6.1 The Advantages of Local SEO and Online Visibility

Several studies have underscored the benefits of implementing local search engine optimization (SEO) strategies within the restaurant industry. According to recent research conducted by Akulshina (2020), implementing effective local SEO strategies has enhanced the presence of restaurants in local search results, thereby augmenting their visibility among prospective customers seeking nearby dining establishments. The improved visibility leads to increased consumer inquiries, internet traffic, and, ultimately, physical visits to the restaurant.

Furthermore, a study by Setiaboedi et al. (2018)demonstrates that local search engine optimization (SEO) strategies can effectively establish customer credibility and trust. When a restaurant consistently appears in local search results and online directories with favorable ratings and accurate information, potential customers are more inclined to select it over its competitors.

6.2 Strategies for Enhancing Local SEO and Online Visibility

Restaurants employ diverse approaches to efficiently leverage local search engine optimization (SEO) to establish a robust online presence. The research conducted by Wiideman (2021) emphasizes the importance of optimizing online listings on directories and search engines such as Google My Business, Yelp, and TripAdvisor. Facilitating a superior user experience is contingent upon providing precise and up-to-date information about the restaurant, encompassing contact details, operational timings, menu offerings, and customer evaluations.

Furthermore, as indicated by the scholarly investigation conducted by Deldjoo et al. (2020), it is recommended that restaurants incorporate location-specific keywords within their website content, meta descriptions, and headings. As a result of implementing this optimization strategy, there is an increased probability that your business will be prominently featured in local search results when prospective clients conduct searches using pertinent phrases such as "finest dining establishments in Dhaka City."

6.3 Optimal Strategies for Local Search Engine Optimization and Online Visibility

It is recommended that restaurants follow the best practices to maximize the benefits of local SEO. De Pelsmacker et al. (2018) underscore the importance of actively managing and responding to online customer evaluations. Restaurants can exhibit their commitment to customer satisfaction by promptly and thoughtfully addressing consumer feedback, augmenting their online reputation and local search rankings.

Moreover, the research conducted by Hanoglu (2021) underscores the significance of obtaining high-quality backlinks from reputable local websites and online directories. Backlinks from reputable websites enhance the search engine credibility of a restaurant, thereby increasing the probability of its higher visibility in local search outcomes.

7. ONLINE ORDERING AND DELIVERY INTEGRATION

Due to the expanding number of meal delivery apps and platforms, online ordering and delivery must be part of restaurants' digital marketing strategy. The literature review in this study evaluates the most important aspects that make restaurant online ordering and delivery successful. This study explores how online order and delivery platforms affect customer satisfaction with new and existing customers.

7.1 Advantages of Integrating Online Ordering and Delivery

Research constantly highlights the benefits of online ordering and delivery for restaurants. Researcher Uzir et al. (2021) found that allowing customers to shop online from home or work improves customer satisfaction. The convenience of this service increases customer retention and repeat business.

According to Traynor et al. (2022), integrating food delivery apps helps companies grow their consumer base and capitalize on meal delivery's rising popularity. Collaborations with delivery platforms allow restaurants to optimize their client base and delivery infrastructure, easing the burden of internal delivery services.

7.2 Approaches for the Integration of Online Ordering and Delivery

Restaurants employ diverse strategies to integrate internet-based ordering and delivery services effectively. The study conducted by F. Li et al. (2021) emphasizes the importance of optimizing the online ordering process to enhance user satisfaction. Customers exhibit higher satisfaction levels when utilizing online ordering systems with convenience and trustworthiness. This can be attributed to user-friendly interfaces, clearly delineated menu options, and secure payment gateways.

Moreover, as indicated by the findings of Presswood (2019), it is recommended that restaurants proactively promote their online ordering and delivery services through various channels, such as their official websites, social media platforms, and email marketing initiatives. Customers can be motivated to explore and utilize multiple online ordering alternatives by implementing visually appealing imagery, persuasive language, and distinctive incentives.

7.3 Optimal Strategies for the Integration of Online Ordering and Delivery

To maximize the benefits of incorporating online ordering and delivery services, restaurants should adhere to established best practices. The research conducted by Srinivas (2020) centers on the importance of punctual and accurate execution of orders. Ensuring the timely creation and delivery of items contributes to heightened customer satisfaction, fostering positive ratings and referrals.

Furthermore, a study conducted by Hartmann & Lussier (2020) underscores the significance of vigilantly monitoring consumer feedback and promptly addressing any issues that may arise. Restaurants must actively listen when addressing client complaints, promptly respond to inquiries, and implement corrective actions. This proactive approach demonstrates a commitment to delivering service of a high standard and ensuring customer satisfaction.

8. DATA ANALYSIS AND PERSONALIZATION

Data analysis and customization have become critical components of a restaurant's digital marketing strategy. By using consumer data and adopting focused marketing tactics, restaurants can improve customer experiences, nurture customer loyalty, and improve business outcomes (Bilgihan et al., 2016). This portion of the chapter thoroughly examines the significance of data analysis and personalization in the restaurant sector. This study investigates the advantages, approaches, and best tactics related to using data personalization and research to improve the success of digital marketing efforts.

8.1 Advantages of Data Analysis and Personalization

Research consistently emphasizes the benefits of data analysis and customization within the context of the restaurant industry. The utilization of data-driven insights enables restaurants to understand their customers' preferences, behaviors, and expenditure patterns, as evidenced by the research conducted by (Alghamdi, 2023). Restaurants can potentially enhance engagement, customer satisfaction, and loyalty by leveraging this data to tailor their marketing communications, promotions, and recommendations to individual customers.

Furthermore, a study by Gilboa et al. (2019) demonstrates that personalized marketing strategies elicit a sense of affiliation and uniqueness among customers, fostering feelings of value and understanding. Customers are more likely to respond positively to promotions relevant to their needs and specifically directed towards them. Consequently, implementing this customized approach has the potential to enhance conversion rates.

8.2 Strategies for Data Analysis and Personalization

Restaurants employ diverse methodologies to utilize data analysis and personalization techniques effectively. The research conducted by Steinhoff & Zondag (2021) underscores the significance of acquiring and evaluating client data from diverse touchpoints, including online ordering platforms, loyalty programs, and website interactions, based on their research findings. This data can provide valuable insights into customer preferences, visit frequency, preferred menu items, and other relevant factors, enabling businesses to customize their marketing strategies accordingly.

Furthermore, the research conducted by Huang & Rust (2021)suggests that segmentation plays a crucial role in implementing personalization strategies. Restaurants can implement customized marketing campaigns and promotional offers that cater to distinct segments of their clientele. This can be achieved by dividing their customer base into different parts, considering demographics, interests, or habits. This strategy enhances the relevance of the material customers receive, thereby leading to higher response and engagement rates.

8.3 Optimal Approaches for Data Analysis and Personalization

Restaurants must employ data analysis best practices and maximize customization. According to Peake et al. (2018), restaurants must be careful when managing customer data, adhere to data protection laws, and have strong security measures.

Scholar Ninh et al. (2022) study stresses consumer data monitoring and analysis. Restaurants may improve their marketing and customer experience by regularly analyzing specialized marketing tactics.

CONCLUSION AND FUTURE RESEARCH

Many different aspects of digital marketing for restaurants were discussed in this chapter. Some things covered were establishing a solid web presence, maximizing local search engine optimization (SEO) and online visibility, integrating online ordering and delivery services, utilizing data analysis software, working with influencers and food bloggers, sending emails to existing customers, etc. In today's information-based economy, restaurant promotion is essential to increase revenue, brand loyalty, and recognition. The chapter highlights the significance of using a variety of digital channels to interact with customers. In the restaurant industry, personalized advertising is a boon. Restaurants can keep their regulars through data analytics and precise advertising.

Each critical topic's characteristics were carefully picked based on their relevance to digital marketing for restaurants and their capacity to offer a thorough grasp of each unique component. The selection process included a study of the available literature on each issue and consideration of the results and suggestions from academic studies, research papers, and expert perspectives. Furthermore, their cohesion identified the link between these elements, contributing to the main topic's ultimate goal. The connection between these elements is that they all play an essential part in establishing a positive online image for a restaurant. This methodical approach guaranteed that the chosen characteristics within each important topic were tightly linked, resulting in a comprehensive comprehension of the subject. We determine these crucial themes based on strict criteria to fulfill the restaurant industry's objectives and provide the most beneficial information for readers. The relevance of the issue to the restaurant industry's digital marketing environment, the potential of the topic to handle the industry's difficulties and possibilities, and the practicality of the insights presented were considered. The essential subjects were also chosen for their ability to provide a well-rounded view of digital marketing, encompassing issues ranging from creating an online presence to leveraging data analysis and customization. Furthermore, upcoming trends and improvements in the digital marketing area were addressed to guarantee that the information remained current and forward-thinking. While there are many possible themes in digital marketing, these specific important issues were picked because they form a complete and beneficial resource for restaurant owners and marketers, assisting them in excelling in the ever-changing digital scene.

Using digital platforms has altered the business model and consumer interaction of restaurants. Using digital resources, restaurants can expand their operations and their online presence. Consumers are more interconnected than ever because of social media, online shopping, and rating and review systems. The literature on the effectiveness of digital marketing for restaurants is quite lengthy. Uncharted territory exists in this field. Possible areas of study include new technological developments, customer habits and choices, digital marketing ethics, performance evaluation and return on investment, mobile marketing, and location-based techniques. As technologies such as AI and voice search become more commonplace, it will be crucial for restaurants to understand how these developments will affect their digital marketing strategies. It's helpful to look into how these technologies can enhance the customer experience, streamline operations, and inspire new ideas. Digital marketing is essential for gaining insight into customer psychology and purchasing decisions. More studies may be done on how customers feel about digital marketing, how much they want personalized experiences, and how they use digital options when choosing a restaurant. The proliferation of smartphones has boosted the significance of mobile marketing and location-based strategies. Users of cutting-edge mobile devices can be reached via proximity marketing, location-based targeting, and mobile marketing. Privacy, openness, and genuineness are three issues that must be addressed in digital marketing. Future research may reveal how data collection, fake online reviews, influencer marketing, and ethical digital marketing affect customer loyalty and trust. Building a profitable digital marketing strategy starts with solid groundwork. Digital marketing for restaurants may be quantified and evaluated in the future. Researchers could aid in the digital marketing of restaurants. Experts in digital marketing could benefit from further study of the topic.

REFERENCES

Akulshina, S. (2020). *Developing and implementing a strategic social media content plan for a local restaurant.* Academic Press.

Al-Abdallah, G. M., Dandis, A., & Al Haj Eid, M. B. (2022). The impact of Instagram utilization on brand management: An empirical study on the restaurants sector in Beirut. *Journal of Foodservice Business Research*, 1–33. doi:10.1080/15378020.2022.2083910

Alghamdi, A. (2023). A hybrid method for customer segmentation in Saudi Arabia restaurants using clustering, neural networks and optimization learning techniques. *Arabian Journal for Science and Engineering*, *48*(2), 2021–2039. doi:10.1007/s13369-022-07091-y PMID:35910042

Allard, T., Dunn, L. H., & White, K. (2020). Negative reviews, positive impact: Consumer empathetic responding to unfair word of mouth. *Journal of Marketing*, *84*(4), 86–108. doi:10.1177/0022242920924389

Bhatt, U., Antorán, J., Zhang, Y., Liao, Q. V., Sattigeri, P., Fogliato, R., Melançon, G., Krishnan, R., Stanley, J., & Tickoo, O. (2021). Uncertainty as a form of transparency: Measuring, communicating, and using uncertainty. *Proceedings of the 2021 AAAI/ACM Conference on AI, Ethics, and Society*, 401–413. 10.1145/3461702.3462571

Bilgihan, A., Kandampully, J., & Zhang, T. (2016). Towards a unified customer experience in online shopping environments: Antecedents and outcomes. *International Journal of Quality and Service Sciences*, *8*(1), 102–119. doi:10.1108/IJQSS-07-2015-0054

Bonfanti, A., Vigolo, V., & Yfantidou, G. (2021). The impact of the Covid-19 pandemic on customer experience design: The hotel managers' perspective. *International Journal of Hospitality Management*, *94*, 102871. doi:10.1016/j.ijhm.2021.102871 PMID:34866744

Cartwright, S., Liu, H., & Davies, I. A. (2022). Influencer marketing within business-to-business organizations. *Industrial Marketing Management*, *106*, 338–350. doi:10.1016/j.indmarman.2022.09.007

Cassar, M. L., Caruana, A., & Konietzny, J. (2020). Wine and satisfaction with fine dining restaurants: An analysis of tourist experiences from user generated content on TripAdvisor. *Journal of Wine Research*, *31*(2), 85–100. doi:10.1080/09571264.2020.1764919

de Lima, M. M., Mainardes, E., & Cavalcanti, A. L. (2019). Influence of social media on restaurant consumers: A case study of Crab island restaurant. *Journal of Foodservice Business Research*, *22*(5), 413–432. doi:10.1080/15378020.2019.1631657

De Pelsmacker, P., Van Tilburg, S., & Holthof, C. (2018). Digital marketing strategies, online reviews and hotel performance. *International Journal of Hospitality Management*, *72*, 47–55. doi:10.1016/j.ijhm.2018.01.003

Deldjoo, Y., Schedl, M., Cremonesi, P., & Pasi, G. (2020). Recommender systems leveraging multimedia content. *ACM Computing Surveys*, *53*(5), 1–38. doi:10.1145/3407190

Etuk, A., & Udonde, U. E. (2023). The Interplay of Digital Marketing Dimensions and Customer's Patronage of Fast Food Industries in Akwa Ibom State, Nigeria. *European Journal of Business and Innovation Research*, *11*(3), 70–97. doi:10.37745/ejbir.2013/vol11n37097

Farrar, S., & Papies, E. K. (2023). How Consumption and Reward Features Affect Desire for Food, Consumption Intentions, and Behaviour. *Retrieved from* Psyarxiv. *Com/Ugvnb*. doi:10.31234/osf.io/ugvnb

Gavilan, D., Avello, M., & Martinez-Navarro, G. (2018). The influence of online ratings and reviews on hotel booking consideration. *Tourism Management*, *66*, 53–61. doi:10.1016/j.tourman.2017.10.018

Gilboa, S., Seger-Guttmann, T., & Mimran, O. (2019). The unique role of relationship marketing in small businesses' customer experience. *Journal of Retailing and Consumer Services*, *51*, 152–164. doi:10.1016/j.jretconser.2019.06.004

Gutierrez, B. V., Kaloostian, D., & Redvers, N. (2023). Elements of Successful Food Sovereignty Interventions within Indigenous Communities in the United States and Canada: A Systematic Review. *Current Developments in Nutrition*, *7*(9), 101973. doi:10.1016/j.cdnut.2023.101973 PMID:37635710

Ha, J., & Jang, S. (2013). Attributes, consequences, and consumer values: A means-end chain approach across restaurant segments. *International Journal of Contemporary Hospitality Management*, *25*(3), 383–409. doi:10.1108/09596111311311035

Hanoglu, I. S. (2021). *Digital Marketing Channels for Organic Growth: Off-Site SEO List View show*. Academic Press.

Hartmann, N. N., & Lussier, B. (2020). Managing the sales force through the unexpected exogenous COVID-19 crisis. *Industrial Marketing Management*, *88*, 101–111. doi:10.1016/j.indmarman.2020.05.005

Huang, M.-H., & Rust, R. T. (2021). A strategic framework for artificial intelligence in marketing. *Journal of the Academy of Marketing Science*, *49*(1), 30–50. doi:10.1007/s11747-020-00749-9

Hung, J. C., & Wang, C.-C. (2021). Exploring the website object layout of responsive web design: Results of eye tracking evaluations. *The Journal of Supercomputing*, *77*(1), 343–365. doi:10.1007/s11227-020-03283-1

Jariangprasert, N., Jaturapataraporn, J., Sivaraks, P., & Luangphaiboonsri, S. (2019). The influence of food information on Facebook fan pages and Instagram affecting generation y in Thailand on restaurant selection. *Veridian E-Journal, Silpakorn University (Humanities, Social Sciences and Arts)*, *12*(2), 620–637.

Jin, Y., Ma, M., & Zhu, Y. (2022). A comparison of natural user interface and graphical user interface for narrative in HMD-based augmented reality. *Multimedia Tools and Applications*, *81*(4), 5795–5826. doi:10.1007/s11042-021-11723-0 PMID:34980945

Khan, M. N. A., & Mahmood, A. (2018). A distinctive approach to obtain higher page rank through search engine optimization. *Sadhana*, *43*(3), 43. doi:10.1007/s12046-018-0812-3

Kumar, V., & Mittal, S. (2020). Mobile marketing campaigns: Practices, challenges and opportunities. *International Journal of Business Innovation and Research*, *21*(4), 523–539. doi:10.1504/IJBIR.2020.105996

Kurdi, B., Alshurideh, M., Akour, I., Alzoubi, H., Obeidat, B., & Alhamad, A. (2022). The role of digital marketing channels on consumer buying decisions through eWOM in the Jordanian markets. *International Journal of Data and Network Science*, *6*(4), 1175–1186. doi:10.5267/j.ijdns.2022.7.002

Lepkowska-White, E., Parsons, A., & Berg, W. (2019). Social media marketing management: An application to small restaurants in the US. *International Journal of Culture, Tourism and Hospitality Research*, *13*(3), 321–345. doi:10.1108/IJCTHR-06-2019-0103

Leung, F. F., Gu, F. F., & Palmatier, R. W. (2022). Online influencer marketing. *Journal of the Academy of Marketing Science*, 1–26.

Li, F., Lu, H., Hou, M., Cui, K., & Darbandi, M. (2021). Customer satisfaction with bank services: The role of cloud services, security, e-learning and service quality. *Technology in Society*, *64*, 101487. doi:10.1016/j.techsoc.2020.101487

Li, H., Meng, F., Jeong, M., & Zhang, Z. (2020). To follow others or be yourself? Social influence in online restaurant reviews. *International Journal of Contemporary Hospitality Management*, *32*(3), 1067–1087. doi:10.1108/IJCHM-03-2019-0263

Li, J., Kim, W. G., & Choi, H. M. (2021). Effectiveness of social media marketing on enhancing performance: Evidence from a casual-dining restaurant setting. *Tourism Economics*, *27*(1), 3–22. doi:10.1177/1354816619867807

Mao, Z., Li, D., Yang, Y., Fu, X., & Yang, W. (2020). Chinese DMOs' engagement on global social media: Examining post-related factors. *Asia Pacific Journal of Tourism Research*, *25*(3), 274–285. doi:10.1080/10941665.2019.1708759

Meek, S., Wilk, V., & Lambert, C. (2021). A big data exploration of the informational and normative influences on the helpfulness of online restaurant reviews. *Journal of Business Research*, *125*, 354–367. doi:10.1016/j.jbusres.2020.12.001

Mohammad Badruddoza Talukder, Firoj Kabir, K. M., & Das, I. R. (2023). Emerging Concepts of Artificial Intelligence in the Hotel Industry: A Conceptual Paper. *International Journal of Research Publication and Reviews, 4*, 1765-1769. doi:10.55248/gengpi.4.923.92451

Nampoothiri, A. (2021). Online Shopping Behaviour: A Study on Exploring the Dependence of Demographics of the People in Kerala on their Behaviour in Online Shopping. *Turkish Journal of Computer and Mathematics Education*, *12*(10), 4153–4161.

Ninh, V.-T., Smyth, S., Tran, M.-T., & Gurrin, C. (2022). Analyzing the performance of stress detection models on consumer-grade wearable devices. *ArXiv Preprint ArXiv:2203.09669.*

Peake, J. M., Kerr, G., & Sullivan, J. P. (2018). A critical review of consumer wearables, mobile applications, and equipment for providing biofeedback, monitoring stress, and sleep in physically active populations. *Frontiers in Physiology*, *9*, 743. doi:10.3389/fphys.2018.00743 PMID:30002629

Phillipov, M., Farmery, A., & Buddle, E. (n.d.). *Media Messages About Sustainable Seafood:# How do Media Influencers affect consumer attitudes?@ Project no. 2017-131*. Academic Press.

Prasetyo, Y. T., Tanto, H., Mariyanto, M., Hanjaya, C., Young, M. N., Persada, S. F., Miraja, B. A., & Redi, A. A. N. P. (2021). Factors affecting customer satisfaction and loyalty in online food delivery service during the COVID-19 pandemic: Its relation with open innovation. *Journal of Open Innovation*, *7*(1), 76. doi:10.3390/joitmc7010076

Presswood, A. L. (2019). *Food Blogs, Postfeminism, and the Communication of Expertise: Digital Domestics*. Lexington Books.

Ruiz-Mafe, C., Chatzipanagiotou, K., & Curras-Perez, R. (2018). The role of emotions and conflicting online reviews on consumers' purchase intentions. *Journal of Business Research*, *89*, 336–344. doi:10.1016/j.jbusres.2018.01.027

Sahni, N. S., Wheeler, S. C., & Chintagunta, P. (2018). Personalization in email marketing: The role of noninformative advertising content. *Marketing Science*, *37*(2), 236–258. doi:10.1287/mksc.2017.1066

Sashi, C. M., Brynildsen, G., & Bilgihan, A. (2019). Social media, customer engagement and advocacy: An empirical investigation using Twitter data for quick service restaurants. *International Journal of Contemporary Hospitality Management*, *31*(3), 1247–1272. doi:10.1108/IJCHM-02-2018-0108

Schultheiß, S., & Lewandowski, D. (2021). "Outside the industry, nobody knows what we do" SEO as seen by search engine optimizers and content providers. *The Journal of Documentation*, *77*(2), 542–557. doi:10.1108/JD-07-2020-0127

Setiaboedi, A. P., Sari, H., & Prihartono, B. (2018). Conceptual model for online marketing strategy to success in the survival phase of small firms. *Proceedings of the International COnference on Industrial Engineering and Operations Management,* 1877.

Srinivas, S. (2020). A machine learning-based approach for predicting patient punctuality in ambulatory care centers. *International Journal of Environmental Research and Public Health*, *17*(10), 3703. doi:10.3390/ijerph17103703 PMID:32456329

Steinhoff, L., & Zondag, M. M. (2021). Loyalty programs as travel companions: Complementary service features across customer journey stages. *Journal of Business Research*, *129*, 70–82. doi:10.1016/j.jbusres.2021.02.016

Talukder, M. B. (2020). The Future of Culinary Tourism: An Emerging Dimension for the Tourism Industry of Bangladesh. *I-Manager's Journal on Management, 15*(1), 27. doi:10.26634/jmgt.15.1.17181

Talukder, M. B., & Bhuiyan, M. L. (2020). An assessment of the roles of the social network in the development of the Tourism Industry in Bangladesh. *International Journalof Business, Law, and Education*, *2*(3), 85–93. doi:10.56442/ijble.v2i3.21

Talukder, M. B., & Hossain, M. M. (2021). Prospects of Future Tourism in Bangladesh: An Evaluative Study. I-Manager's. *Journal of Management*, *15*(4), 1–8. doi:10.26634/jmgt.15.4.17495

Talukder, M. B., Kumar, S., Sood, K., & Grima, S. (2023). Information Technology, Food Service Quality and Restaurant Revisit Intention. *International Journal of Sustainable Development and Planning*, *18*(1), 295–303. doi:10.18280/ijsdp.180131

Tamer, A., & Hussein, M. (2020). The Impact of Digitization on Advertising Effectiveness. *Management Studies and Economic Systems*, *5*(3/4), 117–126. doi:10.12816/0059075

Tranberg, M., Bech, B. H., Blaakær, J., Jensen, J. S., Svanholm, H., & Andersen, B. (2018). Preventing cervical cancer using HPV self-sampling: Direct mailing of test-kits increases screening participation more than timely opt-in procedures-a randomized controlled trial. *BMC Cancer*, *18*(1), 1–11. doi:10.1186/s12885-018-4165-4 PMID:29523108

Traynor, M., Bernard, S., Moreo, A., & O'Neill, S. (2022). Investigating the emergence of third-party online food delivery in the US restaurant industry: A grounded theory approach. *International Journal of Hospitality Management*, *107*, 103299. doi:10.1016/j.ijhm.2022.103299

Uzir, M. U. H., Al Halbusi, H., Thurasamy, R., Hock, R. L. T., Aljaberi, M. A., Hasan, N., & Hamid, M. (2021). The effects of service quality, perceived value and trust in home delivery service personnel on customer satisfaction: Evidence from a developing country. *Journal of Retailing and Consumer Services*, *63*, 102721. doi:10.1016/j.jretconser.2021.102721

Vajjhala, V., & Ghosh, M. (2022). Decoding the effect of restaurant reviews on customer choice: Insights from Zomato. *Journal of Foodservice Business Research*, *25*(5), 533–560. doi:10.1080/15378020.2021.1964417

Valerio, C., William, L., & Noémier, Q. (2019). The impact of social media on E-Commerce decision making process. *International Journal of Technology for Business*, *1*(1), 1–9.

Vo, N. N. Y., Liu, S., Li, X., & Xu, G. (2021). Leveraging unstructured call log data for customer churn prediction. *Knowledge-Based Systems*, *212*, 106586. doi:10.1016/j.knosys.2020.106586

Wiideman, S. (2021). Scaling search engine visibility for franchises: A guide for multi-location brands. *Journal of Digital & Social Media Marketing*, *9*(1), 22–31.

Chapter 10
Digitalization in the Public Management:
Turkish Public Institutions Example

Salim Kurnaz
https://orcid.org/0000-0002-8060-5151
Süleyman Demirel University, Turkey

António Rodrigues
https://orcid.org/0000-0001-5550-5581
Instituto Superior de Gestão, Portugal

Osman Nuri Sunar
https://orcid.org/0000-0003-4405-1945
Istanbul Aydın University, Turkey

ABSTRACT

The digitalization process, which started with the effective use of computers, has become more effective with the use of developing technologies and mobile technologies. The purpose of this research is to examine the way, method, and purposes of digitalization in public institutions in Turkey and the use of e-government and social media tools to reach the citizens. In the first part of the study, internet, social media, artificial intelligence, and e-government applications in the context of digitalization in public institutions have been examined. Also in the first part, corporate communication and the ways public institutions communicate with citizens are examined. In the second part of the study, e-government and social media usage rates and methods of Turkish public institutions are discussed. Finally, in the last part of the study, evaluations regarding the future of social media use by public institutions are included.

DOI: 10.4018/979-8-3693-0855-4.ch010

INTRODUCTION

Due to insufficient investment and lack of capital in private sector, many services have been provided to citizens by public institutions for a long time. Even though many services called public services have been transferred to the private sector today, the public still provides many services to citizens. Public institutions have long been criticized for their rigid management approach and closed management in the twentieth century. Criticisms about the difficulty of accessing public services, the delay of the public in responding to developing events, the difficulty of accessing information in the public sector, and the bureaucratic and time-consuming structure of public transactions have been voiced for a long time. Although the improvement steps taken in response to these criticisms were not effective for a long time, there has been a significant improvement and acceleration in public services recently, especially with the introduction of computers.

With the twenty-first century, public institutions have moved away from the closed, bureaucratic and top-down traditional management approach and moved to the new public management, where citizens participate in management and service efficiency and speed are increased. With this new management approach, public institutions that want to provide faster service to citizens have begun to integrate digital technologies into their daily operations. The digitalization process, which started with the effective use of computers, has become more effective with the use of developing technologies and mobile technologies. In this context, it will be useful to evaluate the digitalization seen in public institutions in the following five stages.

- Internet and Social-Media,
- E Government,
- Artificial Intelligence,
- Corporate Communication,

First of all, it can be said that the digitalization process has started with the invent of computer and internet. The Internet has brought all individuals and institutions together and increased the interaction between individuals and institutions. Later, social media platforms developed on the internet; has become the target of private and public organizations that want to reach their customers and citizens while increasing interaction between individuals. Social media platforms have begun to be used effectively for information sharing and intelligence purposes. Increasing technological developments have made possible artificial intelligence applications that can think or make decisions in certain situations. Today, individuals and societies follow artificial intelligence applications closely. In the twentieth century, public institutions have implemented e-government applications in order to share the information they hold with citizens, reduce the bureaucratic structure and provide faster services to citizens. Finally, this digitalization in public institutions has increased communication between institutions and individuals and increase the interagency communication. In the globalizing world and increasing competition environment, communication is one of the most important concepts of today for individuals, societies, and organizations. While individuals use social media platforms mostly for their own needs and information sharing, public and private businesses use social media networks to inform the public about the products and services they offer, to determine users' expectations and satisfaction levels, to manage customer services or to identify areas of investment.

In light of this information, the purpose of this research is to examine the way, method and purposes of digitalization in public institutions in Turkey and the use of e-government and social media tools to reach the citizens. In the first part of the study internet, social media, artificial intelligence, and e-government applications in the context of digitalization in public institutions have been examined. Also in the first part, corporate communication and the ways public institutions communicate with citizens are examined. In the second part of the study, e-government and social media usage rates and methods of Turkish public institutions are discussed. Finally, in the last part of the study, evaluations regarding the future of social media use by public institutions are included.

BACKGROUND

While public services were previously limited to functions such as ensuring and protecting the safety of life and property, public morality and security, public order, health and welfare within the classical state thought; Nowadays, it is seen that the field of public services has expanded due to the increase in the roles and responsibilities of the state and different forms of service delivery have emerged within this framework. These services are not only at the national level, but also at the regional or local level, is even understood that they are offered by private organizations as well as public institutions.

The desire to provide public services to citizens quickly, practically and easily makes the application of effective service methods inevitable today. In order to eliminate the deficiencies and inadequacies in the traditional way of providing public services, digital applications have been implemented in public services with the development and dissemination of technology. Providing public services digitally directly contributes to the increase in effectiveness and efficiency in public services. Therefore, with the digitalization of public services, business and transactions can be carried out faster, more reliable and with higher quality (Önen & Kahraman, 2022:425).

When the processes of public administration are considered, two approaches come to the fore. These approaches are Traditional Public Management and New public management approaches. First of all, touching on these two approaches will be useful in understanding the subject. Traditional Public Administration is an approach that includes the organization and management of many areas, especially the production structure, organizational order and labor relations in workplaces, in line with the factorization process that started with the industrial revolution (Önen & Kahraman, 2022:426). In traditional public administration, managers are responsible for both maintaining institutional activities effectively and away from external influences and achieving politically determined goals; It tries to fully implement formalities, rules and norms. The implementation process has been regulated in detail, and the discretionary powers of public administrators in implementing policies have been considerably narrowed (Yıldırım, 2010: 840).

The new public management tried to adapt the philosophies and practices of the private sector to the public sector. The roles and responsibilities assumed by management have gone through a radical change process. The restrictive and protective approach of traditional management has been abandoned in order to obtain more practical, faster and appropriate results in managerial decisions and actions. In managerial responsibility, attention is focused on results and performance rather than on strict rules and procedures. Efficiency, effectiveness and economy have become the main principles guiding the managerial process (Yıldırım, 2010: 840).

Within the framework of this understanding, seven basic ideas of the new public service come to the fore (Ayhan and Önder, 2017: 36-40):

- Based on the concept of service to citizens,
- The main purpose is public benefit,
- Giving importance to citizenship,
- Thinking strategically and acting democratically,
- Understanding the importance of accountability,
- Focus on serving,
- Valuing people as well as productivity.

In order to fulfill the goals and expectations of this new management approach, which attaches importance to citizen satisfaction, prioritizes citizens and strives to ensure service efficiency, it has become inevitable to integrate digital technologies into all areas of public institutions. Investments made in this context have caused concepts such as digital government or e-government to come to the fore.

DIGITALIZATION IN PUBLIC MANAGEMENT

When considering the perception of public service in general, closed, top-down, bureaucratic and paper-based transaction models of public sector institutions come to mind, but recently it seems that public services are trying to transition to online or integrated digital applications that encourage a new type of interaction between citizens and government institutions (Önen & Kahraman, 2022: 429). As of the 2000s, due to the increasing population, the information that public services hold and have to manage has become unmanageable with manual methods, so making use of technology in the fields of public service delivery and information management has become inevitable for the rapid and practical management of citizen requests and demands (Gül, 2018:6). In this context, the invention of the computer, the use of the internet, social media environments, artificial intelligence and e-government applications have been the main factors affecting the digitalization seen in public institutions.

At this point, we should not forget the contribution of the Covid-19 pandemic in 2020 to digitalization. The Covid-19 epidemic, which destroyed the usual lifestyle in economic, social, and individual dimensions and caused the largest economic crisis in world history, caused businesses to close and millions of people to become unemployed. Although the Covid-19 pandemic has negatively affected our lives, digital technologies such as remote working, online shopping, e-commerce, and contactless payment have increased the tendency of public and private sector organizations to digital technologies.

Internet and Social-Media

Although the invention of the computer was a big and important step in producing and storing information, it was the invention of the Internet that really increased the importance and use of computers. Internet and web technologies, which add countless values to humanity, will continue to be one of the indispensable technologies of the 21st century and the future, thanks to their features that form the basis of many other technologies and renew themselves at an uninterrupted pace (Gülaslan, 2018:19). The Internet actually allows computers to communicate and interact with each other. In this context, it is necessary

Figure 1. Internet access availability in households and Internet use by individuals, 2012-2023
Source: https://data.tuik.gov.tr/Bulten/Index?p=Hanehalki-Bilisim-Teknolojileri-(BT)-Kullanim-Arastirmasi-2023-49407

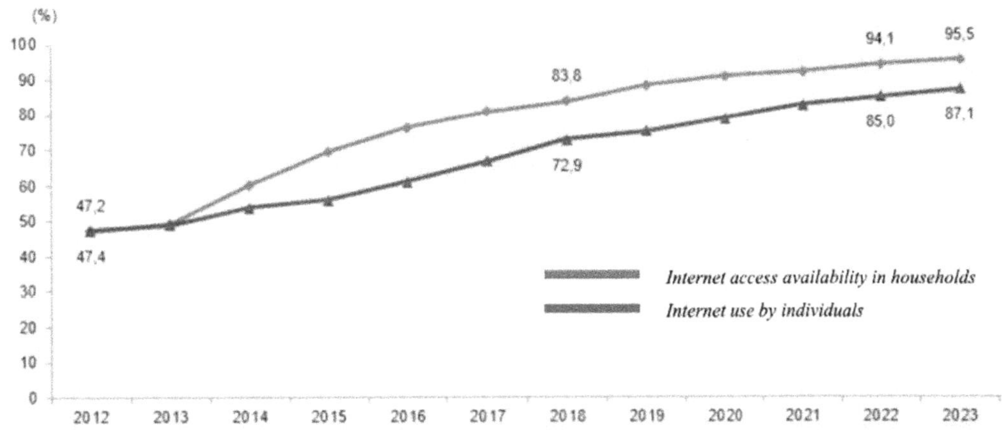

to consider all information technologies together. All kinds of technological tools that ensure the speed of flow of information and thought are called "information and communication technologies"(Güler & Günel, 2022:24). All tools that provide benefits in accessing and creating all kinds of information constitute information and communication technologies. These tools can be visual, auditory, printed or written. Information technologies are the recording and preservation of various data, producing information after certain processes, and then accessing, storing and transferring this information, etc. These are technological developments that enable activities to be carried out effectively, quickly and efficiently (Behan and Holmes, 1990: 1).

In this context, internet access and individual usage figures of individuals in Turkey for the last 10 years are given in Figure 1. As of 2023, %95,5 of individuals in Turkey have internet access in households and %87,1 of individuals have personal internet access over mobile networks. It is clearly seen that the internet access and usage rates of individuals in Turkey are increasing day by day and the internet is an integral part of life.

Internet users worldwide have reached 5.16 billion and the usage rate according to the population is 64.4%. In Turkey, Internet users constitute 83.4% of the population with 71.38 million users. This rate is well above the world average. While the number of social media users worldwide is 4.76 billion, the ratio of this number to the population is 59.4%. In Turkey, active social media users reached 62.55 million people. While the rate of active social media users according to the population in Turkey is 73.1%, the majority of internet users use social media (We Are Social, 2023).

In a country where internet use is so widespread, the fastest way for public and private sector businesses to reach citizens will of course be through digital methods, applications and mobile devices and applications. For this reason, public institutions, like private businesses, should accelerate their investments in digital applications and mobile technologies and reach citizens by creating accounts in social media as soon as possible.

Social media is an environment where people can freely express their opinions, share and produce content. At the same time, people can follow and control the services provided by private and public institutions through social media. In addition, public and private institutions also seriously use social

Figure 2. Most used social media platforms by individuals, Feb 2023
Source: https://www.guvenliweb.org.tr/dosya/HQTLP.pdf

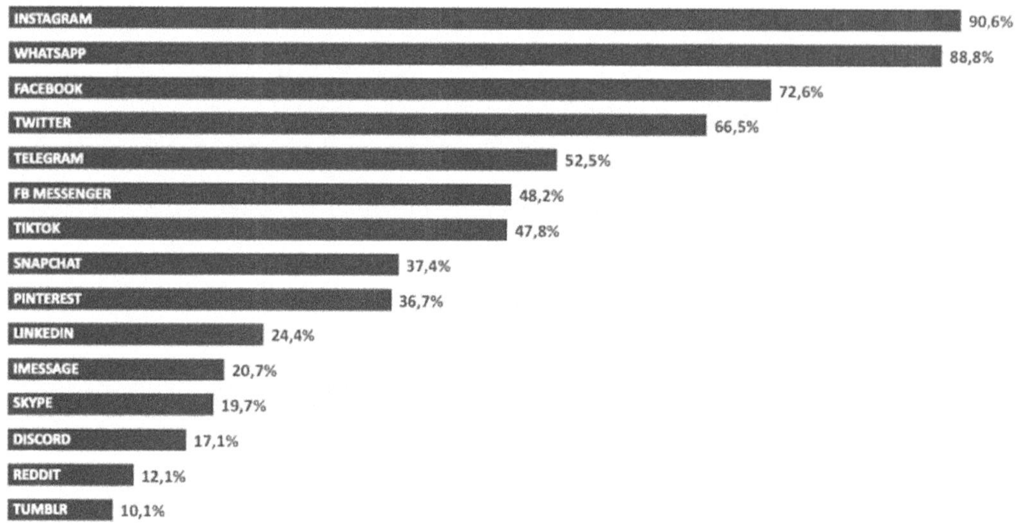

media to express themselves, reach their target audience and provide information about their work and activities. Thus, there is communication and interaction between the institution and the public through social media (Çalışır & Aksoy, 2019:45).

Social media is an effective communication tool due to its three important characteristics. The first of these is that social media presents issues and ideas in a wider area and faster than other traditional media tools. Second, social media creates strong socio-cultural connections between users. Thanks to social media, instant news bulletins, social issues and ideas can be shared very easily. Thirdly, social media has reduced the phenomenon of 'online unknowns' (being present online under different usernames). As 'real networks' (known networks) have moved online, users now need to pay more attention to what they say. Because it can be determined who sent the messages (Çalı, 2012:59).

First of all, it should be determined which social media platforms the users in Turkey use, and public institutions should prioritize their efforts to have a presence on these platforms. In this way, more users can be reached. For this reason the social applications most used by social media users in Turkey are given in Figure 2.

Internet users in Turkey spend an average of 2 hours and 58 minutes on social media. The average number of social media platforms used by social media users monthly is 7.6. Internet users use Instagram the most with 90.6%. Instagram is followed by WhatsApp, Facebook and Twitter respectively. Users spend the most time on Instagram, with an average of 21 hours and 24 minutes per month. Users mostly follow their friends, family and acquaintances on social media accounts. The social media application with the most users in Turkey is YouTube with 57.9 million users (We Are Social, 2023).

E Government

In addition to the use of computers and technological devices in the service concept offered by public institutions, the application that created the main change was the integration into the e-government infra-

Figure 3. E-government number of users by years
Source: https://www.turkiye.gov.tr/edevlet-istatistikleri?kullanici=Istatistikleri

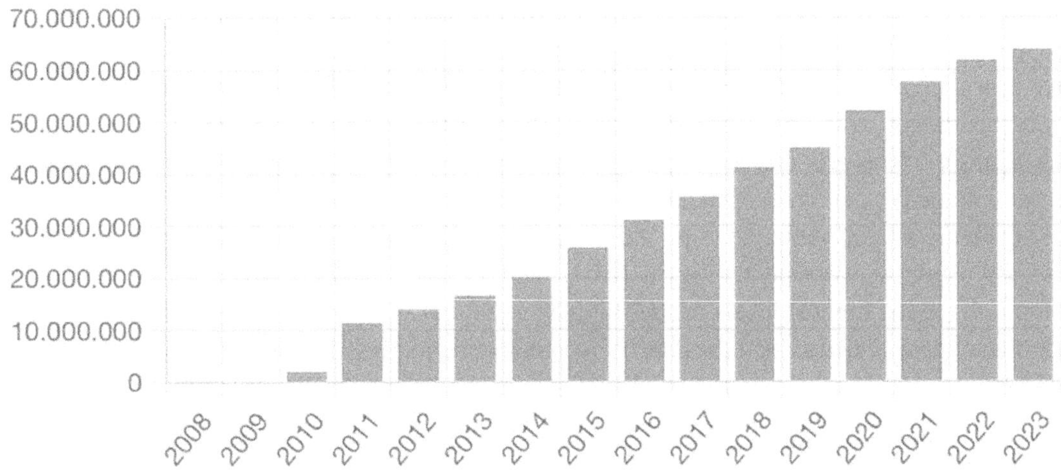

structure of public institutions and the ability to access most of the public services through this platform. In this context, the most concrete form of digital transformation in the delivery of public services is e-government applications (Göçoğlu, 2020: 619).

In definition studies on the concept of e-government, the concept is defined as the use of information technologies (wide area networks, internet and mobile computing) that have the potential to transform the relationship of government bodies with citizens, business and other government organizations (World Bank, 2022). Additionally, e-government is defined by the OECD (2023) as "the use of information and communication technologies (ICT), and in particular the Internet, to provide better governance." In another definition, the electronic transformation of the informatics and services dimension of interaction with online public services, citizens, business world and other public institutions is defined as e-government (United Nations, 2022; Singh & Sharma, 2009).

The concept of e-government in Turkey emerged with the e-government portal introduced in 2008. Login to the e-government portal, whose purpose is to provide public services to all citizens, public institutions and private sector businesses 24/7, is made using the authentication system (Doru, 2022:111). The number of e-government users has increased rapidly and gradually over the years and reached 63.8 million users as of September 2023 (türkiye.gov.tr). The increase in the number of e-government application users over the years is given in Figure 3.

According to e-Government portal user statistics, the number of users in October 2023 is approximately 64 million, of which 30.4 million are women and 33.5 million are men (www.turkiye.gov.tr). The increasing interest of citizens has pushed public institutions to provide more services through the e-government portal. Today, 195 central public institutions, 204 universities, 446 municipalities, 30 water and sewerage administrations and 126 private institutions provide a total of 7,419 different services through e-Government portal (www.turkiye.gov.tr).

E-government portal today is mostly realized by the government sharing information with citizens. Many of the services offered are limited to accessing and making copies of government-held legal and financial information. Presentation of information and documents to government institutions and making legal changes are still done manually and by going to the institution in person.

In the future, it is expected that this interaction will no longer be one-way but will become an environment where the public and citizens interact, and where citizens' requests and expectations are received and met. It is also considered that, thanks to developing identity verification systems, it will be possible to submit documents to public institutions and make legal changes trough e-government portal. The most obvious example of this is banks' attempts to open online accounts. While previously it was necessary to go to a bank branch in person to open a bank account, it has become possible to open an account online.

One of the most important factors provided by e-government is the participation of citizens in management. By using e-government, citizens will be able to convey their feelings, thoughts, expectations and complaints to the highest levels of the state. This mutual interaction strengthens the bond between the state and citizens and also increases the transparency and auditability of the state (Akçaöz & Akçaöz, 2023:3657).

Artificial Intelligence

In today's age of information and technology, computers and other technological devices develop more and more every day and come across new types and many new features. People have easier access to developing technology every day and benefit from it as an indispensable element at every moment of their lives. Rapidly developing technology with the industrial revolution has paved the way for many things used in daily life to be connected to each other via the internet, thus paving the way for the design of fast and smart machines with the development of robotic technology. These developments have developed so dazzlingly today that the concept of artificial intelligence has started to come to the fore in every field. Artificial intelligence, which tries to understand intelligent beings, emerges as a field of study that is based on the programming of computers by taking into account the characteristics of the human mind, and whose impact can be observed in every aspect of human life.

The term artificial intelligence emerged as a sub-branch of computer science and was first used in its modern sense in the 1950s. Today, artificial intelligence constitutes one of the fields of study beyond computer science, cognitive science, philosophy, psychology, economics and even law. Moreover, artificial intelligence is turning into an interdisciplinary research field that has recently attracted special attention from society, politics and the public sector, offering a variety of unique opportunities and creating cataphoric risks (Uzun, et al., 2022:424).

Artificial intelligence is a field that tries to program machines that can think like humans by trying to best describe the human mind and behavior (Önder & Saygılı, 2018:631). Artificial intelligence (AI) is also defined as an artificial entity that can learn, make decisions, influence that environment, and communicate its knowledge and choices to people in a complex, changing environment, in other words, an entity that can think (Gezici, 2023:112).

Applications of Artificial Intelligence, especially in the public sector, which has a guiding, regulatory and encouraging nature, are gradually expanding with studies carried out around the world. The rate of use of Artificial Intelligence is showing serious progress in many areas, especially education programs, public officials' planning of new infrastructure projects, answering citizens' questions and expectations, determining public opinion, creating an advanced level of satisfaction in health services, and social assistance payments (Efe & Özdemir, 2021:35).

Corporate Communication

Communication, in its simplest form, is a phenomenon based on mutual message exchange, sharing and feedback. The main purpose is to convey a message to the relevant target audience, for the target audience to analyze the message and to create the expected behavior accordingly. This flow of information can occur between two people, or between groups or even institutions (Budak &Budak 2014: 84).

Corporate communication has different definitions. First of all corporate communication is defined as a combination of all communication efforts carried out by businesses to implement management strategies in order to achieve their goals (Mert, 2019:1514) Corporate communication is also defined as "a management tool in which all types of internal and external communication, used consciously, are harmonized as effectively and efficiently as possible in order to create a positive understanding with the groups with which the institution has to be in contact." (Van Reil, 1995: 25)

Although it is a fact that corporate communication activities carried out through websites have significant advantages, it is necessary to pay attention to some points while carrying out these studies. First of all, web pages must accurately reflect the corporate identity. Since corporate communication is one of the important elements that reflect corporate identity, correctly designed corporate communication becomes important in conveying the corporate identity correctly and making the image of the institution positive.

DIGITALIZATION OF TURKISH PUBLIC INSTITUTIONS: E-GOVERNMENT AND SOCIAL MEDIA USAGE

Today, as a result of the developments in information and communication technologies, there are changes in all systems, political and economic areas. Therefore, every aspect of society is affected by this change. Especially with the emergence of the internet, it is seen that access has become easier and new types of communication have emerged. Social media, one of these, has become a communication technology product that is used extensively in Turkey and around the world.

As a result of the development of technology and the increased use of digital networks, the transformation of citizens into digital citizens, and the digital transformation occurring throughout society, the state-citizen relationship has been transferred to the digital environment. For this reason, public institutions and organizations must now be in this environment. Not being on these platforms is not a very acceptable situation in this world order. At the same time, it is known that public institutions and organizations on this platform should actively participate. Because active citizens who receive public services and have expectations from the public want to see public institutions and organizations in social media environments (Çalışır & Aksoy, 2019:49).

Social networks, which have a high number of users in social media environments, make serious contributions as long as they are used by public institutions. Through social networks, public institutions can reach a wide range of citizens and inform their target groups about their work and activities. In this way, institutions have the opportunity to measure the quality and efficiency of the services they offer. Because fast communication and feedback can be received through social networks. Therefore, citizens can react very quickly through social networks when evaluating any service provided. At the same time, public institutions can communicate and interact with citizens for the projects they want to realize.

Social media platforms used by public institutions must be managed by experts in line with the principles of transparency and accountability (Erkek, 2016:143). Because social media allows instant

Figure 4. Proportion of individuals using internet in doing interaction with public authorities and activities in the last 12 months for private purpose by sex, 2022, 2023
Source: https://data.tuik.gov.tr/Bulten/Index?p=Hanehalki-Bilisim-Teknolojileri-(BT)-Kullanim-Arastirmasi-2023-49407

(%)

	Total		Male		Female	
Usage of e-government services	2022	2023	2022	2023	2022	2023
Contact/interact with public authorities/public services over the Internet for private purposes	68,7	73,9	76,6	81,3	60,8	66,4
Activities						
Accessed information stored about you by public authorities or public services	64,4	69,6	72,4	77,8	56,4	61,4
Accessed information from public databases or registers	22,0	24,0	27,0	29,1	17,0	19,0
Obtaining information from websites or apps	44,1	48,2	50,3	54,6	37,9	41,8
Downloading/printing official forms	32,4	30,6	38,1	35,8	26,6	25,4
Making any appointment or reservation via a website or app with public authorities or public services	48,5	51,3	53,4	54,9	43,6	47,7
Receiving any official communication/document by public authorities via own account on an website or app	-	18,4	-	23,8	-	13,0
Submitting your tax declaration via a website or app for private purpose	7,2	7,8	10,0	10,5	4,5	5,2
Requesting official documents or certificates (e.g. graduation, birth, marriage, divorce, death, residence certificates, police or criminal records)	21,2	24,7	26,4	29,8	16,0	19,5
Requesting benefits or entitlements (e.g. pension, unemployment, child allowance, enrolment in schools, universities)	9,3	11,9	10,8	13,1	7,9	10,7
Making other requests, claims or complaints (e.g. report theft to the police, launch a legal complaint, request legal aid, initiate a civil claim procedure in front of a court)	4,9	5,6	6,3	6,8	3,5	4,4

TurkStat, Survey on Information and Communication Technology (ICT) Usage in Households and by Individuals, 2023
Since more than one option can be chosen, total may not be 100.
- Denotes magnitude null.

communication and provides an environment where a crisis can arise at any time, it must be managed by a social media expert. Social media accounts to be managed in public institutions should not be a single account. Because the social media accounts used by public institutions may differ depending on the characteristics of the citizens they serve. For example, while young people use Instagram more, middle-aged and older citizens use Facebook more. For this reason, citizens should be segmented, and content should be produced and managed in social media accounts opened accordingly.

When Figure 4 is evaluated in general, it is seen that the rate of those using the internet to communicate with public institutions/organizations for private purposes was 68.7% in 2022, while this rate increased to 73.9% in 2023. It has been determined that in 2023, 24% of citizens used e-government applications to access information from public databases or records, 48.2% used e-government applications to obtain information from websites of public institutions, and 30.6% used e-government applications to download/print official forms.

11.9% of the citizens who used e-government applications in 2023 stated that they used them for reasons such as requesting assistance or rights (pension, unemployment, child allowance, enrollment in schools, universities, etc.), and 5.6% of them stated that they used them for other reasons such as making other requests, claims or complaints (reporting theft to the police, making a legal complaint, requesting legal aid, filing a lawsuit, etc.).

When the data obtained is evaluated in general, it is seen that e-government applications are mostly used to obtain information unilaterally from the state or public institutions. It is expected that e-government applications will turn into a portal in the future where communication will be two-way, and citizens will be able to transfer information, requests and complaints to the state and public institutions as well as extracting information from the state and public institutions.

For these reasons, public institutions should be present in social environments that citizens use significantly. They can use these social media platforms to inform their citizens about their services and respond to citizens' requests and suggestions. In this context, the status of ministries in Turkey on Twitter, the most used social media portal, is given in Figure 5.

Figure 5. Numerical representation of Twitter (X) interaction of the Ministries of Republic of Turkey (October 2023)

	Name of Ministry	Followers	Following	Posts	Subscription Date
1	T.R. Ministry of National Defense	3.2M	29	18,2K	August 2016
2	T.R. Ministry of Interior	2,8M	35	12K	January 2012
3	T.R. Ministry of Education	2,8M	122	10K	October 2013
4	T.R. Ministry of Health	2,7M	21	22,3K	April 2012
5	T.R. Ministry of Foreign Affairs	1,7M	264	26,6K	December 2009
6	T.R. Ministry of Justice	1,3M	31	4,1K	August 2011
7	T.R. Ministry of Family, Labor and Social Services	1M	119	17,8K	September 2012
8	T.R. Ministry of Treasury and Finance	895K	22	2,4K	June 2012
9	T.R. Ministry of Environment and Urbanization and Climate Change	568K	88	9,7K	December 2012
10	T.R. Ministry of Agriculture and Forestry	531K	85	10,6K	May 2012
11	T.R. Ministry of Youth and Sports	527K	107	23,1K	September 2011
12	T.R. Ministry of Industry and Technology	474K	171	16,2K	December 2010
13	T.R. Ministry of Transport and Infrastructure	440,6K	37	18,5K	March 2012
14	T.R. Culture and Tourism Ministry	428K	69	15,3K	January 2011
15	T.R. Energy and Natural Resources Ministry	320K	44	3,5K	October 2013
16	T.R. Ministry of Commerce	285,4K	23	4,9K	August 2016

When Figure 5 is examined in detail, it is seen that ministries in Turkey generally registered their Twitter accounts at the end of 2011 or the first half of 2012. The exceptions to this are the Ministry of Foreign Affairs, which opened its Twitter account in December 2009, and the Ministry of National Defense and Ministry of Commerce, which created their Twitter account in August 2016.

SOLUTIONS AND RECOMMENDATIONS

The impact of digitalization on public services is obvious. It is evaluated that citizens, especially those who want faster and more effective service, want to see more digital solutions in public service delivery. In this context, it is important for public institutions to provide more services through digital means and interact with more citizens via the internet and digital portals. In this context, three methods: More digitalization, more use of social media and more use of artificial intelligence come to the fore.

More digitalization: Since digitalization efforts in public services have started in the last twenty years and are still at the very beginning, we will witness more digitalization and the transfer of more services to digital environments in the coming period. In the future it is expected that more services could be operated over e-government portals.

More use of social media: Nowadays, it is seen that private businesses and public institutions interact more with customers or citizens for reasons such as service improvement and product development. While this interaction was previously carried out via telephone and internet pages, increasing use of social media and citizens spending more time on social media have caused institutions and businesses to turn to social media. Many businesses have started to use social media more actively to inform their customers and promote their products through the social accounts they have created. Recently, the increasing use of social media has caused businesses to move their customer communication channels to social environments. Following this development in the private sector, public institutions have also started to inform citizens about public services through their social media accounts, using the same method. It is considered that in the future, citizens' complaints and expectations from public institutions can be commemorated using social networks.

More use of artificial intelligence: Artificial intelligence products and applications are entering our lives every day. It is evaluated that private enterprises and public institutions will incorporate artificial intelligence applications into their applications in the future. For this reason, it will be useful to evaluate artificial intelligence applications in the investment steps to be taken for the future.

FUTURE RESEARCH DIRECTIONS

It seems that academic studies on digitalization and public administration focus mostly on the current practices of public institutions. Current studies have been carried out on the digital services offered by ministries, public institutions and local governments to their citizens over the internet. In this context, in the future studies on public administration and digitalization; It would be beneficial to build on digital technologies that public institutions can use. Such studies will guide public institutions and facilitate the integration of new applications into public services.

CONCLUSION

Nowadays, in the age of technology and communication, almost all citizens have mobile phones and internet access. When social media usage figures are examined in detail, it is seen that the usage time is increasing rapidly every year. All kinds of communication between individuals have been moved to digital environments. For this reason, it is now a necessity for all public and private sector organizations that want to reach their citizens and inform their citizens and customers about the goods and services they produce, to exist in digital environments.

First of all, examining the status of public institutions regarding digitalization will be guiding in determining the steps to be taken in the future. For this reason, the current digitalization levels of public institutions were examined first in the research. As a result of the identified situation, evaluations regarding future digitalization efforts are included. Digitalization of public services is accelerating day by day as citizens want to receive service faster and public institutions want to provide faster and more effective services. In this context, digitalization is becoming a part of our lives every day.

Three suggestions for the future were developed with the findings obtained within the scope of the study. First of all, it has been observed that more digitalization will be seen in public services and public institutions should accelerate their steps towards digitalization. Secondly, it is considered that public-citizen interaction is increasingly shifting to social networks. Public institutions inform their citizens about public services through both their managers' and corporate accounts. It is considered that in the future, instead of this one-way information, there will be a process in which interaction with citizens will be done bilaterally and citizen expectations and complaints will be received through social accounts. In this context, the importance of public institutions' investments in social accounts is increasing. Finally, it is evaluated that artificial intelligence technologies will rapidly enter our daily lives. For this reason, it is predicted that artificial intelligence investments by public and private sector organizations will gain importance in the coming period.

ACKNOWLEDGMENT

This research received no specific grant from any funding agency in the public, commercial, or not-for-profit sectors.

REFERENCES

Akçaöz, M., & Akçaöz, V. (2023). Kamu Yönetiminde Dijitalleşme ve Türkiye'deki Dijital Devlet Uygulamaları. *Journal of Social Humanities and Administrative Sciences*, *9*(69), 3648–3660. doi:10.29228/JOSHAS.72401

Ayhan, E., & Önder, M. (2017). Yeni Kamu Hizmeti Yaklaşımı: Yönetişime Açılan Bir Kapı. *Gazi İktisat ve İşletme Dergisi*, *3*(2), 19–48.

Behan, K., & Holmes, D. (1990). *Understanding Information Technology*. Prentice Hall.

Budak, G., & Budak, G. (2014). *İmaj Mühendisliği Vizyonundan Halkla İlişkiler* (6th ed.). Nobel Yayıncılık.

Çalı, H. H., & Tombul, F. (2012). Güvenlik ile İlgili Kamu Hizmeti Sunumunda Sosyal Medya. *Türk İdare Dergisi*, *474*, 55–76.

Çalışır, G., & Aksoy, F. (2019). Kamu Kurumlarında Sosyal Medya Kullanımı: Kastamonu İl Kültür ve Turizm Müdürlüğü Örneği. *Alınteri Sosyal Bilimler Dergisi*, *3*(1), 43–65. doi:10.30913/alinterisosbil.503286

Doru, S. (2022). 21. Yüzyılda Türk Kamu Yönetiminin Dönüşümü: Dijitalleşme ve E-Devlet. Siyaset Bilimi ve Kamu Yönetimi Konularında Bilimsel Değerlendirmeler, 105-116.

Efe, A., & Özdemir, G. (2021). Yapay Zekâ Ortamında Kamu Yönetiminin Geleceği Üzerinde Bir Değerlendirme. *Kamu Yönetimi ve Teknoloji Dergisi*, *3*(1), 34-60. Retrieved from https://dergipark.org.tr/tr/pub/kaytek/issue/64162/927834

Erkek, S. (2016). Kamu Kurumlarında Sosyal Medya Kullanımı: Sağlık Bakanlığı Örneği. *Selçuk Üniversitesi Sosyal Bilimler Enstitüsü Dergisi*, *35*, 141–150.

Gezici, H. S. (2023). Kamu Yönetiminde Yapay Zekâ: Avrupa Birliği. *Uluslararası Akademik Birikim Dergisi.*, *6*(2), 111–128.

Göçoğlu, V. (2020). Kamu Hizmetlerinin Sunumunda Dijital Dönüşüm: Nesnelerin İnterneti Üzerine Bir İnceleme. *Manas Sosyal Araştırmalar Dergisi*, *9*(1), 615–628. doi:10.33206/mjss.538784

Gül, H. (2017). Dijitalleşmenin Kamu Yönetimi ve Politikaları ile Bu Alanlardaki Araştırmalara Etkileri. *Yasama Dergisi*, (36), 5–26.

Gülaslan, T. (2018). *Kamu Yönetiminde Sosyal Medya Kullanımı ve Yönetimi: Temel İlkeler ve Öneriler* [Doctoral Thesis]. Hacettepe University Social Science Instıtution, Ankara.

Güler, A., & Günel, Y. (2022). Kamu Kurumlarında Bilgi Teknolojileri ve Sosyal Medya Kullanımının Çalışan Performansına Etkisi. *International Journal of Economic and Administrative Academic Research*, *2*(2), 23–48.

Mert, Y. L. (2019). Kamu Yönetiminde Kurumsal İletişim: Web Siteleri Üzerine Bir Analiz. *Uluslararası Sosyal Araştırmalar Dergisi*, *12*(62), 1513–1522.

OECD. (2023). *Background Paper: Implementing E-Government in OECD Countries Experiences and Challenges.* https://www.oecd.org/mena/governance/36853121.pdf

Önder, M., & Saygılı, H. (2018). Yapay Zekâ ve Kamu Yönetimine Yansımaları. *Türk İdare Dergisi*, *2*(487), 629–670.

Önen, S. M., & Kahraman, N. (2022). Kamu Hizmetlerinin Sunumunda Dijitalleşme Üzerine Bir Değerlendirme. *Uluslararası Akademik Birikim Dergisi*, *5*(5), 424–432.

Singh, A. K. & Sharma, V. (2009). E-Governance and E-Government: A Study of Some Initiatives. *International Journal of eBusiness and eGovernment Studies*, *1*(1), 1-14.

TUİK. (2023). *Hanehalkı Bilişim Teknolojileri Kullanım Araştırması.* https://data.tuik.gov.tr/Bulten/Index?p=Hanehalki-Bilisim-Teknolojileri-(BT)-Kullanim-Arastirmasi-2023-49407

Türkiye E-Devlet Kapısı. (2023). *E-Devlet Kapısı Kullanıcı İstatistikleri.* https://www.turkiye.gov.tr/edevlet-istatistikleri?kullanici=Istatistikleri

United Nations. (2022). *What is e-Government?* https://publicadministration.un.org/egovkb/en-us/About/UNeGovDD-Framework

Uzun, M. M., Yildiz, M., & Önder, M. (2022). Big questions of artificial intelligence (AI) in public administration and policy. SİYASAL. *Journal of Political Science*, *31*(2), 423–442. doi:10.26650/siyasal.2022.31.1121900

Van Riel, C. (1995). *Principles of Corporate Communication*. Prentice Hall.

We Are Social. (2023). *Digital 2023 Turkey.* https://www.guvenliweb.org.tr/dosya/HQTLP.pdf

World Bank. (2022). *What is e-Government?* https://www.worldbank.org/en/topic/digitaldevelopment/brief/e-government

Yıldırım, M. (2010). Kamu Yönetiminde Takdir Yetkisi: Geleneksel ve Yeni Kamu Yönetimi Arasında Karşılaştırmalı Bir İnceleme. *Uluslararas Insan Bilimleri Dergisi*, *7*(2), 839–861.

ADDITIONAL READING

Biswal, S. K. (2020). The Space of Artificial Intelligence in Public Relations: The Way Forward. In A. Kulkarni & S. Satapathy (Eds.), *Optimization in Machine Learning and Applications. Algorithms for Intelligent Systems*. Springer. doi:10.1007/978-981-15-0994-0_11

Leftheriotis, I. G., & Michail, N. (2014). Using Social Media For Work: Losing Your Time Or Improving Your Work? *Computers in Human Behavior*, *31*, 134–142. doi:10.1016/j.chb.2013.10.016

Nduhura, D., & Prieler, M. (2017). When I Chat Online, I Feel Relaxed and Work Better: Exploring the Use of Social Media in The Public Sector Workplace in Rwanda. *Telecommunications Policy*, *41*(7-8), 708–716. doi:10.1016/j.telpol.2017.05.008

Odoom, R., Anning-Dorson, T., & Acheampong, G. (2017). Antecedents of Social Media Usage and Performance Benefits in Small- and Medium-Sized Enterprises (SMEs). *Journal of Enterprise Information Management*, *30*(3), 383–399. doi:10.1108/JEIM-04-2016-0088

Song, Q., Wang, Y., Chen, Y., Benitez, J., & Hu, J. (2019). Impact of The Usage of Social Media in The Workplace on Team and Employee Performance. *Information & Management*, *56*(8), 1–20. doi:10.1016/j.im.2019.04.003

Valle-Cruz, D., Sandoval-Almazan, R., Ruvalcaba-Gomez, E. A., & Ignacio Criado, J. (2019). A Review of Artificial Intelligence in Government and Its Potential from A Public Policy Perspective. *ACM International Conference Proceeding Series*, 91–99. 10.1145/3325112.3325242

Wang, M.-H., Yang, T.-Y., & Chen, Y. S. (2016). How Workers Engage in Social Networking Sites at Work: A Uses and Gratification Expectancy Perspective. *International Journal of Organizational Innovation*, *8*(4), 161–176.

Wirtz, B. W., Weyerer, J. C., & Sturm, B. J. (2020). The Dark Sides of Artificial Intelligence: An Integrated AI Governance Framework for Public Administration. *International Journal of Public Administration*, *43*(9), 818–829. doi:10.1080/01900692.2020.1749851

Yu, L., Cao, X., & Wang, Z. L. J. (2018). Excessive Social Media Use at Work Exploring The Effects of Social Media Overload on Job Performance. *Information Technology & People*, *31*(6), 1091–1112. doi:10.1108/ITP-10-2016-0237

Zavattaro, S. M. (2018). What's in a symbol? Big questions for place branding in public administration. *Public Administration Quarterly*, *42*(1), 90–119.

KEY TERMS AND DEFINITIONS

Corporate Communication: It is the name given to the communication process that takes place for the purpose of information flow, motivation, coordination, organization, training and control between the departments and elements required to achieve the goals and objectives of an institution, a business or an organization and to carry out its activities.

Corporate Reputation: It is the sum of the impressions left on people by the materials related to the visible face of an institution, and the value an institution has in the eyes of the people and institutions it deals with. Corporate reputation can also be defined as the sum of the perceptions of an institution in the minds of shareholders, customers, employees, social institutions, written and oral media and the public.

Digitalization: It is the transformation of traditional business processes, services and products using digital technologies and the adaptation of businesses to these technologies. Digitalization is the process of businesses and society's transition to the digital world and includes the use of technologies such as the internet, mobile devices, artificial intelligence, and cloud computing. With digitalization, information, data, services, and products are processed, stored and shared digitally.

E-Government: It means providing services provided by the government to citizens electronically. In this way, it is aimed to deliver government services to citizens in the easiest and most effective way, in a quality, fast, uninterrupted and safe manner. It is used with authentication tools such as password, e-signature, mobile signature, internet banking and ID card to access personal information through a web browser or mobile application or to access integrated electronic services that require security. Many integrated electronic services can be received from the same web address with a single identity verification (password, e-signature, mobile signature, etc.).

Public Institutions: A public institution is a public legal entity created to perform a specific public service. Another use of public institution is as a government institution. It is a term that covers institutions and organizations working under the state, government, or a ministry.

Social Media: It represents the sum of tools, services and virtual applications that enable individuals to interact with each other using information technologies via the internet. It not only helps people use it for communication purposes, but also allows them to follow local, national and universal developments. It consists of different areas such as social networks, blogs, instant messaging programs, chat sites, and websites established for information purposes. Users can access real information by using these networks.

Chapter 11
Public Relations and AI

Hakan Irak
Iğdır University, Turkey

ABSTRACT

With the increase in technological developments, many innovations have occurred in human life. These innovations have started to facilitate human life by realizing different digital applications of the technology axis that is developing day by day. Artificial intelligence, one of these developments, is undoubtedly one of the most important and useful developments today. With many artificial intelligence-based applications, many conveniences can be obtained in daily life, and it has also been used in public relations applications. In this context, the study examined public relations and artificial intelligence applications, and comments were made about today's applications and their future.

1. INTRODUCTION

Modern public relations has a history of more than one hundred years. Although models, methods, and techniques have evolved due to the possibilities of mass media, it would not be wrong to argue that artificial intelligence technology has brought about a significant change in public relations. This view also stems from the recent increasing trend of academic studies focusing on using artificial intelligence in public relations.

Rapid technological developments and developments in artificial intelligence have also led to changes in the field of public relations. Traditional public relations strategies may no longer meet the business world's demands. The development and use of artificial intelligence present new opportunities and challenges for public relations. This article explores the role and impact of artificial intelligence, focusing on its use in public relations today and how it will affect public relations in the future.

DOI: 10.4018/979-8-3693-0855-4.ch011

2. THEORETICAL FRAMEWORK

2.1. The Concept and History of Artificial Intelligence

Looking at the historical definitions of artificial intelligence, the definitions of artificial intelligence have changed according to people's views, the application areas of artificial intelligence, or the focus of the relevant discipline. As a result, there is still no definitive definition of artificial intelligence.

Definitions of artificial intelligence are related to what is expected from artificial intelligence (Acar, 2020, p. 8). In 1955, John McCarthy provided a conceptual basis for artificial intelligence by claiming that the purpose of artificial intelligence is "to "make a machine behave in a way that can be called intelligent, similar to the behaviour of a human." In this case, artificial intelligence is expected to behave like a human and exhibit behaviours that can be called intelligent. Therefore, the first studies in artificial intelligence seem to have been built on creating machines comparable to human intelligence. Most studies try to find similarities between human and artificial intelligence (Zawacki-Richter et al., 2019: 9). In this context, a general definition of artificial intelligence can be made as follows: "It is the science that studies how we can make artificial systems (with bodies, if necessary) perform any cognitive activity (intelligent or not) that natural systems can perform at an even higher level of performance' " (Say, 2018, p. 83). In the context of this definition, it can be said that by using the phrase "any cognitive activity," artificial intelligence is not limited to specific tasks; rather, artificial intelligence is now evolving to encompass diverse and broad cognitive activities.

Artificial intelligence is classified as strong-general and weak-narrow depending on its stage of development (Kaplan & Haenlein, 2019). Narrow AI performs specific tasks using only one or a portion of human cognitive abilities. In contrast, to narrow AI, broad AI (also referred to as strong AI) can mimic human cognitive abilities and should not be used for specific tasks.

Another definition is transferring artificial intelligence to machines (computers and software) by "*modelling human intelligence's physiological and neurological structure, such as the nervous system, gene structure, and natural events*" (Atalay & Çelik, 2017, p. 158). According to a similar definition, artificial intelligence is the ability of a computer or a computer-controlled robot to perform tasks carried out by intelligent beings. Artificial intelligence is used to develop systems with human characteristics such as inference, reasoning, self-learning, and generalisation (Copeland, 2019). While these definitions view artificial intelligence from a technical perspective, they focus on transferring and appropriating human characteristics into artificial systems. In this case, artificial intelligence can be defined as the ability of computers, robots, or machines to act, think, make decisions, or react like humans through various complex operations. With the advancement of artificial intelligence technologies, the difference between humans and machines is getting smaller daily. Therefore, the definitions of artificial intelligence are becoming more and more diverse. Thus, it is possible to classify the definitions.

It is thought that artificial intelligence systems with different definitions can be examined in a single group that includes artificial intelligence systems that act like humans, think like humans, think logically and act logically. Accordingly, artificial intelligence is "*computer science, where we can create intelligent machines that can act like humans, think like humans and make decisions*"(Özkaya & Pala, 2020, p. 99).

Many distinguished names have played an important role in reaching the current stage of development of artificial intelligence and have contributed to the progress of artificial intelligence with various design and research studies, from the simplest to the most advanced. Alan Turing and John McCarthy were the first to talk about the history of artificial intelligence, which began in the 1950s. Although this situation is very natural, it is perhaps necessary to say that the history of artificial intelligence is also linked to earlier technological innovations. Artificial intelligence, as it is today, cannot be separated from the technologies of that time. Therefore, it is useful to reflect on the "early history of artificial intelligence" to understand how it came to be.

Although the first seeds of artificial intelligence were planted long before the development of modern computers, there is a close connection between the emergence of artificial intelligence and the modern computers of the past. Cohen (1966), McCorduck et al. (1977) say that the first traces of artificial intelligence were found in ancient Greece. According to the historian of Science Mayor, artificial life and robots arose long before technological progress made it possible to produce self-driving devices (Margaryan, 2019). Mayor also points out that artificial intelligence, robots, and self-moving objects appeared in the works of ancient Greek poets Hesiod and Homer between 750 and 650 BC. Homer's Iliad contains examples of artificial beings that serve humans and have various human characteristics (1977: 951)._

The increase of empirical research in Western Europe in the 17th century led to the emergence of various ideas and the decline of alchemy and mysticism. Descartes, Cohen (1966) laid the foundation for the "modern age of autonomy". Descartes holds that the animal body is not different from the machine (Ünal and Kılınç, 2020, p. 55). In other words, it does not see animals as living beings. In 1943, McCulloch and Pitts laid the scientific foundation with their work describing mathematical models of brain cells or neurons. The work of McCulloch and Pitts shows whether neurons fire and how these neurons can learn and change their behaviour over time (Warwick, 2012: 2). These studies (artificial nerve cells) led to the development of one-armed robots in factories.

The terms "computer technologies" and "artificial intelligence" began to be discussed in 1943 when electronic devices for cryptanalysis were developed during World War II. Alan Turing researched the cypher algorithm of the German machine called "Enigma" and then continued his research on cracking cyphers at Bletchley Park in England. "Data processing logic" based on Boolean theory emerged due to the computer models developed by Turing (Sucu & Ataman, 2020, p. 42). Alan Mathison Turing, father of computer science and founder of artificial intelligence (Say, 2018, p. 28), wrote an article titled "Computing Machines and Intelligence" in the journal Mind in 1950, in which he asked the question, "Can machines think?". Turing's article is considered a turning point in the history of artificial intelligence (Buchanan, 2005). Asking "Can machines think?", he was recognised as the founder of artificial intelligence because he developed the "Turing Test" by removing the question from the discussion (Met et al., 2020, pp. 121-122). The Turing test is the first known research on artificial intelligence (Say, 2018, p. 84).

Turing proposed that we assume that a machine capable of successfully passing the following game thinks: a human, whom we call the Inquisitor, corresponds with two players, A and B, in a system that allows text messaging. One of A and B is a woman, and the other is a man. The male player tries convincing the inquisitor that he is the woman, not the other player. Her opponent will argue (rightly) that she is a woman. After a while, the interrogator declares which of the players he has concluded is indeed a woman. The game is played many times. In this scenario, if we replace the male actor with a computer programmed to play the same game (by pretending to be a female), and the interrogator's success rate does not increase, we should conclude that the computer is thinking.

According to Kurzweil (2016), the importance of the Turing test lies not in its applicability but only in its ability to set a specific boundary. This is because human intelligence's finesse, flexibility, and applicability are the only way to imitate the Turing test (2016: 440) successfully. Some studies emphasise that the Turing test is insufficient for understanding, comprehension, and learning. In addition, some studies emphasise that they work with rote learning logic. The most famous of these studies is the work of John Searle, known as the China Room Experiment, to prove that computers cannot think and have consciousness (Nabiyev, 2010: 54).

The exciting developments in the 1960s led to increasing claims that artificial intelligence could mimic human intelligence, and therefore more funding was allocated to research. Despite all these efforts and expectations, the 1970s were a bad year for artificial intelligence in almost every respect. Funding allocated to artificial intelligence was also gradually reduced as it did not produce the expected results (Warwick, 2012: 4). Later, problems such as errors in translations from Russian to English, confusion in artificial intelligence algorithms on complex questions, and the ability to make the best choice among options reduced confidence in artificial intelligence (Say, 2018, p. 88). These advances in artificial intelligence characterised the period between 1974 and 1980 as a dark period and were referred to as the "winter of artificial intelligence" about winter season analysis. In the 1980s, artificial intelligence experienced a resurgence due to several factors. One of them is that researchers following McCarthy continued to develop artificial intelligence systems from a practical perspective. This has involved creating expert systems focusing on specific activities in a particular field. In addition, as the development of robotics technology began to have a positive impact on the development of artificial intelligence, the belief that a computer must perceive the world, have a body, and move to prove that it could be intelligently intensified, and the focus shifted to how a computer could be expected to behave like a human without these capabilities (Warwick, 2012: 6)

Subsequently, the fact that artificial intelligence could compete against a human in chess opened a new door in the history of artificial intelligence. This event took place in 1996 when the artificial intelligence of IBM "Deep Blue" competed against Garry Kasparov; the robot was defeated in the first game, and the robot, which was further developed a year later, defeated Kasparov (Klosky, 2010, p. 205).

2.2. Concept, History, and Goals of Public Relations

According to Sabuncuoğlu (2001), the concept of public relations includes all efforts of an institutional organisation to integrate it into the social structure. Public relations ensures effective communication between an organisation's target audiences and management. The company takes various actions to spread its image in society. Therefore, communication encompasses a wide range of public relations processes. Critical stages and details of communication should be managed by experts (Yurdakul & Coşkun, 2011, p. 10).

Public relations aims to create a suitable environment for individuals to contribute to the decisions of pedestrian institutions. The organisational culture should be suitable for building good relationships with the public. The primary purpose of an organisation's public relations is to create a successful organisational culture (Kozlu, 1986, p. 30). Organisations that are open to the environment and shape their management philosophy with social responsibility operate more efficiently and longer than organisations that focus only on economic goals. Businesses are modern institutions that combine social and organisational interests. When applied and public relations is viewed from a modern perspective, institutions can succeed (Kırdar, 2012, p. 53).

Public relations goals can be divided into institutional and social (Sabuncuoğlu, 2008: 57). Modern companies consider the importance of the public when developing their public relations strategies. The main purpose of developing these strategies is to protect their interests. Nowadays, companies that do not integrate and involve themselves in the stock market will fail. Therefore, companies have high demands on their public relations, especially on the economic content. Examples are providing human resources for the company, increasing marketing effectiveness and studying consumer behaviour (Ataol, 1991, p. 93; Kırdar: 2012).

2.3. Public Relations in the Age of Artificial Intelligence

It is impossible to speak of a day, hour or second when technology does not evolve, change does not occur, and innovations do not emerge. Change and transformation always show their effect in any field. These changes have led to a new process where digital processes are monitored, recorded, analysed, planned and measured by artificial intelligence in a new era called "digitisation", "digital transformation", or "digital age". We are therefore entering an era in which it is no longer sufficient to be digital, but these processes are supported by intelligent machines (the age of artificial intelligence). The developments in artificial intelligence technologies shaping humanity's future are one reason to call this time the age of artificial intelligence. Given the impact of artificial intelligence on large enterprises, these changes are inevitable.

Today, artificial intelligence has drastically changed public relations institutions and processes. In contrast to this change that has taken place with the use of computers and the Internet in the field of public relations, it can be said that public relations has not been moved to a new environment; on the contrary, these environments are very important. Digital platforms such as social media enable the use of artificial intelligence applications. Data is the most important component of artificial intelligence. Therefore, in digitalisation, the communication tools and methods used in public relations are supported by artificial intelligence systems based on machine learning, automation and algorithms. Deep learning, a more advanced system, uses self-learning artificial intelligence technologies such as artificial neural networks.

Institutions strive to obtain more information at each point of contact with the target audience (Gülşen, 2019, p. 418). It is expected that language-based artificial intelligence applications, such as natural language processing, natural language generation, and text and speech, will be used as a new way to interact with target audiences. Shankar (2018:7), using artificial intelligence for business can be discussed in various dimensions, such as understanding and predicting behaviour, personalisation and recommendations, and customer relationship management. Keleş et al. explore the applications of artificial intelligence in four dimensions, defined as "seeing," "understanding," "discovering," "anticipating," and "speaking" (2017, p. 115). "Reactive attitudes" toward these applications are tantamount to impeding progress in the age of AI (Hari, 2018). Aware of this fact, public relations organisations and agencies have begun to accept that artificial intelligence can improve their business units. This acceptance and awareness is an important step for practitioners to reduce their biases toward new technological tools. The next step is recognising, embracing and integrating new technologies into their business and communication processes.

John Bara, president of a major technology company, says that conscious public relations practitioners recognise that AI can provide surprising and data-rich content on important topics, so other experts should not be afraid of AI. It is believed that only in this way can artificial intelligence play an effective role in the field of public relations. Based on research on this topic, Waddington believes that artificial intelligence will significantly change public relations in the coming years. Therefore, research should be conducted on how artificial intelligence can be used in public and private sector organisations (Biswal, 2020, p. 175).

Very little research examines the relationship between public relations and artificial intelligence and determines how artificial intelligence can be used in public relations. However, this situation is beginning to change with the increasing use of artificial intelligence in public relations. For example, three presentations were given on using artificial intelligence technologies in public relations at a recent international public relations conference (Barcelona Critical PR Conference, 2018). In addition to these presentations, various topics such as the ability to monitor the media with artificial intelligence based on natural language processing (Pavlik, 2007), the fact that practitioners can save time and spend more time on creative activities when artificial intelligence applications are used strategically (Yaxley, 2018, p. 147), and the state of ethical issues related to artificial intelligence (Tilson, 2017) were discussed. Following this conference, public relations experts, academics, and professional organisations began to explore artificial intelligence and public relations. In particular, the efforts of the British Institute of Public Relations (CIPR) came to the fore in this context. As part of the #AIinPR panel held in 2018, experts discussed how artificial intelligence is viewed concerning public relations and their views on artificial intelligence. In the said panel, artificial intelligence was defined as "an advanced technology application in which a machine exhibits human cognitive functions such as learning, analysis, and problem-solving" (Valin, 2018, p. 5).

When a general framework is formed on this topic, it can be seen that artificial intelligence applications are creating new areas, standards, and methods in public relations. These new technologies are expected to revolutionise existing public relations practices regarding contextualisation, flexibility, and adaptability. In the age of artificial intelligence, technological applications are tools only public relations professionals can use in their work (Panda et al., 2019, p. 197). As a result, advanced artificial intelligence can be useful in areas such as expert media monitoring and surveillance, content creation, campaign management, reputation management, and crisis communications. At the same time, automated AI can help practitioners perform simple and routine tasks.

Artificial intelligence tools in public relations include technological, relational, and organisational benefits. As a result of artificial intelligence technology's impact on public relations, it is thought that the job descriptions and roles of public relations practice areas and public relations specialists have changed (Galloway & Swiatek, 2018, p. 738). However, the age of artificial intelligence has also changed traditional communication models. The application areas of public relations and the roles of experts have also changed (Guzman & Lewis, 2020, p. 73). In current communication models, a human serves as both the source and receiver of the message and is defined as a communicator. The components or technology used to convey the message are shown. According to Gunkel (2012: 1), computer-mediated communication from human to machine and machine to machine is changing and developing with artificial intelligence tools. Therefore, new theories are required to explain, describe and contain this transformation experienced by artificial intelligence.

However, recent debates about whether artificial intelligence will have human-specific abilities such as creativity, emotional intelligence, intuition, common sense, empathy, trust, and emotion have increased. However, the proliferation of artificial intelligence technologies exposes public relations professionals to ethical and reputational risks. It is thought that artificial intelligence will also affect the machines that control people and affect some or all of the jobs (Chui et al., 2016).

Despite all these global debates, the idea that "artificial intelligence is not a threat but a tool for public relations practitioners" has been widely adopted in public relations. Leveraging AI in public relations enables practitioners to achieve their goals faster than ever, leading to faster and more optimised implementations (Rogers, 2019). However, although artificial intelligence contributes significantly to public relations, human aspects such as judgment, interpretation, experience, trust, empathy, relationship building and humour are not yet automated. It is thought that it is difficult for artificial intelligence to overcome these features (Valin, 2018: 7). Thus, in public relations applications that require these features, artificial intelligence cannot replace humans; these applications require features based on human input.

Public relations conveys the right message to the right target audience at the right time through the right channel (Panda et al., 2019, p. 197). Therefore, it is possible to say that artificial intelligence applications are related to the right concept. AI enables public relations professionals to make quick and strategic decisions at every process stage. With the widespread use of artificial intelligence applications in public relations, it can be said that problems such as creativity, common sense and trust can be solved with artificial intelligence-human cooperation. In addition, the optimal use of artificial intelligence can occur under human control. In addition, professional, legal, moral and personal elements are very important for the future of public relations (Arief & Gustomo, 2020, p. 1071). Therefore, for a public relations professional, professional ethics and integrity form the basis of continuous communication to resolve ethical issues and protect privacy. It can be said that with the protection of this key by the experts using artificial intelligence applications, the problems related to artificial intelligence can be minimised on the axis of human-machine workability.

2.4. Artificial Intelligence Applications and Its Future as a Public Relations Tool

Considering the use of public relations tools, it is seen that the tools have developed in an integrated manner over time. Each new tool has come into use by taking the features of the previous tool or by developing to cover these features. Although traditional communication tools such as newspapers, magazines, brochures, radio and television are still used today, these tools have been transferred to the virtual environment with the emergence of computers and the Internet. With public relations, new media and social media, "fast, effective, independent of time and place, connected, open to participation, dialogic" tools have been obtained. Technology is constantly evolving, and the adoption of these changes by individuals, societies and institutions in a short period leads to the use of new tools in public relations. Therefore, it can be said that artificial intelligence applications are now used as public relations tools.

It can be noted that artificial intelligence tools are integrated into public relations, as in other tools in the past; at least now, both are used together. Artificial intelligence tools with machine learning and deep learning infrastructures provide different opportunities to their users by adapting to social media.

The content and information received from the target audience can be transformed into useful results for the institution, especially by using artificial intelligence tools. However, AI tools allow users to simultaneously build models based on data analytics for predictions, engage with audiences, and increase engagement. The goal of artificial intelligence tools integrated into social media is to learn the thoughts and tendencies of the target audience, analyse their experiences (positive or negative), classify them, and develop them through imitation (Eşitti, 2020, pp. 282-283). It is said that artificial intelligence tools are also successful in creating value. Intellectual, emotional artificial intelligence, which enables one to perceive, analyse and process the emotional states and moods of the target audience, provides appropriate responses to these emotions. In this context, it is believed that these tools are necessary to create personalised experiences (Öztürk, 2020, p. 158).

Artificial intelligence increases the effectiveness and efficiency of agencies. At the same time, it is said that these tools facilitate practitioners' work, improve their ability to experience, and enable them to spend their energy and time on tasks that require creativity (Yılmaz and Iyigun, 2020: 5). For this reason, it can be said that institutions and agencies in many fields have begun to see and benefit from artificial intelligence technologies as a tool, but this process is happening gradually. Canela, a PR agency in Spain, describes AI as "a valuable tool that helps agencies automate routine tasks and execute them more efficiently." The agency claims that artificial intelligence will not remain just a tool for analysing data. Instead, it will enable PR professionals to identify crises on time (Canela, 2019) accurately. Considering how artificial intelligence tools are used in public relations today, it is fair to say that the agency's predictions are correct. Rogers (2019) noted that artificial intelligence is an opportunity for public relations practitioners and can make data faster and more meaningful. At the annual PRSA conference in Boston, a San Francisco entrepreneur said that 90% of the data collected in the last 120 years comes from the last two years. The increase in shares, comments, and interactions, especially on social media, has created an information tsunami that traditional monitoring tools cannot handle. According to Nahas (2017), artificial intelligence has begun to solve these problems and be used in public relations. Data processing in public relations is not a new practice but rather the increasing availability of artificial intelligence tools that process this data and produce meaningful results (Waddington, 2018).

With the development of AI tools, the way public relations practitioners view data collection, analysis, and processing, as well as their communication strategies, is beginning to change. This change occurs concurrently with how practitioners conduct measurement (Ardila, 2020, p.10).

Regarding the change in the field of public relations, it is important to note that, unlike the Internet, the environment in which public relations is conducted has not changed. However, only new tools (e.g., software) have been added to support existing tools. At this point, reference can be made to a misunderstanding regarding artificial intelligence. Although artificial intelligence is now used in various areas of public relations, many practitioners see artificial intelligence only as robots (Galloway & Swiatek, 2018, pp. 735-736). In this case, the idea of professionals becoming robots is seen as a common topic of discussion. It is said that the general perception in this direction could distract practitioners from artificial intelligence. Nowadays, it is used in hospitals, hotels, etc. Although robots are used in important tasks without human control, it is still premature to speak of such advanced robotisation in terms of public relations. For this reason, it should not be overlooked that artificial intelligence technologies are not limited to robots. Artificial intelligence can also be a machine or a software robot.

Deep learning systems, a subset of machine learning, are now going beyond imitation, and machines have begun to learn independently like humans. However, emotional intelligence, sensitivity, creativity, common sense, and ethical practices always require human intervention (Valin, 2018: 5-6). The best way to design, implement, and complete public relations is through human skills supported by artificial intelligence (Biswal, 2020, p. 173). Therefore, artificial intelligence, when used properly, "offers public relations practitioners, with its self-learning capabilities, not only a tool to process vast amounts of data and benefit from insights, but also a new and autonomous system that responds to feedback, posts, questions, complaints, tweets, and other messages in the digital environment" (Panda et al., 2019, p. 2). Both the advantages and disadvantages of artificial intelligence can be discussed. In the decision-making phase, institutions and agencies should focus on the advantages or disadvantages of AI. How institutions will adapt to AI and other technologies is critical in this case. Dealing with ethical issues arising from the use of AI is also very important. At this point, it is assumed that institutions and government agencies can benefit from collaboration between humans and machines in solving problems. Therefore, it can be said that future success depends on the collaboration between humans and artificial intelligence and the synergy that this collaboration will create.

3. CONCLUSION

The development of artificial intelligence in the field of public relations offers new opportunities for public relations professionals. AI can be critical in data analysis, productivity, personalisation, and crisis management. However, ethical issues regarding the interaction between artificial intelligence and humans should not be ignored. For PR, it will be exciting to see how AI and public relations evolve together and how they can use these technologies successfully.

The impact of artificial intelligence on public relations can be twofold: positive and negative. AI saves time by automating routine public relations tasks. This allows PR professionals to focus on more strategic and creative work.

Personalisation and audience relations: Artificial intelligence can personalise marketing and communications strategies. This allows companies to build deeper and more productive relationships with their customers.

Data Analysis and predictive analytics: AI can uncover trends and insights by analysing large amounts of data. This can help businesses make smarter decisions.

However, AI also has some negative implications for outreach: lower human touch: tools like chatbots and automated response systems can reduce human interaction and decrease customers' desire for personalised experiences.

Ethical Issues: When using artificial intelligence, privacy, security, and ethical issues can arise. It is very important to be sensitive about the collection and use of data.

Agencies and institutions that embrace the technology and use it effectively using artificial intelligence as a tool provide an important starting point for how they interact with their stakeholders in their public relations efforts. Therefore, to understand the underlying dynamics of change in public relations, it is important to understand and discuss which areas and tasks artificial intelligence is using. Thus, a general framework for the current and potential use of artificial intelligence tools in public relations should first be established for the study.

REFERENCES

Acar, O. (2020). *Yapay Zekâ Fırsat Mı, Yoksa Tehdit Mi?* Kriter Yayınevi.

Ardila, M. M. (2020). *The Rise of Intelligent Machines: How Artificial Intelligence is Transforming the Public Relations Industry* [Unpublished Master's Thesis]. University of Southern California.

Arief & Gustomo. (2020). Analyzing the Impact of Big Data and Artificial Intelligence on the Communications Profession: A Case Study on Public Relations (PR) Practitioners in Indonesia. Academic Press.

Atalay, M., & Çelik, E. (2017). Büyük Veri Analizinde Yapay Zekâ ve Makine Öğrenmesi Uygulamaları. *Mehmet Akif Ersoy University Journal of Social Sciences Institute*, *9*(22), 155–172. doi:10.20875/makusobed.309727

Ataol, A. (1991). Halkla İlişkiler Örgütlerinin Temsil Edilmesinde Kavramsal Bir Model. Academic Press.

Barcelona P. R. Meeting. (2018). *Critical Intersections: Communication, public relations, and beyond in a time of convergence*. eventum.upf.edu/_files/_event/_17549/_editorFiles/file/BCN%20PR%20 Conference%20Programme.pdf

Biswal, S. K. (2020). The Space of Artificial Intelligence in Public Relations: The Way Forward. In A. Kulkarni & S. Satapathy (Eds.), *Optimization in Machine Learning and Applications. Algorithms for Intelligent Systems*. Springer. doi:10.1007/978-981-15-0994-0_11

Buchanan, B. G. (2005). A (very) brief history of artificial intelligence. *AI Magazine*, *26*(4), 53.

Chui, M., Manyika, J., & Miremadi, M. (2016). *Where machines could replace humans-and where they can't (yet)*. McKinsey & Company. https://www.mckinsey.com/businessfunctions/mckinsey-digital/our-insights/where-machines-could-replace-humans-and-wherethey-cant-yet

Cohen, J. (1966). *Human Robots in Myth And Science*. Geaorge Allen & Unwin LTD.

Copeland, B. J. (2019). *Artificial Intelligence*. https://www.britannica.com/technology/artificial-intelligence

Eşitti, Ş. (2020). Sosyal Medya ve Yapay Zekâ. In Artificial Intelligence Transforms Disciplines – Are We Ready for Change? Ekin Publishing.

Galloway, C., & Swiatek, L. (2018). Public relations and artificial intelligence: It's not (just) about robots. *Public Relations Review*, *44*(5), 734–740. doi:10.1016/j.pubrev.2018.10.008

Gülşen, İ. (2019). İşletmelerde Yapay Zeka Uygulamaları ve Faydaları: Perakende Sektöründe Bir Derleme. *Tüketici ve Tüketim Araştırmaları Dergisi*, *11*(2), 407–436.

GunkelD. J. (2012). Communication and Artificial Intelligence: Opportunities and Challenges for the 21st Century. *Communication +1*, *1*(1). doi:10.7275/R5QJ7F7R

Guzman, A. L., & Lewis, S. C. (2020). Artificial intelligence and communication: A Human–Machine Communication research agenda. *New Media & Society*, *22*(1), 70–86. doi:10.1177/1461444819858691

Haenlein, M., & Kaplan, A. (2019). A brief history of artificial intelligence:on the past, present, and future of artificial intelligence. *California Management Review*, *61*(4), 5–14. doi:10.1177/0008125619864925

Hari, G. (2018). As communicators, we have a responsibility to talk about AI in a positive way. *PR Week*. https://www.prweek.com/article/1519621/as-communicators-responsibility-talk-ai-positive-way

Keleş, A., Keleş, A., & Akçetin, E. (2017). Pazarlama Alanında Yapay Zekâ Kullanım Potansiyeli ve Akıllı Karar Destek Sistemleri. *Turkish Studies*, *12*(11), 109–124. doi:10.7827/TurkishStudies.12022

Kırdar, Y. (2012). *Post Modern Marketing and Consumption Culture*. Moss Publishing House.

Klosky, D. (2010). *The Chess Master and the Computer (R. Diego)*. http://web.mit.edu/6.034/wwwbob/kasparov-article.pdf

Kozlu, C (1986). *Kurumsal Kültür: Amerika, Japonya ve Türkiye: Başarılı Firma Yönetiminde Kurumsal Kültürün Rolü*. İstanbul: Bilkom yayınları.

Kurzweil, R. (2016). *Humanity 2.0: Human Transcending Biology Towards the Singularity* (M. Şengel, Trans.). Alfa Publications.

Margaryan, P. (2019). *Antik Yunan Mitlerinde Yapay Zekâ.* https://arkeofili.com/antik-yunan-mitlerinde-yapay-zeka/

McCorduck, P., Minsky, M., Selfridge, O., & Simon, H. (1977). History of artificial intelligence. *IJCAI Proceedings*, 951-954. https://www.ijcai.org/Proceedings/77-2/Papers/083.pdf

Met, İ., Kabukçu, D., Soyalp, Ü., & Dakdevir, T. (2020). Bilgi Toplumunda Yapay Zekânın Yeri: Akıllı Sohbet Araçları. In Oyunu Değiştiren Güç Yapay Zekâ. Beta Kitap.

Nabiyev, V. (2012). *Yapay Zekâ: İnsan – Bilgisayar Etkileşimi*. Seçkin Yayınları.

Nahas, J. M. (2017). *How Artificial Intelligence is Impacting Public Relations*. https://casacom.ca/en/2017/11/02/how-artificial-intelligence-is-impacting- public-relations/

Özkaya, M., & Pala, F. K. (2020). Artificial intelligence. In Yapay zekâ disiplinleri dönüştürüyor. Değişime hazır mıyız? Ekin Yayınevi.

Öztürk, G. (2020). Yapay Zekâ Teknolojisinin Kullanıldığı Reklamların "Birlikte Değer Yaratma" Kavramı Açısından Değerlendirilmesi. In Oyunu Değiştiren Güç Yapay Zekâ. Beta Kitap.

Panda, G., Upadhyay, A. K., & Khandelwal, K. (2019). Artificial Intelligence: A Strategic Disruption in Public Relations. *Journal of Creative Communications*, *14*(3), 196–213. doi:10.1177/0973258619866585

Pavlik, J. (2007). *Mapping the Consequences of Technology on Public Relations. Institute for Public Relations*. Wieck Media.

Rogers, C. (2019). *How Artificial Intelligence and Big Data will affect the future of PR*. Institute for PR. Available at: https://instituteforpr.org/how-artificial- intelligence-and-big-data-will-affect-the-future-of-pr/

Sabuncuoğlu, Z. (2008). *Public Relations in Business*. Alfa Aktüel Yayınları.

Say, C. (2018). *50 Soruda Yapay Zekâ*. Bilim ve Gelecek Yayınevi.

Shankar, V. (2018). How Artificial Intelligence (AI) Is Resha- ping Retailing. *Journal of Retailing*, *94*(4), 5–11. doi:10.1016/S0022-4359(18)30076-9

Sucu, İ., & Ataman, E. (2020). Dijital Evrenin Yeni Dünyası Olarak Yapay Zekâ Ve Her Filmi Üzerine Bir Çalışma. *Yeni Medya Elektronik Dergisi*, *4*(1), 40–52. doi:10.17932/IAU.EJNM.25480200.2020.4/1.40-52

Tilson, D. J. (2017). From the natural world to artificial intelligence: Public relations as covenantal stewardship. In B. R. Brunner (Ed.), *The moral compass of public relations* (pp. 206–222). Routledge.

Ünal, A., & Kılınç, İ. (2020). *Yapay Zekâ İşletme Yönetimi İlişkisi Üzerine Bir Değerlendirme Yönetim Bilişim Sistemleri*. Academic Press.

Valin, J. (2018). Humans still needed: An analysis of skills and tools in public relations. Discussion paper. London: Chartered Institute of Public Relations.

Waddington, S. (2018). *Tackling the impact of technology and AI on PR.* https://wadds.co.uk/blog/2018/6/26/tackling-the-impact-of-tech-and-ai-on-pr

Warwick, K. (2012). *Artificial Intelligence: The Basics*. Routledge.

Yaxley, H. (2018). Outro. In A. Theaker & H. Yaxley (Eds.), *The public relations strategic toolkit: An essential guide to successful public relations practice* (pp. 147–150). Routledge.

Yurdakul, N. B., & Coşkun, G. (2011). *Teoriden Pratiğe Halkla İlişkiler Projeleri - Ödüllü Örnek Uygulamalar*. Nobel Akademik Yayıncılık.

Zawacki-Richter, O., Marín, V. I., Bond, M., & Gouverneur, F. (2019). Systematic review of research on artificial intelligence applications in higher education – where are the educators? *International Journal of Educational Technology in Higher Education*, *16*(1), 39. doi:10.1186/s41239-019-0171-0

Chapter 12
Crisis Management in the Digital Age

Hasan Yılmaz
İnönü Üniversitesi, Turkey

ABSTRACT

With the rapid development of technology, we are exposed to the ease and challenges of the digital age in all aspects. Technological revolutions are leading to rapid transformations in the global system. These developments can also bring crises. Therefore, it is necessary to be prepared for crises in the digital transformation. Anticipating and taking precautions for crises is one of the most important issues in the digital age. Effective tools are needed to rapidly and effectively solve crises through digital processes. This study will address the management of crises in the digital world and convey important notes to the reader on topics such as management, crisis, leadership, digitalization, and the digital age. The study will conclude with recommendations for solving crises in the digital field.

INTRODUCTION

The digital journey, which began with the transfer of our knowledge and resources to digital environments, is now showing its impact in every field. In the rapidly digitizing world, information and resources are being exchanged, used, and managed as efficiently and quickly as possible. This process brings a new perspective to the concept of management. Traditional management approaches have initiated their digital transformations in order to adapt to the process. In the digital age, management has already taken its place as an important field in management science with its unique structure. However, digitalization in management should have goals such as eliminating managerial challenges and benefiting society.

With the rapid development of technology and increasing technological tools, it is possible to refer to the 21st century as a digital era. In the broadest sense, digitization is the process of sharing information that exists anywhere and at any time in the world through technological tools in electronic environments. In this rapidly developing and changing era, it is inevitable for digital domains to change and transform. The concept of the "digital age" is also becoming commonly used with the rapid development of tech-

DOI: 10.4018/979-8-3693-0855-4.ch012

nology. The digital age is also considered as an area that humanity has been able to explore and is still striving to discover.

The concept of digitization is becoming increasingly in crisis management as one of the most challenging areas for management. Crisis is a situation that emerges unexpectedly and has negative effects. Therefore, digital structures can be more effective than other managerial structures in solving sudden and negative developments due to their speed capabilities, facilitating the solution. In crisis management, the rapid and effective platforms created by digitalization with an effective managerial authority can prevent crises from escalating and even solve them instantly.

In this study, the management of crises in the digitizing world will be discussed, and important notes on management, crisis, leadership, digitization, and the digital age will be conveyed to the reader.

1. CRISIS AND ITS ELEMENTS

Crisis is defined as events that suddenly arise, threaten the existence of the organization, and affect its performance and operation (Karaköse, 2007). The definition of crisis has been described differently by many people. Generally, crisis is expressed as a sudden downturn, crisis, danger, absence, lack, and major problems.

In crisis management, there is a need for strategic planning to control unexpected events and turn their negative effects into positive ones (Thompson & Louie, 2006).

The crisis management process is a process that involves implementing and evaluating appropriate solutions and responses to possible problems and dangers in order to cope with the crisis and take necessary measures. The process, which occurs with the receipt of crisis signals, consists of the following stages. Firstly, it includes receiving crisis signals, preparation and protection, containment, return to normalcy, learning and evaluation stages. During a crisis, the order is temporarily disrupted. Therefore, leadership and managerial skills such as communication are important during these times. Crisis should not always be perceived as negative, but can also be evaluated as the beginning of change. Crisis management is a systematic set of activities. Planned and rational action should be taken to eliminate the crisis (Aksu, 2009).

Conflict, which is defined as any obstacle or negative relationship encountered or witnessed personally in daily life, has become a subject of study for many social science disciplines since the past (Ertekin, 1993).

Conflict is a situation of opposition that occurs when individuals who create effectiveness within an institution or individuals in a department cannot find what they hoped for or take advantage of a potential benefit. Organizational conflict is events that arise from the collaboration of individuals or employees in a department, leading to the termination of activities or effects, or causing current problems (Öztürk, 1992).

The characteristics of a crisis arising from internal or external factors in corporate structures are as follows (Göztaş, 1997):

- The threat to the organization's top-level goals or existence
- Inadequate preventive and forecasting mechanisms of the organization
- The need for urgent intervention and time pressure
- The occurrence of unexpected and sudden changes
- Causing tension in decision makers

- Leading to fear and panic
- Difficulty in controlling
- Being a crucial turning point
- Threatening the organization's image, human resources, financial structure, or natural resources.

Generally, there are elements and factors that stand out in crises. Among these, there are triggering factors. While crises may occur suddenly, there may be social, economic, and political factors behind the scenes. In addition, the state of uncertainty also has an impact. Reputation and image are negatively affected in crises. Communication plays an important role in crises. Crises can have a rapid spreading effect and can spread to a wide area.

2. CRISIS MANAGEMENT

The development stage of an organization can be considered in five stages. These stages are initiation, existence, prosperity, and development, in a certain order. The transition of an organization from one stage to another can create various crises depending on whether the ground is hard or soft. In the initiation stage, the leadership crisis, which should lead to an increase in the organization's productivity level, occurs. In the existence stage, the independence crisis in the organization's management structure occurs. In the growth stage, the bureaucracy crisis developing along with task distribution occurs. And finally, in the development stage, conflicting situations among individuals occur along with growth, which are likely to be encountered in organizations (Ataman, 2001).

There are three types of crises that occur according to the degree level of crises. These are strategic, functional, and financial crises (Müller, 1982). In strategic crises, strategic ambiguity occurs between organizations. This ambiguity arises after problems such as rigidity in their structures, weak surroundings, neglecting the influence of the surroundings, inadequate methods and mistakes, and ignoring the notifications in the surroundings lead to a problem of adaptation between organizations (Dinçer, 1992).

Functional crises occur when organizations fail to achieve their functional goals or when there is a risk of not achieving these goals. Falling short of the goal, ineffective sales strategies, unprofitable production types, or faulty investments lead to functional crises (Müller, 1982).

Financial crises occur when the debts of institutions to the market and banks exceed their assets and deposits, and they are unable to repay their debts. Poor deposit management, mistakes in financial planning, and problems arising from agreements with banks can lead to financial crises.

All these crises vary depending on how institutions deal with the crisis. When institutions are faced with a strategic crisis, they have enough time to take the necessary precautions. However, this time period decreases in the case of a potential functional crisis and is minimized in a financial crisis (Müller, 1982). Moreover, these potential crises are not independent of each other. If necessary measures are not taken on time during crises, other crisis environments are quickly prepared.

Changes and turmoil in the financial environment can lead to crises in institutions. In planned economies, the probability of encountering a crisis is very low unless there is no state intervention or legal change. However, in economies where free market system operates, the probability of encountering a crisis is higher. Additionally, the unplanned nature of economies affects the production quantity of institutions and also affects the selling price of their products (Pira, 2004).

Institutions are affected by the changes in their environments, and this interaction becomes a requirement for their own development. An institution that is detached from society, and institutions that do not adapt to their environment are more likely to face a crisis.

Sometimes organizations face crises due to their own internal structure and functioning. Unsettled institutional culture, oppressive management mentality, negative attitudes of managers, and non-constructive management approaches can create a crisis environment. If this crisis is not intervened in a timely manner, the crisis can grow even bigger, resulting in more serious crisis situations within the organizations (Pira, 2004).

Organizational structures should be in harmony with each other and with the internal and external environment. Unless this necessary harmony is achieved, organizations can still face crises. Managements that do not adapt to internal dynamics and balances or remain indifferent can create a crisis environment (Prokopenko, 1995).

Rapid development and change worldwide play an important role in the improvement of organizations in areas such as production and sales. Organizations that do not adapt to this change can face a crisis. For example, if a company producing goods with its workforce, a competitor has switched to production with robots by adapting to new technology, the other company also needs to adapt to this development. Companies that cannot adapt to this development can also face a crisis (Dinçer, 1992).

Legal and political changes can have a positive or negative impact on the management of institutions. Political instability in the countries where institutions operate is a significant crisis factor for these institutions. The new decisions taken by the leaders of a country that affect institutions can lead to a crisis situation if they have a negative impact on the institutions (Tutar, 2000).

Crisis management is defined as the reaction to problems that arise instead of taking steps to identify and prevent them or limit their consequences. As the definition suggests, it is necessary to predict and prevent crises in advance, or take limiting actions when they occur (Mackenzie, 1995). The key factor in a crisis is management. Crises can be handled with less damage when managed with good management skills. The understanding of effective management plays a crucial role in determining the increase or decrease in the degree of a crisis. In this context, it is necessary to look at the definitions of crisis management to determine what crisis management means (Akdağ and Taşdemir, 2006).

The main characteristics of the crisis period are shrinking demand, rising input costs, and increasing intensity and depth of competition. Organizations try to overcome the crisis by using different methods and techniques in this intense competitive environment (Akat, 2000).

The main features of crisis management are as follows (Haşit, 2000):

a. The perceptual capacities of the individuals managing the crisis play an important role in crisis management. The success in preventing crises can vary depending on how managers perceive crises.
b. Crisis management is a situation that is focused on continuity. There is no before and after. It is appropriate to continuously test and review plans prepared for crises that can be predicted in advance.
c. Crisis management should be created in accordance with the types of crises that arise. Each crisis has its own unique signs and solutions. The solution to one crisis will cause another crisis to become unsolvable.
d. The reward for success in crisis management can be very large. Crisis management that successfully overcomes the crisis can strengthen the confidence and morale of managers. Managers who

have successfully overcome crises are not only consolidating their positions, but also starting a new phase in their careers.

e. Managing a crisis is a very important, necessary, difficult, and even complex process. Therefore, immediate resolution of crises should not be expected. It is a long and laborious journey. Resolving a crisis requires flexibility, creative thinking, objectivity, courage, embracing teamwork, being ready to take action at any moment, and being prepared for any unexpected demands and conditions.
f. Important factors in crisis management include communication, control, cost, culture, regulation, situation planning, the complexity and interdependence of systems. These factors form the crisis prescription for the organization and, of course, are important in directing and resolving crises in accordance with the values and beliefs of the organization.

3. THE DIGITAL AGE

Information is considered as personal and implicit knowledge in its simplest form. In order to have a social contribution, it needs to be encoded, explained, and deciphered through the user. However, the disclosed and deciphered information can be meaningful (Bayram, 2010). Additionally, information, data, and knowledge are commonly used and interconnected concepts. However, there is a process from scattered raw data to information formed by the use of data, and from information to knowledge. Therefore, both the flow and transformation of knowledge in society, as well as its content and formation, are significantly important. When distinguishing our current time from previous eras, it is possible to construct two different periods as "pre-internet and post-internet" (Akgül, 2017). With the integration of the internet into human life, changes and transformations occur in daily life.

The emergence of the internet and the structure based on the "packet switching communication technology" pioneered by Paul Baran rely on the gathering of units within the network at specific points, rather than a center in the newly constructed network. Later, with the help of digital technology, it turned into a network without a centralized control center, which includes not only voice and images but also data. The universality of digital language and the effort to establish networks in communication have prepared the technological conditions for global communication (Castells, 2005).

Digital technology is defined in the literature as the transformation of all types of information, such as data, sound, music, text, photos, and images, into computer language with the help of microprocessors (Değirmencioğlu, 2016). With the widespread use of digital technology, the ability to produce, store, transmit, and distribute information has become easier, and its importance in society has increased. In this context, systems developed with digital technology can reach the public quickly through publishing tools and systems without loss of quality in formats such as sound, text, video, and photos (Törenli, 2005). Moreover, the digitization phenomenon is not a mere duplication of information, but the transformation of information from one format to another (Aktaş, 2014).

The transition to the digital age has had significant effects not only on individuals' lives but also on organizations. Bhatt (2000) describes this era as a period that requires new knowledge, skills, methods, and strategies due to significant changes and transformations.

Firstly, the use of Web 1.0 version started, which brought along some problems and challenges. To find solutions for these issues, a path was taken to open up mutual communication, leading to the adoption of the Web 2.0 version used today. Users have gained access to various alternatives through intra-group and inter-group communication (Taşkıran, 2017).

All economic sectors in a country are affected by digitization, and all sectors undergo changes and developments as a result. Therefore, all employees and management types are affected by digitization. It is stated that digitization also affects the way of doing business, task durations, and skills. Just like all other units in organizations, human resources departments are also affected. In order for organizations to compete with other institutions, they need to follow technological advancements and acquire new knowledge (Güler, 2006).

The invention, development, and widespread use of steam engines in the early 18th century enabled significant changes and privileges in production techniques. This period is referred to as the first industrial revolution. Subsequently, in the late 19th century and early 20th century, the use of electricity and electric technologies, inventions such as the telephone and telegraph, Taylor's scientific management approach, and Henry Ford's assembly line-style mass production revolution are referred to as the second industrial revolution. The third revolution occurred in the early 1970s through the invention of microcomputers and programmable devices, marking the transition from electricity to electronics. Innovations and developments such as programmability and automation systems are inventions that have been heavily invested in since World War II and have had significant effects on the world order. The spread of the internet into people's lives and naturally, into businesses, marks the beginning of the fourth industrial revolution. Although there was a period of over 20 years between the invention of the internet and the use of the term "revolution," Industry 4.0 emerged as a result of the unbelievably rapid development of the internet. The term Industry 4.0 was first used in 2011 at the Hannover Fair as part of the German government's advanced technology-themed project. The first academic study on the topic was conducted by Kagerman et al. (2011), addressing the new era and its components that the world has entered. This new era has also been referred to as the Internet of Things, and it focuses on the era of "smart" factories, directed by computers, which have begun and will continue to spread.

With advancements in technology, the world has been introduced to the Fourth Industrial Revolution and has started to adopt a more flexible structure rather than traditional production factors. With Industry 4.0, quality and efficiency in production have started to increase through cyber-physical systems. Industry 4.0 first emerged in Germany and then became more prominent with the emergence of competitive advantage for developed and powerful economies compared to developing countries. Developed countries transfer their economic resources and experiences to developing countries. Developing countries have gained industrialization advantage by benefiting from these experiences and economic resources. As a result of this interaction, developing countries have lost their competitiveness with developed countries. Developed countries, on the other hand, have needed a new industrial approach like Industry 4.0, as they have lost their competitiveness and faced the reality of increasing social expenses with an aging population. With the leadership of countries like the US and Japan, the Fourth Industrial Revolution aims to reduce the expenses of developed and developing countries, increase productivity, and regain competitiveness in production through digital technology, smart robots, factories, and cloud systems. With Industry 4.0, economic and technological advancements not only impact people's lives but also significantly affect the management and work processes of institutions. The rapid changes in information technology have brought along the necessity for human resources management to adapt to digital transformation in line with the vision and mission of the digitized world. Institutions now contribute to employment with faster recruitment processes in human resources practices, along with digital human resources systems (Bayarçelik, 2020).

With Industry 4.0, it has been observed that situations affecting organizations and individuals have emerged. These include faster and more efficient work, diversity in the activities of organizations, reduc-

Figure 1. Turning points in the industrial revolution
Source: Latinovic (2016)

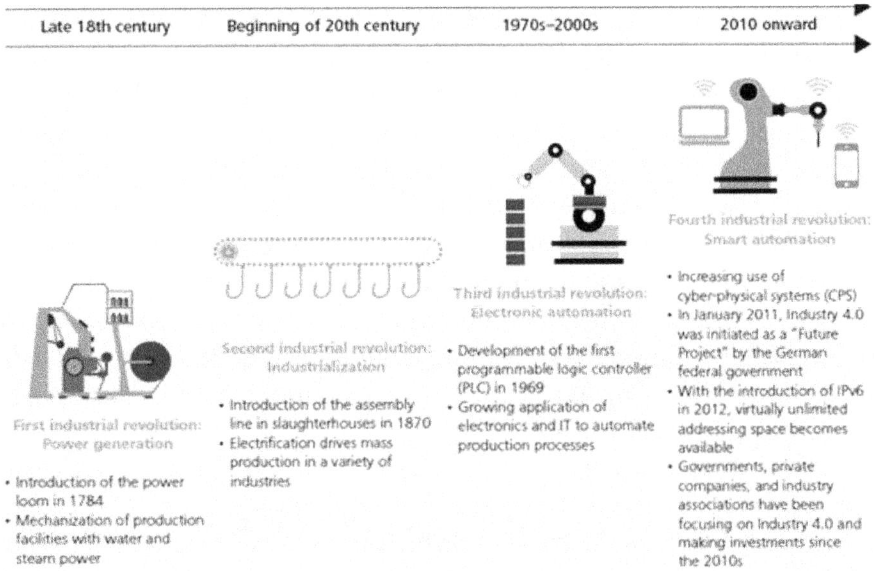

tion in expenses and costs, minimizing errors, and lightening the workload of employees, along with the positive aspects of skilled employees. However, these developments also have some negative effects. These include the decrease in face-to-face human relationships and communication, and the transition from a human state to a digital dimension (Yüksel and Şener, 2017).

Embracing e-technology, which integrates various hardware and software components, is now crucial for successful management. The e-environment is a result of advancements in e-technologies and applications in the corporate work environment. Bill Gates (1999) argued that it is possible to provide a well-integrated flow of information to the right parts of an organization at the right time in order for the organization to become a digital nervous system. With the creation and continuous development of the e-environment, the complexity of organizations is inevitably increasing at a high pace. The defining characteristic of the e-technology era is the transformation of traditional leadership into digital leadership with the advent of e-media.

The technique of digitization means transforming all types of data, such as sound, text, documents, music, images, and moving objects, into computer bits consisting of 0s and 1s, and then sending them to another place through telecommunication technology. In the destination, these codes are decoded very closely to their original form and made available for the recipient's use (Friedman, 2000).

4. MANAGEMENT OF CRISES IN DIGITAL CHANNELS

Crises can have positive outcomes for organizations and employees. After a crisis, organizations go through changes and developments, leading to new beginnings. With effective management, organizations can easily achieve success after a crisis (Silver, 1990).

During a crisis, it is important to inform all members of the organization and establish open communication. This open communication contributes to the trust members have in their leaders. In difficult times, group members are not hesitant to support their trusted leader. This allows organizations to overcome the crisis quickly. Through open communication, leaders also enable individuals to communicate more comfortably with them. When individuals can openly communicate with their leader, they can express their difficulties and negative thoughts without hesitation. This type of communication also prevents the spread of gossip.

In the digital age, a type of leadership called Digital Leadership has been developed to effectively manage crises. Digital leadership is an example of leadership types based on the upper echelon theory (Hambrick and Mason, 1986). According to this theory, leadership decisions based on the actor's interpretation and cognition guide the organization. Digital leadership is a new concept in the literature, open to further development. According to Wasono and Furinto (2018), digital leadership is a concept that combines leadership ability and digital competence to optimize the benefits of digital technologies with the aim of improving job performance.

In particular, in order to resolve conflicts and crises in today's world, managers need to have developed themselves and constantly renew themselves. In today's societies, conflicts and crises cannot be resolved by neglecting or turning a blind eye to them. The success of organizations in achieving their goals depends on how quickly they resolve crises and conflicts and minimize their encounters with them. In cases where the opposite is true, organizations cannot sustain their existence. Conflicts and crises not only affect organizations, but also enable them to identify their weaknesses. These weaknesses can lead to conflicts and conflicts that are not resolved in a timely manner can lead to a crisis environment. However, these two concepts should not only be used in a negative sense. Sometimes crises that emerge can create an opportunity environment in organizations. Organizations that turn crises into opportunities are possible with the presence of a good leader. Therefore, while conflicts and crises are situations that are not desired to be encountered in organizations, utilizing the functional aspect of these two concepts can provide added value to organizations when crises are turned into opportunities. Problems that are not properly and effectively managed in organizations can lead to conflicts, and conflicts can lead to crises. Therefore, in daily life, these two concepts are intertwined and are not independent concepts.

Effectively managing crisis situations helps strengthen public trust in institutions and belief in leadership. On the contrary, failure to manage a crisis successfully can lead to organizational fragmentation, public dissatisfaction, and even leadership change (Dayton, 2009). Managing a crisis in the digital environment can also bring some challenges. Concerns may arise about the accuracy and authenticity of publications made on the internet. In addition, in the digital environment where a lot of information and news are shared, there is a possibility that important information may get lost in the noise. Therefore, it is important to be careful about the accuracy and authenticity of information in the process of crisis management in the digital environment, to prefer information published in a simple and understandable language, and to emphasize important information. In addition, organizations should check the legality and compliance of publications made in the digital environment with ethical rules and, if necessary, seek professional consulting services (Albayrak, 2023).

5. RESULT

With the increasing technology, digitalization is gaining speed and can affect almost every aspect of human life. In addition being able to communicate quickly, various information transfer tools and media outlets can reach these information to masses at the desired scale. However, while doing all of these, individuals' personal information can also be transferred. In some cases, personal information that is shared inadvertently can be easily used for commercial or unofficial purposes. The fact that personal information is stored in third parties and unrelated individuals also includes the risks that may be experienced in the future.

Technology companies create algorithms with artificial intelligence by tracking people's daily lives. They are not doing this secretly. They openly collect and code information from individuals in almost every field such as food, education, culture, art, and daily activities. The sad part is that this situation is portrayed as "individual freedom" in the online environment. In fact, artificial intelligence technologies prepared by these companies with huge amounts are defining a new type of human and by using the information belonging to this newly created "self-feeling free species", needs can be produced and marketed. They can even provide information about that person to their surroundings. Individuals advocating for freedom on the internet, on the other hand, may be aware or unaware of this situation and are watching and sustaining their lives with what this huge power produces.

In digital environments, crisis management requires great attention due to the unlimited nature of the virtual space and its other features. For example, the increasing interest in social media in recent years and the direct or indirect connection of individuals from all walks of life to this media have necessitated following and strategically acting on the work that organizations will do in this environment (Bat and Yurtseven, 2014).

Increased digitization and socialization influence and transform culture as mentioned by Adorno. Individuals with secured positions and fulfilled needs can be susceptible to being directed and controlled (Adorno, 2007). From this perspective, every person has principles of privacy. These principles are the principles and values used in the description of personality. The digital realm pushes boundaries so much that individuals' principles of privacy can also change. In daily life, things that are considered private are easily displayed in the digital environment (especially on social media) and this is considered legitimate. This means that the privacy values freely determined by a person's belief or reason can often involuntarily deteriorate in the face of technology.

An important slogan is used in crisis management: "Prevention is cheaper and easier than paying." Based on this slogan, it is more beneficial to raise necessary precautions to higher levels in areas that can create a crisis instead of bearing the consequences of crises. Preventing crises at their source, before they spread, is also considered a humane behavior.

REFERENCES

Adorno, T. W. (2007). *Kültür Endüstrisi*. İletişim Yayınları.

Akat, Ö. (2000). *Uygulamaya Yönelik İşletme Politikası ve Stratejik Pazarlama*. Ekin Kitabevi.

Akdağ, M., & Taşdemir, E. (2006). Krizden Çıkmanın Yolları: Etkin Bir Kriz İletişimi. *Selçuk İletişim, 4*(2),141-157. https://dergipark.org.tr/en/pub/josc/issue/19011/200778

Akgül, M. (2017). Dijitalleşme ve Din. *Marife, 17*(2), 191–208.

Aksu, A. (2009). Kriz Yönetimi ve Vizyoner Liderlik. *Yaşar Üniversitesi Eğİtim Fakültesi*, 2435-2448.

Aktaş, C. (2014). *QR Kodlar ve İletişim Teknolojisinin Hibritleşmesi*. Kalkedon Yayınları.

Albayrak, O. (2023). Dijital Diplomasi: Diplomasi 3.0. *İstanbul Ticaret Üniversitesi Sosyal Bilimler Dergisi, 22*(46), 493-508. doi:10.46928/iticusbe.1288805

Ataman, G. (2001). *İşletme Yönetimi–Temel Kavramlar & Yeni Yaklaşımlar*. Türkmen Kitabevi.

Bat, M., & Yurtseven, Ç. (2014). Sosyal medyada kurumsal kriz yönetimi: Onur Air örneği. *Gümüşhane Üniversitesi İletişim Fakültesi Elektronik Dergisi, 2*(3), 197–223. doi:10.19145/guifd.74720

Bayarçelik, E. (2020). Dijital Dönüşümün İnsan Kaynakları Yönetimi. *İstanbul Gelişim Üniversitesi Yayınları*, 59-77.

Bayram, H. (2010). *Bilgi Toplumu ve Bilgi Yönetimi*. Etap Yayınevi.

Bhatt, G. D. (2000). Information Dynamics, Learning And Knowledge Creation In Organizations. *The Learning Organization, 7*(2), 89–98. doi:10.1108/09696470010316288

Castells, M. (2005). *"Enformasyon Çağı: Ekonomi, Toplum ve Kültür, Ağ Toplumunun Yükselişi", Çev. Ebru Kılıç, 1*. Baskı, İstanbul Bilgi Üniversitesi Yayınları.

Dayton, B. W. (2009). Crisis management. In International Encyclopedia of Peace. Oxford University Press.

Değirmencioğlu, G. (2016). Dijitalleşme Çağında Gazeteciliğin Geleceği ve İnovasyon Haberciliği. *TRT Akademi, 1*(2), 590–606.

Dinçer, Ö. (1992). *Stratejik Yönetim ve İşletme Politikası*. Timaş Basım Ticaret Sanayi A.Ş.

Ertekin, Y. (1993). Stres ve Yönetim. *TODAİE Yayınları*, 253.

Friedman Thomas, L. (2000). *Lexus ve Zeytin Ağacı Küreselleşmenin Geleceği*. Boyner Holding Ya.

Gates, B. (1999). Dijital Sinir Sistemiyle Düşünce Hızında Çalışmak. Doğan Kitap.

Göztaş. (1997). *Aylin* Kriz Yönetimi ve Halkla İlişkiler. Ege Yayıncılık.

Güler, E. (2006). İşletmelerin e-insan Kaynakları Yönetimi ve e-işe Alım Süreçlerindeki Gelişmeler. *Ege Akademik Bakış Dergisi, 6*(1), 17–23.

Hambrick, D. C., & Mason, P. A. (1986). Upper echelens: The organizations as a reflection of its Top Management. *Academy of Management Review, 9*(2), 193–206. doi:10.2307/258434

Haşit, G. (2000). İşletmelerde Kriz Yönetimi ve Türkiyenin Büyük Sanayi İşletmeleri Üzerinde Yapılan Araştırma Çalışması. Eskişehir: Anadolu Üniversitesi Açık Öğretim Fakültesi Yayınları.

Karaköse, T. (2007). Örgütler ve kriz yönetimi. *Akademik bakış, 13*, 1-15.

Latinovic, T. (2016). *Big Data As The Basis For The İnnovative Development Strategyof The Industry 4.0.* https://www.researchgate.net/publication/331187513_Big_Data_as_the_basis_for_the_innovative_development_strategy_of_the_Industry_40

Mackenzie, A. (1995). *Başarı ve Zaman.* Bilim Teknik Yayınevi.

Müller, R. (1982). *Krisenmanegement in Der Unternehmung, Kölner Schriften Zur betriebswirtschaft und Organization-5* (V. E. Grochla, Ed.). Lang Verlag.

Öztürk, A. (1992). Örgütlerde Çatışma ve Yönetimi: İşletme Yönetiminde Güncel Konular. *Çukurova Üniversitesi İktisadi ve İdari Bilimler Fakültesi İşletme Bölümü Yayınları, 1*, 35-40.

Pira, A. (2004). Kriz Yönetimi Halkla İlişkiler Açısından Bir Değerlendirme. İletişim yayınları.

Prokopenko, J. (1995). *Verimlilik Yönetimi.* Yayını.

Silver, A. D. (1990). Taban Çöktüğü Zaman. Form Yayınları No:6.

Taşkıran, İ. (2017). *Sosyal Medyada Haber Var.* Der Yayınları.

Thompson, D. F., & Louie, R. P. (2006). Cooperative Crisis Management and Avian Influenza. A Risk Assessment Guide for International Contagious Disease Prevention and Risk Mitigation. National Defense University Center for Technology and National Security Policy.

Törenli, N. (2005). *Yeni Medya, Yeni İletişim Ortamı.* Bilim ve Sanat Yayınları.

Tutar, H. (2000). *Kriz ve Stres Ortamında Yönetim.* Hayat Yayıncılık.

Wasono, L. W. (2018). The effect of digital leadership and innovation management for incumbent telecommunication company in the digital disruptive era. *IACSIT International Journal of Engineering and Technology, 7*(2.29), 125–130. doi:10.14419/ijet.v7i2.29.13142

Yüksel, A., & Şener, E. (2017). The reflections of digitalization at organizational level: industry 4.0 in Turkey. *Journal of Business, Economicsand Finance, 6*(3), 291-300.

KEY TERMS AND DEFINITIONS

Crisis: Sudden deterioration, depression, danger, absence, absence are expressed as major problems.

Crisis Management: It is defined as reacting to potential problems when they occur, rather than taking steps to detect them in advance, prevent them, or limit their consequences.

Digital Age: It is the historical period formed by the widespread advancement of digital technologies, including computers and the internet.

Leadership: It is the process of directing and managing a group or organization.

Chapter 13
Mitigating Reputational Damage in Corporate Crises:
An Examination of Apology Strategies

Elanor Colleoni
https://orcid.org/0000-0001-7176-0638
IULM University, Italy

Grazia Murtarelli
https://orcid.org/0000-0002-6602-8503
IULM University, Italy

Stefania Romenti
IULM University, Italy

Francesca Dodini
IULM University, Italy

ABSTRACT

This study addresses the critical role of organizational apologies in crisis management, focusing specifically on their impact on corporate reputation and stakeholder behavior. Recognizing that crises can severely damage an organization's reputation and legitimacy, the research explores the complexities of using apologies as a crisis response strategy. It builds upon existing scholarship that has predominantly analyzed the legal and financial aspects of organizational apologies to delve into the nuances of their effectiveness. The study's scope is narrowed down to crises for which the organization is highly culpable, as perceived by public opinion shaped by news media. The research thereby offers granular insights into the strategic utility of varying apology categories, particularly in situations where the organization faces intense media scrutiny and stakeholder skepticism.

DOI: 10.4018/979-8-3693-0855-4.ch013

INTRODUCTION

Every organization will experience soon or later a crisis impacting the organization's operations and potentially damaging its reputation. Crisis threatens stakeholders' expectations about how an organization should act and may result in the questioning of the organization's legitimacy, affect how stakeholders interact with the organization and damage the organization's reputation intended as: "a global perception of the extent to which an organization is held in high esteem or regard." (Weiss et al., 1999, p. 75). Because reputation is crucial to an organization's success and enables the development of strong relationships with stakeholders, the use of communication strategies to help organizations managing threats to reputation is being deeply studied by scholars (Coombs, 2004). Apologies are a particular type of crisis response strategy and the debate concerning its components and beneficial implications is evolving in the literature (Bentley, 2015). Organizational apologies can enhance a company's reputation by benefiting stakeholders and empathizing with the victims through the expression of sympathy. Although they may not be able to completely restore the harm brought on by a crisis, apologies can help victims find peace and enhance an organization's reputation as they represent conciliatory gestures frequently implied by individuals to de-escalate confrontations (O'Connor, 2011). Nevertheless, when it comes to organizational apologies, the discussion often focuses on the legal dimension of apologies and the associated financial costs. The debate regarding apology as a crisis response strategy lacks clarity concerning the specific elements characterizing an effective apology and focusing in particular on the need to include the acknowledgment of responsibility by the organization in order to fully benefit from the reputational advantages of apologies (Benoit, 2015). Indeed, since an apology involving a simple expression of sympathy requires a different commitment from one requesting the organization to admit its guilt, often referred as full apology (Patel & Reinsch, 2003), we lack full understanding on the possible similar or different effects that different categories of apologies may have on protecting the organization's reputation and on stakeholders' behavioral intentions.

As a remedy, this chapter seeks to investigate the effectiveness of different categories of apologies in a specific crisis scenario in which the organization is perceived as highly responsible for the crisis, in protecting the corporate reputation of a company.

In doing so, this research provides insights on the effects of these crisis response strategies in a crisis scenario in which the company is directly accused by news media of causing an internal crisis within the organization.

THEORETICAL BACKGROUND

Crisis Communication Management

From a corporate perspective, a crisis can be defined as "the perception of an unpredictable event that threatens important expectancies of stakeholders related to health, safety, environmental and economic issues and can seriously affect an organization's performance and generate negative outcomes". (Coombs, 2004, p.19). A crisis can violate expectations that stakeholders hold about how organizations should act. These expectations may be motivated by worries about one's physical well-being, personal safety, the environment, or the economy. It is easy to reason that a crisis alerts the audience to the possibility that the organization is not upholding the appropriate norms of accountability and legitimacy. This violation can impact the perception that stakeholders have of the firm, and it explains why crises are considered dangerous to organizations' reputations. Consequences related to a crisis may have severe effects for stakeholders. Crises can harm stakeholders on a physical, emotional and financial level; also, a wide array of stakeholders are adversely affected by a crisis including community members, employees, customers, suppliers and stockholders. In addition, a crisis is an incident that has the potential to disrupt organizational operations and potentially tear down the organization (Barton, 2001). It obstructs routine company operations and, in the worst-case scenario, might endanger the organization's existence (Fearn-Banks, 2001) because if a business is disrupted, an organization will most likely suffer financial losses. However, crisis adverse effects go beyond monetary loss and besides including injury to stakeholders' health or mortality, may involve structural or property damage, deterioration of reputation, harm to a brand, and environmental destruction (Coombs, 2004).

In order to prevent reputational damage, it is important to manage effectively a crisis, but to do so effective communication is required. Much of the research on crisis communication looks at the rhetorical tactics that businesses employ to protect and rebuild the reputation and the relationship with stakeholders after a crisis (Benoit, 2015). The choice of the correct strategic communicative response can be effective to protect the organization's reputation, therefore crisis managers need to understand how crisis communication can be used in an effective way by selecting the crisis response strategy more appropriate for the crisis.

The most prominent crisis management tool is the Situation Crisis Communication Theory developed by Coombs (2004) which describes a set of guidelines to help managers select the correct crisis response in order to maximize reputational protection. SCCT is rooted in attribution theory (Weiner, 2006), which claims that people frequently attribute the actions of others to internal or external, constant or erratic, and controlled or uncontrollable variables. When someone believes that a person or an organization did something unintentionally or that an act did not truly depict the actor's true personality, they are less likely to criticize them; instead, when people think that the actor was in control of the action or when the action looks typical of the person, they rate bad acts more severely. Therefore, regarding organizations, the amount of reputation damage suffered by a firm is related to how much responsibility stakeholders attribute to it.

Based on the level of crisis responsibility attributed by stakeholders, crisis managers select the appropriate crisis response strategy. A crisis response approach should be chosen by the crisis manager in accordance with the potential reputational damage that the crisis could cause: the stronger the potential reputational damage, the more the crisis response strategy must try to accommodate the victim or victims negatively affected by the crisis. In this sense, when high responsibility is attributed to the company, companies are expected to adopt an accommodative strategy through apology, taking responsibility for the consequences of their actions.

Types of Apologies

According to Hearit (2006) apologies have common ritualistic foundations, regardless of the type of crisis an institution is facing. Organizations must confront their transgression during this ritualistic occasion, admit their guilt in front of the public, and then ask to be accepted back into society. Apologies are a particular type of crisis communication strategy. By apologizing and taking corrective action, organizations demonstrate their regret and gain the community's forgiveness.

Despite the great number of definitions, there are some common elements repeating themselves in several studies. In particular, the acknowledgement of responsibility is the one which has been discussed most frequently, especially within the debate of which elements constitute a so-called full apology. Indeed, Pace et al. (2010) make a distinction between a full apology and a partial apology, which is characterized mainly by the absence of guilt admission. Based on the author's perspective, immediately following an incident, partial apologies such as expressing regret and sympathy, are considered appropriate techniques to employ, especially in the case of an unclear crisis scenario. The relationship might be repaired, and the parties involved could move on after the statement of regret since stakeholders will have a more favorable opinion of the company knowing that the organization regrets its conduct (Patel & Reinsch, 2003).

In a crisis situation, choosing a partial apology, like the expression of sympathy, rather than a full apology, has been supported by Coombs and Holladay (2008). The two scholars compared the effects of a full apology, intended as an admission of responsibility and a request for forgiveness, with the effects of a straightforward statement of sympathy and with the effects of the offer of compensation on participants' perceptions. According to the study, there were no significant variations between participants' attitudes or intentions toward the organization in the three cases. Indeed, Schlenker (as cited in Pace & Botero 2010) argued that the simple phrase "I am sorry" can be perceived as an expression of sympathy or an apology based on the context. Even though there is no formal declaration of taking responsibility for the organization's acts, it is assumed that when an organization apologizes, it is also accepting responsibility for its actions. Furthermore, Coombs (2015) affirms that although companies make non-apologies, when they express sympathy or regret without the admission of guilt, stakeholders often accept these non-apologies as true apologies. Despite showing sympathy for victims can be classified as an information-adjustment approach rather than a reputation-management one, it demonstrates a high degree of accommodation (Coombs & Holladay, 2008).

In a similar way, compensation is recognized by scholars as an effective strategy in crisis communication. Compensation, in the form of money or aid, helps victims to lessen their suffering (Coombs & Holladay, 2008). Hearit (2006) suggested that organizations were generally avoiding full apologies, but stakeholders were satisfied as long as organizations paid what they owed to crisis victims, stating that "due to liability concerns in the current form of contemporary apologetic speech, the acknowledgement of the wrongdoing comes not in the apology but instead in the compensation" (p. 210).

Finally, there are also apologies which could be defined as pseudo-apologies (Bentley, 2015). Pseudo-apologies, also known as non-apologies (Kampf, 2009) have been observed to be increasing, according to scholars (Lazare, 2005). Bentley (2015) suggests that phrases like "I'm sorry" or "I apologize" can be used in pseudo-apologies, which differ from genuine apologies in a number of ways. False apologies could downplay the seriousness of an offence or convey sympathy without accepting responsibility (Lazare, 2005). Pseudo-apologies do not include one or more of the crucial components that characterize sincere ones. Lazare (2005) outlined several typical issues with pseudo-apologies:

- offering a vague and incomplete acknowledgement;
- using the passive voice;
- making the offense conditional;
- questioning whether the victim was damaged;
- minimizing the offense;
- using the empathic "I'm sorry";
- apologizing to the wrong party; and

- apologizing for the wrong offense. (p. 160)

Indeed, he argues that the absence of one or more of the elements of an effective apology often indicates a lack of sincerity: for example, making affirmations like "I'm apologizing for the conduct that it was alleged I did" fails to identify a specific wrongful act and result in an insincere apology perceived as strategic. The concept of insincere apologies and the ability of victims to discriminate between sincere and insincere apologies have been studied deeply by O'Connor (2011) in the context of marriage and spouse abusers. The scholar identifies the inclusion of argumentative language as another element showing a lack of remorse in the attempt to justify the conduct. For instance, it appears that the transgressor is not sorry for not mowing the lawn when a spouse apologizes saying "I'm sorry that I didn't mow the lawn, but I wanted to watch the game"; instead, it seems like the spouse is making an effort to defend the behavior as reasonable. Apologies are often carefully examined for subtle signs of sincerity. Given that recipients of apologies frequently check them for appropriateness, context is crucial for establishing the necessary timing, form, elaborateness, and word choice. Nonverbal signs include eye contact, breathing, posture, facial emotions, pace of speech, tone of voice, and facial complexion.

In sum, as shown through this review, there is a lack of clarity in the definition of which specific components characterize an apology. Different types or categories of apologies are mentioned and investigated in literature distinguishing full apologies from partial apologies (Pace et al., 2010) and pseudo apologies (O'Connor 2011; Bentley 2015).

It is therefore critical to empirically assess which type of apology could be more effective to protect the reputation of a company during a crisis. In particular, the following research questions are formulated:

RQ 1 - When the organization is accused of high responsibility for a crisis, can different apologies have different effects in protecting the organizational reputation and which apology can be considered the most effective?

RQ2 - Can the effects of different apologies in protecting the organizational reputation during a crisis be influenced by the credibility attributed to the accusation of high responsibility moved toward the organization?

Lastly, the literature suggests how a positive pre-crisis reputation can represent also a defense mechanism during a crisis (Fombrun & Van Riel, 2004). In a similar way, however, a negative pre-crisis reputation, characterized by a history of crisis, can have a negative impact on reputation (Coombs, 2004) and worsen the overall judgment of stakeholders towards the organization. Therefore, it is possible that if the crisis history of an organization has an impact on the current reputation, it will also influence the effectiveness of apologies as crisis response strategies. Therefore, the last research question will be:

RQ3 - Can the effects of different apologies in protecting the organizational reputation during a crisis be influenced by the crisis history of the organization accused of high responsibility for a new crisis?

METHODOLOGY

We answer our research questions using a pre-post between-subjects experiment with 5 conditions (full apology vs sympathy vs compensation vs insincere vs no apology as control) to isolate the effects of the different types of apologies on the corporate reputation drop in the aftermath of a crisis. This type of design fits our research purposes as it allows us to statistically assess the mitigating effects of the different apology responses. The outcome (dependent) variable is the relative change in corporate reputation before and after the exposure to the corporate response strategy. The case we chose is that of an Italian nursing home for the elderly that found itself at the center of a journalistic and judicial investigation following the publication of a few news media articles accusing the organization of being highly responsible for the deaths of elderly residents in the facility during the Covid-19 epidemic. The organization was accused of mishandling and negligence in the management of the emergency, which led to the spread of the virus in the structure and the contagion of its residents.

Survey

The questionnaire was developed using the platform Qualtrics and was distributed from the 14th of December 2022 to the 9th of January 2023 through word-of-mouth of the first respondents and social media, for example Facebook groups for research purposes. The benefits of conducting surveys online include the speed with which they can be shared and answered as well as the fact that the results can be easily entered into spreadsheet or statistical software for data analysis. A total of 300 respondents have been collected; nevertheless, the number of subjects considered for the statistical analysis amounts to 203; the subjects excluded were the ones that did not complete in its entirety the survey. The questionnaire was administered entirely in Italian, in order to be able to reach a larger sample and facilitate the comprehension of the text to the subjects; this made it possible to distribute the survey to older subjects who would have been excluded in the case of an English-only questionnaire, due to language barriers. Furthermore, this was a particularly important factor in being able to ensure the participation of a sample of people who were familiar with the organization analyzed, located in Lombardy, Italy. A sample of subjects was recruited with a focus on factors of willingness and readiness to participate, in order to ensure a sufficient number of responses. This method is coherent with a non-probability kind of sampling defined "convenience sampling" (Stacks, 2017). In particular, for this research, convenience sampling has been used since it was possible to reach only people willing to participate to the survey, meaning that they were the only available subjects. For this reason, it was particularly important to collect sociodemographic data in order to have a clear understanding of the characteristics of the sample reached. The majority of the items of the survey were measured with Likert scales, asking the subjects to express their level of agreement regarding a statement on a scale from 1, meaning "strongly disagree", and 7, meaning "strongly agree". The Likert scale was selected as method of evaluation of subjects' beliefs and opinions because of its high usage in the field of social studies and its efficacy in email and online surveys (Stacks, 2017) since subjects can quickly understand and choose the predesignated response.- Some items did not require the use of a Likert scale since they measured only the presence, absence, or frequency of certain characteristics of the subjects.

The survey's structure was designed in three blocks, starting with an initial section in which the subject's familiarity with the structure was tested and the evaluations of the variables of interest collected. After the first part, subjects were assigned randomly to one of the five experimental conditions (full apology, sympathy, compensation, insincere, no apology). All conditions involved first the presentation of a written stimulus, consisting of an extract from an article accusing the organization of being responsible for the crisis, followed by the presentation of a hypothetical statement of the organization in response to the crisis, which varied based on the different apology categories. Subjects were not aware of the existence of multiple conditions other than the one that they were randomly assigned to, in order to avoid possible biases. Following these two elements, subjects were presented again with the same questions presented in the first block. This structure allowed to study changes in the evaluation of subjects between T0, before the presentation of the stimulus article and the organization's statement and after at T1. At the end, in the final block, all subjects responded to a set of questions concerning socio-demographic and personal aspects.

Manipulation

The stimulus presented after the first block started with an extract of an article in which the organization was briefly identified and accused of being responsible for the crisis. This text is adapted from a real article written by an Italian columnist and was selected after an in-depth analysis of the media coverage of the crisis conducted specifically for this research. This article can be considered the starting point of the crisis involving the organization. It represents in fact a harsh and severe indictment against the organization and its management methods, judged insufficient to contrast the diffusion of the virus in the structure. Participants to the experiment were presented the original title, subtitle and a few lines of context taken from the article in order to offer a better and immediate understanding of the situation while taking into account the subject's difficulty in maintaining attention while reading a long text. The reason behind the choice of this article lies in the necessity to present subjects with a short content characterized by a news media framing positioning the crisis in a preventable cluster and attributing a high responsibility to the organization.

Since the nature of the crisis studied mainly concerns the news media sphere, it was decided to present a public-oriented response, offering a statement characterized by specific components of the different types of apologies of interest in the study. The statements were conceptualized and constructed around specific characteristics of each type of apology that were traced in the literature and adapted to the crisis situation under investigation.

Full Apology

The full apology statement is characterized by the identification of the wrongful act and the acknowledgment of responsibility, the expression of regret and sympathy towards what happened, the promise of an effort to avoid future damage and an offer to repair the damage (Scher & Darley 1997; Massersmith, 2012; O'Connor, 2011).

Full apology Statement

"The management of the Pio Albergo Trivulzio would like to express its sympathy to the families of the patients who have died during this difficult period due to the covid-19 virus. The care and assistance of the most vulnerable people has always been our priority and we are devastated by what is happening in the world in these months. What happened inside our organization is very serious, the measures we took were inadequate in combating the spread of the Covid-19 virus, an emergency we underestimated. In order to prevent this from happening again in the future, a task force has been set up to develop and define new and effective management methods to counter the spread of the virus, to be applied from now on in our organization, and on which all healthcare personnel will be trained. Finally, compensation will be granted to the families of patients who have been missing due to the Covid-19 pandemic and, in addition to the cash sum, free access to 20 psychological support sessions. We remain at your disposal for any needs."

Partial Apologies

Partial apologies are characterized mainly by the absence of guilt admission, expressing regret and sympathy ("sympathy" apology) or the offer of repairing in the form of money or aid ("compensation" apology). (Pace et al 2010; Patel & Reinsch 2003; Hearit 2006; Coombs & Holladay, 2008).

"Compensation" statement. "The management of the Pio Albergo Trivulzio, in view of what has happened in recent weeks, intends to guarantee compensation to the families of patients who have died as a result of the Covid-19 infection. In addition to the cash sum, the families will be guaranteed free access to 20 psychological support sessions. We remain at your disposal for any needs."

"Sympathy" statement. "The management of the Pio Albergo Trivulzio would like to express its sympathy to the families of the patients who have died during this difficult period due to the Covid-19 virus. The care and assistance of the most vulnerable people has always been our priority and we are devastated by what is happening in the world in these months. We extend our sympathy to the families of those who have passed away and to their grief."

Pseudo Apologies

Pseudo apologies or insincere, differ from the other more genuine apologies in several ways including not only the expression of sympathy without the acceptance of responsibility but mainly in failing the identification of the wrongful act, minimizing the offence and including justifications for the conduct. (O'Connor, 2011; Bentley, 2015; Kampf, 2009).

"Insincere" statement. "The management of the Pio Albergo Trivulzio regrets the accusations made against the organization regarding incorrect management of measures to contain the spread of the Covid-19 virus. We are close to all those who have lost a family member due to the pandemic and wish to reiterate our long-standing commitment to providing help and assistance to our patients. During the pandemic, the management of the Pio Albergo Trivulzio and the medical staff managed the extremely complex situation with the utmost professionalism, adhering to the instructions of the Region and the Protection and Health Agency."

For the control condition, no statement of apology was presented and the subjects' beliefs and opinions about the organization were re-evaluated at T1.

Variables

Corporate Reputation

The dependent variable of interest is the corporate reputation, which was measured using the four questions of the RepTrak Pulse scale (Ponzi et al., 2011). Subjects had to indicate their level of disagreement and agreement on a 7-point scales where 1 = strongly disagree and 7 = strongly agree.

Covariates

Furthermore, two variables were identified in order evaluate their possible effect on the changes in reputation: knowledge of past crisis history of the organization and credibility of the accusation. These variables were all investigated after the re-evaluation of dependent variables, in order to prevent possible biases regarding subjects' beliefs and opinions about the organization.

Knowledge of Crisis History

The subjects' knowledge of past crisis history of the organization was measured using the item "Are you aware of any other crises involving the Pio Albergo Trivulzio in past years? Please indicate which of the following crises have occurred in the past"; the subjects were presented with a list of four real past crises of the organization and could choose how many of them they knew, or if they knew none.

Credibility of the Accusation

The subjects' perception of credibility of accusation towards the organization presented the news article was also measured, asking "How credible do you think this accusation is?", to which subjects could respond on a Likert scale ranging from 1 ("with no credibility") to 7 ("very credible").

At the end of the questionnaire, several basic socio-demographic questions were included in order to have an overview of the sample main characteristics, such as age, gender, level of education, area of profession or study as well as questions related with the familiarity with the structure and its activities.

Statistical Analysis

In order to answer the research questions, the statistical analysis employed in the research mainly focuses on the use of the one-way Analysis of Variance (ANOVA). The one-way ANOVA is used when testing differences in relationships between more than two groups of an independent variable on a dependent variable (Stacks, 2017). Additionally, the statistical method ANCOVA was used to test if variables other than the group conditions could influence the effect on the dependent variables. For this analysis the variables were put as covariates in the one-way ANOVA model in order to control the results obtained for these variables. The one-way ANCOVA (analysis of covariance) can be thought of as an extension of the one-way ANOVA one or more covariates variables.

FINDINGS

In Table 1 the reputational changes after the exposure to the different forms of apology are reported.

As it can be seen from table 1, subjects assigned to the condition full apology showed a trend opposite to all other conditions of apologies concerning changes in perception of reputation. Indeed, while for compensation, insincere, sympathy and no apology groups the perception of reputation worsened from T0 to T1 only for the condition full apology the perception of reputation improved.

Overall, the deterioration in the perception of reputation was a predictable result as subjects were exposed to a crisis scenario, which tests the company's reputation and usually causes a decrease of reputation evaluation. For this reason, the effect of full apology could be even more surprising if confirmed by the statistical analysis.

To test the hypothesis that changes in perception of reputation after being exposed to a crisis may depend on the effect of apologies and to establish whether this effect is influenced by the type of apology statement to which one is exposed, a one-way analysis of variance (ANOVA) was conducted with categories of apologies as the independent variable and changes in the perception of a reputation as the dependent variable.

Looking at Table 2, it can be noted that the effect of the independent variable on the dependent variable is statistically significant with an alpha of 0.1, since $F\ (4, 198) = 2.205$, $p = 0{,}07$. It is possible therefore to accept the alternative hypothesis H1: the independent variable *apologies* has a significant

Table 1. Changes in reputation of the five conditions of apology

Condition of Apology	Change in Reputation Perception (%)
Full Apology	9%
Sympathy	-3%
Compensation	-13%
Insincere	-14%
No Apology	-16%

Table 2. Tests of between-subjects effects

Dependent Variable: Delta_reputation					
Source	Type III Sum of Squares	df	Mean Square	F	Sig.
Corrected Model	1.681[a]	4	.420	2.205	**.070**
Intercept	1.142	1	1.142	5.990	.015
Apologies	1.681	4	.420	2.205	.070
Error	37.743	198	.191		
Total	40.497	203			
Corrected Total	39.424	202			
a. R Squared =, 043 (Adjusted R Squared =, 023)					

Table 3. Pairwise comparisons

Dependent Variable: Delta_reputation						
(I) Group_Value	(J) Group_Value	Mean Difference (I-J)	Std. Error	Sig.[b]	95% Confidence Interval for Difference[b]	
					Lower Bound	Upper Bound
Sympathy	Insincere	-.104	.097	.286	-.294	.087
	Compensation	-.011	.098	.914	-.205	.183
	Full apology	-.223*	.098	.024	-.417	-.029
	No apology	.024	.100	.806	-.172	.221
Insincere	Sympathy	.104	.097	.286	-.087	.294
	Compensation	.093	.095	.328	-.094	.280
	Full apology	-.119	.095	.209	-.306	.068
	No apology	.128	.096	.184	-.061	.317
Compensation	Sympathy	.011	.098	.914	-.183	.205
	Insincere	-.093	.095	.328	-.280	.094
	Full apology	-.212*	.096	.029	-.402	-.022
	No apology	.035	.098	.720	-.157	.228
Full apology	Sympathy	.223*	.098	**.024**	.029	.417
	Insincere	.119	.095	.209	-.068	.306
	Compensation	.212*	.096	**.029**	.022	.402
	No apology	.247*	.098	**.012**	.055	.440
No apology	Sympathy	-.024	.100	.806	-.221	.172
	Insincere	-.128	.096	.184	-.317	.061
	Compensation	-.035	.098	.720	-.228	.157
	Full apology	-.247*	.098	.012	-.440	-.055
Based on estimated marginal means						
b. Adjustment for multiple comparisons: Least Significant Difference (equivalent to no adjustments).						

effect on the dependent variable changes in perception of reputation and the mean values of *changes in perception of reputation* of at least two conditions of apologies are statistically different.

By observing the Pairwise comparisons (Table 3) resulted from the ANOVA analysis, we can identify those comparisons with a p value < 0,1.

From the table, we note how only the mean value of the full apology condition shows a statistically significant difference with the mean value of "no apology" ($p = 0.012$). Therefore, we can affirm that a full apology is the only apology effective in protecting the reputation after a crisis. Furthermore, as we have seen at the beginning of the analysis, a full apology allows not only to protect the perception of reputation, but also to improve it since the mean value of changes in reputation for this condition is positive. Overall results demonstrated that, in this particular form of crisis, only a full apology, which implies the acknowledgement of responsibility, the expression of sympathy towards what happened, the promise of an effort to avoid future damage and an offer to repair the damage (O'Connor, 2011), can safeguard the company's reputation and the relationship with stakeholders in terms of behavioral intentions. The study's outcomes also revealed how the implementation of a full apology as a crisis response strategy could not only protect the organization's reputation and relationship with stakeholders but enhance and strengthen them as well. This is coherent with Gaultier-Gaillard and Louisot (2006) considerations suggesting that a crisis can represent a possible turning point for those organizations capable of managing it while maintaining a positive image.

For what concerns the other apology conditions the table of Pairwise Comparisons confirmed the statistical difference of the mean value for *Delta reputation* between full apology and sympathy ($p = 0.024$), and full apology and compensation ($p = 0.029$). Nevertheless, these differences are not useful for the purpose of this research since no statistical difference was found between sympathy and no apology or between compensation and no apology. This means that it cannot be established that they are more effective than offering no statement of apology.

CONCLUSION

This study aimed to analyze and compare the effects of the different types of apologies in protecting the organization's reputation after a crisis. While extant research has shown the relevance of apologies when companies are perceived as highly responsible for the crisis, to out knowledge, no prior study has systematically compared the different forms of apologies and their ability to protect a corporate reputation. The results showed that, when an organization is publicly accused by the news media of being seriously responsible for a crisis occurring within the organization, full apology is the only type of apology capable of protecting both the organization's reputation and stakeholder-organization relationship. This implies that in crisis situations where companies are portrayed by the media as significantly responsible, they should consider issuing a comprehensive, full apology. This strategy can help safeguard their reputation and preserve relationships with key stakeholders, which could be critical for their long-term success.

REFERENCES

Barton, L. (2001). *Crisis in organizations II* (2nd ed.). College Divisions South-Western.

Benoit, W. L. (2015). *Accounts, excuses, and apologies* (2nd ed.). State University of New York.

Bentley, J. M. (2015). Shifting identification: A theory of apologies and pseudo-apologies. *Public Relations Review*, *41*(1), 22–29. doi:10.1016/j.pubrev.2014.10.011

Coombs, W. T. (2004). Impact of past crises on current crisis communication: Insights from situational crisis communication theory. *Journal of Business Communication*, *41*(3), 265–289. doi:10.1177/0021943604265607

Coombs, W. T., & Holladay, S. J. (2008). Comparing apology to equivalent crisis response strategies: Clarifying apology's role and value in crisis communication. *Public Relations Review*, *34*(3), 252–257. doi:10.1016/j.pubrev.2008.04.001

Fearn-Banks, K. (2001). Crisis communication: A review of some best practices. In R. Heath (Ed.), *Handbook of public relations* (pp. 479–485). SAGE Publications. doi:10.4135/9781452220727.n40

Fombrun, C. J., & van Riel, C. (2004). *Fame & Fortune: How Successful Companies Build Winning Reputations*. Prentice Hall/Financial Times.

Gaultier-Gaillard, S., & Louisot, J.-P. (2006). Risks to reputation: A global approach. *The Geneva Papers on Risk and Insurance. Issues and Practice*, *31*(3), 425–445. doi:10.1057/palgrave.gpp.2510090

Hearit, K. M. (2006). *Crisis management by apology: Corporate response to allegations of wrongdoing*. Routledge. doi:10.4324/9781410615596

Kampf, Z. (2009). Public (non-) apologies: The discourse of minimizing responsibility. *Journal of Pragmatics*, *41*(11), 2257–2270. doi:10.1016/j.pragma.2008.11.007

Kim, Y. (2016). Understanding publics' perception and behaviors in crisis communication: Effects of crisis news framing and publics' acquisition, selection, and transmission of information in crisis situations. *Journal of Public Relations Research*, *28*(1), 35–50. doi:10.1080/1062726X.2015.1131697

Lazare, A. (2005). *On apology*. Oxford University Press.

Liu, B. F., & Kim, S. (2011). How organizations framed the 2009 H1N1 pandemic via social and traditional media: Implications for US health communicators. *Public Relations Review*, *37*(3), 233–244. doi:10.1016/j.pubrev.2011.03.005

O'Connor, E. (2011). Organizational Apologies: BP as Case Study. *Vanderbilt Law Review*, *64*(6), 1957–1992.

Pace, K. M., Fediuk, T. A., & Botero, I. C. (2010). The acceptance of responsibility and expressions of regret in organizational apologies after a transgression. *Corporate Communications*, *15*(4), 410–427. doi:10.1108/13563281011085510

Patel, A., & Reinsch, L. (2003). Companies can apologize: Corporate apologies and legal liability. *Business Communication Quarterly*, *66*(1), 9–25. doi:10.1177/108056990306600103

Quarantelli, E. L. (2005). A social science research agenda for the disasters of the 21st century. In R. W. Perry & E. L. Quarantelli (Eds.), *What is a disaster? New answers to old questions* (pp. 325–296). Xlibris.

Scher, S. J., & Darley, J. M. (1997). How effective are the things people say to apologize? Effects of the realization of the apology speech act. *Journal of Psycholinguistic Research*, *26*(1), 127–140. doi:10.1023/A:1025068306386

Stacks, D. W. (2016). *Primer of public relations research*. Guilford Publications.

Weiner, D. (2006). Crisis communications: managing corporate reputation in the court of public opinion. *Ivey Business Journal*, *70*(4).

Weiss, A. M., Anderson, E., & MacInnis, D. J. (1999). Reputation Management as a Motivation for Sales Structure Decisions. *Journal of Marketing*, *63*(4), 74–89. doi:10.1177/002224299906300407

Chapter 14
Cat Diplomacy:
A New Approach to Digital Public Diplomacy Through Politicians' Cat-Related Social Media Posts

Ayten Bengisu Cansever
https://orcid.org/0000-0002-1165-7273
Institute of Social Sciences, Istanbul University, Turkey

ABSTRACT

The rise of digitalization has brought significant changes across various fields, including diplomacy. This has given rise to the concept of "digital diplomacy," which combines traditional diplomatic practices with digital tools and social media platforms. Digital diplomacy leverages social media's ubiquity to enable politicians to not only reach their constituents but also shape their public image effectively. This phenomenon offers politicians new avenues to enhance public relations, craft their image, and engage voters. Recently, a global trend known as "digital diplomacy" has emerged, with politicians using cat-related posts on social media platforms as a novel approach. In this study, researchers analyze the cat-related social media posts of politicians in Turkey, examining their potential roles in creating a charming image, influencing the audience, or garnering societal attention. The study employs content analysis and delves into socio-political contexts to explore this intriguing phenomenon further.

INTRODUCTION

The field of political science, international relations, public relations, and international communication, which intersect in the realm of "public diplomacy," has undergone a significant transformation in conjunction with the impact of digitization. Particularly in the early 2000s, the developments in information and communication technologies not only altered interpersonal communication but also had an influence on communication between the public and the state. In this context, public diplomacy evolved to effectively utilize new media tools, giving rise to a novel phenomenon known as digital public diplomacy in the literature. Digital public diplomacy can be described as a concept that merges traditional public

DOI: 10.4018/979-8-3693-0855-4.ch014

diplomacy with digital communication tools and social media platforms. According to the principles of digital public diplomacy, social media platforms that permeate everyday life and micro-level relationships have become highly effective means for politicians to reach voters and shape their images. The landscape has shifted, the sphere of influence has expanded, mutual interaction rates have increased, and instant, unmediated communication has become a significant factor. New media tools are now seen as an indispensable component of diplomatic communication within the context of digital diplomacy and are even being positioned as a new form of diplomatic mechanism.

This situation, a product of digital diplomacy, presents politicians with new opportunities to strengthen their public relations, shape their images, and capture the attention of voters. This study aims to map how political leaders in the Republic of Turkey, specifically during the 2023 Presidential elections, integrated the "cat" image into their digital diplomacy efforts and constructed their image among the electorate. In this context, the research question guiding the study is: "How have political leaders in Turkey integrated the 'cat' image into their digital diplomacy efforts, especially during the 2023 Presidential elections, and how have they shaped their images among the electorate?" In recent years, globally, it has been observed that politicians have adopted a new approach called digital diplomacy through "cat-themed" posts on new media platforms. From a socio-psychological perspective, cats, in addition to being widely popular and endearing creatures worldwide, hold a special place in Turkey's streets and in the hearts of its people. However, it can be noted that cats, especially starting from 2018, began to appear more frequently on the Turkish political stage and became an important tool of digital public diplomacy. In Turkey, political leaders and figures not only make cat-themed posts on their personal social media accounts but also participate in interviews with cats on television and in newspapers. In fact, the cat can be regarded as one of the nation branding strategies of the Turkish government. In Turkey, cats hold a special place in the culture and society, influenced by both religious and historical contexts.

Firstly, the respect and affection for cats in Islamic religion are supported by narratives in religious texts. Hadiths that suggest the Prophet Muhammad had a positive attitude towards cats indicate that this affection has a religious foundation. Historically, Istanbul's centrality in sea trade increased the cat population in the city. Sailors carried cats on their ships to combat rats, leading to the spread of cats in Istanbul. Because cats were effective in controlling the rat population, interest in these animals grew during the Ottoman Empire era. The role of cats in maintaining the city's cleanliness was appreciated by the public, and the respect for cats was supported by religious beliefs. During this period, while cats in medieval European cities faced ill-treatment, cats in Ottoman Empire territories were protected thanks to charitable institutions established by the religious. With the establishment of the Republic of Turkey, support for cat welfare was further enhanced. There is legal legislation in Turkey that ensures the protection of cats. In 2004, in parallel with state policies regarding the capture, neutering, and subsequent release or adoption of cats, an animal protection law was approved. This law formalizes a positive attitude towards cats.

Many people in Turkey express their interest in cats by placing food and water bowls on the streets, offering cats a chance to eat, and allowing them to sleep on their doorsteps. In this way, people feel responsible for the welfare of cats. Is it possible to consider that the cat phenomenon, shaped by religious, historical, and cultural factors, is now being used in politics as a new form of soft power? Based on this question that forms the problem statement of the study, it is assumed that the cat, which has become a part of Turkey's cultural and social fabric, is being employed as a new form of soft power in recent times, especially in politics. In this context, it is believed that the cat posts, which are the subject of the study, are made for various purposes, such as creating a cute and friendly image for politicians, influencing their follower base, or attracting the attention of society. Therefore, in the 2023 Presidential elections in the Republic of Turkey, where the peak of influencing the public and creating a positive impression on the masses is reached, the posts made by leading political leaders will be discussed, as well as what they conveyed to the electorate. In this regard, cat-themed posts on the social media platforms of the President of the Republic of Turkey and the Chairman of the ruling Justice and Development Party (Ak Party), Recep Tayyip Erdoğan, the Chairman of the main opposition Republican People's Party (CHP), Kemal Kılıçdaroğlu, the Chairwoman of the Good Party (İyi Party), Meral Akşener, the Chairman of the Future Party (Gelecek Party), Ahmet Davutoğlu, the Chairman of the Felicity Party (Saadet Party), Temel Karamollaoğlu, and the Chairman of the Democracy and Progress Party (DEVA Party), Ali Babacan, between 2018 and 2023, were selected as examples for the study. The selected posts were analyzed using content analysis, and the data sets obtained were discussed with a holistic perspective, considering the socio-political context. This study is expected to make a significant contribution to the literature due to its relevance to the field of digital public diplomacy.

The first section of the study outlines a conceptual framework that combines digital public diplomacy, soft power, and animal diplomacy concepts to guide cat diplomacy practices. Secondly, using content analysis, cat-themed posts made by Turkish political leaders in the five-year period leading up to the 2023 Presidential elections were included in the sample and analyzed.

CONCEPTUAL FRAMEWORK

From Traditional Diplomacy to Digital Diplomacy

In contemporary society, there has been a profound change in the field of information communication. Starting from the era of the industrial society, technological advancements have evolved into the network society with the rise of information technologies. In the 21st century, referred to as the "Network Age" by Van Dijk, networks have become the neural system of societies. These networks have formed information highways where information flows more effectively than traditional means (Van Dijk, 2018). Van Dijk (2018) defines the network society as a form of society where relationships in media networks increasingly organize, replacing or complementing face-to-face communication. According to Castells (2005), networks shape the new social morphology of our societies and have become the fundamental units of modern society. Throughout history, knowledge has represented power, and having access to and mechanisms for producing knowledge has always held a valuable and powerful position. Therefore, Castells (2005) argues that instead of calling our era the "information society," the term "network society" can be used to distinguish it from others. According to him, information should be considered as the fundamental paradigm, and emphasizing this pivotal role of information is important in understanding contemporary society. Castells posits that people in our time live in a social structure surrounded by networks connected through computer tools. A notable feature of these networks is the absence of central authority. Therefore, it is not possible to seize or occupy control of these networks. Each node of the network is part of this social structure and fulfills its function. However, nodes that cannot keep up with the speed or dynamics of these networks or adapt to changing conditions may be excluded by the system or may attempt to reconfigure themselves to conform to the system. In this context, capturing or disabling a node within the network does not bring down the entire network because the network is composed of independent nodes and continues to exist. In other words, attacks on the network can only affect specific nodes but cannot destroy the entire network. Therefore, understanding the complexity and resilience of the network society is crucial.

In the traditional information communication order, information was usually conveyed in a one-way manner, from top to bottom or from the source to the masses. However, today, every segment of society, including individuals, can contribute to information flow from the bottom up or from different directions. This signifies a fundamental change in the information communication order. With the development of social media applications and digitalization, instant access to information has become possible. This has not only affected information consumption but has also had a significant impact on politics by enabling direct, unmediated communication between politicians and citizens. Politicians can now reach their constituents and share their views not through traditional media but directly through social media platforms. Through social media, politicians can monitor instant reactions, answer questions from voters, and convey policy proposals. This encourages greater citizen participation in political processes and makes politics more accessible. Therefore, it can be stated that the digital transformations in the field of public diplomacy have changed the communication between the state and its citizens, rendering intermediary actors obsolete, and in this context, states have begun to experiment with new ways to expand the boundaries and scope of their soft powers.

Edward Murrow, the director of the United States Information Agency (USIA), coined the term "public diplomacy" in 1963. This idea extends beyond the standard definition of diplomacy, denoting a field that is not restricted to governing a government's dealings with other governments. Public diplomacy is a broad category of public relations and communication operations intended at introducing, explaining, and promoting a country's ideals, policies, and cultural traits to other people and the public. It tries to communicate with all parts of the public, not only other governments. Public diplomacy is viewed as a means of improving a country's diplomatic relations and international reputation. It can encompass efforts such as cultural diplomacy, educational initiatives, media relations, and language training in this context. In an era when international relations are becoming more complex, public diplomacy emphasizes states' efforts to influence their own populations as well as the populations of other countries. Furthermore, as information and communication technology have advanced, the effect and value of public diplomacy have grown. A country's public relations strategy, within this context, include efforts to influence foreign public opinion through communication tools and digital media platforms.

Public diplomacy, which is regarded as "one of the most prominent issues in political communication, is used by political scientists to increase soft power in nation-states. (Melissen, 2008; van Ham, 2008; Snow & Taylor, 2009; Keohane & Nye, 2012). According to Nye (2008, p. 95), public diplomacy is "a tool used by governments to communicate with foreign publics, to attract them, and to activate soft power resources." In today's world, effective public diplomacy relies on the efficient use of media tools. Consequently, it is possible to talk about governments engaging in dialogue by bypassing intermediary actors, both at the national and transnational levels, by using media platforms. Public relations theorists have used the concept of public diplomacy within the framework of strategic communication, country image construction, and managing relationships with national and transnational citizens (Zaharna, 2000; Fitpatrick, 2007; Fitzpatrick, Fullerton, & Kendrick, 2013; Buhmann & Ingenhoff, 2015; Zaharna, 2016; Ingenhoff, White, Buhmann, & Kiousis, 2019). Gilboa (2016, p. 1) defines public diplomacy as "interactions from person to person, in common or conflicting national and global interests, in a post-truth society."

Concepts such as strategic communication and soft power constitute the fundamental components of public diplomacy, encompassing efforts to access the thoughts and feelings of the public and influence and win them over (Yücel, 2016). Governments, moving beyond traditional methods, seek to gain the consent of the public through content and activities aimed at establishing emotional connections with the public in new media environments. Manuel Castells' theory of informationalism, based on information technologies, explains the background of the concept of digital diplomacy. According to this theory, a knowledge-based society has emerged, and individuals play a central role in knowledge production. Interpersonal knowledge flow takes place continuously and seamlessly through networks. This implies a societal structure where politics and diplomacy are conducted through networks (Ekşi, 2016).

As a result of digitalization, states have begun to explore new ways to enhance their soft power. By using platforms like social media, they have strategically branded their political leaders as influential figures among their populations (Uysal & Schroeder, 2019). For example, leaders like US President Donald Trump and Russian President Vladimir Putin have strategically used social media to create strong leader images. The theory of personality cult, which entails elevating leaders to be perceived as flawless and faultless figures, is based on Weber's concept of charismatic authority (Cassiday & Johnson, 2010). The multimedia features, easy accessibility, and ability to reach large audiences provided by social media have facilitated the expansion of the public discourse of political leaders and the strengthening of their personal brands.

Animal Diplomacy: An Interesting and Effective Component of Digital Public Diplomacy

Diplomatic utilization of animals has a longstanding history, dating back to ancient times. In this context, historical documents such as the Amarna Letters allow us to trace the evolution of animal diplomacy from ancient times to the present. Leira and Neuman's (2015) studies shed light on how, particularly since ancient times, diplomacy has been conveyed through the exchange of gifts and tributes involving animals. Examples of such diplomatic relations range from Nubia sending giraffes to the capital of Egypt during the Tutankhamun era, to the Assyrians receiving horses and cattle as tributes, and even the Tang Dynasty gifting pandas to neighboring countries as a means to foster good relations. In the past, the size and power of gifts exchanged among rulers played a significant role in reflecting the depth and respect within relationships. While riding animals were commonly preferred in exchanges between officials and ordinary citizens, voluminous animals like elephants and giraffes presented to rulers carried diplomatic messages beyond mere ostentatious gestures. For instance, the noteworthy diplomatic gesture of Mamluk Sultan Baybars presenting Arabian horses, parrots, monkeys, and weaponry to Berke Khan symbolized power and wealth. In the history of diplomacy, animals have played a crucial role not only in relationships between rulers but also in strengthening bonds of friendship and collaboration between states. Even in the present day, instances of animal diplomacy can be observed. An illustrative example is Zimbabwean President Mugabe's directive to create an ark for every animal in the country in exchange for Siberian tigers gifted to China, showcasing a contemporary manifestation of this traditional diplomatic practice.

Building upon this, animal diplomacy can be characterized as a means for a state to enhance its national image, presenting itself favorably in the eyes of the public and portraying a positive image to foreign countries. As a long-standing practice, animal diplomacy refers to the "use of live native fauna (…) for diplomatic purposes" and to most importantly "increase repute and standing" (Cushing & Markwell, 2009, p. 255; Hartig, 2013, p. 52). Animal diplomacy, as highlighted by examples like China's "panda diplomacy", Australia's "platypus diplomacy" and Russia's "dog diplomacy" is an intriguing and effective phenomenon within the realm of public diplomacy. In this regard, examining the widely recognized example of China's 'panda diplomacy' in the context of 'animal diplomacy,' it can be argued that starting from the twentieth century, pandas have been strategically employed by the Chinese government as a national branding strategy. The history of China's panda diplomacy can be divided into three distinct periods: (1) Between 1957 and 1982, China 'gifted' pandas to neighboring countries with whom it sought to maintain good relations; (2) From 1982 to 1994, the 'loan' method was employed for the preservation and continuation of the panda species; (3) After 1994, China realized the economic benefits it could gain from pandas and developed the 'leasing' method. Indeed, the selection of the panda as the official mascot for the 2022 Beijing Winter Olympics can be interpreted as a strategic communication move within the framework of animal diplomacy (Olympic Committee, 2022). In this context, according to Xing (2010, p. 32), it is believed that the Chinese government's use of pandas for political and diplomatic purposes involves a strong ideological propaganda and sincere friendship. The global appeal of pandas, with their cute appearance, is utilized to create a reputable state image as an actor of China's soft power. Furthermore, besides being playful and adorable creatures, the non-aggressive nature of pandas contributes to portraying a sympathetic image of the state (Xing, 2010, p. 19-20). In fact, the reason for choosing 'pandas' over another significant symbol of soft power, the 'dragon,' is to present a softer and more positive image on the international stage (Wang, 2008, p. 258). Pandas, having become diplomatic objects, also evoke China as a national symbol.

Another example in the field of animal diplomacy is Australia's 'platypus diplomacy' (Cushing & Markwell, 2009). The choice of the platypus, among iconic animals like kangaroos or koalas, is closely related to how Australia aims to create its national image. The platypus, a mammal known for its rare venomous features and unique structures, has captured attention. However, the difficulty of domesticating platypuses and their inability to thrive in captivity for extended periods made them unsuitable for display in zoos. In 1943, inspired by the interest of British Prime Minister Churchill, a diplomatic move was made by sending platypuses abroad to live at least during the research period (Yıldırım, 2021). This introduced a new dimension to public diplomacy using Australia's symbolic animal. This diplomatic move, made in goodwill and effort between two close nations, facilitated the acceptance of Australia's symbol by the United Kingdom. Following the success of this diplomatic initiative, platypuses were gifted to the United States in 1947. It was perceived as a gesture reflecting Australia's political stance, and platypus diplomacy became a part of inter-country relations. During this period, platypuses were not only considered for diplomatic gestures but also for introducing them to citizens of countries interested in seeing them. However, over time, policies changed, and from 1958 onwards, the export of animals was prohibited. Factors such as species conservation, increasing maintenance costs, and survival rates played a role in this shift. Additionally, with Australia cultivating an image of greater concern for animal rights, a more cautious policy regarding animal exports was adopted.

Another noteworthy example is the 'dog diplomacy' that took place in Sochi. It is a known fact that Angela Merkel is afraid of dogs, and Vladimir Putin bringing his dog alongside during Merkel's visit was interpreted as an attempt to influence her in some way. The role of dogs in diplomacy is particularly crucial for Russia. In 2010, Russia gifted two puppies to the President of Austria. Bulgarian Prime Minister Borisov also presented a Bulgarian Shepherd Dog to Russia, a gesture previously extended to B. Obama and George Bush. During the early years of Kyrgyzstan's independence, U.S. Secretary of State James Baker received a horse as a diplomatic gesture. After Putin received an Akita dog from Japan, Russia pledged to reciprocate by gifting a Siberian cat (von Twickel, 2012). In 2012, Putin presented a black Terrier to Cuban leader H. Chavez and expressed the intention to send a dog to France in place of a police dog killed in the Charlie Hebdo attack (Neumann & Leira, 2015, p. 355).

Compared to other forms of cultural diplomacy, animal diplomacy can be more efficacious due to its lack of language barriers (Xing, 2010, s. 24). It is possible to observe how countries utilize animals for the exercise of soft power. Turkey, for instance, has gained recognition with its "cat diplomacy". This type of diplomacy carries the potential to evoke positive emotions in people, often owing to the inherent cuteness and innocence of animals.

Hartig (2013, s. 53) delineates three primary manifestations of animal diplomacy: gifts, diplomatic gestures, and the loan of animals. For optimal success, the chosen animal must possess a positive 'visual identity' and have an easily accessible 'natural distribution' to effectively 'win hearts' for diplomatic purposes (Hartig 2013, 55). To exert influence on the actions of others, an animal must exhibit traits that are universally perceived as cute and have the ability to capture media attention (Hartig 2013, 55). In addition to the characteristics mentioned, Lorenz (1943) stated that animals employed in diplomacy should possess specific traits. These traits include a high forehead, a broad head, huge eyes, a round face, and short, thin limbs. Lorenz (1943), based on the characteristics he mentioned, introduced the concept of "*kindchenschema*" (baby schema); according to this concept, the perception of features like "a large head, a round face, and big eyes forming a set of infantile physical features" as cute, and the motivation of caregiving behavior in others, serves an evolutionary function of increasing the chances of survival for offspring. As indicated by Lorenz (1943) and further emphasized by Gould (1979, p.34) and Schaller (1994, p. xvi), these characteristics frequently generate positive emotions in people and activate mechanisms for releasing these emotions.

With the impact of digitization, animal diplomacy has also undergone change and transformation, beginning to manifest itself in the online environment. Limited studies have addressed this phenomenon. Moreover, it is observed that in this limited literature, the emphasis is mostly on China's digital panda diplomacy. According to Huang and Wang (2020, p. 5), this situation is closely related to China's initiation of digital public diplomacy, which is in line with the government's efforts to "innovate and develop online propaganda" to "guide public opinion." In this way, the Chinese government has started to release "panda-themed tweets", which align with the ideas of soft power and panda diplomacy (Huang 2020, p. 1). Although Twitter is banned for ordinary citizens in China, the government has some platforms that mimic the concept of Twitter. Huang and Wang's study (2020) confirmed that these tweets "promote and strengthen not only Sino-foreign relations using digital public diplomacy but also show that Chinese media follow the principles of constructive journalism to transfer positive emotions". In Huang and Wang's (2019) another study titled "The New 'Cat' of the Internet: China's Panda Diplomacy on Twitter", the authors investigate how the Chinese government utilizes the panda image on Twitter within the context of digital diplomacy. The study aims to understand how this usage contributes to enhancing the cognitive impact of China's national treasure and softening its national image. Notably, the work by Huang and Wang (2019) is the first study to employ a multi-method approach to demonstrate the effectiveness of China's digital public diplomacy on Twitter. According to the findings of the study, the Chinese government strategically employs tweets through media organizations, incorporating content featuring pandas. This strategic communication approach serves the purpose of reconstructing China's 'soft' image and promoting the nation's brand. The study sheds light on the intricate ways in which China leverages its digital presence on Twitter for diplomatic objectives, particularly in enhancing its global image and national identity. Yıldırım (2021) examined the historical context of China's panda diplomacy and discussed examples of panda diplomacy in digital environments in his study. Aranceta-Reboredo (2022) conducted a comparative case analysis of China's panda diplomacy and Australia's koala diplomacy using the method of animal-based soft power practice.

Particularly in recent years, cat diplomacy has gained notoriety in Turkey. Cats are adored by many people and are generally thought to be good. As a result, politicians and governments use cats as a political communication tool to improve their public relations. Politicians may project a more empathetic, personal, and inviting image by using cats' charming characteristics. The charm of cats contributes to the perception of leaders as more approachable and accessible figures in the eyes of the public. Political leaders have seized the opportunity to expand their follower base, attract attention, and build a positive image by frequently featuring cats on social media platforms. Cat-related posts serve the purpose of increasing a leader's social media presence and growing their follower count. Furthermore, when the cuteness of cats is utilized as part of communication strategies, it often generates a positive and endearing atmosphere. This potential fosters the ability of leaders to evoke positive emotions and generate sympathy among their followers.

METHODOLOGY

In this study, it is believed that the impact of digital transformations in the field of public diplomacy has altered the communication between the state and its citizens. The study suggests that intermediary actors between the state and citizens have been sidelined, prompting governments to explore new avenues to enhance the boundaries and scope of their soft power. One of these emerging soft power activities involves political leaders strategically using social media platforms to construct their image actively.

Through their postings on these platforms, political leaders aim not only to present themselves as "strong authoritative figures" but also as relatable, genuine, and humane individuals, thereby seeking to cultivate sympathy among the citizens. One of the most notable examples of this effort to build sympathy is observed in "cat-themed" posts. From a social psychological perspective, cats are charming and appealing creatures that have gained immense popularity on social media. In the context of this study, cat-themed posts are believed to serve various purposes, such as helping politicians create an amiable and approachable image, influencing their follower base, or capturing the attention of the public.

Through the prism of the idea of soft power, this study seeks to assess how Turkish political leaders' cat-themed posts are used for digital public diplomacy. In this context, the research question guiding the study is: "How have political leaders in Turkey integrated the 'cat' image into their digital diplomacy efforts, especially during the 2023 Presidential elections, and how have they shaped their images among the electorate?" As Turkey prepares for the 2023 Presidential Election, the research focuses on political figures in Turkey and chooses cat-related posts from the previous five years.

Electoral outcomes, current affairs, and cultural dynamics can all have an impact on a political leader's popularity and influence. However, as of 2023, a broad evaluation was conducted to identify the most well-known and significant political figures in Turkish politics. The political leaders included in the sample in this study are as follows:

1. **Recep Tayyip Erdoğan:** In 2003, Erdoğan was appointed Prime Minister of Turkey before being elected President. He has long been recognized as one of the most important people in Turkish politics. His inclusion on this list as the founder of the AK Party is owing to the party's electoral triumphs and the influence it has had on Turkish domestic and foreign policy.
2. **Kemal Kılıçdaroğlu:** As the leader of the Republican People's Party (CHP), Kemal Kılıçdaroğlu has a substantial political influence. He has the responsibility of denouncing the policies of the

administration as the leader of the largest opposition party. Additionally, the fact that CHP's cat, Şero, has a social media account might be used as an illustration of how Kılıçdaroğlu operates.[1]

3. **Meral Akşener:** Meral Akşener is the Chairwoman of the Good Party (İyi Party) and one of the founding leaders of the party. She is considered an influential figure in the Turkish political agenda. Her efforts to alter the political dynamics in Turkey since the establishment of the Good Party (İyi Party) and her leadership within the party are among the reasons for her inclusion in this list.
4. **Temel Karamollaoğlu:** Temel Karamollaoğlu, the leader of the Felicity Party (Saadet Party), ensures the party's presence in Turkish politics within an ideological framework. The unique policy proposals of the Felicity Party (Saadet Party) and its performance in elections, along with Karamollaoğlu's cat-related social media posts, support his inclusion in this list.
5. **Ali Babacan:** Ali Babacan, the leader of the Democracy and Progress Party (DEVA Party), is one of the founding leaders of his party. As a new political formation, DEVA Party offers a different option in Turkish politics. One reason for including Babacan in this list is to examine the evolving image engineering through his cat, Çakıl, related posts.
6. **Ahmet Davutoğlu:** An important political figure who held a significant role during the AK Party era, Ahmet Davutoğlu served as the Prime Minister of Turkey from 2014 to 2016. In 2019, he established the Future Party after parting ways with the Justice and Development Party (AK Party). Davutoğlu's founding and leadership of the Future Party (Gelecek Party) contributed to the emergence of a new political formation in Turkish politics and had an impact on the party's political structure. Being part of this new political formation led to a reshaping of Davutoğlu's image and a change in his target audience. Hence, he is included in the study's sample.

In this study, the social media accounts of the political leaders other than those included in the sample were examined. The Nationalist Movement Party (MHP), which has the power to influence public opinion and is one of the most recognized parties in Turkey, is led by Devlet Bahçeli. All Devlet Bahçeli's social media accounts were scrutinized, and no cat-related posts were found within the relevant dates. Therefore, he was not included in the sample. While the reasons for the absence of cat-related posts in Devlet Bahçeli's social media accounts are not known with certainty, it should be considered that such personal or animal-related posts may vary depending on the communication strategies and personal preferences of political leaders. The decision not to make cat-related posts by Devlet Bahçeli may be due to personal preferences or a choice not to reflect his political image or message.

Cat-related posts on the social media accounts of the included political leaders were identified and subjected to content analysis in this study. The relevant contents were noted by individually scanning each leader's social media platform. No specific social media platform was selected, as each leader sometimes shares the same content on all platforms, while at other times, they may make more specific posts in line with the spirit of a particular platform. In this context, the analysis of cat-related posts was not directly tied to a particular social media platform, and both recurring and non-recurring content were listed.

During the analysis, factors such as the frequency, dates, content, and interactions of these posts were taken into consideration. Furthermore, similarities and differences in cat-related posts of each political leader were determined. It is believed that this will provide valuable information about how political leaders shape their social media strategies and images. However, it should be noted that the study's focus on the posts of specific political leaders within specific time frames limits its scope. The research can expand its sample in future studies, considering a broader time frame and including posts from local governments, allowing for a more in-depth understanding of this subject.

Table 1. Cat-related posts of Turkish political party leaders between 2018-2023

Political Leader	Social Media Platform	Date of Posting	Caption	Likes Count
Recep Tayyip Erdoğan	Instagram	September 19, 2019	15 years ago today... On September 19, 2004, we traveled from Istanbul to Malatya with our lovely Van Cat friend... #Istanbul #Malatya #Van #Turkey #Cat #tbt	507.494
	Facebook			42K
	Instagram	Semptember 26, 2021	My dear granddaughter Aybike's cat, Pıt Pıt Şeker... Quite curious about current events (cat emoji)	94,9K
	Twitter			
	BİP	January 12, 2021	Hello (with cat photo)	-
	Instagram	January 6, 2023	Today, we reopened the historic New Mosque in Eminönü for worship, following the completion of its restoration works. I congratulate the institutions, architects, artists, and workers who contributed to the revitalization of this unique masterpiece, and I extend my heartfelt gratitude to them.	216.287
Kemal Kılıçdaroğlu	Twitter/X	On February 17, 2019	It is our responsibility to make our cities and all living spaces livable for you. Happy World Cat Day. May the end of March bring you spring as well! #WorldCatDay	6.148
	Twitter/X	October 4, 2021	We are looking forward to the beautiful days ahead.	55,7K
	Facebook	October 5, 2021		35K
	Instagram			71.677
	Twitter/X	March 12, 2023	I promised Şero today that when I come to power, I will make canned food affordable.	71.714
	Instagram	March 12, 2023	We met with our old friend Şero at the CHP Headquarters. Şero, born in 2005, became known to our people as the 'social democrat cat.' You know, cats claim their space. And in a cat's eyes, everything belongs to the cat. Şero is the one who claims this place the most. The doors are always open to him. You see, cats don't like closed doors. He enters and exits wherever he wants; he has the freedom of endless travel. He roams where he wants, rests where he wants, lies down where he wants. He does whatever he pleases. Sometimes he appears on TV with us, sometimes he interrupts our meetings. He always attracts attention. Cats are wise creatures anyway. Şero has also turned into a politician. Today, I told him about our latest work. Today, I made a promise to Şero. When we come to power, we will make wet cat food affordable. We will wholeheartedly love everyone who has walked with us on this journey, everyone, young and old, cats, flowers, insects, because compassion is a virtue	281,4K
Meral Akşener	Twitter/X	February 19, 2018	Our cat, who has been through tough times, is now in its new home. We will organize a topic on animal rights protection and take deterrent measures against cruelty, abuse, and ill-treatment of animals. God's silent servants will hopefully be well too	13.4K
	Facebook			6.7K
	Twitter/X	July 12, 2018	We can make a difference to dozens of unnoticed lives with just a bowl of water and food. Please #SpeakUpForStreetAnimals	6,9K
	Instagram			13K
	Instagram	June 6, 2018	We prioritize protecting our voiceless animals and trees that cannot protect themselves. #TurnYourFaceToTheSunTurkey	13.7K
	Twitter/X			4,4K
	Twitter/X	August 8, 2018	As an individual from a nation that always values the creatures it shares the world with and with the consciousness that loving cats comes from faith. Happy #InternationalCatDay	4.426
	Facebook			1.151
	Twitter/X	April 4, 2019	"This world is better with them; let's not forget. #WorldStrayAnimalsDay	5.436
	Twitter/X	August 8, 2019	Cats are entrusted silent orphans to us. Protecting them and nature altogether is to instill a love for nature in our children, which is the real value.	4.784
	Facebook			4,8K
	Instagram			49.866

Continued on following page

Table 1. Continued

Political Leader	Social Media Platform	Date of Posting	Caption	Likes Count
	Facebook	April 4, 2020	In these days when we stay at home due to the pandemic, let's not forget our friends who share our streets, neighborhoods, and cities; let's not leave a bowl of food and a bowl of water missing from our doorsteps. #WorldStrayAnimalsDay	3.369
	Twitter/X			7K
	Twitter/X	August 8, 2020	Today; it is the day of Tekir, Durmuş, Şeker, Paşa, and Minnoş... Happy #InternationalCatDay to our cute but equally vigilant and silent friends.	17,4K
	Facebook			9,5K
	Twitter/X	February 19, 2020	I said, 'We will wear out our shoes, not our seats, and we will be the voice of the silent masses in our country.' We are visiting Edirne district by district. Our next stop is Uzunköprü.	2.7K
	Twitter/X	April 4, 2021	One of the values that make us human is the virtue of sharing the world with all its inhabitants. Let's remember our friends who are part of our streets, neighborhoods, and lives not only on #WorldStrayAnimalsDay but every day. Let's lend our ears to their silence with love.	5.846
	Instagram			23.721
	Facebook			3,608
	Instagram	July 1, 2022	#Pasaklı	102,3K
	Instagram/Story	August 28, 2022	In the story, I'm answering the question "Do you have a pet?" The answer is: "Yes, I have many.	-
	Instagram	January 18, 2021	While enjoying the snow covering our country, let's not forget our cute friends living on the streets; remember to put out a bowl of water and food in front of our homes, leave the doors of our apartment buildings open, and always check between the wheels before starting our cars.	20.953
	Twitter/X			6,920
	Facebook			5.798
	Instagram	January 9, 2021	To protect our adorable friends from the cruelty of merciless hearts... To make Turkey a happy home for them too... We are closely following the Animal Rights Law.	19.420
Ali Babacan	Twitter/X	December 5, 2020	There has been interest in seeing our cat who was a guest in the background of today's broadcast. Let's introduce our cat, Çakıl. You can watch the program where I answered your questions through the following link: https://youtu.be/2MZjAPSwI6M	13,2K
Temel Karamollaoğlu	Instagram	March 13, 2023	Let me introduce you to @Kilicdarogluk; this is our cat, Duman. He occasionally visits the Party Headquarters. He's not very interested in politics, but I think he shares the same opinion as Şero when it comes to wet food.	26K
	Twitter/X	October 4, 2019	Let's never withhold our love, compassion, and mercy from our friends with whom we share the same world. On #WorldAnimalProtectionDay, I hope it reminds us of our responsibilities towards innocent and adorable companions.	1.6K
	Facebook			970
	Instagram	October 4, 2019	They are entrusted to us, life is beautiful with them.	3.696
	Instagram	March 2, 2019	I answered Ruhat Mengi's questions.	3.719
Ahmet Davutoğlu	Twitter/X	April 4, 2020	We love the created for the sake of the Creator. Happy #WorldStrayAnimalsDay..	2.513
	Facebook			2,9K
	TikTok			6010
	Instagram			5.3K

In this context, the selected political leaders, the social media platforms they use, the dates of cat-related posts, the descriptions of these posts, and the number of likes are provided in Table 1.

In the context of the problem that this study addresses, one of the most significant reasons for selecting Turkey as the population and sample is that, unlike many other countries worldwide, Turkey has a dense cat population. It is noteworthy that political leaders in Turkey use cats in their election campaigns

Figure 1. Harold Lasswell's communication model

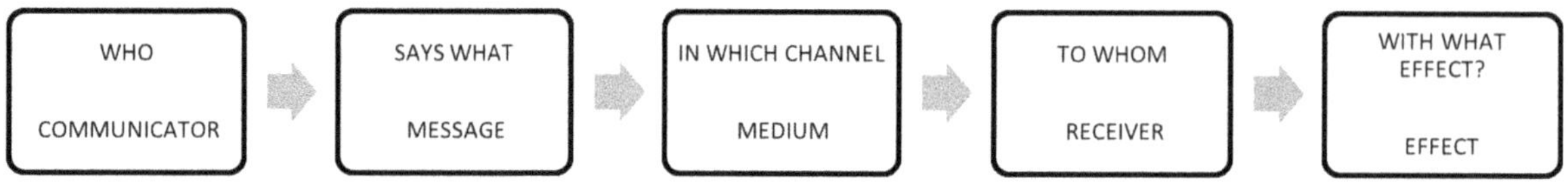

and during election periods as part of their image-building efforts. Particularly, for mature leaders who have been at the helm of political parties in Turkey for a long time, it can be argued that the use of cat-related posts in their campaigns is a strategy adopted to appeal to voters under the age of 40. Within this context, these relevant political leaders and parties employ various promises, gestures, facial expressions, and behaviors to reach voters under the age of 40. The use of cats as an election strategy can be seen as an inclusive move that appeals to both the young and the elderly, does not undermine the institutional identity, and is in harmony with the personality of mature politicians.

In this study, without selecting a specific social media platform, an attempt has been made to interpret repeated or diversified cat-related content on various social media platforms. A total of 48 cat-related content pieces were identified for analysis in this context. The findings obtained from these 48 cat-related contents have been discussed under different headings for each political leader.

Content analysis has been employed as the method in this study. The content analysis method consists of interpreting quantitative and qualitative analyses. Harold Laswell's formula "who?, says what?, in which channel?, to whom?, with what effect?" which he derived from his studies on communication, has shaped the structure of content analysis (Yıldırım, 2015).

The findings were thematically coded and discussed in consideration of context and meaning. In this context, the usage of cats in the photos, the captions in the posts, the choice of words in the captions, and the posting dates were considered to discuss the use of cats in the image construction of political leaders within the sample.

FINDINGS AND DISCUSSION

In this section, the findings of the 'cat' posts made by Turkish political leaders on their social media platforms within the scope of the study's problem statement have been discussed. These findings provide important insights into the social media strategies and communication styles of political leaders. Without directly selecting a specific social media platform, the study aimed to make sense of repeated or varied cat content on each social media. In this context, a total of 48 cat-related contents were identified for analysis. The findings from these 48 cat-related contents have been discussed under different headings for each political leader.

Frequency and Distribution of Political Leaders' Cat Posts: A General Overview

In the study, when examining the frequency and distribution of 'cat' posts made by the political leaders included in the sample on their social media accounts, it can be noted that the results are presented as shown in the following figure.

Figure 2. Distribution graph of cat-related posts on social media accounts of political leaders in Turkey from 2018 to 2023

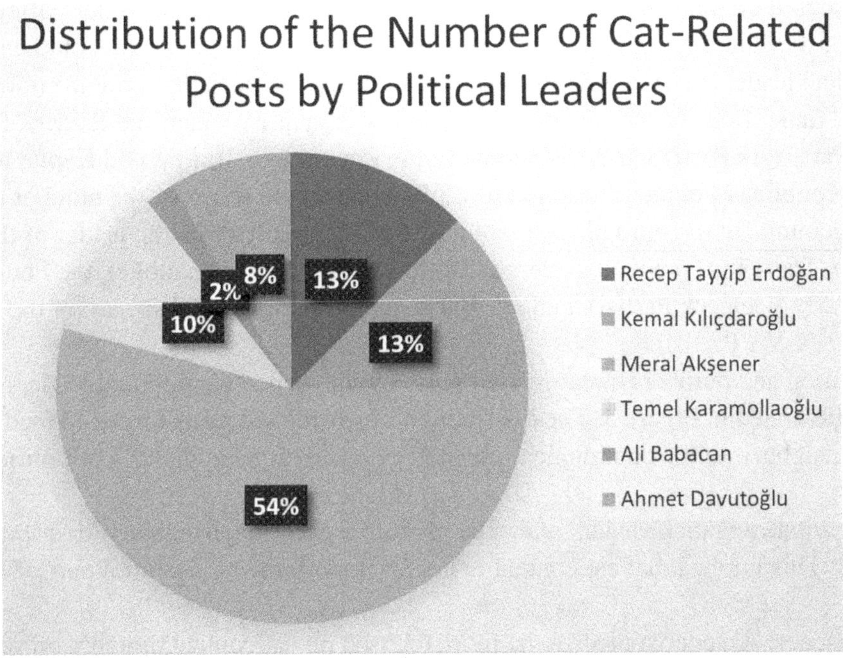

Figure 3. Distribution of cat-related posts by political leaders on social media platforms

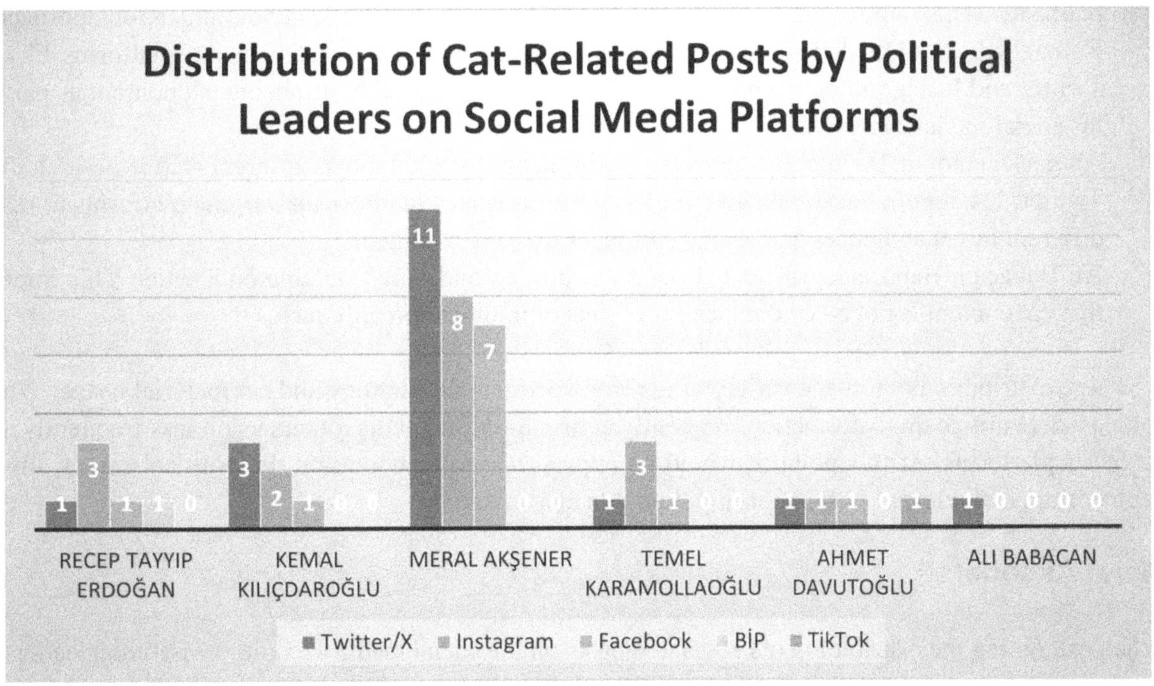

Based on the findings obtained from the study, it can be observed that cat-related posts were made at regular intervals, although there were differences in the frequency of these posts among the leaders. Some leaders shared cat-related content more frequently, while others did so less often. In the context of the sample of the study, when looking at the distribution of cat-related posts on the social media accounts of political leaders in Turkey from 2018 to 2023, it can be seen that İyi Parti (Good Party) leader Meral Akşener ranks first. In the second place, Recep Tayyip Erdoğan, the leader of the Justice and Development Party (Ak Parti) and the President of the Republic of Turkey, and Kemal Kılıçdaroğlu, the leader of the Republican People's Party (CHP), follow closely in terms of the number of posts on their social media accounts. In the third place, there is Temel Karamollaoğlu, the leader of the Felicity Party (Saadet Partisi). These four political leaders are followed by Ahmet Davutoğlu, the Founding Chairman of the Future Party (Gelecek Partisi), and Ali Babacan, the Founding Chairman of the Democracy and Progress Party (DEVA Partisi).

The distribution and numbers of cat-related posts by the respective political leaders on social media platforms are illustrated in Figure 3. The distribution of cat-related posts on social media platforms can provide some insights into the communication strategies and target audiences of political leaders:

1. Recep Tayyip Erdoğan: Erdoğan's cat-related posts are few and irregularly distributed across many platforms. This implies that cat content is not an important and a central part of his social media strategy.
2. Meral Akşener: Akşener appears to be more focused on cat content, notably on social media platforms such as Twitter, Instagram, and Facebook, where she frequently shares cat-related posts. This suggests that Akşener purposefully employs cat content in order to attract a larger target audience.
3. Temel Karamollaoğlu: Karamollaoğlu's cat-related posts are few and dispersed unevenly across many platforms. This implies that cat content is not a key component of his communication approach.
4. Kemal Kılıçdaroğlu: Kılıçdaroğlu's cat-related posts appear on social media platforms like as Twitter and Instagram on a regular basis. This suggests that he is still using cat content as part of his social media campaign.
5. Ahmet Davutoğlu: Davutoğlu's cat-related posts are diversified across different platforms, including Twitter, Instagram, Facebook, and TikTok. This indicates that he uses various platforms to reach different target audiences and to make broader use of cat content.
6. Ali Babacan: Babacan's cat-related posts are limited and only available on Twitter. This implies that cat content is not a key component of his communication approach.

These distributions show the variety of leaders' social media strategy and cat material usage. While some leaders utilize this information frequently across multiple media, others use it less frequently and on fewer platforms. At this point, it would be appropriate to elaborate on the political career, image engineering, and relevant posts of each political leader in detail.

Meral Akşener

When examining the distribution of cat-related posts on the social media accounts of political leaders in Turkey, it is observed that İyi Party Chairman Meral Akşener ranks first. Akşener served as the Minister of Internal Affairs in the 54th Government of Turkey and also held the position of Deputy Speaker of the Grand National Assembly of Turkey (TBMM). Additionally, she commenced her early political career by

Figure 4. Cat-related posts by Meral Akşener

serving in the True Path Party (DYP) and continued her career within the Nationalist Movement Party (MHP) until 2016. Although she was initially involved in the establishment of the Justice and Development Party (AKP), she later joined the MHP, believing that they continued the line of National Vision (Millî Görüş). In the November 2015 elections, as the MHP lost votes and became the fourth party represented in the parliament, Akşener became a candidate for the party leadership. However, when the MHP headquarters did not recognize this decision, internal conflicts within the party emerged, leading to Akşener's departure from the party. Subsequently, in 2017, she founded the İyi Party.

The political image constructed through Meral Akşener's social media platforms can be described as a figure who embraces everyone, operating in the supposedly masculine field of politics like a "man" but at the same time possessing the compassion of a "mother." Indeed, female politicians in male-dominated political arenas can face challenges. Female politicians may need to strike a delicate balance between conforming to societal gender expectations embedded in their cultural codes and assuming a strong leadership role in shaping their images. It can be pointed out that in this complex balancing act, Akşener sometimes conforms to stereotypes of "acting like a man" or displaying "motherly care." In the literature, this situation is considered a "gender performance," where female politicians may find themselves having to conform to gender roles. These performances can influence the impact and perceptions of female politicians on voters. The political leader, who is the central figure in political communication and directly addresses the target audience at some point, must be trustworthy for persuasion. At this point, even the gender of the source can determine the level of trust. For example, in some societies, women may not be considered as trustworthy as men in terms of leadership. Such gender-based biases can affect the credibility of female politicians. In some cases, gender biases may include perceptions that "feminine" figures are not associated with leadership and determination. These perceptions can increase doubts about the leadership abilities of female politicians. The "Political Representation of Women in Politics Research" conducted by KONDA in 2011 revealed the lack of trust in female politicians in Turkey. In this context, to exist in this masculine field, Akşener's body language, discourse, clothing, and appearance tend to align with a more masculine image.

Furthermore, when evaluating Meral Akşener's past political experiences and her position as the Chairperson of the İyi Party, it can be noted that she emphasizes nationalism, aligns with a center-right ideology, believes in the supremacy of justice and democracy, and demonstrates a sensitive stance towards women's and animal rights. It can also be stated that all these elements contribute to the construction of her political image. Moreover, it can be observed that these narratives resonate with her target audience. Particularly regarding the cat-related posts, which are the subject of this study, it can be said that Akşener shares more posts compared to other political leaders, and these posts often convey a sense of maternal care.

In this context, Meral Akşener's cat-related posts can be examined under three categories: (1) cat posts that combine maternal care with a conservative nationalist discourse, (2) cat posts aimed at strengthening her leadership image, (3) reminder posts for the needs of street cats.

In the first category of posts, Akşener addresses her target audience with a more compassionate stereotype based on the image of "motherhood," particularly in sensitive areas such as animal rights. These posts, where the maternal stereotype and compassion intersect with a nationalist conservative discourse, can be categorized as posts from February 19, 2018, June 6, 2018, August 8, 2019, August 8, 2020, and July 1, 2020.

As shown in Figure 1, Akşener frequently utilizes the maternal care emphasis and relates it to cats in her posts, which can be a part of her political image. Such posts reflect an image built upon qualities like sensitivity, compassion, and love for people. Furthermore, when combined with a nationalist discourse, these posts can be perceived as an expression of patriotism and respect for national values. Emphasizing animal rights, in particular, can help the leader be known as a sympathetic figure in society and reinforce the idea that the defenseless should be safeguarded. Such tweets can also be linked to the leader's religious beliefs, presenting her as a political figure who shares religious and moral values. Meral Akşener's cat-related posts have the ability to build her political identity while also conveying a message of empathy and love to people, potentially forming a good image in the eyes of voters. Furthermore, these posts can help to shape the leader's image as a more approachable political figure.

Meral Akşener's second series of cat-related posts, described as seeking to boost her leadership image, contains features that stand out. The tweet dated February 19, 2020, in which Akşener shares an encounter with a stray cat during her election campaign and uses it as a symbol of her relationship with the public, is particularly remarkable. This message illustrates her efforts to engage voters directly and her desire to look genuine and pleasant to people. Some of her caption lines, such as "being the voice of the silent masses" and "wearing out shoes, not seats," can be construed as criticisms of the current leadership. The leader emphasizes the insufficiency of the current administration for the people and the necessity for change with these words. Furthermore, her claim to be the people's voice displays her leadership qualities and awareness to societal challenges. Such posts have the potential to have a favorable impact on voters by stressing Meral Akşener's leadership capabilities and serving as part of a strategy to demonstrate her excellent leadership talents.

Meral Akşener's cat-related posts fall into the last group, consisting of content aimed at reminding people of the needs of street cats. Such posts serve the purpose of raising awareness among people about animal welfare and the living conditions of street cats. Through these posts, Akşener aims to encourage

Figure 5. Meral Akşener's cat-related post on February 19, 2020

society to help street animals and increase sensitivity towards animal rights. Expressions such as "A bowl of water and food" or "Let's not forget them on cold days" specifically call on people to assist street cats. These reminder posts can contribute to Akşener being perceived as a humane and compassionate figure and can be considered part of a strategy aimed at supporting animal rights advocacy.

Kemal Kılıçdaroğlu

When looking at the distribution of cat-related posts on social media platforms, the second political leader who shares the most cat-related content is Kemal Kılıçdaroğlu, the Chairman of the Republican People's Party (CHP) in Turkey. The CHP positions itself as a center-left political party based on social

Figure 6. Meral Akşener's cat-related posts

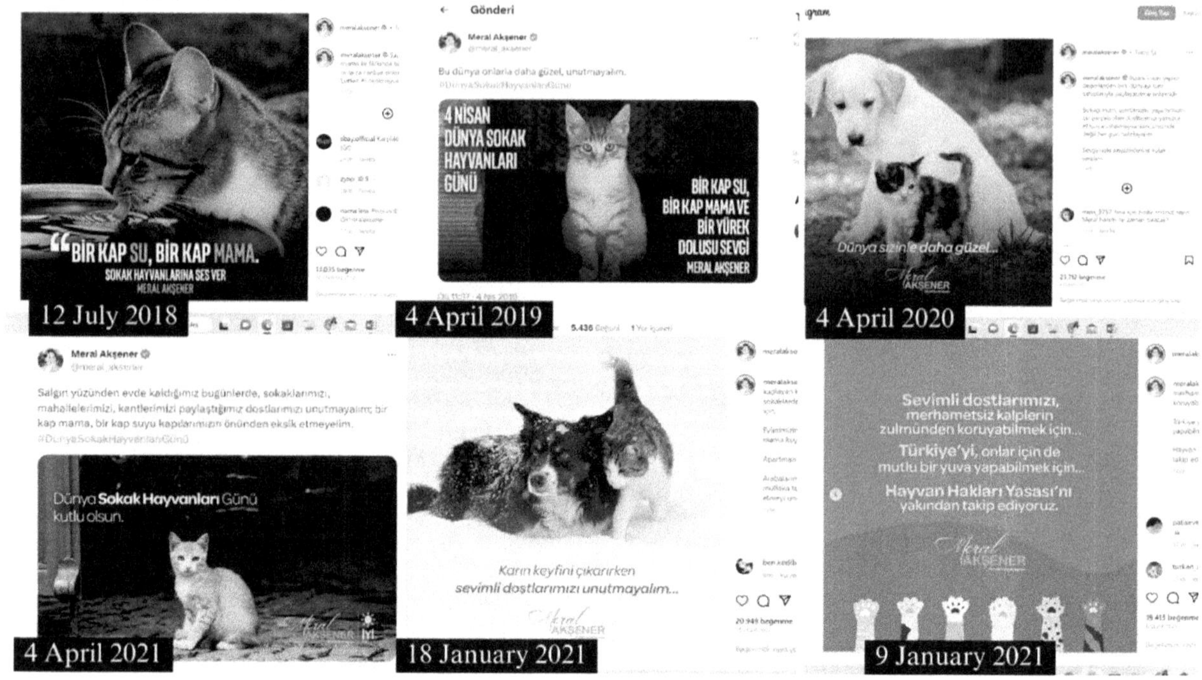

democracy and Kemalism. Kılıçdaroğlu has been the Chairman of the CHP since 2010 and is also the leader of the main opposition in Turkey. He became a Member of Parliament for the Istanbul 2nd Electoral District in the Turkish Grand National Assembly in the general elections held between 2002 and 2015. In June 2015, he was re-elected as a Member of Parliament for the Izmir 2nd Electoral District, a position he held until 2023. Kılıçdaroğlu's political image is constructed on a variety of discourses and themes, including a feeling of justice and equality, social awareness, secularism, the protection of republican values, inclusivity, and the use of kind language. Kılıçdaroğlu appeals to many elements of society by promoting justice and equality. He identifies himself as a leader who is sensitive to societal inequalities by constantly utilizing the theme of justice. Furthermore, he frequently touches on social awareness topics, paying attention to concerns like as social justice, poverty reduction, and education, showing his attempts to promote society's total welfare. He communicates his political battle to preserve and defend these ideas by constantly highlighting secularism and the protection of republican norms. A significant part of Kılıçdaroğlu's political image is built upon being an inclusive leader who embraces and protects everyone. He aims to eliminate the divisive "us vs. them" rhetoric used by those in power. He emphasizes that he embraces citizens from different ethnic backgrounds, sects, and beliefs and defends their rights. Therefore, he frequently uses a language of affection in his communication style, attempting to establish a more intimate relationship with the people and make them feel emotionally close to him. In general, when looking at Kılıçdaroğlu's personal and political background, his family origins, and his political stance, these are all essential elements forming the basis of this image. Kılıçdaroğlu's background as coming from a Zaza-Alevi family reinforces the perception that he stands against discrimination towards different sects and cultures in Turkey and that he embraces everyone. By combining these characteristics with his political identity and leadership style, he has successfully created a positive image among

Figure 7. Kemal Kılıçdaroğlu's cat-related post on February 17, 2019

the public. Therefore, strategies like Kılıçdaroğlu's cat-related posts on social media platforms can be considered as part of his political image. Additionally, Kılıçdaroğlu has a cat named "Şero" living in the CHP's Ankara Headquarters. He frequently shares posts featuring Şero, which has turned Şero into an important icon in Turkish politics. [2] On social media platforms, Kılıçdaroğlu often builds a political image that emphasizes justice and equality, generally aiming to be an inclusive and protective leader. The reflections of his political image, which is constructed around social justice, equality, social awareness, secularism, and the protection of republican values, can also be seen in his cat-related posts.

From this perspective, it can be argued that in his cat-related post on February 17, 2019, Kılıçdaroğlu employed an attention-grabbing communication strategy by combining his political image with his party's local election campaign slogan. In this post, while celebrating World Cat Day, he successfully conveyed

Figure 8. Kemal Kılıçdaroğlu's cat-related post on October 4, 2021

a political message by using CHP's slogan, "Martın sonu bahar!" (The end of March is spring!), simultaneously. This post aimed to portray Kılıçdaroğlu as both a sincere leader and a candidate committed to his party's values by combining it with his "embracing everyone" rhetoric, which emphasizes his political identity. Such posts provide an example of digital diplomacy that political leaders can utilize to strengthen their personal and party images.

Another example can be seen in the post-dated October 4, 2021, where Kılıçdaroğlu is pictured with Şero. With this post, it can be inferred that Kılıçdaroğlu aims to emphasize the image of a hardworking and responsible leader while also highlighting his love for animals and his closeness to people. In the post, Kılıçdaroğlu is shown busy at his desk in the CHP Headquarters, indicating his engagement in politics and portraying him as a responsible leader. Additionally, the pose with Şero emphasizes Kılıçdaroğlu's affection for animals and his image as an approachable, friendly leader. Such posts provide an example

Figure 9. Kemal Kılıçdaroğlu's post from March 12, 2023

of an effective communication strategy that political leaders use to strengthen various aspects of their image among voters and evoke positive emotions.

The post shared by Kılıçdaroğlu with Şero on March 12, 2023, both in its visual content and accompanying caption, vividly illustrates the contours of his political image. In the visual, Kılıçdaroğlu's presence alongside Şero conveys the leader's sincerity and human closeness. The humorous portrayal of Şero as a "social democrat cat" elevates the feline into a political symbol with a touch of wit. The caption strategically employs universal themes such as the freedom and wisdom of cats to emphasize Kılıçdaroğlu's leadership qualities and his compassion for people. The promise of coming to power reflects a societal idea by transforming canned cat food from a luxury into an accessible necessity. By emphasizing their commitment to loving everyone and highlighting the virtue of compassion, this post aims to establish an emotional connection with the voters. This share contributes to the perception of the leader as approachable and empathetic within the realm of politics, thereby enhancing his political image.

We met with our beloved Şero at the CHP Headquarters. Şero, born in 2005, is known to the public as the "social democrat cat." As you may know, cats tend to claim their space. In a cat's eyes, everything belongs to the cat. Şero has claimed this place the most. The doors are always open to him. You know, cats don't like closed spaces. He goes in and out wherever he pleases, enjoying boundless travel freedom.

He roams where he wants, rests where he desires, and lounges wherever he pleases. He does whatever he wants. Sometimes, he makes an appearance on TV beside us, and sometimes, he interrupts our meetings. He always manages to capture everyone's attention. Cats are wise creatures by nature. Şero has now become a political sage, coming and going as he pleases. Today, I shared our latest work with him. I made a promise to Şero today. When we come to power, we will make canned cat food affordable. We will love everyone wholeheartedly, whether they are with us on this journey, young or old, cats, flowers, or insects. Because compassion is a virtue.

Recep Tayyip Erdoğan

In the realm of social media, another prominent leader known for sharing cat-related content is the President of the Republic of Turkey and the Chairman of the AK Party, Recep Tayyip Erdoğan. Firstly, it can be stated that the AK Party, under Erdoğan's leadership, adheres to conservative and right-wing populist ideologies, aligning with a right-wing political orientation. Erdoğan served as Turkey's Prime Minister for 11 years from 2003 to 2014 and has been in the position of the President of Turkey for three terms. In his early political career, Erdoğan was associated with the National Salvation Party and the Welfare Party. During the 1994 local elections, an opinion poll was conducted within the Welfare Party to determine its Istanbul Metropolitan Municipality mayoral candidate, with Erdoğan and Temel Karamollaoğlu involved. Subsequently, Welfare Party Chairman Necmettin Erbakan announced that Erdoğan would be the mayoral candidate for Istanbul. Erdoğan won the elections, securing 25.19% of the vote, and became the Mayor of Istanbul Metropolitan Municipality.

On December 6, 1997, during an open-air meeting in Siirt, Erdoğan recited a portion of Ziya Gökalp's poem "Asker Duası" (Soldier's Prayer), which includes the line: "Minarets are bayonets, domes are helmets, mosques are barracks, believers are soldiers." As a result, a legal process was initiated. The reason behind this legal investigation, according to statements from the competent authorities, was the belief that Erdoğan, through his speech in Siirt, kept the tension alive between religious and non-religious segments of society. The Yargıtay (Court of Cassation) deemed this poem, as read by Erdoğan for the sake of national unity and faith, to have the nature of a "call to war." The Diyarbakır State Security Court Prosecutor's Office filed a lawsuit against Erdoğan, accusing him of "openly inciting the people to hatred and enmity based on religious and racial differences." In this case, Erdoğan was found guilty and sentenced to one year in prison, along with a heavy fine. Subsequently, considering Erdoğan's behavior and attitude during the trial, the sentence was converted to 4 months and 10 days of imprisonment and a fine. As a result of this process, Erdoğan was subject to a political ban, preventing him from participating in elections as a member of any party or as an independent candidate.

After the Welfare Party was permanently closed by the Constitutional Court, the independent members of parliament were divided into two factions known as the "traditionalists" and the "innovators." The "National Vision" faction, under the leadership of Recai Kutan, established the Felicity Party (Saadet Partisi) on July 20, 2001, while the "change-oriented" faction, led by Erdoğan, founded the Justice and Development Party (Ak Party) on August 14, 2001, with Erdoğan becoming the party's chairman. Erdoğan heralded this new era with the statement, "We have changed our shirt" (Sarıkaya, 2003). The newly formed Justice and Development Party won the 2002 elections, becoming the first party. However, Erdoğan was unable to participate in the elections and was not elected as a member of parliament due to his political ban. The 58th Government, under the leadership of Abdullah Gül, was formed after the

Figure 10. Recep Tayyip Erdoğan's cat-related post on January 6, 2023

elections. During this government's tenure, a bill was introduced to the Turkish Grand National Assembly to lift Erdoğan's political ban. Although this legislative change was approved by the Grand National Assembly of Turkey with a majority vote, President Ahmet Necdet Sezer vetoed it, citing that the law was "subjective, specific, and personal." Later, the same law was reapproved by the parliament without any changes, and President Sezer approved the legislative change this time. With the acceptance of this law, there were no legal obstacles left for Erdoğan to become a member of parliament. Following Erdoğan's election as a member of parliament, then-Prime Minister Abdullah Gül submitted his resignation to President Sezer, paving the way for Erdoğan to become the Prime Minister. Sezer entrusted Erdoğan with forming the government, and approximately three months after the general elections, the 59th Government was formed under Erdoğan's leadership. In the general elections held on July 22, 2007, the Justice and Development Party, receiving 46.6% of the votes and securing 341 members of parliament, brought Recep Tayyip Erdoğan to the Prime Minister's seat for the second time (Yüksek Seçim Kurulu, 2007). On June 12, 2011, in the 2011 general elections, the party increased its vote percentage to 49.83%, receiving a total of 21,399,082 votes nationwide and securing 327 members of parliament. This victory marked Erdoğan's third term as the head of a government (Hürriyet, 2011). As seen, the political image of Recep Tayyip Erdoğan, a long-standing influential political leader in Turkey, has been constructed based on different characteristics in various periods. However, his personal and political experiences have played a significant role in shaping this image.

In this context, one of the key factors contributing to Erdogan's political success during his leadership can be attributed to his ability to cope with challenging economic periods, particularly the 2001 economic crisis in Turkey. The country experienced an unanticipated economic slowdown as a result of the 2001 economic crisis, and under Recep Tayyip Erdoğan's leadership throughout this crisis, he was able to stabilize the economy and stimulate growth, building trust in voters. However, Erdoğan's distinct style and manner are also important factors in his political success. Erdoğan has earned the title of "man of the people" by taking a different approach than previous political leaders. Unlike previous leaders, Erdoğan repeatedly shown his capacity to develop emotional ties. This concept is demonstrated by three prominent examples: first, his emotional display and tears during his mother's death; second, his outburst at the Davos summit; and third, his words following the July 15 coup attempt. These occurrences contributed to Erdoğan establishing a true relationship with his supporters and being viewed as a member of the people. In this perspective, Erdoğan's leadership can be defined not just by his economic successes, but also by his personal style and honesty. These three occurrences aided in transforming his image from that of a politician as an inhuman figure to that of a "man of the people". This research spans the years 2018 to 2023. Erdoğan's political image is built on Islamic origins, conservative identity, nationalism, national unity, charismatic leadership, and political determination. Since the beginning of his political career, Erdoğan has been associated with a conservative identity, winning support from religious and conservative people, which led to their acceptance of his leadership. Erdoğan has been recognized with a conservative identity since the early days of his political career, gaining support from religious and conservative voters, which led to their acceptance of his leadership. Erdoğan's close relations with the Middle East and the Islamic world, along with his nationalist rhetoric and efforts to defend the interests of the Turkish nation, are also integral components of his political image. Another element is Erdoğan's political determination and willpower. Particularly during coup attempts and political crises, his resolute stance has been positively evaluated by his target audience. Finally, the implementation of social policies such as increasing social assistance and providing support to the impoverished segments of society during Erdoğan's time in power has strengthened the government's image of being sensitive to social welfare. This political image, built upon these factors, has been reflected in his cat-related posts on new media platforms in two ways. The first of these images, as seen in the January 6, 2023 post, involves the usage of "cats" as a national branding strategy to supplement the charismatic leader image. President Recep Tayyip Erdoğan shared a photo of himself praying after inaugurating Istanbul's recently rebuilt New Mosque in this post. A cat, a symbol of Istanbul, is also shown in the frame on the stairs of the mosque. The purpose of this post is to further build President Recep Tayyip Erdoğan's leadership image and concrete his perception as a charismatic leader. The appearance of the cat, which is considered a symbol of Istanbul, in the photo shot at the mosque's opening ceremony reflects Erdoğan's status as the spiritual head of Istanbul and the country. The appearance of the cat in the photograph is intended to emphasize Erdoğan's commitment to and depiction of religious and national ideals. Furthermore, the cat's popularity and reputation as a beloved animal among people creates the idea that the leader is more approachable and personable, which, when paired with his charismatic leadership abilities, creates the perception that the leader is more approachable and personable. This post tries to present the leader as someone who is truthful, charismatic, and a strong figure who is committed to both national and spiritual principles.

Another instance of this issue can be found in President Erdoğan's January 12, 2021 post. President Erdoğan aimed to build a more personable and friendlier leader image with this post-dated January 12, 2021, by sharing a cat photo with only a "Hello" greeting. Such posts might be regarded to highlight the leader's personal and compassionate side. Cats are creatures associated with charming and entertaining social media content; thus, cat-related posts assist develop a more intimate relationship with followers and depict the leader as a more approachable personality. In this context, the "Hello" message indicates the leader's willingness to communicate in a straightforward and genuine manner. Such posts are an efficient communication method for increasing the leader's popularity, effectively reaching a larger audience, and establishing an emotional connection with followers.

Figure 11. Recep Tayyip Erdoğan's cat-related post on January 12, 2021

Recep Tayyip Erdoğan's cat-related posts can be considered as part of his efforts on the political scene to show his humanitarian side. These posts intend to demonstrate that the leader is more than simply a political figure; he also acts like an ordinary person in daily life, adoring cute and human-friendly critters such as cats. Particularly, the cat-related throwback photo he shared on September 19, 2019, following the #tbt tradition, intends to reflect the human dimension of his image beyond the political sphere. Such content aims to create a more intimate and accessible impact on the leader's voter base. Additionally, by

Figure 12. President Recep Tayyip Erdoğan's cat-related post on September 19, 2019

generating sympathy at the international level, it contributes to the strategy of nation branding. These types of posts serve as an effective communication strategy used by the leader to expand his voter base, establish stronger connections with supporters, and be perceived as a more influential leader both nationally and internationally.

Recep Tayyip Erdoğan's photograph taken with his granddaughter Aybike's cat, Pıt Pıt Şeker, on September 26, 2021, can be said to aim at creating a humane image by emphasizing his family ties and personal life. In the photograph, Erdoğan is not only seen as a political leader but also as a family elder. Playing with his granddaughter's cat while reading a newspaper reflects the human aspect of his daily life and aims to show voters that he is a closer and more intimate leader. Such posts help the leader establish a warmer relationship with his voter base and add a human dimension beyond his political identity.

Temel Karamollaoğlu

The three political leaders who share the distinction of making the most cat-related posts on social media platforms are followed by Temel Karamollaoğlu, the Chairman of the Felicity Party (Saadet Partisi). The Felicity Party, led by Karamollaoğlu, tends to lean towards right-wing views and embraces the ideologies of National Vision (Milli Görüş/Erbakancılık) and Islamism. Karamollaoğlu's political image is structured

Figure 13. President Recep Tayyip Erdoğan's cat-related post on September 26, 2021

around Islamism, religiosity, nationalism, a calm and measured progressive approach. It is worth noting the following: Erdogan and Karamollaoğlu's political careers can be said to have started from a similar point due to their initial involvement in the same political parties. Both of them have actively served in parties with Islamic roots such as the National Salvation Party, the Welfare Party, and the Virtue Party. However, there is an important distinction: Erdogan continued his political career with the AK Party and has been governing Turkey through this party for many years. The AK Party is defined as a center-right and conservative party and has followed a different political line under Erdogan's leadership. On the other hand, Temel Karamollaoğlu, especially since 2018, has cooperated with the opposition front by participating in agreements such as the "Nation Alliance" (Millet İttifakı) or "Table of Six" (Altılı Masa) and has continued his political career as the leader of the Felicity Party. The Felicity Party embraces an Islamist ideology and represents a conservative line in Turkish politics. Therefore, both politicians may have a similar political background, but the direction of their political careers and their political parties are different. As a result, Karamollaoğlu's transition to the opposition front after 2018 and his inclusion in the Nation Alliance (Millet İttifakı) marked a significant turning point in his political career and led to the adoption of a different political position. In this context, it can be said that Karamollaoğlu uses cat-related posts to appear more "likable" to the target audience he addresses through these alliances. An example of this is the post-dated March 2, 2019. Karamollaoğlu announced his interview with Ruhat Mengi through a cat-related post. He included visuals of him petting a cat during the interview. This can be seen as an example of Karamollaoğlu using cat-related posts to construct his political image in a more intimate and warm manner.

Figure 14. Temel Karamollaoğlu's cat-related post on March 2, 2019

However, nuances of his own image construction within the themes of conservatism and Islam can still be observed in the relevant posts. In this context, his post-dated October 4, 2019, where Karamollaoğlu stated that "[God] entrusted them to us" serves as an example. In this particular post, it is evident that compassion and mercy towards cats are portrayed as religious values. This can be seen as an example of how Karamollaoğlu, while addressing conservative voters, associates his love for animals with religious and moral values.

Temel Karamollaoğlu's post on March 13, 2023, may appear to be a cute and lighthearted content at a superficial glance, but upon deeper examination, it can be considered as part of a communication strategy that subtly reflects support for the Nation Alliance. The characteristics of this post reflect a different approach from the cat-related posts of other political leaders. Firstly, the reference to CHP Chairman Kemal Kılıçdaroğlu and tagging Kılıçdaroğlu in the post may signify an affiliation with the Nation Alliance. This could imply the support or collaboration of Temel Karamollaoğlu with this alliance. Additionally, Karamollaoğlu freely allowing his cat to roam around the Saadet Party General Headquarters and entering Karamollaoğlu's room could convey the message that the leader can easily move in political spaces and communicate with everyone. This might be an effort to strengthen the leader's image as approachable and down-to-earth. At the end of the post, there is the expression, "I think I agree with Şero on the issue

Figure 15. Temel Karamollaoğlu's cat-related post on October 4, 2019

of canned food." This could reflect a message of partnership or solidarity not only with cats but also with those in need of assistance in general.

Ahmet Davutoğlu

One other political leader who shares a significant number of cat-related posts on social media is Ahmet Davutoğlu. Davutoğlu is a former Minister of Foreign Affairs, former Deputy Prime Minister, the 2nd Chairman of the AK Party, and the 26th Prime Minister of Turkey. He served as the Chairman of the AK Party and as the Prime Minister from 2014 to 2016. Prior to these roles, he held the position of Minister of Foreign Affairs in the 60th and 61st Turkish Governments, both of which were established by Recep Tayyip Erdoğan between 2009 and 2014. He worked as a foreign policy advisor to Erdoğan, who was Prime Minister at the time, and Abdullah Gül from 2003 until 2009. On May 22, 2016, he resigned as Prime Minister and Chairman of the AK Party. Davutoğlu's resignation as Prime Minister is regarded as an important turning point in Turkish politics, and it is linked to the "Pelican Files" investigation. Tensions between Ahmet Davutoğlu and Recep Tayyip Erdoğan caused the process that led to Davutoğlu's departure. In 2016, the Central Decision and Executive Board (MKYK) of the AK Party, wanting more authority in appointing provincial and district chairmen, had taken this authority from Davutoğlu, which had led to frequent rumors in the media that Davutoğlu would resign. Additionally, there were rumors of differing views between Davutoğlu and Erdoğan on Turkey's political future and intra-party governance,

Figure 16. Temel Karamollaoğlu's cat-related post on March 13, 2023

leading to tensions between the two political figures. A critical phase of Davutoğlu's resignation process was a private meeting between Recep Tayyip Erdoğan and Ahmet Davutoğlu. As a result of this meeting, instead of resigning directly, Davutoğlu decided to take the AK Party to an extraordinary congress and it was agreed that he would not be a candidate for the party leadership again. Consequently, Davutoğlu announced his resignation on May 5, 2016. This process was a significant event reflecting internal dynamics and intra-party conflicts in Turkish politics and is recorded as one of the firsts in Turkey's political history. In 2019, he founded the Future Party, which is positioned as a party that embraces liberal conservatism, pro-European Union stances, and parliamentarism. It is inclined towards center-right ideology. Davutoğlu, due to his stance against Erdoğan during the AK Party era and his political election campaigns, is thought to have wanted to attract both the audience he appealed to during the AK Party era to his new party's voter base and to gain support from opposition parties, referred to as the "Table of Six" and the "Nation Alliance," in his new target audience. Especially given Ahmet Davutoğlu's long

Figure 17. Temel Karamollaoğlu's cat-related post on April 4, 2020

years of collaboration with Recep Tayyip Erdoğan under the AK Party umbrella, it can be challenging for him to reach out to a new voter base as an opposition leader. Voters may hesitate to accept someone they previously saw in power as an opposition leader. Therefore, Davutoğlu creating a more sympathetic and amicable image and establishing a new political identity can help him be more effective with voters. This is where cat-related posts can be seen as contributing to Davutoğlu's ability to appear more likable to his audience. Hence, these posts may be part of Davutoğlu's new political strategy.

In this context, on April 4, 2020, Davutoğlu shared the same cat-related video content on four different platforms with the caption "We love the created because of the Creator. Happy #WorldStrayAnimalsDay." It can be assumed that through this content, Davutoğlu aimed to present himself as more sympathetic to his voters. While trying to maintain his former voter base, he also aimed to influence new ones. In the related cat-related post, Davutoğlu is seen with his wife Sare Davutoğlu giving water and food to a street cat and petting it. Additionally, Davutoğlu emphasizes the idea that "these beings are entrusted to us by

God, and we should love the created because of the Creator," thus incorporating moderate conservative discourse into the content. This indicates that Davutoğlu is attempting to construct his political image as a more humane, religious, and socially responsible leader.

Ali Babacan

Ali Babacan, the Founder Chairman of the DEVA Party, is another political leader who shares cat-related content most frequently on social media platforms. Similar to Davutoğlu, Babacan worked within the AK Party under the leadership of Recep Tayyip Erdoğan for many years and then founded his own political party after parting ways with the AK Party in 2019. Babacan served as Turkey's Foreign Minister and Economy Minister for 13 years, from 2002 to 2015. The rift between Babacan and the AK Party dates back to 2010, and it can be attributed to differences in economic approaches between Erdoğan and Babacan. After his resignation process, Babacan, alongside the DEVA Party, adopted a stance against Erdoğan and the AK Party. He aimed to attract his former voters to his new party while also creating positive associations in the minds of the voters on the new opposition side by constructing an image quite different from his previous one. In this context, it can be said that Babacan's image is built upon themes such as emphasizing economic and financial stability, improving diplomacy and foreign policy relations, maintaining a calm and composed demeanor, promoting advanced democracy and judicial independence. Although the DEVA Party's ideology is believed to be center-right, Babacan hopes to appeal to opposition voters now that he is a member of the opposition. As a result, his party can be described as more moderate than extreme. Babacan's decision to back Kemal Kılıçdaroğlu's presidential campaign against Erdoğan's within the Nation Alliance (Millet İttifakı) in 2023 is a significant step that underlines his political position and aspirations. In this approach, Babacan contributes significantly to gaining a new voter base and transforming his formerly unfavorable image into a good one. Babacan's political image, electoral speeches, and social media posts reflect all of these situations. It should be mentioned that Babacan employs a variety of techniques to attract both existing and new voters and establish a positive image for himself, such as light-hearted content on social media platforms such as cat-related messages. These techniques reflect Babacan's political identity as well as the DEVA Party's center-right ideology, while also assisting him in projecting himself as a more moderate and conciliatory leader.

In this context, consider Babacan's December 5, 2020 post, in which he uploaded a photo of himself with his cat and stated, "There have been those who wanted to see our guest cat in the background of today's broadcast." Let's meet our cat, Çakıl," has been included in the sample. During this live broadcast, Babacan spoke with Ruşen Çakır, and viewers saw his cat, Çakıl, come in the frame at various points. The post, which pointed viewers to the relevant broadcast's recording link and included a photo of Babacan with Çakıl, can be called a communication technique. Such posts could be intended to represent Babacan as a more intimate, kind, and affectionate leader. Furthermore, these posts might be considered as part of Babacan's efforts to reach out to a broader audience and influence other voting groups.

Figure 18. Ali Babacan's cat-related post on December 5, 2020

CONCLUSION

This research looks at how digitalization and communication technology have changed and transformed public diplomacy, especially during the 2000s. The advancement of information and communication technologies has had an impact not only on interpersonal communication but also on communication between nations and states. A new phenomena known as digital public diplomacy has evolved in this setting, combining traditional diplomacy with digital communication tools and social media platforms. Social media platforms have evolved into powerful tools for politicians to reach out to voters and create their public image. These new platforms have become an essential aspect of diplomatic communication, even being seen as a new diplomatic process.

The purpose of this research is to look into how the "cat" image utilized by political leaders on social media platforms in the context of the Republic of Turkey's 2023 Presidential elections has been integrated into digital diplomacy and how it has established an image among voters. In recent years, politicians have embraced this new approach by posting "cat-themed" content, particularly on social media sites. Cats are not only adorable and appealing all over the world, but they are also extremely popular in Turkey. Cats have a special position in Turkish society and have played an essential role in religious and cultural contexts, it has been highlighted. It has been argued that politicians employ cats as part of their national branding strategy in this regard. According to this study, cat-related posts are utilized for a variety of goals, including presenting a warm and welcoming image among politicians' followers and garnering public attention.

This study looks at how well-known political figures in Turkey have shaped and bolstered their political personas between 2018 and 2023, especially with cat-related social media posts. These posts have been examined using content analysis while considering the socio-political setting. It has come to light those leaders like Recep Tayyip Erdoğan, Temel Karamollaoğlu, Ahmet Davutoğlu, Ali Babacan, Kemal Kılıçdaroğlu, and Meral Akşener want to give their fans the impression that they are a more personal and approachable kind of leader through adorable and humanitarian content.

Recep Tayyip Erdoğan's cat-related posts have shown him as a charismatic leader who is loyal to religious principles and is seen as a people's leader. He also sought to project a humanitarian image by highlighting his family ties and personal life. Temel Karamollaoğlu has emphasized religiosity, nationalism, and human values in his cat-themed posts in order to position himself as a more personal leader. Ahmet Davutoğlu has utilized animal welfare to establish a humanitarian image, which he has combined with moderate conservatism. Ali Babacan has utilized cat-themed messages to reach out to old supporters and attract new supporters. Kemal Kılıçdaroğlu's cat-related posts have attempted to create a warmer and more intimate leadership image, attempting to make an emotional connection with people and humanize his political identity. In her cat-related posts, Meral Akşener, on the other hand, has highlighted both conservative and human principles in order to seem as a more intimate and caring leader. Her content has also been heavily influenced by nationalism.

In conclusion, political leaders in Turkey have embraced cat-themed posts as an effective communication tactic to define their political identities beyond simply offering cute stuff. These blogs attempt to showcase these leaders' humane and caring qualities, fit with national and religious ideals, and reach a diverse variety of voters. In this light, cat-themed posts have played an essential role as a communication tool in modern politics, helping to the creation of political images.

Future research can look at similar communication tactics used by political leaders in different countries, analyze their impact on voters, and investigate the impact of digital public diplomacy on international relations. Furthermore, additional research can be undertaken on how political leaders use digital media platforms efficiently and their effects on political success. More research will be needed to understand how political leaders' usage of social media contributes to democratic processes and public dialogue. Furthermore, in an era of fast evolving digital communication technologies, it is critical to watch the shifting effects of social media on political communication and diplomacy. Providing current data and analysis on how new platforms and communication technologies affect political leaders' strategies will be a significant addition to future research.

REFERENCES

Aranceta-Reboredo, O. (2022). And What About the Animals? A Case Study Comparison Between China's Panda Diplomacy and Australia's Koala Diplomacy. *Animal Ethics Review*, *2*(1), 78–93.

Buhmann, A., & Ingenhoff, D. (2015). Advancing the Country Image Construction From a Public Relations Perspective: From Model to Measurement. *Journal of Communication Management (London)*, *19*(1), 62–80. doi:10.1108/JCOM-11-2013-0083

Cassiday, J., & Johnson, E. (2010). Cassiday, J., & Johnson, E. (2010). Putin, putiniana and the question of a post-soviet cult of personality. *Slavonic and East European Review, 88*(4), 681-707. Von https://www.jstor.org/stable/41061898abgerufen

Castells, M. (2005). *Enformasyon Çağı: Ekonomi, Toplum ve Kültür: Ağ Toplumunun Yükselişi* (E. Kılıç, Trans.). İstanbul Bilgi Üniversitesi Yayınları.

Cushing, N., & Markwell, K. (2009). Platypus diplomacy: Animal gifts in international relations. *Journal of Australian Studies*, *33*(3), 255–271. doi:10.1080/14443050903079664

Dolea, A. (2015). The Need for Critical Thinking in Country Promotion. In J. L'Etang (Ed.), *The Routledge Handbook of Critical Public Relations* (pp. 274–288). Routledge, Taylor & Francis Group.

Ekşi, M. (2016). Türk Dış Politikasında Diplomasinin Yeni İletişimsel Boyutları ve Mekanizmaları: Dijital Diplomasi. In B. Cankurtaran-Sunar (Ed.), *Uluslararası İlişkilere Disiplinlerarası Bir Yaklaşım: Uluslararası İletişim Perspektifi*. Röle Akademik Yayıncılık.

Fitpatrick, K. R. (2007). Advancing the New Public Diplomacy: A Public Relations Perspective. *The Hague Journal of Diplomacy*, *2*(3), 187–211. doi:10.1163/187119007X240497

Fitzpatrick, K. R., Fullerton, J., & Kendrick, A. (2013). Public Relations and Public Diplomacy: Conceptual and Practical Connections. *The Public Relations Journal*, *7*(4), 1–21.

Gilboa, E. (2016). Public Diplomacy. In G. Mazzoleni, K. G. Barnhurst, K. Ikeda, R. Maia, & H. Wessler (Eds.), *The International Encyclopedia of Political Communication* (pp. 1–9). American Cancer Society., doi:10.1002/9781118541555.wbiepc232

Gould, S. J. (1979). Mickey Mouse meets Konrad Lorenz. *Natural History*, *88*(5), 30–36.

Hartig, F. (2013). Panda Diplomacy: The Cutest Part of China's Public Diplomacy. *The Hague Journal of Diplomacy*, 49-78. doi:10.1163/1871191X-12341245

Huang, Z., & Wang, R. (2020). Panda Engagement in China's Digital Public Diplomacy. *Asian Journal of Communication*, *30*(2), 1–23. doi:10.1080/01292986.2020.1725075

Huang, Z. A., & Wang, R. (2019). The New "Cat" of the Internet: China's Panda Diplomacy on Twitter. *Advances in Public Relations and Communication Management*, 69-85. doi:10.1108/S2398-391420190000004006

Hürriyet. (2011). *2011 Yılı Türkiye Genel Seçim Sonuçları*. Abgerufen am 20. August 2023 von Hürriyet: https://www.hurriyet.com.tr/secim2011/default.html

Ingenhoff, D., White, C., Buhmann, A., & Kiousis, S. (2019). *Bridging Disciplinary Perspectives of Country Image, Reputation, Brand, and Identity*. Routledge, Taylor & Franscis Group.

Keohane, R. O., & Nye, J. S. (2012). *Power and Interdependence*. Longman.

KONDA. (2011). Abgerufen am 16. August 2023 von https://konda.com.tr/uploads/2011-04-konda-siyasette-kadin-temsili-raporu-2ad240366fc77a679627647b8504cb4c44bfb56d04a461fd1e0c6593b2777af9.pdf

Lorenz, K. (1943). Die angeborenen Formen möglichen Verhaltens. *Zeitschrift für Tierpsychologie*, *5*(2), 235–409. doi:10.1111/j.1439-0310.1943.tb00655.x

Melissen, J. (2008). The New Public Diplomacy: Between Theory and Pratice. In J. Melissen (Ed.), *The New Public Diplomacy: Soft Power in International Relations* (pp. 3–28). Palgrave Macmillan.

Neumann, I., & Leira, H. (2015). Beastly Diplomacy. *The Hague Journal of Diplomacy*, *12*(4), 337–359. doi:10.1163/1871191X-12341355

Nye, J. S. Jr. (2008). Public Diplomacy and Soft Power. *The Annals of the American Academy of Political and Social Science*, *616*(1), 94–109. doi:10.1177/0002716207311699

Olympic Committee. (2022). *Beijing 2022: The Mascot*. Abgerufen am 17. November 2023 von https://olympics.com/en/olympic-games/beijing-2022/mascot

Sarıkaya, M. (2003). *Millî görüş gömleğimizi değiştirdik*. Abgerufen am 16. September 2023 von Sabah Gazetesi: https://arsiv.sabah.com.tr/2003/05/28/s1812.html

Schaller, G. B. (1994). *The Last Panda*. University of Chicago Press.

Snow, N., & Taylor, P. M. (2009). *Routledge Handbook of Public Diplomacy*. Routledge.

Songster, E. (2018). *Panda Nation: The Construction and Conservation of China's Modern Icon*. Oxford University Press. doi:10.1093/oso/9780199393671.001.0001

Uysal, N., & Schroeder, J. (2019). Turkey's Twitter Public Diplomacy: Towards a "new" cult of personality. *Public Relations Review*, *45*(5), 101837. doi:10.1016/j.pubrev.2019.101837

Van Dijk, J. (2018). *Ağ Toplumu*. Epsilon.

van Ham, P. (2008). Power, Public Diplomacy, and The Pax Americana. In J. Melissen (Ed.), *The New Public Diplomacy: Soft Power in International Relations* (pp. 46–66). Palgrave Macmillan.

von Twickel, N. (2012). *Puppy Diplomacy: Putin Gets Pets Wrapped With a Bow*. Abgerufen am 19. November 2023 von The Moscow Times: https://www.themoscowtimes.com/2012/08/02/puppy-diplomacy-putin-gets-pets-wrapped-with-a-bow-a16752

Wang, Y. (2008). Public Diplomacy and the Rise of Chinese Soft Power. *The Annals of the American Academy of Political and Social Science*, *616*(1), 257–273. doi:10.1177/0002716207312757

Xing, Y. (2010). *China's Panda Diplomacy: The Power of being Cute*. University of Southern California.

Yıldırım, B. (2015). İçerik Çözümlemesi Yönteminin Tarihsel Gelişimi Uygulama Alanları ve Aşamaları. In B. Yıldırım (Ed.), *İletişim Araştırmalarında Yöntemler*. Literatürk Academia.

Yıldırım, U. (2021). Çin'in Panda Diplomasisi. *Bölgesel Araştırmalar Dergisi*, *5*(1), 48–86.

Yücel, G. (2016). Dijital Diplomasi. *TRT Akademi Dergisi, 1*(2).

Yüksek Seçim Kurulu. (2007). *Türkiye Geneli Partilerin Kazandıkları Milletvekilleri Sayıları*. Von Yüksek Seçim Kurulu: https://web.archive.org/web/20071030213029/http://www.ysk.gov.tr/ysk/docs/2007secim/turkiye/milletvekilisayisi.htm abgerufen

Zaharna, R. S. (2000). Intercultural Communication and International Public Relations: Exploring Parallels. *Communication Quarterly*, *42*(1), 85–100. doi:10.1080/01463370009385582

Zaharna, R. S. (2016). Beyond the Individualism-collectivism Divide to Relationalism: Explicating Cultural Assumptions In The Concept of "Relationships". *Communication Theory*, *26*(2), 190–211. doi:10.1111/comt.12058

ENDNOTES

1 On November 4, 2023, during the 38th Ordinary Congress of the Republican People's Party (CHP), he lost the election to his opponent Özgür Özel, concluding his tenure as the leader of the party. On November 8, 2023, he officially handed over his duties. However, this situation does not directly impact the study as it falls outside the timeframe of the research.

2 Furthermore, Şero also has a Twitter account. However, since this study focuses on the posts of politicians within the sample, the analysis of Şero's posts could be the subject of another research.

Chapter 15
An Examination of Diplomatic Entities' Digital Communication:
A Case Study of the U.S. Embassy in Bishkek's Use of Instagram

Onur Kaya
Southern Federal University, Russia

ABSTRACT

In today's world, technology has become central to human life, leading to the popularity of social media applications. Consequently, the interdisciplinary concept of communication has evolved and transformed. This transformation has rapidly integrated diplomatic practices into the digital world, contributing to the expansion and implementation of the concept of public diplomacy. States and non-state actors have actively used social media applications to bring cultural diplomacy activities, one of the tools of public diplomacy, into the digital realm to influence individuals and communities, change negative perceptions into positive ones, shape an image, create attraction, or convey desired messages. In this study, cultural activities shared on the Instagram official account of the U.S. Embassy in Bishkek (@usembassybishkek) are examined in the context of cultural diplomacy. The findings are evaluated based on the shared posts, interaction results, participation, and conclusions are drawn.

INTRODUCTION

With globalization and technology, the importance of communication has increased in the changing world. Communication practices of today's societies have undergone significant changes. For instance, in the past, people had limited communication using home telephones and information transmission was delayed accordingly. In contrast, today, people can communicate anytime, anywhere using mobile phones. Traditional communication methods have been replaced by email and instant messaging applications that allow individuals to communicate with anyone they desire at any time and place. Technology has not only affected individual communication but has also made significant advancements in mass

DOI: 10.4018/979-8-3693-0855-4.ch015

communication. Social media applications play a crucial role in mass communication, allowing governments, non-governmental organizations, politicians, institutions, celebrities, influencers, and others to communicate with the masses from anywhere and at any time. Another advantage of technology is the cost-effective access it provides to the target audience. In this context, the concept of public relations has rapidly evolved with technology, leading to new approaches and practices, expanding the application field, and making it easier. The widespread use of social media has led governments and non-state actors to extend their public relations activities to social media. They create positive perceptions they want to create through social media content, seeking to influence emotions, thoughts, and ideas or ideologies, and shape individuals and societies. Public relations activities conducted by governments or non-state actors are contextually related to public diplomacy activities. Public diplomacy primarily aims to create positive perceptions and attraction on societies or individuals targeted for activities. As defined by Edmund Gullion, whose first used the concept of public diplomacy and regarded it as "the transnational flow of information and ideas," public diplomacy addresses the influence of public attitudes on the formulation and implementation of foreign policies (Kocabıyık, 2019)

The Concept of Public Relations

There are several definitions regarding the field of public relations. The general and widely accepted definitions, as presented by Aşkun, are as follows: "The actions of an enterprise, union, public organization, or a similar organization to adapt itself to its surroundings and interpret its situation to the public, to establish and maintain consistent and efficient relationships with specific sections of the public such as customers, employees, or partners, and the actions taken to maintain these relationships" (Aşkun, 1990, p.8).

The modern definition of public relations was first formulated by Edward Bernays, often referred to as the father of public relations, at the beginning of the 20th century. He defined public relations as "a management function that includes the plans, procedures, policies, and behaviours created by managers to gain the public's interest" (Yıldırım, 2020, p.138).

To understand what public relations is, it's essential to delve into its history. The question of what public relations is has been addressed in the works of both Bernays and Lee in the past. While modern researchers acknowledge that public relations have a somewhat "tarnished" image in the eyes of the public, Lee's "Declaration of Principles" was based on ethical values and included various functions of public relations. Lee argued that public relations provide information and do not simply engage in promotional activities for customers (Yıldırım, 2020, p.135).

Although public relations are rooted in communication sciences and draws from various social science disciplines, it has a broad application field that extends beyond communication. In the context of international relations, public diplomacy studies and their concepts and tools are closely related to public relations (Özkan, 2009, p.14). Public relations activities encompass diverse areas, including media relations, crisis management, lobbying, reputation management, promotion, marketing, organization, and communication. As communication methods have evolved and technology has advanced, public relations has adapted to these changes, giving rise to new concepts, practices, and approaches.

For example, when examining public diplomacy studies within the context of international relations, it becomes evident how closely related they are to the discipline of public relations. The wide range of fields in which public relations operates, such as crisis management, reputation management, issue management, event management, lobbying, image management, sponsorship, and social responsibility practices, makes it challenging to arrive at a single, shared definition (Özkan, 2009, p.14).

According to Bıçakçı (2000), the concept of public relations is fundamentally rooted in the practice and empirical aspects of public relations as a management function. This field is primarily characterized by individual skills and abilities, which often take precedence over the scientific aspect. Although public relations draw from various scientific fields such as psychology, sociology, and communication, in terms of both theory and practice, it is more of an art. Some argue that public relations are on its way to becoming an independent science.

The multifaceted nature of the field of public relations allows for a broad range of applications, and the development of technology has facilitated its implementation due to the wider reach to the masses.

The Concept of Soft Power

In the realm of diplomacy, there are three fundamental sources of power. This study focuses on the element of "soft power." The use of soft power is essentially about engaging in activities that lead to gains against a target country where diplomatic pressure is applied, all based on the country's willingness and consent. Public diplomacy activities can be seen as a tool of soft power, aiming to shape the public opinions of target countries by relying on sympathy and appeal.

According to Kömür (2020), "soft power" is the ability to achieve one's objectives by attracting others to their side without resorting to brute force or financial incentives. Soft power relies on the appeal of a country's values and its ability to influence and shape the desires of others. In essence, it means achieving the results you desire while also persuading others to want the same results, all without coercion.

The relationship between the use of soft power and cultural diplomacy, which serves as a practical tool for public diplomacy, can be described as follows. While soft power is a concept related to the practice of diplomacy, its application can be seen in the use of cultural diplomacy as a means of achieving these objectives. States that take cultural diplomacy seriously establish various institutions to strengthen their presence and synchronize their policies in this field. By the late 1980s, Joseph Nye coined the term "soft power" to encompass all public diplomacy activities, including cultural diplomacy, as a means to gain influence in the international arena, with a focus on obtaining what a state desires through non-coercive means (Ünalmış, 2019, p.138).

The Concept of Public Diplomacy

The concept of public diplomacy was first introduced by Edward R. Murrow, who served as the United States' Deputy President during the Kennedy administration. According to Murrow, public diplomacy encompasses not only efforts involving foreign governments but also interactions that target civil society organizations and civilians. These interactions represent not only the government's views but also various personal perspectives (Altincik and Koçak, 2022, p.139).

In simpler terms, public diplomacy can be described as a comprehensive set of communication and public relations activities aimed at influencing foreign governments in achieving predefined goals by positively shaping the perceptions and attractiveness of a country's public opinion. The term "public diplomacy" was first coined in 1965 by Edmund Gullion, the Dean of the Fletcher School of Law and Diplomacy at Tufts University. Gullion provided a broad definition of public diplomacy as follows: "It has to do with the influence of public attitudes on the formation and execution of foreign policies. It encompasses dimensions of international relations beyond traditional diplomacy; the range of institutions, processes, and information by which a nation conducts its relations with other nations – ranging from 'cultured' efforts to bring information to an interested foreign public, in an attempt to improve understanding and advance national objectives, to the 'new' and 'old' media efforts that support international broadcasting" (Ünal, 2016: 16).

In the context of public diplomacy, there are several tools available for conducting diplomatic activities, including:

- Education Diplomacy
- Faith Diplomacy
- Health Diplomacy
- Sports Diplomacy
- Citizen Diplomacy
- Culinary Diplomacy
- Tourism Diplomacy
- Cultural Diplomacy

Cultural diplomacy is one of the most frequently used tools for influencing international public opinion in the execution of public diplomacy activities. It's important to note that public diplomacy activities are often considered a form of "soft power" in the realm of diplomacy.

Cultural Diplomacy as a Tool of Public Diplomacy

Culture is the fundamental foundation of societies. It encompasses a nation's or a community's religion, customs, way of life, moral structure, and is regarded as a cultural heritage passed down from generation to generation. Because cultural diplomacy has a wide range of application, it is considered an effective tool for creating positive perceptions and sympathy among broad populations in the implementing country.

In the context of cultural diplomacy, implementation can cover various aspects such as the history, language, archaeological richness, art, and education of the implementing country. Cultural diplomacy can also serve as a platform for demonstrating the economic and political power of the implementing countries. According to Yağmurlu (2019), nation-states have tried to showcase their differences, levels of development, and reputation through cultural diplomacy. In the 17th and 18th centuries, French culture played a dominant role in the European landscape. During the colonial era, Western countries made efforts to disseminate their cultures to the entire world. After World War II, the United States entered the field of cultural diplomacy and initiated the Marshall Plan for the reconstruction of Europe and Japan. The years of the Cold War were significant for cultural diplomacy, as, in a bipolar world order led by the United States and the USSR, both superpowers sought to showcase their soft power to the world through exhibitions, radio programs, student exchanges, music, and other cultural elements.

The connection between cultural diplomacy and public relations can be established through the fact that all these activities are executed using communication strategies and channels. Therefore, cultural diplomacy and public relations are intertwined as they both involve the use of communication methods and channels.

Research Questions

This study aims to address the following main research questions:

1. In what area does the U.S. Embassy in Bishkek emphasize its cultural diplomacy activities on its Instagram account (@usembassybishkek)?
2. Does the U.S. Embassy in Bishkek conduct cultural diplomacy activities on its Instagram account (@usembassybishkek)? If so, to what extent does it receive engagement?

Data Collection Method

In this study, data was collected through document analysis and the examination of cultural activities shared on the Instagram account (@usembassybishkek) of the U.S. Embassy in Bishkek over the past six months. The findings were obtained by examining these activities and used to draw conclusions.

Classification and Analysis of Data

The collected data was classified within the scope of cultural diplomacy activities and their application areas. The analysis will be conducted using a "content analysis" approach, and the findings will be used to make conclusions.

Findings

As of the time of the research, the @usembassybishkek Instagram page had a total of 1,519 posts and 103,000 followers. All findings of this study were based on a review of cultural activities shared on the Instagram account (@usembassybishkek) of the U.S. Embassy over the past six months. The results of the examination are as follows:

A total of 16 different content categories were identified in cultural diplomacy activities, including Language Teaching (10), Afro-American History (5), Book Translation (2), Important Days (14), Historical & Cultural Competitions (3), Student Exchange Program (7), Teacher Exchange Program (3), Language Competition (2), Native Language Competition (1), Native Language Activity (1), Scholarship Program (13), Citizen Exchange Program (4), Cultural Elements (2), Art Activities (5), Song & Music Competitions (2), and Other Cultural Activities (2). In total, 76 content posts related to cultural diplomacy were created and shared.

The content category "Language Teaching" received the highest number of likes in the field of cultural diplomacy, with 10 posts. The total likes and comments reached 38,845 likes and 1,687 comments.

The content category "Important Days" had the highest number of posts with 14. The total likes and comments for this category were 19,835 likes, 727 comments, and 10,235 live stream views for the New Year's live broadcast.

The content category with the lowest likes and comments in the context of cultural diplomacy was "Song Competition," with only 2 posts. It received 557 likes and 27 comments.

Other totals for content categories include Book Translation (1,972 likes and 95 comments), Historical & Cultural Competitions (2,328 likes and 69 comments), Student Exchange Program (7,624 likes, 247 comments, and 28,870 live stream views), Teacher Exchange Program (1,494 likes and 21 comments),

Language Competition (836 likes and 10 comments), Native Language Competition (980 likes and 17 comments), Native Language Activity (1,370 likes and 327 comments), Scholarship Program (9,249 likes and 260 comments, with 24,035 live stream views), Citizen Exchange Program (1,944 likes and 30 comments), Cultural Elements (6,105 likes and 147 comments), Art Activities (2,887 likes and 142 comments), and Other Cultural Activities (732 likes and 6 comments).

The data gathered quantitatively from the past six months of cultural diplomacy-related posts are as described above. These findings will be analyzed to draw conclusions in the results section of the study.

CONCLUSION

Based on the research questions, the following conclusions were drawn from this study, which examined the cultural diplomacy-related posts on the official Instagram account (@usembassybishkek) of the U.S. Embassy in Bishkek over the past six months:

- Examination of the findings revealed that the U.S. Embassy in Bishkek actively shares posts on Instagram, with a significant and variable frequency based on the period.
- The primary reason for the highest engagement in the posts was identified as the sympathy and admiration for the embassy staff featured in the content. Throughout the shared content, young people and women were highlighted, and their value was emphasized.
- It was observed that the general interaction of followers with the posts was predominantly through likes and views, while the interaction involving comments was relatively low.
- In line with cultural diplomacy efforts, the embassy staff took the lead in the posts, engaging with followers in Kyrgyz and making efforts to establish a friendly connection. It was observed that they received reciprocation from their followers.
- A significant portion of the followers displayed a high motivation to embrace American sympathy and attractiveness, along with a strong desire to visit the United States.
- In the comment interactions, followers tended to use emojis more frequently to express their feelings and thoughts, and the number of comments was significantly lower compared to the number of likes. This created the perception that the activities did not fully motivate engagement.

In response to the research questions:

1. Does the U.S. Embassy in Bishkek conduct cultural diplomacy activities on its Instagram account (@usembassybishkek)? If so, to what extent does it receive engagement?

Yes, it conducts cultural diplomacy activities. While the engagement is moderate to low based on the existing number of followers, it is evident that there is an effort to establish a connection with followers through sympathy.

2. In what area does the U.S. Embassy in Bishkek emphasize its cultural diplomacy activities on its Instagram account (@usembassybishkek)?

The U.S. Embassy in Bishkek primarily focuses its cultural diplomacy activities on Scholarship Programs (13), Language Teaching (10), and exchange programs (Student Exchange Program (7), Teacher Exchange Program (3), Citizen Exchange Program (4)

REFERENCES

Ahmet Nafiz, Ü. (2019). Yumuşak Gücün Tesis Edilmesinde Kültürel Diplomasinin Önemi ve Bir Uygulayıcı Olarak Yunus Emre Enstitüsü. *Bilig - Turk DunyasI Sosyal Bilimler Dergisi, 91*, 137–159.

Altincik, H., & Koçak, P. G. (2022). *Kamu Diplomasısı ve Halkla İlişkilerde Kullanılan Araçlar.* Kamu Diplomasisi Alanında Çalışan Akademisyenlerin Değerlendirmeleri Van Yüzüncü Yıl Üniversitesi İktisadi ve İdari Bilimler Fakültesi.

Aşkun. (1990). Eskişehir Anadolu Üniversitesi iktisadi ve idari Bilimler Fak. Academic Press.

Kocabiyik. (2019). Değişen Diplomasi Anlayışı, Kamu Diplomasisi ve Türkiye. Avrasya Etüdleri.

Kömür, G. (2020). Yumuşak Güç Unsuru Olarak Kamu Diplomasisi. *International Journal of Politics and Security, 2*(3), 89-115.

Özkan, A. (2009). Halkla İlişkiler Yönetimi. İstanbul: Sosyal Yayınlar.

Ünal. (2016). Uluslararası Stratejik İletişim Yönetimi Olarak Kamu Diplomasisinin Ülke İmajına Etkileri. İstanbul Ticaret Üniversitesi Sosyal Bilimler Enstitüsü.

Yağmurlu, A. (2019). *Kültürel Diplomasi: Kuram ve Pratikteki Çerçevesi.* Ankara Üniversitesi İletişim Fakültesi.

Yildirim, A. (2020). Halkla İlişkilerin Kavramsal Tanımlamaları Üzerine Bir İnceleme. Jandarma ve Sahil Güvenlik Akademisi, Türkiye. *İletişim Çalışmaları Dergisi, 6*(2), 133-150. doi:10.17932/IAU.ICD.2015.006/icd_v06i2001

Chapter 16
Exploring the Associations Between Acculturative Stress, Well-Being, Life Satisfaction, and Social Media Use Among Turkish Refugees in Norway

Ali Acilar
Independent Researcher, Norway

ABSTRACT

The main aim of this study is to explore the associations between acculturative stress, well-being, life satisfaction, and social media use among Turkish refugees in Norway. This study examines the results of an online survey of Turkish refugees living in Norway. The snowball sampling method was used to recruit respondents. A correlational analysis was used to explore the associations between variables. The study found that the level of acculturative stress was negatively correlated with both the level of well-being and the level of satisfaction with life. The level of well-being was found to be positively correlated with the level of satisfaction with life. The female refugee participants reported higher levels of acculturative stress than males. Another finding of the study was that being employed was positively correlated with the level of well-being. No significant correlation was observed between social media use intensity and other variables.

INTRODUCTION

A considerable number of people have had to leave their countries in recent years. According to the United Nations Refugee Agency UNHCR, there were 89.3 million forcibly displaced people worldwide at the end of 2021 (UNHCR, 2022). The refugee crisis has been one of the global issues in the last decades, and the number of refugees has been increasing. After the Russian invasion of Ukraine, the refugee crisis came to the fore again.

DOI: 10.4018/979-8-3693-0855-4.ch016

Norway has become a country of immigration in recent decades (Sam et al., 2017). In 2022, Norway's immigrant population was reported as 819,356 by Statistics Norway (SSB, 2022). With Norwegian-born children to immigrant parents, they are making up 18.9% of the country's total population. Statistics Norway reported the five largest immigrant groups in Norway are from Poland, Lithuania, Sweden, Syria and Somalia. In Norway, total number of immigrants from Turkey was reported as 13,727.

This article focuses on the Turkish asylum seekers and refugees in Norway. People from Turkey form one of the largest groups of refugees and asylum seekers in Norway in the recent years following the coup attempt in 2016. Following the failed coup attempt in July 2016, large-scale political purges have been carried out by the Turkish government that have affected almost all areas of Turkish society (NOAS, 2021). Journalists, lawyers, judges, teachers, academicians, police and military personnel have lost their jobs, and the purges have driven many Turks to flee to Europe (NOAS, 2021). According to the Norwegian Directorate of Immigration (UDI), In 2018, 765 Turkish citizens applied for asylum in Norway, making them the largest asylum-seeking group (UDI, n.d.; NTB, 2018). Asylum seekers from Turkey represented the second-largest group of asylum seekers in Norway in 2019. Turkish citizens have continued to seek asylum in Norway; In 2021, Turkish citizens constituted the fifth largest group of asylum seekers (UDI, n.d.).

Social media use has been increasingly popular all over the world and this technological and social phenomenon has also affected the migration and acculturation process. Leading social network sites and apps (Facebook, YouTube, WhatsApp, Instagram) have more than 1 billion active users (Statista, 2022). Among them, the most popular social network site, Facebook, has reach 2.9 billion users. Internet and internet based social technologies, such as social media, have transformed the transnational interactions and mobilities of everyone, including forcibly displaced refugees (Jauhiainen et al., 2022).

Information and communication technologies (ICTs), especially the internet, have been an integral part of modern society. These technologies have radically affected societies and also transformed the experience of international migration (Charmarkeh, 2013). Smartphones, the internet and social media platforms are crucial for refugees. These technologies help refugees access information and communication through the whole migration process. With having communication and social features, social media platforms are critically important for refugees.

Studies show that these technologies help refugees and immigrants in a wide range of context, such as contact family and old and new friends, receive news about the country of origin, the host country and the potential destination countries, and search for and access humanitarian assistance, employment, education, health needs, and entertainment (Jauhiainen et al., 2022).

This study explores the associations between acculturative stress, well-being, life satisfaction, and social media use among the Turkish refugees in Norway. Although there are a number of studies about the use of social media among refugees and immigrants, there is a lack of research exploring the relationships between these variables (Du and Lin, 2019; Pottie et al., 2020).

ACCULTURATIVE STRESS

Acculturation and resettlement within a host country pose a complex array of social and psychological challenges for refugees (Lumley et al., 2018). Regardless of the reasons for relocation, immigrants are often faced with the challenge of adapting to the new culture of host country (Var et al., 2013). Two broad forms of change, behavioral changes and acculturation stress, occur when individuals move to another culture (Berry, 1992).

Berry (2005) defined acculturation as "the dual process of cultural and psychological change that takes place as a result of contact between two or more cultural groups and their individual members." Acculturation often occurs at different rates and sometimes this process leads increased stress and conflict as well as more difficult adaptations (Berry, 2005). Acculturative stress takes place when individuals move to another culture (Berry, 1992). During the acculturation process several changes occur at the group level and individual level (Berry, 1992). "The concept of acculturative stress refers to one kind of stress, that in which the stressors are identified as having their source in the process of acculturation" (Berry et al., 1987). Acculturative stress is related to experiences that cause stress among refugees and immigrants, such as unfamiliarity with daily tasks, difficulties in finding job, learning the host country's language, discrimination, and a feeling of not belonging in one's new environment (Hameed et al., 2018).

Berry et al. (1987) states a number of factors can modify the acculturation-stress relationship, such as nature of the larger society, type of acculturating group, modes of acculturation, demographic and social characteristics of individual and psychological characteristics of individual. Uncertainty in the new society and cultural concerns can cause heightened levels of depression and of anxiety (Berry, 2006a). Acculturation often proceeds at different rates within families and among family members and this can lead to increase in conflict and stress and to more difficult adaptations (Berry, 2005). Individual's demographic, social and psychological characteristics, such as education, age, gender, cognitive style, prior intercultural experiences, and contact experiences, can modify the acculturation - stress relationship (Berry et al., 1987). Different levels of acculturation stress can manifest as a result of acculturation experience and stressors (Berry et al., 1987). Acculturation strategies have been shown to have substantial relationships with positive adaptation: integration is usually the most successful; marginalization is the least; and assimilation and separation strategies are intermediate (Berry, 2006b).

WELL-BEING

According to Diener and Ryan (2009) "subjective well-being is an umbrella term used to describe the level of wellbeing people experience according to their subjective evaluations of their lives". Many asylum seekers and refugees face stressful experiences during forced migration, and during resettlement in host countries and this can profoundly affect their mental health, including high rates of depression, anxiety and posttraumatic stress disorder (van der Boor et al., 2020; Turrini et al., 2017). Immigrants and refugees often face great challenges of adapting to the new country which can affect their health and wellbeing (Var et al., 2013).

Starting to live in a new country involves many challenges. Refugees and immigrants have several stressors related to language, culture, education, and employment. These factors affect well-being of these individuals. The process of acculturation can be stressful and problematic; a low level of acculturation is often associated with higher levels of acculturative stress, loneliness, and depression (Du and Lin, 2019). The hardships in the host country which immigrants face, such as the absence of significant others, cultural disparities, language limitations, and social degradation, affect their happiness negatively (Hendriks, 2015).

Social media has important potentials to support refugees and immigrants by providing online network and communication tools. Zaher (2020) explored how newcomer women to Canada use social media for social support and reported that they mostly use social media for receiving information, followed by esteem support, networking, and emotional support. There are different types of social media and their active and passive use affects differently to well-being of users (Masciantonio et al., 2021).

Overall life satisfaction and personal well-being have been found to be generally correlated (Var et al., 2013). "WHO defines Quality of Life as an individual's perception of their position in life in the context of the culture and value systems in which they live and in relation to their goals, expectations, standards and concerns." (WHO, n.d.). Paparusso (2021) found that self-reported life satisfaction among immigrants living in Europa strongly depends on immigrants' demographic characteristics and human capital factors, such as age, marital status, current economic situation and perceived financial well-being. Prapas and Mavreas (2019) found that three factors contributed to quality of life and wellbeing of immigrants in Greece: ethnicity, heritage dimension of acculturation and gender. Jun et al. (2021) reported high levels of smartphone use and social media use were significantly related to a high level of social support from friends and a high level of social media use was significantly related to a high level of life satisfaction among Korean immigrant elders in the USA. A characteristic of social network sites that increases negative feelings is the availability of upward targets for social comparisons (Wirtz et al., 2021). Therefore, it is possible that social comparison with people living better conditions in the host country can affect refugees' wellbeing, especially at the beginning of their new lives in the host country.

SOCIAL MEDIA

Social media can be defined as "Internet-based applications that allow users to create, exchange, or simply consume user-generated content, that is, content created by individuals themselves" (Valentini, 2018). Social media includes communication websites that facilitate relationship formation among users of diverse backgrounds, thus creating a rich social structure (Kapoor et al., 2018). Facebook, WhatsApp, Twitter, YouTube, LinkedIn, Pinterest, and Instagram are among the most known social media platforms (Kapoor et al., 2018). Social media platforms can be used on smartphones and on PCs, and they are generally free to use. Whiting and Williams (2013) identified ten uses and gratifications for using social media such as social interaction, information seeking, pass time, entertainment, relaxation, communicatory utility, convenience utility, expression of opinion, information sharing, and surveillance/knowledge about others.

Social media platforms play an important role in the entire immigration process; before leaving the homeland, during the journey and after arriving in the new host country. Social media have become increasingly popular channels of information on which migrants base their decisions about whether to migrate and where to settle (Dekker et al., 2018). While in the homeland, social media help refugees to get information and to contact people living in the country which they plan to reach. In the new host country, social media allows refugees to maintain contact with people (relatives and friends) living in the homeland and also establish new networks in the new country with same ethnic background and other people.

Mobile phones and the internet technologies help refugees in wide range of areas: maintaining the bonding ties with family and friends in home country and generating new bridging ties in new host country, receiving news about the country of origin, the host country and the potential destination countries, and searching for and accessing humanitarian assistance, employment, education, health needs, and entertainment (Jauhiainen et al., 2022). With the widespread use of online media, social media have become increasingly important for people seeking and providing social support (Zaher, 2020).

Social media usage has been recognized as an important part of immigrants' acculturation experience (Ju et al., 2021). Immigrants engage in various types of social communication, which can have an impact on their acculturation (Ju et al., 2021). The use of internet and social media can help immigrants and refugees both to resist and assist in the new host culture (Croucher, 2011). On the one hand, social networking sites affect immigrants' interactions with the host dominant culture and help to foster relationships with members of their new host country, on the other hand, these social technologies can decrease acculturation if immigrants use these technologies mainly among same social group they belong (Croucher, 2011). Social media platforms not only help people to maintain their existing social networks and establish new social network relationships but also provides opportunities and platforms for them to understand and learn about different cultures (Yuan and Li, 2021).

Using social media can assist intercultural adaptation in various ways, such as by learning about other cultures and countries, communicating with others, and staying informed about events (Alamri, 2018). Social media can facilitate integration of immigrant and refugees to the host society. Social media particularly important for these individuals for acquiring language and cultural competences, as well as to build bonding and bridging social capital (Alencar, 2018). Erdem (2018) found that social media plays an important role in the integration of immigrants to society in the USA in terms of acquiring language, cultural competencies and bridging social capital.

Anderson and Daniel (2020) explored social media usage among young refugees living in Norway and found that refugees use social media mainly for communication, access to information, and learning. They reported that social media offered five related capabilities for the refugees, such as effective communication, social connectedness, participation in learning opportunities, access to information, and expression of self. Harde (2018) interviewed young Syrian and Afghan refugees in Germany, and reported that they used social media for contacting family members and friends, generating new social connections, gathering information and news, and engaging in online discourse.

PURPOSE OF THIS STUDY

This study attempts to explore the associations between acculturative stress, well-being, life satisfaction and social media use among Turkish refugees living in Norway.

METHODOLOGY

In this study, we used an online survey which was developed and administered by using SurveyXact. The survey link was distributed by WhatsApp and e-mail. The snowball sampling method was used to recruit the respondents. The participants were requested to send the survey link to other Turkish refugees living in Norway. Participation in the survey was anonymous and voluntary. The invitation to participate in the online questionnaire was sent in December 2021 via WhatsApp and e-mail with a link to the survey. Data collection was completed on February 28, 2022.

Survey Instrument

The survey consisted of questions related to the demographic variables of the respondents (gender, age, marital status, education level, legal status, length of time lived in Norway, Norwegian language proficiency), acculturative stress, mental well-being, life satisfaction and social media usage. The survey participants were asked to indicate the social media platforms they use and the average daily social media usage time. The survey was translated to Turkish and tested with ten Turkish refugees, before distribution.

Measures

Acculturative Stress

The multidimensional acculturative stress scale (Jibeen and Khalid, 2010) was adapted to measure acculturative stress among the respondents. The original scale included 24 items that were developed to measure acculturative stress among Pakistani immigrants in Toronto, Canada. The items were reworded in the context of Turkish refugees in Norway. The scale items range from strongly disagree to strongly agree on a five-point Likert-type scale. The following item in the scale was not used "I am treated differently b/c of my race or skin color". The multidimensional acculturative stress scale has five subscales including discrimination, threat to ethnic identity, lack of opportunities for occupational and financial mobility, homesickness and language-barrier.

Well-Being

The short Warwick–Edinburgh mental well-being scale was used to assess participants' wellbeing. The scale includes seven items about feelings and thoughts that range from none of the time to all of the time on five-point Likert-type scale. This scale was widely used in the literature.

Satisfaction With Life Scale

The satisfaction with life scale was developed by Diener et al. (1985) and consists of five items with five-point Likert-type scale ranging from strongly disagree to strongly agree. Higher scores show greater levels of wellbeing and satisfaction with life.

Social Media Use

The scale was adapted originally from the social media use integration scale (Jenkins-Guarnieri et al., 2013) to measure social media use intensity. The response items were ranging from strongly disagree to strongly agree on a five-point Likert type scale. The scale has two subscales: social routine integration subscale and emotional connection subscale. Besides social media use intensity scale items, the survey includes several questions about social media usage. The survey participants were asked to indicate the social media platforms they use and the average daily social media usage time.

Demographic Variables

In the survey, the participants were asked to report following demographic characteristics: gender, age, marital status, education level, employment status, legal status in Norway, length of time lived in Norway, Norwegian language proficiency in speaking, writing, listening, and reading.

RESULTS

Demographics of the Participants

The participants of the study consisted of 124 Turkish refugees in Norway. Only completed surveys were analyzed. Table 1 shows the demographic characteristics of the respondents. 73.4 percent of the participants were male, and the remaining were female. The age of the participants ranged from 19 to 62 years old (Mean= 37.1, SD= 8.1). 65.3 percent of the participants were between 19 and 40 years old, and the remaining were 41-62 years old. 88 percent of the participants were married, 10.5 percent were single, and 1.6 percent were divorced.

Most of the participants (87.9%) had a higher education degree, with 62.9 percent having a bachelor's degree, 19.4 percent had a master's degree, and one participant had a doctoral degree. Of the 124 respondents, 37 percent were employed. The majority of the participants (92.7%) have been granted asylum. The participants had been living in Norway between less than 6 months and 5 years at the time of the data collection. Over half of the participants (56.4%) indicated that they have lived in Norway between 3 years to 5 years.

Regarding Norwegian language proficiency, the participants were asked to indicate their Norwegian language skills in speaking, writing, listening, and reading with using five-point Likert type scale (1 = Very poor, 5 = Very good). Mean and standard deviations of the responses are shown on Table 1. The mean values for speaking, writing, and listening were approximately midpoint of the scale. The results show that the respondents considered their Norwegian language proficiency were not good. Language can be a challenging issue for refugees and immigrants in the host country. Language is an important factor in acculturation and related to acculturative stress (Nasirudeen et al., 2019; Poppitt and Frey, 2007; Lumley et al., 2018; Yako and Biswas, 2014; Jun et al., 2021).

In the questionnaire, the participants were asked to indicate which social media platforms they used. Among the participants, the most commonly used social media platform was WhatsApp (100.0 percent), followed by YouTube (86.29 percent), and Facebook (76.61 percent). WhatsApp is one of the most popular social media platforms among refugees (Briggs, 2021). Table 2 shows the social media platforms used by the respondents.

Table 3 shows the average daily social media usage by the respondents. Most of the respondents indicated that they used social media less than two hours a day. 41 percent of the respondents' average social media usage was one to two hours daily.

Data Analysis

An exploratory factor analysis with Varimax rotation was performed on items of the scales in the survey using IBM SPSS (version 25). Table 4 presents the summary statistics of the scales. Cronbach's alpha

Table 1. Demographic characteristics of the respondents

Variables	Category	Frequency	Percentage
Gender	Female	33	26.6
	Male	91	73.4
Age	19-25	7	5.65
	26-30	22	17.74
	31-35	30	24.19
	36-40	22	17.74
	41-45	22	17.74
	46-50	17	13.71
	50+	4	3.23
Marital status	Married	109	87.9
	Single (Never married)	13	10.5
	Divorced	2	1.6
Level of education	Less than high school degree	2	1.6
	High school degree or equivalent	13	10.5
	Vocational school of higher education (2 years)	6	4.8
	Bachelor's degree (4 years or more)	78	62.9
	Master's degree	24	19.4
	Doctoral degree	1	0.8
Employment status*	Introduction programme	73	58.87
	Unemployed	14	11.29
	Studying (high school, university, etc.)	22	17.74
	Employed (full-time, part-time or self-employed)	46	37.10
	Other	2	1.61
Legal status (Asylum status)	Asylum seeker	9	7.3
	have been granted asylum	115	92.7
Length of time lived in Norway	Less than 6 months	6	4.8
	6 months to less than 1 year	3	2.4
	1 year to less than 2 years	16	12.9
	2 years to less than 3 years	29	23.4
	3 years to less than 4 years	66	53.2
	4 years to less than 5 years	4	3.2
		Mean	**Std. Deviation**
Language proficiency	Speaking	3.03	0.945
	Writing	3.22	0.851
	Listening	3.12	0.898
	Reading	3.69	0.820

Table 2. Social media platforms used by respondents

	Frequency	Percentage
WhatsApp	124	100.00
YouTube	107	86.29
Facebook	95	76.61
Instagram	77	62.10
Twitter	72	58.06
LinkedIn	30	24.19
Pinterest	12	9.68
Snapchat	10	8.06
TikTok	5	4.03
Other	2	1.61

Table 3. Daily social media usage

	Frequency	Percentage
Less than 30 min.	5	4.03
30 min to less than 1 h	22	17.74
1 h to less than 2 h	51	41.13
2 h to less than 3 h	31	25.00
3 h to less than 4 h	11	8.87
4 h to less than 5 h	3	2.42
More than 5 h	1	0.81

coefficient values were used to assess the reliability of the scales. Cronbach's alpha values were over the acceptable level. Based on the factor analysis results, one item in the social media intensity scale and four items in the acculturative scale were excluded from further analysis because of factor loadings. Factor loadings are presented at the attachment.

A Pearson bivariate correlation analysis was conducted to examine the associations among demographic variables (age, gender, marital status, education level, time spent in Norway, employment status, Norwegian language proficiency, acculturative stress, the level of satisfaction with life, the level of well-being and the level of social media use intensity. Table 5 presents the correlational analysis of the study.

The study identified negative correlations between the level of acculturative stress and well-being ($r = -.445$, $p < .01$), life satisfaction ($r = -.368$, $p < .01$), and gender ($r = -.243$, $p < .01$). Specifically, higher acculturative stress was associated with lower levels of well-being and life satisfaction. As the level of acculturative stress increases, there is a corresponding decrease in both well-being and life satisfaction. Female participants reported higher level of acculturative stress than males.

As expected, Norwegian language proficiency is positively correlated with time spent in Norway ($r = .484$, $p < .01$). Employment status was found to be positively correlated with time spent in Norway

Table 4. Summary statistics of the scales

	Min	Max	Mean	St Dev.	α
Social media use intensity total scale	18.00	44.00	28.35	5.59	0.779
Social routine integration subscale	9.00	30.00	17.48	4.63	0.790
Emotional connection subscale	6.00	15.00	10.86	1.96	0.602
Acculturative stress total scale	17.00	79.00	50.47	10.67	0.818
Discrimination subscale	.00	25.00	11.91	4.09	0.789
Threat to ethnic identity subscale	1.00	21.00	11.44	4.32	0.742
Lack of opportunities for occupational and financial mobility subscale	0.00	15.00	8.11	3.21	0.664
Homesickness subscale	0.00	15.00	10.77	3.17	0.727
Language-barrier subscale	2.00	10.00	8.23	1.46	0.707
Short Warwick–Edinburgh mental well-being scale	16.00	35.00	26.00	4.03	0.847
Satisfaction with life scale	5.00	24.00	14.90	3.70	0.817

Table 5. Correlational analysis

	(1)	(2)	(3)	(4)	(5)	(6)	(7)	(8)	(9)	(10)
(1) Age	-									
(2) Gender	.153	-								
(3) Marital status	.371**	-.111	-							
(4) Education level	-.023	.036	.286**	-						
(5) Time spent in Norway	.271**	.099	.158	.058	-					
(6) Employment status	-.036	.349**	-.022	.173	.275**	-				
(7) Language proficiency	-.075	.089	-.001	.112	.484**	.271**	-			
(8) Acculturative stress	-.147	-.243**	.019	-.078	-.027	-.166	-.076	-		
(9) Well-being	-.029	.059	-.049	.128	.018	.224*	.150	-.445**	-	
(10) Satisfaction with life	-.049	-.125	-.016	-.041	.026	.097	.135	-.368**	.581**	-
(11) Social media use intensity	-.088	-.084	-.026	-.097	-.061	-.090	-.039	.162	-.060	-.172

*p < 0.05, **p < 0.01. Gender: O = Female, 1 = Male, Marital status: 0 = not married, 1 = married, Employment status: 0 = not employed, 1 = employed

($r = .275$, $p < .01$), Norwegian language proficiency ($r = .271$, $p < .01$), and well-being ($r = .224$, $p < .05$). Employed participants reported higher levels of well-being and language proficiency.

The study found that the level of well-being was positively correlated with employment status ($r = .224$, $p < .05$), the level of satisfaction with life ($r = .581$, $p < .01$) and negatively correlated the level of acculturative stress ($r = -.445$, $p < .01$). The level of satisfaction with life was found to be positively correlated with the level of well-being and negatively correlated with the level of acculturative stress.

The level of well-being is highly positively correlated the level of satisfaction with life. No statistically significant correlations were found between social media use intensity and other variables.

DISCUSSION AND CONCLUSION

This study explored the associations between acculturative stress, well-being, life satisfaction, and social media use among Turkish refugees in Norway. The study found that the level of acculturative stress was negatively correlated with both the level of well-being and the level of satisfaction with life. Well-being and life satisfaction decreases with higher levels of acculturative stress. Stuart et al. (2016) reported the same result that decreased life satisfaction was associated with acculturative stress. This finding is also consistent with findings of (Suh et al., 2016).

Consistent with the literature, the level of well-being was found to be positively correlated with the level of satisfaction with life. Higher levels of life satisfaction were correlated with higher levels of well-being. Overall life satisfaction and personal well-being have been found to be generally correlated (Var et al., 2013). Subjective well-being includes assessment of all aspects of a person's life (Diener, 1984).

The findings of this study show that female refugees have higher level of acculturative stress than males. Female refugees were found to be more vulnerable in the host country. This result shows that female refugees need more social and psychological supports. Among refugees, females are more likely to suffer from mental distress than males (Hameed et al., 2018). Nasıroğlu and Çeri (2016) reported being female as a factor associated with depression among Yazidi refugees in Turkey. Fang et al. (2021) found that acculturative stress was positively associated with depressive symptoms among both males and females among Chinese immigrants in the USA.

Another finding of the study was that being employed was positively correlated with the level of well-being. However, employment status did not correlate with the life satisfaction. This result is consistent with that of (Walther et al., 2020). They stated that the expectations of refugees regarding the norm of being employed might be the reason behind the lack of a link between employment and life satisfaction. Being employed was also found to be positively correlated with time spent in Norway and Norwegian language proficiency. On the other hand, no significant correlation was observed between social media use intensity and other study variables.

The limitations of this current study should be acknowledged in interpreting the results. The snowball sampling method was used to recruit the respondents. The sample size was limited. The study sample may not be fully representative of the Turkish refugee population in Norway. An online survey was used for data collection. Other significant variables such as income have not been collected. Interviews can give a deeper understanding of acculturative stress, well-being, life satisfaction, and social media usage among refugees. Future studies can also consider comparative studies between different refugee groups.

REFERENCES

Alamri, B. (2018). The Role of Social Media in Intercultural Adaptation: A Review of the Literature. *English Language Teaching*, *11*(12), 77–85. doi:10.5539/elt.v11n12p77

Alencar, A. (2018). Refugee integration and social media: A local and experiential perspective. *Information Communication and Society, 21*(11), 1588–1603. doi:10.1080/1369118X.2017.1340500

Anderson, S., & Daniel, M. (2020). Refugees and social media in a digital society. *The Journal of Community Informatics, 16*, 26–44. doi:10.15353/joci.v16i0.3473

Berry, J. W. (1992). Acculturation and adaptation in a new society. *International Migration (Geneva, Switzerland), 30*(s1), 69–85. doi:10.1111/j.1468-2435.1992.tb00776.x

Berry, J. W. (2005). Acculturation: Living successfully in two cultures. *International Journal of Intercultural Relations, 29*(6), 697–712. doi:10.1016/j.ijintrel.2005.07.013

Berry, J. W. (2006a) Stress perspectives on acculturation. The Cambridge Handbook of Acculturation Psychology, 1, 43-56.

Berry, J. W. (2006b). Stress perspectives on acculturation. In D. L. Sam & J. W. Berry (Eds.), *The Cambridge handbook of acculturation psychology* (pp. 43–57). Cambridge University Press. doi:10.1017/CBO9780511489891.007

Berry, J. W., Kim, U., Minde, T., & Mok, D. (1987). Comparative Studies of Acculturative Stress. *The International Migration Review, 21*(3), 491–511. doi:10.1177/019791838702100303

Briggs, D. (2021) *WhatsApp refugees? A reflexive account of the methodological use of WhatsApp with newly arrived refugees in Europe.* Available at: https://pjp-eu.coe.int/documents/42128013/47261623/YKB-27-WEB.pdf/dbab979b-75ff-4ee8-b3da-c10dc57650d5

Cain, J. A., & Imre, I. (2021). Everybody wants some: Collection and control of personal information, privacy concerns, and social media use. *New Media & Society, 24*(12), 2705-2724. doi: 10.1177/14614448211000327.

Charmarkeh, H. (2013). Social Media Usage, Tahriib (Migration), and Settlement among Somali Refugees in France. *Refuge: Canada's Journal on Refugees, 29*(1), 43–52. doi:10.25071/1920-7336.37505

Croucher, S. M. (2011). Social Networking and Cultural Adaptation: A Theoretical Model. *Journal of International and Intercultural Communication, 4*(4), 259–264. doi:10.1080/17513057.2011.598046

Dekker, R., Engbersen, G., Klaver, J., & Vonk, H. (2018). Smart Refugees: How Syrian Asylum Migrants Use Social Media Information in Migration Decision-Making. *Social Media + Society, 4*(1), 2056305118764439. doi:10.1177/2056305118764439

Diener, E. (1984). Subjective well-being. *Psychological Bulletin, 95*(3), 542–575. doi:10.1037/0033-2909.95.3.542 PMID:6399758

Diener, E., Emmons, R. A., Larsen, R. J., & Griffin, S. (1985). The Satisfaction With Life Scale. *Journal of Personality Assessment, 49*(1), 71–75. doi:10.1207/s15327752jpa4901_13 PMID:16367493

Diener, E., & Ryan, K. (2009). Subjective well-being: A general overview. *South African Journal of Psychology. Suid-Afrikaanse Tydskrif vir Sielkunde, 39*(4), 391–406. doi:10.1177/008124630903900402

Du, X., & Lin, S. (2019). Social media usage, acculturation and psychological well-being: A study with Chinese in New Zealand. *International Communication of Chinese Culture*, *6*(3), 231–245. doi:10.1007/s40636-019-00160-2

Erdem, B. (2018). How Can Social Media Be Helpful for Immigrants to Integrate Society in the US. *European Journal of Multidisciplinary Studies*, *3*(3), 74–79. doi:10.26417/ejms.v3i3.p74-79

Fang, C. Y., Handorf, E. A., Rao, A. D., Siu, P. T., & Tseng, M. (2021). Acculturative Stress and Depressive Symptoms Among Chinese Immigrants: The Role of Gender and Social Support. *Journal of Racial and Ethnic Health Disparities*, *8*(5), 1130–1138. doi:10.1007/s40615-020-00869-6 PMID:33000431

Hameed, S., Sadiq, A., & Din, A. U. (2018). The Increased Vulnerability of Refugee Population to Mental Health Disorders. *Kansas Journal of Medicine*, *11*(1), 1–12. PMID:29844851

Harde A (2018) *A Qualitative Study on How Refugees Use Technology after Arriving in Germany.* Reportno.

Hendriks, M. (2015). The happiness of international migrants: A review of research findings. *Migration Studies*, *3*(3), 343–369. doi:10.1093/migration/mnu053

Jauhiainen, J. S., Özçürümez, S., & Tursun, Ö. (2022). Internet and social media uses, digital divides, and digitally mediated transnationalism in forced migration: Syrians in Turkey. *Global Networks*, *22*(2), 197–210. doi:10.1111/glob.12339

Jenkins-Guarnieri, M. A., Wright, S. L., & Johnson, B. (2013). Development and validation of a social media use integration scale. *Psychology of Popular Media Culture*, *2*(1), 38–50. doi:10.1037/a0030277

Jibeen, T., & Khalid, R. (2010). Development and Preliminary Validation of Multidimensional Acculturative Stress Scale for Pakistani Immigrants in Toronto, Canada. *International Journal of Intercultural Relations*, *34*(3), 233–243. doi:10.1016/j.ijintrel.2009.09.006

Ju, R., Hamilton, L., & McLarnon, M. (2021). *The Medium Is the Message: WeChat.* YouTube, and Facebook Usage and Acculturation Outcomes.

Jun, J. S., Galambos, C., & Lee, K. H. (2021). Information and Communication Technology Use, Social Support, and Life Satisfaction among Korean Immigrant Elders. *Journal of Social Service Research*, *47*(4), 537–552. doi:10.1080/01488376.2020.1848969

Kapoor, K. K., Tamilmani, K., Rana, N. P., Patil, P., Dwivedi, Y. K., & Nerur, S. (2018). Advances in Social Media Research: Past, Present and Future. *Information Systems Frontiers*, *20*(3), 531–558. doi:10.1007/s10796-017-9810-y

Lumley, M., Katsikitis, M., & Statham, D. (2018). Depression, Anxiety, and Acculturative Stress Among Resettled Bhutanese Refugees in Australia. *Journal of Cross-Cultural Psychology*, *49*(8), 1269–1282. doi:10.1177/0022022118786458

Masciantonio, A., Bourguignon, D., Bouchat, P., Balty, M., & Rimé, B. (2021). Don't put all social network sites in one basket: Facebook, Instagram, Twitter, TikTok, and their relations with well-being during the COVID-19 pandemic. *PLoS One*, *16*(3), e0248384. doi:10.1371/journal.pone.0248384 PMID:33705462

Nasıroğlu, S., & Çeri, V. (2016). Posttraumatic stress and depression in Yazidi refugees. *Neuropsychiatric Disease and Treatment*, *12*, 2941–2948. doi:10.2147/NDT.S119506 PMID:27881919

Nasirudeen, A., Josephine, K. W. N., & Adeline, L. L. C. (2019). Acculturative stress among Asian international students in Singapore. *Journal of International Students*, *4*(4), 363–373. doi:10.32674/jis.v4i4.455

NOAS. (2021). *Landprofiler: Tyrkia*. Available at: https://noas.no/riketstilstand/2021-2/landprofiler/tyrkia/

NTB. (2018). *Én av fire asylsøkere i år kommer fra Tyrkia*. Available at: https://www.nettavisen.no/nyheter/innenriks/n-av-fire-asylsokere-i-ar-kommer-fra-tyrkia/s/12-95-3423545013

Paparusso, A. (2021). *Immigrants' Self-reported Life Satisfaction in Europe. In Immigrant Integration in Europe: A Subjective Well-Being Perspective*. Springer International Publishing.

Poppitt, G., & Frey, R. (2007). Sudanese Adolescent Refugees: Acculturation and Acculturative Stress. *Australian Journal of Guidance & Counselling*, *17*(2), 160–181. doi:10.1375/ajgc.17.2.160

Pottie, K., Ratnayake, A., Ahmed, R., Veronis, L., & Alghazali, I. (2020). How refugee youth use social media: What does this mean for improving their health and welfare? *Journal of Public Health Policy*, *41*(3), 268–278. doi:10.1057/s41271-020-00231-4 PMID:32690862

Prapas, C., & Mavreas, V. (2019). The Relationship Between Quality of Life, Psychological Wellbeing, Satisfaction with Life and Acculturation of Immigrants in Greece. *Culture, Medicine and Psychiatry*, *43*(1), 77–92. doi:10.1007/s11013-018-9598-3 PMID:30097834

Sam, D. L., Vetik, R., & Makarova, M. (2017). Intercultural Relations in Norway. In J. W. Berry (Ed.), *Mutual Intercultural Relations* (pp. 105–124). Cambridge University Press. doi:10.1017/9781316875032.006

SSB. (2022). *Immigrants and Norwegian-born to immigrant parents*. Available at: https://www.ssb.no/en/befolkning/innvandrere/statistikk/innvandrere-og-norskfodte-med-innvandrerforeldre

Statista. (2022). *Social media - Statistics & Facts*. Available at: https://www.statista.com/topics/1164/social-networks/

Stuart, J., Ward, C., & Robinson, L. (2016). The influence of family climate on stress and adaptation for Muslim immigrant young adults in two Western countries. *International Perspectives in Psychology : Research, Practice, Consultation*, *5*(1), 1–17. doi:10.1037/ipp0000043

Suh, H., Rice, K. G., Choi, C.-C., van Nuenen, M., Zhang, Y., Morero, Y., & Anderson, D. (2016). Measuring acculturative stress with the SAFE: Evidence for longitudinal measurement invariance and associations with life satisfaction. *Personality and Individual Differences*, *89*, 217–222. doi:10.1016/j.paid.2015.10.002

Turrini, G., Purgato, M., Ballette, F., Nosè, M., Ostuzzi, G., & Barbui, C. (2017). Common mental disorders in asylum seekers and refugees: Umbrella review of prevalence and intervention studies. *International Journal of Mental Health Systems*, *11*(1), 51. doi:10.1186/s13033-017-0156-0 PMID:28855963

UDI. (n.d.). *Statistics on immigration*. Available at: https://www.udi.no/en/statistics-and-analysis/statistics/?year=0&filter=42&page=3

UNHCR. (2022). *Forced displacement hit record high in 2021 with too few able to go home*. Available at: https://www.unhcr.org/news/stories/2022/6/62a9ccb54/forced-displacement-hit-record-high-2021-few-able-home.html

Valentini, C. (2018). *Social Media*. The International Encyclopedia of Strategic Communication.

van der Boor, C. F., Amos, R., Nevitt, S., Dowrick, C., & White, R. G. (2020). Systematic review of factors associated with quality of life of asylum seekers and refugees in high-income countries. *Conflict and Health*, *14*(1), 48. doi:10.1186/s13031-020-00292-y PMID:32699551

Var, S., Poyrazli, S., & Grahame, K. M. (2013). Personal Well-being and Overall Satisfaction of Life of Asian Immigrant and Refugee Women. *Asia Taepyongyang Sangdam Yongu*, *3*(1), 77–90. doi:10.18401/2013.3.1.6

Walther, L., Fuchs, L. M., Schupp, J., & von Scheve, C. (2020). Living Conditions and the Mental Health and Well-being of Refugees: Evidence from a Large-Scale German Survey. *Journal of Immigrant and Minority Health*, *22*(5), 903–913. doi:10.1007/s10903-019-00968-5 PMID:31974927

Whiting, A., & Williams, D. (2013). Why people use social media: A uses and gratifications approach. *Qualitative Market Research*, *16*(4), 362–369. doi:10.1108/QMR-06-2013-0041

WHO. (n.d.). *WHOQOL: Measuring Quality of Life*. Available at: https://www.who.int/tools/whoqol

Wirtz, D., Tucker, A., Briggs, C., & Schoemann, A. M. (2021). How and Why Social Media Affect Subjective Well-Being: Multi-Site Use and Social Comparison as Predictors of Change Across Time. *Journal of Happiness Studies*, *22*(4), 1673–1691. doi:10.1007/s10902-020-00291-z

Yako, R. M., & Biswas, B. (2014). "We came to this country for the future of our children. We have no future": Acculturative stress among Iraqi refugees in the United States. *International Journal of Intercultural Relations*, *38*, 133–141. doi:10.1016/j.ijintrel.2013.08.003

Yuan, S., & Li, H. (2021) Ethnic Identity, Acculturation and Life Satisfaction of the Yi in the Context of social media: Moderating and Mediating Effects. In *2021 5th International Conference on Business and Information Management*. Association for Computing Machinery.

Zaher, Z. (2020). Examining How Newcomer Women to Canada Use Social Media for Social Support. *Canadian Journal of Communication*, *45*(2), 122–220. doi:10.22230/cjc.2020v45n2a3541

APPENDIX: FACTOR LOADINGS AND THE SUMMARY STATISTICS OF THE SCALES

Table A1. Acculturative stress scale

	Min	Max	Mean	St Dev	Factor Loading	α
Acculturative stress total scale	17.00	79.00	50.47	10.67		0.818
Discrimination subscale	0.00	25.00	11.91	4.09		0.789
1. Norwegians treat me like a foreigner.					.674	
3. I am constantly reminded of my minority status.					.773	
4. I think that many opportunities are denied to me because I am Turkish.					.738	
5. I think that Norwegian society discriminates against me just I am Turkish.					.676	
6. I feel that Norwegians do not treat me with respect.					.703	
7. People from other ethnic groups try to stop me from advancing.					.406	
Threat to ethnic identity subscale	1.00	21.00	11.44	4.32		0.742
8. I worry that my children/next generation will become very broad minded.					.712	
9. I feel as if I am divided between Pakistan (Turkey) and Canada (Norway).					.636	
10. I worry that my children/next generation will not adopt follow Turkish beliefs and customs.					.697	
11. I feel that I am neither Turkish nor Norwegian.					.673	
12. I am losing my Turkish identity.					.643	
Lack of opportunities for occupational and financial mobility subscale	0.00	15.00	8.11	3.21		0.664
14. My job/my work (situation) is uncertain.					.673	
15. I have few opportunities to earn more income.					.803	
17. I am disappointed that my standard of living is not what I hoped for before coming to Norway.					.498	
Homesickness subscale	0.00	15.00	10.77	3.17		0.727
19 I miss my country and my people.					.733	
20 I am living far away from my family members, relatives and friends.					.724	
21 I miss my family members, relatives and friends.					.801	
Language-barrier subscale	2.00	10.00	8.23	1.46		0.707
23 I have difficulty understanding Norwegian in some situations.					.857	
24 Due to language differences, it is difficult for me to express my ideas.					.782	

Table A2. The short Warwick–Edinburgh mental well-being scale

	Min	Max	Mean	St Dev	Factor Loading	α
Short Warwick–Edinburgh mental well-being total scale	16.00	35.00	26.00	4.03		0.847
1. I've been feeling optimistic about the future.					.758	
2. I've been feeling useful.					.746	
3. I've been feeling relaxed.					.796	
4. I've been dealing with problems well.					.815	
5. I've been thinking clearly.					.794	
6. I've been feeling close to other people.					.582	
7. I've been able to make up my own mind about things.					.600	

Table A3. The satisfaction with life scale

	Min	Max	Mean	St Dev	Factor Loading	α
Satisfaction with life total scale	5.00	24.00	14.90	3.70		0.817
1. In most ways my life is close to my ideal.					.763	
2. The conditions of my life are excellent.					.775	
3. I am satisfied with my life					.775	
4. So far I have gotten the important things I want in life.					.795	
5. If I could live my life over, I would change almost nothing.					.713	

Table A4. Social media use intensity scale

	Min	Max	Mean	St Dev	Factor Loading	α
Social media use intensity total scale	18.00	44.00	28.35	5.59		0.779
Social routine integration subscale	9.00	30.00	17.48	4.63		0.790
1. I feel disconnected from friends when I have not logged into my social media sites.					.615	
2. I would like it if everyone used social media sites to communicate.					.798	
3. I would be disappointed if I could not use social media sites at all.					.669	
4. I get upset when I cannot log on to my social media sites.					.605	
5. I prefer to communicate with others mainly through social media sites.					.650	
6. Social media sites play an important role in my social relationships.					.720	
Emotional connection subscale	6.00	15.00	10.86	1.96		0.602
7. I enjoy checking my social media site accounts.					.649	
8. I do not like to use social media sites. (Reversed)					.781	
9. Using social media sites is part of my everyday routine.					.739	

Chapter 17

Influence of Instagram as a Social Media Platform on Academic Routine and Schedule of Students

Pritesh Pradeep Somani
https://orcid.org/0000-0002-0039-0358
Balaji Institute of International Business, Sri Balaji University, Pune, India

Vishwanathan Iyer
https://orcid.org/0009-0007-1469-2369
Balaji Institute of International Business, Sri Balaji University, Pune, India

Ushmita Gupta
https://orcid.org/0000-0002-6442-1248
Balaji Institute of International Business, Sri Balaji University, Pune, India

Nitesh Behare
https://orcid.org/0000-0002-9338-8563
Balaji Institute of International Business, Sri Balaji University, Pune, India

Rashmi Mahajan
https://orcid.org/0000-0001-9082-6874
Balaji Institute of International Business, Sri Balaji University, Pune, India

Meenakshi Singh
https://orcid.org/0009-0006-9505-8214
Balaji Institute of International Business, Sri Balaji University, Pune, India

ABSTRACT

Social media platforms have become an integral part of the lives of students worldwide. Among these platforms, Instagram stands out as one of the most popular and influential. This chapter delves into the pervasive impact of Instagram on the academic routines and schedules of students, shedding light on the multifaceted ways in which this visually driven platform can both positively and negatively affect students' educational routine. In the digital age, Instagram has emerged as a powerhouse of social connectivity and self-expression. Its primary feature, image sharing, encourages users to present an idealized version of their lives to the world. This constant exposure to carefully curated content can inadvertently affect students' academic lives.

DOI: 10.4018/979-8-3693-0855-4.ch017

INTRODUCTION

What is social media? If this is raised as a general question to group of people, they will list down different social media platforms like Facebook, Instagram and Twitter but it will be a challenge to find set of people who can come up with on a concrete definition of a social media platform. The term "Social Media" refers to internet services that creates opportunities for users to showcase their participation across various online communities or even allowing them to generate their own content and make it available for public viewing. Social media majorly comprises of blogs, social bookmarking, social networking sites and virtual connections platforms.

Social media is a key parameter in how individuals are changing their lifestyles (Asough, 2012). Social media comprises blogging and social networking services that enable quick connections between users. Social networking has become an integral part of the day-to-day lifestyle of people. An ideal definition of Social Networking is given as "the use of websites and other internet services to communicate with other people and make friends" (Shivkumar, 2006) The foundation of social networking is the idea that individuals should engage and get to know one another. It empowers people to share, fostering greater connectivity and global openness. Social networking has a significant influence across or daily routine as it is so helpful in all spheres of life, including the political, economic, and educational spheres. However, the chapter attempts to highlight the usage of social media in education and evaluate its influence across the academic routine of students. Nowadays, social networking has emerged as one of the most vital platforms for communication. However, social networks exist on websites on the Internet where millions of individuals have common interests in particular fields. Members of these networks can access a variety of shared data, images, and videos, as well as write blogs, send messages, and have in-person chats. These networks are referred to as social since they enable contact with friends and colleagues while fostering relationships amongst them in the online community.

INSTAGRAM: THE POWERFUL SOCIAL MEDIA TOOL

"Network is equal to Net worth" a common phrase shared by all the successful entrepreneurs and top-level management people. The concept of networking has been reinvented and redefined with passage of time. With limited resources available, people connected to each other but the geographical constraints limited the expansion of the network. A few people who knew each other would catch up with each other and spend time after the work. While men enjoyed the meetings with a dose of drink to make life pleasurable, the women would spend lots of time garnishing it with heavy of gossips. The ultimate motive was sharing of information. Any activity of a certain household, good or bad, would become talk of the time within a short period of time. This was the power of network. Without modern amenities, information reached far and wide through proper networking channels. The concept of monetisation of network was conceptualised much later.

Social media changed the way people communicated, and revolutionised the way individuals connected regardless of the location (Saiku, et al., 2019). With growth of networks, the technology also grew and concepts of Social networking, and Internet of Things (IOT) has evolved. Social media primarily broke all geographical barriers and made the entire world a small market place. People belonging to any country could communicate, coordinate and execute their business with any person in the world. It also played a pivotal role in improvement of networking channels. This growth of networking gave wings to people to soar high in the sky. The major reason for success was pinpointed as the networking culture. Many businesses built on the concept of networking proved to be a highly successful venture. Due to this, more and more people were attracted towards this kind of business model.

Multilevel marketing was evolving and growing at a faster pace in India and consequently, becoming more powerful and popular attracting more people to it (Salem, 2019). The rise of social media played a positive role in this monetisation of the networking. The concept of "Direct Selling' or referred to as "multi-level marketing" found its feet due to widespread usage of social media. Many M.L.M. companies like Amway, Avon, MaryKay, Forever Living are flourishing by exploring the world of social networking.

In the olden days networking was possible by attending conferences, seminars or through known references. The development of communication systems revolutionised this powerful tool for leaders in the industry. In the modern world, anyone can connect across any other person virtually thereby making globalisation a true reality. The geographical borders are no more barriers to networking. Social media has played a pivotal role in this breakthrough innovation. YouTube gets the credit of being the oldest social media content publisher. However, with the introduction of 'Facebook' and the micro-blogging site 'Twitter' the traffic got diverted; as a result it was diluted as well. The success of Facebook induced brilliant minds to understand the needs of younger generation and 'Instagram' was born. (Sharma, et.al., 2022) The concept of Instagram was sharing picture stories. However, the younger generation liked this concept so much that they welcomed it wide arms and it became an integral part of their lives. The usage of Instagram is more indulgent than a need. The mental health issues are generally pushed in the backburner in our country.

Taking a cue from the trend and the increasing acceptance of Instagram, many corporates appointed Influencers to promote their products and/or services. This gave a boost to sales of the organisations and the influencers got a platform. This proved to be a win-win situation for both the parties. In other words, the marketing strategy was revolutionised and Instagram played a pivotal role in this aspect. According to leading statistical data base Statista as of February, 2023 39% of the organisations have worked with approximate 10 influencers while there were 12% organisations who have worked with more than 1000 plus influencers which showcases the importance of influencers as far as brand promotions are concerned.

Influencer marketing was a great tool to create awareness of new products (Kabilan, 2023). However influencers play a substantial role only during the preliminary stages, the final decision of consumers depends on many other factors as well. The study concluded that male consumers were more influenced by Influencers as compared to other consumers.

The role and impact of Instagram on the lives of a common man changed from just sharing pictures to a powerful marketing tool within a short span of time. It was a 'trending' tool and naturally, the young generation were attracted to it. Instagram also helped in connecting people all over the world and networking was very easy for everyone. The features of Instagram were youth centric and there was a constant effort by the company to keep it 'young' and 'lively'.

Instagram intelligently included the features of Snapchat and Pinterest (Industry Competitors) so effectively that it rose to the No.1 position in the market (Chaturvedi, 2018). In just over a decade, Instagram had over 800 million active users which was utilised by companies perfectly. The SWOT analysis on Instagram suggested a few important changes to be included in Instagram. The 'privacy' was a weak link for the Instagram users. However, the option to upload photos and videos instantly gave the young users the spontaneity feature and acceptance across. Hence, the use of Instagram as a channel act as a double-edged sword, the benefits were largely available but each benefit came with a cost as well (Daryl, et al.2018). It was a subjective tool which put the responsibility on the user to make use of Instagram to their advantage. Instagram addiction primarily happens due to recognition needs, social needs and entertainment needs (Foroughi, 2021). The physical activity has a moderating role in the effect of social needs and entertainment needs. There was strong evidence of negative impact of Instagram on academic performance and positive impact of Instagram on social anxiety and depression. Addictions consists of a number of distinct components (salience, mood modification, tolerance, withdrawal, conflict, and relapse) and addictions are a part of biopsychosocial process and there is growing evidence that excessive behaviours have commonalities. Such commonalities have implications for both treatment and general perception of public for such behaviours (Mark & Griffiths, 2005).

STUDENTS: ANOTHER POWERFUL FORCE

The role of Youth has been recognised and appreciated by many stalwarts not only in India but even abroad (Wilson, 2017). Our late President, Bharat Ratna, Shri Dr Abdul Kalam sir in his historic speech at IIT Madras quoted, "While children are struggling to be unique, the world around them is trying all means to make them look like everybody else." Our current Prime Minister, Shri Narendra Modiji, has also given emphasis to the fact that India is feared by all countries because we are the most youthful nation. Not only youthfulness, it is very important that the youth must be educated. The power of youth multiplies when they are empowered with education. In the words of South African President, Mr. Nelson Mandela, "Education is the great engine of personal development. It is through education that the daughter of a peasant can become a doctor, that the son of a mine worker can become the head of the mine; that a child of farm workers can become the president of a great nation. It is what we make out of what we have, not what we are given, that separates one person from another.

Education is a broad term. Academic education is one part of this larger term. An academic education is imparted through a systematic manner. The syllabus to be covered by a particular course is decided by a group of experts in the respective field. Thereafter, the entire syllabus is taught in a phased manner through lectures by an eminent team of academicians. To check whether the knowledge has reached proper destination, exams are conducted at the end of the term. After clearing one term, the student qualifies for the next term. This continues till the student clears all the terms and obtains the relevant degree. To get this degree, there are a few processes that every regular student follows. These processes are not clearly defined but are implemented with different degree of differences from institute to institute, city to city, and state to state. These can be collectively called as "Academic Routine."

There is no appropriate definition available in connection with the term Academic Routine and it varies from stream to stream. For a Science student, practical at laboratories are an indispensable part of Academic routine whereas such practical do not exist for Commerce or Arts or any other degree course. So, to define an Academic Routine may be difficult. However, one aspect is true that every student needs to define the needs of the course and set up the academic routine accordingly. Through an interview with few sets of parents on the condition of anonymity it was found Typically, an academic routine would include attending 6-8 hours of learning at school or college, 2 -3 hours of revision or homework at home and additional 2-3 hours for self-study. Typically, an academic routine involves 10 hours of learning – formally and informally. The amount of time invested and hard work undertaken converts a youth to a student. Only after such perseverance, the 'Youth' becomes an asset to serve the country, directly or indirectly, with the knowledge earned. The process of the youth becoming student is very important as they further go on to become the important asset of the country i.e., being a part of the work force of the Country.

INSTAGRAM: A BOON OR A CURSE?

Before understanding the boon and bane of Instagram, a research paper that highlights on the thought process of Instagram uses need to considered. Hemley (2013) advocated that an Instagram follower likes different types of posts. As per his study, customer centric posts, employee centric posts, Instagram contest photos, product photos, service photos are welcomed by the Instagram users widely. This simple knowledge of the variety of posts can help the company derive maximum advantage.

Based on his study, everyone can plan the purpose of posts on Instagram. If the posts are to be done for commercial purpose then a few more pointers needed to be taken care of. Further, in this modern world where time is costlier than money, the timings of the post carry a huge weightage. (Wahid, et,al., 2020) opined that the analysis of posting timing on Instagram would benefit social media managers and brands associated with food industry in Indonesia. However, the authors pointed out that the outcome of this study can differ for different industries as well as countries of other demographics as well. The disclaimer also pointed out that the timing may work only on Instagram and other social media platforms like facebook, snapchat may have a different algorithm. Herman (2019) through his research came up with the various benefits associated with usage of Instagram being summarised below:

a) ***High Presence in the Online world*** – Within no time, Instagram has become 2nd largest social media platform and has a global reach. The best part is that the reach is increasing each passing day.
b) ***Viral Marketing*** – Since the Instagram users are young minds, a post that is attractive can be viewed, liked and commented by millions of viewers within the first few hours.
c) ***High visibility of posts*** – With huge number of user base, the posts that lure the youth have high visibility.
d) ***High levels of engagement*** – The concept of reposting makes a post with sound, colours trending. The higher the rate of likes and comments, the higher will be the reposting of the same post. Hence the engagement levels are pretty higher and instant than compared to any other form of social media.
e) ***Targeted Audience*** – the concept of target audience is better defined in Instagram than compared to a Facebook. The posts can be prepared with specific audience in mind. Hence, the interaction is faster, and better creating a connect with the existing as well as future audience.
f) ***Emotional Connect*** – The picture and videos posted by the company are able to create a emotional connect with the end user. Hence, Instagram provides that extra edge as compared to other social media sites.

On the other hand in a separate research Barot (2019) through his article has emphasized on the disadvantages that erupted due to this Instagram and they can be summarised as:

a) **Technological limitations:** The algorithm of Instagram is created in such a manner that it is compatible with Android or IOS phones. Those companies which wish to post on Instagram must design their online post must ensure these aspects are to be considered before the post is created.

b) **Copyright issues**: The marketing experts and the social media users are expected to know and understand the Copyright Law. One cannot post anything or everything; likewise they cannot post about anyone or everyone.
c) **Fake accounts:** Like every social media, there is a high possibility of fake accounts of con artists, companies or even consumers in the Instagram. So the onus is on the creator to be aware of such fake accounts and ensure that proper precautions are taken.
d) **Addiction**: The Instagram addiction is an integral part of the social media which is in turn a part of the Internet addiction. The medical professionals have warned against the negative impact of these addictions at different levels and this would negatively impact the sales expected through Instagram marketing.

Mircea (2019) supported interesting statistics for the corporate world to optimise their cost-revenue ratio. In the research conducted, they emphasized on the importance of setting up profile for their own advantage. Likewise, they highlighted the important moments of the day, and days of the week are most efficient. The paper also pointed out several elements when the Instagram users appreciated certain posts.

With company armed with the trends from the experts through proper research, the students find themselves at crossroads many times with regards to use of Instagram. The researchers also have a diverse opinion regarding well-being of students and use of Instagram. While most of the studies related to use of Instagram has reported an adverse effect on well-being (Fioravanti et al., 2020) while Tekin, et al. (2022) through their research have concluded that there is a positive influence of wellness and Instagram. Such confusing statistical reports add to the existing confusion of students.

THE 'TEEN' AGE CONFUSION

A day in a students' life is very interesting and entertaining. The natural growing age of students adds to the confusing thought process. They are not in a state of mind to reach to logical conclusions easily. Add to it the peer pressure, the parents' expectation and their career aspirations; their life becomes complicated.

From a student's point of view, Instagram comes with a lot of opportunities for them (Wright and Yasar, 2022). They can connect and network with anyone and everyone in the world so easily. Instagram provides virtual spaces for people to create profiles, share updates, exchange messages, and engage in various forms of online communication related to their personal or professional life too. Instagram allows them to connect with friends, family, acquaintances, and even strangers from any corner of the world (Constine, 2018). They can search for and add contacts, allowing them to expand their social circle beyond physical limitations. Instagram is their main source of entertainment. They spend majority of the time watching the reels trending on the 'gram'. The algorithm of Instagram is so powerful that it keeps the user glued to the screen for hours together (Pitman & Reich, 2016). The backend throws all the short videos which the user likes or is regularly involved with in day-to-day life. Instagram has proved to be a single application which serves to the needs of the young minds and heart.

The unique aspect of Instagram is allowing every user to post a photo or video instantly. This helps many upcoming talented people to showcase their hidden talents and the world to take a note of the same instantly (Handayani, 2015). They get instant gratification and many students look forward to the same. The 'likes' and 'shares' gives them the kick to move ahead in life. Likewise, the number of 'followers' in their account makes them feel special. The simple logic of 'number begets number' works largely in the algorithm of Instagram.

The next most important aspect to be considered regarding Instagram is the nature of tasks and challenges they are exposed to. Instagram has given rise to a new concept known as following the trend where in users are performing different task or challenges which are sometimes dangerous for them (Highfield and Leaver, 2015). The dreadful part is students are further facing another dilemma of Fear of Missing Out (FOMO) and the peer pressure resulting out of such challenges forces many of the people to perform challenges even if they don't know about the same which further leads to loss of emotional well-being, lack of bonding with their near and dear ones and the most important feeling of negative attitude towards things thereby severely damaging their self-respect.

ACADEMIC ROUTINE AND INSTAGRAM

Singh et al. (2020) quoted the dietary routine activity and physical activities had significant association with the levels of stress. They further emphasized that a daily routine helped the youngsters to live a stress-free life. Hence, their ultimate concluding remarks were that planning and executing a daily schedule was the best option to create a positive attitude during stressful conditions (Akanksh, et al., 2020). The number of students getting addicted to Instagram is increasing. The rate is alarming and a cognizance of the same is to be taken on immediate basis The more worrying factor is that Instagram addiction has a negative impact on the academic performance (Foroughi, et al., 2021). The impact of social media on undergraduate students' academic performance is significant to be considered (Emmanuel, et al., 2018).

LIFE OF A STUDENT: BIRD EYE VIEW

A typical day of a student involve the time of waking up, doing physical activities, revising the concepts taught in the classroom, getting ready physically and mentally to attend the academic institution, spend the next few hours for learning at the institution, following a passion, spending time with family members, have dinner and proper sleep for the day. This routine requires unforced 'discipline'. It is followed day in and day out without any coercion. However, the sequence of these activities may differ for each individual student depending on the geographical area, the academic qualification pursued, the nature of learning and many other factors – personal and professional. These activities ensure the holistic development of a student. It includes a range of activities and the time invested for different activities is subjective depending upon the personality of the student, the family environment, the society, the peers and other psychological factors as well. When such routine is followed consistently, many issues related to psychology like depression, emotional turmoil can be avoided. In other words, a routine can help a student become healthy physically as well as mentally. The contribution of mental well-being is more important than physical well-being. In the modern world, a majority of students face mental stress due to inconsistent routines.

Out of these activities, those activities which can be purely aligned with the academic goals of a student can be considered as an 'Academic routine.' Though not specifically defined, an academic routine can include the normal processes a student goes through during the passage of a day related to academics only. It would primarily involve travel, physically and mental attendance at the institution, sessions related to academic syllabus, revision, doing homework regularly. This academic routine also undergoes a lot of variation. During the examination times, the entire routine of a student revolves around academics and all other aspects of life (passion, health) go for a toss. On the contrary, during regular times, the academic routine finds minimum time allotment and passion and/or health finds more time and money commitment.

This routine has been disrupted largely. Many reasons can be attributed to such disruption. In the earlier days, the major reason for disruption was lack of interest in academics. Students spent their time lazing around without any productive work due to lack of interest in the subject concerned. No other form of entertainment caused a strain in the concentration level of students. However, the internet age proved to be a major cause of disruption. To begin with the flourishing of the dotcom era brought along with it a lot of technological advancement for the country but it also opened up plethora of information to the students. The access to information and conversion of the same to data was a breakthrough disruption. Many IT companies took advantage of the mass media exposure and the concept of Social media dawned. Initially, the social media utilization was limited to a few hours for entertainment purpose. However, the availability of internet and exposure to the social media trigged the creative minds. Invention of Facebook allowed intervening into other people's life for free, and it also gave a peep into the world a person created by him. The friend requests poured from all corners of the world but it still gave one control of adding people known to the person directly or indirectly. Hence the scope of the world could be defined by the person creating his own virtual world. Also, it gave the power to a person to restrict the people who could view the post and write comments related to the same.

While restriction was an advantage as to controlling and welcomed by people in their mid-age (parents), the children found the restriction more restrictive in nature and a newer platform without any restriction was created. This was the age of "Instagram" where connectivity was thrown wide open to everyone across the globe. There was definitely a controlled version available to the account holder but many students found the "Open" version more worthy of exploring. Hence, many of the Instagram accounts had open access to their accounts. This means that anyone being at any place could access the account of any one at any place. This proved to be a major advantage for the Instagram holders and it was an overnight success. This concept was welcome by the teenagers with open arms.

Naturally, this disturbed academic routine of students in a big way. The entire academic routine was thrown into disarray. The time table or the routine was compromised to a great extent. The discipline ceased to exist. The "catch" of the eye was nothing but Instagram. Scrolling the screen and enjoying posts, photos, and videos was a part of the routine. Before a student could realize countless hours were down the drain. The student's feeble mind had no control on their activity. The more he understood there was wastage of time, the more he enjoyed being with himself. He was in a drugged state of affairs. The maximum he could feel was a sense of 'being guilty'. However, even the guilt was short-lived and unknowingly he was attracted to the screen back without his self-permission. This continued for hours together which converted days to weeks which culminated to months at a stretch. The students got out of control and finally, when the realisation drew upon them, it was beyond their control. The only solution they feel is to run away from the existing problems or feel nervous, stressful to an extent that quitting life seems to be the only viable option.

The side effect of scrolling the screen is dangerous in one more aspect. The entire communication system of the individual is broken to a large extent. The person stays alone all the time and in the process stops communication with family members, friends and society at large. This makes them feel alone all times and they feel lack of a shoulder to support them emotionally when needed. In a nutshell, Instagram has been a ruiner from students' academic point of view. Many lives have been put on the edge of the knife because of carelessness and irresponsible behaviour of the students. The onus of control lies in the hands of the user only but unfortunately the realisation dawns after the loss has taken place. It is very similar to the 'Big C'. If the diagnosis happens at the elementary stage, then the patient can be saved. However, if the diagnosis happens a bit late, then trying to save the patient is the only option available with the doctors and relatives. An Instagram or rather a social media affected student is mentally and emotionally drained into the system to such an extent that retrieving them into regular world will not be less than a 'magic'. It would require a strong will of the student supported by doctors, parents and teachers to a great extent.

ROLE OF PARENTS/TEACHERS IN THE AGE OF SOCIAL MEDIA EXPLOSION

Parenting styles specifically warmth and control, influence adolscents' media literacy and ability to criticize media. Higher the warmth of parenting, the higher is the children's ability to criticize the media (Riesmeyer, et.al.,2019). A parent happily takes his child to watch a 'live' show of carnivorous animals like lion, tiger and huge animals like elephants without any fear in mind. The reason behind this is a simple logic that the animals are trained and they are seated in the grand stand which is at a distance that gives them the feeling of being safe. The intention of the parent is to expose his child to the animals which are seen in the jungle only and read by the children in books or has seen in movies. The 'live' show is an enhancement of knowledge and the feeling is exciting.

The analogy of a natural zoo is applicable to the world of internet. All kinds of animals exist in this habitat. However, they are not trained nor are any kind of fencing available that will make the existence in this habitat safe. A parent has to be very careful when they expose their child to this world of internet. It is impossible to have individual supervision over the activities of the children every time they log into the internet world. The personal attention sometimes may ruin the communication system between the child and the parent. Hence, a balanced approach is required. Parental supervision of children on social media must be done properly by balancing child's needs with creativity. Social media can provide a platform to explore the child's talents under proper parental supervision - Mohamad Ali Syaifudin. Parents' privacy self-efficacy did not play a role in parents' sharing of either personal or children-related content (Giulia, et.al., 2020).

The parental control apps that have emerged in the market help parents to keep a tab on access and control over children's online activities as a means of protecting them from the harms of the internet risks – Parental Control: advice for parents, researchers and industry. Tools which provide more stricter vigilance over the child by the parents who 'hover' around wittingly and unwittingly at all cost are not welcome by the child (Clark, 2013; Haddon & Livingstone, 2014). Also, such tools create a negative impact in the minds of the children. This is a kind of over-controlling or a over protective parent and has a negative impact on the development of the child (Janssens, et al, 2015). On the contrary, the open discussion method between the parent and child establishing appropriate and inappropriate contents brings about better results (Hashish, Bunt and Young, 2014).

A role of teacher is similar to a 'compass' that helps the child to reach the destination in a vast ocean. The 'Ocean' is the world of internet, where the turbulent waves hit the child consistently. Understanding the knowledge acquired by the student, the teacher regulates the exposure and the speed of exploring the internet. The negative factors attract the mind and the chance of a child getting deviated from the core purpose is very high and natural. The role of a teacher is more 'balanced' than compared to a parent. While possessiveness of a parent may act as a negative factor, the balanced view of a teacher can provide the required cover and act as a positive factor.

A teacher influencer can use Instagram as a form of commodification and commerce simultaneously (Summer Davis et al, 2022). A game-based learning approach for IOT had a positive impact on the learning process and integration of educational games into common learning management practices for extending common formal learning models (Luca Petrovic, 2022). Instagram in education had greater advantage due to its ease in use, and daily use of mobile phones by students. (D. Stojanovic, et al, 2019).

Figure 1. We try to present below a conceptual model towards understanding the influence of social networking platform Instagram over the academic performance of students
Source: Compilation from Review of Literature

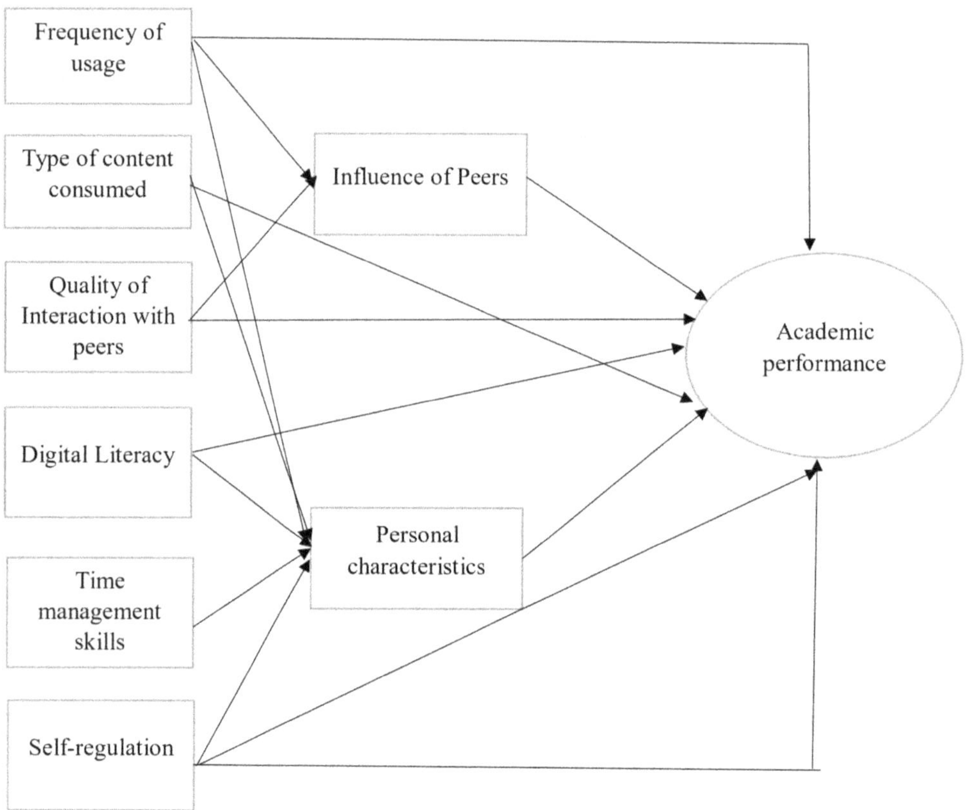

INTERPRETATION OF THE MODEL

The above model tries to explain the influence of different independent variables like Frequency of usage, type of content consumed by them across social networking channel, quality of interaction with peers, Digital literacy possessed by the students, their time management skills along with a self-regulation play a key role in influencing the Academic performance. The frequency of usage across social networking platform plays a key role as the increase in frequency of usage of social network will keep the students away from their academics and thereby influencing their academic scores. The frequency of usage is further affected by influence of peer to a great extent, peer support is a key dimension as it has the power to influence the time spend by user across social networking platforms.

The quality of interaction with peers is another significant parameter influencing academic performance as it will influence the time spend across different networking platforms. Type of peers a student will come across will influence the time they spend across social networking portals.

Content consumption play an important role towards influencing academic performance of students as the student community comes across different types of content which keeps them engrossed to their screens and thereby affecting their academic performance. Hence Content consumption is a key connection towards academic performance of students.

Digital Literacy play an important role towards academic performance of students if a student is aware about the digital set up there are chances of having an academic performance which may not be up to the mark as he or she may be spending more time across different networking platforms and may not be ensuring academic progress. Academic performance may be heavily influenced by the level of digital literacy carried by the student further digital literacy is also influenced by the personal characteristics which further influences the performances of students.

Time management skills also play a key role towards academic performance, if the students community spend excessive amount of time across social networking channels their academic performance will be influenced which is further moderated by personal characteristics of people. It is essential to watch out for time management so the academic performance is not influenced and results are in favor of students

Finally, it is all about self-regulation if a particular student is able to regulate himself and ensure proper division of time towards usage of social networking the academic performance will not be affected and the student will be able to effectively utilize their time across social networking as well as academics.

CONCLUSION

Many youngsters log in 'Instagram' in search of motivation. However, motivation is like a cola 'fizz' which disappears sooner than expected. After watching a few motivational reels, the AI directs the nature of watching and the student forgets the purpose of starting the Instagram and before realisation, a lot of time is wasted.

For the youngsters, the better source of motivation can be a real life 'inspiration. An inspiration from a close relative or a neighbour can help the students correlate the real life struggle and the success achieved. It would create a realisation factor for the students and the trust factor would be high.

Also, the 'routine' inculcates a 'discipline' in life which is a better source to achieve success than watching motivational videos. In simple words, an academic routine though boring is a better recipes of success whereas a motivational video can be a reason for distraction.

Instagram has a lot of advantages with regards to exposure of students to the world at large, becoming an instant sensation and trending element, explore newer market avenues, increased emotional quotient. However, these advantages come at a huge cost. The cost involved is not in terms of money but in terms of time. The emotional maturity is very important with regards to the call to stop. This is because the algorithm of Instagram is so powerful that it can keep a person of any age engaged for a long period of time. Influencers who gain monetary gain are smart enough to restrict their screen time, likewise, experienced and matured people keep a check on the screen time. The most likely scape goats are inexperienced, young, and enthusiastic adolescents who are unable to control their emotions and they get addicted. The students are unable to manage their academic routine and hence, end up losing the basic qualification and get lost in the starry world of influencers and the world of Instagram.

It may not be wrong to say that Instagram affects the Academic routine in a big way if it is not controlled. A 'balanced' approach is the need of the hour.

REFERENCES

Ahmed, M. S., Rony, R. J., Ashhab, M. M., & Ahmed, N. (2020). An Empirical Study to Analyze the Impact of Instagram on Students' Academic Results. *2020 IEEE Region 10 Symposium (TENSYMP)*, 666-669.

Akanksh, S. S., D'souza, L., & Manish, S. (2020). The effect of Instagram addiction on quality of life among undergraduate students in Mysuru. *International Journal of Indian Psychology*, *8*(4), 1324–1330.

Barot, H. (2019). *Drawbacks of Instagram on Today's Society.* https://www.justwebw-orld.com/drawbacks-instagram-todays-society/

Berlatsky, N. (2014). *Are social networking sites harmful?* Greenhaven Publishing LLC.

Borgatti, S. P., Everett, M. G., & Johnson, J. C. (2013). Analyzing social networks. *Sage (Atlanta, Ga.)*.

Chaturvedi, C. (2018). *Instagram vs. Snapchat vs. Pinterest - What should be your pick* [Infographic]. A1 Future Technologies. https://www.a1future.com/blog/instagram-snapchat-pinterest-infographic/

Clark, L. S. (2013). *The parent app: Understanding families in the digital age*. Oxford University Press.

Coman, C., Meseşan-Schmitz, L., Ţîru, L.G., Grosseck, G., & Bularca, M.C. (2021). *Dear student, what should I write on my wall? A case study on academic uses of Facebook and Instagram during the pandemic*. Academic Press.

Constine, J. (2018). *Instagram hits 1 billion monthly users, up from 800M in September*. TechCrunch.

Davis, S., & Yi, J. H. (2022). Double tap, double trouble: Instagram, teachers, and profit. *E-Learning and Digital Media*, *19*(3), 320–339. doi:10.1177/20427530211064706

Diker, E., & Gencer, Z. (2019). A Study About the Habits Of Using Instagram By Academicians. *Online Academic Journal of Information Technology.*, *18*(4), 18–24. doi:10.5824/1309-1581.2019.3.007.x

Fioravanti, G., Prostamo, A., & Casale, S. (2020). Taking a short break from Instagram: The effects on subjective well-Being. *Cyberpsychology, Behavior, and Social Networking*, *23*(2), 107–112. doi:10.1089/cyber.2019.0400 PMID:31851833

Floros, G., & Siomos, K. (2013). The relationship between optimal parenting, Internet addiction and motives for social networking in adolescence. *Psychiatry Research*, *209*(3), 529–534. doi:10.1016/j.psychres.2013.01.010 PMID:23415042

Foroughi, B., Griffiths, M., Iranmanesh, M., & Salamzadeh, Y. (2021). Associations Between Instagram Addiction, Academic Performance, Social Anxiety, Depression, and Life Satisfaction Among University Students. *International Journal of Mental Health and Addiction*, *20*, 1–22.

Green, D. J. (2019). *Instagram Marketing: The Guide Book for Using Photos on Instagram to Gain Millions of Followers Quickly and to Skyrocket Your Business*. Influencer and Social Media Marketing.

Green & Martinez. (2018). In a World of Social Media: A Case Study Analysis of Instagram. *American Research Journal of Business and Management, 4*(1), 1-8.

Haddon, L., & Livingstone, S. (2014). *The meaning of online problematic situations for children: The UK report*. London: EU Kids Online, LSE.

Handayani, F. (2015). Instagram as a teaching tool? Really? *Proceedings of ISELT FBS Universitas Negeri Padang*, *4*(1), 320–327.

Hasfi, Mau, & Farid. (2022). Instagram Accounts for Parenting Education: A New Culture. *Proceedings of the 3rd International Conference on Linguistics and Cultural (ICLC),* 198-207.

Hashish, Y., Bunt, A., & Young, J. E. (2014). Involving children in content control: A collaborative and research. *Communication Yearbook*, *29*, 35–47.

Hemley, D. (2013). *Instagram for business tips*. https://www.so-cialmediaex-am-iner.com/instagram-for-business-tips/

Herman, J. (2019). *The 8 Advantages of Using Instagram for Business.* https://nealschaffer.com/advan-tages-using-instagrambusiness

Highfield, T., & Leaver, T. (2015). A methodology for mapping Instagram hashtags. *First Monday*, *20*(1), 1–11.

Janssens, A., Goossens, L., van den Noortgate, W., Colpin, H., Verschueren, K., & van Leeuwen, K. (2015). Parents' and adolescents' perspectives on parenting: Evaluating conceptual structure, measure-ment in variance and criterion validity. *Assessment*, *22*(4), 473–489. doi:10.1177/1073191114550477 PMID:25225229

Jayasekara, Maniyangama, Vithana, Weerasinghe, Wijekoon, & Panchendrarajan. (2022). AI-Based Child Care Parental Control System. *4th International Conference on Advancements in Computing (ICAC),* 120-125.

Johnson, J., & Henderson, A. (2024). *Conceptual models: Core to the Design of Interactive Applica-tions*. Springer.

Kabilan, S. (2023). A Study on Impact of Social Media On Consumer Purchasing Behaviour In Chen-nai City With Special Reference To Instagram Influencers. *Indian Journal of Psychology*, *02*, 59–64.

Karagiannis, D., Mayr, H. C., & Mylopoulos, J. (2016). *Domain-Specific conceptual modeling: Concepts, Methods and Tools*. Springer. doi:10.1007/978-3-319-39417-6

Laksana, I., Wahyuni, E., & Aditya, C. (2023). Game Design for Mobile App-Based IoT Introduction Education in STEM Learning. *Jurnal RESTI*, *7*, 688–696.

Mark, G. (2005). A 'components' model of addiction within a biopsychosocial framework. *Journal of Substance Use*, *10*(4), 191–197. doi:10.1080/14659890500114359

Mircea. (2019). The Rise Of Instagram - Evolution, Statistics, Advantages And Disadvantages. *Revisita Economics, 71*(4), 53-63.

Obadara & Olaopa. (2018). *Social Media Utilisation, Study Habit and Undergraduate Students' Academic Performance in a University of Education in Nigeria*. Academic Press.

Pittman, M., & Reich, B. (2016). Social media and loneliness: Why an Instagram picture may be worth more than a thousand Twitter words. *Computers in Human Behavior*, *62*, 155–167. doi:10.1016/j.chb.2016.03.084

Ranzini, G., Newlands, G., & Lutz, C. (2020). Sharenting, Peer Influence, and Privacy Concerns: A Study on the Instagram-Sharing Behaviors of Parents in the United Kingdom. *Social Media + Society*, *6*(4). Advance online publication. doi:10.1177/2056305120978376

Riesmeyer, C., Abel, B., & Großmann, A. (2019). The family rules. The influence of parenting styles on adolescents' media literacy. MedienPädagogik. *Zeitschrift Für Theorie Und Praxis Der Medienbildung*, *35*, 74–96. doi:10.21240/mpaed/35/2019.10.20.X

Robiatul, A., & Rachmawati, Y. (2021). Parenting Program to Protect Children's Privacy: The Phenomenon of Sharenting Children on social media. *Pendidikan Usia Dini*, *15*(1), 162–180. doi:10.21009/JPUD.151.09

Sadiku, M., Omotoso, A., & Musa, S. (2019). Social Networking. *International Journal of Trend in Scientific Research and Development.*, *3*(-3), 126–128. doi:10.31142/ijtsrd21657

Saleem, P. (2019). A Study on Growth Rate of Multi-Level Marketing In India, A Paradigm Shift in Banking. *Marketing and HRM.*, *1*, 70–74.

Sharma, A., Sanghvi, K., & Churi, P. (2022). The Impact of Instagram on young Adult's social comparison, colourism and mental health: Indian perspective. Academic Press.

Singh, C., Bhnwaria, D., Nengzaching, E., Kaur, G., Haokip, H., Jani, H., Sharma, M. C., & Sk, M. (2020). A Descriptive study to access daily routine activities and level of stress among students of BSc (Hons.) Nursing students at AIIMS, Jodhpur. *International Journal of Nursing Education and Research.*, *8*(1), 13–18. doi:10.5958/2454-2660.2020.00003.4

Social Networking. (2023b). https://dictionary.cambridge.org/dictionary/english/social-networking

Statista. (2023). *Number of influencers brands worked with worldwide 2023*. Author.

Stojanovic, D., Bogdanovic, Z., & Despotovic, M. (2019). An approach to using Instagram in secondary education. University of Bucharest, Faculty of Matematics and Informatics.

Syaifudin, M. A. (2021). The Role of Parents in the Use of Children's Social Media Under Age. *Ilmu Hukum.*, *12*(1), 15–27. doi:10.58471/justi.v12i1.97

Tekin, I., & Aydın, S. (2022). Well-Being and Instagram Use Among University Students. *International Journal of Adult Education and Technology.*, *4*(3), 18–23. doi:10.4018/IJAET.310074

Wahid, R., & Wadud, M. (2020). Social Media Marketing on Instagram: When Is the Most Effective Posting Timing? *International Journal of Multidisciplinary Research, 14*(4), 312–321.

Wilson, T. (2017). *A.P.J. Abdul Kalam: "Evolution of a unique you", address to students IIT Madras - 2010*. Speakola. https://speakola.com/motivate/apj-abdul-kalam-iit-madras-2010

Wright, G., & Yasar, K. (2022, December 12). *Social networking*. WhatIs. https://www.techtarget.com/whatis/definition/social-networking

Zaman, B., & Nouwen, M. (2016). *Parental controls: Advice for parents, researchers and industry*. Academic Press.

Chapter 18
Competitive Data Use, Analysis, and Big Data Applications in Online Advertising

Sinan Akseki
Iğdir Üniversitesi, Turkey

ABSTRACT

In the advertising industry, based on data, the reasonable application of big data analysis means that accurate internet advertising can promote the display of advertising marketing, and then truly achieve accurate positioning and marketing. Consideration should be given to the difficulties faced by organizations in accessing expensive data storage and the difficulties in sharing data with commercial and international partners due to the availability of data platforms that are considered insecure. It is safe to say that now is the right time to invest in advertising solutions specifically designed to handle big data. Big data may need to be rethought to be clearer not only in terms of the direct effects of advertising messages on individuals, but also on the profound, if indirect, consequences of the self-transformation of advertising industries.

INTRODUCTION

Today, the proliferation of digital environments is rapidly changing the application areas and capabilities of the advertising industry. The analysis of big data, business intelligence and analysis, like the application layer, represent data science, which offers a set of processes and plays a role in extracting innervisions from structured or unstructured big data. Nowadays, by the help of big data solutions, advertising companies can comprehend consumer routines better and gain in-depth information about their behavior.

Big data solutions not only predict what customers want to hear from advertisements, but also incorporate the effectiveness of high-load systems and thus can become a key component of a results-oriented advertising system. Late innovations of technology and growing interest in the big data potential can enable chances to create competitive pros for companies all the way through multiple industries.

DOI: 10.4018/979-8-3693-0855-4.ch018

Analyzing large amounts of data on the fly can enable advertisers to apply insights into customer segmentation models to improve customer engagement strategies and increase the valuation of customer interactions. The solutions could transmit traditional advertising models and practices and improve how core marketing functions are carried out. Data analytics has a positive impact on all pieces of the chain of data value and increases business opportunities via business intelligence and analyses whilst benefiting both society and citizens (Curry, et al. 2021).

The big data concept first appeared in a paper written by Francis X. Diebold in August 2000 (Gürsakal, 2013). The big data concept was discussed in the paper titled Big Data Dynamic Factor Models for Macroeconomic Measurement and Forecasting at the 8th World Econometrics Congress held in Seattle (Gülsoy, 1999). The company called Meta Group, which is now part of Gartner, made statements about the diversity, volume and speed of big data in 2001 (Laney, 2019).

Gahi et al. (2016) expresses big data as follows: They are a set of technologies and techniques that require new ways of adapting to discover hidden values from diverse, complex, and large-scale large data sets. Google, Facebook, E-Bay are the first companies to use big data software and new technologies. These companies have large and growing amounts of data to store and analyze. However, there is no software or tool that can be used to handle such a large capacity. As a matter of fact, when there is too much data, there will be other organizations and companies that encounter the same problem. As a result, organizations and companies have helped develop new data mining facilities and transfer these facilities to the computer environment in order not to lose their competitive advantage and to help them gain it.

Schönberger, Mayer and Cukier (2013) state that there is no clear definition of big data. Initially, people thought that if the amount of information was too large, the amount of data analyzed would not fit in the computer's memory for processing. Engineers needed to change the tools and resources they used to examine all the data. Today, these tools are the source of new processing technologies, such as Google's MapReduce and Hadoop, and can be considered tools equivalent to the open software that emerged at Yahoo and can handle more data than before. The data used in these techniques does not need to be in sequential rows or in classical database tables. With big data, many things that could never be stored, measured, shared and analyzed in the past have started to become data (Schönberger, Mayer and Cukier, 2013).

PURPOSE - SCOPE AND METHOD OF THE RESEARCH

About big data, their organizational structure and their orientation on how they have the necessary talents for it are discussed in the context of digital advertising. It shows the digital advertising, management and analysis processes of the technology platforms in question, mediated by big data. The representation of the analysis of big data techniques used in digital advertising industry platforms is stated in terms of process and transaction stages. It is so significant for managers and researchers who are interested in big data to understand the role of data analytics, especially big data analytics, and the role of technology in big data system quality when trying to achieve success in developing new products.

This research is designed according to the areas where technologies at the conceptual frontier relate to big data and digital advertising. In this way, it was tried to ensure "consistent application of analytical procedures and standards" (Krippendorff, 2003: 88).

Advertising has evolved into a rather complicated and interconnected global ecosystem including various technologies and applications that are led by automated systems and data analytics applications. (Vlist ve Helmond, 2021).

Another aim of the research is to analyze the operating model of digital advertising in the big data environment and provide a space to connect discussions on how they structure big data. The results of this research are expected to provide managers of manufacturing companies with insight into making better decisions that increase product or service success, which includes providing personalized services to customers, thereby helping the business achieve goals and competitiveness.

THE COMPETITIVE TOOL OF ONLINE ADVERTISING: BIG DATA

Big data is a large data set that cannot be used, stored, processed, retrieved, analyzed and examined by evaluating the techniques and assumptions of traditional databases (Cox and Ellsworth, 1997: 235). While big data processes, organizes and analyzes data, it transforms it into a useful form that we call information (Konya, 2019). According to another literature, data is raw information that is meaningless or cannot be used alone. However, knowledge and information need to be associated, grouped, explained, and analyzed (Forest et al., 2014).

Big data helps improve transaction efficiency by meeting buyers' requirements, improving customers' services and products, increasing market share, and preventing excess costs. Teradat, IBM, HP, Oracle and similar companies provide different data warehouses and software to help organizations accumulate and process their data (Aktan, 2018: 1-22).

Large volumes of data sets that ensure unparalleled point of view into user profiles and mores are a key input to the functioning of the entire digital economy as a whole and online advertising in particular. Because the data sets in question are the basic parameters of what type of ads will be shown to people who view the ad in aimed advertising that composes an important part of online advertising. The better the consumers to whom ads will be displayed are aimed, the more advertisers are willing to pay for the relevant advertising space, so it converts consumer data into income for online platforms. (BUITEN M. C. (2020), "Exploitative Abuses in Digital Markets: Between Competition Law and Data Protection Law", Journal of Antitrust Enforcement, Vol. 9, No: 2, s. 271.).

That's why issues such as the sorts of data collected/processed in online advertising, the power gained by enterprises within the framework of the data they collect, by what means utilizer data is collected, how data are utilized in the aimed advertising, the behavior of consumers and reactions to their data being used in aimed advertising are one of the main matters which need to be dealt in order to reveal the significance of data in terms of rivalry in the online advertising market. These issues are discussed respectively below.

Studies that replace subjective evaluations in traditional advertising with analytical findings based on information obtained as a result of data analysis can be added to the literature. Different applied studies can be done which could assist drive digital strategy and shape fairly aimed campaigns by connecting data to human experience. More research is needed from the perspective of advertising professionals to gain insight and a deeper understanding of advertising professionals.

Phenomena such as big data, predictive analysis, personalized content, behavioral targeting, which are the future predictions of advertising analytics and ideas about the future effects of current strategies, shape the advertising industry day by day. As the insights, actions, research and academic debates gained from big data continue, the data-driven creative industry will develop further than it is today.

Big data is exactly the invisible side of the iceberg. You can see a small part of it on the surface, but underneath it is the larger and most important part. Companies that attach particular importance to innovation have perceived the importance of big data and strive to emphasize it in every environment (Schönberger and Cukier, 2013).

If data is a value that shapes the future, companies should make data useful in predicting and implementing new business models (Rotella, 2012). The option value of the data represents the set of all possible formats in which the data can be applied. In the Big Data Era, data continues to add value for a long time after it is used (Schönberger and Cukier, 2013).

The way for businesses to understand the value that will be created by utilizing big data is to analyze their "big data business motivations". Companies can use data types to provide new and important information to business processes and improve decision-making processes. These can be explained as follows (Konya, 2019; Akıncı, 2019; Bayrakçı, 2015).

BIG DATA SOURCES USED IN DIGITAL ADVERTISING

Today, people produce data regularly. Using big data applications, large amounts of valuable information can be obtained, which is collected, analyzed and visualized. Thanks to this information, big data may give idea as to not only who potential customers are, but also where they are, what they want, and how and when they want to be contacted (Hasimova, 2016: 13).

Integration of any big data-mediated system means that it can integrate different types of data such as voice, transactional, video and clickstream. A system's accessibility determines the level at which administrators can access an analytics platform with guaranteed scalability and convenience. Additionally, the response time of a system determines the responsiveness and timeliness of an analytics platform (Aljumah, et al., 2021).

Digital data is described as data generated via services supplied by the internet (e.g. search and click data) and on the net, man interaction with others (e.g. the data from social media, blogs, community forums and incentivized referrals) (Kumar et al., 2013)

Clickstream data is created by cataloging a customer's clicking behavior when they access a web page. Analyzing clickstream data could supply the chance to understand visitor traffic by collecting a wealth of knowledge about the behavior of the customer and can be of different structures and types, involving yet not limited to the number of page views, visits frequency, items characteristics viewed and visit duration (Moe and Fader, 2004).

As well as unstructured data such as log files, video, audio, images, internet of things (IoT), social media and more, data sources may involve structured data like the data of the customer. Advertisers use the data of a customer to define who need to be aimed at with which marketing. Target audiences are selected from pools of customer data using characteristics such as demographics, geography, values, or interests. Gandomi and Harder argue how analytics of big data has drawn attention of business and government leaders by breaking down big data analytics into text analytics, audio analytics, video analytics, social media analytics, and predictive analytics (Gandomi, and Haider, 2015).

By using digital footprints of unprecedented customer identifiers (e.g., email addresses, phone numbers, social media logins, etc.) to reach individuals, data brokers play a central role in modern "people-based marketing" (Vlist and Helmond, 2021).

Structured and unstructured data provide cues and specimens about the behavior of a consumer. The science of big data analytics which is applied to a great number of unstructured data is used to make innovation advertising campaigns (Jobs et al., 2016).

The skill to sort and analyze structured and unstructured data helps digital advertisers find out new relationships, detect arising movements and models, and get actionable innervisions which provide a competitive pros. This enables traditional advertising to speedily transform into the field of personalized and fairly aimed online and mobile advertisements, that is, data-based marketing (Chandramouli, 2022, p. 95).

In the digital advertising and marketing industry, sourcing (or accessing) and using data through partnership agreements is common. These types of data partnerships occur since data is a strategic entity for many companies, supporting advertising-based business models, data-driven business operations, and artificial intelligence (AI)-based tools, products, and services that all rely on (access to) data in large volumes (Vlist and Helmond, 2021).

Any internet user leaves a "digital footprint". Digital devices, smartphones, and smart devices at home collect data about our lives to show the advertising products we need (Verhoef et al. 2016).

In addition to these objects, data sets within big data mostly come from different sources for instance social media, sensors (signal receivers and transmitters), scientific applications, monitoring data (surveillance), video and visual archives, internet texts and documents, internet browsing indexes, medical records, business activity records consist of large volumes of data flowing very quickly (Power, 2015).

Personalized and targeted advertising all results in constantly revealing large amounts of data about what users do, say, like, share, and where they go via our mobile devices. These are data obtained from sources like photos, videos and social media posts. However, they could not be analyzed by traditional methods. These data can now be captured, stored and analyzed using big data analysis platforms (Chandramouli, 2022, p. 98).

In conclusion, digital advertisers derive new and relevant information from raw chaotic data. The subheadings of this section specify the data sorts and data sources used in big data-mediated digital advertising.

TYPES OF DATA COLLECTED/PROCESSED IN ONLINE ADVERTISING

Online advertising uses various technologies to process big data and present it to advertisers. Additionally, data mining creates economic value for the online behavioral advertising industry, enabling its rapid growth and development. Such a large advertising revenue essentially shows that users are under the influence of more online advertising, that is, more online behavioral advertising and data mining (Hunt, 2016: 57-59).

In short, online advertising is now based on online behavioral advertising and data mining. Big data content includes texts, emails, videos, documents, images, system logs, clickstreams, social network interactions, scientific data, health records, sensors and smartphones, government and private sector records, and other components. The combination of data obtained using these components can provide a wide range of results. Because, in the cholera epidemic of 1854, the mapping method is represented as big data basis and today it could be done with search engines. These data can be obtained according to the density of Google searches in a certain area (Lokke, 2018: 61).

For this reason, it can be said that Google can even detect the potential for disease transmission by recording who you call and where you search at the same time as official health institutions. Online behavioral advertising still has a very privileged place today. On the one hand, it is very important for the formation of digital advertising, but on the other hand, it also leads to changes in the target audience that today's advertising is trying to reach. This is also of great value to advertisers and is at the center of privacy debates such as security and privacy. In this way, its important and special status comes from various components. This phenomenon is partly driven by different parties, including consumers, advertisers, policy makers, computer scientists, and the interdisciplinary nature of the field (Boerman; Kruikemeier; Borgesius, 2017: 364).

Although online behavioral advertising itself is considered an advertising practice, it is defined differently; It is also called a system, a specific form of targeted advertising, data collection practices and a new form of advertising (Smith; Noort; Voorveld, 2014; McDonald and Cranor, 2009; Kim, 2014). In general, online behavioral advertising is expressed as a method of creating online advertising in the world of digital advertising, and its investments are gradually increasing. However, that this type of advertising goes far beyond ordinary methods and will become a part of advertising in the future is stated. Actually, the definition of online behavioral advertising involves the expression "a new phenomenon" (Boerman; Kruikemeier; Borgesius, 2017:363).

The case for online behavioral advertising in digital advertising relates to its use as a targeting method. Behavioral objectives are one of several types of objectives and form the basis of online behavioral advertising. It simply "gets benefits from users' web browsing behavior to improve advertising effects" (Chen and Stallaert, 2014: 430). To summarize; Online behavioral advertising is advertising that has its own signature and rules. It is an important method used in digital and online advertising applications, which is especially popular among advertisers. Because of this, it has a special position unlike many advertisements in this respect.

Accessing Unstructured Data

Data whose format or structure is unknown is classified as unstructured data. Approximately 80% of existing data, consisting of videos, graphics, web pages, e-mails, PDF files, PowerPoint presentations and Wikipedia entries, is unstructured (Tanwar, Duggal and Khatri, 2015: 1-4). Unstructured data is the largest type of structure and is becoming more abundant. Simply analyzing data from social media can provide more insight and support businesses with new ideas. If we take the data obtained from Twitter as an example, it is examined by transforming it into structured data to reveal the behavior of users (Alkan, 2015).

Unstructured data constitutes the most of the volume of the big data conception. Unstructured data, whose volume increases with the use of developing technology, does not allow working with conventional methods. This problem has led to the development of data mining and text mining and the formation of NoSQL (Not only SQL-more than relational) database (Oracle, 2011: 5-6).

When unstructured data is combined with structured data, the resulting data after analyzing the data can be used to obtain important information. Unstructured data, such as data from social media, electronic devices and smartphones or sensors, can provide different angles and indicators, supporting consumers to better understand products and markets (Desouza and Jacob, 2017: 4-7; Tanwar, Duggal and Khatri, 2015: 1 -4).

Unstructured Data is the most difficult data to process and categorize among data sets. Audio files, videos, images and text files are examples of such data. Businesses and organizations cannot benefit from these data sets without the help of data analysts. These data sets are made available only through analysis and processing (Orgaz et al. 2015).

Unstructured data is used to refer to data which haven't got a predefined data model or cannot be adapted to a predefined model. Although it is generally text-oriented, it can also contain different types of data such as date, number, coordinate data. Unstructured data contains information that needs to be labeled and organized. This data is mostly used to analyze the content which is generated by users. Data can come from various places (review sites, social media, business listings) and different media (texts, images, short video clips, chat responses) (Yu, 2022: 195).

These types of data, also called Third Party Data, can analyze holistic performance through aggregated, cross-platform analytics that integrate local, proprietary, and third-party metrics. Contrary to third-party application developers and self-service advertisers, just cooperators could automate the creation, management and measurement of advertisements and aiming of data-based audiences by means of CRM software integrations. In addition, just cooperators could analyze the performance of advertisement campaign throughout channels of media distribution using custom dashboards (Vlist and Helmond, 2021).

Unstructured data is readily accessible from websites operated by third parties too. Unstructured and semi-structured data are all other data, accounting for approximately 95% of all data (Gandomi and Haider, 2015), it includes dates, numbers, and images and videos that are not readily classified into columns, rows, or fields, and are often text-heavy. Structured data is knowledge which has a predefined data model and could be organized in a predetermined manner, for instance, into a predefined field – Gender, age, occupation, marital status, etc. - is properly created customer data (Marr, 2016).

Semi-Structured Data

Semi Structured Data: They are used to define data sets in which some of the data within the concept of semi-structured data is structured and some of it is unstructured. Semi-structured data consists of a mixture of existing data in databases and new data sets, and it is not clear how they will be stored. Semi-structured data is defined as a structured data format that is not organized like the structure in relational databases and contains elements that can separate the data into various hierarchies (Ebenderu, 2016, p. 46).

Data exchanged between third-party aggregators using web services is semi-structured data. Semi-structured data is a structured data format that is not organized like the structure in relational databases (Bendle and Wang, 2016).

Digital advertising is subject to the capability to get, integrate and analyze data both from internal and external resources. That 80% of this data is "unstructured or chaotic" is the challenge. This data is obtained from sources like photos, videos and social media posts (they are data that says a lot about us) however, they could not be analyzed by traditional methods (Kees et al. 2017. P. 144-150).

Companies could now obtain, store and analyze the whole collected data, both structured and unstructured utilizing big data analytics platforms. In conclusion, digital advertisers could derive fresh and relevant innervisions from raw chaotic data. Actionable information that informs marketing decisions and strategies can be obtained (Hashimova, 2016).

This data needs to be properly structured and cleaned. Only after this data is processed can it be transformed into real business insights. With the rapid data analytics technology and the capability to process new data sources, organizations could quickly analyze knowledge and make informed decisions based upon what they learn. It is used as a model which converts this unstructured raw log-level data into clear and transparent knowledge to understand advertising performance better (Ma et al., 2014: 515).

Semi-structured data could include both forms of data. We could see semi-structured data structured in the form. It is a type of structured data, but its structure is not suitable for a strict data model. For example, Word Processing Software includes metadata that indicates the name of the person who created the text and the time it was created, but the majority of documents are unstructured text. In e-mails, date, time, sender, recipient, other fixed fields, content of the e-mail and attachments are added to unstructured data. Images, graphs, dates, and places are used to mark keywords so that we can organize and find graphs (Beal, 1997).

Semi-structured data has an understandable system but is not useful in form (Franks, 2012: 14). Although semi-structured data can be used alone, like structured data, it may produce different results when analyzed. Markup languages such as Extensible Markup Language (XML) are shown as examples of this type of data. The development of big data has allowed data to undergo transformation. Thus, useful information can be obtained by collecting difficult to understand data in a table (Alkan, 2015: 5).

Structured Data

In its most general definition, structured data means organized (structured) data. Structured data refers to traditional data that is stored in the database and can be easily edited and applied (Desouza and Jacob, 2017: 4).

Structured Data basically mentions the data that consists of certain structures and is easy to access and process. These data, which are in the form of rows and columns and can be displayed in spreadsheets, include addresses, names, etc. Simply put, structured data refer to data circulating in fixed areas (Orgaz et al. 2015).

Structured data displays a view that contains various fields and shows how these fields are related to each other. Involving name, surname, address, age, phone number, etc., a consumer databas can be shown as an example of structured data.

Unstructured data, however, is a sort of data that does not suit a specific model and should be processed by algorithms to turn into commercial value, and mostly created by people and contains person-oriented content.

Structured data is defined as data that is simpler to understand compared to other types of data. Structured data has an understandable structure that is well explained in databases or spreadsheets. Processing, maintaining and reviewing data is simple. For example, we can consider an Excel file containing all customer records.

Structured data is managed using a programming language (Structured Query Language (SQL)) built to manage and query data in relational database management systems. It was first developed by IBM in the early 1970s and later by Relational Software, Inc.. It is currently being developed commercially by Oracle Corporation (Beal, 1997).

Microsoft SQL Server, Access, SAP, Oracle Excel etc. Conventional applications have been sufficient to store and use data. There is no need for complex algorithms or long-term analyzes to process this data (Bayrakçı, 2015: 8).

This type of data is already organized, it just needs to be recorded and analyzed. For example, those who will integrate a big data platform into an existing lead distribution service will benefit from additional speed and more detailed analysis. This is because each piece of information already comes with a label like name, age, country, etc. Within structured data, it is clear which data is located where and in what format. Therefore, when any information is needed between data sets, it is very easy to obtain this information quickly. Summarization and reporting operations can be carried out quickly within data stacks. To query structured data sets, SQL (Structured Query Language) program is generally used (Vargiu, 2012: 48).

Data that remains within the modified boundaries of a record or document is known as organized data. Customer data refer to behavioral and demographic knowledge as to customers which businesses and marketers gather to comprehend and connect with their customers. Customer data is the basis of any succeeding business strategy, and data-driven organizations are taking the required steps to collect sufficient customer data which will allow them to develop customer experience and fine-tune business operations (Atley and Nepikelov, 2014).

Access to Real-Time Data

It is very important for companies to produce data at the right time to get use of opportunities. Nowadays, consumers attach great importance to the process of obtaining a product or service. Companies generally face difficulties such as consumers appearing and disappearing suddenly. For this reason, companies have difficulty in influencing consumers' purchasing decisions (Bayrakçı, 2015).

Predictive Analysis

Integration of existing data with predictive analysis is crucial, otherwise the data will be of no relevance. Analysis of the data provided can ensure companies to foresee future events from different perspectives. The data could be used as a guide and may reveal some precautions which should be taken. Predictive analysis can provide speed to gain an advantage in business-to-business competition. Having used predictive analysis to make up personalized services or products could enhance customer acquisition and retention, increasing income chances for companies. Thus, it allows the company to stand out and gain a better position. Predictive analysis can provide insight into possibilities by interpreting harms and challenges (Franks, 2012; Ohlhorst, 2012).

DATA COLLECTION MANAGEMENT TECHNOLOGIES USED IN DIGITAL ADVERTISING

The Technologies of big data analytics enable to find the actionable data which could be utilized in media planning and marketing and also advertising. Big data can be collected from various sources like social media, website traffic and clicks, emails, video and presentations and obtain actionable and meaningful data from that. Big data technologies make it possible not only to collect and store larger data sets, but also to analyze them to reveal new and precious innervisions with new instruments which address the whole data management loop. Usually, big data processing covers an extensive data run, from collecting coarse data to consuming actionable knowledge. The process of analysis, data collection and cleaning of data within Big Data has gained importance with the increasing effectiveness of digital platforms and social networks in user profiles (Assad and Gomez, 2011: 115-118).

Producing rich interaction data that are known as behavioral data, nowaday, customers interact with brands across an increasingly larger digital and offline footprint. In conclusion, marketers and customer experience teams need to work with more than one tools to interact with these customers and to aim them at contact points. Big data makes it possible to collect and analyze consistent and personalized data from multiple sources like web, mobile apps, email, live chat and even in-store interactions.(Berkgvist, 2015: 70).

The foundations of big data analytics consist of mathematics, statistics, engineering, program interface, computer science and information technology. Big data analytics techniques involve a very diverse mathematical, statistical and modeling techniques. (Sun et al., 2015). However, in advertising, big data is used with a range of applications, involving real-time planning, optimization and "micro-moments" (Gibson, 2018: 42) marketing. as well as cookies, application programming interfaces (APIs), and software development kits (SDKs), business software technology tools, takes place at the centre of the digital advertising ecosystem. Software needed to make programmatic advertising 'work' to a great extent, development and integration efforts are faciliated (Vlist and Helmond, 2021).

Cookie

Objective and advertising cookies are technology specially designed to collect knowledge from internet users' devices for the purpose of displaying advertisements on topics of interest. A cookie is described as a file which is saved on computers to help identify unique utilizers and store preferences (Moore, 2021).

Advertisers put those cookies on a website with the permission of the website operator. Cookies in digital advertizing help attract customers with aimed ads and also can share with other advertisers so that this kind of aimed ads can be observed and measured. Cookies can also help create user profiles and provide the most appropriate advertisements to users by monitoring data on websites (Couto, 2015).

By storing information in an identification link, websites and servers could recall preferences or distinguish web browsers from one visit to the next or from one website to another. This identification process is called "third party" cookies, and they may be designed to pursue a user's online activities over time, creating a database of personal interests and other details. (Wingfield, 2010).

When a visitor reaches the site, Google Analytics puts a cookie on the computer, then that cookie traces future action on the website by anonymously recording certain technological and geographical information in browsing logs. An advertisement cookie basically is nothing more than a little piece of data which catalogs the behaviours of all the users in a certain website. However, when implemented correctly, this simple information can store the user's login information, which pages they visited, how long they stayed on the page, the device they used, the time zone, and what language they used. This information is crucial for the digital efforts of any website. Thanks to the information obtained from cookies, the chances of success of the campaigns of businesses and organizations increase (Cooper et al., 2021).

Information contained in cookies; suggests a more personalized user experience since it recollects previous internet transactions such as login information, location settings, items added to cart and more. Advertisers get benefit of cookies to obtain data (such as the websites you visit) that will help them deliver the most relevant and aimed content to certain spectators (Jagetheesan, 2013).

Web Beacon

Web Beacons technology is a technology that provides proximity-based triggers and movements in both the physical and digital world. Beacon advertising is an advertising technique which is used to aim consumers that are based on their physical location. This is made possible through a small device called a beacon that is battery-powered and installed in a physical location (for example, a retail store counter). These beacons later send messages or advertisements to consumers' mobile phones by means of bluetooth. The targeting radius can be specific to the consumer's location or expanded to a certain range (Khofi and Minet, 2018, p. 750).

There might be pursuing devices like web "beacons" which have code pieces embedded in the page and can track the visiters' clicks and even record their keystrokes. It will track where every piece of content, every image, video or piece of text on a visited web page comes from on the internet. This feature pays particular attention to content coming from "third-party" internet addresses, that is, addresses different from what the utiliser views in the address bar at the top of the browser (Wingfield, 2010).

This technology helps you understand the effect and effectiveness of your search advertisements by registering real store visits from your search advertisements. By collecting as much data as possible about marketing activities, businesses and organizations can better understand what works and what does not, and the marketing strategy can be adapted according to this information (Sie and Kou, 2017: 335).

Ad Attribution APIs

API is a technology that emerged from the initials of the definition meaning "Application Programming Interface" in Turkish. Application Programming Interface is designed for the developers who represent the third parties that have technical knowledge and the advertisers that give big advertisements. These are an important Technologies that involve other online marketing professionals and manage agecies, search engine marketers, big companies and more than one customer accounts.

APIs are a significant infrastructure control technology for platform owners. Users' positions in the digital ecosystem are strategically important since they signal and supply concessionary access to private data of social media or services conducted via technical boundry resources and partnerships (Vlist and Helmond, 2021).

Open Application Programming Interfaces (APIs) have been defined as a significant way forward (for example third-party innovation, via sharing data). Additionally, it is possible for projects to concentrate on reusability and devices to cutback potential obstacles or blanks resulting from big data devices influencing end users. Performance is designed to support extensive data collection systems from all projects and to have a methodology of measurement. Performance watching was carried out for two-thirds of the project time at least (Zillner et al., 2021).

APIs aren't necessarily the tools which take the data out, however, they provide programmatic access to data based servises of another platform (for example targeting the aimed group, campaign optimization etc.). Subsidiary "social" verge resources co-ordinate and manage coactions between platforms and complements, involving developer directives and policies (Vlist and Helmond, 2021).

The API offers most of the functionality of the ad console while enabling programmatic management letting advertisers manage advertisements or advertisement groups based on predefined conditions. The Ad API is a robust tool for managing application and versioning updates for users with development resources (van Dijck et al, 2019).

By using their public (open) APIs to access certain data and services, application developers could interface with social media. In turn, copartners could access marketing data of social media and services utilizing business-specific APIs. These possibilities facilitate programmatic tools, products, and services by enabling these partners integrating enterprise software platforms and business solutions with social media platforms (Sun et al., 2015).

APIs also provide a way to optimize and scale ads. Through the API, which provides programmatic access for campaign reporting and management, for sponsored products, sponsored brands, and the sponsored display network, performance data and campaign are provided. That's one reason why many of the most popular Application Programming Interfaces, or APIs, in the advertising industry are offered by industry giants like Facebook, Google, Verizon, and Amazon. The Advertising category includes hundreds of secure options to support advertising programs or monetized apps, including ad network engagement, mobile advertising, affiliate ad management, app marketplace ads, and ad analytics (Acker and Kreisberg, 2017: 107).

Ad Attribution SDKs

SDK is defined as a type of Software Development Kit designed for use when placing ads on resources that are applications for mobile devices (Zillner et al., 2021).

A well-applied SDK could enhance the worth of mobile application stock and make up a far more dynamic in-app advert experience. SDK (Software Development Kit) is a range of software improvement device which assist improvers make up applications for a certain software platform like İOS or Android. SDK may include APIs (Application Programming Interfaces), technical documents, specimen code and other devices which assist an improver complement their job (Sie and Kou, 2017: 335).

Ads are significant to augment income for mobile applications or games. Another terminology which is widely utilized in the world of mobile advertising is API that stands for Application Programming Interface. An API is not a kit, just an explicit set of rules or protocols for interacting with a system. A programmer can manage the tasks they want to complete on the platform successfully provided they know how to use the right protocols (Li, et al. 2015).

A mobile software development kit or SDK is a piece of code which lets mobile applications contact the third party services and technologies. Developers integrating a mobile SDK can access different devices like analytics or re-engagement, or contact advert networks to serve in-app advertisements. Unlike APIs, which act more as bridges, SDKs are embedded in an application more deeply, allowing for a richer range of technological capabilities and providing a more comprehensive toolset.

BIG DATA ANALYSIS IN DIGITAL ADVERTISING AND DIGITAL ADVERTISING ASSOCIATION MODELS BASED ON BIG DATA

In digital advertising, many of the benefits of big data relate to better understanding the factors that drive successful campaigns. This model supports capabilities to integrate, manage and apply quantitative computational operations to data. Practitioners of this model should be told that they need to establish good relationships with data scientists who deal with quantitative concepts and advertisers who are asked to "tell a story with data" (Davenport and Dyché 2013: 14).

It is assumed that the applicability of the model will be more possible when the big data analysis and technology capabilities applied by the data scientist are combined with the creative intelligence and artistic talents of the advertisers. In this way, advertising broadcasting, which are digital advertising applications in which big data analytics can play a significant role, can be combined with customer behavior insight, behavioral targeting, and statistical analysis, reporting and data mining capabilities, which are the applications of data analysts.

In order to offer the most suitable product to their customers, digital advertisers need to collect and analyze in real time the customer's reactions to the advertisements presented to them while browsing any website. This situation requires the development of process-specific methods in processing big data. Historical data and real-time analysis occurs with the help of applications based on target analysis (Osman, 2019).

With big data analytics, unprecedentedly complex platforms, frameworks, and algorithms can be developed to shift traditional information extraction methods to new dimensions (Osman, 2019). Thanks to data cleaning, effective advertising campaigns and sales channels can be clearly identified and you can get rid of inefficient ones (Nazarov, 2019).

Data Mining: Data Collection

Advertisers use third-party cookies to take a look at a user's activity on a particular web browser. Cookies are one of many identifiers and can collect countless data for marketers to deliver effective advertising. In this part of the model, the data that needs to be collected for digital advertising management can be discussed as follows. Device and browser knowledge: This is technical knowledge about the device or browser you utilize to reach adverts. More specifically, this knowledge covers: Cookies, Pixels help conduct advert context on websites. Pixels work with ranges of cookies to record interactions of utilizers with websites and adverts (Grether, 2016).

Since mobile advertising identifiers do not contain cookies in mobile applications, data may be collected depending on the operating system of the device. IP Address, browser type, operating system, and device brand may be collected from where a device interacts with a mobile application to improve advert serving and aiming capabilities. Advertising data may be used to track how well our ads and campaigns are performing, including the number of times the ad was presented and if you clicked on or you interacted with the advert or not. Involving mobile web, desktop, web analytics tools, mobile applications, CRM, sale point, social, online video, offline, and even TV, big data technologies could gather unstructured spectators data from any source. Data mining is utilized to make a valid estimation of these properties for as many online utilizers as possible (Grether, 2016).

Essentially, unstructured data is data which are not easily stored and indexed in traditional databases or formats. Social media posts, photos, video context, audio recordings, sounds, etc. are included. This dispersed and complicated data can be combined with others (Marr, 2015). Collected datasets can sometimes contain a lot of unnecessary or unneeded data, which unessentially enhances storage space and influences following data analysis (Chen et al., 2017).

After the raw data is collected, during big data collection an efficient transport mechanism need to be utilized to transmit this data to a suitable storage management system to back up various analytical applications. Finally, data that should not be collected at this stage of the model should be applied within the framework of International Data Protection Laws (e.g. data limited by the General Data Protection Regulation (GDPR) of the European Union). The data should not be collected from such international personally identifiable information. While applying this model; must not gather or utilize any data which recognizes an individual straight, like name, address, telephone number, government identity, credit card knowledge, knowledge of bank account, and telephone or cellphone number.

In digital environments, collected data can have very different structures and exist in multiple environments. It is dedicated to storing and managing all this collected data to make it ready for analysis. Servers, which represent the collection of digital resources, and the cloud system, which represents the data being located online, are basic tools for data storage systems. Through these systems, physical or digital data sources are placed in virtual environments, virtual storages and virtual networks. This shows that data storage locations can also serve as a data source for the big data environment. (Davenport and Dyché 2013).

These virtual resources are managed and controlled by Network/Resource Orchestration according to user demand (Suciu, et al., 2013). To create accurate customer profiles and nurture customer relationships, their data can be stored for long periods of time and then shared with any system that needs it. Therefore, data is stored in relational databases structured in tables, which can be combined with other data carefully and in specified methods. Thus, data storages fulfill their role in the business model by using data from data collection technologies and storing historical data to provide traditional business intelligence and results of analytics. The pure speed and data accessibility moved to the cloud and available anywhere on any device is important to the data analyst or advertising professional. Making data at the critical need point or decision making and actionable in real time is where data is not only great but also highly effective (Couldry and Turow, 2014: 1714).

Advertisers can store data over long periods of time to create detailed and accurate customer profiles that can be utilized to nurture customer relationships. The storage infrastructure must provide knowledge storage services with safe storage space; However, it should supply a powerful interface of access for questioning and analyzing large amount of data (Chen et al., 2014).

Because data could have different formats and structures, companies should think different systems of storage depending on the sort of data they need to collect. As a matter of fact, this issue is a requirement under the EU GDPR (Vlis and Helmond, 2021). Finally, in collaboration with advertisers, data analyst teams can help define data storage standards that streamline workflows around analytics, deep learning models and machine learning.

Analyzing

"Working with big data is about trying to predict what will happen rather than waiting for it to happen." Big data analysis methods basically include software based on technology applications obtained through analytical methods. One of the most essential qualifications in the big data era is big data analysis, and this stage opens up brand new horizons for advertising marketing and advertisers (Chen, 2022).

Data analysing deals with determining the raw data abtained and facilitating the usage for the purposes specific to the field. Therefore, it is the effective management of data throughout its lifecycle to ensure that it meets the data quality requirements necessary for its efficient use (Hassan and Curry, 2021).

Data analysis means using appropriate statistical methods for analyzing large amounts of first-hand data and second-hand data, concentrating, extracting and refining beneficial data hidden in a pile of chaotic data, and determining the natural law of the matter. Data analysis plays a tremendous guiding role in comprehending customer wishes and estimating the market trend by businesses in order to improve the data's functions to the fullest extent and maximize the data's value, (Chen, et al., 2014).

Extract, Transform, Load is one of the basic processes that conduct ETL data storages. It cleans up the work model and loading necessities for data extraction, transformation and compatibility from external sources in the repository. ETL is not only a process of data transfer but also a tool of data preparation (Hashimova, 2016).

It covers business objectives that necessitate reach to data and its analysis, and the devices required to integrate analysis into decision-making (Hassan and Curry, 2021). At this point, analysis programs will process the raw data to establish both temporal relationships and semantic connections between multiple data sources. Analyzes can be performed both in batch mode and based on interactive input. Analytics application technologies include matching data with keywords and preserving only the most popular attributes through feature selection (Chandramouli, et al., 2012).

Since the big data analysis phase prosporeously serves the aimed spectators, interests, needs and activities of consumers, it could be said that big data is a tool that advertisers should use to predict user behavior. During the big data analytics phase, data collected from data sources can be used by digital advertisers and data analysts to learn what their customers' options are, how often they purchase products, and what can be done with the data collected from digital environments. After you know what types of data are available and have access to that data, it is necessary to leverage analytics programs to obtain beneficial information from the data that can support to answer strategic questions.

As a result, big data analytics applicable to this model is generally categorized as consumer aiming and segmentation, management of customer relationship, media optimization, measurement and sales effect. Data ready for analysis should be of high quality so that only the most accurate data can be used in your marketing efforts. (Broussard, 2016).

Targeting: Segmentation

Big data lets advertisers to compile, explore and analyze diversified channels of behavioral criteria, how people utilize their outputs and labours, just as societary and demographical elements. One of the most significant quests that advertisers must reply when advertising in these model stages is "to whom should we show the services?" and How does advertising convert into insights and activate to drive results?". Big data allows intelligent segmentation. In this way, the target audience can be successfully segmented to increase advertising performance. This part of the model involves the advertising unit and data scientists working together to capture users and cluster users and customer segmentation to obtain characteristics of target customers that can be used in potential customer mining (Cheng et al., 2016).

Segmentation of customer is a strong approach in advertisement. The whole advertisers utilize a structure of segmentation to aim their advertisements. Since advertising campaign offers, ad creatives, text, images and other factors affecting conversion will differ, people who may be interested in offers from different segments can be selected for each segment, and advertisements created through digital channels can be delivered in different ways.

A data management system with a permanent, unified database that combines data from many channels and sources to create a unified profile is ideal. This data help personalize marketing messages. By connecting a user's desktop activity to their mobile browsing habits, it can provide a better view of a person's online activities. By connecting similar profiles, a target audience can be created that will receive the same marketing messages. Advertisers can increase their sales by determining their offers and presenting them to their target audiences by bringing all this information together.

In the data era, mass consumer behavior data allows businesses to better segment the market based on consumer behavior routines and classify those with the same behavioral traits through sorting devices in big data mining. Customer segmentation is a form of marketing in big data-based advertising where all decisions are made on the basis of data analysis and flexible segmentation of customers. When using descriptive data, we often use it to identify approximate versions, which are then utilized to classify or estimate. Customers are divided into several segments based upon analysis of data collected about customers and their demands are estimated (Hashimova, 2016).

By collecting, arranging, and sharing data, it helps advertisers lay out aimed advertising campaigns, reach similar prospects beyond known customers, and provide more customised, interchannel interactions. In this way, advantages such as developing more effective advertising programs that will pave the way for more customers to shop can be achieved. A user's online profile ensures a summary of their online interests and preferences and is the basis of behavioral aiming of ads which can increase response rates (Gibson, 2018).

It needs to create right models from behavioral profiles based upon historical knowledge as to ad activity. Image advertisement utilises Behavioral Targeting (BT) to choose adverts for utilizer based upon former searches, page looks, etc. (Chandramouli, et al., 2012).

Specific ads are more likely to be relevant based on the time of the day you might be most interested in seeing them based on the interests previously related to the devices users own. Therefore, consumers' online behavioral traces make up a vital source of data about their knowledge necessities and are inevitable in delivering customised advert content (Liu-Thompkins and Malthouse 2017).

Automatic classification of user tags can be performed according to users' browsing behavior and shopping history (Deng et al., 2019). Behavioral segmentation often depends on browsing data which is connected with online behavior, which can involve browsing routines, spending routines, buying routines, brand commitment, former interactions, and more.

Big data can give idea as to not only who your customers are but also where they are, what they would like, how and when they would like to be contacted. Intelligent personalized advertisements should be developed which could personalize advertisement context automatically according to the needs of individual consumers (Deng et al., 2019).

To personalize the ad according to customers' interests and increase the ad performance, the ad accurately positions the target audience based on its analysis with a high-performance combination (Ge and Wu, 2021).

Advertising Combination-Advertising Broadcast

Correct advertising positioning has a constructive and prosperous influence on the practice and carrying out of the thorough advertising shedule strategy. It is necessary to run ads on the right media platforms to increase engagement and reduce overall customer acquisition costs by understanding where the target audience interacts the most. It is claimed that at this stage of the model, taking into account the advertising context and user characteristics, one should select the best match along with creative inserts from the potential advertising library, and then the advertising campaign can be launched. The more accurate the product preferences and segmentation of consumers through data collection and analysis in the previous stages of the model, the more successful the advertising broadcast can be. The more accurate the ad is, the better the advertising impact will be (Chen, 2022).

Ad Display Platform

Productivity can be increased with workflows that enable ads, reporting, and optimization across multiple platforms. It can be possible to estimate the consumer needs of different groups, rightly segmenting ad display platforms by combining quantitative and qualitative methods (Chen, 2022).

Optimizations can be enhanced with cross-digital platform insights based on source-of-truth measurement and native platform data. Briefly, what needs to be considered at this point is the necessity of combining data with advertising technology and advertising space.

Measurement an Evaluation

This stage includes the correct placement method of the advertisement and the assessment of the advertising impact based upon the technology of big data. It is necessary to show how it can bring the target audience closer to the advertisement and to evaluate the advertisements before, during and after they appear. Big data can integrate all influence evaluation methods to improve the relevance and accuracy of advertising influence evaluation so that the entire advertising influence can be seen. Advertisers may think that they can initiate the correct advertising process according to user needs, but when advertising results and reports are evaluated, target audience interaction will emerge. Viable managerial resolutions taken for sustained advertisement activities of digital advertisement are achieved by adequately providing appropriate and excellent information to the organization (Hashimova 2016).

In this way, customer value mediated by big data can be calculated. It is possible to look at the purchasing patterns to see what a commercial customer will buy later (Davenport ve Dyché 2013). To get the best customer experience, advertisers can more easily achieve their goals by tweaking the pieces that have worked in the past. With ad campaign results, Optimum marketing spend can be specified over multiple channels and by means of testing, measurement and analysis, marketing programs can be continually optimized. Previous stages of the model can be linked to the data collected and analyzed, so ads could be aimed, limited and sorted across different devices, and campaign effeciency can be measured and analyzed.

The target of the phase is to understand the contacts between the advert itself and the customer's reply. The meaning of the results can be clearly conveyed and explained to decision makers and stakeholders at all levels of technical understanding and illustrated with examples. Also to provide innervisions into how their adverts are performing and learn about their customers, reporting may involve advertising metrics like effects, clicks, and conversions. These data let an advertiser specify if an advert is performing well so that the advertiser can view these data and update the advertisement. Number of visits could be utilized to assess attention. Number of clicks, number of ad views, device utilized and other factors that specify which keywords and clicks are most efficient in obtaining conclusions etc., number of customer interactions are utilized to assess the degree of connection, and number of customer buyings are used to assess the degree (Ge and Wu, 2021).

Creating correct models from behavioral profiles which are based upon historical knowledge about advertisement effeciency can provide predictable information for the number of clicks and effects. Historical data could be stored in an allocated file system like HDFS or Cosmos to scale ad positioning, (Chandramouli et al., 2012). Using these technologies makes it possible to measure and evaluate the effects of advertising in order to monitor the effects of advertising in real time, ensures prompt feedback to advertisers, makes prompt refinement and also performs precise placement of adverts.

Big data allows advertisers to measure campaign performance. Data-driven distribution process, helps track ad information clicks in real time. This phase of the model can also provide insight into how to resolve collaboration issues with advertising agencies and other members of data science team, such as analysts of data business, IT architects, engineers of data, and developers of application. In this way, by understanding which advertising measurement and evaluation stage insights and decisions affect and/or inform the customer, better strategies could be improved which address the basic needs and motivations of consumers.

Visualization

Visualization techniques, a significant piece of big data analysis, can be done in figure, table or multimedia format to capture information patterns and insights for decision-making purposes. Big data analytics includes ad metrics, current or historical data, and visualization. Data visualization plays a significant role in exploring and comprehending big data effectively. Visual analysis makes analytical argument backed up by interacting utilizer interfaces. With creative advertising components, advertisements are delivered to end users through multi-device reports and dashboards (traditional or innovative) that include a variety of media formats for the end user, stringing out from text and graphics to dynamic 3D and possibly enhanced media (Curry et al., 2021).

It can be possible to transform insights into data visualizations that could be understood and acted upon easily and quickly. It is harder to make up data visualizations when the first output is a model that is based on multiple variable prediction; people have difficulty comprehending more than two dimension visualizations. (Davenport ve Dyché 2013).

A few data visualization devices now choose the most suitable visual representation for the data sort and number of variables (Davenport ve Dyché 2013). Data measurement and evaluation allows advertisers to understand which product is better for which segments and on which platforms. Advertisers can identify changes in customer behavior and peaks of shopping periods with the help of measurement and evaluation.

Hadoop Application

Simple programming models are a frame that lets data clusters be processed among the computer clusters dispersed. However, advertising or marketing outputs such as insight or behavioral targeting to be obtained from big data in the field of advertising require the inclusion of programs created from software languages in the process. For effective and efficient processing and analysis of data streams (data in motion) in the context of big data, especially integration with inactive data and advances in databases, parallel processing and analysis (e.g. Apache Hadoop, Apache Spark, Apache Flink, Apache Kafka) programs are available. Apps are necessary to take full advantage of all capabilities (Curry, et al. 2021:131).

Additionally, Hadoop big data offers a fully flexible application domain providing the analytical power they should extract meaningful knowledge from unstructured data to deliver actionable innervisions and competitive cons to digital advertisers. The programme is devised with one presenter each one offering local calculating and storing to scale for thousand of machines. Hadoop is a system that helps distribute large data sets to different computers or disks and produces results by merging operations on the data after running them in a distributed manner. Hadoop Distributed File System (HDFS) is a system which is created to store big files in a machine cluster HDFS. HDFS performs data chunking and distributes data among different machines (Hadoop, 2022).

Mapping and reduction (MapReduce)is programming model which was designed to process the dispersed data which divides the work into a range of duty stored in parallel (Hadoop, 2022). Hadoop similarly can combine basic data outputs that can fill data stores for the next analyses. (Davenport and Dyché 2013). Hadoop and cloud technology are reliable platforms to reduce the difficulties of big data and to store and process data (Osman, 2019).

Hadoop is used to not only store but also process data transformations and integrate heterogeneous data faster and more effectively than ever before. It includes various hardware/software architectures, involving clustered parallel servers using Hadoop, in-memory analytics, in-database processing, etc. The whole of these technologies are highly faster than the previous generation technologies for management of data and analysis. The program can perform analyzes in seconds that might have taken hours or days in the past (Davenport and Dyché 2013).

Many platforms in digital media uses offline analyse architecture based on Hadoop to make a reduction of the price of converting data format and to augment the efficiency. (Chen, v.d. 2014).

Hadoop was introduced to provide a platform and programming models to enable distributed rooms of large data sets across different clusters. By using appropriate software, algorithms and technologies on big data, it has become possible to process the collected data, detect the relationships between them, identify associations and extract patterns. At this point, Hadoop serves with two main components, Hadoop Distributed File System and MapReduce, which are connected to each other closely (Hashem, 2016).

Hadoop – The product from Apache is mostly used by many data scientists due to its processing power and extensive software library. It is updated regularly and can be said to be the most suitable program for processing large amounts of data.

Apple Analytics App

Continued investment in implementation, research and development, and marketing and advertising is believed to be critical to the improvement and sale of innovative products and technologies. The key to Apple's success is its use of consumer knowledge to affect consumer purchasing behavior in its marketing campaigns. Consumer behavior is utilised when it comes to marketing, not in the production of Apple products. Consumers and the target audience requires access to the decision-making process. Apple obtains its information from people who purchase its products (Apple, 2022).

When a consumer buys any apple product or downloads iTune, Apple gets Access to their information and the company uses the information to discover the tastes of the customer and the urging power of the consumer's behaviour. The company utilizes this innervision to get a competitive pros over its competitors (Zheng, Phelps, and Pimentel, 2019).

They learn everything that they could as to their consumers and how they decide to develop advertising that targets this consumer base. The platform is directed by the necessities of consumers, making its products far more natural for the market. Apple has found out that advertising its products should not be as to the product and its usages, but as to the core values of the Apple Company. According to Jobs, Apple's advertising "passionate people can change the world for the better" (Addison and Adelaide, 2022). Most income of Apple's comes from the sales of hardware devices that creates an emotional user experience and perceived as superior to its competitors (Schultz, et al. 2011).

Apple's customer experience strategy focuses on the marketing that persuades considerably to make up a strong Apple customer commitment. Since customer experience is the most important thing for Apple throughout the entire customer lifecycle, it offers the best customer experience by planning innovative software, hardware and innovative products every year. Apple has many relevant data sources that could be utilized as input for online services (Tucker and Wellford, 2014). Apple utilizes knowledge from consumers to get access to the consumer's emotional system, cognition, and the consumer's environment. Later the platform utilizes this information to produce advertisements and marketing designs that appeal to the aimed audience and guide the consumer's decisions and information structure. Advertisements served by Apple could appear in the App Store, Apple News and Stock Exchange (Apple, 2022).

The advertisements served cannot get to data in another environment. In order to show the advertisement mentioned in App Store and Apple News, search and download history is utilised. Ads on Apple News and Stocks are served based in part upon what the user reads and follows. This includes publishers who have notifications enabled and the types of broadcast subscriptions they have.

Apple's advertising platform protects information and is designed to give the user control over how they use the information (Apple, 2022). The advertisement platform of Apple doesn't share the information that might cause being known individually with third parties. The advertisement platform of Apple doesn't follow the user. This means that there is no connection between utilizer or device data collected by its applications and user or device data collected from third-party applications for the purpose of targeting ads and ad measurement. Utilizer or data of device is not shared with data agents. Apple's Safari is arranged in advance to prevent all third-party indentifying information in terms of privacy of user (Wingfield, 2010).

Google Analytics App

Google gets billions of search demands on its search engine every day, besides accessing utilizer knowledge via its Chrome browser and Gmail products. The company utilizes these data to be better at basic search duties such as training its algorithms, distinguishing sentences, correct spelling mistakes and to understand what a user tries to look for (Google, 2022).

Besides Google uses the data that provide users with automatic completion services, and the data related to the past and current search terms to offer search suggestions before they finish typing. Google has acquired and delivered this demand through several previously independent firms that provide "ad technology" services necessary to make it easier for advertisers to place ads on publishers' websites (Google, 2022). Google created a data cluster fort he services of ad technology that uses user data that come from search engine and other qualifications related to customers (Google Maps, Gmail etc.) to gain a high ability in that it aims for the advertisements (Morton and Dinielli, 2020).

Meta Analysis Application

Meta offers two different ad targeting options for broad target audiences, to reach consumers who have not yet shopped or reviewed the site but may have shown interest in the types of products or services offered, and for retargeting, to reach consumers who have shown interest in certain products on the site or application. A Meta Pixel is a piece of code you place on your site to allow you to measure how effective your ads are by understanding what people are doing on your site. By using the Meta Pixel, you can ensure that ads are shown to the right people, sales can be increased, and the results of the ads are measurable (Meta, 2022).

Meta offers performance to advertisers where they can view traffic, Shopping Behaviors, Sales on Facebook, and Site Events; discovery, where users can see traffic statistics for the location they browsed before coming to the store; tagged content where one can see conversion metrics by specific products and product types, as well as by format; catalog where one can view statistics regarding products or collections; target audience reports where customers can see where they browsed the store, their gender, age and the languages they speak (Meta, 2022).

Meta provides access to its users' age and gender information verified by their login data and achieves tremendous reach through a variety of devices. The basic data can be fully conveyed to the target group of the ad. Age and gender are very suitable criteria for targeting, especially in video advertising used to increase brand awareness (Grether, 2016).

This feature makes advertising efforts more targeted to potential customers. On meta platforms, the second form of advertisement is free form, in which companies make up a fan page on that social network. Facebook and Instagram utilizers could like the pages of the brands they like and, accordingly, become fans of these brands. These fan pages' social media directors, to keep customers updated on the company's products and services and to have them more contacted and engaged with the brands they admire, continue to publish news about their brand on these fan pages. Everyone that uses a Meta partner can link partner account to platforms and can configure the advert or make up target audiences based upon pixels, application events or conversion APIs (Vlist ve Helmond, 2021).

Facebook and Instagram ads provide utilizer or consumers with the chance to interact actively with advertisements on their pages, allowing them to "like" and "share" and besides see who else or which of their friends has liked or shared the same advertisements (Dehghani and Tumer, 2015). 'As one of Facebook's first API partners, AdParlor claims that he 'understands Facebook ads better than anyone else in the industry' owing to his strategic API pros (Vlist and Helmond, 2021).

Algorithm Learning and Optimization Meta's machine learning-based algorithms are designed to serve users with content (including ads) that is relevant to their personality or lifestyle (Wang, 2011). Sufficient data must be collected to determine which members of the target population are most likely to engage with the ad before the algorithms used to distribute ads can become effective (Hazelwood, 2018). Meta adjusts ad spend to stay within budget for the entire ad time frame (Meta, 2022).

CONCLUSION AND EVALUATIONS

More comprehensive and application-oriented studies can be carried out to increase the effectiveness and natural value of big data in advertising, for targeted advertising management and to fully benefit from its economic potential. The data types and analytics discussed and suggested in this research can be used effectively in many areas such as defense systems, fraud detection and cyber traffic monitoring, apart from the digital advertising industry service that is at the center of the research. To take full advantage of the chances suggested by big data and effectively use its potential, government, industry, academic institutions and non-profit organizations must work together to implement this initiative. Ideal future business models for data analytics management require a security model across processes, and to supply business valuation to an organization, security and data privacy issues need to be examined from a systems perspective (Hashem, 2016).

With the opening of the web age in the future, big data or data itself will become a lot more valuable and data management in digital advertising will become increasingly comprehensive. The core ideas of what data is, who owns it, and who controls access to it are predominantly directed at service providers, data repositories, and sector-specific data users (scientific and/or commercial). The rise of digital and mobile communications has made way for the world to be more contacted, networked and trackable; this has often led to the availability of such large-scale datasets (Rainie and Wellman, 2012). So far, consumers have owned trusted companies such as Google, Amazon, Facebook, Apple, and Microsoft to collect and utilize their personal data in exchange for free services (Zillner et al., 2021).

Thus, users are enabled to participate in digital platforms with online and offline applications in social, commercial, scientific and government fields. The view and idea that big data is not just software refers to the impact of what can be done with data on human behavior and the articulation of the results of human behavior as output. Big data collection tools are increasingly present in our daily lives, covering mining digital medical records for scientific and economic information, through social media mapping relationships, holding individuals' speech and movements through sensors, tracking movements in space, and shaping police and security policies. (Zook et al., 2017).

Constant recording of digital activity points to rapidly increasing ethical problems such as surveillance that comes with factory settings, decreased privacy, diappearance of anonymity, theft of digital identity, and data safety. For this reason, it is believed that the foundations of this future are laid today and here (with people using the data correctly at the right time) whether the humanity's future is positive or dystopian (Leonhard, 2018).

In particular, in the field of advertising, studies are expected to be carried out knowing that individuals have the right to data portability and the right to data deletion, as stated in the GDPR, which will be the driving force for large data collectors to explore new business models for personal data access (Zillner, et al. 2021).

It can be said that with the opening of network services integrated with 5G and artificial intelligence in the future, the operation of big data in business environments will become increasingly comprehensive. Semantic data management with semantic data-oriented artificial intelligence integration is an academically and sectorally well-established but also rapidly developing field. Significant media apps like "smart personal assistants" and artificial intelligence applications such as Siri and Cortana and Alexa will be supported by big data analysis technology (Lippell, 2016).

As platforms become accustomed to micro or macro targeting from advertisers and digital advertising becomes part of their daily lives, they will look for ways how publishers can take advantage of this dynamic. Different brands or institutions from various sectors will begin to change their brand images in digital environments according to what they want visitors to know about, with more easily accessible digital advertising applications (Couldry and Turow, 2014).

More comprehensive and application-oriented studies can be carried out to increase the effectiveness and natural value of big data in advertising, for targeted advertising management and to fully benefit from its economic potential. The data types and analytics discussed and suggested in this research can be used effectively in many areas such as defense systems, fraud detection and cyber traffic monitoring, apart from the digital advertising industry service that is at the center of the research.

REFERENCES

Addison, M. (2022). Brand Development and marketing strategies in USA: A Case of Apple Inc. *Journal of Marketing Communications*, *5*(1), 1–8. doi:10.53819/81018102t2055

Agarwal, S. (2013). Data mining: Data mining concepts and techniques. *International Conference on Machine Intelligence and Research Advancement*, 203-207. 10.1109/ICMIRA.2013.45

Aggarwal, C. C. (2011). *An introduction to social network data analytics*. Springer. doi:10.1007/978-1-4419-8462-3

Ahmed, M. (2019). Novel big data analytics framework for smart cities. *Future Generation Computer Systems*, *91*, 620–633. doi:10.1016/j.future.2018.06.046

Ahmed, M., & Osman, S. A. (2019). Novel big data analytics framework for smart cities. *Future Generation Computer Systems*, *91*, 620–633. doi:10.1016/j.future.2018.06.046

Ahrholdt, D., Greve, G., & Hopf, G. (2019). Online-Marketing-Intelligence. New York: Springer.

Akıncı, A. N. (2019). *Personal Data Privacy in Big Data Applications* [Expert Thesis]. General Directorate of Sectors and Public Investments, Ankara.

Akter, S., Wamba, S. F., Gunasekaran, A., Dubey, R., & Childe, S. J. (2016). How to improve firm performance using big data analytics capability and business strategy alignment? *International Journal of Production Economics*, *182*, 113–131. doi:10.1016/j.ijpe.2016.08.018

Aljumah, A., Nuseir, M., & Alam, M. M. (2021). Traditional Marketing Analytics, Big Data Analytics and Big Data System Quality and the Success of New Product Development. *Business Process Management Journal*, *27*(4), 1108–1125. doi:10.1108/BPMJ-11-2020-0527

Alkan, S. (2015). *The Future of the Data World: Big Data (Big Data)*. Linkedin. https://www.linkedin.com/pulse/verid%C3%BCnyas%C4%B1n%C4%B1ngelece%C4%9Fi-b%C3%BCy%C3%BCk-big-data-seydi-alkan/

Allouche, G. (2014). *Big Data Use Case: Digital Advertising*. http://cmsreport.com/articles/big-data-use-case-digital-advertising-8225

Amazon. (2021). *Amazon Gizlilik Bildirimi*. https://www.amazon.com.tr/gp/help/customer/display.html?nodeId=GX7NJQ4ZB8MHFRNJ

Amazon (2022). *What is AWS*? https://aws.amazon.com/tr/what-is-aws/

Anyoha, R. (2017). *The History of Artificial Intelligence*. Harvard University The Graduate School of Arts and Sciences. https://sitn.hms.harvard.edu/flash/2017/history-artificial-intelligence/

Apple. (2022). *Apple gizlilik politikası*. https://www.apple.com/legal/privacy/tr/

Arandilla, R. (2012). Rise and fall of online advertising. Academic Press.

Arribas-Bel, D. (2014). Accidental, open and everywhere: Emerging data sources for the understanding of cities. *Applied Geography, 49*, 45-53. doi:10.1016/j.apgeog.2013.09.012

Ashton, K. (2009). That 'Internet of Things' Thing. *Rfid Journal.* https://www.rfidjournal.com/articles/view?4986

Barlow, M. (2013). *Real Time Big Data Analytics: Emerging Arthitecture.* O'Reilly Media.

Barnes, S. J. (2002). Wireless digital advertising: Nature and implications. *International Journal of Advertising, 21*(3), 399–420. doi:10.1080/02650487.2002.11104939

Bartlett, L., & Vavrus, F. (2017). Rethinking case study research. Routledge.

Baskin, M., & Coburn, N. (2001). Two tribes divided by a common language? *International Journal of Market Research, 43*(2), 137.

Baskin, M., & Pickton, D. (2003). Account planning from genesis to revelation. *Marketing Intelligence & Planning, 21*(7), 416–424. doi:10.1108/02634500310504250

Bayrakçı, S. (2015). *Use of Big Data in Academic Studies in Social Sciences* [Unpublished Master's Thesis]. Marmara University SSI.

Beal, A. (1997). A generalization of Fermat's last theorem: Beal's conjecture and the reward problem. *Notices of the American Mathematical Society, 44*(11).

Bellman, S., Potter, R. F., Treleaven-Hassard, S., Robinson, J. A., & Varan, D. (2011). The effectiveness of branded mobile phone apps. *Journal of Interactive Marketing, 25*(4), 191–200. doi:10.1016/j.intmar.2011.06.001

Bendle, N. T., & Wang, X. (2016). Uncovering the message from the mess of big data. Amsterdam: Elsevier Science BV.

Berman, J. (2015). *Principles of Big Data: Preparing, Sharing, and Analyzing Complex Information.* Morgan Kaufmann.

Boerman, S. C., Kruikemeier, S., & Zuiderveen Borgesius, F. J. (2017). Online Behavioral Advertising: A Literature Review and Research Agenda. *Journal of Advertising, 46*(3), 363–376. doi:10.1080/00913367.2017.1339368

Bollen, J., & Huina, M. (2011). Twitter Mood predicts the stock market. *Journal of Computational Science, 2*(1), 1–8. doi:10.1016/j.jocs.2010.12.007

Booz Allen Hamilton. (2015). *Understanding the DNA of data science.* https://www.boozallen.com/s/insight/publication/field-guide-to-data-science.html doi:10.1016/j.drugpo.2016.02.022

Boyd, D., & Crawford, K. (2012). Crıtıcal questıons for bıg data. *Information Communication and Society, 15*(5), 662–679. doi:10.1080/1369118X.2012.678878

Broussard, G. (2016). Enriching media data: A special report from the U.S. coalition of ınnovative media measurement. *Journal of Advertising Research, 56*(1), 25–55. doi:10.2501/JAR-2016-010

Bühler, J., Baur, A. W., Bick, M., & Shi, J. (2015). Big data, big opportunities: Revenue sources of social media services besides advertising. In. Lecture Notes in Computer Science: Vol. 9373. *Open and big data management and ınnovation.* Springer. doi:10.1007/978-3-319-25013-7_15

Buiten, M. C. (2020). Exploitative Abuses in Digital Markets: Between Competition Law and Data Protection Law. *Journal of Antitrust Enforcement*, *9*(2), 271.

Campbell, C., & Leyland, F. (2011). Understanding Consumer Conversations Around Ads in a Web 2.0 World. *Journal of Advertising*, *40*(1), 87–102. doi:10.2753/JOA0091-3367400106

Cao, Q., & Schniederjans, M. J. (2004). Empirical study of the relationship between Operations Strategy and Information Systems Strategic Orientation in an e-Commerce Environment. *International Journal of Production Research*, *42*(15), 2915–2939. doi:10.1080/00207540410001691884

Cauberghe, V., & De Pelsmacker, P. (2010). Advergames. *Journal of Advertising*, *39*(1), 5–18. doi:10.2753/JOA0091-3367390101

Cavanillas, J. M., Curry, E., & Wahlster, W. (2016). New horizons for a data-driven economy: A roadmap for usage and exploitation of big data in Europe. New York: Springer. doi:10.1007/978-3-319-21569-3

Ceccagnoli, M., Forman, C., & Huang, P. (2012). Cocreation of value in a platform ecosystem: The case of enterprise software. *MIS Quarterly, 36*(1), 263–290.10.1109/ICDE.2012.55

Chandramouli, B., & Goldstein, J., & Duan, S. (2012). Temporal Analytics on Big Data for Web Advertising. *2012 IEEE 28th International Conference on Data Engineering*, 90-101. 10.1109/ICDE.2012.55

Chang, H., & Rizal, H. (2013). The determinants of consumer behavior towards email advertisement. *Internet Research*, *23*(3), 316–337. doi:10.1108/10662241311331754

Charney, S. (2012). *Trustworthy Computing Next (Version 1.01)*. Microsoft Corporation Trustworthy Computing.

Chazal, F., & Michel, B. (2021). An introduction to topological data analysis: Fundamental and practical aspects for data scientists. *Frontiers in Artificial Intelligence*, *4*, 1–28. doi:10.3389/frai.2021.667963 PMID:34661095

Chen, H. ve Zhou, L. (2017). The myth of big data: Chinese advertising practitioners' perspective. *International Journal of Advertising*, 1-17. http://www-tandfonline-com.ezp01.library.qut.edu.au/doi/full/10.1080/02650487.2017.1340865

Chen, H., & Zhou, L. (2018). The myth of big data: Chinese advertising practitioners' perspective. *International Journal of Advertising*, *37*(4), 633–649. doi:10.1080/02650487.2017.1340865

Cheng, X. (2016) Big data assisted customer analysis and advertising architecture for real estate. *16th International Symposium on Communications and Information Technologies (ISCIT),* 312-317. 10.1109/ISCIT.2016.7751642

Curry, E., Metzger, A., Berre, A. J., Monzón, A., & Boggio-Marzet, A. (2021). The elements of big data value. Springer.

Davenport, T. (2018). *Big Data @Work. (Çev. M. Çavdar)*. Türk Havayolları Yayınları.

Davenport, T. H., & Dyché, J. (2013). Big data in big companie. International Institute for Analytic. SAS Institute Inc.

Dehghani, M., & Tumer, M. (2015). A research on effectiveness of Facebook advertising on enhancing purchase intention of consumers. *Computers in Human Behavior, 49*, 597-600. doi:10.1016/j.chb.2015.03.051

Deng, S., Tan, C.-W., Wang, W., & Pan, Y. (2019). Smart generation system of personalized advertising copy and ıts application to advertising practice and research. *Journal of Advertising*, *48*(4), 356–365. do i:10.1080/00913367.2019.1652121

Desouza, K. C., & Jacob, B. (2017). Big Data in the Public Sector: Lessons for Practitioners and Scholars. *Administration & Society*, *49*(7), 1043–1064. doi:10.1177/0095399714555751

Dhar, V. (2013). Data science and prediction. *Communications of the ACM*, *56*(12), 64–73. doi:10.1145/2500499

Dolata, U. (2017). *Apple, Amazon, Google, Facebook, Microsoft: Market concentration-competition-innovation strategies 1.* Stuttgarter Beitrage zur Organisations-und Innovations forschung, SOI Discussion Paper. https://www.econstor.eu/bitstream/10419/152249/1/ 880328606.pdf

Du, R. Y., Hu, Y., & Damangir, S. (2015). Leveraging trends in online searches for product features in market response modeling. *Journal of Marketing*, *79*(1), 29–43. doi:10.1509/jm.12.0459

Duncan, T. (2005). *Principles of Advertising & IMC* (2nd ed.). Taylor & Francis.

Franks, B. (2012). *Taming the Big Data Tidal Wave: Finding Opportunities in Huge Data Streams with Advanced Analytics*. John Wiley & Sons, Inc. doi:10.1002/9781119204275

Gaille, B. (2015). *18 Key Apple Target Market Demographics.* http://brandongaille.com/18- apple-target-market-demographics/

Gandomi, A., & Haider, M. (2015). Beyond the hype: Big data concepts, methods, and analytics. *International Journal of Information Management*, *35*(2), 137–144. doi:10.1016/j.ijinfomgt.2014.10.007

García, R. A. (2021). The elements of big data value. Springer. doi:10.1007/978-3-030-68176-0

Ge, T., & Wu, X. (2021). Accurate delivery of online advertising and the evaluation of advertising effect based on big data technology. *Mobile Information Systems*, *10*, 1–10. Advance online publication. doi:10.1155/2021/1598666

Glazer, H. (2012). Likes' are lovely, but do they lead to more logins? *College & Research Libraries News*, *73*(1), 18–22. doi:10.5860/crln.73.1.8688

Google. (2022). *Google Gizlilik Politikası.* https://policies.google.com/privacy?hl=tr

Google. (2023). *Google Ads İle İşinizi Büyütün.* https://ads.google.com/intl/tr_tr/home/

Google Inc. (2021). *Google Trends Help*. https://support.google.com/trends/?hl=ko#topic=6248052

Grant, R. (2012). *How to React to Halved Reach on Facebook.* http://wearesocial.net/blog/2012/10/reacthalved-reach-facebook/

Grether, M. (2016). Using big data for online advertising without wastage: wishful dream, nightmare or reality? *Online Advertising, 8*(2). doi:10.1515/gfkmir-2016-0014

Grossberg, K. A. (2016). The new marketing solutions that will drive strategy implementation. *Strategy and Leadership*, *44*(3), 20–26. doi:10.1108/SL-04-2016-0018

Gry, K., & Kjeldgaard, D. (2014). Online reception analysis: Big data in qualitative marketing research. In Consumer culture theory: Research in consumer behavior (Vol. 16, pp. 217–42). Academic Press.

Haq, Z. (2009). E-mail advertising: A study of consumer attitude toward e-mail advertising among Indian users. *Journal of Retail & Leisure Property*, *8*(3), 207–223. doi:10.1057/rlp.2009.10

Harvard. (2022). *History Artificial Intelligence*. https://sitn.hms.harvard.edu/flash/2017/history-artificial-intelligence/

Hashem, I., Chang, V., Anuar, N., Adewole, K., Yaqoob, I., Gani, A., Ahmed, E., & Chiroma, H. (2016). The role of big data in smart city. *International Journal of Information Management*, *36*(5), 748–758. doi:10.1016/j.ijinfomgt.2016.05.002

Hashimova, K. K. (2016). The role of big data in ınternet advertising problem solution. *International Journal of Education and Management Engineering*, *6*(4), 10–19. doi:10.5815/ijeme.2016.04.02

Hassan, U., & Curry, E. (2021). Stakeholder analysis of data ecosystems. In The elements of big data value. Springer. doi:10.1007/978-3-030-68176-0_2

Hunt, K. (2016). CookieConsumer: Tracking Online Behavioural Advertising in Australia. *Computer Law & Security Report*, *32*(1), 55–90. doi:10.1016/j.clsr.2015.12.006

Jobs, C. G., Gilfoil, D. M., & Aukers, S. M. (2016). How marketing organizations can benefit from big data advertising analytics. *Academy of Marketing Studies Journal*, *20*(1), 18.

Kaya, İ., Ateş, S., Akbulut, D., & Köksal, A. (2017). Accounting Education in the Light of Big Data, Data Analytics and Data Analysis: A Research on Course Contents. *36th Accounting Education Symposium Book, Matsis printing press*, İstanbul.

Kumar, S. (2020). Data mining based marketing decision support system using hybrid machine learning algorithm. *Journal of Artificial Intelligence and Capsule Networks*, *2*(3), 185–193. doi:10.36548//jaicn.2020.3.006

Laney, D. (2001). *3D data management: Controlling data volume, velocity and variety*. META Group Research Note, 6.

Liu, P., & Yi, S. (2017). Pricing policies of green supply chain considering targeted advertising and product green degree in the big data environment. *Journal of Cleaner Production*, *164*, 1614–1622. doi:10.1016/j.jclepro.2017.07.049

Lokke, E. (2018). *Privacy: Private Life in the Digital Society* (D. Başak, Trans.). Koç University Publications.

Manyika, J. (2011). *Big data: The next frontier for innovation, Competition, and productivity*. McKinsey Global Institute.

Mikalef, P., Boura, M., Lekakos, G., & Krogstie, J. (2020). The role of information governance in big data analytics driven innovation. *Information & Management*, *57*(7), 103361. doi:10.1016/j.im.2020.103361

Moe, W. W., & Fader, P. S. (2004). Capturing evolving visit behavior in clickstream data. *Journal of Interactive Marketing*, *18*(1), 5–19. doi:10.1002/dir.10074

Moorthi, K., Dhiman, G., Arulprakash, P., Suresh, C., & Srihari, K. (2020). (Article in press). A survey on impact of data analytics techniques in E-commerce. *Materials Today: Proceedings*.

Nakip, M., & Yaraş, E. (2017). *SPSS Uygulamalı Pazarlamada Araştırma Teknikleri, 4.Basım*. Seçkin.

Phillips-Wren, G., & Hoskisson, A. (2015). An analytical journey towards big data. *Journal of Decision Systems*, *24*(1), 87–102. doi:10.1080/12460125.2015.994333

Porter, M. E., & Heppelmann, J. E. (2014). How smart, connected products are transforming competition. *Harvard Business Review*, *92*(11), 64–88.

Richardson, C. (2017). *7 Great Benefits of Big Data in Marketing*. https://www.smartdatacollective.com/benefits-big-data-in-marketing/

Rosoff, M. (2015). *Every type of tech product has gotten cheaper over the last two decades-except for one*. https://www.businessinsider.com/historical-price-trends-for-tech-products-2015-10

Sathi, A. (2014). *Engaging customers using big data: how Marketing analytics are transforming business*. Palgrave Macmillan. doi:10.1057/9781137386199

Schönberger. (2013). *Viktor Mayer and Kenneth Cukier. Big Data – A Revolution That Will Transform the Way We Live, Work and Think* (B. Erol, Trans.). Paloma.

Todor, R.D. (2016). Blending traditional and digital marketing. *Bulletin of the Transilvania University of Braşov, Series V: Economic Sciences, 9*(58), 51-56.

Tyhkheev, D. (2018). *Big data in marketing*. Saimaa University of Applied Sciences, Business Administration.

Vlist, V. D. F. N., & Helmond, A. (2021). How partners mediate platform power: Mapping business and data partnerships in the social media ecosystem. *Big Data & Society*, *8*(1). Advance online publication. doi:10.1177/20539517211025061

Xu, Z. (2016). Three essays on big data analytics, traditional marketing analytics, knowledge discovery, and new product performance. *Open Access Theses & Dissertations*, 781.

Xu, Z., Frankwick, G.L. & Ramirez, E. (2015). Effects of big data analytics and traditional marketing analytics on new product success: A knowledge fusion perspective. *Journal of Business Research, 59*(2016), 1562-1566.

Yeni İş Fikirleri. (2019). *Büyük Veri Nedir ve Nasıl Analiz Edilir?* https://www.yeniisfikirleri.net/buyuk-veri-nedir-ve-nasil-analiz-edilir/

Chapter 19
A Ludological and Narrotological Analysis of Crime Representations in Digital Games

Feridun Nizam
https://orcid.org/0000-0002-4215-6973
Fırat University, Turkey

ABSTRACT

For a long time, the representation of crime in various media channels has been the subject of many studies. The studies conducted are mainly on news content. However, crime is represented not only in the news but also in many different media and content. One of these channels is digital games. According to the latest data released by Statista, 3.24 billion people are currently playing games worldwide. It is also stated that 48% of computer owners currently use the device to play video games. It is understood that digital games have a very important place in the process—they evolved from analogue games to digital games—and the market share they have and the size of the audience they can reach. Digital games, which have many categories and can reach a large number of people, produce and present representations of crime like other media types. There are not many studies on crime representations in digital games, which is an important branch of new media. This study aims to reveal the ways of production and presentation of crime representations in digital games.

INTRODUCTION

For a long time, the representation of crime in various media channels has been the subject of many studies. The studies conducted are mainly on news content. However, crime is represented not only in the news but also in many different media and content. One of these channels is digital games. According to the latest data released by Statista, 3.24 billion people are currently playing games worldwide. It is also stated that 48 per cent of computer owners currently use the device to play video games. It is

DOI: 10.4018/979-8-3693-0855-4.ch019

understood that digital games have a very important place in the process of they evolved from analogue games to digital games - and the market share they have and the size of the audience they can reach. Digital games, which have tens of categories and can reach a large number of people, produce and present representations of crime like other media types. There are not many studies on crime representations in digital games, which is an important branch of new media. This study aims to reveal the ways of production and presentation of crime representations in digital games.

Since long before modern times, stories about major crimes and criminals have always attracted attention, and their punishment has been widely followed by the masses. Executions in front of large crowds were a common practice in medieval Europe. Masses of people would go to watch these executions with their families as if they were going to a theatre (Foucault, 1975:5-6). Today, with television news broadcasts, infotainment programmes, films, radio broadcasts, daily tabloids, magazine articles, internet blogs and digital games, the factual and fictional media sources that bring the remote microcosm of crime and criminal punishment into the privacy of our safe and comfortable living rooms are more widespread than ever before (Cheliotis, 2010:4). For a long time, the representation of crime in various media channels has been the subject of many studies. The studies conducted are mainly on news content. However, crime is represented not only in the news but also in many different media and content. One of these channels is digital games. According to the latest data released by Statista, 3.24 billion people are currently playing games worldwide. According to the 2021 gaming statistics research in Wepc, the computer game industry is expected to reach $ 70 billion by 2023. It is also stated that 48 per cent of computer owners currently use the device to play video games. It is understood that digital games have a very important place in the process of transition and transformation from traditional media to new media, both in terms of the transformation they have experienced within themselves - considering the process in which they evolved from analogue games to digital games - and the market share they have and the size of the audience they can reach. Digital games, which have tens of categories and can reach a large number of people, produce and present representations of crime like other media types. There are not many studies on crime representations in digital games, which is an important branch of new media. This study aims to reveal the ways of production and presentation of crime representations in digital games.

The population of this study consists of crime representations in all digital games. The sample of the study consists of the computer game GTA V (Grand Theft Auto V). Grand Theft Auto V is a 2013 open-ended action-adventure video game developed by Rockstar North and published by Rockstar Games. GTA V is set in the fictional state of San Andreas, based on Southern California, and its single-player story follows the efforts of the three main characters - former bank robber Michael De Santa, street gang member Franklin Clinton, and drug dealer Trevor Philips - as they attempt to pull off heists while under pressure from a corrupt government agency and powerful criminals (Bachchan, 2020). GTA V is the second best-selling video game of all time with 140 million copies sold and is one of the most financially successful entertainment products of all time with worldwide revenues of approximately $6 billion. These qualities that make GTA V stand out among other computer games, the fact that the subject of the game is about crime and the characters in the game are designed in the criminal profile are the main reasons for choosing GTA V as a sample.

Early studies on crime representations in the media were conducted in the light of influence theories. However, in the following periods, it was revealed that the findings obtained from the researches conducted with theories of influence were not healthy. After the theories of influence were abandoned, crime representations were tried to be understood through content analysis. However, this method has also been subjected to a lot of criticism due to the limitations of content analysis itself - such as the possibility of searching for the content that the researcher wants to find and therefore cannot provide a fully objective perspective (Reiner, 2007:379-380). In these days when digital games are frequently the subject of academic research, there are serious debates about which approach digital games should be handled. This debate has been going on for about fourteen years between ludologists and narratologists. Henry Jenkins (2004), Brenda Laurel (1991) and Janet H. Murray (1997), the main representatives of narratology, argue that games belong to the same ecology as narrative-based media such as drama, film and novels. This approach argues that analytical tools of existing narrative media can be used in the study of games due to their relevance, adjusting them according to empirical evidence when necessary (Raessens, 2006, p. 55). In contrast, the general view of major representatives of ludology, including Espen Aarseth (1997), Jesper Juul (2001), Markku Eskelinen (2001), and Gonzalo Frasca (2003), is that to claim that there is no difference between narrative and games is to reduce both media. Games and narratives are fundamentally different, despite the similarities and commonalities between them, and therefore the theoretical tools of existing disciplines are inadequate for the analysis of games. A semiotic perspective would allow research in the field to focus on the similarities (as they more or less share the narrative) and differences (they have different degrees of interactivity) between games and traditional narrative forms, leading to a better understanding of the hybrid nature of the gaming medium (Kokonis, 2014:171). In this study, the method of semiotic analysis was chosen as a method that both perspectives can work together.

1. CONCEPTUAL FRAMEWORK

1.1. Narratology

Digital game studies have an interdisciplinary feature. Research, which is generally within the scope of media and traditional game studies, has spread over a wide area due to certain features of digital games. Digital games have features related to fields such as technology, art, culture, industry and education, and therefore they have been examined with the approaches of all these fields. In the 1980s and 1990s, digital games were examined in the fields of psychology and health, and in the late 1990s and early 2000s, they were shaped by media studies, and in the continuation of these studies, many research areas became prominent in digital game studies (Wolf and Konzack, 2012: 672-674).

The broadest definition of narrative in the context of linguistics and semiotics was made by Rifat. "*Narrative is an oral or written discourse that narrates an event or a series of events; the organization formed by the articulation relations of real or fictional events that are the subject of this discourse, narrative text. In this second sense, narrative falls within the field of analysis of narrative theorists who are directly concerned with content. Therefore, in semiotics, narrative is understood as a narrative syllabus (narrative program) that includes people (narrative persons) who perform certain actions in a certain space and time, and thus contains a plot*" (Rifat, 2013:12).

Of course, the roots of the narrative are laid with the history of humanity. All written or verbal works can be called "narrative". However, narrative, in its meaning, evokes an intellectual effort, in other words, any work of art. In this context, "*narration is always present in drama, myth, tragedy, comedy, pantomime, painting, cartoons, ordinary news, speech, and cinema*" (Barthes, 2009: 101).

Narrative, as Barthes puts it, is life itself. "*Whether international, transhistorical, or transcultural, narrative is always present, just like life. There are too many narratives in the world to count. First of all, there is a surprising number of species; these genres, too, are dispersed into different substances, as if each material was suitable for man to be able to trust and reveal his narratives. The basis of the narrative can be articulated language (spoken or written), image (static or dynamic), hand-arm-head movement, and a regular mix of all these substances. There is always narrative in myth, legend, fable, tale, long story, epic, story, tragedy, drama, pantomime, painting, stained glass, cinema, cartoons, ordinary newspaper news, speech. Moreover, in these infinitely many forms, narrative exists in all times, in all places, in all societies. The narrative begins with human history itself; There is not, and never has been, a people without a narrative anywhere in the world. All classes, all human societies have narratives*" (Barthes, 1993:83).

Narrative, a sub-branch of social sciences, is considered as a part of the return to language in social sciences. The theories until the period when the term narratology was used are called narrative theory. Narrative is the transmission of two or more events that are logically connected, realised over time and connected into a whole with a stable subject (Mutlu: 1998,41). According to Chatman, narrative is the language conveyed through the words (paroles) of concrete oral communication or other means of communication (Chatman: 2009, 21).

The origins of narratology can be traced back to Plato and Aristotle. Narrative theory is based on Plato and Aristotle's distinction between "mimesis" and "diegesis". Mimesis is the understanding of representation based on imitation and emulation in Ancient Greek rhetoric. With Plato and Aristotle, it transformed into a view of reflecting nature and reality. In contrast to the difficulty of using a single meaning or expression to express mimesis; it is to express any phenomenon, to simply tell something, to depict something, and in the meantime to imitate it. It first appears in Plato's State as a concept in which the meanings of delusion and deception are attributed (Kıyar and Karkın, 2013:13). Diegesis is related to the concept of narration. It refers to all the words that can be attributed to the author. In diegesis, the author narrates the story; in other words, the author is the narrator who presents to his readers the thoughts of his characters and everything he or they imagine. Narrative studies based on the distinction between mimesis and diegesis developed firstly with the theoretical analyses of Friedrich Spielhagen and Otto Ludwig on the novel at the end of the 1800s, and then in the early 20th century when linguists such as Charles Bally and Fritz Karph began to address issues related to narrative and to use linguistic categories in narrative analyses. Another important distinction is based on Aristotle's Poetics. The distinction between "the sum total of the events taking place in the world depicted" and the plot (muthos) constitutes one of the main foundations of narrative theory. "Muthos" refers to the set of events selected and organised by taking into account aesthetic considerations and logical requirements, i.e. the plot. It is the phenomenon of selecting and presenting the events that take place in the real world (Dervişcemaloğlu, 2014:16-17).

In order to investigate a structure or to offer a structural explanation, the narratologist breaks narrative events into their component parts and then tries to identify functions and relationships. Practically all narrative theories distinguish between "what" is told - the story - and "how" it is told - the discourse. According to Jahn, anything that tells a story, of whatever genre, constitutes a narrative. Anything that tells or presents a story through text, painting, performance or a combination of these is a narrative. Accordingly, novels, plays, films, comic books are also narrative genres. A series of events involving characters make up stories. Events include both natural and unnatural events, such as floods and car accidents. Characters are involved in an event as agents as the person who causes it, victims or beneficiaries as the person affected by it. Linguists have approached narrative from a deeper perspective (Jahn, 2005: 23).

The other major influence on narrative theory and the linguistic turn came from the Swiss linguist Ferdinand de Saussure. Saussure's structural linguistics has been described as a Copernican revolution in the social sciences because of the way it completely influenced how language was seen in Western thought. Although it was accepted before Saussure that language was an important tool in human rationality, Saussure went beyond this logic and put signs at the centre of social reality (Harris & Taylor, 2005, p. 210). According to Swiss linguist Ferdinand de Saussure, any sign consists of a 'signifier' and a 'signified', that is, basically a form and a meaning. For a narrative text, which is a complex signifier, the signifier is a 'discourse', that is, a mode of presentation. The signified is a 'story', i.e. a sequence of actions.

According to linguists, therefore, narratological research usually follows one of two basic orientations:

'Discourse narratology' analyses the stylistic choices that determine the form or realisation of a narrative text or, in the case of films and plays, performance. Also of interest are pragmatic features that contextualise the text or performance within the social and cultural framework of a narrative act.

'Storytelling', on the contrary, focuses on the units of action that 'facilitate' and organise a flow of events according to themes, motifs and plot (Jahn, 2005: 27).

After the classical period, interdisciplinarity has gained great importance in the field of narratology. Many approaches attempt to bridge the gap between narratology and disciplines such as linguistics, cognitive psychology, literature, cultural history, cultural theory and philosophy. The revival of interest in cultural and philosophical issues of history and ideology due to the critiques of both deconstructionists and postmodernists and other scholars, combined with the systematicism of structuralists, has led to the emergence of many new approaches. Beginning in the late 1960s and continuing at an intense pace, narrative thought has penetrated almost every discipline and profession. No longer the sole specialisation of literary science, the study of narrative is interdisciplinary and does not fit within the boundaries of any one scientific field. The 'narrative turn' has found its place in history, anthropology and folklore, psychology, society, linguistics and communication studies, and sociology (Riessman and Quinney, 2005:392). Sociology, psychology, anthropology, education and similar social science disciplines have long treated narrative as a cognitive and discursive tool for making sense of and organising human life experiences. The premise of their treatment of narrative as a tool is that narratives are social products produced by people in the context of specific social, historical and cultural positions. Accordingly, people are related to the experiences they have in their lives, but they are not transparent carriers of these experiences. Rather, they are interpretative tools that enable people to represent themselves both to themselves and to others (Lawler, 2002: 242). These disciplines have consequently developed their own methodological tools for analysing narrative. These tools include thematic analysis, structural analysis, dialogue/performance analysis and visual analysis (Riessman: 2008).

1.2. Ludology

As an academic study area "ludology" (from the latin *ludus*, meaning game) is the academic study of games. Ludologists assert that games should be understood on their own terms rather than as narratives which can be studied using traditional forms of narrative analysis. "ludology is, like the games it studies, is not about story and discourse at all but about actions and events".

It is also determined "an approach within videogame studies emphasizing the ludic elements of gaming over its narrative elements". The word ludology was born from the combination of two terms, one Latin and the other Greek. Ludus means game in Latin, while logos means knowledge in Greek. In summary, Ludology means the science of play. Similarly, in a broad sense, Ludology focuses on interaction, structure and play in simulation and play (Frasca, 2003a). Ludologists generally argue that the fidelity, immersion and "reality" of the experience are more important than narrative elements. Aarseth, on the other hand, argued that new empirical evidence predominantly proves that narratology is not really a good model for studying and understanding computer games and that we are witnessing "a transitional phase, a paradigm shift" (Raessens, 2006, p. 55).

Some game scholars have argued that simulations and games are not narratives because their characteristics are incompatible with existing definitions of narratology (Frasca, 2003b). Ryan argues that games are games and stories are stories, and that such cultural artefacts offer entirely different essences (Ryan, 2001, p. 6). The overriding goal of traditionalist narratology is to achieve interactivity, a goal shared by game scholars, and expansionist narratologists deconstruct and challenge one of the most popular methods of ludology, that of narrative structure and plot (McManus and Feinstein, 2006:365).

Digital games are now among the favourite leisure activities. Billions of people around the world nowadays utilise their leisure time with digital game battles. In his introduction to the first issue of Game Studies, Espen Aarseth describes 2001 as "the first year of computer game studies" when the first peer-reviewed journal on game studies was launched and the first international academic conference on games was held. The transformation of game studies into an *(inter)discipline* is the result of a struggle in which Aarseth himself took part, and the aim of this struggle is to ensure that games are taken seriously by the academy and to reveal who (which individuals, disciplines and institutions) and how (under whose supervision and primarily with the theoretical/conceptual tools of which disciplines) digital games will be studied (Karadeniz, 2007: 60).

At the research level, a rivalry has developed between two rival groups of critics, resulting in an ongoing debate that has lasted for almost a decade on the most appropriate methodological approach for the study of computer games. On the one hand, narratologists (or narrators) find affinities between computer games and the storytelling arts and approach games in terms of their narrative dimensions; on the other hand, game scientists focus their attention on the mechanics of computer game functions and reject the analysis of computer games as narrative (Kokonis, 2014: 173). According to ludologists, the story elements in a game, if any, are of no real importance as the player is least interested in them; his main concern is with the game itself, i.e. how to win the game. On the other hand, narratologists argue that some games have nothing to do with stories, but that the most popular ones, i.e. those released as blockbuster games, have a strong narrative element or share common features with Hollywood blockbuster films, and as a result, they start to investigate aspects such as visual representation, the concept of movement, narrative space and time, character narration, animation techniques, etc. (King and Krzywinska 2002, 3).

Janet H. Murray (2005) made a similar criticism in her DIGRA 2005 paper the last in his keynote speech titled Word on Ludology v Narratology in Game Studies does. The ludologists, whom Murray calls play essentialists, are the ones who focus on formal approaches. They wanted to privilege the experience of the game because they wanted the game experience to have "a sense of immersion, violence the staging of sexual or sexual events, the performative dimension of the play and even to ignore important aspects such as "the personal experience of winning and losing they are ready. According to this understanding, a researcher who studies games is expected to analyse the emotional, narrative and symbolically highly loaded objects with only "abstract play functions" must have a winter spirit that can see.

2. METHODOLOGY

2.1. Purpose

The main purpose of this study, which is based on the axis of Narratology-Ludology discussions, is to reveal the differences and similarities between the crime representations presented in traditional and new media by making use of Narratology and Ludology disciplines together, and to reveal the factors that determine how the crime representations presented in both media tools will be presented. The work of Çelik and Davulcu in the literature is also in line with this aim of our work. As a matter of fact, Çelik and Davulcu reveal that the hostility object and criminal motivations of the New Zealand Attack of 15 March 2019 and the Call of Duty computer game are the same (Çelik and Davulcu, 2022:321).

The most famous current debate in game studies is ostensibly about digital narrative the problem of narratology. "Ludology versus narratology" (playformers vs. narratologists theorists), in the debate expressed as a discussion of the game form as something in itself ludologists, who believe that games should be analysed as narratives. against the so-called narratologists, who claim to be able to analyse emerged.

2.2. Population and Sample of Study

Analysing the computer game GTA V (Grand Theft Auto V) with semiotic analysis technique. Grand Theft Auto V is a 2013 open-ended action-adventure video game developed by Rockstar North and published by Rockstar Games. GTA V is set in the fictional state of San Andreas, based on Southern California, and its single-player story follows the efforts of the three main characters - former bank robber Michael De Santa, street gang member Franklin Clinton, and drug dealer Trevor Philips - to pull off a heist while under pressure from a corrupt government agency and powerful criminals (Bachchan, 2020). The game broke sales records, grossing $800 million on its first day and $1 billion in its first three days, becoming the entertainment product to reach these numbers in the shortest time (Nayak, 2013). It was praised for its character designs, open world, presentation, and gameplay, but was controversial for its use of torture devices in one mission, excessive violence, and depiction of women (web.archive.org). The Australian division of Target Corporation removed the game from its 300 stores after a Change.org campaign claimed that the game "encourages players to commit sexual violence and kill women". GTA V is the second best-selling video game of all time, with 140 million copies sold, and one of the most financially successful entertainment products of all time, with worldwide revenues of approximately $6 billion. These qualities that make GTA V stand out among other computer games, the fact that the subject of the game is about crime and that the characters in the game are designed in the criminal profile are the main reasons for choosing GTA V as the sample.

2.3. Assumption

The basic assumption of the study is that with this study, which makes use of Narratology and Ludology disciplines together, it is claimed that both disciplines can be used together in terms of crime representations in digital media, leaving aside the existing debates between narratology and ludology.

2.4. Method

From a purely pragmatic point of view, what the player is confronted with on the screen are only some shapes, colours, designs, objects and movements. Playing the game means attributing a meaning to each of them, structuring the output, i.e. treating them as signs to be interpreted. In combination with each other they give rise to other signs that need to be interpreted as part of an ongoing process in the semiotic chain of signs; what C. S. Pierce calls the semiosis spiral. When we approach a computer game from a semiotic point of view, we observe that meaning is derived or produced by a process of signs that, when interpreted, stimulate the player to further action (Kokonis:2014,180). The game as text is presented for scrutiny as a field in which interpretation and action must always be seen in a closely coordinated working relationship, as signs are both the result and the basis of any action. Semiotics in Computer Game Studies has not been applied until recently, either because computer games are a relatively new cultural form or because members of the international semiotic community initially thought that hybrid, technology-based computer games would not constitute a de facto object of study. However, some semioticians believe that, given the appropriate semiotic model, computer games can also be subjected to semiotic analysis (Compagnio and Coppock 2009, 9).

In some games we find a lot of meaning, in others the meaning is very abstract, we may even find games that are almost meaningless. Note, however, that there is no connection between the quality of the game (the meaning of a game for certain players) and the semantic meaning of the game, because the game may have its own meaning, which cannot be measured from outside the game. But even if we find narratives in games, they must first of all function as a game, otherwise the game fails. All semantic meanings of the game are secondary to the primary gameological structure of the game. Signs that carry meaning are actually superficial, but they still help to give the game a perspective. Two games may have exactly the same gameplay, but they carry different meanings because they have different decorative signs and narratives (such as pictures, sounds and/or text). Here we find the semantic meaning of the computer game. This can best be analysed using semiotics (Konzak: 2002,95).

Semiotic analysis method, one of the qualitative research methods, was used in the study. Semiotics deals with the signification of signs in the communication process (Rıfat, 2013:99). The meanings contained in the indicator are formed by the arrangement of common codes (Geray, 2014:168). In this respect, semiotics aims to analyse the common codes in the most accurate way and to reach the most accurate meaning (Tekinalp and Uzun, 2013:139). Semiotics analyses these structures that express meaning in messages (Fiske, 2017:130). In summary, semiotics works for the most accurate expression of the messages that the meaning-laden indicator strings in our environment want to give in the communication dimension.

3. FINDINGS

3.1. Lamar's Pulls a Gun on a Member of the Los Santos Vagos Gang Scene

Episode: Repossession

Mission: You need to get in the car with Lamar and go to the place on the map. When you get out of the vehicle and jump over the iron gate and search for the engine in the closed garages and enter the last garage, at the end of an intense conflict with the Los Santos Vagos gang, kill the person with the motorbike and take the engine and go to the car wash on the map to finish the mission.

When analysed in terms of Barthes's plain meaning, the character Lamar is dressed in comfortable clothes and is pointing a gun at a white person. The person standing behind Lamar is Franklin, one of the main characters of the play. The person pointing the gun has tattoos on his arm. This person is a gang member. It is understood that the place where the scene takes place is the garage of a house.

When considered in Barthes' connotation dimension, the fact that Lamar and Franklin are black and that Lamar points his gun at a white person gives the message that black people are criminal people. Lamar's choice of clothing is in the style of black people who have committed crimes before or who are thought to be prone to crime. Franklin's staying behind Lamar also expresses that he is a novice in this kind of crime. Franklin learns how to commit a crime by watching Lamar. The fact that the white gang member pointing a gun does not have a gun in his hand is presented to strengthen the perception that white people are innocent. The fact that the characters are black is in line with the fact that the majority of criminal characters in traditional media representations of crime are black people.

3.2. Bank Robbery Scene

Episode: Prologue

Mission: 9 years ago, a bank robbery took place in North Yankton. Aim the gun at the hostages and scare them. The frightened hostages go into the back room. Explode the safe and take the money. Conflict with the police.

When analysed in terms of Barthes's plain meaning dimension, it is seen that the character Brad points the shotgun in his hand at the bank customer. The character Trevor is waiting behind Brad in front of the bank security room with an automatic rifle in his hand. A sign above the point where Trevor is waiting with the inscription "all visitors must report to security" adds irony to the scene. Both Brad and Trevor have masks on their faces.

When analysed in Barthes' connotation dimension, it is understood that the season is winter from the mask Brad and Trevor wear and the snow goggles they use, the parka on the hostage and the beret on his head. Although the characters have gloves on their hands, the snow goggles they wear leave part of their faces exposed, giving the message that the robbers are novices. In front of the security room with the sign "all visitors must report to security", the robbers with long-barreled guns pointing a gun at a hostage gives the impression that banks are not as well protected as thought and that it is not very difficult to rob a bank.

3.3. Destroy the Evidence Scene

Episode: Crystal Maze

Mission: Kill all the men who appear in the distance with the sniper gun. After that, kill everyone in the building, take the petrol canister in the basement, pour it on the ground as shown on the radar and get out of the house and shoot with a gun and get away.

When analysed in Barthes' plain meaning dimension, we see a two-storey wooden house on fire. During the explosion, pieces of the house fly in the air. Michael, having completed his mission, walks away from the house.

When considered in Barthes' connotation dimension, it is shown that the wooden house in the image starts to burn as a result of an explosion, giving the message that the evidence left behind after the crime is committed by fire or burning can be destroyed in this way. The character Michael walks confidently, showing that he experiences the pleasure of eliminating the evidence. The dull expression in Michael's eyes depicts that he has lost his feelings because of the crimes he committed.

Narratologically, the images subject to the research contain many messages. Such as that committing a crime is not very difficult, or that getting into a conflict is not as scary as it is thought to be. It is also possible to see the suggestion that black people can be potential criminals. In ludological terms, when the visuals in question are considered, it can be said that the game graphics are very successful and quite similar to real life. Committing the crimes in the visuals is just an activity for the player to spend free time or to have fun.

The most famous current debate in game studies is ostensibly about digital narrative the problem of narratology. "Ludology versus narratology" (playformers vs. narratologists theorists), in the debate expressed as a discussion of the game form as something in itself ludologists, who believe that games should be analysed as narratives. against the so-called narratologists, who claim to be able to analyse emerged.

REFERENCES

Bachchan, V. (2020). *All GTA games ranked in order of release date*. www.sportskeeda.com

Barthes, R. (1993). *Göstergebilimsel Serüven (The Semiotic Challenge), 1. Baskı, (Çev. M. Rifat ve S. Rifat)*. YKY.

Barthes, R. (2009). *Göstergebilimsel Serüven (The Semiotic Challenge) (Çev. M. Rifat ve S. Rifat)*. Yapı Kredi Yayınları.

Çelik, F., & Davulcu, E. (2022). İslamofobi'nin post hakikat dönemde görünümü: Yeni Zelanda Saldırısı'nda dijital oyun izleri (Islamophobia Image in the Post-Truth Age: Traces of Digital Game in New Zealand Attack). *Medya ve Din Araştırmaları Dergisi*, *5*(2), 315–340.

Chatman, S. (2009). *Öykü ve Söylem: Filmde ve Kurmacada Anlatı Yapısı (Story and Discourse: Narrative Structure in Fiction and Film), (Çev. Özgür Yaren)*. De Ki Basım Yayın.

Compagnio, D., & Coppock, P. (2009). Introduction: Computer Games: Between Text and Practice. E |C Journal (Serie Speciale). Associazione di Studi Semiotica. *Anno*, *III*(5), 5–11.

Dervişcemaloğlu, B. (2014). *Anlatıbilime Giriş, (Introduction to Narratology)*. Dergâh Yayınları.

Fiske, J. (2017) İletişim Çalışmalarına Giriş (Introduction to Communication Studies). (Translated by Süleyman İrvan). 5. Basım. Bilim ve Sanat Yayınları, Ankara.

Frasca, G. (2003a). Simulation versus Narrative: Introduction to Ludology. In M. J. P. Wolf & B. Perron (Eds.), *Video/Game/Theory*. Routledge.

Frasca, G. (2003b). Ludologists love stories, too: notes from a debate that never took place. *Digital Game Research Conference 2003 Proceedings*.

Geray, H. (2014). *İletişim Alanından Örneklerle Toplumsal Araştırmalarda Nicel ve Nitel Yöntemlere Giriş (Introduction to Quantitative and Qualitative Methods in Social Research with Examples from the Field of Communication)*. Umuttepe Yayınları, Kocaeli.

Harris, R., & Taylor, H. (2005). Landmarks in Linguistic Thought I: The Western Tradition from Socrates to Saussure (2nd ed.). Routledge.

Jahn, M. (2005). Narratology: A guide to the theory of narrative. English Department, University of Cologne.

Karadeniz, O. Ö. (2017). Oyun İncelemelerinde Ludoloji - Narratoloji Tartışması ve Alternatif Kuramsal Arayışlar (Ludology - Narratology Debate and Alternative Theoretical Searches in Game Studies). *Galatasaray Üniversitesi İletişim Dergisi*, *27*(27), 57–78. doi:10.16878/gsuilet.373236

King, G., & Krzywinska, T. (2002). *ScreenPlay: Cinema / Videogames / Interfaces*. Wallflower Press.

Kıyar, N. & Karkın, N. (2013). Mimesis'in Yapıbozumsal Dönüşümleri (Deconstructive Transformations of Mimesis). *İnönü Üniversitesi Sanat ve Tasarım Dergisi, 3*(7).

Kokonis, M. (2014). Intermediality between games and fiction: The "ludology vs. narratology" debate in computer game studies: A response to Gonzalo Frasca. Acta Universitatis Sapientiae. *Film and Media Studies*, (09), 171–188.

Konzack, L. (2002, June). Computer game criticism: A method for computer game analysis. *CGDC Conference.*

Lawler, S. (2002). Narrative in Social Research. In Qualitative Research in Action. Sage.

McManus, A., & Feinstein, A. H. (2006). Narratology and ludology: Competing paradigms or complementary theories in simulation. In *Developments in Business Simulation and Experiential Learning: Proceedings of the Annual ABSEL conference* (*Vol. 33*). Academic Press.

Mutlu, E. (1998). *İletişim Sözlüğü (Dictionary of Communication)*. Bilim-Sanat Yayınları.

Raessens, J. (2006). Playful Identities, or the Ludification of Culture. *Games and Culture*, *1*(1), 52–57. doi:10.1177/1555412005281779

Riessman, C. K. (2008). *Narrative methods for the human sciences*. Sage Pub.

Riessman, C. K., & Quinney, L. (2005). Narrative in social work: A critical review. *Qualitative Social Work: Research and Practice*, *4*(3), 391–412. doi:10.1177/1473325005058643

Rifat, M. (2013). Açıklamalı Göstergebilim Sözlüğü, (Kavramlar- Yöntemler- Kuramcılar- Okullar) (Annotated Semiotics Dictionary, (Concepts- Methods- Theorists- Echols). Türkiye İş Bankası Kültür Yayınları, İstanbul.

Ryan, M. L. (2001). Beyond Myth and Metaphor: The Case of Narrative in Digital Media. *Game Studies*, 1.

Tekinalp, Ş., & Uzun, R. (2013). İletişim Araştırmaları ve Kuramları (Communication Research and Theories). Derin Yayınları, İstanbul.

Chapter 20
Machine Learning and Virtual Reality:
Enabling Safety in Social Media Websites

N. Ambika
https://orcid.org/0000-0003-4452-5514
St. Francis College, India

ABSTRACT

The study focuses on data produced by social media users. It applies the El Saddik communication structure between a digital twin and a physical twin to the setting of understanding and personality identification in people. Depending on the requirements, real twins use sensors to mimic their senses of sight, hearing, taste, smell, and touch. Users' posting and liking activities may be tracked in online social networks to get a sense of and an understanding of their personalities. Digital twins should have a deep learning-enhanced controller to act quickly and wisely on behalf of their physical counterparts. The approach combines user content posting and like behavior for personality prediction. Depending on the application, digital twins can be represented virtually as a social humanoid robot or a software element without a physical replica. The status messages uploaded by each user are pooled as a document. The work enhances security by 17.4%.

INTRODUCTION

Social media (Kaplan & Mazurek, 2018; Mayfield, 2008) refers to digital platforms and technologies that facilitate the creation, sharing, and exchange of user-generated content, ideas, information, and interactions within virtual communities and networks. These platforms enable individuals and organizations to connect, communicate, and engage with each other globally through various forms of multimedia content, such as text, images, videos, and audio.

Social media has become a significant part of modern communication and has implications for personal connections, entertainment, news dissemination, activism, marketing, and more. However, it also raises concerns about privacy, misinformation, and the impact of excessive screen time on mental well-being.

DOI: 10.4018/979-8-3693-0855-4.ch020

The core features of social media include:

1. **User Profiles**: Users create personal or business profiles that represent their identity, interests, and activities on the platform.
2. **Content Sharing**: Users can share a wide range of content, including posts, photos, videos, links, and more, often with the option to add captions, hashtags, and tags.
3. **Interactions**: Social media platforms allow users to engage with content by liking, commenting, sharing, retweeting, or reacting to posts. This interaction encourages conversations and connections.
4. **Networking**: Users can connect with others by sending friend requests, following profiles, subscribing to channels, or joining groups and communities.
5. **Real-time Communication**: Many platforms offer instant messaging, live chat, and video calling features to facilitate real-time communication between users.
6. **Discovery and Exploration**: Users can explore new ideas, topics, and trends through algorithms that recommend content based on their interests and interactions.
7. **Collaboration**: Social media platforms often provide tools for collaborative work, allowing users to collaborate on projects, documents, and shared content.
8. **Personalization**: Platforms use user data to personalize content and recommendations, enhancing the user experience.
9. **Broadcasting**: Some platforms support live streaming, enabling users to broadcast themselves or events in real time.
10. **Community Building**: Social media fosters the creation of online communities centered around shared interests, hobbies, or affiliations.
11. **Marketing and Promotion**: Businesses and individuals can use social media to promote products, services, events, and ideas to a broad audience.
12. **Feedback and Insights**: Users and businesses can receive feedback and insights from their audience, helping them refine their content and strategies.

Some of the social media websites include

- **Facebook** (Wilson, Gosling, & Graham, 2012): One of the largest social media platforms, allowing users to connect with friends and family, share updates, photos, and videos, and join groups based on interests.
- **Instagram** (Mattern, 2016): A visual-focused platform where users share photos and short videos, along with captions and hashtags. It's widely used for personal and business purposes.
- **Twitter** (Murthy, 2018): A microblogging platform where users share short messages called "tweets." It's known for its real-time updates and the use of hashtags to follow trends and topics.
- **LinkedIn** (Van Dijck, 2013): A professional networking platform designed for connecting with colleagues, industry professionals, and potential employers. It's commonly used for career-related activities.
- **Snapchat** (Vaterlaus, Barnett, Roche, & Young, 2016): This platform focuses on sharing ephemeral photos and videos that disappear after a short time. It's popular among younger users for its playful features and filters.

- **TikTok** (Li, Guan, Hammond, & Berrey, 2021): A short-form video platform where users can create and share engaging videos, often set to music. It gained significant popularity for its entertaining and creative content.
- **Pinterest** (Gilbert, Bakhshi, Chang, & Terveen, 2013): A visual discovery platform where users can find and save ideas for various topics such as recipes, fashion, home decor, and more.
- **Reddit** (Proferes, Jones, Gilbert, Fiesler,, & Zimmer, 2021): A discussion platform organized into various communities called "subreddits." Users can post text, links, and images and engage in discussions on a wide range of topics.
- **YouTube**: While primarily a video-sharing platform, YouTube also has social features like commenting, subscribing to channels, and interacting with content creators.
- **WhatsApp**: A messaging app that enables users to send text messages, voice messages, make voice and video calls, and share media with their contacts.
- **Telegram**: Another messaging app known for its security features and the ability to create large groups and channels for discussions.
- **Discord**: Originally focused on gaming, Discord is now used for various interest-based communities and offers features like text, voice, and video chat in servers.
- **Tumblr**: A microblogging platform that allows users to share multimedia content and short blog posts. It's often used for creative expression and connecting with like-minded users.
- **Vkontakte (VK)**: A popular social network in Russia and neighboring countries, offering features similar to Facebook.
- **WeChat**: A Chinese multi-purpose messaging, social media, and mobile payment app that integrates various features like messaging, social networking, and online shopping.

Designers consider many facts and information during the product design stage of production, including gadgets, product sales, and customer feedback data. These data are enormous and dispersed among several locations. The incorporation of data is easier in digital twin technology (Ambika, 2023; Batty, 2018; Chaudhary, Khari, & Elhoseny, 2021), which helps designers swiftly update their product designs.

The previous study (Sun, Tian, Fu, Geng, & Liu, 2021) focuses on data produced by social media users. It applies the El Saddik communication structure between a digital twin and a physical twin to the setting of understanding and personality identification in people. Depending on the requirements, real twins use sensors to mimic their senses of sight, hearing, taste, smell, and touch. Users' posting and liking activities may be tracked in online social networks to get a sense of and an understanding of their personalities. Digital twins should have a deep learning-enhanced controller to act quickly and wisely on behalf of their physical counterparts. The approach combines user content posting and like behavior for personality prediction. Depending on the application, digital twins can be represented virtually as a social humanoid robot or a software element without a physical replica. The status messages uploaded by each user are pooled as a document, where digital twins use a virtual human representation to analyze human nature by timely watching users' posting and like behavior. Then, illogical punctuation and stop words are eliminated. Then, each word vector in the user document is obtained using the pre-trained Glove-vector (GloVE) file. The suggestion aims to understand the behaviour of the communicating party by using virtual reality and machine learning. This methodology helps the client to be safe by 17.4% from harmful parties.

BACKGROUND

Machine learning (Zhou, 2021) is a subset of artificial intelligence (AI) (Michalski, Carbonell, & Mitchell, 2013) that involves the development of algorithms and models that enable computer systems to learn and improve from experience without being explicitly programmed. In other words, machine learning systems can analyze data, identify patterns, and make informed decisions or predictions based on the patterns they've learned. Machine learning has a wide range of applications, including image and speech recognition, natural language processing, recommendation systems, fraud detection, medical diagnosis, autonomous vehicles, and more. It's a rapidly evolving field that continues to advance as more sophisticated algorithms and techniques are developed.

Key components of machine learning include:

1. **Data**: Machine learning algorithms require large amounts of data to learn from. This data can be structured (in databases or spreadsheets) or unstructured (like text, images, audio).
2. **Training**: During the training phase, the machine learning model is exposed to the data and learns from it. It adjusts its internal parameters to recognize patterns and relationships within the data.
3. **Features**: Features are specific characteristics or attributes extracted from the data that the model uses to make predictions or classifications. Feature engineering involves selecting and transforming relevant features.
4. **Algorithms**: Machine learning algorithms are the mathematical and computational techniques that process the data and learn patterns. Different algorithms are used for various tasks, such as classification, regression, clustering, and more.
5. **Model Evaluation**: After training, the model's performance is evaluated on new, unseen data. This helps assess how well the model generalizes its learned patterns to new instances.
6. **Predictions or Decisions**: Once trained and evaluated, the model can make predictions, classifications, or decisions about new data it hasn't seen before, based on the patterns it learned.
7. **Feedback Loop**: Models can be improved over time by continually updating them with new data and refining their algorithms. This process is known as "iterative learning."

Types of machine learning include:

1. **Supervised Learning**: The model learns from labeled data, where input examples are paired with correct output labels. It learns to map inputs to correct outputs, making predictions based on new, unseen inputs.
2. **Unsupervised Learning**: In this type, the model analyzes data without explicit output labels. It identifies patterns or structures within the data, often used for tasks like clustering and dimensionality reduction.
3. **Semi-Supervised Learning**: A combination of supervised and unsupervised learning, using a small amount of labeled data along with a larger amount of unlabeled data.
4. **Reinforcement Learning**: The model learns by interacting with an environment. It receives feedback in the form of rewards or penalties based on its actions, learning to optimize its decisions.

Using Images to Understand Human Behaviour

1. **Neuroimaging and Human Behavior**: Neuroimaging techniques such as fMRI (functional Magnetic Resonance Imaging) and PET (Positron Emission Tomography) allow researchers to observe brain activity while individuals engage in different behaviors or tasks. These images provide insights into how the brain responds to various stimuli, experiences, and emotions. For example, studies have used neuroimaging to understand the brain regions involved in decision-making, memory recall, emotional responses, and more.
2. **Facial Expression Analysis**: Images of human faces can provide valuable information about emotions and behavior. Facial expression analysis involves using computer vision techniques to analyze facial features and determine emotions like happiness, sadness, anger, and surprise. This information can be used in fields like marketing, user experience design, and psychology to understand how people respond to different stimuli.
3. **Eye Tracking and Attention**: Eye tracking technology records the movement of a person's gaze as they view images or interact with their environment. By analyzing where a person's eyes linger and how they move, researchers can gain insights into attentional patterns, preferences, and cognitive processes. This information is often used in fields like advertising, usability testing, and educational research.
4. **Physiological Responses to Visual Stimuli**: Images can evoke physiological responses in humans, such as changes in heart rate, skin conductance, and pupil dilation. These responses can be used to study emotional reactions and arousal levels in response to different visual stimuli. For instance, horror movies leads to increased heart rate and heightened arousal compared to calming nature scenes.
5. **Neuroaesthetics**: This field explores how the brain processes and responds to artistic and aesthetic experiences, including visual stimuli. Researchers use neuroimaging and physiological measurements to understand the neural mechanisms underlying preferences for different types of visual art, architecture, and design.
6. **Advertising and Consumer Behavior**: The use of images in advertising plays a significant role in shaping consumer behavior. Understanding how specific visual elements affect people's emotions and decisions can help advertisers create more effective campaigns.
7. **Nonverbal Communication**: Images and body language are essential components of nonverbal communication. Researchers study how people interpret and convey messages through visual cues, which can include gestures, postures, and facial expressions. These cues play a role in forming impressions, conveying emotions, and establishing social connections.
8. **Virtual Reality and Immersive Experiences**: Virtual reality (VR) technology allows researchers to create immersive environments that can elicit specific behaviors and emotions. Studies using VR have explored topics such as phobias, empathy-building, and social interactions in controlled virtual environments.
9. **Cultural and Cross-Cultural Influences**: Human behavior and responses to images can vary based on cultural backgrounds and societal norms. Researchers analyze how cultural factors shape the perception of images, symbols, and visual representations.

Overall, the intersection of physiology, images, and human behavior is a rich and multidisciplinary field that offers insights into how the brain processes visual information, how emotions are evoked, and how people respond to various stimuli in their environment. It has applications ranging from psychology and marketing to design and education.

Social Media With Virtual Reality

Social media integrated with virtual reality (VR) (Bri, García, Coll, & Lloret, 2009) has the potential to revolutionize how we connect and engage with others online. This combination can create immersive and interactive experiences that go beyond traditional text and images. Here's how social media and VR can work together:

1. **Immersive Social Interaction**: With VR, users can create avatars and immerse themselves in virtual environments. Instead of just scrolling through a feed, users can physically "meet" in virtual spaces, attend events, and interact in a more natural and immersive way.
2. **Virtual Hangouts and Events**: Social media platforms in VR can host virtual events, gatherings, parties, and conferences. Friends and colleagues from around the world can join these events using their avatars, making interactions feel more personal and engaging.
3. **Shared Experiences**: Imagine being able to virtually visit a museum, travel destination, or concert with friends in real time. VR-enhanced social media can provide shared experiences, enabling users to explore together even when physically apart.
4. **Virtual Workspaces**: VR can transform remote work by creating collaborative virtual workspaces. Social media integrated with VR can provide a more interactive and engaging environment for team discussions, presentations, and brainstorming sessions.
5. **Content Sharing in 3D**: Instead of just sharing photos and videos, users could share 3D models, immersive panoramas, and VR experiences. It could revolutionize storytelling and content creation on social platforms.
6. **Enhanced Communication**: VR can add a sense of presence to communication. Imagine having a conversation where you can see the other person's gestures, facial expressions, and body language, making online interactions feel more authentic.
7. **Personalized Environments**: Users can personalize their virtual spaces reflect their personalities, interests, and moods. It could create a more intimate and meaningful connection between users.
8. **Virtual Marketplaces**: Social media VR platforms could include virtual marketplaces where users can browse and purchase products. It could offer new possibilities for e-commerce and advertising.
9. **Virtual Tourism**: VR-enabled social media could allow users to virtually explore different places, cultures, and historical sites, offering a unique way to experience travel without leaving home.
10. **New Forms of Expression**: VR can enable users to express themselves creatively in new ways. Artists could create immersive VR galleries, musicians could perform in virtual concert halls, and writers could share stories in three-dimensional environments.
11. **Privacy and Ethical Considerations**: As with any technology, there are concerns about privacy and ethics. VR social media platforms would need to carefully consider issues related to data security, consent, and user tracking to ensure user safety.

Incorporating virtual reality into social media opens up exciting possibilities for more engaging and immersive online interactions. However, it also requires overcoming technical, ethical, and user experience challenges to create a seamless and enjoyable integration.

Social Media with Virtual Reality and Machine Learning

The convergence of social media, virtual reality (VR), and machine learning can lead to a transformative online experience, offering highly personalized and immersive interactions. Here's a closer look at how these three elements can come together:

1. **Personalized VR Social Spaces**: Social media platforms in VR can leverage machine learning to analyze user preferences, behaviors, and interactions. This data can then be used to create personalized virtual spaces, events, and experiences that cater to individual interests and connections.
2. **Immersive Content Recommendation**: Machine learning algorithms can analyze users' past interactions and behaviors to recommend VR content that aligns with their preferences. For instance, a VR social media platform could suggest VR experiences, virtual hangouts, or events based on users' interests and engagement history.
3. **Avatar Customization and Emotion Analysis**: Machine learning can enhance the personalization of avatars within VR social platforms. Users' expressions, gestures, and even emotions can be analyzed in real-time to make avatars more realistic and emotionally responsive, enhancing the sense of presence during interactions.
4. **Real-time Language Translation**: VR social media platforms can utilize machine learning to offer real-time translation of conversations between users who speak different languages. This fosters cross-cultural connections and enables more inclusive communication within the VR environment.
5. **Enhanced Content Creation and Sharing**: Machine learning algorithms can assist users in generating and sharing content within VR. Whether it's automatically converting spoken conversations into text or suggesting VR-friendly multimedia elements for storytelling, machine learning can enhance content creation.
6. **Immersive Ads and Product Placement**: Advertisers can leverage machine learning to create immersive and non-intrusive advertising experiences within VR social spaces. By analyzing user preferences and behaviors, VR ads and product placements can be tailored to align with users' interests.
7. **Social Behavior Prediction**: Machine learning can predict social behaviors within VR environments based on historical data. This prediction can help in organizing events, allocating resources, and optimizing user engagement strategies for better community interactions.
8. **Emotionally Aware Interactions**: Machine learning algorithms can interpret users' emotional cues through voice, text, and even VR gestures. This enables more emotionally aware and empathetic interactions within the virtual social space.
9. **Virtual Education and Training**: Integrating machine learning into VR

Different Kinds of Tweets

- **Text Updates:** These are simple text-based tweets where users share updates about their day, thoughts, opinions, or any other text-based content.
- **Links to Articles or Websites:** Users often share links to news articles, blog posts, websites, or other online resources they find interesting or informative.
- **Quotes:** Sharing quotes from famous individuals, authors, or personal thoughts is a common type of tweet.

- **Retweets (RTs):** Users can share tweets from others on their own timeline. It shares content you find interesting or important with your followers.
- **Replies:** Replies are tweets in response to another user's tweet. It is used for conversations, discussions, or engaging with other users.
- **Hashtags:** Tweets with hashtags are used to categorize content and make it more discoverable. Users can search for or click on hashtags to find related tweets.
- **Mentions and Tags:** Users can tag other users using the "@" symbol. It is used to include someone in a conversation or bring their attention to a specific tweet.
- **Images and GIFs:** Including images, GIFs, or short videos in tweets can add visual appeal and enhance the message.
- **Polls:** Twitter allows users to create polls where followers can vote on a specific question or topic.
- **Promotional Tweets:** Individuals and businesses often use Twitter to promote products, services, events, or special offers.
- **Live Tweeting:** Users can provide real-time commentary on events, shows, conferences, and more by tweeting their thoughts and reactions as things unfold.
- **Personal Updates:** People often share updates about their personal lives, achievements, milestones, and experiences.
- **Humor and Memes:** Many tweets are humorous or share memes, jokes, and relatable content.
- **Thoughts and Opinions:** Users often share their thoughts, opinions, and perspectives on various topics, ranging from politics to entertainment.
- **Educational Tweets:** Many users share educational content, facts, tips, and insights on various subjects.
- **Inspiration and Motivation:** Tweets with inspirational quotes, messages, or stories are quite popular.
- **Contests and Giveaways:** Brands and individuals may use Twitter to host contests and giveaways, encouraging engagement and interaction.
- **Shoutouts:** Users often give shoutouts to other users, businesses, or causes to show appreciation or support.
- **Announcements:** Businesses, organizations, and individuals may use Twitter to make official announcements about new products, events, or news.
- **Support and Assistance:** Companies often use Twitter for customer support, responding to inquiries, and assisting users with issues.

LITERATURE SURVEY

The previous study (Sun, Tian, Fu, Geng, & Liu, 2021) focuses on data produced by social media users. It applies the El Saddik communication structure between a digital twin and a physical twin to the setting of understanding and personality identification in people. Depending on the requirements, real twins use sensors to mimic their senses of sight, hearing, taste, smell, and touch. Users' posting and liking activities may be tracked in online social networks to get a sense of and an understanding of their personalities. Digital twins should have a deep learning-enhanced controller to act quickly and wisely on behalf of their physical counterparts. The approach combines user content posting and like behavior for personality prediction. Depending on the application, digital twins can be represented virtually as a social humanoid robot or a software element without a physical replica. The status messages uploaded by each user are pooled as a document, where digital twins use a virtual human representation to analyze human nature by timely watching users' posting and like behavior. Then, illogical punctuation and stop words are eliminated. Then, each word vector in the user document is obtained using the pre-trained Glove-vector (GloVE) file.

The paper (Arasu, Seelan, & Thamaraiselvan, 2020) presents a machine learning-driven approach to improving the effectiveness of social media marketing strategies. The paper addresses the challenge of optimizing social media marketing efforts to achieve better engagement, reach, and conversion rates. The authors propose a machine learning-based approach to enhance the effectiveness of these strategies. The study applies various machine learning techniques to analyze social media data and make informed marketing decisions. These techniques likely include predictive modeling, classification, and data analysis. The authors gather data from social media platforms and employ machine learning algorithms to analyze user behavior, preferences, and interactions. This data-driven approach aims to uncover patterns and insights that can inform marketing strategies. One focus of the paper is likely on how machine learning can be used to personalize marketing content and target specific audience segments. By analyzing user data, the authors suggest ways to tailor content to individual preferences and characteristics. The paper likely discusses how machine learning algorithms can optimize social media marketing strategies. This could involve automated decision-making for content scheduling, campaign timing, and platform selection based on data-driven insights. The article likely presents the results of applying the machine learning approach to social media marketing and discusses the benefits observed, such as improved engagement rates, increased click-through rates, or enhanced conversion rates. The authors likely provide insights into how businesses and marketers can implement machine learning-based strategies in their social media marketing campaigns, potentially offering guidelines or recommendations for implementation. The paper likely contributes to the growing field of data-driven marketing, specifically focusing on how machine learning techniques can be leveraged to enhance social media marketing efforts. By demonstrating how data analysis and automation can lead to improved marketing outcomes, the authors likely provide insights that are valuable for both researchers and practitioners in the field of marketing.

The paper (Dhaoui, Webster, & Tan, 2017) examines and compares two approaches—lexicon-based sentiment analysis and machine learning-based sentiment analysis—for analyzing sentiment in social media data. It addresses the task of sentiment analysis, which involves determining the emotional tone or sentiment expressed in social media posts, comments, or other textual content. Sentiment analysis is important for understanding public opinion, brand perception, and customer sentiment. The authors discuss the use of lexicons, which are dictionaries containing words associated with different sentiment polarities (positive, negative, neutral). Lexicon-based sentiment analysis assigns sentiment scores to text based on the presence of words from the lexicon. The study explores the use of machine learning algorithms for sentiment analysis. Machine learning models are trained on labeled data to learn patterns and relationships between words and sentiment labels, enabling them to predict sentiment in new texts. It likely presents a comparison between the lexicon-based approach and machine learning-based approach. This comparison could cover aspects such as accuracy, robustness.

The paper (Chavan & Shylaja, 2015) likely discusses machine learning techniques to identify and detect cyber-aggressive comments made by peers on social media networks. Cyber-aggressive comments refer to negative, offensive, or harmful remarks that individuals might post online, which can contribute to online harassment and toxicity. In this context, the authors may have proposed a machine learning-based approach that involves analyzing text-based content on social media platforms to automatically identify and flag comments that display aggressive or harmful behavior. The approach could involve training machine learning models on labeled data to recognize patterns associated with cyber-aggressive language. These models could then be used to analyze new comments and determine whether they exhibit cyber-aggressive behavior. The goal of such research is to develop tools and methods to create a safer and more positive online environment by detecting and addressing instances of cyberbullying, harassment, and other negative behaviors on social media platforms.

The recommendation (Abd El-Jawad, Hodhod, & Omar, 2018) focuses on the application of machine learning techniques to perform sentiment analysis on social media networks. Sentiment analysis known as opinion mining, involves using computational methods to determine the sentiment or emotional tone expressed in text data, such as social media posts, reviews, and comments. In this context, the authors may have explored how machine learning algorithms can automatically categorize social media posts into positive, negative, or neutral sentiments. It can involve training machine learning models on labeled data where each post is associated with its corresponding sentiment. The trained models could then be used to predict sentiment labels for new and unseen social media posts. Data Preprocessing discusses of techniques used to clean and prepare the social media text data for analysis, including removing noise, special characters, and irrelevant content. Feature Extraction explains methods for transforming the textual content into numerical features that machine learning algorithms can process. ITmight involve techniques like bag-of-words, word embeddings, or other natural language processing (NLP) approaches. Model Selection discusses the machine learning algorithms used for sentiment analysis, such as support vector machines, decision trees, random forests, or neural networks. Evaluation Metrics explains how the authors evaluated the performance of their sentiment analysis models, including metrics like accuracy, precision, recall, F1-score, and possibly ROC curves. Presentation of the outcomes of the sentiment analysis experiments. It includes insights into the effectiveness of the machine learning models on predicting sentiment in social media data.

The suggestion (Habernal, Ptáček, & Steinberger, 2013) applies supervised machine learning techniques to perform sentiment analysis on social media data in the Czech language. It introduces the problem of sentiment analysis, explaining its significance and relevance in the context of social media data. Data Collection and Preprocessing Details collected social media data in Czech, such as tweets or posts, for their sentiment analysis task. This section might also discuss preprocessing steps like tokenization, stemming, and removing stop words. Feature Extraction explains how the textual data is transformed into numerical features that machine learning algorithms can use. It includes techniques like n-grams, word embeddings, or other linguistic features. Supervised Machine Learning describes machine learning algorithms employed for sentiment analysis. It involves explaining the chosen classifier (e.g., support vector machines, naive Bayes, etc.), the training process, and model evaluation methods. It discusses how the authors obtained labeled data for training and evaluating their sentiment analysis models. Annotation of sentiment labels is crucial for supervised learning in sentiment analysis.

The work (Chancellor, Baumer, & De Choudhury, 2019)addresses the ethical and human-centered considerations when using machine learning to predict mental health outcomes based on social media data. The authors might explore how machine learning models can predict mental health states or conditions by analyzing individuals' online behaviors and language on social media platforms. The authors introduce the topic of using social media data for predicting mental health outcomes. They may highlight the potential benefits and challenges of such an approach. Fairness, Accountability, and Transparency (FAT) handles these issues by viewing them as contained within the data, methodologies, and algorithmic representations, and then employing statistical or mathematical techniques as a solution. Engineering solutions for algorithms adhere to these ideals, such as fairness, justice, and equality in prediction tasks. It provided conception of human-centeredness. It created two sets of search terms—one for social media and the other for mental health—to be used in pairs. It conducted a keyword search across 41 English-language venues in the multidisciplinary field of social media prediction of mental health.

PREVIOUS STUDY

The study by (Sun, Tian, Fu, Geng, & Liu, 2021)focuses on utilizing the concept of digital twins and the communication structure between digital and physical twins to understand and predict personality traits in individuals based on their online social media activities. The approach involves using sensors to mimic the sensory experiences of real individuals and employing deep learning-enhanced controllers within digital twins to mimic real-world behaviors and decisions.

Key points from the study include:

1. **Digital Twins and Communication Structure**: The study leverages the concept of digital twins, where a digital twin represents a virtual counterpart of a physical entity (in this case, individuals). The communication structure between the digital twin and physical twin is inspired by El Saddik's model. This structure enables the digital twin to analyze the online behavior of the physical twin and make informed decisions on their behalf.
2. **Data Collection and Analysis**: Sensors are used to mimic the sensory experiences (sight, hearing, taste, smell, touch) of the physical individuals, which helps gather data for analysis. The study collects data from users' posting and liking activities on social media platforms. These activities are analyzed to gain insights into users' personalities.
3. **Personality Prediction**: The study employs a deep learning-enhanced controller within the digital twin to quickly and wisely simulate the behavior of the physical twin. This simulation includes analyzing users' content posting and liking behaviors to predict their personality traits.
4. **Data Processing and Analysis Techniques**:
    - The study uses textual data from status messages uploaded by users. These messages are treated as documents for analysis.
    - Natural language processing techniques are applied, including eliminating illogical punctuation and stop words to enhance data quality.
    - Word vectors are generated using pre-trained GloVe (Global Vectors for Word Representation) vectors, which encode semantic relationships between words.
        1. **Representation of Digital Twins**: Depending on the application, digital twins can be virtually represented as social humanoid robots or software elements without a physical replica. These digital twins leverage the insights gained from users' online behaviors to mimic human nature and behavior.
        2. **Personality Prediction Approach**: The study combines user content posting and like behavior to predict personality traits. By analyzing users' online interactions, the digital twin can infer patterns and characteristics that correlate with different personality traits.
        3. **Application Areas**: The approach has potential applications in understanding human behavior, psychology, and personalized services. It could also be used to develop AI-driven virtual assistants that simulate human-like interactions.

The study proposes a novel application of digital twins and communication structures to predict personality traits based on online social media activities. By integrating sensory data, deep learning techniques, and behavioral analysis, this approach demonstrates the potential of understanding human behavior and decision-making in digital environments.

PROPOSED WORK

Virtual reality (VR) is a powerful technology. It deeply influences human behavior across a wide range of contexts. Here are several ways in which virtual reality can impact human behavior:

1. **Behavioral Immersion**: VR creates highly immersive environments that can make users feel physically present in a different world. This immersion can lead to more realistic reactions and behaviors within the virtual environment. For example, in a VR simulation of a job interview, users might experience similar levels of nervousness and excitement as they would in an interview.
2. **Experiential Learning**: VR provides a safe and controlled space for individuals to learn and practice new skills. It includes anything from medical training to flight simulation. Users can engage in hands-on experiences that mimic real-world situations, enabling them to learn and refine behaviors in a risk-free environment.
3. **Therapeutic Applications**: Virtual reality has shown promise in therapeutic contexts. It helps them confront and manage their fears or traumatic experiences.
4. **Social Interaction and Empathy**: VR can facilitate social interactions and enable individuals to experience different perspectives and cultures. Virtual reality environments can encourage users to interact with avatars or other users, influencing their social behaviors and communication skills. VR experiences can also promote empathy by allowing individuals to see the world from someone else's point of view.
5. **Behavioral Research**: Researchers can use VR to study human behavior in controlled and repeatable environments. This is particularly useful in fields such as psychology, sociology, and neuroscience. By manipulating virtual scenarios, researchers can observe how individuals react, make decisions, and interact with their surroundings.
6. **Entertainment and Gaming**: VR gaming platforms provide immersive experiences that can impact users' emotions, reactions, and behaviors. Game designers can create environments that evoke excitement, fear, or curiosity, influencing players' behaviors and emotions within the game world.
7. **Cognitive Rehabilitation**: VR has been explored as a tool for cognitive rehabilitation, helping individuals recover cognitive functions after brain injuries or strokes. Virtual reality exercises can engage users in activities that challenge memory, attention, and problem-solving skills.
8. **Training and Skill Development**: Beyond professional training, VR can be used for skill development in various fields, including sports. Athletes can practice techniques, analyze their performance, and make adjustments within a virtual training environment.
9. **Architectural and Urban Planning**: VR allows architects and urban planners to create interactive visualizations of buildings and urban spaces. Users can explore and interact with these environments, providing feedback that can influence design choices and human behavior within these spaces.
10. **Behavioral Change and Exposure**: VR can be used as a tool for behavior modification, such as helping individuals overcome fears, manage stress, or develop healthier habits. By exposing users

Table 1. Algorithm to used to analyse the words tweeted to draw the profile

Step 1 – Create a dictionary with tweets T_i mapping to different category C_i of tweets.
Step 2 – Create profile pics P_i of different categories (mild to extreme)
Step 3 - Input the tweets
Step 4- keep a benchmark B_i for the number of tweets of a particular category
Step 5 – Change the profile pic according to the benchmark

to controlled scenarios, VR can facilitate desensitization and gradual habituation to challenging situations.

CASE STUDY

The work uses Kaggle dataset. Tweets exchanged are used to create the profile pic of the individual. The system uses virtual reality with machine learning to derive the profile pic of the communicating party. The phrases exchanged are classified into –

- **Harassment:** Continuously sending hurtful, threatening, or derogatory messages to a person or group.
- **Hate Speech:** Using language that promotes discrimination, prejudice, or hostility based on factors like race, ethnicity, gender, religion, sexual orientation, etc.
- **Bullying:** Targeting an individual to cause emotional distress or harm.
- **Personal Attacks:** It is Making derogatory or malicious remarks about someone's appearance, character, or personal life.
- **Trolling:** Posting deliberately provocative or offensive content to provoke reactions or upset others.
- **Doxxing:** Sharing someone's private or personal information without their consent, leading to potential harm or harassment.
- **Threats:** It is Posting messages that include threats of physical harm or violence.
- **Cyberbullying:** Engaging in bullying behavior online, including through tweets, to target and harass someone.
- **Misinformation and Disinformation:** Sharing false or misleading information to cause harm or confusion.
- **Defamation:** It is Posting false and damaging statements about a person or entity that can harm their reputation.

SECURITY

The users are more safer using the suggested system by 17.4% compared to (Sun, Tian, Fu, Geng, & Liu, 2021).

Figure 1. Comparison of security in both the systems

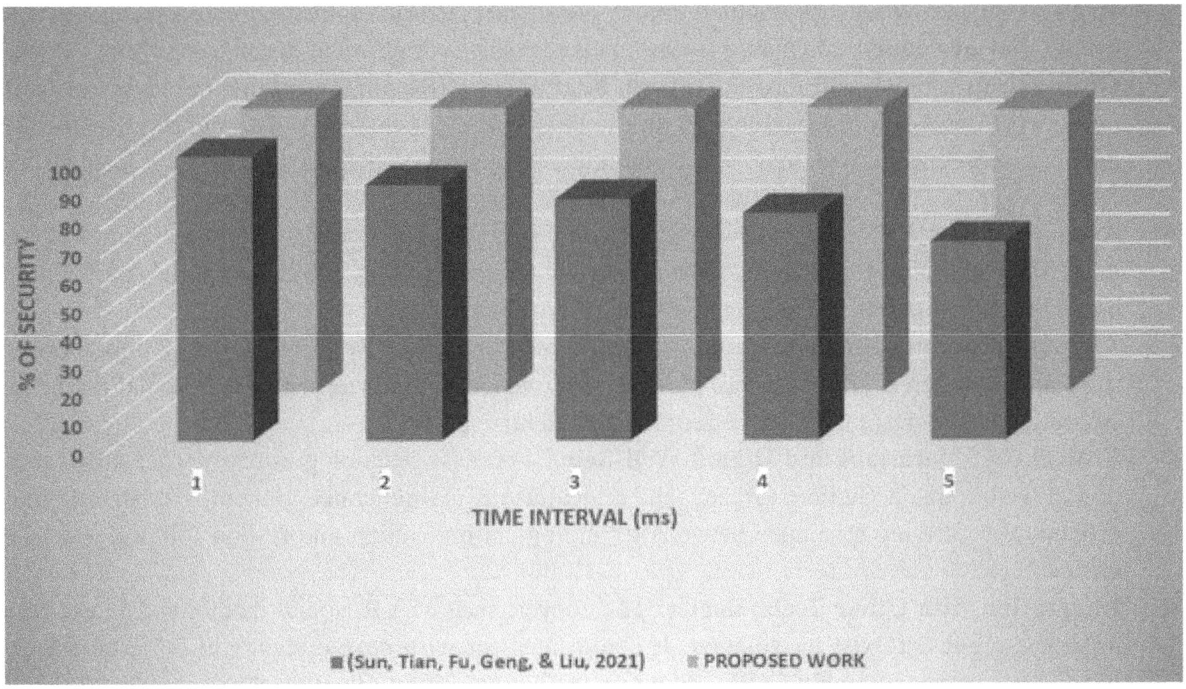

FUTURE SCOPE

The fusion of social media, virtual reality (VR), and future advancements holds immense potential for reshaping how we interact, communicate, and experience digital spaces. As we look ahead, here's how these elements might come together to create a transformative future:

- **Total Immersion and Presence**: Future VR technologies could offer even more immersive experiences, blurring the lines between physical and virtual realities. Users might be able to experience social media content and interactions as if they were happening right in front of them, fostering a deeper sense of presence.
- **Holographic Avatars and Augmented Reality Integration**: Holographic avatars could provide a level of realism and interactivity that goes beyond current VR. Augmented reality (AR) could also play a role, allowing users to overlay digital information and interactions onto their physical environment, enabling seamless integration of social media into daily life.
- **Neural Interfaces and Brain-Computer Interaction**: The future might bring advancements in neural interfaces that allow direct communication between the brain and digital devices. This could enable users to interact with social media platforms, navigate VR environments, and communicate with others using their thoughts and emotions.
- **Synthetic Reality and Personalized Worlds**: Advanced AI and machine learning could create synthetic reality environments tailored to individuals' preferences and desires. Social media interactions could take place in fully customizable worlds, offering unique and personalized experiences for each user.

- **Shared Virtual Experiences**: Imagine sharing virtual experiences with friends and family as if you were physically present together. Future VR-social platforms could facilitate shared activities, events, and adventures, enhancing social bonds regardless of physical distance.
- **Global Connectivity and Cross-Cultural Exchanges**: VR-enhanced social media could facilitate deeper cross-cultural interactions and understanding. Users might be able to virtually visit distant places, engage with diverse communities, and gain new perspectives without leaving their homes.
- **AI-Generated VR Content**: Advanced AI could generate highly realistic and dynamic VR content, from landscapes to characters to entire environments. This could lead to an explosion of creative possibilities for content creators and users alike.
- **Virtual Economies and Commerce**: Virtual reality could give rise to new forms of digital economies and commerce. Users might buy, sell, and trade virtual assets within VR social platforms, creating novel opportunities for entrepreneurs and businesses.
- **Ethical Considerations and Digital Well-Being**: As these technologies evolve, questions about digital well-being, addiction, privacy, and ethical use of AI-generated content will become more pronounced. Striking a balance between technological innovation and responsible usage will be critical.
- **Integration with Other Technologies**: The convergence of VR, social media, and future technologies might not exist in isolation. It could intersect with developments in 5G connectivity, blockchain, extended reality (XR), and more, further amplifying its impact.

The future of social media integrated with virtual reality holds both exciting possibilities and complex challenges. It will require careful consideration of user needs, ethical implications, and the responsible development of technology to ensure a positive and inclusive digital landscape.

CONCLUSION

The combination of social media, machine learning, and virtual reality has the potential to create a highly immersive and personalized online experience. Machine learning algorithms can analyze users' preferences, behaviors, and interactions on social media platforms. It can curate and deliver highly personalized content, including text, images, videos, and even VR experiences. This personalization enhances user engagement and satisfaction. Machine learning generates and enhances content for social media and VR. Text-to-speech, image generation, and video synthesis models can help users create multimedia content effortlessly. It could lead to a surge in user-generated content and creativity. The work enhances security by 17.4%.

REFERENCES

Abd El-Jawad, M. H., Hodhod, R., & Omar, Y. M. (2018). Sentiment analysis of social media networks using machine learning. In *14th International Computer Engineering Conference (ICENCO)* (pp. 174-176). Cairo, Egypt: IEEE.

Ambika, N. (2023). Smart System Engineering-Digital Twin. In *Digital Twins and Healthcare: Trends, Techniques, and Challenges* (pp. 215–228). IGI.

Arasu, B. S., Seelan, B. J., & Thamaraiselvan, N. (2020). A machine learning-based approach to enhancing social media marketing. *Computers & Electrical Engineering*, *86*, 106723. doi:10.1016/j.compeleceng.2020.106723

Batty, M. (2018). Digital twins. *Environment and Planning. B, Urban Analytics and City Science*, *45*(5), 817–820. doi:10.1177/2399808318796416

Chancellor, S., Baumer, E. P., & De Choudhury, M. (2019). Who is the" human" in human-centered machine learning: The case of predicting mental health from social media. *Proceedings of the ACM on Human-Computer Interaction*, *3*(CSCW), 1–32. doi:10.1145/3359249

Chaudhary, G., Khari, M., & Elhoseny, M. (2021). *Digital Twin Technology*. CRC Press. doi:10.1201/9781003132868

Chavan, V. S., & Shylaja, S. S. (2015). Machine learning approach for detection of cyber-aggressive comments by peers on social media network. In *International Conference on Advances in Computing, Communications and Informatics (ICACCI)* (pp. 2354-2358). Kochi, India: IEEE. 10.1109/ICACCI.2015.7275970

Dhaoui, C., Webster, C. M., & Tan, L. P. (2017). Social media sentiment analysis: Lexicon versus machine learning. *Journal of Consumer Marketing*, *34*(6), 480–488. doi:10.1108/JCM-03-2017-2141

Gilbert, E., Bakhshi, S., Chang, S., & Terveen, L. (2013). need to try this"? a statistical overview of pinterest. In SIGCHI Conference on Human Factors in Computing Systems (pp. 2427-2436). Paris France: ACM.

Habernal, I., Ptáček, T., & Steinberger, J. (2013). Sentiment analysis in czech social media using supervised machine learning. In *4th workshop on computational approaches to subjectivity, sentiment and social media analysis* (pp. 65-74). Association for Computational Linguistics.

Kaplan, A., & Mazurek, G. (2018). Social media. In Handbook of media management and economics (pp. 273-286). Taylor and Francis. doi:10.4324/9781315189918-17

Li, Y., Guan, M., Hammond, P., & Berrey, L. E. (2021). Communicating COVID-19 information on TikTok: A content analysis of TikTok videos from official accounts featured in the COVID-19 information hub. *Health Education Research*, *36*(3), 261–271. doi:10.1093/her/cyab010 PMID:33667311

Mattern, J. (2016). *Instagram*. ABDO.

Mayfield, A. (2008). *What is social media*. NDU PRESS.

Murthy, D. (2018). *Twitter*. Polity Press.

Proferes, N., Jones, N., Gilbert, S. F. C., & Zimmer, M. (2021). Studying reddit: A systematic overview of disciplines, approaches, methods, and ethics. *Social Media + Society*, *7*(2). doi:10.1177/20563051211019004

Sun, J., Tian, Z., Fu, Y., Geng, J., & Liu, C. (2021). Digital twins in human understanding: A deep learning-based method to recognize personality traits. *International Journal of Computer Integrated Manufacturing*, *7-8*(7-8), 860–873. doi:10.1080/0951192X.2020.1757155

Van Dijck, J. (2013). 'You have one identity': Performing the self on Facebook and LinkedIn. *Media Culture & Society*, *35*(2), 199–215. doi:10.1177/0163443712468605

Vaterlaus, J. M., Barnett, K., Roche, C., & Young, J. A. (2016). Snapchat is more personal": An exploratory study on Snapchat behaviors and young adult interpersonal relationships. *Computers in Human Behavior*, *62*, 594–601. doi:10.1016/j.chb.2016.04.029

Wilson, R. E., Gosling, S. D., & Graham, L. T. (2012). A review of Facebook research in the social sciences. *Perspectives on Psychological Science*, *7*(3), 203–220. doi:10.1177/1745691612442904 PMID:26168459

Compilation of References

Abd El-Jawad, M. H., Hodhod, R., & Omar, Y. M. (2018). Sentiment analysis of social media networks using machine learning. In *14th International Computer Engineering Conference (ICENCO)* (pp. 174-176). Cairo, Egypt: IEEE.

Addison, M. (2022). Brand Development and marketing strategies in USA: A Case of Apple Inc. *Journal of Marketing Communications*, *5*(1), 1–8. doi:10.53819/81018102t2055

Adorno, T. W. (2007). *Kültür Endüstrisi*. İletişim Yayınları.

Adorno, T. W., & Horkheimer, M. (2002). The culture industry: Enlightenment as mass deception. In G. Schmid Noerr (Ed.), *Dialectic of Enlightenment: Philosophical Fragments* (pp. 94–156). Stanford University Press.

Agarwal, S. (2013). Data mining: Data mining concepts and techniques. *International Conference on Machine Intelligence and Research Advancement*, 203-207. 10.1109/ICMIRA.2013.45

Aggarwal, C. C. (2011). *An introduction to social network data analytics*. Springer. doi:10.1007/978-1-4419-8462-3

Agostino, D., Arnaboldi, M., & Calissano, A. (2019). How to Quantify Social Media Influencers: An Empirical Application at The Teatro Alla Scala. *Elsevier. Heliyon*, *5*(5), 1–7. doi:10.1016/j.heliyon.2019.e01677

Ahmad, I. (2018). The Influencer Marketing Revolution. *Social Media Today*, *15*(2), 22–26.

Ahmed, M. S., Rony, R. J., Ashhab, M. M., & Ahmed, N. (2020). An Empirical Study to Analyze the Impact of Instagram on Students' Academic Results. *2020 IEEE Region 10 Symposium (TENSYMP)*, 666-669.

Ahmed, M. (2019). Novel big data analytics framework for smart cities. *Future Generation Computer Systems*, *91*, 620–633. doi:10.1016/j.future.2018.06.046

Ahmet Nafiz, Ü. (2019). Yumuşak Gücün Tesis Edilmesinde Kültürel Diplomasinin Önemi ve Bir Uygulayıcı Olarak Yunus Emre Enstitüsü. *Bilig - Turk DunyasI Sosyal Bilimler Dergisi*, *91*, 137–159.

Ahrholdt, D., Greve, G., & Hopf, G. (2019). Online-Marketing-Intelligence. New York: Springer.

Akanksh, S. S., D'souza, L., & Manish, S. (2020). The effect of Instagram addiction on quality of life among undergraduate students in Mysuru. *International Journal of Indian Psychology*, *8*(4), 1324–1330.

Akat, Ö. (2000). *Uygulamaya Yönelik İşletme Politikası ve Stratejik Pazarlama*. Ekin Kitabevi.

Akçaöz, M., & Akçaöz, V. (2023). Kamu Yönetiminde Dijitalleşme ve Türkiye'deki Dijital Devlet Uygulamaları. *Journal of Social Humanities and Administrative Sciences*, *9*(69), 3648–3660. doi:10.29228/JOSHAS.72401

Akdağ, M., & Taşdemir, E. (2006). Krizden Çıkmanın Yolları: Etkin Bir Kriz İletişimi. *Selçuk İletişim*, *4*(2),141-157. https://dergipark.org.tr/en/pub/josc/issue/19011/200778

Akgül, M. (2017). Dijitalleşme ve Din. *Marife, 17*(2), 191–208.

Akıncı, A. N. (2019). *Personal Data Privacy in Big Data Applications* [Expert Thesis]. General Directorate of Sectors and Public Investments, Ankara.

Aksu, A. (2009). Kriz Yönetimi ve Vizyoner Liderlik. *Yaşar Üniversitesi Eğİtim Fakültesi*, 2435-2448.

Aktaş, A., & Şener, G. (2019). Nüfuz Pazarlamasında (Influencer Marketing) Mesaj Stratejileri. *Erciyes İletişim Dergisi, 6*(1), 399–422. doi:10.17680/erciyesiletisim.477592

Aktaş, C. (2014). *QR Kodlar ve İletişim Teknolojisinin Hibritleşmesi*. Kalkedon Yayınları.

Akter, S., Wamba, S. F., Gunasekaran, A., Dubey, R., & Childe, S. J. (2016). How to improve firm performance using big data analytics capability and business strategy alignment? *International Journal of Production Economics, 182*, 113–131. doi:10.1016/j.ijpe.2016.08.018

Aktop, A. & Seferoğlu, F. (2014). Sportif performans açısından nöro-geribildirim. *Spor ve Performans Araştırmaları Dergisi, 5*(2).

Akulshina, S. (2020). *Developing and implementing a strategic social media content plan for a local restaurant*. Academic Press.

Al-Abdallah, G. M., Dandis, A., & Al Haj Eid, M. B. (2022). The impact of Instagram utilization on brand management: An empirical study on the restaurants sector in Beirut. *Journal of Foodservice Business Research*, 1–33. doi:10.1080/15378020.2022.2083910

Alamri, B. (2018). The Role of Social Media in Intercultural Adaptation: A Review of the Literature. *English Language Teaching, 11*(12), 77–85. doi:10.5539/elt.v11n12p77

Albayrak, O. (2023). Dijital Diplomasi: Diplomasi 3.0. *İstanbul Ticaret Üniversitesi Sosyal Bilimler Dergisi, 22*(46), 493-508. doi:10.46928/iticusbe.1288805

Albert, N., & Merunka, D. (2015). Role of Brand Love in Consumer Brand Relationships. In M. Fetscherin & T. Heilmann (Eds.), *Consumer Brand Relationships Meaning, Measuring, Managing* (pp. 15–30). Palgrave Macmillan.

Alencar, A. (2018). Refugee integration and social media: A local and experiential perspective. *Information Communication and Society, 21*(11), 1588–1603. doi:10.1080/1369118X.2017.1340500

Alghamdi, A. (2023). A hybrid method for customer segmentation in Saudi Arabia restaurants using clustering, neural networks and optimization learning techniques. *Arabian Journal for Science and Engineering, 48*(2), 2021–2039. doi:10.1007/s13369-022-07091-y PMID:35910042

Aljumah, A., Nuseir, M., & Alam, M. M. (2021). Traditional Marketing Analytics, Big Data Analytics and Big Data System Quality and the Success of New Product Development. *Business Process Management Journal, 27*(4), 1108–1125. doi:10.1108/BPMJ-11-2020-0527

Alkan, S. (2015). *The Future of the Data World: Big Data (Big Data)*. Linkedin. https://www.linkedin.com/pulse/verid%C3%BCnyas%C4%B1n%C4%B1ngelece%C4%9Fi-b%C3%BCy%C3%BCk-big-data-seydi-alkan/

Allard, T., Dunn, L. H., & White, K. (2020). Negative reviews, positive impact: Consumer empathetic responding to unfair word of mouth. *Journal of Marketing, 84*(4), 86–108. doi:10.1177/0022242920924389

Allouche, G. (2014). *Big Data Use Case: Digital Advertising*. http://cmsreport.com/articles/big-data-use-case-digital-advertising-8225

Alpay, N., Karşıdağ, Ç., & Kükürt, R. (2005). Transkranyal manyetik stimülasyon (TMS). *Dusunen Adam : Bakirkoy Ruh Ve Sinir Hastaliklari Hastanesi Yayin Organi, 18*(3), 136–148.

Alsharif, A. H., Md Salleh, N. Z., Baharun, R., & Yusoff, M. E. (2021). Consumer behaviour through neuromarketing approach. *Journal of Contemporary Issues in Business and Government, 27*(3), 344–354.

Amazon (2022). *What is AWS*? https://aws.amazon.com/tr/what-is-aws/

Amazon. (2021). *Amazon Gizlilik Bildirimi*. https://www.amazon.com.tr/gp/help/customer/display.html?nodeId=GX7NJQ4ZB8MHFRNJ

Amazon. (2023). *Playback & DRM Overview*. https://developer.amazon.com/docs/music/playback_overview.html

Ambika, N. (2023). Smart System Engineering-Digital Twin. In *Digital Twins and Healthcare: Trends, Techniques, and Challenges* (pp. 215–228). IGI.

Anderson, C. W. (2018). *Apostles of Certainty*. Oxford University Press. doi:10.1093/oso/9780190492335.001.0001

Anderson, S., & Daniel, M. (2020). Refugees and social media in a digital society. *The Journal of Community Informatics, 16*, 26–44. doi:10.15353/joci.v16i0.3473

Anyoha, R. (2017). *The History of Artificial Intelligence*. Harvard University The Graduate School of Arts and Sciences. https://sitn.hms.harvard.edu/flash/2017/history-artificial-intelligence/

Appelgren, E. (2018). An ıllusion of ınteractivity. The paternalistic side of data journalism. *Journalism Practice, 12*(3), 308–325. doi:10.1080/17512786.2017.1299032

Appelgren, E., Lindén, C., & van Dalen, A. (2019). Data journalism research: Studying a maturing field across journalistic cultures, media markets and political environments. *Digital Journalism (Abingdon, England), 7*(9), 1191–1199. doi:10.1080/21670811.2019.1685899

Apple Newsroom. (2023). *Celebrating 100 million songs*. https://www.apple.com/newsroom/2022/10/celebrating-100-million-songs/

Apple. (2022). *Apple gizlilik politikası*. https://www.apple.com/legal/privacy/tr/

Aranceta-Reboredo, O. (2022). And What About the Animals? A Case Study Comparison Between China's Panda Diplomacy and Australia's Koala Diplomacy. *Animal Ethics Review, 2*(1), 78–93.

Arandilla, R. (2012). Rise and fall of online advertising. Academic Press.

Arasu, B. S., Seelan, B. J., & Thamaraiselvan, N. (2020). A machine learning-based approach to enhancing social media marketing. *Computers & Electrical Engineering, 86*, 106723. doi:10.1016/j.compeleceng.2020.106723

Arnold, C., & Blackman, S. (2021). Retrieving and repurposing: A grounded approach to hyperlocal working practices through a subcultural lens. *Digital Journalism (Abingdon, England)*. Advance online publication. doi:10.1080/21670811.2021.1880330

Arribas-Bel, D. (2014). Accidental, open and everywhere: Emerging data sources for the understanding of cities. *Applied Geography, 49*, 45-53. doi:10.1016/j.apgeog.2013.09.012

Ashton, K. (2009). That 'Internet of Things' Thing. *Rfid Journal*. https://www.rfidjournal.com/articles/view?4986

Aşkun. (1990). Eskişehir Anadolu Üniversitesi iktisadi ve idari Bilimler Fak. Academic Press.

Ataman, G. (2001). *İşletme Yönetimi–Temel Kavramlar & Yeni Yaklaşımlar*. Türkmen Kitabevi.

Ausserhofer, J., Gutounig, R., Oppermann, M., Matiasek, S., & Goldgruber, E. (2020). The datafication of data journalism scholarship: Focal points, methods, and research propositions for the ınvestigation of data-ıntensive newswork. *Journalism*, *21*(7), 950–973. doi:10.1177/1464884917700667

Aw, E. C. X., & Agnihotri, R. (2023). Influencer marketing research: Review and future research agenda. *Journal of Marketing Theory and Practice*, 1–14. doi:10.1080/10696679.2023.2235883

Ayhan, E., & Önder, M. (2017). Yeni Kamu Hizmeti Yaklaşımı: Yönetişime Açılan Bir Kapı. *Gazi İktisat ve İşletme Dergisi*, *3*(2), 19–48.

Aytekin, B. A. (2019). İzleyici ve içerik etkileşimi bağlamında yeni bir youtube fenomeni olarak otonom duyusal meridyen tepki (ASMR) etkisinin deri iletkenliği ölçümü (GSR) tekniği ile incelenmesi. *OPUS–Uluslararası Toplum Araştırmaları Dergisi*, *10*(17), 1568–1600. doi:10.26466/opus.533789

Bachchan, V. (2020). *All GTA games ranked in order of release date.* www.sportskeeda.com

Bae, S., & Lee, T. (2011). Gender Differences in Consumers' Perception of Online Consumer Views. *Electronic Commerce Research*, *11*(11), 201–214. doi:10.1007/s10660-010-9072-y

Baines, D. (2010). Hyper-local: Glocalised rural news. *The International Journal of Sociology and Social Policy*, *30*(9/10), 581–592. doi:10.1108/01443331011072316

Bakker, D. (2018). Conceptualising influencer marketing. *Journal of Emerging Trends in Marketing and Management*, *1*(1), 79-87.

Barlow, M. (2013). *Real Time Big Data Analytics: Emerging Arthitecture*. O'Reilly Media.

Barnes, S. J. (2002). Wireless digital advertising: Nature and implications. *International Journal of Advertising*, *21*(3), 399–420. doi:10.1080/02650487.2002.11104939

Barnett, S., & Townend, J. (2015). Plurality, policy and the local. *Journalism Practice*, *9*(3), 332–349. doi:10.1080/17512786.2014.943930

Barot, H. (2019). *Drawbacks of Instagram on Today's Society.* https://www.justwebw-orld.com/drawbacks-instagram-todays-society/

Barthes, R. (1993). *Göstergebilimsel Serüven (The Semiotic Challenge), 1. Baskı, (Çev. M. Rifat ve S. Rifat)*. YKY.

Barthes, R. (2009). *Göstergebilimsel Serüven (The Semiotic Challenge) (Çev. M. Rifat ve S. Rifat)*. Yapı Kredi Yayınları.

Bartlett, L., & Vavrus, F. (2017). Rethinking case study research. Routledge.

Barton, L. (2001). *Crisis in organizations II* (2nd ed.). College Divisions South-Western.

Baş, T. & Tüzün, H. (2014). Tüketicileri (Kullanıcıları) ve ürün kullanımlarını analiz etmek için göz izleme yönteminin kullanılması. *Tüketici Yazıları*, (4), 217 – 234.

Baskin, M., & Coburn, N. (2001). Two tribes divided by a common language? *International Journal of Market Research*, *43*(2), 137.

Baskin, M., & Pickton, D. (2003). Account planning from genesis to revelation. *Marketing Intelligence & Planning*, *21*(7), 416–424. doi:10.1108/02634500310504250

Bat, M., & Yurtseven, Ç. (2014). Sosyal medyada kurumsal kriz yönetimi: Onur Air örneği. *Gümüşhane Üniversitesi İletişim Fakültesi Elektronik Dergisi*, *2*(3), 197–223. doi:10.19145/guifd.74720

Batty, M. (2018). Digital twins. *Environment and Planning. B, Urban Analytics and City Science*, *45*(5), 817–820. doi:10.1177/2399808318796416

Bayarçelik, E. (2020). Dijital Dönüşümün İnsan Kaynakları Yönetimi. *İstanbul Gelişim Üniversitesi Yayınları*, 59-77.

Bayrakçı, S. (2015). *Use of Big Data in Academic Studies in Social Sciences* [Unpublished Master's Thesis]. Marmara University SSI.

Bayram, H. (2010). *Bilgi Toplumu ve Bilgi Yönetimi*. Etap Yayınevi.

Beal, A. (1997). A generalization of Fermat's last theorem: Beal's conjecture and the reward problem. *Notices of the American Mathematical Society*, *44*(11).

Bebko, C., Sciulli, L. M., & Bhagat, P. (2014). Using eye-tracking to assess the ımpact of advertising appeals on donor behavior. *Journal of Nonprofit & Public Sector Marketing*, *26*(4), 354–371. doi:10.1080/10495142.2014.965073

Behan, K., & Holmes, D. (1990). *Understanding Information Technology*. Prentice Hall.

Bellman, S., Potter, R. F., Treleaven-Hassard, S., Robinson, J. A., & Varan, D. (2011). The effectiveness of branded mobile phone apps. *Journal of Interactive Marketing*, *25*(4), 191–200. doi:10.1016/j.intmar.2011.06.001

Bendle, N. T., & Wang, X. (2016). Uncovering the message from the mess of big data. Amsterdam: Elsevier Science BV.

Benkler, Y. (2006). *The wealth of networks: How social production transforms markets and freedom*. Yale University Press.

Benoit, W. L. (2015). *Accounts, excuses, and apologies* (2nd ed.). State University of New York.

Bentley, J. M. (2015). Shifting identification: A theory of apologies and pseudo-apologies. *Public Relations Review*, *41*(1), 22–29. doi:10.1016/j.pubrev.2014.10.011

Berlatsky, N. (2014). *Are social networking sites harmful?* Greenhaven Publishing LLC.

Berman, J. (2015). *Principles of Big Data: Preparing, Sharing, and Analyzing Complex Information*. Morgan Kaufmann.

Berry, J. W. (2006a) Stress perspectives on acculturation. The Cambridge Handbook of Acculturation Psychology, 1, 43-56.

Berry, J. W. (1992). Acculturation and adaptation in a new society. *International Migration (Geneva, Switzerland)*, *30*(s1), 69–85. doi:10.1111/j.1468-2435.1992.tb00776.x

Berry, J. W. (2005). Acculturation: Living successfully in two cultures. *International Journal of Intercultural Relations*, *29*(6), 697–712. doi:10.1016/j.ijintrel.2005.07.013

Berry, J. W. (2006b). Stress perspectives on acculturation. In D. L. Sam & J. W. Berry (Eds.), *The Cambridge handbook of acculturation psychology* (pp. 43–57). Cambridge University Press. doi:10.1017/CBO9780511489891.007

Berry, J. W., Kim, U., Minde, T., & Mok, D. (1987). Comparative Studies of Acculturative Stress. *The International Migration Review*, *21*(3), 491–511. doi:10.1177/019791838702100303

Betancourt, M. (2015). *The critique of digital capitalism*. Punctum Books.

Bhatt, G. D. (2000). Information Dynamics, Learning And Knowledge Creation In Organizations. *The Learning Organization*, *7*(2), 89–98. doi:10.1108/09696470010316288

Bhatt, U., Antorán, J., Zhang, Y., Liao, Q. V., Sattigeri, P., Fogliato, R., Melançon, G., Krishnan, R., Stanley, J., & Tickoo, O. (2021). Uncertainty as a form of transparency: Measuring, communicating, and using uncertainty. *Proceedings of the 2021 AAAI/ACM Conference on AI, Ethics, and Society*, 401–413. 10.1145/3461702.3462571

Bilgihan, A., Kandampully, J., & Zhang, T. (2016). Towards a unified customer experience in online shopping environments: Antecedents and outcomes. *International Journal of Quality and Service Sciences*, *8*(1), 102–119. doi:10.1108/IJQSS-07-2015-0054

Blazquez-Resino, J. J., Gutierrez-Broncano, S., & Gołąb-Andrzejak, E. (2022). Neuroeconomy and neuromarketing: The study of the consumer behaviour in the Covid-19 context. *Frontiers in Psychology*, *13*, 13. doi:10.3389/fpsyg.2022.822856 PMID:35369189

Blinowska, K., & Durka, P. (2006). *Electroencephalography (EEG)*. Wiley Encyclopedia of Biomedical Engineering. doi:10.1002/9780471740360.ebs0418

Bobkowski, S. P., Jiang, L., Peterlin, L. J., & Rodriguez, N. J. (2018). Who gets vocal about hyperlocal. *Journalism Practice*. Advance online publication. doi:10.1080/17512786.2017.1419827

Boerman, S. C., Kruikemeier, S., & Zuiderveen Borgesius, F. J. (2017). Online Behavioral Advertising: A Literature Review and Research Agenda. *Journal of Advertising*, *46*(3), 363–376. doi:10.1080/00913367.2017.1339368

Bollen, J., & Huina, M. (2011). Twitter Mood predicts the stock market. *Journal of Computational Science*, *2*(1), 1–8. doi:10.1016/j.jocs.2010.12.007

Bonfanti, A., Vigolo, V., & Yfantidou, G. (2021). The impact of the Covid-19 pandemic on customer experience design: The hotel managers' perspective. *International Journal of Hospitality Management*, *94*, 102871. doi:10.1016/j.ijhm.2021.102871 PMID:34866744

Booz Allen Hamilton. (2015). *Understanding the DNA of data science*. https://www.boozallen.com/s/insight/publication/field-guide-to-data-science.html doi:10.1016/j.drugpo.2016.02.022

Borgatti, S. P., Everett, M. G., & Johnson, J. C. (2013). Analyzing social networks. *Sage (Atlanta, Ga.)*.

Borges-Rey, E. (2016). Unravelling data journalism: A study of data journalism practice in british newsrooms. *Journalism Practice*, *10*(7), 833–843. doi:10.1080/17512786.2016.1159921

Borges-Rey, E. (2020). Towards an epistemology of data journalism in the devolved nations of the United Kingdom: Changes and continuities in materiality, performativity and reflexivity. *Journalism*, *21*(7), 915–932. doi:10.1177/1464884917693864

Boulos, M. N., Wheeler, S., Tavares, C., & Jones, R. (2011). How smartphones are changing the face of mobile and participatory healthcare: An overview, with example from eCAALYX. *Biomedical Engineering Online*, *10*(1), 1–14. doi:10.1186/1475-925X-10-24 PMID:21466669

Bourdieu, P. (1993). *The field of cultural production*. Colombia University Press.

Boyd, D. (2008). Why youth (heart) social network sites: The role of networked publics in teenage social life. In D. Buckingham (Ed.), Youth, identity, and digital media (pp. 119-142). The MIT Press.

boyd, d. (2010). Social network sites as networked publics: Affordances, dynamics, and implications. In Z. Papacharissi (Ed.), *Networked self: Identity, community, and culture on social network sites* (pp. 39-58). Routledge.

Boyd, D. M. (2014). *It's complicated: The social lives of networked teens*. Yale University Press.

Boyd, D., & Crawford, K. (2012). Crıtıcal questıons for bıg data. *Information Communication and Society*, *15*(5), 662–679. doi:10.1080/1369118X.2012.678878

Boyles, J. L. (2020). Strength in numbers. In A. Gulyas & D. Baines (Eds.), *The routledge companion to local media and journalism* (pp. 389–397). Routledge. doi:10.4324/9781351239943-44

Boyles, J. L., & Meyer, E. (2016). Letting the data speak. *Digital Journalism (Abingdon, England)*, *4*(7), 944–954. doi:10.1080/21670811.2016.1166063

Braatz, L. (2017). *#Influencer Marketing on Instagram: Consumer Responses Towards Promotional Posts: The Effects of Message Sidedness, Responses* [Master thesis]. University of Twente.

Briggs, D. (2021) *WhatsApp refugees? A reflexive account of the methodological use of WhatsApp with newly arrived refugees in Europe*. Available at: https://pjp-eu.coe.int/documents/42128013/47261623/YKB-27-WEB.pdf/dbab979b-75ff-4ee8-b3da-c10dc57650d5

Briggs, R., Krishnan, R., & Borin, N. (2005). Integrated multichannel communication strategies: Evaluating the return on marketing objectives—the case of the 2004 Ford F-150 launch. *Journal of Interactive Marketing*, *19*(3), 81–90. doi:10.1002/dir.20045

Broussard, G. (2016). Enriching media data: A special report from the U.S. coalition of ınnovative media measurement. *Journal of Advertising Research*, *56*(1), 25–55. doi:10.2501/JAR-2016-010

Brown, D., & Hayes, N. (2008). *Influencer marketing*. Routledge. doi:10.4324/9780080557700

Bruns, A. (2008). *Blogs, Wikipedia, second life, and beyond: From production to produsage*. Peter Lang.

Budak, G., & Budak, G. (2014). *İmaj Mühendisliği Vizyonundan Halkla İlişkiler* (6th ed.). Nobel Yayıncılık.

Bühler, J., Baur, A. W., Bick, M., & Shi, J. (2015). Big data, big opportunities: Revenue sources of social media services besides advertising. In. Lecture Notes in Computer Science: Vol. 9373. *Open and big data management and ınnovation*. Springer. doi:10.1007/978-3-319-25013-7_15

Buhmann, A., & Ingenhoff, D. (2015). Advancing the Country Image Construction From a Public Relations Perspective: From Model to Measurement. *Journal of Communication Management (London)*, *19*(1), 62–80. doi:10.1108/JCOM-11-2013-0083

Buiten, M. C. (2020). Exploitative Abuses in Digital Markets: Between Competition Law and Data Protection Law. *Journal of Antitrust Enforcement*, *9*(2), 271.

Bustamante, E. (2004). Cultural industries in the digital age: Some provisional conclusions. *Media Culture & Society*, *26*(6), 803–820. doi:10.1177/0163443704047027

Cain, J. A., & Imre, I. (2021). Everybody wants some: Collection and control of personal information, privacy concerns, and social media use. *New Media & Society*, *24*(12), 2705-2724. doi: 10.1177/14614448211000327.

Çalı, H. H., & Tombul, F. (2012). Güvenlik ile İlgili Kamu Hizmeti Sunumunda Sosyal Medya. *Türk İdare Dergisi*, *474*, 55–76.

Çalışır, G., & Aksoy, F. (2019). Kamu Kurumlarında Sosyal Medya Kullanımı: Kastamonu İl Kültür ve Turizm Müdürlüğü Örneği. *Alınteri Sosyal Bilimler Dergisi*, *3*(1), 43–65. doi:10.30913/alinterisosbil.503286

Camaj, L. (2016). From 'window dressing'to 'door openers'? Freedom of ınformation legislation, public demand, and state compliance in south east europe. *Government Information Quarterly*, *33*(2), 346–357. doi:10.1016/j.giq.2016.03.001

Campbell, C., & Farrell, J. (2020). More Than Meets The Eye: The Functional Components Underlying İnfluencer Marketing. *Business Horizons*, *63*(4), 469–479. doi:10.1016/j.bushor.2020.03.003

Campbell, C., & Leyland, F. (2011). Understanding Consumer Conversations Around Ads in a Web 2.0 World. *Journal of Advertising*, *40*(1), 87–102. doi:10.2753/JOA0091-3367400106

Campbell, R., Martin, C., & Bettina, F. (2014). *Media & culture mass communication in a digital age*. McMillan Learning.

Cao, Q., & Schniederjans, M. J. (2004). Empirical study of the relationship between Operations Strategy and Information Systems Strategic Orientation in an e-Commerce Environment. *International Journal of Production Research*, *42*(15), 2915–2939. doi:10.1080/00207540410001691884

Carroll, B. A., & Ahuvia, A. C. (2006). Some antecedents and outcomes of brand love. *Marketing Letters*, *17*(2), 79–89. doi:10.1007/s11002-006-4219-2

Carson, A., Muller, D., Martin, J., & Simons, M. (2016). A new symbiosis? Opportunities and challenges to hyperlocal journalism in the digital age. *Media International Australia, Incorporating Culture & Policy*, *161*(1), 132–146. doi:10.1177/1329878X16648390

Carter, D. (2016). Hustle and Brand: The Sociotechnical Shaping of Influence. *Social Media + Society*, *2*(3), 1–12. doi:10.1177/2056305116666305

Cartwright, S., Liu, H., & Davies, I. A. (2022). Influencer marketing within business-to-business organizations. *Industrial Marketing Management*, *106*, 338–350. doi:10.1016/j.indmarman.2022.09.007

Cassar, M. L., Caruana, A., & Konietzny, J. (2020). Wine and satisfaction with fine dining restaurants: An analysis of tourist experiences from user generated content on TripAdvisor. *Journal of Wine Research*, *31*(2), 85–100. doi:10.1080/09571264.2020.1764919

Cassiday, J., & Johnson, E. (2010). Cassiday, J., & Johnson, E. (2010). Putin, putiniana and the question of a post-soviet cult of personality. *Slavonic and East European Review*, *88*(4), 681-707. Von https://www.jstor.org/stable/41061898abgerufen

Castells, M. (2005). *"Enformasyon Çağı: Ekonomi, Toplum ve Kültür, Ağ Toplumunun Yükselişi", Çev. Ebru Kılıç, 1.* Baskı, İstanbul Bilgi Üniversitesi Yayınları.

Castells, M. (2005). *Enformasyon Çağı: Ekonomi, Toplum ve Kültür: Ağ Toplumunun Yükselişi* (E. Kılıç, Trans.). İstanbul Bilgi Üniversitesi Yayınları.

Cauberghe, V., & De Pelsmacker, P. (2010). Advergames. *Journal of Advertising*, *39*(1), 5–18. doi:10.2753/JOA0091-3367390101

Cavanillas, J. M., Curry, E., & Wahlster, W. (2016). New horizons for a data-driven economy: A roadmap for usage and exploitation of big data in Europe. New York: Springer. doi:10.1007/978-3-319-21569-3

Ceccagnoli, M., Forman, C., & Huang, P. (2012). Cocreation of value in a platform ecosystem: The case of enterprise software. *MIS Quarterly*, *36*(1), 263–290.10.1109/ICDE.2012.55

Çelik, F., & Davulcu, E. (2022). İslamofobi'nin post hakikat dönemde görünümü: Yeni Zelanda Saldırısı'nda dijital oyun izleri (Islamophobia Image in the Post-Truth Age: Traces of Digital Game in New Zealand Attack). *Medya ve Din Araştırmaları Dergisi*, *5*(2), 315–340.

Chadha, M. (2016). The neighborhood hyperlocal. *Digital Journalism (Abingdon, England)*, *4*(6), 743–763. doi:10.1080/21670811.2015.1096747

Chancellor, S., Baumer, E. P., & De Choudhury, M. (2019). Who is the" human" in human-centered machine learning: The case of predicting mental health from social media. *Proceedings of the ACM on Human-Computer Interaction*, *3*(CSCW), 1–32. doi:10.1145/3359249

ChandonP.HutchinsonJ. W.BradlowE. T.ScottH. (2007). *Measuring the value of point-of-purchase marketing with commercial eye-tracking data.* Faculty and Research Working Paper. Available at: https://ssrn.com/abstract=1032162

Chang, H., & Rizal, H. (2013). The determinants of consumer behavior towards email advertisement. *Internet Research, 23*(3), 316–337. doi:10.1108/10662241311331754

Charmarkeh, H. (2013). Social Media Usage, Tahriib (Migration), and Settlement among Somali Refugees in France. *Refuge: Canada's Journal on Refugees, 29*(1), 43–52. doi:10.25071/1920-7336.37505

Charney, S. (2012). *Trustworthy Computing Next (Version 1.01).* Microsoft Corporation Trustworthy Computing.

Chatman, S. (2009). *Öykü ve Söylem: Filmde ve Kurmacada Anlatı Yapısı (Story and Discourse: Narrative Structure in Fiction and Film), (Çev. Özgür Yaren).* De Ki Basım Yayın.

Chaturvedi, C. (2018). *Instagram vs. Snapchat vs. Pinterest - What should be your pick* [Infographic]. A1 Future Technologies. https://www.a1future.com/blog/instagram-snapchat-pinterest-infographic/

Chaudhary, G., Khari, M., & Elhoseny, M. (2021). *Digital Twin Technology.* CRC Press. doi:10.1201/9781003132868

Chavan, V. S., & Shylaja, S. S. (2015). Machine learning approach for detection of cyber-aggressive comments by peers on social media network. In *International Conference on Advances in Computing, Communications and Informatics (ICACCI)* (pp. 2354-2358). Kochi, India: IEEE. 10.1109/ICACCI.2015.7275970

Chazal, F., & Michel, B. (2021). An introduction to topological data analysis: Fundamental and practical aspects for data scientists. *Frontiers in Artificial Intelligence, 4*, 1–28. doi:10.3389/frai.2021.667963 PMID:34661095

Chen, H. ve Zhou, L. (2017). The myth of big data: Chinese advertising practitioners' perspective. *International Journal of Advertising*, 1-17. http://www-tandfonline-com.ezp01.library.qut.edu.au/doi/full/10.1080/02650487.2017.1340865

Cheng, X. (2016) Big data assisted customer analysis and advertising architecture for real estate. *16th International Symposium on Communications and Information Technologies (ISCIT),* 312-317. 10.1109/ISCIT.2016.7751642

Chen, H., & Zhou, L. (2018). The myth of big data: Chinese advertising practitioners' perspective. *International Journal of Advertising, 37*(4), 633–649. doi:10.1080/02650487.2017.1340865

Chen, N. N., Ognyanova, K., Zhang, C., Wang, C., Ball-Rokeach, S. J., & Parks, M. (2017). Causing ripples in local power relations. *Journalism Studies, 18*(6), 710–731. doi:10.1080/1461670X.2015.1078738

Choudhury, M., Mishra, B. B., & Mohanty, P. K. (2019). An empirical study of brand evangelism for recommending cars-a qualitative & Systematic review of literature. *International Journal of Technical Research & Science, 4*(3), 1–12. doi:10.30780/IJTRS.V04.I03.001

Çinay & Sezerel. (2020). Ferzan Özpetek Filmlerinde Gösterge Olarak Yemek: Mine Vaganti/Serseri Mayınlar Üzerine Bir İnceleme. *Journal Of Tourism And Gastronomy Studies,* (8), 111-136.

Claesson, A., & Liungberg, N. (2018). *Consumer Engagement on Instagram: Viewed through the Perspectives of Social Influence and Influencer marketing* [Master thesis]. University of Lund, Lund, Sweden.

Clark, L. S. (2013). *The parent app: Understanding families in the digital age.* Oxford University Press.

Coddington, M. (2015). Clarifying journalism's quantitative turn. *Digital Journalism (Abingdon, England), 3*(3), 331–348. doi:10.1080/21670811.2014.976400

Compagnio, D., & Coppock, P. (2009). Introduction: Computer Games: Between Text and Practice. E |C Journal (Serie Speciale). Associazione di Studi Semiotica. *Anno, III*(5), 5–11.

Constine, J. (2018). *Instagram hits 1 billion monthly users, up from 800M in September.* TechCrunch.

Cook, C., Geels, K., & Bakker, P. (2016). *Hyperlocal revenues in the Europe and UK.* Nesta.

Coombs, W. T. (2004). Impact of past crises on current crisis communication: Insights from situational crisis communication theory. *Journal of Business Communication*, *41*(3), 265–289. doi:10.1177/0021943604265607

Coombs, W. T., & Holladay, S. J. (2008). Comparing apology to equivalent crisis response strategies: Clarifying apology's role and value in crisis communication. *Public Relations Review*, *34*(3), 252–257. doi:10.1016/j.pubrev.2008.04.001

Cormican, M. (2013). Kültürlerarası Etkileşimde Sinemanın Rolü: Ferzan Özpetek Ve Fatih Akın Filmlerinde Kültürlerarasılık. *International Journal of Science Culture and Sport,* (1), 340-349.

Corporate Executives. (2020). *Deezer*. https://corporate-executives.com/companies/deezer/

Coşkun, T. (2019). *Hedonik Ve Faydacı Tüketim Davranışları İle Tüketici Etnosentrizmi Arasındaki İlişki: Kuşaklara Yönelik Bir Araştırma* [Doktora tezi]. Muğla Sıtkı Koçman Üniversitesi.

Craig, D., Ketterer, S., & Yousuf, M. (2017). To post or not to post: Online discussion of gun permit mapping and the development of ethical standards in data journalism. *Journalism & Mass Communication Quarterly*, *94*(1), 168–188. doi:10.1177/1077699016684796

Croucher, S. M. (2011). Social Networking and Cultural Adaptation: A Theoretical Model. *Journal of International and Intercultural Communication*, *4*(4), 259–264. doi:10.1080/17513057.2011.598046

Cummings, J. N., Sproull, L., & Kiesler, S. B. (2002). Beyond hearing: Where real-world and online support meet. *Group Dynamics*, *6*(1), 78–88. doi:10.1037/1089-2699.6.1.78

Curry, D. (2023). *Apple Music Revenue and Usage Statistics (2023)*. Business of Apps. https://www.businessofapps.com/data/apple-music-statistics/#:~:text=Statistics%2C%20Company%20data-,Apple%20Music%20users,million%20on%20the%20previous%20year

Curry, E., Metzger, A., Berre, A. J., Monzón, A., & Boggio-Marzet, A. (2021). The elements of big data value. Springer.

Cushing, N., & Markwell, K. (2009). Platypus diplomacy: Animal gifts in international relations. *Journal of Australian Studies*, *33*(3), 255–271. doi:10.1080/14443050903079664

Darley, A. (2000). *Visual digital culture*. Routledge.

Davenport, T. H., & Dyché, J. (2013). Big data in big companie. International Institute for Analytic. SAS Institute Inc.

Davenport, T. (2018). *Big Data @Work. (Çev. M. Çavdar)*. Türk Havayolları Yayınları.

Davis, S., & Yi, J. H. (2022). Double tap, double trouble: Instagram, teachers, and profit. *E-Learning and Digital Media*, *19*(3), 320–339. doi:10.1177/20427530211064706

Dayton, B. W. (2009). Crisis management. In International Encyclopedia of Peace. Oxford University Press.

de Lima, M. M., Mainardes, E., & Cavalcanti, A. L. (2019). Influence of social media on restaurant consumers: A case study of Crab island restaurant. *Journal of Foodservice Business Research*, *22*(5), 413–432. doi:10.1080/15378020.2019.1631657

De Pelsmacker, P., Van Tilburg, S., & Holthof, C. (2018). Digital marketing strategies, online reviews and hotel performance. *International Journal of Hospitality Management*, *72*, 47–55. doi:10.1016/j.ijhm.2018.01.003

De Veirman, M., Cauberghe, V., & Hudders, L. (2017). Marketing through Instagram influencers: The impact of number of followers and product divergence on brand attitude. *International Journal of Advertising*, *36*(5), 798–828. doi:10.1080/02650487.2017.1348035

Değirmencioğlu, G. (2016). Dijitalleşme Çağında Gazeteciliğin Geleceği ve İnovasyon Haberciliği. *TRT Akademi*, *1*(2), 590–606.

Dehghani, M., & Tumer, M. (2015). A research on effectiveness of Facebook advertising on enhancing purchase intention of consumers. *Computers in Human Behavior*, *49*, 597-600. doi:10.1016/j.chb.2015.03.051

Dekker, R., Engbersen, G., Klaver, J., & Vonk, H. (2018). Smart Refugees: How Syrian Asylum Migrants Use Social Media Information in Migration Decision-Making. *Social Media + Society*, *4*(1), 2056305118764439. doi:10.1177/2056305118764439

Deldjoo, Y., Schedl, M., Cremonesi, P., & Pasi, G. (2020). Recommender systems leveraging multimedia content. *ACM Computing Surveys*, *53*(5), 1–38. doi:10.1145/3407190

de-Limas-Santos, S., M., A. K. & Bruns, A. (2020). Out-of-the-box versus in-house tools: How are they affecting data journalism in australia? *Media International Australia*, 1–15. doi:10.1177/1329878X20961569

Deng, S., Tan, C.-W., Wang, W., & Pan, Y. (2019). Smart generation system of personalized advertising copy and ıts application to advertising practice and research. *Journal of Advertising*, *48*(4), 356–365. doi:10.1080/00913367.2019.1652121

Dervişcemaloğlu, B. (2014). *Anlatıbilime Giriş, (Introduction to Narratology)*. Dergâh Yayınları.

Desouza, K. C., & Jacob, B. (2017). Big Data in the Public Sector: Lessons for Practitioners and Scholars. *Administration & Society*, *49*(7), 1043–1064. doi:10.1177/0095399714555751

Deuze, M. (2006). Participation, remediation, bricolage: Considering principal components of a digital culture. *The Information Society*, *22*(2), 63–75. doi:10.1080/01972240600567170

Deuze, M. (2007). Media work. *Polity*.

Dey, B. L., Yen, D., & Samuel, L. (2020). Digital consumer culture and digital acculturation. *International Journal of Information Management*, *51*, 102–157. doi:10.1016/j.ijinfomgt.2019.102057

Dhaoui, C., Webster, C. M., & Tan, L. P. (2017). Social media sentiment analysis: Lexicon versus machine learning. *Journal of Consumer Marketing*, *34*(6), 480–488. doi:10.1108/JCM-03-2017-2141

Dhar, V. (2013). Data science and prediction. *Communications of the ACM*, *56*(12), 64–73. doi:10.1145/2500499

Diener, E. (1984). Subjective well-being. *Psychological Bulletin*, *95*(3), 542–575. doi:10.1037/0033-2909.95.3.542 PMID:6399758

Diener, E., Emmons, R. A., Larsen, R. J., & Griffin, S. (1985). The Satisfaction With Life Scale. *Journal of Personality Assessment*, *49*(1), 71–75. doi:10.1207/s15327752jpa4901_13 PMID:16367493

Diener, E., & Ryan, K. (2009). Subjective well-being: A general overview. *South African Journal of Psychology. Suid-Afrikaanse Tydskrif vir Sielkunde*, *39*(4), 391–406. doi:10.1177/008124630903900402

Diker, E., & Gencer, Z. (2019). A Study About the Habits Of Using Instagram By Academicians. *Online Academic Journal of Information Technology.*, *18*(4), 18–24. doi:10.5824/1309-1581.2019.3.007.x

Dinçer, Ö. (1992). *Stratejik Yönetim ve İşletme Politikası*. Timaş Basım Ticaret Sanayi A.Ş.

Doksat, M. K., & Aslan, S. (2006). Tekrarlanan transkraniyal manyetik stimulasyon (rTMS) ve depresyon tedavisi. *New/Yeni Symposium Journal*, *44*(2), 92-99.

Dolata, U. (2017). *Apple, Amazon, Google, Facebook, Microsoft: Market concentration-competition-innovation strategies 1.* Stuttgarter Beitrage zur Organisations-und Innovations forschung, SOI Discussion Paper. https://www.econstor.eu/bitstream/10419/152249/1/ 880328606.pdf

Dolea, A. (2015). The Need for Critical Thinking in Country Promotion. In J. L'Etang (Ed.), *The Routledge Handbook of Critical Public Relations* (pp. 274–288). Routledge, Taylor & Francis Group.

Dömbekci, H., & Erişen, M. A. (2022). Nitel Araştırmalarda Görüşme Tekniği. *Anadolu Üniversitesi Sosyal Bilimler Dergisi*, (22), 141–160. doi:10.1177/20563051166663

Dorschel, R. (2021). Reconsidering digital labour: Bringing tech workers into the debate. *New Technology, Work and Employment*, *37*(2), 288–307. doi:10.1111/ntwe.12225

Doru, S. (2022). 21. Yüzyılda Türk Kamu Yönetiminin Dönüşümü: Dijitalleşme ve E-Devlet. Siyaset Bilimi ve Kamu Yönetimi Konularında Bilimsel Değerlendirmeler, 105-116.

Doss, S. K., & Carstens, D. S. (2014). Big five personality traits and brand evangelism. *International Journal of Marketing Studies*, *6*(3), 13–22. doi:10.5539/ijms.v6n3p13

Downham, S., & Murray, R. (2020). The hyperlocal 'renaissance' in Australia and New Zealand. In G. Agnes & D. Baines (Eds.), *The routledge companion of local media and journalism* (pp. 255–264). Routledge.

Duncan, T. (2005). *Principles of Advertising & IMC* (2nd ed.). Taylor & Francis.

Du, R. Y., Hu, Y., & Damangir, S. (2015). Leveraging trends in online searches for product features in market response modeling. *Journal of Marketing*, *79*(1), 29–43. doi:10.1509/jm.12.0459

Dutta-Bergman, M. J. (2004). Complementarity in consumption of news types across traditional and new media. *Journal of Broadcasting & Electronic Media*, *48*(1), 41–60. doi:10.1207/s15506878jobem4801_3

Du, X., & Lin, S. (2019). Social media usage, acculturation and psychological well-being: A study with Chinese in New Zealand. *International Communication of Chinese Culture*, *6*(3), 231–245. doi:10.1007/s40636-019-00160-2

Earle, A. (2022). *High Fidelity (HiFi).* Deezer. https://support.deezer.com/hc/en-gb/articles/115004588345-High-Fidelity-HiFi-

Efe, A., & Özdemir, G. (2021). Yapay Zekâ Ortamında Kamu Yönetiminin Geleceği Üzerinde Bir Değerlendirme. *Kamu Yönetimi ve Teknoloji Dergisi*, *3*(1), 34-60. Retrieved from https://dergipark.org.tr/tr/pub/kaytek/issue/64162/927834

Ekşi, M. (2016). Türk Dış Politikasında Diplomasinin Yeni İletişimsel Boyutları ve Mekanizmaları: Dijital Diplomasi. In B. Cankurtaran-Sunar (Ed.), *Uluslararası İlişkilere Disiplinlerarası Bir Yaklaşım: Uluslararası İletişim Perspektifi.* Röle Akademik Yayıncılık.

Ellison, N. B., Steinfield, C., & Lampe, C. (2007). The benefits of Facebook "friends:" Social capital and college students' use of online social network sites. *Journal of Computer-Mediated Communication*, *12*(4), 1143–1168. doi:10.1111/j.1083-6101.2007.00367.x

Erdem, B. (2018). How Can Social Media Be Helpful for Immigrants to Integrate Society in the US. *European Journal of Multidisciplinary Studies*, *3*(3), 74–79. doi:10.26417/ejms.v3i3.p74-79

Erkek, S. (2016). Kamu Kurumlarında Sosyal Medya Kullanımı: Sağlık Bakanlığı Örneği. *Selçuk Üniversitesi Sosyal Bilimler Enstitüsü Dergisi*, *35*, 141–150.

Ertekin, Y. (1993). Stres ve Yönetim. *TODAİE Yayınları*, 253.

Etuk, A., & Udonde, U. E. (2023). The Interplay of Digital Marketing Dimensions and Customer's Patronage of Fast Food Industries in Akwa Ibom State, Nigeria. *European Journal of Business and Innovation Research*, *11*(3), 70–97. doi:10.37745/ejbir.2013/vol11n37097

Ewers, N. (2017). *#Sponsored –Influencer Marketing on Instagram An Analysis of the Effects of Sponsorship Disclosure, Product Placement, Type of Influencer and their Interplay on Consumer Responses* [Master thesis]. University of Twente, Enschede, Holland.

Fairfield, J., & Shtein, H. (2014). Big data, big problems: Emerging ıssues in the ethics of data science and journalism. *Journal of Mass Media Ethics*, *29*(1), 38–51. doi:10.1080/08900523.2014.863126

Fang, C. Y., Handorf, E. A., Rao, A. D., Siu, P. T., & Tseng, M. (2021). Acculturative Stress and Depressive Symptoms Among Chinese Immigrants: The Role of Gender and Social Support. *Journal of Racial and Ethnic Health Disparities*, *8*(5), 1130–1138. doi:10.1007/s40615-020-00869-6 PMID:33000431

Farrar, S., & Papies, E. K. (2023). How Consumption and Reward Features Affect Desire for Food, Consumption Intentions, and Behaviour. *Retrieved from* Psyarxiv. *Com/Ugvnb*. doi:10.31234/osf.io/ugvnb

Fearn-Banks, K. (2001). Crisis communication: A review of some best practices. In R. Heath (Ed.), *Handbook of public relations* (pp. 479–485). SAGE Publications. doi:10.4135/9781452220727.n40

Femenia-Serra, F., & Gretzel, U. (2020). Influencer marketing for tourism destinations: Lessons from a mature destination. In *Information and Communication Technologies in Tourism 2020: Proceedings of the International Conference in Surrey, United Kingdom, January 08–10, 2020* (pp. 65-78). Springer International Publishing.

Fetscherin, M., & Conway Dato-on, M. (2012). Brand love: Investigating two alternative love relationships. In *Consumer-brand relationships: Theory and practice* (pp. 151-164). Routledge.

Fioravanti, G., Prostamo, A., & Casale, S. (2020). Taking a short break from Instagram: The effects on subjective well-Being. *Cyberpsychology, Behavior, and Social Networking*, *23*(2), 107–112. doi:10.1089/cyber.2019.0400 PMID:31851833

Fisher, E. (2010). *Media and new capitalism in the digital age*. Palgrave Macmillan. doi:10.1057/9780230106062

Fiske, J. (2017) İletişim Çalışmalarına Giriş (Introduction to Communication Studies). (Translated by Süleyman İrvan). 5. Basım. Bilim ve Sanat Yayınları, Ankara.

Fitpatrick, K. R. (2007). Advancing the New Public Diplomacy: A Public Relations Perspective. *The Hague Journal of Diplomacy*, *2*(3), 187–211. doi:10.1163/187119007X240497

Fitzpatrick, K. R., Fullerton, J., & Kendrick, A. (2013). Public Relations and Public Diplomacy: Conceptual and Practical Connections. *The Public Relations Journal*, *7*(4), 1–21.

Floros, G., & Siomos, K. (2013). The relationship between optimal parenting, Internet addiction and motives for social networking in adolescence. *Psychiatry Research*, *209*(3), 529–534. doi:10.1016/j.psychres.2013.01.010 PMID:23415042

Fombrun, C. J., & van Riel, C. (2004). *Fame & Fortune: How Successful Companies Build Winning Reputations*. Prentice Hall/Financial Times.

Forbes. (2023). *Martin Lorentzon*. https://www.forbes.com/profile/martin-lorentzon/

Foroughi, B., Griffiths, M., Iranmanesh, M., & Salamzadeh, Y. (2021). Associations Between Instagram Addiction, Academic Performance, Social Anxiety, Depression, and Life Satisfaction Among University Students. *International Journal of Mental Health and Addiction*, *20*, 1–22.

Forristal, L. (2022). *YouTube Music and Premium top 80 million paid subscribers*. Tech Crunch. https://techcrunch.com/2022/11/09/youtube-music-and-premium-top-80-million-paid-subscribers/?guccounter=1&guce_referrer=aHR0cHM6Ly93d3cuZ29vZ2xlLmNvbS8&guce_referrer_sig=AQAAAMAcNflnvqgfUUFdV-l2EQvA05k0QkQPi8b9Uo-R6eo1sKUzTdi-1NBSz1m1111CnbwvSo9O_HA-gCRNVDFPuxkg8631tNhyRTwsIfl8RDxOFtYnqe8GkbKTJ0mlca-NpUMMyXMbwpBimh9KMjmOFBXhRsxglnSiBuOLXRM_UfOr_c

Fortune. (2021). *A Quick Guide to Apple Music, Spotify, and More Top Music Streaming Services*. https://fortune.com/2017/09/11/spotify-apple-music-tidal-streaming/

Franklin, B. (2006). *Local journalism and local media:Making the local news*. Routledge. doi:10.4324/9780203969205

Franks, B. (2012). *Taming the Big Data Tidal Wave: Finding Opportunities in Huge Data Streams with Advanced Analytics*. John Wiley & Sons, Inc. doi:10.1002/9781119204275

Frasca, G. (2003b). Ludologists love stories, too: notes from a debate that never took place. *Digital Game Research Conference 2003 Proceedings*.

Frasca, G. (2003a). Simulation versus Narrative: Introduction to Ludology. In M. J. P. Wolf & B. Perron (Eds.), *Video/Game/Theory*. Routledge.

Freberg, K., Graham, K., McGaughey, K. A., & Freberg, L. (2011). Who are the Social Media Influencers? A Study of Public Perceptions of Personality. *Public Relations Review*, *37*(1), 90–92. doi:10.1016/j.pubrev.2010.11.001

Friedman Thomas, L. (2000). *Lexus ve Zeytin Ağacı Küreselleşmenin Geleceği*. Boyner Holding Ya.

Friedman, H. H., & Friedman, L. (1979). Endorser Effectiveness by Product Type. *Journal of Advertising Research*, *19*(5), 63–71.

Fuchs, C. (2010). Labor in informational capitalism and on the internet. *The Information Society*, *26*(3), 179–196. doi:10.1080/01972241003712215

Fuchs, C. (2014a). *Digital labour and Karl Marx*. Routledge. doi:10.4324/9781315880075

Fuchs, C. (2014b). Karl Marx and the study of media and culture today. *Culture Unbound*, *6*(1), 39–76. doi:10.3384/cu.2000.1525.14639

Fuchs, C. (2019). *Dijital Emek ve Karl Marx. Kalaycı, T. E. ve Oğuz, S. (Trans.)*. NotaBene Yayınları.

Fuchs, C. (2020). *Communication and capitalism: A critical theory*. University of Westminster Press.

Fuchs, C., & Sandoval, M. (2014c). Digital workers of the world unite! A framework for critically theorising and analysing digital labour. *TripleC*, *12*(2), 486–563. doi:10.31269/triplec.v12i2.549

Fuchs, C., & Sevignani, S. (2013). What is digital labour? What is digital work? What's Their difference? And why do these questions matter for understanding social media? *TripleC*, *11*(2), 237–293. doi:10.31269/triplec.v11i2.461

Fuller, Z. (2018). *Spotify, Apple Music and Ad-Supported Streaming*. Midia Research. https://midiaresearch.com/blog/spotify-apple-music-and-ad-supported-streaming

Fumagalli, A., Lucarelli, S., Musolino, E., & Rocchi, G. (2018). Digital labour in the platform economy: The case of Facebook. *Sustainability*, *10*(1757), 1-16.

Gaille, B. (2015). *18 Key Apple Target Market Demographics*. http://brandongaille.com/18- apple-target-market-demographics/

Gamage, T., & Ashill, N. (2023). Sponsored-influencer marketing: Effects of the commercial orientation of influencer-created content on followers' willingness to search for information. *Journal of Product and Brand Management, 32*(2), 316–329. doi:10.1108/JPBM-10-2021-3681

Gandomi, A., & Haider, M. (2015). Beyond the hype: Big data concepts, methods, and analytics. *International Journal of Information Management, 35*(2), 137–144. doi:10.1016/j.ijinfomgt.2014.10.007

García, R. A. (2021). The elements of big data value. Springer. doi:10.1007/978-3-030-68176-0

Gates, B. (1999). Dijital Sinir Sistemiyle Düşünce Hızında Çalışmak. Doğan Kitap.

Gaultier-Gaillard, S., & Louisot, J.-P. (2006). Risks to reputation: A global approach. *The Geneva Papers on Risk and Insurance. Issues and Practice, 31*(3), 425–445. doi:10.1057/palgrave.gpp.2510090

Gavilan, D., Avello, M., & Martinez-Navarro, G. (2018). The influence of online ratings and reviews on hotel booking consideration. *Tourism Management, 66*, 53–61. doi:10.1016/j.tourman.2017.10.018

Geray, H. (2014). *İletişim Alanından Örneklerle Toplumsal Araştırmalarda Nicel ve Nitel Yöntemlere Giriş (Introduction to Quantitative and Qualitative Methods in Social Research with Examples from the Field of Communication)*. Umuttepe Yayınları, Kocaeli.

Gerber, R. (2019). *The Freemium Model Is Coming To Music*. Forbes. https://www.forbes.com/sites/greatspeculations/2019/08/14/the-freemium-model-is-coming-to-music/

Gere, C. (2002). *Digital culture*. Reaktion Books.

Ge, T., & Wu, X. (2021). Accurate delivery of online advertising and the evaluation of advertising effect based on big data technology. *Mobile Information Systems, 10*, 1–10. Advance online publication. doi:10.1155/2021/1598666

Gezici, H. S. (2023). Kamu Yönetiminde Yapay Zekâ: Avrupa Birliği. *Uluslararası Akademik Birikim Dergisi., 6*(2), 111–128.

Gilbert, E., Bakhshi, S., Chang, S., & Terveen, L. (2013). need to try this"? a statistical overview of pinterest. In SIGCHI Conference on Human Factors in Computing Systems (pp. 2427-2436). Paris France: ACM.

Gilboa, E. (2016). Public Diplomacy. In G. Mazzoleni, K. G. Barnhurst, K. Ikeda, R. Maia, & H. Wessler (Eds.), *The International Encyclopedia of Political Communication* (pp. 1–9). American Cancer Society., doi:10.1002/9781118541555.wbiepc232

Gilboa, S., Seger-Guttmann, T., & Mimran, O. (2019). The unique role of relationship marketing in small businesses' customer experience. *Journal of Retailing and Consumer Services, 51*, 152–164. doi:10.1016/j.jretconser.2019.06.004

Gillespie, T. (2018). *Custodians of the Internet: Platforms, content moderation, and the hidden decisions that shape social media*. Yale University Press.

Gitnux. (2023). *The Most Surprising Deezer Statistics And Trends in 2023*. https://blog.gitnux.com/deezer-statistics/#:~:text=With%20over%2016%20million%20monthly,library%20of%2073%20million%20tracks

Glazer, H. (2012). Likes' are lovely, but do they lead to more logins? *College & Research Libraries News, 73*(1), 18–22. doi:10.5860/crln.73.1.8688

Glucksman, M. (2017). The rise of social media Influencer marketing on lifestyle branding: A case study of Lucie Fink. *Elon Journal of Undergraduate Research in Communications, 8*(2), 77–78.

Gmachi, S. (2017). Der Einfluss von Influencer-Marketing auf die Generation Y. *Psychology & Marketing*, 32-55.

Göçoğlu, V. (2020). Kamu Hizmetlerinin Sunumunda Dijital Dönüşüm: Nesnelerin İnterneti Üzerine Bir İnceleme. *Manas Sosyal Araştırmalar Dergisi*, *9*(1), 615–628. doi:10.33206/mjss.538784

Göktürk, D. (2004). Yüksel Yavuz's Kleine Freiheit / A Little Bit of Freedom. *TRANSIT, 1*(1)

Goldfayn, A. L. (2011). *Evangelist marketing: What Apple, Amazon, and Netflix understand about their customers (That your company probably doesn't)*. Benbella Books.

Gönülşen, G. (2020). Olumlu Marka İmajı Yaratmada Influencer Pazarlama Stratejisinin Marka Algısı Üzerindeki Etkisi: Foreo Türkiye Markasının Uygulamalarına Yönelik Bir Araştırma. *Akdeniz Üniversitesi Sosyal Bilimler Enstitüsü Dergisi*, (8), 9–34.

Google Inc. (2021). *Google Trends Help*. https://support.google.com/trends/?hl=ko#topic=6248052

Google. (2022). *Google Gizlilik Politikası*. https://policies.google.com/privacy?hl=tr

Google. (2023). *Google Ads İle İşinizi Büyütün*. https://ads.google.com/intl/tr_tr/home/

Gould, S. J. (1979). Mickey Mouse meets Konrad Lorenz. *Natural History*, *88*(5), 30–36.

Göztaş. (1997). *Aylin* Kriz Yönetimi ve Halkla İlişkiler. Ege Yayıncılık.

Grant, R. (2012). *How to React to Halved Reach on Facebook*. http://wearesocial.net/blog/2012/10/reacthalved-reach-facebook/

Green & Martinez. (2018). In a World of Social Media: A Case Study Analysis of Instagram. *American Research Journal of Business and Management, 4*(1), 1-8.

Green, D. J. (2019). *Instagram Marketing: The Guide Book for Using Photos on Instagram to Gain Millions of Followers Quickly and to Skyrocket Your Business*. Influencer and Social Media Marketing.

Grether, M. (2016). Using big data for online advertising without wastage: wishful dream, nightmare or reality? *Online Advertising, 8*(2). doi:10.1515/gfkmir-2016-0014

Grossberg, K. A. (2016). The new marketing solutions that will drive strategy implementation. *Strategy and Leadership*, *44*(3), 20–26. doi:10.1108/SL-04-2016-0018

Gross, J., & Wangenheim, F. V. (2018). The big four of Influencer marketing: A typology of Influencers. *Marketing Review St. Gallen*, (2), 30–38.

Gry, K., & Kjeldgaard, D. (2014). Online reception analysis: Big data in qualitative marketing research. In Consumer culture theory: Research in consumer behavior (Vol. 16, pp. 217–42). Academic Press.

Gülaslan, T. (2018). *Kamu Yönetiminde Sosyal Medya Kullanımı ve Yönetimi: Temel İlkeler ve Öneriler* [Doctoral Thesis]. Hacettepe University Social Science Instıtution, Ankara.

Güler, A., & Günel, Y. (2022). Kamu Kurumlarında Bilgi Teknolojileri ve Sosyal Medya Kullanımının Çalışan Performansına Etkisi. *International Journal of Economic and Administrative Academic Research*, *2*(2), 23–48.

Güler, E. (2006). İşletmelerin e-insan Kaynakları Yönetimi ve e-işe Alım Süreçlerindeki Gelişmeler. *Ege Akademik Bakış Dergisi*, *6*(1), 17–23.

Gül, H. (2017). Dijitalleşmenin Kamu Yönetimi ve Politikaları ile Bu Alanlardaki Araştırmalara Etkileri. *Yasama Dergisi*, (36), 5–26.

Gutierrez, B. V., Kaloostian, D., & Redvers, N. (2023). Elements of Successful Food Sovereignty Interventions within Indigenous Communities in the United States and Canada: A Systematic Review. *Current Developments in Nutrition, 7*(9), 101973. doi:10.1016/j.cdnut.2023.101973 PMID:37635710

Habernal, I., Ptáček, T., & Steinberger, J. (2013). Sentiment analysis in czech social media using supervised machine learning. In *4th workshop on computational approaches to subjectivity, sentiment and social media analysis* (pp. 65-74). Association for Computational Linguistics.

Haddon, L., & Livingstone, S. (2014). *The meaning of online problematic situations for children: The UK report*. London: EU Kids Online, LSE.

Ha, J., & Jang, S. (2013). Attributes, consequences, and consumer values: A means-end chain approach across restaurant segments. *International Journal of Contemporary Hospitality Management, 25*(3), 383–409. doi:10.1108/09596111311311035

Halvorsen, L. S., & Bjerke, P. (2019). All seats taken? Hyperlocal online media in strong print newspaper surroundings. *Nordicom Review, 40*(2), 115–128. doi:10.2478/nor-2019-0030 PMID:33907698

Hambrick, D. C., & Mason, P. A. (1986). Upper echelens: The organizations as a reflection of its Top Management. *Academy of Management Review, 9*(2), 193–206. doi:10.2307/258434

Hameed, S., Sadiq, A., & Din, A. U. (2018). The Increased Vulnerability of Refugee Population to Mental Health Disorders. *Kansas Journal of Medicine, 11*(1), 1–12. PMID:29844851

Handayani, F. (2015). Instagram as a teaching tool? Really? *Proceedings of ISELT FBS Universitas Negeri Padang, 4*(1), 320–327.

Hanoglu, I. S. (2021). *Digital Marketing Channels for Organic Growth: Off-Site SEO List View show*. Academic Press.

Haq, Z. (2009). E-mail advertising: A study of consumer attitude toward e-mail advertising among Indian users. *Journal of Retail & Leisure Property, 8*(3), 207–223. doi:10.1057/rlp.2009.10

Harde A (2018) *A Qualitative Study on How Refugees Use Technology after Arriving in Germany.* Reportno.

Harrell, E. (2019). Neuromarketing: What you need to know. *Harvard Business Review, 97*(4), 64–70.

Harris, R., & Taylor, H. (2005). Landmarks in Linguistic Thought I: The Western Tradition from Socrates to Saussure (2nd ed.). Routledge.

Harris, J. M., Ciorciari, J., & Gountas, J. (2018). Consumer neuroscience for marketing researchers. *Journal of Consumer Behaviour, 17*(3), 239–252. doi:10.1002/cb.1710

Hart, J. A. (2010). *Toward a political economy of digital culture: From organized mass consumption to attention rivalry.* https://www.academia.edu/22951072/Toward_a_Political_Economy_of_Digital_Culture_From_Organized_Mass_Consumption_to_Attention_Rivalry

Harte, D., Turner, J., & Williams, A. (2016). Discourses of enterprise in hyperlocal community news in the UK. *Journalism Practice, 10*(2), 233–250. doi:10.1080/17512786.2015.1123109

Harte, D., Williams, A., & Turner, J. (2017). Reciprocity and the hyperlocal journalist. *Journalism Practice, 11*(2-3), 160–176. doi:10.1080/17512786.2016.1219963

Hartig, F. (2013). Panda Diplomacy: The Cutest Part of China's Public Diplomacy. *The Hague Journal of Diplomacy*, 49-78. doi:10.1163/1871191X-12341245

Hartmann, N. N., & Lussier, B. (2020). Managing the sales force through the unexpected exogenous COVID-19 crisis. *Industrial Marketing Management*, *88*, 101–111. doi:10.1016/j.indmarman.2020.05.005

Harvard. (2022). *History Artificial Intelligence*. https://sitn.hms.harvard.edu/flash/2017/history-artificial-intelligence/

Hasfi, Mau, & Farid. (2022). Instagram Accounts for Parenting Education: A New Culture. *Proceedings of the 3rd International Conference on Linguistics and Cultural (ICLC)*, 198-207.

Hashem, I., Chang, V., Anuar, N., Adewole, K., Yaqoob, I., Gani, A., Ahmed, E., & Chiroma, H. (2016). The role of big data in smart city. *International Journal of Information Management*, *36*(5), 748–758. doi:10.1016/j.ijinfomgt.2016.05.002

Hashimova, K. K. (2016). The role of big data in ınternet advertising problem solution. *International Journal of Education and Management Engineering*, *6*(4), 10–19. doi:10.5815/ijeme.2016.04.02

Hashish, Y., Bunt, A., & Young, J. E. (2014). Involving children in content control: A collaborative and research. *Communication Yearbook*, *29*, 35–47.

Haşit, G. (2000). İşletmelerde Kriz Yönetimi ve Türkiyenin Büyük Sanayi İşletmeleri Üzerinde Yapılan Araştırma Çalışması. Eskişehir: Anadolu Üniversitesi Açık Öğretim Fakültesi Yayınları.

Hassan, U., & Curry, E. (2021). Stakeholder analysis of data ecosystems. In The elements of big data value. Springer. doi:10.1007/978-3-030-68176-0_2

Hearit, K. M. (2006). *Crisis management by apology: Corporate response to allegations of wrongdoing*. Routledge. doi:10.4324/9781410615596

Hemley, D. (2013). *Instagram for business tips*. https://www.so-cialmediaex-am-iner.com/instagram-for-business-tips/

Hendriks, M. (2015). The happiness of international migrants: A review of research findings. *Migration Studies*, *3*(3), 343–369. doi:10.1093/migration/mnu053

Herman, J. (2019). *The 8 Advantages of Using Instagram for Business*. https://nealschaffer.com/advantages-using-instagrambusiness

Hess, K., & Waller, L. (2016). Community anf hyperlocal journalism. A "sustainable model". In B. Franklin & S. A. Eldridge II, (Eds.), *The routledge companion to digital journalism studies* (pp. 194–204). Routledge. doi:10.4324/9781315713793-20

Hess, K., & Waller, L. (2017). *Local journalism in a digital world*. Palgrave. doi:10.1057/978-1-137-50478-4

Hıdıroğlu & Yıldırım. (2018). Fatih Akın Filmlerinde Geleneksel Simgelerin Temsili. *Atatürk Üniversitesi Sosyal Bilimler Enstitüsü Dergisi*, (3), 1369-1385.

Highfield, T., & Leaver, T. (2015). A methodology for mapping Instagram hashtags. *First Monday*, *20*(1), 1–11.

Hoffman, D. L., & Fodor, M. (2010). Can you measure the ROI of your social media marketing? *MIT Sloan Management Review*, *52*(1).

Hoşçan, Ç. (2015). *Arzu ve İktidar: Ferzan Özpetek Sineması Üzerinden Eleştirel bir Bakış*. Doğu Kitabevi.

Huang, Z. A., & Wang, R. (2019). The New "Cat" of the Internet: China's Panda Diplomacy on Twitter. *Advances in Public Relations and Communication Management*, 69-85. doi:10.1108/S2398-391420190000004006

Huang, M.-H., & Rust, R. T. (2021). A strategic framework for artificial intelligence in marketing. *Journal of the Academy of Marketing Science*, *49*(1), 30–50. doi:10.1007/s11747-020-00749-9

Huang, Z., & Wang, R. (2020). Panda Engagement in China's Digital Public Diplomacy. *Asian Journal of Communication, 30*(2), 1–23. doi:10.1080/01292986.2020.1725075

Hung, J. C., & Wang, C.-C. (2021). Exploring the website object layout of responsive web design: Results of eye tracking evaluations. *The Journal of Supercomputing, 77*(1), 343–365. doi:10.1007/s11227-020-03283-1

Hunt, K. (2016). CookieConsumer: Tracking Online Behavioural Advertising in Australia. *Computer Law & Security Report, 32*(1), 55–90. doi:10.1016/j.clsr.2015.12.006

Hür, Ş. & Kumbasar, S. (2011). Göz hareketlerine dayalı araştırma çözümleri eye-tracking teknolojisi. *Araştırmada Yenilikler Konferansı.*

Hürriyet. (2011). *2011 Yılı Türkiye Genel Seçim Sonuçları.* Abgerufen am 20. August 2023 von Hürriyet: https://www.hurriyet.com.tr/secim2011/default.html

Ilya, L., & Mamlok, D. (2021). Culture and society in the digital age. *Information (Basel), 12*(2), 1–13.

Ingenhoff, D., White, C., Buhmann, A., & Kiousis, S. (2019). *Bridging Disciplinary Perspectives of Country Image, Reputation, Brand, and Identity.* Routledge, Taylor & Franscis Group.

Işıkoğlu, D. (2005). Kültürlerin Kesişimi, Aksanlı Sinema ve Almanya'daki 2. ve 3. Kuşak Türk Yönetmenlerin Sinemasal Üretimi (Yayımlanmamış Yüksek Lisans Tezi). İstanbul Üniversitesi, Radyo, İstanbul, Türkiye.

Ivanov, A. E. (2012). The Internet's impact on integrated marketing communication. *Procedia Economics and Finance, 3*, 536–542. doi:10.1016/S2212-5671(12)00192-X

Jahn, M. (2005). Narratology: A guide to the theory of narrative. English Department, University of Cologne.

Janssens, A., Goossens, L., van den Noortgate, W., Colpin, H., Verschueren, K., & van Leeuwen, K. (2015). Parents' and adolescents' perspectives on parenting: Evaluating conceptual structure, measurement in variance and criterion validity. *Assessment, 22*(4), 473–489. doi:10.1177/1073191114550477 PMID:25225229

Jariangprasert, N., Jaturapataraporn, J., Sivaraks, P., & Luangphaiboonsri, S. (2019). The influence of food information on Facebook fan pages and Instagram affecting generation y in Thailand on restaurant selection. *Veridian E-Journal, Silpakorn University (Humanities, Social Sciences and Arts), 12*(2), 620–637.

Jauhiainen, J. S., Özçürümez, S., & Tursun, Ö. (2022). Internet and social media uses, digital divides, and digitally mediated transnationalism in forced migration: Syrians in Turkey. *Global Networks, 22*(2), 197–210. doi:10.1111/glob.12339

Jayasekara, Maniyangama, Vithana, Weerasinghe, Wijekoon, & Panchendrarajan. (2022). AI-Based Child Care Parental Control System. *4th International Conference on Advancements in Computing (ICAC),* 120-125.

Jenkins-Guarnieri, M. A., Wright, S. L., & Johnson, B. (2013). Development and validation of a social media use integration scale. *Psychology of Popular Media Culture, 2*(1), 38–50. doi:10.1037/a0030277

Jenkins, H. (2006). *Convergence culture: Where old and new media collide.* NYU Press.

Jenkins, H., Ford, S., & Green, J. (2013). *Spreadable media: Creating value and meaning in a networked culture.* NYU Press.

Jibeen, T., & Khalid, R. (2010). Development and Preliminary Validation of Multidimensional Acculturative Stress Scale for Pakistani Immigrants in Toronto, Canada. *International Journal of Intercultural Relations, 34*(3), 233–243. doi:10.1016/j.ijintrel.2009.09.006

Jin, Y., Ma, M., & Zhu, Y. (2022). A comparison of natural user interface and graphical user interface for narrative in HMD-based augmented reality. *Multimedia Tools and Applications, 81*(4), 5795–5826. doi:10.1007/s11042-021-11723-0 PMID:34980945

Jobs, C. G., Gilfoil, D. M., & Aukers, S. M. (2016). How marketing organizations can benefit from big data advertising analytics. *Academy of Marketing Studies Journal, 20*(1), 18.

Johnson, J., & Henderson, A. (2024). *Conceptual models: Core to the Design of Interactive Applications*. Springer.

Jun, J. S., Galambos, C., & Lee, K. H. (2021). Information and Communication Technology Use, Social Support, and Life Satisfaction among Korean Immigrant Elders. *Journal of Social Service Research, 47*(4), 537–552. doi:10.1080/01488376.2020.1848969

Ju, R., Hamilton, L., & McLarnon, M. (2021). *The Medium Is the Message: WeChat*. YouTube, and Facebook Usage and Acculturation Outcomes.

Kabilan, S. (2023). A Study on Impact of Social Media On Consumer Purchasing Behaviour In Chennai City With Special Reference To Instagram Influencers. *Indian Journal of Psychology, 02*, 59–64.

Kacmaz, E. G., & Yilmaz, T. (2014). Fatih Akin Filmlerinde Gercekligin Temsili Representing Reality in Fatih Akin Films. Betonart: Concrete. *Architectural Design*, (41), 54–59.

Kampf, Z. (2009). Public (non-) apologies: The discourse of minimizing responsibility. *Journal of Pragmatics, 41*(11), 2257–2270. doi:10.1016/j.pragma.2008.11.007

Kaplan, A., & Mazurek, G. (2018). Social media. In Handbook of media management and economics (pp. 273-286). Taylor and Francis. doi:10.4324/9781315189918-17

Kaplan, A. M., & Haenlein, M. (2010). Users of the world, unite! The challenges and opportunities of Social Media. *Business Horizons, 53*(1), 59–68. doi:10.1016/j.bushor.2009.09.003

Kapoor, K. K., Tamilmani, K., Rana, N. P., Patil, P., Dwivedi, Y. K., & Nerur, S. (2018). Advances in Social Media Research: Past, Present and Future. *Information Systems Frontiers, 20*(3), 531–558. doi:10.1007/s10796-017-9810-y

Karadeniz, O. Ö. (2017). Oyun İncelemelerinde Ludoloji - Narratoloji Tartışması ve Alternatif Kuramsal Arayışlar (Ludology - Narratology Debate and Alternative Theoretical Searches in Game Studies). *Galatasaray Üniversitesi İletişim Dergisi, 27*(27), 57–78. doi:10.16878/gsuilet.373236

Karaganis, J. (2007). The ecology of control: Filters, digital right management and trusted computing. In J. Karaganis (Ed.), *Structures of participation in digital culture* (pp. 256–280). Colombia University Press.

Karagiannis, D., Mayr, H. C., & Mylopoulos, J. (2016). *Domain-Specific conceptual modeling: Concepts, Methods and Tools*. Springer. doi:10.1007/978-3-319-39417-6

Karakaya, H. (2018). Türk Sinemasında Din Adamı Tiplemesi. *Munzur üniversitesi Sosyal Bilimler Dergisi*, (12), 48-70.

Karaköse, T. (2007). Örgütler ve kriz yönetimi. *Akademik bakış, 13*, 1-15.

Karataş, M., & Eti, H. (2022). Dijital Pazarlama Çağında Instagram Fenomenlerinin Tüketici Satın Alma Davranışlarına Etkisi. *Academic Journal of Information Technology, 13*(50), 184–219. doi:10.5824/ajite.2022.03.005.x

Katz, E., Blumler, J. G., & Gurevitch, M. (1974). Utilization of mass communication by the individual. In J. G. Blumler & E. Katz (Eds.), *The uses of mass communications: Current perspectives on gratifications research* (pp. 19–32). Sage.

Kawasaki, G. (2015). The art of evangelism. *Harvard Business Review*, 108–111.

Kaya, İ., Ateş, S., Akbulut, D., & Köksal, A. (2017). Accounting Education in the Light of Big Data, Data Analytics and Data Analysis: A Research on Course Contents. *36th Accounting Education Symposium Book, Matsis printing press*, İstanbul.

Kazancı, P. (2022). *Influencer Marketing Uygulamalarının Üniversite Öğrencilerinin Satın Alma Niyeti Üzerine Etkisi* [Doktora tezi]. Selçuk Üniversitesi.

Kehya, R. Ö. (2023). Alman-Türk Sinemasında Bir Entegrasyon Yönetmeni: Buket Alakuş. *Diyalog*, 34-50.

Keohane, R. O., & Nye, J. S. (2012). *Power and Interdependence*. Longman.

Khan, M. N. A., & Mahmood, A. (2018). A distinctive approach to obtain higher page rank through search engine optimization. *Sadhana*, *43*(3), 43. doi:10.1007/s12046-018-0812-3

Kietzmann, J. H., Hermkens, K., McCarthy, I. P., & Silvestre, B. S. (2011). Social media? Get serious! Understanding the functional building blocks of social media. *Business Horizons*, *54*(3), 241–251. doi:10.1016/j.bushor.2011.01.005

Kim, Y. (2016). Understanding publics' perception and behaviors in crisis communication: Effects of crisis news framing and publics' acquisition, selection, and transmission of information in crisis situations. *Journal of Public Relations Research*, *28*(1), 35–50. doi:10.1080/1062726X.2015.1131697

Kim, Y., Chae, Y., & Kim, Y. (2022). Doing community: Digital hyperlocal media as care. *Digital Journalism (Abingdon, England)*, 1–15. Advance online publication. doi:10.1080/21670811.2022.2145330

King, G., & Krzywinska, T. (2002). *ScreenPlay: Cinema / Videogames / Interfaces*. Wallflower Press.

Kıyar, N. & Karkın, N. (2013). Mimesis'in Yapıbozumsal Dönüşümleri (Deconstructive Transformations of Mimesis). *İnönü Üniversitesi Sanat ve Tasarım Dergisi, 3*(7).

Kleinman, B. Z. (2019). *A brief history of Apple's iTunes*. BBC News. https://www.bbc.com/news/technology-48511006

Klinenberg, E., & Benzecry, C. (2005). Cultural production in a digital age. *The Annals of the American Academy of Political and Social Science*, *597*(1), 6–18. doi:10.1177/0002716204270420

Kocabiyik. (2019). Değişen Diplomasi Anlayışı, Kamu Diplomasisi ve Türkiye. Avrasya Etüdleri.

Koçak & Tüplek. (2018). Yönetmen Ferzan Özpetek'in İstanbul Kırmızısı Filminin Türkiye Tanıtımı Çerçevesinde İncelenmesi: Göstergebilimsel Bir İnceleme. *BUJSS,* (11), 546-86.

Kokonis, M. (2014). Intermediality between games and fiction: The "ludology vs. narratology" debate in computer game studies: A response to Gonzalo Frasca. Acta Universitatis Sapientiae. *Film and Media Studies*, (09), 171–188.

Kömür, G. (2020). Yumuşak Güç Unsuru Olarak Kamu Diplomasisi. *International Journal of Politics and Security, 2*(3), 89-115.

KONDA. (2011). Abgerufen am 16. August 2023 von https://konda.com.tr/uploads/2011-04-konda-siyasette-kadin-temsili-raporu-2ad240366fc77a679627647b8504cb4c44bfb56d04a461fd1e0c6593b2777af9.pdf

Konzack, L. (2002, June). Computer game criticism: A method for computer game analysis. *CGDC Conference.*

Kotler, P., Kartajaya, H., Setiawan, I. (2021), *Pazarlama 4.0 Gelenekselden Dijitale Geçiş* (Çev. Özata, N.). Optimist Yayıncılık.

Kotler, P., Kartajaya, H., Setiawan, I. (2022), *Pazarlama 5.0 Gelenekselden Dijitale Geçiş* (Çev. Taner, G.). Nişantaşı Üniversitesi Yayınları.

Kula, H., & Süer, C. (2006). Kısa süreli egzersizin antrene sporcularda deri iletkenliğine etkisi. *Saglik Bilimleri Dergisi*, *15*(2), 107–115.

Kültür, N. (2017). Aksanlı Sinema ve Fatih Akın. *Maltepe Üniversitesi İletişim Fakültesi Dergisi*, (2), 3-17.

Kumar, S. (2020). Data mining based marketing decision support system using hybrid machine learning algorithm. *Journal of Artificial Intelligence and Capsule Networks*, *2*(3), 185–193. doi:10.36548//jaicn.2020.3.006

Kumar, V., & Mittal, S. (2020). Mobile marketing campaigns: Practices, challenges and opportunities. *International Journal of Business Innovation and Research*, *21*(4), 523–539. doi:10.1504/IJBIR.2020.105996

Kurdi, B., Alshurideh, M., Akour, I., Alzoubi, H., Obeidat, B., & Alhamad, A. (2022). The role of digital marketing channels on consumer buying decisions through eWOM in the Jordanian markets. *International Journal of Data and Network Science*, *6*(4), 1175–1186. doi:10.5267/j.ijdns.2022.7.002

Kurpius, D., Metzgar, E., & Rowley, K. (2010). Sustaining hyperlocal media. *Journalism Studies*, *11*(3), 359–376. doi:10.1080/14616700903429787

Lacy, S. R., Daniel, R., Esther, T., & Margaret, D. (2009). Examining the features, policies, and resources of citizen journalism: Citizen news sites and blogs. *Web Journal of Mass Communication Research*, *15*(1), 1–20.

Laksana, I., Wahyuni, E., & Aditya, C. (2023). Game Design for Mobile App-Based IoT Introduction Education in STEM Learning. *Jurnal RESTI*, *7*, 688–696.

Laney, D. (2001). *3D data management: Controlling data volume, velocity and variety*. META Group Research Note, 6.

Latinovic, T. (2016). *Big Data As The Basis For The İnnovative Development Strategyof The Industry 4.0*. https://www.researchgate.net/publication/331187513_Big_Data_as_the_basis_for_the_innovative_development_strategy_of_the_Industry_40

Latzer, M., Hollnbuchner, K., Just, N., & Saurwein, F. (2016). *The economics of algorithmic selection on the Internet*. Springer. doi:10.4337/9780857939852.00028

Lawler, S. (2002). Narrative in Social Research. In Qualitative Research in Action. Sage.

Lazare, A. (2005). *On apology*. Oxford University Press.

Lazzarato, M. (1996). Immaterial labour. In P. Virno & M. Hardy (Eds.), *Radical Thought in Italy: A Potential Politics* (Vol. 7, pp. 132–146). University of Minnesota Press.

Ledbetter, A. M., & Meisner, C. (2021). Extending the personal branding affordances typology to parasocial interaction with public figures on social media: Social presence and media multiplexity as mediators. *Computers in Human Behavior*, *106610*(115), 106610. doi:10.1016/j.chb.2020.106610

Leonard, D. (2015). *Why Jay Z's Tidal Streaming-Music Service Has Been a Disaster*. Bloomberg. https://www.bloomberg.com/news/features/2015-05-28/why-jay-z-s-tidal-streaming-music-service-has-been-a-disaster

Lepkowska-White, E., Parsons, A., & Berg, W. (2019). Social media marketing management: An application to small restaurants in the US. *International Journal of Culture, Tourism and Hospitality Research*, *13*(3), 321–345. doi:10.1108/IJCTHR-06-2019-0103

Leung, F. F., Gu, F. F., & Palmatier, R. W. (2022). Online influencer marketing. *Journal of the Academy of Marketing Science*, *50*(26), 226–251. doi:10.1007/s11747-021-00829-4

Lewis, S. C., Holton, A. E., & Coddington, M. (2014). Reciprocal Jjournalism. *Journalism Practice*, *8*(2), 229–241. doi:10.1080/17512786.2013.859840

Li, S., Luo, Q., & Qiu, L. (2016). The Optimal Pricing Model of Digital Music: Subscription, Ownership or Mixed? SSRN *Electronic Journal, 1*(1), 1–60. doi:10.2139/ssrn.2884252

Li, C., & Suh, A. (2015). Factors influencing information credibility on social media platforms: Evidence from Facebook pages. *Proceedings of the Association for Information Science and Technology*, *52*(1), 1–4. doi:10.1002/pra2.2015.145052010030

Lievrouw, L. A., & Livingstone, S. (Eds.). (2006). *Handbook of new media: Social shaping and social consequences*. Sage.

Li, F., Lu, H., Hou, M., Cui, K., & Darbandi, M. (2021). Customer satisfaction with bank services: The role of cloud services, security, e-learning and service quality. *Technology in Society*, *64*, 101487. doi:10.1016/j.techsoc.2020.101487

Li, H., Meng, F., Jeong, M., & Zhang, Z. (2020). To follow others or be yourself? Social influence in online restaurant reviews. *International Journal of Contemporary Hospitality Management*, *32*(3), 1067–1087. doi:10.1108/IJCHM-03-2019-0263

Li, J., Kim, W. G., & Choi, H. M. (2021). Effectiveness of social media marketing on enhancing performance: Evidence from a casual-dining restaurant setting. *Tourism Economics*, *27*(1), 3–22. doi:10.1177/1354816619867807

Lim, W. M. (2018). Demystifying neuromarketing. *Journal of Business Research*, *91*, 205–220. doi:10.1016/j.jbusres.2018.05.036

Li, S., Sung, B., Linc, Y., & Mitas, O. (2022). Electrodermal Activity Measure: A Methodological Review. *Annals of Tourism Research*, *96*, 103460. Advance online publication. doi:10.1016/j.annals.2022.103460

Liu, B. F., & Kim, S. (2011). How organizations framed the 2009 H1N1 pandemic via social and traditional media: Implications for US health communicators. *Public Relations Review*, *37*(3), 233–244. doi:10.1016/j.pubrev.2011.03.005

Liu, P., & Yi, S. (2017). Pricing policies of green supply chain considering targeted advertising and product green degree in the big data environment. *Journal of Cleaner Production*, *164*, 1614–1622. doi:10.1016/j.jclepro.2017.07.049

Li, Y., Guan, M., Hammond, P., & Berrey, L. E. (2021). Communicating COVID-19 information on TikTok: A content analysis of TikTok videos from official accounts featured in the COVID-19 information hub. *Health Education Research*, *36*(3), 261–271. doi:10.1093/her/cyab010 PMID:33667311

Lokke, E. (2018). *Privacy: Private Life in the Digital Society* (D. Başak, Trans.). Koç University Publications.

Loosen, W., Reimer, J., & de Silva-Schmidt, F. (2020). Data-driven reporting: An on-going (r)evolution? An analysis of projects nominated for the data journalism awards 2013–2016. *Journalism*, *21*(9), 1246–1263. doi:10.1177/1464884917735691

Lorenz, K. (1943). Die angeborenen Formen möglichen Verhaltens. *Zeitschrift für Tierpsychologie*, *5*(2), 235–409. doi:10.1111/j.1439-0310.1943.tb00655.x

Lowrey, W., Broussard, R., & Sherrill, L. A. (2019). Data journalism and black-boxed data sets. *Newspaper Research Journal*, *40*(1), 69–82. doi:10.1177/0739532918814451

Lumley, M., Katsikitis, M., & Statham, D. (2018). Depression, Anxiety, and Acculturative Stress Among Resettled Bhutanese Refugees in Australia. *Journal of Cross-Cultural Psychology*, *49*(8), 1269–1282. doi:10.1177/0022022118786458

Mackenzie, A. (1995). *Başarı ve Zaman*. Bilim Teknik Yayınevi.

Mair, J., & Keeble, R. B. (2014). *Data Journalism: Mapping the Future*. Abramis.

Malapragada, M. (2006). An interdisciplinary approach to the study of cybercultures. In D. Silver & A. Massanari (Eds.), *Critical Cyber Studies* (pp. 194–204). New York University Press.

Mangold, W. G., & Faulds, D. J. (2009). Social media: The new hybrid element of the promotion mix. *Business Horizons*, *52*(4), 357–365. doi:10.1016/j.bushor.2009.03.002

Manyika, J. (2011). *Big data: The next frontier for innovation, Competition, and productivity*. McKinsey Global Institute.

Mao, Z., Li, D., Yang, Y., Fu, X., & Yang, W. (2020). Chinese DMOs' engagement on global social media: Examining post-related factors. *Asia Pacific Journal of Tourism Research*, *25*(3), 274–285. doi:10.1080/10941665.2019.1708759

Marcuse, H. (2004). Some social implications of modern technology. In D. Kellner (Ed.), *Technology war and fascism* (pp. 39–66). Routledge. doi:10.4324/9780203208311-6

Mark, G. (2005). A 'components' model of addiction within a biopsychosocial framework. *Journal of Substance Use*, *10*(4), 191–197. doi:10.1080/14659890500114359

Masciantonio, A., Bourguignon, D., Bouchat, P., Balty, M., & Rimé, B. (2021). Don't put all social network sites in one basket: Facebook, Instagram, Twitter, TikTok, and their relations with well-being during the COVID-19 pandemic. *PLoS One*, *16*(3), e0248384. doi:10.1371/journal.pone.0248384 PMID:33705462

Mattern, J. (2016). *Instagram*. ABDO.

Matzler, K., Pichler, E., & Hemetsberger, A. (2007). Who is spreading the word? The positive ınfluence of extraversion on consumer passion and evangelism. In *AMA Winter educator's conference proceedings marketing theory and applications* (pp. 1-22). American Marketing Association.

Mayfield, A. (2008). *What is social media*. NDU PRESS.

McManus, A., & Feinstein, A. H. (2006). Narratology and ludology: Competing paradigms or complementary theories in simulation. In *Developments in Business Simulation and Experiential Learning: Proceedings of the Annual ABSEL conference* (*Vol. 33*). Academic Press.

Meek, S., Wilk, V., & Lambert, C. (2021). A big data exploration of the informational and normative influences on the helpfulness of online restaurant reviews. *Journal of Business Research*, *125*, 354–367. doi:10.1016/j.jbusres.2020.12.001

Meijer, I. (2013). When news hurts: The promise of participatory storytelling for urban problem neighbourhoods. *Journalism Studies*, *14*(1), 13–28. doi:10.1080/1461670X.2012.662398

Melissen, J. (2008). The New Public Diplomacy: Between Theory and Pratice. In J. Melissen (Ed.), *The New Public Diplomacy: Soft Power in International Relations* (pp. 3–28). Palgrave Macmillan.

Mencütekin, M. (2010). Sinema Dili, Film Retoriği ve İmgelenen Anlama Ulaşma. *Arel Üniversitesi İletişim Fakültesi*, (34), 259-266.

Mersey, R. D. (2009). Online news users' sense of community: Is geography dead? *Journalism Practice*, *3*(3), 347–360. doi:10.1080/17512780902798687

Mert, Y. L. (2019). Kamu Yönetiminde Kurumsal İletişim: Web Sitelerí Üzerine Bir Analiz. *Uluslararası Sosyal Araştırmalar Dergisi*, *12*(62), 1513–1522.

Mert, Y. T. (2018). Dijital Pazarlama Ekseninde Influencer Marketing Uygulamaları. *Gümüşhane Üniversitesi İletişim Fakültesi Ekonomi Dergisi*, *6*(2), 1300–1328. doi:10.19145/e-gifder.431622

Metzgar, E. T., Kurpius, D. D., & Rowley, K. M. (2011). Defining hyperlocal media: Proposing a framework for discussion. *New Media & Society*, *13*(5), 772–787. doi:10.1177/1461444810385095

Mihaela, O. O. E. (2015). The influence of the integrated marketing communication on the consumer buying behaviour. *Procedia Economics and Finance*, *23*, 1446–1450. doi:10.1016/S2212-5671(15)00446-3

Mihart, C. (2012). Modelling the influence of integrated marketing communication on consumer behaviour: An approach based on hierarchy of effects concept. *Procedia: Social and Behavioral Sciences*, *62*, 975–980. doi:10.1016/j.sbspro.2012.09.166

Mikalef, P., Boura, M., Lekakos, G., & Krogstie, J. (2020). The role of information governance in big data analytics driven innovation. *Information & Management*, *57*(7), 103361. doi:10.1016/j.im.2020.103361

Mileti, A., Guido, G., & Prete, M. I. (2016). Nanomarketing: A new frontier for *Neuromarketing. Psychology and Marketing*, *33*(8), 664–674. doi:10.1002/mar.20907

Miller, V. (2020). *Understanding digital culture*. Sage Publications.

Mircea. (2019). The Rise Of Instagram - Evolution, Statistics, Advantages And Disadvantages. *Revisita Economics*, *71*(4), 53-63.

Moe, W. W., & Fader, P. S. (2004). Capturing evolving visit behavior in clickstream data. *Journal of Interactive Marketing*, *18*(1), 5–19. doi:10.1002/dir.10074

Mohammad Badruddoza Talukder, Firoj Kabir, K. M., & Das, I. R. (2023). Emerging Concepts of Artificial Intelligence in the Hotel Industry: A Conceptual Paper. *International Journal of Research Publication and Reviews*, *4*, 1765-1769. doi:10.55248/gengpi.4.923.92451

Moorthi, K., Dhiman, G., Arulprakash, P., Suresh, C., & Srihari, K. (2020). (Article in press). A survey on impact of data analytics techniques in E-commerce. *Materials Today: Proceedings*.

Morin, C. (2011). Neuromarketing: The new science of consumer behaviour. *Society*, *48*(2), 131–135. doi:10.1007/s12115-010-9408-1

Mowery, D. C., & Simcoe, T. (2002). Is the Internet a US invention? An economic and technological history of computer networking. *Research Policy*, *31*(8-9), 1369–1387. doi:10.1016/S0048-7333(02)00069-0

Müller, R. (1982). *Krisenmanegement in Der Unternehmung, Kölner Schriften Zur betriebswirtschaft und Organization-5* (V. E. Grochla, Ed.). Lang Verlag.

Murthy, D. (2018). *Twitter*. Polity Press.

Mutlu, E. (1998). *İletişim Sözlüğü (Dictionary of Communication)*. Bilim-Sanat Yayınları.

Nakip, M., & Yaraş, E. (2017). *SPSS Uygulamalı Pazarlamada Araştırma Teknikleri, 4.Basım*. Seçkin.

Nampoothiri, A. (2021). Online Shopping Behaviour: A Study on Exploring the Dependence of Demographics of the People in Kerala on their Behaviour in Online Shopping. *Turkish Journal of Computer and Mathematics Education*, *12*(10), 4153–4161.

Nasıroğlu, S., & Çeri, V. (2016). Posttraumatic stress and depression in Yazidi refugees. *Neuropsychiatric Disease and Treatment*, *12*, 2941–2948. doi:10.2147/NDT.S119506 PMID:27881919

Nasirudeen, A., Josephine, K. W. N., & Adeline, L. L. C. (2019). Acculturative stress among Asian international students in Singapore. *Journal of International Students*, *4*(4), 363–373. doi:10.32674/jis.v4i4.455

Negreira-Rey, M.-C., & López-García, X. (2021). A decade of research on hyperlocal media: An international approach to a new media model. *Online Journal of Communication and Media Technologies, 11*(3), e202111. doi:10.30935/ojcmt/11082

Neumann, I., & Leira, H. (2015). Beastly Diplomacy. *The Hague Journal of Diplomacy, 12*(4), 337–359. doi:10.1163/1871191X-12341355

Ninh, V.-T., Smyth, S., Tran, M.-T., & Gurrin, C. (2022). Analyzing the performance of stress detection models on consumer-grade wearable devices. *ArXiv Preprint ArXiv:2203.09669.*

NOAS. (2021). *Landprofiler: Tyrkia.* Available at: https://noas.no/riketstilstand/2021-2/landprofiler/tyrkia/

NTB. (2018). *Én av fire asylsøkere i år kommer fra Tyrkia.* Available at: https://www.nettavisen.no/nyheter/innenriks/n-av-fire-asylsokere-i-ar-kommer-fra-tyrkia/s/12-95-3423545013

Nye, J. S. Jr. (2008). Public Diplomacy and Soft Power. *The Annals of the American Academy of Political and Social Science, 616*(1), 94–109. doi:10.1177/0002716207311699

O'Connor, E. (2011). Organizational Apologies: BP as Case Study. *Vanderbilt Law Review, 64*(6), 1957–1992.

Obadara & Olaopa. (2018). *Social Media Utilisation, Study Habit and Undergraduate Students' Academic Performance in a University of Education in Nigeria.* Academic Press.

Obar, J. A., & Wildman, S. (2015). Social media definition and the governance challenge: An introduction to the special issue. *Telecommunications Policy, 39*(9), 745–750. doi:10.1016/j.telpol.2015.07.014

OECD. (2023). *Background Paper: Implementing E-Government in OECD Countries Experiences and Challenges.* https://www.oecd.org/mena/governance/36853121.pdf

Olympic Committee. (2022). *Beijing 2022: The Mascot.* Abgerufen am 17. November 2023 von https://olympics.com/en/olympic-games/beijing-2022/mascot

Önder, M., & Saygılı, H. (2018). Yapay Zekâ ve Kamu Yönetimine Yansımaları. *Türk İdare Dergisi, 2*(487), 629–670.

Önen, S. M., & Kahraman, N. (2022). Kamu Hizmetlerinin Sunumunda Dijitalleşme Üzerine Bir Değerlendirme. *Uluslararası Akademik Birikim Dergisi, 5*(5), 424–432.

Özdoğan, F. B. (2008). Göz izleme ve pazarlamada kullanılması üzerine kavramsal bir çalışma. *Gazi Üniversitesi Ticaret ve Turizm Eğitim Fakültesi Dergisi, 2*, 134-147.

Özgün Kehya, R. (2023). Alman-Türk Sinemasında Bir Entegrasyon Yönetmeni: Buket Alakuş. *Diyalog Interkulturelle Zeitschrift Für Germanistik, 11*(1), 34 – 50.

Özkan, A. (2009). Halkla İlişkiler Yönetimi. İstanbul: Sosyal Yayınlar.

Özkaya, B. (2015). Marka yönetiminde araştırma: Fonksiyonel manyetik rezonans görüntüleme tekniği. *Maltepe Üniversitesi İletişim Fakültesi Dergisi, 2*(1), 24–47.

Özkoçak, Y. (2019). Göçmen Ve Sinema Avrupa Göçmen Sineması Ve Türk Asıllı Yönetmenler. *Stratejik ve Sosyal Araştırmalar Dergisi*, (3), 431-452.

Öztürk, A. (1992). Örgütlerde Çatışma ve Yönetimi: İşletme Yönetiminde Güncel Konular. *Çukurova Üniversitesi İktisadi ve İdari Bilimler Fakültesi İşletme Bölümü Yayınları, 1*, 35-40.

Pace, K. M., Fediuk, T. A., & Botero, I. C. (2010). The acceptance of responsibility and expressions of regret in organizational apologies after a transgression. *Corporate Communications, 15*(4), 410–427. doi:10.1108/13563281011085510

Panda, M., & Mishra, A. (2022). *Digital marketing*. https://www. researchgate. net/publication/358646409

Papa, M. J., Singhal, A., & Papa, W. H. (2000). *Organizing for social change: A dialectical journey of theory and praxis*. Sage Publications.

Paparusso, A. (2021). *Immigrants' Self-reported Life Satisfaction in Europe. In Immigrant Integration in Europe: A Subjective Well-Being Perspective*. Springer International Publishing.

Pasick, A. (2022). *The magic that makes Spotify's Discover Weekly playlists so damn good*. Quartz. https://qz.com/571007/the-magic-that-makes-spotifys-discover-weekly-playlists-so-damn-good

Patel, A., & Reinsch, L. (2003). Companies can apologize: Corporate apologies and legal liability. *Business Communication Quarterly*, *66*(1), 9–25. doi:10.1177/108056990306600103

Paulussen, S., & D'Heer, E. (2013). Using citizens for community journalism. *Journalism Practice*, *7*(5), 588–603. doi:10.1080/17512786.2012.756667

Peake, J. M., Kerr, G., & Sullivan, J. P. (2018). A critical review of consumer wearables, mobile applications, and equipment for providing biofeedback, monitoring stress, and sleep in physically active populations. *Frontiers in Physiology*, *9*, 743. doi:10.3389/fphys.2018.00743 PMID:30002629

Percy, L., & Elliott, R. (2016). *Strategic advertising management*. Oxford University Press.

Perrin, A. (2015). *Social Media Usage: 2005-2015*. Pew Research Center. Retrieved from http://www. pewinternet. org/2015/10/08/social-networking-usage-2005-2015

Phillipov, M., Farmery, A., & Buddle, E. (n.d.). *Media Messages About Sustainable Seafood:# How do Media Influencers affect consumer attitudes?@ Project no. 2017-131*. Academic Press.

Phillips-Wren, G., & Hoskisson, A. (2015). An analytical journey towards big data. *Journal of Decision Systems*, *24*(1), 87–102. doi:10.1080/12460125.2015.994333

Picard, R. G. (2014). Twilight or new dawn of journalism? Evidence from the changing news ecosystem. *Journalism Practice*, *8*(5), 488–498. doi:10.1080/17512786.2014.905338

Piccarozzi, M., Silvestri, C., & Morganti, P. (2021). COVID-19 in management studies: A systematic literature review. *Sustainability (Basel)*, *13*(7), 3791. doi:10.3390/su13073791

Pira, A. (2004). Kriz Yönetimi Halkla İlişkiler Açısından Bir Değerlendirme. İletişim yayınları.

Pittman, M., & Reich, B. (2016). Social media and loneliness: Why an Instagram picture may be worth more than a thousand Twitter words. *Computers in Human Behavior*, *62*, 155–167. doi:10.1016/j.chb.2016.03.084

Ponirah, A. (2020). Influencer Marketing as a Marketing Strateg. *Journal of Economicate Studies*, (04), 11–16.

Poppitt, G., & Frey, R. (2007). Sudanese Adolescent Refugees: Acculturation and Acculturative Stress. *Australian Journal of Guidance & Counselling*, *17*(2), 160–181. doi:10.1375/ajgc.17.2.160

Porcu, L., del Barrio-García, S., Alcántara-Pilar, J. M., & Crespo-Almendros, E. (2019). Analyzing the influence of firm-wide integrated marketing communication on market performance in the hospitality industry. *International Journal of Hospitality Management*, *80*, 13–24. doi:10.1016/j.ijhm.2019.01.008

Porcu, L., del Barrio-García, S., Kitchen, P. J., & Tourky, M. (2020). The antecedent role of a collaborative vs. a controlling corporate culture on firm-wide integrated marketing communication and brand performance. *Journal of Business Research*, *119*, 435–443. doi:10.1016/j.jbusres.2019.10.049

Porter, M. E., & Heppelmann, J. E. (2014). How smart, connected products are transforming competition. *Harvard Business Review*, *92*(11), 64–88.

Pottie, K., Ratnayake, A., Ahmed, R., Veronis, L., & Alghazali, I. (2020). How refugee youth use social media: What does this mean for improving their health and welfare? *Journal of Public Health Policy*, *41*(3), 268–278. doi:10.1057/s41271-020-00231-4 PMID:32690862

Prapas, C., & Mavreas, V. (2019). The Relationship Between Quality of Life, Psychological Wellbeing, Satisfaction with Life and Acculturation of Immigrants in Greece. *Culture, Medicine and Psychiatry*, *43*(1), 77–92. doi:10.1007/s11013-018-9598-3 PMID:30097834

Prasetyo, Y. T., Tanto, H., Mariyanto, M., Hanjaya, C., Young, M. N., Persada, S. F., Miraja, B. A., & Redi, A. A. N. P. (2021). Factors affecting customer satisfaction and loyalty in online food delivery service during the COVID-19 pandemic: Its relation with open innovation. *Journal of Open Innovation*, *7*(1), 76. doi:10.3390/joitmc7010076

Presswood, A. L. (2019). *Food Blogs, Postfeminism, and the Communication of Expertise: Digital Domestics*. Lexington Books.

Proferes, N., Jones, N., Gilbert, S. F. C., & Zimmer, M. (2021). Studying reddit: A systematic overview of disciplines, approaches, methods, and ethics. *Social Media + Society*, *7*(2). doi:10.1177/20563051211019004

Prokopenko, J. (1995). *Verimlilik Yönetimi*. Yayını.

Punathambekar, A., & Mohan, S. (2019). Digital platforms, globalization, and culture. In J. Curran & D. Hesmondhalgh (Eds.), *Media and Society* (pp. 207–224). Bloomsbury Publishing. doi:10.5040/9781501340765.ch-011

Putnam, R. D. (2000). *Bowling alone: The collapse and revival of American community*. Simon and Schuster.

Quarantelli, E. L. (2005). A social science research agenda for the disasters of the 21st century. In R. W. Perry & E. L. Quarantelli (Eds.), *What is a disaster? New answers to old questions* (pp. 325–296). Xlibris.

Radcliffe, D. (2012). *Here and now: UK hyperlocal media today*. Nesta. https://media.nesta.org.uk/documents/here_and_now_uk_hyperlocal_media_today.pdf

Raessens, J. (2006). Playful Identities, or the Ludification of Culture. *Games and Culture*, *1*(1), 52–57. doi:10.1177/1555412005281779

Ranzini, G., Newlands, G., & Lutz, C. (2020). Sharenting, Peer Influence, and Privacy Concerns: A Study on the Instagram-Sharing Behaviors of Parents in the United Kingdom. *Social Media + Society*, *6*(4). Advance online publication. doi:10.1177/2056305120978376

Read, G. L., & Innis, I. J. (2017). Electroencephalography (EEG). The İnternational Encyclopedia of Communication Research Methods, 1-18. doi:10.1002/9781118901731.iecrm0080

Reed, T. V. (2019). *Digitized lives: Culture power and social change in the internet era*. Routledge.

Reinhardt, B. (2013). *Gold by Thomas Arslan: Always on the move but why, and where?* World Socialist Web Site.

Resnick, M. & Albert, W. (2014). The impact of advertising location and user taskon the emergence of banner ad blindness: An eye-tracking study. *Intl. Journal of Human–Computer Interaction*, *30*, 206–219. doi:10.1080/10447318.2013.847762

Richardson, C. (2017). *7 Great Benefits of Big Data in Marketing*. https://www.smartdatacollective.com/benefits-big-data-in-marketing/

Riesmeyer, C., Abel, B., & Großmann, A. (2019). The family rules. The influence of parenting styles on adolescents' media literacy. MedienPädagogik. *Zeitschrift Für Theorie Und Praxis Der Medienbildung*, *35*, 74–96. doi:10.21240/mpaed/35/2019.10.20.X

Riessman, C. K. (2008). *Narrative methods for the human sciences*. Sage Pub.

Riessman, C. K., & Quinney, L. (2005). Narrative in social work: A critical review. *Qualitative Social Work: Research and Practice*, *4*(3), 391–412. doi:10.1177/1473325005058643

Rifat, M. (2013). Açıklamalı Göstergebilim Sözlüğü, (Kavramlar- Yöntemler- Kuramcılar- Okullar) (Annotated Semiotics Dictionary, (Concepts- Methods- Theorists- Echols). Türkiye İş Bankası Kültür Yayınları, İstanbul.

Ritzer, G. (2009). *Enchanting a disenchanted world: Continuity and change in the cathedrals of consumption*. SAGE Publication.

Roberts, S. J., & David, M. E. (2020). *The social media party: Politics in a Facebook world*. Oxford University Press.

Robiatul, A., & Rachmawati, Y. (2021). Parenting Program to Protect Children's Privacy: The Phenomenon of Sharenting Children on social media. *Pendidikan Usia Dini*, *15*(1), 162–180. doi:10.21009/JPUD.151.09

Robins, K., & Webster, F. (2002). Prospects of a virtual culture. *Science as Culture*, *11*(2), 235–256. doi:10.1080/09505430220137261

Rodgers, S. (2017). Roots and fields: Excursions through place, space, and local in hyperlocal media. *Media Culture & Society*, *40*(6), 856–874. doi:10.1177/0163443717729213

Rosoff, M. (2015). *Every type of tech product has gotten cheaper over the last two decades-except for one*. https://www.businessinsider.com/historical-price-trends-for-tech-products-2015-10

Ruiz-Mafe, C., Chatzipanagiotou, K., & Curras-Perez, R. (2018). The role of emotions and conflicting online reviews on consumers' purchase intentions. *Journal of Business Research*, *89*, 336–344. doi:10.1016/j.jbusres.2018.01.027

Ryan, M. L. (2001). Beyond Myth and Metaphor: The Case of Narrative in Digital Media. *Game Studies*, 1.

Rys, D. (2016). *Tidal Claims Three Million Global Subscribers, Finally Releases Kanye's 'Pablo' Stream Numbers*. Billboard. https://www.billboard.com/pro/tidal-three-million-global-subscribers-kanye-west-pablo-streams/

Sadiku, M., Omotoso, A., & Musa, S. (2019). Social Networking. *International Journal of Trend in Scientific Research and Development.*, *3*(-3), 126–128. doi:10.31142/ijtsrd21657

Sahni, N. S., Wheeler, S. C., & Chintagunta, P. (2018). Personalization in email marketing: The role of noninformative advertising content. *Marketing Science*, *37*(2), 236–258. doi:10.1287/mksc.2017.1066

Saleem, P. (2019). A Study on Growth Rate of Multi-Level Marketing In India, A Paradigm Shift in Banking. *Marketing and HRM.*, *1*, 70–74.

Sam, D. L., Vetik, R., & Makarova, M. (2017). Intercultural Relations in Norway. In J. W. Berry (Ed.), *Mutual Intercultural Relations* (pp. 105–124). Cambridge University Press. doi:10.1017/9781316875032.006

Santos, R. O. (2015). Eye tracking in neuromarketing: A research agenda for marketing studies. *International Journal of Psychological Studies*, *7*(1). doi:10.1080/13683500.2014.1003797

Sarıkaya, M. (2003). *Millî görüş gömleğimizi değiştirdik*. Abgerufen am 16. September 2023 von Sabah Gazetesi: https://arsiv.sabah.com.tr/2003/05/28/s1812.html

Sashi, C. M., Brynildsen, G., & Bilgihan, A. (2019). Social media, customer engagement and advocacy: An empirical investigation using Twitter data for quick service restaurants. *International Journal of Contemporary Hospitality Management*, *31*(3), 1247–1272. doi:10.1108/IJCHM-02-2018-0108

Sathi, A. (2014). *Engaging customers using big data: how Marketing analytics are transforming business.* Palgrave Macmillan. doi:10.1057/9781137386199

Schaller, G. B. (1994). *The Last Panda.* University of Chicago Press.

Scher, S. J., & Darley, J. M. (1997). How effective are the things people say to apologize? Effects of the realization of the apology speech act. *Journal of Psycholinguistic Research*, *26*(1), 127–140. doi:10.1023/A:1025068306386

Schönberger. (2013). *Viktor Mayer and Kenneth Cukier. Big Data – A Revolution That Will Transform the Way We Live, Work and Think* (B. Erol, Trans.). Paloma.

Schudson, M. (2010). Political observatories, Databases & news in the emerging ecology of public ınformation. *Daedalus*, *139*(2), 100–109. doi:10.1162/daed.2010.139.2.100

Schultheiß, S., & Lewandowski, D. (2021). "Outside the industry, nobody knows what we do" SEO as seen by search engine optimizers and content providers. *The Journal of Documentation*, *77*(2), 542–557. doi:10.1108/JD-07-2020-0127

Šerić, M., Gil-Saura, I., & Ruiz-Molina, M. E. (2014). How can integrated marketing communications and advanced technology influence the creation of customer-based brand equity? Evidence from the hospitality industry. *International Journal of Hospitality Management*, *39*, 144–156. doi:10.1016/j.ijhm.2014.02.008

Setiaboedi, A. P., Sari, H., & Prihartono, B. (2018). Conceptual model for online marketing strategy to success in the survival phase of small firms. *Proceedings of the International COnference on Industrial Engineering and Operations Management,* 1877.

Seyyid, T. A., & Mehmood, F. (2023). Brand–SMI Collaboration in İnfluencer Marketing Campaigns: A transaction cost economics. *Technological Forecasting and Social Change*, *192*, 1–15. doi:10.1016/j.techfore.2023.122580

Shajan, A. (2023). Digital Culture and Digi-Relations. In S. Chakraborty (Ed.), *Dynamics of dialogue, cultural development, and peace in the metaverse* (pp. 30–39). IGI Global.

Shaker, L. (2014). Dead newspapers and citizens' civic engagement. *Political Communication*, *31*(1), 131–148. doi:10.1080/10584609.2012.762817

Sharma, A., Sanghvi, K., & Churi, P. (2022). The Impact of Instagram on young Adult's social comparison, colourism and mental health: Indian perspective. Academic Press.

Sharma, M., Kacker, S., & Sharma, M. (2016). A Brief Introduction and Review on Galvanic Skin Response. *International Journal of Medical Research Professionals*, *2*(6), 13–17. doi:10.21276/ijmrp.2016.2.6.003

Silver, A. D. (1990). Taban Çöktüğü Zaman. Form Yayınları No:6.

Singh, A. K. & Sharma, V. (2009). E-Governance and E-Government: A Study of Some Initiatives. *International Journal of eBusiness and eGovernment Studies*, *1*(1), 1-14.

Singh, C., Bhnwaria, D., Nengzaching, E., Kaur, G., Haokip, H., Jani, H., Sharma, M. C., & Sk, M. (2020). A Descriptive study to access daily routine activities and level of stress among students of BSc (Hons.) Nursing students at AIIMS, Jodhpur. *International Journal of Nursing Education and Research.*, *8*(1), 13–18. doi:10.5958/2454-2660.2020.00003.4

Singh, N. (2015). Evangelism marketing: The evolution of consumer fidelity. *Journal of Marketing Communications*, *11*(1), 5–16.

Şirin, Y. (2019). *Oryantalizm Bağlamında Ferzan Özpetek Sineması (Yayımlanmamış Yüksek Lisans Tezi).* Maltepe Üniversitesi, Radyo, Sinema ve Televizyon.

Snapes, L., & Sweney, M. (2018). *YouTube to launch new music streaming service.* The Guardian. https://www.theguardian.com/music/2018/may/17/youtube-music-new-streaming-service-launch

Snow, N., & Taylor, P. M. (2009). *Routledge Handbook of Public Diplomacy.* Routledge.

Social Networking. (2023b). https://dictionary.cambridge.org/dictionary/english/social-networking

Songster, E. (2018). *Panda Nation: The Construction and Conservation of China's Modern Icon.* Oxford University Press. doi:10.1093/oso/9780199393671.001.0001

Spotify. (2023). *About Spotify.* https://newsroom.spotify.com/company-info/

Srinivas, S. (2020). A machine learning-based approach for predicting patient punctuality in ambulatory care centers. *International Journal of Environmental Research and Public Health, 17*(10), 3703. doi:10.3390/ijerph17103703 PMID:32456329

SSB. (2022). *Immigrants and Norwegian-born to immigrant parents.* Available at: https://www.ssb.no/en/befolkning/innvandrere/statistikk/innvandrere-og-norskfodte-med-innvandrerforeldre

Stacks, D. W. (2016). *Primer of public relations research.* Guilford Publications.

Stalph, F. (2020). Evolving Data Teams: Tensions Between Organisational Structure and Professional Subculture. *Big Data & Society, 7*(1), 1–13. doi:10.1177/2053951720919964

Stalph, F., Hahn, O., & Liewehr, D. (2023). Local data journalism in germany: Data-driven reporting amidst local communities and authorities. *Journalism Practice, 17*(9), 1882–1901. doi:10.1080/17512786.2021.2019089

Statista. (2022). *Social media - Statistics & Facts.* Available at: https://www.statista.com/topics/1164/social-networks/

Statista. (2023). *Number of influencers brands worked with worldwide 2023.* Author.

Steinhoff, L., & Zondag, M. M. (2021). Loyalty programs as travel companions: Complementary service features across customer journey stages. *Journal of Business Research, 129*, 70–82. doi:10.1016/j.jbusres.2021.02.016

Stojanovic, D., Bogdanovic, Z., & Despotovic, M. (2019). An approach to using Instagram in secondary education. University of Bucharest, Faculty of Matematics and Informatics.

Stuart, J., Ward, C., & Robinson, L. (2016). The influence of family climate on stress and adaptation for Muslim immigrant young adults in two Western countries. *International Perspectives in Psychology : Research, Practice, Consultation, 5*(1), 1–17. doi:10.1037/ipp0000043

Stubb, C. (2019). *The Gray Zone in Marketing Consumer Responses to Influencer Marketing.* Abo Akademi University.

Suh, H., Rice, K. G., Choi, C.-C., van Nuenen, M., Zhang, Y., Morero, Y., & Anderson, D. (2016). Measuring acculturative stress with the SAFE: Evidence for longitudinal measurement invariance and associations with life satisfaction. *Personality and Individual Differences, 89*, 217–222. doi:10.1016/j.paid.2015.10.002

Sun, J., Tian, Z., Fu, Y., Geng, J., & Liu, C. (2021). Digital twins in human understanding: A deep learning-based method to recognize personality traits. *International Journal of Computer Integrated Manufacturing, 7-8*(7-8), 860–873. doi:10.1080/0951192X.2020.1757155

Sürmeli, Z. (2017). *Sinemada Oryantalist ve Oksidentalist Fatih Akın Filmleri Örneği (Yayımlanmamış Yüksek Lisans Tezi).* Ordu Üniversitesi, Sinema ve Televizyon.

Susic, P. (2023). *31+ Fresh Amazon Music Statistics 2023: Revenue, Users, Subs*. HeadphonesAddict. https://headphonesaddict.com/amazon-music-statistics/#:~:text=How%20many%20people%20use%20Amazon,has%20around%2082.2%20million%20users

Syaifudin, M. A. (2021). The Role of Parents in the Use of Children's Social Media Under Age. *Ilmu Hukum.*, *12*(1), 15–27. doi:10.58471/justi.v12i1.97

Talukder, M. B. (2020). The Future of Culinary Tourism: An Emerging Dimension for the Tourism Industry of Bangladesh. *I-Manager's Journal on Management, 15*(1), 27. doi:10.26634/jmgt.15.1.17181

Talukder, M. B., & Bhuiyan, M. L. (2020). An assessment of the roles of the social network in the development of the Tourism Industry in Bangladesh. *International Journalof Business, Law, and Education*, *2*(3), 85–93. doi:10.56442/ijble.v2i3.21

Talukder, M. B., & Hossain, M. M. (2021). Prospects of Future Tourism in Bangladesh: An Evaluative Study. I-Manager's. *Journal of Management*, *15*(4), 1–8. doi:10.26634/jmgt.15.4.17495

Talukder, M. B., Kumar, S., Sood, K., & Grima, S. (2023). Information Technology, Food Service Quality and Restaurant Revisit Intention. *International Journal of Sustainable Development and Planning*, *18*(1), 295–303. doi:10.18280/ijsdp.180131

Tamer, A., & Hussein, M. (2020). The Impact of Digitization on Advertising Effectiveness. *Management Studies and Economic Systems*, *5*(3/4), 117–126. doi:10.12816/0059075

Tandoc, E. Jr, & Oh, S.-K. (2017). Small departures, big continuities? Norms, values, and routines in the guardian's big data journalism. *Journalism Studies*, *18*(8), 997–1015. doi:10.1080/1461670X.2015.1104260

Taşkıran, İ. (2017). *Sosyal Medyada Haber Var*. Der Yayınları.

Tekinalp, Ş., & Uzun, R. (2013). İletişim Araştırmaları ve Kuramları (Communication Research and Theories). Derin Yayınları, İstanbul.

Tekin, I., & Aydın, S. (2022). Well-Being and Instagram Use Among University Students. *International Journal of Adult Education and Technology.*, *4*(3), 18–23. doi:10.4018/IJAET.310074

Tenor, C. (2018). Hyperlocal News And Media Accountability. *Digital Journalism (Abingdon, England)*, *6*(8), 1064–1077. doi:10.1080/21670811.2018.1503059

Tenor, C. (2019). Logic of an effectuating hyperlocal: Entrepreneurial processes and passions of online news start-ups. *Nordicom Review*, *40*(2), 129–145. doi:10.2478/nor-2019-0031

Terranova, T. (2000). Free labor: Producing culture for the digital economy. *Social Text*, *18*(2), 33-58.

Thompson, D. F., & Louie, R. P. (2006). Cooperative Crisis Management and Avian Influenza. A Risk Assessment Guide for International Contagious Disease Prevention and Risk Mitigation. National Defense University Center for Technology and National Security Policy.

Thomson, M., MacInnis, D. J., & Park, C. W. (2005). The ties that bind: Measuring the strength of consumers' emotional attachments to brands. *Journal of Consumer Psychology*, *15*(1), 77–91. doi:10.1207/s15327663jcp1501_10

Todor, R.D. (2016). Blending traditional and digital marketing. *Bulletin of the Transilvania University of Braşov, Series V: Economic Sciences, 9*(58), 51-56.

Toffler, A. (1980). *The third wave*. William Morrow and Company, Inc.

Törenli, N. (2005). *Yeni Medya, Yeni İletişim Ortamı*. Bilim ve Sanat Yayınları.

Törnberg, P., & Uitermark, J. (2022). Tweeting ourselves to death: The cultural logic of digital capitalism. *Media Culture & Society*, *44*(3), 574–590. doi:10.1177/01634437211053766

Trainor, K. J. (2012). Relating social media technologies to performance: A capabilities-based perspective. *Journal of Personal Selling & Sales Management*, *32*(3), 317–331. doi:10.2753/PSS0885-3134320303

Tranberg, M., Bech, B. H., Blaakær, J., Jensen, J. S., Svanholm, H., & Andersen, B. (2018). Preventing cervical cancer using HPV self-sampling: Direct mailing of test-kits increases screening participation more than timely opt-in procedures-a randomized controlled trial. *BMC Cancer*, *18*(1), 1–11. doi:10.1186/s12885-018-4165-4 PMID:29523108

Traynor, M., Bernard, S., Moreo, A., & O'Neill, S. (2022). Investigating the emergence of third-party online food delivery in the US restaurant industry: A grounded theory approach. *International Journal of Hospitality Management*, *107*, 103299. doi:10.1016/j.ijhm.2022.103299

Tredinnick, L. (2008). *Digital information culture: The individual and society in the digital age*. Chandos Publishing. doi:10.1533/9781780631677

Tremblay, G. (2015). Cultural industries, the creative economy, and the information society. In L. A. Albornoz (Ed.), *Power media culture: Global transformations in media and communication research* (pp. 73–95). Palgrave Macmillan. doi:10.1057/9781137540089_4

Tufekci, Z. (2017). *Twitter and tear gas: The power and fragility of networked protest*. Yale University Press.

TUİK. (2023). *Hanehalkı Bilişim Teknolojileri Kullanım Araştırması*. https://data.tuik.gov.tr/Bulten/Index?p=Hanehalki-Bilisim-Teknolojileri-(BT)-Kullanim-Arastirmasi-2023-49407

Tunalı, S. B., Ömer, G., & Göktuğ, Ö. (2016). Pazarlama ve Reklam Araştırmalarında Nöropazarlama Üzerine Yapılmış Araştırmaların İncelenmesi ve Etik Boyutunun Tartışılması. *Kurgu*, *24*(2), 1–8.

Tuncel, H. (2009). Halkla İlişkiler Anlayişiyla Bütünleşik Pazarlama İletişimi. İstanbul Üniversitesi İletişim Fakültesi Dergisi, (35), 115-136.

Türkiye E-Devlet Kapısı. (2023). *E-Devlet Kapısı Kullanıcı İstatistikleri*. https://www.turkiye.gov.tr/edevlet-istatistikl eri?kullanici=Istatistikleri

Turner, J. (2021). Someone should do something: Exploring public sphere ıdeals in the audiences of uk hyperlocal media facebook Pages. *Journalism Studies*, *22*(16), 2236–2255. doi:10.1080/1461670X.2021.1991837

Turrini, G., Purgato, M., Ballette, F., Nosè, M., Ostuzzi, G., & Barbui, C. (2017). Common mental disorders in asylum seekers and refugees: Umbrella review of prevalence and intervention studies. *International Journal of Mental Health Systems*, *11*(1), 51. doi:10.1186/s13033-017-0156-0 PMID:28855963

Tutar, H. (2000). *Kriz ve Stres Ortamında Yönetim*. Hayat Yayıncılık.

Tyhkheev, D. (2018). *Big data in marketing*. Saimaa University of Applied Sciences, Business Administration.

UDI. (n.d.). *Statistics on immigration*. Available at: https://www.udi.no/en/statistics-and-analysis/statistics/?year=0&f ilter=42&page=3

Ünal. (2016). Uluslararası Stratejik İletişim Yönetimi Olarak Kamu Diplomasisinin Ülke İmajına Etkileri. İstanbul Ticaret Üniversitesi Sosyal Bilimler Enstitüsü.

UNHCR. (2022). *Forced displacement hit record high in 2021 with too few able to go home*. Available at: https://www.unhcr.org/news/stories/2022/6/62a9ccb54/forced-displacement-hit-record-high-2021-few-able-home.html

United Nations. (2022). *What is e-Government?* https://publicadministration.un.org/egovkb/en-us/About/UNeGovDD-Framework

Uysal, N., & Schroeder, J. (2019). Turkey's Twitter Public Diplomacy: Towards a "new" cult of personality. *Public Relations Review*, *45*(5), 101837. doi:10.1016/j.pubrev.2019.101837

Uzir, M. U. H., Al Halbusi, H., Thurasamy, R., Hock, R. L. T., Aljaberi, M. A., Hasan, N., & Hamid, M. (2021). The effects of service quality, perceived value and trust in home delivery service personnel on customer satisfaction: Evidence from a developing country. *Journal of Retailing and Consumer Services*, *63*, 102721. doi:10.1016/j.jretconser.2021.102721

Uzun, M. M., Yildiz, M., & Önder, M. (2022). Big questions of artificial intelligence (AI) in public administration and policy. SİYASAL. *Journal of Political Science*, *31*(2), 423–442. doi:10.26650/siyasal.2022.31.1121900

Vaganti, M. (2021). *Mine Vaganti (Losse Cannons)*. Tr Beca Film Festival.

Vajjhala, V., & Ghosh, M. (2022). Decoding the effect of restaurant reviews on customer choice: Insights from Zomato. *Journal of Foodservice Business Research*, *25*(5), 533–560. doi:10.1080/15378020.2021.1964417

Valentini, C. (2018). *Social Media*. The International Encyclopedia of Strategic Communication.

Valerio, C., William, L., & Noémier, Q. (2019). The impact of social media on E-Commerce decision making process. *International Journal of Technology for Business*, *1*(1), 1–9.

van der Boor, C. F., Amos, R., Nevitt, S., Dowrick, C., & White, R. G. (2020). Systematic review of factors associated with quality of life of asylum seekers and refugees in high-income countries. *Conflict and Health*, *14*(1), 48. doi:10.1186/s13031-020-00292-y PMID:32699551

Van Dijck, J. (2013). 'You have one identity': Performing the self on Facebook and LinkedIn. *Media Culture & Society*, *35*(2), 199–215. doi:10.1177/0163443712468605

Van Dijk, J. (2013). *The culture of connectivity, a critical history of social media*. Oxford University Press. doi:10.1093/acprof:oso/9780199970773.001.0001

Van Dijk, J. (2018). *Ağ Toplumu*. Epsilon.

van Ham, P. (2008). Power, Public Diplomacy, and The Pax Americana. In J. Melissen (Ed.), *The New Public Diplomacy: Soft Power in International Relations* (pp. 46–66). Palgrave Macmillan.

Van Riel, C. (1995). *Principles of Corporate Communication*. Prentice Hall.

Var, S., Poyrazli, S., & Grahame, K. M. (2013). Personal Well-being and Overall Satisfaction of Life of Asian Immigrant and Refugee Women. *Asia Taepyongyang Sangdam Yongu*, *3*(1), 77–90. doi:10.18401/2013.3.1.6

Vaterlaus, J. M., Barnett, K., Roche, C., & Young, J. A. (2016). Snapchat is more personal": An exploratory study on Snapchat behaviors and young adult interpersonal relationships. *Computers in Human Behavior*, *62*, 594–601. doi:10.1016/j.chb.2016.04.029

Vlist, V. D. F. N., & Helmond, A. (2021). How partners mediate platform power: Mapping business and data partnerships in the social media ecosystem. *Big Data & Society*, *8*(1). Advance online publication. doi:10.1177/20539517211025061 von Twickel, N. (2012). *Puppy Diplomacy: Putin Gets Pets Wrapped With a Bow*. Abgerufen am 19. November 2023 von The Moscow Times: https://www.themoscowtimes.com/2012/08/02/puppy-diplomacy-putin-gets-pets-wrapped-with-a-bow-a16752

Vo, N. N. Y., Liu, S., Li, X., & Xu, G. (2021). Leveraging unstructured call log data for customer churn prediction. *Knowledge-Based Systems*, *212*, 106586. doi:10.1016/j.knosys.2020.106586

Wahid, R., & Wadud, M. (2020). Social Media Marketing on Instagram: When Is the Most Effective Posting Timing? *International Journal of Multidisciplinary Research*, *14*(4), 312–321.

Walther, L., Fuchs, L. M., Schupp, J., & von Scheve, C. (2020). Living Conditions and the Mental Health and Well-being of Refugees: Evidence from a Large-Scale German Survey. *Journal of Immigrant and Minority Health*, *22*(5), 903–913. doi:10.1007/s10903-019-00968-5 PMID:31974927

Wang, Y. (2008). Public Diplomacy and the Rise of Chinese Soft Power. *The Annals of the American Academy of Political and Social Science*, *616*(1), 257–273. doi:10.1177/0002716207312757

Ward, S. J. A. (2014). Radical media ethics. *Digital Journalism (Abingdon, England)*, *2*(4), 455–471. doi:10.1080/21670811.2014.952985

Wasono, L. W. (2018). The effect of digital leadership and innovation management for incumbent telecommunication company in the digital disruptive era. *IACSIT International Journal of Engineering and Technology*, *7*(2.29), 125–130. doi:10.14419/ijet.v7i2.29.13142

We Are Social. (2023). *Digital 2023 Turkey*. https://www.guvenliweb.org.tr/dosya/HQTLP.pdf

Weiner, D. (2006). Crisis communications: managing corporate reputation in the court of public opinion. *Ivey Business Journal*, *70*(4).

Weiss, A. M., Anderson, E., & MacInnis, D. J. (1999). Reputation Management as a Motivation for Sales Structure Decisions. *Journal of Marketing*, *63*(4), 74–89. doi:10.1177/002224299906300407

Wellman, B. (2001). Physical place and cyberplace: The rise of personalized networking. *International Journal of Urban and Regional Research*, *25*(2), 227–252. doi:10.1111/1468-2427.00309

Wellman, B., Haase, A. Q., Witte, J., & Hampton, K. (2001). Does the Internet increase, decrease, or supplement social capital? Social networks, participation, and community commitment. *The American Behavioral Scientist*, *45*(3), 436–455. doi:10.1177/00027640121957286

Whiting, A., & Williams, D. (2013). Why people use social media: A uses and gratifications approach. *Qualitative Market Research*, *16*(4), 362–369. doi:10.1108/QMR-06-2013-0041

Whittier, J. B. (2007). *Representatıons Of Germans And The Use Of Language In Turksıhgerman Fılms By Fatıh Akın And Thomas Arslan* [Thesis]. The University of Georgia.

WHO. (n.d.). *WHOQOL: Measuring Quality of Life*. Available at: https://www.who.int/tools/whoqol

Wiideman, S. (2021). Scaling search engine visibility for franchises: A guide for multi-location brands. *Journal of Digital & Social Media Marketing*, *9*(1), 22–31.

Wikström, P. (2022). *The Music Industry in an Age of Digital Distribution*. OpenMind. https://www.bbvaopenmind.com/en/articles/the-music-industry-in-an-age-of-digital-distribution/

Wiley, S. K. (2021). The grey area: How regulations ımpact autonomy in computational journalism. *Digital Journalism (Abingdon, England)*, *11*(6), 889–905. doi:10.1080/21670811.2021.1893199

Williams, R. (1960). *Culture & Society 1780-1950*. Anchor Book.

Williams, R., & Edge, D. (1996). The social shaping of technology. *Research Policy*, *25*(6), 865–899. doi:10.1016/0048-7333(96)00885-2

Wilson, T. (2017). *A.P.J. Abdul Kalam: "Evolution of a unique you", address to students IIT Madras - 2010*. Speakola. https://speakola.com/motivate/apj-abdul-kalam-iit-madras-2010

Wilson, R. E., Gosling, S. D., & Graham, L. T. (2012). A review of Facebook research in the social sciences. *Perspectives on Psychological Science*, *7*(3), 203–220. doi:10.1177/1745691612442904 PMID:26168459

Wirtz, D., Tucker, A., Briggs, C., & Schoemann, A. M. (2021). How and Why Social Media Affect Subjective Well-Being: Multi-Site Use and Social Comparison as Predictors of Change Across Time. *Journal of Happiness Studies*, *22*(4), 1673–1691. doi:10.1007/s10902-020-00291-z

World Bank. (2022). *What is e-Government?* https://www.worldbank.org/en/topic/digitaldevelopment/brief/e-government

Wright, G., & Yasar, K. (2022, December 12). *Social networking*. WhatIs. https://www.techtarget.com/whatis/definition/social-networking

Xing, Y. (2010). *China's Panda Diplomacy: The Power of being Cute*. University of Southern California.

Xu, Z. (2016). Three essays on big data analytics, traditional marketing analytics, knowledge discovery, and new product performance. *Open Access Theses & Dissertations*, 781.

Xu, Z., Frankwick, G.L. & Ramirez, E. (2015). Effects of big data analytics and traditional marketing analytics on new product success: A knowledge fusion perspective. *Journal of Business Research, 59*(2016), 1562-1566.

Yako, R. M., & Biswas, B. (2014). "We came to this country for the future of our children. We have no future": Acculturative stress among Iraqi refugees in the United States. *International Journal of Intercultural Relations*, *38*, 133–141. doi:10.1016/j.ijintrel.2013.08.003

Yalçın, H. (2022). Bir Araştırma Deseni Olarak Fenomenoloji. *Anadolu Üniversitesi Sosyal Bilimler Dergisi*, *22*(2), 213–232. doi:10.18037/ausbd.1227345

Yassin, D., & Yassin, D. (2021). *A brief history of streaming services*. The Michigan Daily. https://www.michigandaily.com/music/brief-history-steaming-services/

Yeni İş Fikirleri. (2019). *Büyük Veri Nedir ve Nasıl Analiz Edilir?* https://www.yeniisfikirleri.net/buyuk-veri-nedir-ve-nasil-analiz-edilir/

Yildirim, A. (2020). Halkla İlişkilerin Kavramsal Tanımlamaları Üzerine Bir İnceleme. Jandarma ve Sahil Güvenlik Akademisi, Türkiye. *İletişim Çalışmaları Dergisi, 6*(2), 133-150. doi:10.17932/IAU.ICD.2015.006/icd_v06i2001

Yıldırım, A., & Şimşek, H. (2005). *Sosyal Bilimlerde Nitel Araştırma Yöntemleri*. Seçkin Yayıncılık.

Yıldırım, B. (2015). İçerik Çözümlemesi Yönteminin Tarihsel Gelişimi Uygulama Alanları ve Aşamaları. In B. Yıldırım (Ed.), *İletişim Araştırmalarında Yöntemler*. Literatürk Academia.

Yıldırım, M. (2010). Kamu Yönetiminde Takdir Yetkisi: Geleneksel ve Yeni Kamu Yönetimi Arasında Karşılaştırmalı Bir İnceleme. *Uluslararas Insan Bilimleri Dergisi*, *7*(2), 839–861.

Yıldırım, U. (2021). Çin'in Panda Diplomasisi. *Bölgesel Araştırmalar Dergisi*, *5*(1), 48–86.

Young, M. L., Hermida, A., & Fulda, J. (2018). What makes for great data journalism? A content analysis of data journalism awards finalists 2012–2015. *Journalism Practice*, *12*(1), 115–135. doi:10.1080/17512786.2016.1270171

Yuan, S., & Li, H. (2021) Ethnic Identity, Acculturation and Life Satisfaction of the Yi in the Context of social media: Moderating and Mediating Effects. In *2021 5th International Conference on Business and Information Management*. Association for Computing Machinery.

Yücel, G. (2016). Dijital Diplomasi. *TRT Akademi Dergisi, 1*(2).

Yüksek Seçim Kurulu. (2007). *Türkiye Geneli Partilerin Kazandıkları Milletvekilleri Sayıları*. Von Yüksek Seçim Kurulu: https://web.archive.org/web/20071030213029/http://www.ysk.gov.tr/ysk/docs/2007secim/turkiye/milletvekilisayisi.htm abgerufen

Yüksel, A., & Şener, E. (2017). The reflections of digitalization at organizational level: industry 4.0 in Turkey. *Journal of Business, Economicsand Finance, 6*(3), 291-300.

Zaharna, R. S. (2000). Intercultural Communication and International Public Relations: Exploring Parallels. *Communication Quarterly*, *42*(1), 85–100. doi:10.1080/01463370009385582

Zaharna, R. S. (2016). Beyond the Individualism-collectivism Divide to Relationalism: Explicating Cultural Assumptions In The Concept of "Relationships". *Communication Theory*, *26*(2), 190–211. doi:10.1111/comt.12058

Zaher, Z. (2020). Examining How Newcomer Women to Canada Use Social Media for Social Support. *Canadian Journal of Communication*, *45*(2), 122–220. doi:10.22230/cjc.2020v45n2a3541

Zaman, B., & Nouwen, M. (2016). *Parental controls: Advice for parents, researchers and industry*. Academic Press.

Zamenopoulos, T., Alexiou, K., Alevizou, G., Chapain, C., Sobers, S., & Williams, A. (2016). Varieties of Creative Citizenship. In I. Hargreaves & J. Hartley (Eds.), *The Creative Citizen Unbound* (pp. 103–128). Polity. doi:10.2307/j.ctt1t89gk8.11

Zengin Demirbilek, E. (2021). *Pazarlamanın Dijital Dönüşümü: Influencer Marketing Üzerine Bir Uygulama* [Doktora tezi]. İstanbul Üniversitesi.

About the Contributors

Michael (Mihalis) Kuyucu, a Turkish academic and media professional of Greek descent, received his bachelor's degree in the English Department of Istanbul University, his master's degree in Marketing at Yeditepe University – MBA and his PhD in Media Economics and Management from Marmara University Communication Departments. Kuyucu, who received the title of associate professor in the field of communication applications, has been working as a manager and radio & TV programmer in the media industry since 1994. Michael Kuyucu, who has been a faculty member of Istanbul Aydın University for fifteen years since its establishment, has worked as a manager and radio programmer in radios such as Alem Fm – Radyo D – Süper Fm – Metro Fm – Radyo Klas – Radyo Mega – Number One Türk – TRT Radyoları – Best Fm – RS FM and CRI TÜRK. Kuyucu started his television career at Eko TV in 1997 and worked as a television programmer in channels such as TRT Müzik – Number One TV – Flying Bird TV – EkoTürk (economy).

* * *

Ali Acilar is an associate professor of Management Information Systems. He graduated from the Department of Business Administration at Hacettepe University, Ankara, Turkey, received his MS in Operation Research and Statistics from Rensselaer Polytechnic Institute (RPI), Troy, NY, USA, and obtained his Ph.D. in Business Administration from Dumlupınar University, Kütahya, Turkey in 2007. His research interest includes the use of information and communication technologies (ICTs) by individuals and organizations, information society, issues in ICT use, digital inequalities.

Nitesh Behare is an accomplished author with a wealth of knowledge and 15 years of experience in the academic field. He currently holds the position of Associate Professor at the Balaji Institute of International Business (BIIB), Sri Balaji University Pune (SBUP). Throughout his career, Dr. Behare has made significant contributions to the academic world through the publication of numerous research papers and book chapters, establishing himself as a recognized authority in his field.

Cihan Çakır graduated from Selcuk University, Faculty of Communication, Department of Journalism in 2012. He completed his master's degree in Selcuk University, Institute of Social Sciences, Department of Journalism in 2015 with his thesis titled "Sports Media as a Field where Hegemonic Masculinity is Reproduced: An Analysis on Masculinity Discourses in Sports News". He completed his doctorate in 2023 with his thesis titled "The Social Capital Creation Potential of Virtual Spaces: An Analysis on Social Media" at the same university. Again in 2023, he became an assistant professor at Avrasya University,

Faculty of Communication, Department of New Media and Communication. Currently, he continues his studies in the fields of social media, media and psychology, virtual spaces, computers and technology in human behavior, gender, masculinity, mobile media, family communication, and digital journalism.

Ayten Cansever graduated as the top student from the Department of Public Relations and Publicity at Marmara University's Faculty of Communication. She also completed a double major program in Sociology (in English) at the same university with honors. After completing her undergraduate studies, she started her master's degree in the Department of Interpersonal Communication at the Faculty of Communication at Marmara University's Social Sciences Institute, defending her thesis titled "Biopolitical Discourse and Narrative in Digital Games: The Case of The Sims 4" and graduating. She is currently pursuing her doctoral studies in the Public Relations and Publicity program at Istanbul University's Social Sciences Institute. Simultaneously, she works as a research assistant in the Faculty of Fine Arts, Communication, and Design at Istanbul Gelişim University. In 2023, she obtained the title of Family Counselor by completing the Family Counseling Certificate Program offered by Marmara University's Continuing Education Center. Her academic interests revolve around digital game research, communication sociology, communication psychology, new media studies, and critical media studies.

Iva Rani Das is a dynamic individual, currently pursuing her MPhil in the Marketing Department of Dhaka University. Alongside her academic pursuits, she holds key positions as an Assistant Director at the Daffodil Institute of Technology and serves as Guest Faculty in the Business Faculty at the Asian Institute of Business and Technology. Her scholarly achievements extend beyond the classroom, with publications in esteemed national and international journals. Iva's dedication to education and research makes her a driving force in the fields of business and marketing.

Mustafa Gülsin was born in Muş in 1985. After completing primary and high school here, he completed his undergraduate education at Karadeniz Technical University, Faculty of Economics and Administrative Sciences, Department of Business Administration in 2011, and his Master's degree in Communication Sciences at İnönü University in 2020. After completing his undergraduate education, he worked as a teacher at the Ministry of National Education for 1 year and at a financial institution for 1 year, and then started working as a lecturer at Muş Alparslan University Malazgirt Vocational School in 2015. He is currently performing this duty and continues his PhD studies at Erzurum Atatürk University, Social Sciences Institute, Department of Communication. His areas of interest include cinema, film analysis and advertising analysis, and he conducts academic studies in the fields of cinema and communication.

Ushmita Gupta is a seasoned academic visionary with over 15 years of experience, specializing in subjects such Economics & Economic theory. With an unwavering passion for education, my current role as a Senior Assistant Professor at Sri Balaji University Pune is a testament to my commitment to shaping the future of students. My academic journey began at Avadh Girls' Degree College, Lucknow in 2008. A pivotal moment in my academic voyage was the completion of my Ph.D. at the University of Lucknow in 2012, Participation in national and international seminars & conferences has been a cornerstone of my career, providing me with the platform to present research papers, engage in meaningful discussions, and contribute to the intellectual growth of my peers and students. Beyond teaching and research, I've made significant contributions through publications. Notably, I've co-authored books," reflecting my expertise and commitment to creating valuable educational resources. My dedication to education extends to various administrative roles. My journey as an educator and researcher continues, promising more years of enriching the lives of students and shaping the academic landscape.

Vishwanathan Iyer is an Asst Professor with Sri Balaji University Pune. He is a research enthusiast and contributes for research paper regularly. Many of this research papers are published and presented in various National and international conferences. He has one Patent registered in his name.

Sanjeev Kumar is an accomplished expert in Food and Beverage. He currently holds the positions of Professor at the Lovely Professional University, Punjab, India. With over a decade of experience in the field, food Service Industry, his research focuses on Alcoholic beverages, Event management and Sustainable Management Practices, Metaverse and Artificial Intelligence. He has published more than 35 research papers, articles and chapters in Scopus Indexed, UGC Approved and peer reviewed Journals and books. Dr. Sanjeev Kumar participated and acted as resource person in various National and International conferences, seminars, research workshops and industry talks and his work has been widely cited.

Salim Kurnaz is an Associate Professor at Süleyman Demirel University, School of Civil Aviation with 22 years of experience in aviation. He worked as a maintenance technician, quality control technician and maintenance instructor in the Turkish Armed Forces between 1997-2020. He worked at Joint Force Command (JFCBS) Brunssum/Netherlands between 2010-2013. He received bachelor's degree on Public Management in 2005 and on Aviation Management in 2022 from Anadolu University; master's degree in International Relations from Oklahoma University Oklahoma/USA in 2013 and in Business Management from Malatya Inonu University in 2018. He received his doctorate degree on management Sciences in 2019 from Malatya Inonu University. He continues his studies in the fields of aviation management, contemporary management systems, strategic management, and behavioral sciences. He is currently working as visiting Associate Professor at Kazimiero Simonaviciaus University Vilnius, Lithuania for his Post-Doctorate Research on Crisis Management in Aviation Sector which is supported by The Scientific and Technological Research Council of Türkiye (TÜBİTAK).

Ambika N. is an MCA, MPhil, Ph.D. in computer science. She completed her Ph.D. from Bharathiar university in the year 2015. She has 16 years of teaching experience and presently working for St.Francis College, Bangalore. She has guided BCA, MCA and M.Tech students in their projects. Her expertise includes wireless sensor network, Internet of things, cybersecurity. She gives guest lectures in her expertise. She is a reviewer of books, conferences (national/international), encyclopaedia and journals. She is advisory committee member of some conferences. She has many publications in National & international conferences, international books, national and international journals and encyclopaedias. She has some patent publications (National) in computer science division.

António Rodrigues obtained a PhD in Management and Marketing at the University of Seville in Spain. He is currently a professor and researcher at the ISG-Business & Economics School (Lisbon, Portugal). He has teaching experience in undergraduate and master's degrees in Aeronautical Management. He is the author of several opinion articles and scientific articles. Professionally, he has experience in the financial, marketing and general management areas. He is certified in Sustainable Finance (ESG Advisor) by EFPA The European Financial Planning Association.

Pritesh Pradeep Somani is an eminent academician specializing in the field of Marketing and Research with a keen interest in the field of Statistical analysis. He is credited with 2 International patents in his name Registered across Republic of South Africa.

Osman Nuri Sunar is an assistant professor at Istanbul Aydın University, Anadolu Bil Vocational School, Department of Transportation Services, with approximately 30 years of aviation experience. Between 1993 and 2022, he worked as an aircraft flight and maintenance technician, quality control, maintenance instructor, flight and maintenance standardization control personnel in various units of the Turkish Armed Forces. He received bachelor's degree on Public Management in 2003 and on Aviation Management in 2020 from Anadolu University; master's degree in Business Management from Kutahya Dumlupinar University in 2008. He received his doctorate degree on Management Sciences in 2021 from Malatya Inonu University. He conducts studies and research in the fields of aviation management, contemporary management systems, strategic management and behavioral sciences.

Mohammad Badruddoza Talukder is an Associate Professor and head of the Department of Tourism and Hospitality Management, Daffodil Institute of Information Technology (at the National University), Dhaka, Bangladesh. He completed his Ph.D. in Hotel Management at the School of Hotel Management and Tourism, Lovely Professional University, India. He holds a bachelor's and a master's degree in Hotel Management from India. He has been teaching various courses in the Department of Tourism and Hospitality at various universities in Bangladesh since 2009. His research areas include tourism management, hotel management, hospitality management, food and beverage management, and accommodation management, where he has published research papers in well-known journals in Bangladesh and abroad. Dr. Talukder is one of the executive members of the Tourism Educators Association of Bangladesh. He has led training and counseling for various hospitality organizations in Bangladesh. As an administrator, Dr. Talukder served as a debate advisor at the University coordinator for courses and exams in the Department of Tourism and Hotel Management. He has experience as a manager in various business-class hotels in Bangladesh. He is one of the certified trainers for the food and beverage service department of the SIEP project from Bangladesh. He became an honorary facilitator at Bangladesh Tourism Board's Bangabandhu International Tourism and Hospitality Training Institute.

Index

F

G

H

I

L

M

N

O

P

R

S

T

U

V

W

www.ingramcontent.com/pod-product-compliance
Lightning Source LLC
LaVergne TN
LVHW082346011026
849160LV00024B/1198

9798369344583